THE PRACTICAL SKEPTIC

READINGS IN SOCIOLOGY

Fourth Edition

Lisa J. McIntyre

Washington State University

 **McGraw-Hill**
Higher Education

Boston   Burr Ridge, IL   Dubuque, IA   New York   San Francisco   St. Louis
Bangkok   Bogotá   Caracas   Kuala Lumpur   Lisbon   London   Madrid   Mexico City
Milan   Montreal   New Delhi   Santiago   Seoul   Singapore   Sydney · Taipei   Toronto

**McGraw-Hill
Higher Education**

THE PRACTICAL SKEPTIC: READINGS IN SOCIOLOGY, FOURTH EDITION

Published by McGraw-Hill, an imprint of The McGraw-Hill Companies, Inc., 1221 Avenue of the Americas, New York, NY 10020. Copyright © 2009, 2006, 2002, 1999. All rights reserved. No part of this publication may be reproduced or distributed in any form or by any means, or stored in a database or retrieval system, without the prior written consent of The McGraw-Hill Companies, Inc., including, but not limited to, in any network or other electronic storage or transmission, or broadcast for distance learning.

This book is printed on acid-free paper.

2 3 4 5 6 7 8 9 0 DOC/DOC 0 9 8

ISBN: 978-0-07-338003-2
MHID: 0-07-338003-2

Editor-in-Chief: *Michael Ryan*
Publisher: *Frank Mortimer*
Sponsoring Editor: *Gina Boedeker*
Marketing Manager: *Leslie Oberhuber*
Developmental Editor: *Larry Goldberg*
Production Editor: *David Blatty*
Designer: *Andrei Pasternak*
Production Supervisor: *Tandra Jorgensen*
Composition: *10/12 Book Antiqua by ICC Macmillan Inc.*
Printing: *45# New Era Matte, R. R. Donnelley & Sons/Crawfordsville, IN*

Cover Photo: © Ryan McVay/Getty Images

Library of Congress Cataloging-in-Publication Data
The practical skeptic : readings in sociology / [edited by] Lisa McIntyre. — 4th ed.
  p. cm.
 Includes bibliographical references.
 ISBN-13: 978-0-07-338003-2 (alk. paper)
 ISBN-10: 0-07-338003-2 (alk. paper)
 1. Sociology. 2. Social problems. 3. United States—Social conditions. I. McIntyre, Lisa J.
 HM585 .P73 2009
 301—dc22   2007028364

The Internet addresses listed in the text were accurate at the time of publication. The inclusion of a Web site does not indicate an endorsement by the authors or McGraw-Hill, and McGraw-Hill does not guarantee the accuracy of the information presented at these sites.

www.mhhe.com

PREFACE

There are dozens of anthologies available for introductory-level sociology classes, but I think that this one is different. It's different because as I compiled and edited these articles, I kept the needs of introductory students in mind. That's important. When sociologists write for their professional colleagues, they take for granted (as they should) that their readers are equipped with a great deal of knowledge. Student readers, by contrast, generally lack this sort of preparation; consequently, many students find that reading the works of sociologists is not so much a challenge as an onerous chore. I suspect that beginning students assigned to read sociology feel much like the theatergoer who stumbles into a foreign film that lacks subtitles. No matter how dramatic or comedic the action, unless one can follow the dialogue, the movie is boring.

In this volume, I have tried to bridge the gap between the sociologists who wrote these articles and the students who will read them. Each article begins with a brief introduction to help orient students to the author's aims and point of view, includes footnotes containing explanations of concepts that are likely to be unfamiliar to novice sociologists, and concludes with some questions that will help students sort through and make sense of what they have read. My goal is to replace boredom with intellectual challenge, to make sociology not "easy," but accessible.

Both classic and contemporary articles were selected because they help to illustrate the importance of understanding the social contexts through which people move and to highlight some of the core concepts that sociologists and other social observers use to make sense of the social world. The classic articles especially were selected to illustrate the foundational concepts that most contemporary writers take for granted. But while these fundamentals might seem old hat to professional sociologists, they still contain important revelations for beginners.

New to This Edition

In the final selection in this edition, Randall Collins suggests that the core of sociology is not a "set of texts or ideas." It is, he tells us, "an activity." This fourth edition of the reader continues to emphasize articles that provide students the opportunity to do the activity that sociologists do: to reexamine the familiar and to rethink conventional understandings of these understandings. Moreover, I want to invite students to contemplate in new ways their own participation in the social world.

Supplements for Text and Reader

Visit our Online Learning Center Web site at www.mhhe.com/mcintyre4 for robust student and instructor resources. This is a combined Web site for both *The Practical Skeptic: Core Concepts in Sociology* and its companion reader, *The Practical Skeptic: Readings in Sociology*.

FOR STUDENTS

Student resources for the *Core Concepts* text include self-quizzes, defined key concepts, practical applications, and other chapter study aids.

FOR INSTRUCTORS

The password-protected instructor portion of the Web site includes the *Core Concepts* text instructor's manual (written by the author), containing discussion questions and activities, examples of lectures, tips specifically targeting new instructors, a comprehensive test bank and computerized test bank, and all the tools available to students. Also included are a separate test bank and computerized test bank for the reader with multiple choice, true/false, and essay questions for each reading.

The Practical Skeptic: Core Concepts in Sociology

Created to serve as a companion to the reader, *The Practical Skeptic: Readings in Sociology,* this text focuses on core concepts as the central building blocks for understanding sociology. Written in a lively, conversational style, this text includes numerous pedagogical features to help students grasp key sociological concepts.

ACKNOWLEDGMENTS

The fourth edition was reviewed by the following people, who responded with suggestions and pointed out necessary revisions, for which I am deeply grateful: Chris Adamski-Mietus, Western Illinois University; James Cassell, Henderson State University; Lindsay Custer, Bellevue Community College; Martha Doyle, Mercy College of Health Sciences; Yasmiyn Irizarry, Indiana University; Christine K. Oakley, Washington State University; Kennon Rice, Albright College; and Elizabeth Underwood, Eastern Kentucky University.

I would like to thank the reviewers of the third edition for their insightful feedback: Deborah A. Abowitz, Bucknell University; Jarl Ahlkvist, University of Colorado-Colorado Springs; Cheryl Albers, Buffalo State College; Sue Cox, Bellevue Community College; Derek Greenfield, Highline Community College; Tiffany Hayes, Green River Community College; Louise Hull, Green River Community College; Barbara Karcher, Kennesaw State University; John Poindexter, West Shore Community College; Susan Ross, Lycoming College; Ericka Stange, Central Washington University; Ann S. Stein, College of Charleston; Deborah Thorne, Ohio University; and Jamee K. Wolfe, Roanoke College.

For the second edition, the following individuals provided thoughtful reviews and recommendations: Deborah J. Baiano Berman, Framingham State College; Jerry Barrish, Bellevue Community College; Valerie S. Brown, Cuyahoga Community College; Margo Rita Capparelli, Framingham State College; Debra Cornelius, Shippensburg University; Jamie Dangler, SUNY Cortland; Laurel R. Davis, Springfield College; Gloria Y. Gadsden, Fairleigh Dickinson University; Alan G. Hill, Delta College; Susan E. Humphers-Ginther, Moorhead State University; Katherine Johnson, Niagara County Community College; Barbara Karcher, Kennesaw State University; Debra C. Lemke, Western Maryland College; Patricia A. Masters, George Mason University; Susan McWilliams, University of Southern Maine; Kristy McNamara, Furman University; Dan Pence, Southern Utah University; Marcella Thompson, University of Arkansas; and Brenda S. Zicha, Charles Stewart Mott Community College.

The following colleagues reviewed the manuscript and choice of articles for the first edition and made many helpful suggestions: Sheila Cordray, Oregon State University; Rebecca Erickson, University of Akron; Allen Scarboro, Augusta State University; and Martha L. Shockey, St. Ambrose University.

Lisa J. McIntyre

CONTENTS

Part Two   *THE RESEARCH CRAFT*

What do men and women really want in potential mates? Davis suggests that using unobtrusive research methods can help us get beyond the "politically correct" to find the real answers.

According to many professors, student absenteeism can be a problem. We wonder, "What's wrong with those students? Don't they care about their education?" But, is missing class really just a "personal trouble"? Or, is something else going on? Professor Wyatt did what sociologists do best—some research.

In recent years, the work of social researchers has come under increasing scrutiny. In her paper, McIntyre discusses the sometimes scandalous history of research and explores what it means today to be an ethical social researcher.

As Meyer recounts, Stanley Milgram's research on obedience taught us a great deal about the extent to which everyday people will do as they are told—even when what they are told to do is repulsive. But, was gaining this knowledge worth the emotional price paid by Milgram's subjects?

Part Three   *CULTURE*

What is culture? How does it affect our lives? How is culture different from society? In this classic piece, anthropologist Kluckhohn explains how social scientists define and use the concept of culture.

Now, here's an important question: Why do women spend so much time in the bathroom?

Besides the "Three R's," just what is being taught to primary school students? If you've been listening to some of the political debates, the answers may just surprise you.

Every society has them—occupations that are socially necessary but looked down upon as tainted. How do people cope with doing work that is stigmatized?

How difficult is it to turn ordinary boys into professional killers? Apparently, it's not that hard, as long as you know what buttons to push.

"A prison sentence constitutes a 'massive assault' on the identity of those imprisoned." What happens to the self in prison? Can the self ever really be reclaimed once someone gets out of prison?

Sociologists frequently stress the power of social roles to shape individuals' behavior. Zimmer finds that, under some circumstances, individuals can shape social roles.

1

THE PROMISE

C. Wright Mills

"The Promise," published in 1959 by C. Wright Mills, is probably the most famous essay ever written by a modern sociologist. In this article, Mills captures the essential lesson of sociology: To truly understand people's behavior, we must look beyond those individuals to the larger social contexts in which they live. Individuals make choices, to be sure, but their choices are constrained by social, historical, cultural, political, and economic factors. Most important, people frequently do not even realize the extent to which their lives are affected by things that are external to them and outside of their control. Mills's point is that if we are to understand people's behavior, we must take into account these nonindividual factors. (This is not an especially easy article to read, but it is fundamental. You might find it helpful to read the section on Mills in *The Practical Skeptic: Core Concepts in Sociology,* chapter 2, before you tackle this reading.)

Nowadays men often feel that their private lives are a series of traps. They sense that within their everyday worlds, they cannot overcome their troubles, and in this feeling, they are often quite correct: What ordinary men are directly aware of and what they try to do are bounded by the private orbits in which they live; their visions and their powers are limited to the close-up scenes of job, family, neighborhood; in other milieux[1] they move vicariously and remain spectators. And the more aware they become, however vaguely, of ambitions and of threats which transcend their immediate locales, the more trapped they seem to feel.

Underlying this sense of being trapped are seemingly impersonal changes in the very structure of continent-wide societies. The facts of contemporary history are also facts about the success and the failure of individual men and women. When a society is industrialized, a peasant becomes a worker; a feudal lord is liquidated or becomes a businessman. When classes rise or fall, a man is employed or unemployed; when the rate of investment goes up or down, a man takes new heart or goes broke. When wars happen, an insurance salesman becomes a rocket launcher; a store clerk, a radar man; a wife lives alone; a child grows up without a father. Neither the life of an individual nor the history of a society can be understood without understanding both.

[1]*Milieux* is French; it means "social environments." (*Milieux* is plural; *milieu* is singular.)—Ed.

Yet men do not usually define the troubles they endure in terms of historical change and institutional contradiction.[2] The well-being they enjoy, they do not usually impute to the big ups and downs of the societies in which they live. Seldom aware of the intricate connection between the patterns of their own lives and the course of world history, ordinary men do not usually know what this connection means for the kinds of men they are becoming and for the kinds of history-making in which they might take part. They do not possess the quality of mind essential to grasp the interplay of man and society, of biography and history, of self and world. They cannot cope with their personal troubles in such ways as to control the structural transformations that usually lie behind them.

Surely it is no wonder. In what period have so many men been so totally exposed at so fast a pace to such earthquakes of change? That Americans have not known such catastrophic changes as have the men and women of other societies is due to historical facts that are now quickly becoming "merely history." The history that now affects every man is world history. Within this scene and this period, in the course of a single generation, one sixth of mankind is transformed from all that is feudal and backward into all that is modern, advanced, and fearful. Political colonies are freed; new and less visible forms of imperialism installed. Revolutions occur; men feel the intimate grip of new kinds of authority. Totalitarian societies rise, and are smashed to bits—or succeed fabulously. After two centuries of ascendancy, capitalism is shown up as only one way to make society into an industrial apparatus. After two centuries of hope, even formal democracy is restricted to a quite small portion of mankind. Everywhere in the underdeveloped world, ancient ways of life are broken up and vague expectations become urgent demands. Everywhere in the overdeveloped world, the means of authority and of violence become total in scope and bureaucratic in form. Humanity itself now lies before us, the super-nation at either pole concentrating its most coordinated and massive efforts upon the preparation of World War Three.

The very shaping of history now outpaces the ability of men to orient themselves in accordance with cherished values. And which values? Even when they do not panic, men often sense that older ways of feeling and thinking have collapsed and that newer beginnings are ambiguous to the point of moral stasis. Is it any wonder that ordinary men feel they cannot cope with the larger worlds with which they are so suddenly confronted? That they cannot understand the meaning of their epoch for their own lives? That—in defense of selfhood—they become morally insensible, trying to remain altogether private men? Is it any wonder that they come to be possessed by a sense of the trap?

It is not only information that they need—in this Age of Fact, information often dominates their attention and overwhelms their capacities to assimilate it. It is not only the skills of reason that they need—although their struggles to acquire these often exhaust their limited moral energy.

---

[2]Mills is using the term *institution* in its sociological sense—which is a bit different from the way this term is used in everyday or conventional speech. To the sociologist, institution refers to *a set of social arrangements, an accepted way of resolving important social problems.* Thus, the institution of the family is our society's way of resolving the important social problem of raising children. The institution of the economy is how we resolve the problem of distributing goods and services (for example, in the case of the United States, capitalism). The concept of institutional contradiction refers to situations in which the demands of one institution are not compatible with the demands of another institution. For example, there is institutional contradiction when the institution of the family is based on the norm that dad goes to work and mom stays home with the kids but the institution of the economy is such that it takes two employed adults to support a family. You will find more examples of institutional contradictions in reading 2 by Stephanie Coontz. You can read more about the nature of institutions in *The Practical Skeptic: Core Concepts in Sociology,* chapter 9, "Society and Social Institutions."—Ed.

What they need, and what they feel they need, is a quality of mind that will help them to use information and to develop reason in order to achieve lucid summations of what is going on in the world and of what may be happening within themselves. It is this quality, I am going to contend, that journalists and scholars, artists and publics, scientists and editors are coming to expect of what may be called the sociological imagination.

1

The sociological imagination enables its possessor to understand the larger historical scene in terms of its meaning for the inner life and the external career of a variety of individuals. It enables him to take into account how individuals, in the welter of their daily experience, often become falsely conscious of their social positions. Within that welter, the framework of modern society is sought, and within that framework the psychologies of a variety of men and women are formulated. By such means the personal uneasiness of individuals is focused upon explicit troubles and the indifference of publics is transformed into involvement with public issues.

The first fruit of this imagination—and the first lesson of the social science that embodies it—is the idea that the individual can understand his own experience and gauge his own fate only by locating himself within his period, that he can know his own chances in life only by becoming aware of those of all individuals in his circumstances. In many ways it is a terrible lesson; in many ways a magnificent one. We do not know the limits of man's capacities for supreme effort or willing degradation, for agony or glee, for pleasurable brutality or the sweetness of reason. But in our time we have come to know that the limits of "human nature" are frighteningly broad. We have come to know that every individual lives, from one

generation to the next, in some society; that he lives out a biography, and that he lives it out within some historical sequence. By the fact of his living he contributes, however minutely, to the shaping of this society and to the course of its history, even as he is made by society and by its historical push and shove.

The sociological imagination enables us to grasp history and biography and the relations between the two within society. That is its task and its promise. . . . And it is the signal of what is best in contemporary studies of man and society.

No social study that does not come back to the problems of biography, of history and of their intersections within a society has completed its intellectual journey. Whatever the specific problems of the classic social analysts, however limited or however broad the features of social reality they have examined, those who have been imaginatively aware of the promise of their work have consistently asked three sorts of questions:

1. What is the structure of this particular society as a whole? What are its essential components, and how are they related to one another? How does it differ from other varieties of social order? Within it, what is the meaning of any particular feature for its continuance and for its change?

2. Where does this society stand in human history? What are the mechanics by which it is changing? What is its place within and its meaning for the development of humanity as a whole? How does any particular feature we are examining affect, and how is it affected by, the historical period in which it moves? And this period—what are its essential features? How does it differ from other periods? What are its characteristic ways of history-making?

3. What varieties of men and women now prevail in this society and in this period?

And what varieties are coming to prevail? In what ways are they selected and formed, liberated and repressed, made sensitive and blunted? What kinds of "human nature" are revealed in the conduct and character we observe in this society in this period? And what is the meaning for "human nature" of each and every feature of the society we are examining?

Whether the point of interest is a great power state or a minor literary mood, a family, a prison, a creed—these are the kinds of questions the best social analysts have asked. They are the intellectual pivots of classic studies of man in society—and they are the questions inevitably raised by any mind possessing the sociological imagination. For that imagination is the capacity to shift from one perspective to another—from the political to the psychological; from examination of a single family to comparative assessment of the national budgets of the world; from the theological school to the military establishment; from considerations of an oil industry to studies of contemporary poetry. It is the capacity to range from the most impersonal and remote transformations to the most intimate features of the human self—and to see the relations between the two. Back of its use there is always the urge to know the social and historical meaning of the individual in the society and in the period in which he has his quality and his being.

That, in brief, is why it is by means of the sociological imagination that men now hope to grasp what is going on in the world, and to understand what is happening in themselves as minute points of the intersections of biography and history within society. In large part, contemporary man's self-conscious view of himself as at least an outsider, if not a permanent stranger, rests upon an absorbed realization of social relativity and of the transformative power of history. The sociological imagination is the most fruitful form of this self-consciousness. By its use men whose mentalities have swept only a series of limited orbits often come to feel as if suddenly awakened in a house with which they had only supposed themselves to be familiar. Correctly, or incorrectly, they often come to feel that they can now provide themselves with adequate summations, cohesive assessments, comprehensive orientations. Older decisions that once appeared sound now seem to them products of a mind unaccountably dense. Their capacity for astonishment is made lively again. They acquire a new way of thinking, they experience a transvaluation of values; in a word, by their reflection and by their sensibility, they realize the cultural meaning of the social sciences.

2

Perhaps the most fruitful distinction with which the sociological imagination works is between "the personal troubles of milieu" and "the public issues of social structure." This distinction is an essential tool of the sociological imagination and a feature of all classic work in social science.

Troubles occur within the character of the individual and within the range of his immediate relations with others; they have to do with his self and with those limited areas of social life of which he is directly and personally aware. Accordingly, the statement and the resolution of troubles properly lie within the individual as a biological entity and within the scope of his immediate milieu—the social setting that is directly open to his personal experience and to some extent his willful activity. A trouble is a private matter: values cherished by an individual are felt by him to be threatened.

Issues have to do with matters that transcend these local environments of the individual and the range of his inner life. They have to do with the organization of many such milieux into the institutions of an historical society as a whole, with the ways in which various milieux overlap and interpenetrate to form the larger structure of social and historical life. An issue is a public matter: some value cherished by publics is felt to be threatened. Often there is a debate about what that value really is and about what it is that really threatens it. This debate is often without focus if only because it is the very nature of an issue, unlike even widespread trouble, that it cannot very well be defined in terms of the immediate and everyday environments of ordinary men. An issue, in fact, often involves a crisis in institutional arrangements, and often too it involves what Marxists call "contradictions" or "antagonisms."

In these terms, consider unemployment. When, in a city of 100,000, only one man is unemployed, that is his personal trouble, and for its relief we properly look to the character of the man, his skills, and his immediate opportunities. But when in a nation of 50 million employees, 15 million men are unemployed, that is an issue, and we may not hope to find its solution within the range of opportunities open to any one individual. The very structure of opportunities has collapsed. Both the correct statement of the problem and the range of possible solutions require us to consider the economic and political institutions of the society, and not merely the personal situation and character of a scatter of individuals.

Consider war. The personal problem of war, when it occurs, may be how to survive it or how to die in it with honor; how to make money out of it; how to climb into the higher safety of the military apparatus; or how to contribute to the war's termination. In short, according to one's values, to find a set of milieux and within it to survive the war or make one's death in it meaningful. But the structural issues of war have to do with its causes; with what types of men it throws up into command; with its effects upon economic and political, family and religious institutions, with

the unorganized irresponsibility of a world of nation-states.

Consider marriage. Inside a marriage a man and a woman may experience personal troubles, but when the divorce rate during the first four years of marriage is 250 out of every 1,000 attempts, this is an indication of a structural issue having to do with the institutions of marriage and the family and other institutions that bear upon them.

Or consider the metropolis—the horrible, beautiful, ugly, magnificent sprawl of the great city. For many upper-class people, the personal solution to "the problem of the city" is to have an apartment with private garage under it in the heart of the city, and forty miles out, a house by Henry Hill, garden by Garrett Eckbo, on a hundred acres of private land. In these two controlled environments—with a small staff at each end and a private helicopter connection—most people could solve many of the problems of personal milieux caused by the facts of the city. But all this, however splendid, does not solve the public issues that the structural fact of the city poses. What should be done with this wonderful monstrosity? Break it all up into scattered units, combining residence and work? Refurbish it as it stands? Or, after evacuation, dynamite it and build new cities according to new plans in new places? What should those plans be? And who is to decide and to accomplish whatever choice is made? These are structural issues; to confront them and to solve them requires us to consider political and economic issues that affect innumerable milieux.

In so far as an economy is so arranged that slumps occur, the problem of unemployment becomes incapable of personal solution. In so far as war is inherent in the nation-state system and in the uneven industrialization of the world, the ordinary individual in his restricted milieu will be powerless—with or without psychiatric aid—to solve the troubles this system or lack of system imposes upon him. In so far as the family as an institution turns women into darling little slaves and men into their chief providers and unweaned dependents, the problem of a satisfactory marriage remains incapable of purely private solution. In so far as the overdeveloped megalopolis and the overdeveloped automobile are built-in features of the overdeveloped society, the issues of urban living will not be solved by personal ingenuity and private wealth.

What we experience in various and specific milieux, I have noted, is often caused by structural changes. Accordingly, to understand the changes of many personal milieux we are required to look beyond them. And the number and variety of such structural changes increase as the institutions within which we live become more embracing and more intricately connected with one another. To be aware of the idea of social structure and to use it with sensibility is to be capable of tracing such linkages among a great variety of milieux. To be able to do that is to possess the sociological imagination. . . .

Questions

1. What is the sociological imagination? (You might begin with quoting Mills's definition, but try to describe this phenomenon in your own words as well.)

2. In brief, what kinds of questions are asked by those who possess a sociological imagination?

3. What are "personal troubles of milieu"? What are "public issues of social structure"? Why does Mills say that the distinction between troubles and issues is "an essential tool of the sociological imagination"?

2

HOW HISTORY AND SOCIOLOGY CAN HELP TODAY'S FAMILIES

Stephanie Coontz

In this 1997 article (the introductory chapter to her book *The Way We Really Are*), Stephanie Coontz demonstrates the sociological imagination as she discusses the nature of relations between men and women and between parents and kids. Again, these issues *seem* personal; but Coontz demonstrates how taking the larger—sociological and historical—view is very important if we want to find practical answers to such crucial questions as "What's wrong with male–female relationships in modern society?" and "What's happening to today's youth?"

When lecture audiences first urged me to talk about how family history and sociology were relevant to contemporary life, I wasn't sure I wanted to abandon the safety of my historical observation post. But my experiences in recent years have convinced me that people are eager to learn whether historians and social scientists can help them improve their grasp of family issues. And I've come to believe that it's our responsibility to try.

I don't want to make false promises about what history and sociology offer. I can't give you five tips to make your relationship last. I don't have a list of ten things you can say to get your kids to do what *you* want and make them think it's what *they* want. Nor can I give kids many useful pointers on how to raise their parents.

But a historical perspective can help us place our personal relationships into a larger social context, so we can distinguish individual idiosyncrasies or problems from broader

dilemmas posed by the times in which we live. Understanding the historical background and the current socioeconomic setting of family changes helps turn down the heat on discussion of many family issues. It can alleviate some of the anxieties of modern parents and temper the recriminations that go back and forth between men and women. Seeing the larger picture won't make family dilemmas go away, but it can reduce the insecurity, personal bitterness, or sense of betrayal that all of us, at one time or another, bring to these issues. Sometimes it helps to know that the tension originates in the situation, not the psyche.

Putting Teen–Parent Conflicts in Perspective

Consider the question of what's happening to American youth. It's extremely difficult for parents today to look at a specific problem they may have with their teenager, whether that is sneaking out at night or experimenting with alcohol and drugs, without seeing it as a sign of the crisis we are told grips modern youth. Parents tell me they are terrified by headlines about the "epidemic" of teen suicide and by chilling television stories about kids too young to drive a car but old enough to carry an AK-47.

Concerns over adolescent behavior are not entirely new. "Let's Face It," a *Newsweek* cover story of September 6, 1954, declared: "Our Teenagers Are Out of Control." The 1955 film, *Blackboard Jungle,* claimed that teens were "savage" animals because "gang leaders have taken the place of parents." Still, there *are* new structural and historical changes in American life that have recently complicated the transition from early adolescence to young adulthood, making youth–adult relations seem more adversarial.

It doesn't help us understand these changes, however, when people exaggerate the problems of today's teens or turn their normal ups and downs into pathologies. Most teens do not get involved in violence, either as criminals or victims. While teen suicide rates have indeed been increasing, any growth from a low starting point can sound dramatic if presented as a percentage. For example, a 1995 report from the Centers for Disease Control stated that suicides among 10- to 14-year-old youths had "soared" between 1980 and 1992. What this meant in real figures, points out researcher Mike Males, was that 1 in 60,000 youths in this age group killed themselves in 1992, compared to 1 in 125,000 in 1980. The actual death rate among teens from firearms and poisoning has scarcely changed since the 1950s, but the proportion attributed to suicide has risen dramatically, while the proportion attributed to accident has declined (Holinger 1994; Males 1996).

Furthermore, many "teen" suicide figures are overstated because they come from a database that includes people aged 15 to 24. Suicide rates for actual teenagers, aged 13 to 19, are among the lowest of any age group. In fact, notes Kirk Astroth, "teens as a whole are *less likely* to commit suicide than any other age group *except* preteens. . . . Occupational surveys consistently show that parents and teachers are *twice* as likely, counselors and psychologists are *four* times as likely, and school administrators are *six* times as likely to commit suicide as are high school students" (Astroth 1993, 413). (When I read this statistic to a teenage acquaintance of mine, he told me dourly, "Yeah, but they'll just say we drove them to it.")

It's not that we have more bad parents or more bad kids today than we used to. It's not that families have lost interest in their kids. And there is no evidence that the majority of today's teenagers are more destructive or irresponsible than in the past. However, relations between adults and teens are especially strained today, not because youths have lost their childhood, as is usually suggested, but because they are not being adequately prepared for the new requirements of adulthood. In some ways, childhood has actually been prolonged, if it is measured by dependence on parents and segregation from adult activities. What many young people have lost are clear paths for gaining experience doing responsible, socially necessary work, either in or out of the home, and for moving away from parental supervision without losing contact with adults.

The most common dilemma facing adolescents, and the one that probably causes the most conflicts with adults, is their "rolelessness" in modern society. A rare piece of hard data in all the speculation about what makes adolescents tick is that young people do better on almost every level when they have meaningful involvement in useful and necessary tasks. This effect exists independently of their relationships with parents and friends. Teens also benefit from taking responsibility for younger or less-fortunate children. As one author observes, teens "need some experience of being older, bigger, stronger, or wiser" (Hamburg 1992, 201; Maton 1990, 297).

But today's adolescents have very few opportunities to do socially necessary work. The issue of rolelessness has been building for eighty years, ever since the abolition of child labor, the extension of schooling, and the decline in farm work that used to occupy many youths in the summer. The problem has accelerated recently, as many of the paths that once led teenagers toward mastery of productive and social roles have turned into dead ends. Instead of having a variety of routes to adulthood, as was true for most of American history, most youngsters are now expected to stay in high school until age 17 or 18.

High schools were originally designed for the most privileged sector of the population. Even now they tend to serve well only that half of the high school population that goes on to college. Non-college-bound students often tell me they feel like second-class citizens, not really of interest to the school. And in recent decades a high school degree has lost considerable value as a ticket to a stable job. Even partial college work confers fewer advantages than in the past. Because of these and other trends, researcher Laurence Steinberg claims, adolescence "has become a social and economic holding period" (1992, 30).

Parents are expected to do the holding. In 1968, two researchers commented that most teen–parent conflicts stemmed from the fact that "readiness for adulthood comes about two years *later* than the adolescent claims and about two years *before* the parent will admit" (Stone and Church 1968, 447; emphasis added). There is some evidence that the level of miscalculation has widened for *both* parents and kids.

From the point of view of parents, it is more necessary than ever for kids to stay in school rather than seek full-time work, and to delay marriage or pregnancy. After all, the age at which youths can support themselves, let alone a *family,* has reached a new high in the past two decades. From the kids' point of view, though, this waiting period seems almost unbearable. They not only know a lot more than their folks about modern technology but they feel that they also know more

about the facts of life than yesterday's teens. Understandably, they strain at the leash.

The strain is accentuated by the fact that while the age of economic maturation has been rising, the age of physical maturation has been falling. The average age of puberty for girls, for instance, was 16 in 1820, 14 in 1900, and 13 in 1940. Today it is 12, and may still be dropping. For boys, the pace and timing of pubertal development is the most important factor in determining the age at which they first have sex; the influence of parents, friends, income, and race is secondary. Although parents and friends continue to exert considerable influence on the age at which girls begin to have sex, there are obvious limits to how long parents can hold their teenagers back (Nightingale and Wolverton 1988, 1994).

And even as the job market offers fewer and fewer ways for teens to assert their independence and show that they are more grown up than younger kids, consumer markets and the media offer more and more. Steinberg points out that while teens "have less autonomy to pursue societally-valued *adult* activities" than in the past, they "have more autonomy than did their counterparts previously in matters of leisure, discretionary consumption, and grooming." As a result, adolescents "find it easier to purchase illicit drugs than to obtain legitimate employment" (Steinberg 1992, 30).

Another problem for parent–child relations is society's expectation that teens abide by rules and habits that grown-ups have abandoned, and that parents ought to be able to *make* them do so. In preindustrial societies most kids were integrated into almost all adult activities, and right up until the twentieth century there were few separate standards or different laws for teens and adults. For centuries, youth and adults played the same games by the same rules, both literally and figuratively. From "blind man's bluff" to "follow the leader," games we now leave to children were once played by adults as well. There were few special rules or restrictions that applied solely to teens. *All* premarital sex was supposedly out of line in the nineteenth century; teen sex was not singled out as a special problem. In fact, as late as 1886, the "age of consent" for girls was only 10 in more than half the states in the union (Luker 1996). However, girls or women who *did* consent to premarital sex were ostracized, regardless of their age.

Today's adults have moved on to new amusements and freedoms, but we want teens to play the old games by the old rules. There may be some good reasons for this, but any segregated group soon develops its own institutions, rules, and value systems, and young people are no exception.

Sports is virtually the only adult-approved and peer-admired realm where teens can demonstrate successive gains in competency, test their limits, and show themselves bigger, stronger, and better than younger children. But for teens who aren't good at sports, or those who reject it as busywork designed to keep them out of trouble, what's left? Music, clothes, drugs, alcohol—the choices differ. Many kids experiment and move on. Others get caught in the quagmire of seeking their identity through consumption. What we often call the youth culture is actually adult marketers seeking to commercially exploit youthful energy and rebellion. But sometimes consumerism seems the only way teens can show that they are growing up and experimenting with new social identities while adults try to keep them suspended in the children's world of school or summer camp.

Of course, many teens get a lot out of school and summer camp. But the dilemmas of rolelessness often put adolescents and their parents on a collision course. Young people feel that adults are plying them with make-work or asking them to put their lives on hold as they mature. They're pretty sure we didn't put *our* lives on hold at comparable levels of maturity, so they suspect us of hypocrisy. Often, they have a point.

On the other hand, while many parents recognize that risk taking among teenagers hasn't changed much since their own youth, they feel that there are more serious consequences for those behaviors than there used to be, given the presence of AIDS (acquired immune deficiency syndrome), high-tech weapons, and new potent drugs. So adults are not necessarily being hypocritical when they hold kids to higher standards than they met themselves. Many of us fear that the second chances and lucky breaks we got may not be available to the next generation.

Balancing the legitimate fears of adults against the legitimate aspirations of teens is not easy. But it helps for both teens and adults to realize that many of their conflicts are triggered by changes in social and economic arrangements, not just family ones. The best way I've found to personally confirm the sociological studies of rolelessness is to ask older men to talk about their life histories. Some of the most interesting discussions I've had over the past few years have been with men over age 60, whose memories extend beyond the transitional period of the 1960s and 1970s to what teen life was like in the 1930s, 1940s, or early 1950s.

The conversations usually start with comments on irresponsible behavior by today's teenage males. "I'd have had my hide tanned if I'd been caught doing that," someone always says, which generally leads to examples of how they got "whomped" or "taught a lesson." Soon, though, the subject switches to the things these upstanding men *didn't* get caught doing in their youth. And most of the time, it turns out the first lesson they learned by getting whomped was how not to get caught.

When they talk about what *really* set them on the right path, almost every older man I've talked with recalls his first job. "I was supporting myself when I was 17" (16, 18, 19, even 15), or "I was in the army with a job to do," the stories go: "What's the matter with today's kids?"

And soon they provide their own answers. The typical job a teenager can get today provides neither the self-pride of economic independence nor the socializing benefits of working alongside adult mentors. Teens work in segregated jobs where the only adult who ever comes around is the boss, almost always in an adversarial role. Few jobs for youth allow them to start at the bottom and move up; the middle rungs of the job ladder have been sawed off. Marking time in dead-end jobs that teach no useful skills for the future, teens remain dependent on their parents for the basic necessities of life, simultaneously resenting that dependence and trying to manipulate it.

The stories older men tell about their first jobs are quite different from those told by today's teens. Even men who later became businessmen or highly educated professionals say that their first jobs were in construction, factory work, or some menial setting where they worked beside older men who were more skilled or highly paid. The senior men teased the youngsters, sending them out for a left-handed hammer or making them the butt of sometimes painful practical jokes, but they also showed kids the ropes and helped protect them from the foreman or boss. And they explained why "putting up with the crap" was worth it. After older men talk for a while about what these work experiences meant to them, they are almost always surprised to find themselves agreeing that the loss of nonparental male mentoring may be a bigger problem for boys today than the rise of single-mother homes.

Even allowing for nostalgia, such work relations seem to have been critical experiences for the socialization of many young men in the past. Such jobs integrated youths into adult society, teaching skills they would continue to use as they aged, instead of segregating them in a separate peer culture. As late as 1940, about 60 percent of employed adolescents aged 16–17 worked in traditional workplaces, such as farms, factories, or construction sites. The jobs

they did there, or at least the skills they used, might last well into their adult lives. By 1980, only 14 percent worked in such settings (Greenberger and Steinberg 1986).

Girls, who were excluded from many such jobs, have lost less in this arena of life. Up through the 1960s an adolescent girl typically had more responsibilities at home, from washing dishes to taking care of siblings, than she does today. While such tasks may have prepared girls for adult roles as wives and mothers, they also held girls back from further education or preparation for future work outside the home. The change in work patterns for girls has thus made it *easier* for them to see that they have paths toward adult independence. On the other hand, it raises a different set of tensions between girls and their parents. The decline of the sexual double standard, without an equal decline in economic and social discrimination against women, leads parents to worry that their daughters may have too much opportunity, too early, to engage in sexual risk taking for which girls still pay a far higher price than boys.

Another issue facing teens of both sexes is their increasing exclusion from public space. People talk about how kids today are unsupervised, and they often are; but in one sense teens are under *more* surveillance than in the past. Almost anyone about the age of 40 can remember places where young people could establish real physical, as opposed to psychic, distance from adults. In the suburbs it was undeveloped or abandoned lots and overgrown woods, hidden from adult view, often with old buildings that you could deface without anyone caring. In the cities it was downtown areas where kids could hang out. Many of these places are now gone, and only some kids feel comfortable in the malls that have replaced them.

Much has been written about the gentrification of public space in America, the displacement of the poor or socially marginal from their older niches, followed by fear and indignation from respectable people suddenly forced to actually see the homeless doing what they always used to do. Over the years we have also seen what I think of as an "adultification" of public space. Kids are usually allowed there, as long as they're young enough to be in their parents' charge. But where in your town are teenagers welcome on their own?

Teens today have fewer opportunities than in the past for gradual initiation into productive activities, both at home and in public, and fewer places to demonstrate their autonomy in socially approved ways. At the same time, though, they have more access to certain so-called adult forms of consumption than ever before. This makes it hard for adults to avoid the extremes of overly controlling, lock-'em-up positions on the one hand and frequent breakdowns of supervision on the other. Some parents clearly underprotect their kids. We've all seen parents who are too stressed to monitor their kids effectively or who have had their limits overrun so many times that they have given up. Other parents, however, overprotect their kids, trying to personally compensate for the loss of wider adult contacts and of safe retreats. Both extremes drive kids away. But, in most cases, both are reactions to structural dilemmas facing parents and teens rather than abdications of parental responsibility.

What Social Science Tells Us About Male–Female Conflicts

The same kind of perspective can be useful in sorting through conflicts between modern couples. I vividly remember the first people who forced me to bring my historical and social analysis down to individual cases. Following one of my talks, a couple stood up and described a conflict they were having in their marriage. She complained about how unappreciative he was of the effort she took in making gourmet dinners and keeping the house clean. He said: "Hang on a minute. I never asked her to do any of those things. I can't help it if she has higher standards than I do. I don't *care* what we have for dinner. I don't *care* if the floor gets mopped twice a week." They wanted me to comment on their situation.

This is not fair, I thought, as I tried to wriggle out of doing so. I've just summed up the history of family diversity and changing gender roles since colonial times and they want me to settle a marital argument—over housework, of all things? I'm not a counselor; I don't know anything about mediating these issues. I tried to change the subject, but they wouldn't let up, and the audience was clearly on their side. You think family history is relevant, they seemed to be saying. Prove it.

Trapped, but unwilling to pretend I had therapeutic expertise, I cast about for something in my own research or training that might by any stretch of the imagination be helpful. The only thing that came to mind was a concept I had read about in an academic journal. "So," I said, feeling a bit silly, "perhaps the problem we have here lies in what social scientists would call your 'situated social power'" (Wartenberg 1988).

It sounded very academic, even downright pompous, but the more we talked about it, the more I realized this *was* a useful concept for them. In plain English it means that various groups in society have unequal access to economic resources, political power, and social status, and these social differences limit how fair or equal a personal relationship between two individuals from different groups can really be. Such social imbalances affect personal behavior regardless of sincere intentions of both parties to "not let it make a difference."

Teachers, for example, have social power over students. I tell my students that I want them to speak their minds and express their disagreements with me. And I mean it. But often I don't even notice that they continue to defer until someone finally gets angry at me for "dominating the discussion." Even after all these years, my initial reaction is usually indignation. "I told you to speak up," I want to say; "it's not my fault if you hold back." Then I remind myself that in any situation of unequal power, it's the party with the most power who always assumes that other people can act totally free of outside constraints.

When a person with power pretends not to have it, people with less power feel doubly vulnerable. Although they continue to be unequal, they are now asked to put aside the psychological defenses they have constructed against that inequality, including a certain amount of self-protective guardedness. So they clam up or get sore, which leaves the more powerful person feeling that his or her big-hearted gestures are being rebuffed. This tension arises between people of different races and classes, between employees and supervisors, and between men and women, as well as between my students and me.

With this awareness, I try to remember that my students are never going to feel as free criticizing my work as I'm going to feel criticizing theirs. I have to adjust the structure of my class to facilitate discussion. I need to institute protected spaces for criticism, such as providing anonymous evaluation forms for assessing my performance. But I also have to recognize that our power imbalance will always create tensions between us. I should neither blame my students for that nor feel that I've failed to communicate my "authentic self" to them. None of us exists independently of the social relations in which we operate.

Remembering how helpful this concept is to me in depersonalizing conflicts with students, I reminded the couple that men and women have different options in our society, outside and independent of their personal relationships. Research shows that men are happiest in a relationship when they don't have to do much housework and yet meals get made, clothes get

ironed, and the house looks good. This doesn't mean they are chauvinist pigs. Who *wouldn't* be happier under those conditions?

But the wives of such men tend to be depressed. A wife may feel, especially if she jeopardized her earning power by taking time off to raise children, that she can't give up the domestic services she performs, because if her husband *does* get dissatisfied, she has fewer options than he does in the work world, and will be far worse off after a divorce.

Consciously or not, the wife in this particular marriage seemed to be assessing the risk of not keeping a nice house or putting delicious meals on the table, and finding it too high to just relax and let the housework go. But she was also resenting her husband's unwillingness to help out. This very common pattern of seemingly voluntary sacrifice by the woman, followed by resentment for the man's failure to reciprocate, originates outside the individual relationship. The man was probably completely sincere about not caring if the work got done, but he was missing the point. His wife had looked around, seen what happened to wives who failed to please their husbands, and tried extra hard to make her husband happy. He could not understand her compulsion, and resented being asked to participate in what he saw as unnecessary work. Counseling and better communication might help, but would probably not totally remove the little kernel of fear in the wife's heart that stems from her perfectly reasonable assessment of the unequal social and economic options for men and women.

Similarly, two people trying to raise a child while they both work full-time are going to get stressed or angry. Part of the problem may be that the man isn't doing enough at home (on average, research shows, having a man in the house *adds* hours to a woman's workday) (Brace, Lloyd, and Leonard 1995; Hartmann 1981). Part of the problem may be that the woman is sabotaging her own stated desire to have the man do more—treating him as an unskilled assistant, refusing to relinquish her control over child-raising decisions, and keeping her domestic standards too high for him to meet. But another part of the problem will remain even if they are the most enlightened individuals in the world.

There's no nonstressful way to divide three full-time jobs between two individuals. Better communication can make the sacrifices more fair, or help clear away the side issues that get entangled with the stress, but the strains are a social problem existing outside the relationship. The solution does not lie in Martians learning to talk Venusian or Venusians being tolerant of the cultural oddities of Martians, as one pop psychologist describes the differences between men and women, but in changing the job structures and social support networks for family life. Until businesses and schools adjust their hours and policies to the realities of two-earner families, even the best-intentioned couples are going to have difficult times.

Improving communication or using the shortcuts offered by self-help books can alleviate some of the conflicts between men and women in this period of rapidly changing roles and expectations. But addressing communication problems alone ignores the differing social options and the patterned experiences of inequality that continually *re-create* such problems between men and women. So people move from one self-help book to another; they try out new encounter groups and memorize new techniques; they slip back and must start all over again. They are medicating the symptoms without solving the problem.

For example, the Venusian–Martian reference comes from best-selling author John Gray, who has found a strikingly effective analogy for getting men and women to realize that they bring different assumptions and experiences to relationships: Men and women, he says, come from different planets. They need to learn each other's culture and language. Gray tells women why men's periodic

withdrawals from communication do not mean lack of interest in a relationship. Martians, he says, like to retreat to caves in times of stress, while Venusians tend to crowd around, offering each other support and empathy. He explains to men that women are often just asking for reassurance, not trying to control men's lives, when they pursue subjects past the male comfort zone (Gray 1992).

But Gray doesn't urge either sex to make any big changes, merely to take "tiny steps toward understanding the other." He offers women hints on how to ask their partners for help without antagonizing them or making them feel manipulated, but he doesn't demand that men share housework or that women accept the responsibilities that go with egalitarian relationships. For Gray, a healthy relationship exists "when both partners have permission to ask for what they want and need, and they both have permission to say no if they choose." This is certainly better than no one feeling free to ask, but it leaves a rather large set of issues unresolved (Gray 1992, 265; Peterson 1994).

The problem is that many advice books refuse to ask hard questions about the division of household work and decision-making power. In a section called "scoring points with the opposite sex," for example, Gray's advice to women revolves around issues such as not criticizing men for their driving or choice of restaurants. Men, by contrast, are advised: "offer to make dinner," "occasionally offer to wash the dishes," "compliment her on how she looks," "give her four hugs a day," and "don't flick the remote control to different channels when she is watching TV with you" (Gray 1992; Sen 1983).

Now, most women will say that the book would be worth its weight in gold if their husbands would just follow that last tip, but the fact remains that the unequal bargaining power and social support systems for men and women are not addressed, *or even acknowledged,* in this kind of advice. In the long run, failure to address the roots of gender differences perpetuates the problem of communication, or merely replaces one set of misunderstandings with another. As therapist Betty Carter writes, communicating about feelings rather than addressing issues of power and daily behavior can lead to manipulation that eventually degenerates into mutual blame and psychological name-calling (Carter 1996).[1] If we're going to think of men and women as being from different planets, they need more than guidebooks and language translations; we must make sure that the social, economic, and political treaties they operate under are fair to both parties.

It's not only women's dissatisfactions that are addressed by a historical and sociological perspective. Men often complain that feminists ignore male insecurities and burdens, and they have a point. Men *do* feel injured and alienated, despite their economic and political advantages over women of the same social group. But history and sociology can identify the sources of men's pain a lot more accurately than myths about the loss of some heroic age of male bonding when Australian aborigines, Chinese sun kings, and Greek warriors marched to their own drumbeat. Going "back to the woods" makes a nice weekend retreat, but it doesn't help men restructure their long-term relationships or identify the social, economic, and political changes they need to improve their family lives (Bly 1990).[2]

Male pain is the other side of male power. Not all men, contrary to the rhetoric of masculinity, can be at the top of the pyramid. The contrast between rhetoric and reality is very painful for men whose race, class, health, or even height does not allow them to wield power, exercise authority, or just cut a figure imposing enough to qualify as a "real man." Even successful men pay a high price for their control and authority. The competitive, hierarchical environments men are encouraged to operate in cut them off from intimacy and penalize them for letting down their guard. The myth that male power is all individually achieved, not socially structured, means masculinity can be lost if it is not constantly proven in daily behavior (Brines 1994; Lehne 1989).

Structural analysis helps us get beyond the question of "who hurts more" to explore the different rewards and penalties that traditional gender roles impose on today's men and women. For girls, societal pressures descend heavily at about age 11 or 12, penalizing them for excelling and creating a sharp drop in their self-esteem. There is overwhelming evidence, for example, that girls are treated in ways that hinder their academic and intellectual development. But sometimes this discrimination takes the form of too easy praise and too little pressure to complete a task, leading boys to feel that "girls get off easy." And almost any parent can testify that boys are subject to a much earlier, more abrupt campaign to extinguish the compassion, empathy, and expression of feelings that young boys initially display as openly as girls. The list of derogatory words for boys who don't act masculine is miles longer than the list of disparaging words for girls who don't act feminine. Boys who don't get the message quickly enough are treated brutally. Those who do get the message find that the very success of their effort to "be a man" earns mistrust and fear as well as admiration. In an article that my male students invariably love, Eugene August points out that people always talk about "innocent women and children" in describing victims of war or terrorism. Is there no such thing as an innocent man? (August 1992; Gilligan and Brown 1992;

---

[1]As Andrew Greeley points out (1989), women's morale has declined far more significantly than men's. Unless their frustrations with the marriage bargain are addressed more directly, not just placated, men and women *could* end up on different planets.

[2]For a critique of Bly's point of view, see Connell 1992.

Gilligan, Lyons, and Hammer 1990; Kann 1986; Orenstein 1994; Sadker and Sadker 1994).

It's good to get past caricatures of female victims and male villains, but it is too simplistic to say that we just have to accept our differences. A man's fear of failure and discomfort with intimacy, for example, come from his socially structured need to constantly have others affirm his competence, self-reliance, or superiority. This is the downside of what he must do to exercise power and privilege. For women, lack of power often leads to fear of *success*. The downside of women's comfort with intimacy is discomfort with asserting authority.

As three researchers in the psychology of gender summarize the tradeoffs, boys "get encouraged to be independent and powerful, possibly at the cost of distancing themselves from intimacy." The result is that boys "tend to be overrepresented in the psychopathologies involving aggression." Girls, by contrast, "get rewarded for being compliant and for establishing intimate relations, possibly at the cost of achieving autonomy and control over their choices." This may be why girls are "overrepresented in the psychopathologies involving depression" (Cowan, Cowan, and Kerig 1993, 190).

The solution suggested by historical and social analysis is not for men and women to feel each other's pain but to equalize their power and access to resources. That is the only way they can relate with fairness and integrity, so that unequal and therefore inherently dishonest relations do not deform their identities. Men must be willing to give up their advantages over women if they hope to build healthy relationships with either sex. Women must be willing to accept tough criticism and give up superficial "privileges" such as being able to cry their way out of a speeding ticket if they hope to develop the inner resources to be high achievers. . . .

References

Astroth, Kirk. 1993. "Beyond Ephebiphobia: Problem Adults or Problem Youths?" *Phi Delta Kappan,* January.

August, Eugene. 1992. "Real Men Don't: Anti-Male Bias in English." Pp. 131–141 in Melita Schaum and Connie Flanagan (eds.), *Gender Images: Reading for Composition.* Boston: Houghton Mifflin.

Bly, Robert. 1990. *Iron John: A Book About Men.* Reading, MA: Addison-Wesley.

Brace, Judith, Cynthia Lloyd, and Ann Leonard, with Patrice Engle and Niev Duffy. 1995. *Families in Focus: New Perspectives on Mothers, Fathers, and Children.* New York: The Population Council.

Brines, Julie. 1994. "Economic Dependency, Gender, and the Division of Labor at Home." *American Journal of Sociology* 100.

Carter, Betty. 1996. *Love, Honor, and Negotiate: Making Your Marriage Work.* New York: Pocket Books.

Connell, R. W. 1992. "Drumming Up the Wrong Tree." *Tikkun* 7.

Cowan, Philip A., Carolyn Pape Cowan, and Patricia K. Kerig. 1993. "Mothers, Fathers, Sons and Daughters: Gender Differences in Family Formation and Parenting Styles" in Philip Cowan et al., (eds.), *Family, Self, and Society: Toward a New Agenda for Family Research.* Hillsdale, NJ: Erlbaum.

Gilligan, Carol, and Lynn Mickel Brown. 1992. *Meeting at the Crossroads: Women's Psychology and Girls' Development.* Cambridge, MA: Harvard University Press.

Gilligan, Carol, Nona Lyons, and Trudy Hammer. 1990. *Making Connections: The Relational World of Adolescent Girls at Emma Willard School.* Cambridge, MA: Harvard University Press.

Gray, John. 1992. *Men Are from Mars, Women Are from Venus.* New York: HarperCollins.

Greeley, Andrew. 1989. "The Declining Morale of Women." *Sociology and Social Research* 73.

Greenberger, Ellen, and Laurence Steinberg. 1986. *When Teenagers Work: The Psychological and Social Costs of Adolescent Employment.* New York: Basic Books.

Hamburg, David. 1992. *Today's Children: Creating a Future for a Generation in Crisis.* New York: Times Books.

Hartmann, Heidi. 1981. "The Family as the Locus of Gender, Class and Political Struggle: The Example of Housework." *Signs* 6.

Holinger, Paul. 1994. *Suicide and Homicide Among Adolescents.* New York: Guilford.

Kann, Mark. 1986. "The Costs of Being on Top." *Journal of the National Association for Women Deans* 49.

Lehne, Gregory. 1989. "Homophobia Among Men: Supporting and Defining the Male Role." Pp. 416–429 in Michael Kimmel and Michael Messner (eds.), *Men's Lives.* New York: Macmillan.

Luker, Kristin. 1996. *Dubious Conceptions: The Politics of Teenage Pregnancy.* Cambridge, MA: Harvard University Press.

Maddrick, Jeffrey. 1995. *The End of Affluence: The Causes and Consequences of America's Economic Dilemma.* New York: Random House.

Males, Mike. 1996. *The Scapegoat Generation: America's War on Adolescents.* Monroe, ME: Common Courage Press.

Maton, Kenneth. 1990. "Meaningful Involvement in Instrumental Activity and Well-Being: Studies of Older Adolescents and At Risk Urban Teen-Agers." *American Journal of Community Psychology* 18.

Nightingale, Elena, and Lisa Wolverton. 1988. "Adolescent Rolelessness in Modern Society." Working paper, Carnegie Council on Adolescent Development, September.

———. 1994. "Sex and America's Teenagers." New York: Alan Guttmacher Institute.

Orenstein, Peggy. 1994. *School Girls: Young Women, Self-Esteem, and the Confidence Gap.* New York: Doubleday.

Peterson, Karen. 1994. "A Global Ambassador Between the Sexes." *USA Today,* March 28.

Sadker, Myra, and David Sadker. 1994. *Failing at Fairness: How American Schools Cheat Girls.* New York: Scribner.

Sen, Amartya. 1983. "Economics and the Family." *Asian Development Review* 1.

Steinberg, Laurence. 1992. "The Logic of Adolescence." In Peter Edelman and Joyce Ladner (eds.), *Adolescence and Poverty: Challenge for the 1990s.* Washington, DC: Center for National Policy Press.

Stone, L. J., and J. Church. 1968. *Childhood and Adolescence: A Psychology of the Growing Person.* New York: Random House.

Wartenberg, Thomas. 1988. "The Situated Concept of Social Power." *Social Theory and Practice* 14.

Questions

1. Would Mills conclude that Coontz has a sociological imagination? Why or why not?

2. What is "rolelessness"? As a teenager, did you experience (or are you now experiencing) this phenomenon? Explain.

3. What is "situated social power"? Describe an example of situated social power that you have experienced or witnessed personally.

4. Consider the concept of "adultification." To what extent did it exist in the place(s) where you grew up? Explain. How might this problem be resolved?

3
HERNANDO WASHINGTON

Lisa J. McIntyre

One of the things that sets sociologists apart from ordinary people is their concern for the social. In their professional lives, sociologists tend to ignore individual cases and focus on aggregates or groups. For example, Émile Durkheim studied suicide in order to discover what factors contributed to fluctuations in the overall rates of suicide; he had no interest in what might lead particular individuals to take their lives.

Professional sociologists study *social* facts simply because these are interesting (at least to us). But to the layperson trying to live life in society, social facts may seem irrelevant. Why a society's crime rate goes up and down seems much less intriguing than why *my* house was robbed, or why *I* was mugged on the street. Likewise, the social forces that propel the unemployment rate are not nearly as interesting as the matter of why I am having a difficult time finding a job.

As C. Wright Mills pointed out, however, having a sociological imagination allows us to make connections between individuals and the societies in which they live. And, for the student of sociology, the acquisition of this imagination brings with it an enhanced ability to make sense of the behavior of individuals. Recall what Mills stressed as the "first fruit" of the sociological imagination: "the idea that the individual can understand his own experience and gauge his own fate only by locating himself within his period." It was in this sense that Stephanie Coontz (in the previous reading) brought to bear the sociological concept of "situated social power" to help her understand her own relationships with her teaching assistants, as well as the personal troubles of the woman whose husband did not appreciate her heroic housework.

From the viewpoint of the professional sociologist, the following reading may seem out of place in a sociology reader, because its focus is on an individual and how he responded to his immediate social milieu. But I have included it for the benefit of nonsociologists; written in 1999, it provides an example of how having an understanding of the impact of the social milieu can help us to understand the all-too-frequently unintelligible behaviors of individuals in our environment.

To get a Ph.D., one has to write something called a dissertation. It's essentially a research paper, and sometimes a very long research paper. Mine, for example, ended up being two hundred plus pages. I wrote my dissertation on public defenders—those attorneys who are paid by the state to defend people who are accused of crimes but can't afford to hire their own lawyer. The basic question was this: How can these attorneys defend individuals they know are guilty of crimes, especially if they are terrible crimes? Ultimately, I arrived at my answer by looking not just at the private consciences of the public defenders but also

18

at what Mills would have called their social milieux or surroundings.

I met a number of murderers in the course of my research, but Hernando was my first one; and in part because he was my first, he left a large impression on me. But this crime also made a big impression on me because it seemed so bizarre. It never should have happened the way it did. But you can judge for yourself. I will tell you the story as I learned it.

Warning: The first time I heard this story, I remember being shocked. I remember, in fact, feeling nauseous. It's not because anyone showed me terrible pictures of the crime scene; it's just because the whole thing seemed so awful. And it *seemed* so awful because it *was* awful. That led me to wonder, Should I share this story with college students? Possibly, no one is (or should be) worldly enough to hear about this sort of thing.

The Case

This story takes place in Chicago. The major player in the story is a man named Hernando Washington. At various times, his nicknames included the Reverend and the Deacon, because he was president of the youth choir. His other nickname was Prince, because he was so charming and good-looking.

Before I get to the story, let me tell you a bit about the neighborhood in which Hernando lived, or as Mills would put it, his *social milieu*. It was on the South Side of Chicago. In a song from the 1970s, Jim Croce called the South Side of Chicago "the baddest part of town." That was an astute observation. It is the baddest part of town; chances are, if you lived on the South Side, you'd never be able to get a cab driver to take you home at night; some cabs won't even venture there in the daytime.

The police refer to a murder that involves a man and woman on the South Side as a "South Side divorce." A great deal of its reputation involves the fact that the South Side of Chicago is heavily populated by people who are poor—mostly African Americans. Perhaps that's why the police tend to disrespect the people who live there. The police often call murders that involve African American killers and victims as "63rd Street misdemeanors." Police also take much longer to respond to calls on the South Side. The clear message to the people who live there is that they really aren't a part of the community that the Chicago police are pledged to "serve and to protect." This, I think, is an important fact.

On April 1, 1978, Hernando "Prince" Washington was arrested and charged with robbery, aggravated kidnapping, rape, and murder. His victim, 29-year-old Sarah Gould, was the wife of a physician and the mother of a small child. Sarah Gould had the great misfortune to be one of the 787 people in Chicago and one of the 20,432 people in the United States who were murdered that year.

When I say that Sarah had the "great misfortune" to be murdered, I mean that. Statistically, she should not have been a murder victim. Nationally, the murder rate for white women in 1978 was 2.8 per 100,000 population. For white men, it was 9.0; for black women, 12.8; and for black men, 58.1. Not only was Sarah white, but she was killed by a stranger. And in 1978, most murder victims were killed by people they knew—friends, lovers, family members, acquaintances, or neighbors. Of all the recorded acts of criminal violence—batteries, assaults, murders—in 1978, less than a third were committed by strangers. This was especially true for women: When the violent act was committed by a stranger, the victim was typically male.

Finally, Sarah Gould was white while Hernando was black. This was one of the more unusual aspects of the case. Most violence, and certainly most murders, involve persons of the same race.

So, the odds were really against Sarah Gould being murdered—however you want to look at it.

That year, April 1, April Fool's Day, fell on a Saturday. The story actually begins two days earlier. That Thursday afternoon, Hernando went out to do his sister Leah a favor. She had just bought a car, a used two-year-old Oldsmobile Cutlass, and the dealer had called the day before to tell her it was ready to be picked up. Hernando offered to do this for her, partly because he wanted to drive the car. His sister, who is ten years older than Hernando, said that would be fine as long as Hernando came to pick her up when she was done with work. Leah worked at the post office and got off work ten minutes before midnight.

Hernando picked up the car, but of course he didn't drive it straight home. Instead, he cruised around his South Side neighborhood for a while. However, he didn't see any of his friends, so he decided to cruise up to the north part of the city.

For Sarah Gould, that was a fatal decision.

Hernando later said he didn't have any particular plan, but eventually he admitted that just maybe, in the back of his mind, he thought he might rob someone. But it was nothing definite. He would simply drive around and see what happened.

Once up north, he drove to Northwestern University's hospital parking lot. He got out of his car and sat on the steps of a nearby building.

ROBBERY AND ABDUCTION

Around 7:30 P.M., Hernando saw a woman getting out of a reddish-orange VW Rabbit. He approached her, gun in hand, and demanded her money. Sarah gave him $25, explaining that it was all the money she had, but he grabbed her by the arm, dragged her back to his car, and shoved her inside.

Later, when asked why he did that, he told his lawyers that he'd noticed a bunch of people walking toward them and he didn't want them to know that he had just robbed this woman. He said he was afraid that she'd scream or run or something.

Once Hernando got Sarah into the car, he was still afraid that she'd somehow make trouble, so he ordered her to take off her slacks and underpants. He threw her clothing underneath her car and then drove off.

In his confession to the police, Hernando had this to say:

> She was real excited, you know, asking me not to hurt her and I was constantly telling her I wouldn't hurt her, that all I want is money. She was sitting in the front seat alongside of me. We drove off, and she asked me, "What are you going to do to me?" and I told her that I would take her away from the area, so I would have a chance, you know, to get away without being caught.

He kept assuring her that he would not hurt her.

THE PHONE CALL

After Hernando drove around for several hours, Sarah said that he should let her go because her husband and son would be getting worried about her. He considered this for a while and then asked her if she'd like to call home. He stopped at a gas station that was closed for the evening but it had a phone booth.

Sarah's husband, who was indeed worried about her, later told police that she had said something to the effect that she was okay. He asked her, "When are you coming home?" There was a pause, and then he could hear Sarah asking someone when she'd be home. In the background, he heard a male voice saying "an hour." He then asked, "Where are you?" She asked, "Where are we?" Her husband heard the answer: "You'll be home in an hour, bitch, come on."

After the phone call, Hernando told police,

> I turned from the phone, going around the car and at this time, when I, you know, walked around to my car, she broke and ran. I was running after her. I asked her, I said, "Why are you acting like that? I have not hurt you, I told you I will let you go, I just want to make it as safe for me as you want it safe for yourself."

Then, as it was approaching midnight, Hernando pulled the car into a dark alley. He explained to Sarah that he had to go pick someone up and that she couldn't stay in the front seat of the car while he did this. Perhaps for a moment Sarah thought he was going to let her go, but instead, he forced her into the trunk telling her that if she was quiet, everything would be okay.

At exactly 11:50 P.M., Hernando was where he was supposed to be—in the car in front of the main post office. His sister Leah came out and got into the front seat with him. As he drove her home, they talked about the sorts of things that you would expect a brother and sister to talk about—mostly about the new car.

When they got home, Hernando waited in the car until Leah was inside the house. He had always been very concerned about her safety.

A few years earlier, Leah had been raped on her way home from work. Two men grabbed her, dragged her into an alley, stripped off her clothes, and raped her repeatedly. Afterwards, she crawled out of the alley and was relieved to see a police car there. The two officers looked at her, a black woman with her face bleeding and her clothes torn up, and said "Get home by yourself, bitch." Maybe they didn't want her to mess up the back of their patrol car.

Usually, Hernando met his sister after work—but that night he'd had a bike accident and was running late.

Indeed, Hernando's family had not had a great deal of luck when it came to dealing with the police. A few years earlier, Hernando's brother James had been at a party when he was shot by one of the neighborhood guys. Some of James's friends took *him to the emergency room, but they were afraid to stay with him because gunshot wounds tend to attract attention. They left him in the emergency room, where he bled to death before the medical staff got to him. "Everyone knew" who had shot Hernando's brother, but for some reason the police didn't take him into custody. It was at that point that Hernando bought his first gun.*

Then Hernando drove a few blocks away, stopped, and let Sarah out of the trunk. She reminded him of his promise to let her go, but he said they'd have to go back and get her clothes, because he didn't want to let her go until she was fully dressed again. He drove back to the hospital parking lot, but her clothes were gone; by now, the police had them.

When Sarah had driven into that parking lot earlier in the evening, she was on her way to a Lamaze class she was supposed to teach that night. Eventually, her students became worried about her, called her husband, and found out that she wasn't home. And, of course, he thought she was in class. Next, the class notified hospital security, which investigated and found Sarah's car in the parking lot. When they saw her keys in the ignition and her pants and underpants under the car, the security officers were naturally concerned. They called her husband, who immediately called the police to file a missing person's report.

Finding the clothes missing from under the car scared Hernando. Sarah told him that it didn't matter, that she could go home without them—she was covered enough, she said, by her long raincoat. But he was adamant that he wasn't going to let her go until he'd found her something to wear or, as he put it, until she was "decent" again. He said, "I've got to think of somewhere to get you some clothes."

THE RAPE

By now, it was well past midnight. Hernando thought it was much too late to go to a friend's house and borrow some clothes, so instead, he drove them back down to the South Side. On the way, he stopped and bought a pint of rum, leaving Sarah alone in the car for a moment. Then, he drove to a motel, got out of the car (again leaving Sarah in the front seat alone), registered for a room—in his name. He later told police, "I let her wash up. First she was kind of skeptical. I guess she was frightened. I kept reassuring her that I would not do anything to her. After a while, she went into the bathroom and washed up." Then, he told police, they both went to sleep.

But that was a lie. What really happened next, as Hernando admitted to his attorneys, was that he raped Sarah.

The next morning, Hernando left Sarah alone in the room while he checked out. After they left the motel, he stopped the car and put her back into the trunk. Then he drove to his parents' house to get a change of clothing for himself.

A few blocks later, Hernando let Sarah out of the trunk. Then he drove to a northwestern suburb where he had an appointment. On the way, he again stopped in an alley and forced her into the trunk while he "took care of some business."

What was this urgent appointment? Hernando's "appointment" was in one of the felony trial courtrooms in Cook County, Illinois. At the time all this was going on, Hernando was out on bail. A year earlier, Hernando had been arrested on charges of rape and aggravated kidnapping. His parents had taken out a loan, paid his bail, and hired him a private lawyer, who told Hernando that he would probably beat the rap and not to worry.

In any case, that Friday, March 31, was the scheduled trial date for the year-old rape case. When the case was called, however, the prosecutor requested a continuance, which the judge granted. Feeling good, Hernando walked out of the courtroom a relatively free

man; he even offered his lawyer's assistant a ride back downtown.

When Hernando got back to his car, he saw a couple of people standing near it, seemingly talking to his trunk. Hernando told them to get lost and sped away. But one of the people got Hernando's license plate number and called it in to the police. The dispatcher who took the call about a "woman in the trunk" relayed the message to the detective division; someone placed it on a detective's desk.

Unfortunately, that particular detective had taken off—unannounced—for the weekend, and so no one found the message until the next morning. By then, it was too late. Sarah was dead.

Hernando let Sarah out of the trunk and told her he was disappointed that she'd tried to get help. After all, hadn't he told her that he wasn't going to hurt her and that he would let her go as soon as she got some clothes?

Hernando drove around for a while, and then, as he later told his lawyers, he noticed how dirty her raincoat was. Once again, he told Sarah that he just had to find some decent clothes for her. And once again, she protested that it really wasn't necessary, that she could get home without being fully dressed. Instead, Hernando went to the home of an old girlfriend to borrow some clothes. But he ended up not getting any clothes, claiming that he just didn't quite know how to ask and that her boyfriend was home and he didn't want the boyfriend to hear.

So he released Sarah from the trunk and drove around some more.

As evening approached, Hernando put Sarah back into the trunk of the car and went to meet some friends at a bar. Actually, they ended up going to several bars. He was, he said, getting pretty tired, but he liked being with his friends. And he was "reluctant" to go back to his car because he knew he'd have to deal with this problem. Finally, well after midnight, he returned to the car.

At this point, as they were listening to Hernando tell his story, one of his attorneys asked him, "If you were beginning to be uncomfortable about your situation, why didn't you just let her go, then and there?" Hernando said, "Because the neighborhood I was in wasn't a safe neighborhood for a white woman to be alone in."

Instead of letting her go, he took Sarah to another motel and again raped her. Details about the rape are sketchy because Hernando was a "little shy," as he put it, when it came to talking about "sex." And that's how he referred to the rapes—as sex.

THE MURDER

Early the next morning, Hernando checked out of the motel, drove around for about an hour, and then came to a decision: Clothing or no clothing, it was time to let Sarah go. He parked the car on a residential street, gave her some change, and told her to get on the bus. He said he told her, "All you got to do is walk straight down the street there and get on the bus. Go straight home."

And Sarah, as Hernando always emphasized when he got to this part of the story, Sarah Gould *promised* him that she would get on the bus and go straight home. And, of course, she *promised* not to tell the police.

Hernando let Sarah out of the car, and as he drove away, she was walking toward the bus stop. But, as soon as he was out of sight, she changed her course, walked up to a house, and rang the doorbell.

The house belonged to a Chicago firefighter, who was getting ready for work. He opened the door and saw Sarah—messy, dirty, bruised, and distraught. She told him that she needed help; he told her that he would call the police and that she should stay right there on the porch. Then he closed the door and went to phone the police.

Meanwhile, Hernando had begun to wonder whether Sarah had kept her promise and gotten on the bus. So he doubled back to where he had left her. He saw Sarah standing on the porch of that house; he saw the firefighter talking to her; he saw the firefighter close the door.

As Hernando recounted it, he felt betrayed—she had broken her promise to him. He parked and got out of the car. He said that he called out to her. In Hernando's words, here's what happened next:

> I called to her and she came down. I took her by the arm and around the corner to the alley.
>
> I said, "What are you doing? All you had to do was get on the bus. You promised that you would get on the bus."
>
> She protested that I was hurting her, that I was going to kill her.
>
> I said, "No. All you had to do was get on the bus!"
>
> She screamed, "You are going to kill me!"
>
> I said, "No, you said you was going to get on the bus. All you had to do was to get on the bus. Stop screaming. I'm not going to hurt you."
>
> She said, "You are going to kill me."
>
> I said, "I am not going to kill you, shut up, stop screaming."
>
> She said, "You are going to kill me. You are going to kill me."
>
> I said, "I am not going to kill you."
>
> She said, "You are going to kill me. I know you are going to kill me."
>
> So I shot her. Then I shot her again. She fell. I looked at her, then I broke and ran to my car.

The Chicago firefighter kept his promise and called the police, but they were too late to save Sarah. Around one of her wrists was a cloth stamped with Hernando's father's name. When the police asked the firefighter why he didn't let Sarah into his home, he said that when he saw how beat up she was and saw a black man out on the street calling to her, he assumed it was a domestic dispute and didn't want to get in the middle of it.

Shortly thereafter, the police found Hernando at his parents' home, washing the trunk of his car. At first, he denied everything. Then, when police confronted him with the fact that witnesses had said he had a woman in the trunk of his car, he said it was a prostitute. He varied his story every time the police introduced more information. The police were gentle with him; they read him his Miranda rights, they offered him food and drink. But they confused him with their questions, and it didn't take too long for Hernando to confess to having robbed, kidnapped, and murdered Sarah.

But when police asked Hernando to sign the confession, he refused, saying that it might make his attorney mad. It didn't matter. That attorney didn't really want to have anything to do with Hernando the murderer, and besides, his parents had no money left to pay him.

Before his trial, his new attorneys—public defenders—persuaded him that his only chance to beat the death penalty was to plead guilty. This was one of those cases that defense attorneys in Chicago, not without a certain amount of irony, call a "dead bang loser case"—one in which "the state has everything but a videotape of the crime." At first, Hernando didn't want to plead guilty; he didn't want his parents to know that he was guilty. But ultimately, in hopes of saving his own life, he did plead guilty.

It didn't work. In January 1980, Hernando was sentenced to death. Finally, on March 25, 1995, after his appeals were exhausted, Hernando was executed by lethal injection.

Hernando's lawyers spend a lot of time trying to find some explanation for what happened. Maybe if they could understand what had been going on in his mind, it would help to save his life. But Hernando couldn't really say. What he kept saying, in essence, was, "What is the big deal? Why is everyone so upset with me?" It was not that, in his mind, Hernando did not understand that robbery, kidnapping, rape, and murder are against the law. The fact that he at first denied doing them helped to prove that. So, Hernando was not legally insane—in the sense that he didn't know right from wrong. It was simply that he could not understand why everyone was so worked up about what he had done.

This is difficult for most of us to understand. Why would someone be surprised at getting into really serious trouble for robbing, kidnapping, raping, and murdering another human being? At first, I could not make any sense of Hernando's confusion on this point. But eventually, as my horror receded, I was able to bring a more sociological perspective to bear on the whole subject. In other words, I had to call upon my sociological imagination—I had to look for the general in the particular.

Let me begin my explanation with an analogy. Last semester, in my introductory class, two students decided to turn in the same paper. They weren't in the same section, so I guess they thought they could get away with it. Unfortunately for them, in my department the professors discuss the papers because we want to be sure that we are all grading consistently. We noticed that the two students had submitted the same paper, so we called them in and said, "Hey, you cheated. And, as it says in the syllabus, if you cheat, you flunk."

At first, in each case, the students denied the accusation. However, when confronted with positive proof (copies of the papers with their names on them), they admitted what they had done. But, they said, our reaction was way out of line. Yes, they had read in the syllabus that getting caught cheating meant flunking the course. But flunking was simply *too much* punishment. In one case, flunking meant more than getting an F; it meant losing scholarship and loan money.

Hernando's reaction was much the same: "Okay, I did this, but you shouldn't punish me; certainly you shouldn't punish me this much."

You may be thinking that my analogy isn't really appropriate, that there is no way to compare students who cheat with people who murder. And, of course, I would not compare the behaviors. What I am comparing is how the individuals thought about their acts, and especially their reactions to the punishment.

Both the murder and the cheating were done in hopes of not getting caught; and in neither case did the perpetrators plan on getting caught. Furthermore, when they were caught, each thought the punishment was way out of proportion to the crime. In the case of the students, they argued that the consequences were much too severe, that cheating on a paper wasn't that bad and that losing a scholarship is unfair. In part, too, I think the students were shocked to find that we actually were going to flunk them. I suspect that to the degree they thought about it in advance, they expected to be given another chance, or to receive some lesser punishment. It's possible that they knew of other students who had been caught but not punished for cheating. In any case, their view was that punishment was unfair.

Hernando's reaction was much the same. He acted as if he thought that people were simply too worked up over his deeds. Being sentenced to death was just not acceptable to him. Like our students, he showed no real remorse for what he had done. He was only sorry that he had been caught and had to deal with the consequences.

Again, I suspect that some of you won't like my analogy. Perhaps you can understand why the students might feel that the punishment for cheating was too harsh. But you might wonder how Hernando could think that he should not be given the more serious punishment for what he'd done wrong.

This is where having a sociological imagination becomes helpful. The students felt abused because they did not see cheating as such a horrendous crime. After all, cheating happened all the time, and in any case, it was only a class paper.

The same kind of logic can be used to explain Hernando's reaction. Recall that Hernando had grown up on Chicago's South Side, where, when a husband killed his wife, it was jokingly referred to by police as a "South Side divorce." That sort of attitude from officials teaches people that life is not very valuable. And, as I mentioned previously, Hernando had learned some more personal, and painful, lessons about the low value placed on life. When his sister was raped, the police would not help her; they would not even give her a ride home. Also, when his brother was murdered, no one moved to identify the killer, much less to arrest him.

What I did not stress was the degree to which Hernando himself had committed violent acts against others. I did mention that he was out on bail on a rape and kidnapping charge, but in addition to that, he had raped at least three other women. No charges were brought in any of those cases—perhaps because they were not reported, for his victims knew there would be little point. *Those* victims also lived on the South Side.

What about the one charge he did have against him? Hernando's parents had mortgaged their home to get him a private lawyer, who told him he would beat the rape charge. Again, Hernando got the same message: His acts had no consequences. As a result of his life experiences, Hernando had learned that human life doesn't count for too much and that it's okay to take what you want. That's why he was so surprised that he was in so much trouble.

Let's look at what two psychiatrists had to say about Hernando.

> He appeared to mask any signs of strong emotions and states that "this is typical for me." He gave an example of—if he were upset about something and it pertained mostly to himself, he wouldn't reveal it to anyone. He would give the impression that he didn't have any feelings, and that he does not reveal his real emotions. . . .
> He shows a recall of dates and times not in

synchrony with reality—this, together with his difficulty with complex problem solving and concept formation—shows impairment, possibly indicative of minimal brain dysfunction. . . .

The evaluation of this man indicates that he is suffering from a borderline personality disorder with episodic deterioration in reality testing and thought processes with episodic psychotic thinking. There is the impression of someone who may be seen as withdrawn or aloof, with a superficial intellectual achievement in the use of language which masks a lowered intellectual achievement. There is also the indication of a minimal brain damage, which combined with his psychological profile, would indicate that at times of stress (as existed prior to the commission of the alleged offense) he lacks the ability to plan and to comprehend to the consequences of action.

He has at best a fragile purchase on reality. He feels overwhelmed by external stimulation and must constantly narrow his perceptual field in order to manage it. These overwhelmed feelings include those of inferiority and paranoia. While he generally stays close to the normal bounds of reality, he does occasionally lapse into abnormal perception and thinking. His capacity to recover from such lapses is the major reason for forgoing a diagnosis of schizophrenia. In general, his thinking and perception are idiosyncratic. He often does not see what others see. The mode of this distortion is to experience and understand the world in ways that are egocentric and sociopathic. . . . [The results of projective tests] present a picture of a highly impoverished internal world where fantasy and imagination are often enacted according to the most basic laws of "kill or be killed," or "eat or be eaten."

Note that this second psychiatrist stressed his expert opinion that *Hernando did not have much of a grasp of reality.* The psychiatrist made that judgment because Hernando persisted in seeing the world as a jungle in which the rule is to kill or be killed.

If this psychiatrist had possessed a sociological imagination, he might have realized that Hernando actually had an uncannily accurate grasp of reality. The understanding of his world as one in which the most basic law was kill or be killed was no delusion or misunderstanding; that was the way things worked on the South Side of Chicago. The very structure of social life in that part of the city meant that people were vulnerable—without help from the police, they had only themselves to fall back on.

But Hernando, too, lacked a sociological imagination—the ability to see beyond his own immediate social milieu, to understand that there are different rules for different people in places like Chicago. On the South Side, where the population is mostly poor and mostly African American, people don't have much power to call on "the establishment" to help them, so life is like a jungle. But on the North Side, things are different. When Hernando drove his sister's car to the North Side of Chicago, he made a fatal error because he drove into a part of the world where life does have value.

On the face of it, we seemingly can never understand what Hernando did. However, it is easier to understand if we use our sociological imagination (as Mills told us to do) and look past Hernando to his social milieu or environment. Then, things begin to make sense.

Don't get me wrong! I'm not saying that we should excuse Hernando for what he did because of the harsh environment in which he grew up. That's not the point. And certainly, that's not the *sociological* point. The goal of sociology is to understand and make predictable people's behavior, to explain what can lead people to act as they do.

What's the benefit of this sort of sociological thinking? What if it were your job to help prevent such crimes? Wouldn't you want to understand how the social environment affects people so that you could, if possible, make changes in that environment? Wouldn't you want to have a sociological imagination?

Mini-Glossary

borderline personality disorder a personality disorder characterized by a long-standing pattern of instability in mood, interpersonal relationships, and self-image. Frequently severe enough to cause extreme distress or interfere with social and occupational functioning.

egocentric centered around and focused on the self.

idiosyncratic a personal reaction (not shared by other people).

minimal brain dysfunction a relatively mild impairment of brain function which has subtle effects on perception, behavior, and academic ability.

psychotic a form of thinking in which the individual has inaccurate perceptions. Specific symptoms of psychosis include delusions, hallucinations, markedly incoherent speech, disorientation, and confusion. Psychotic individuals generally do not know that they are confusing reality and fantasy.

sociopathic like "psychopathic," a term for what is now usually called "antisocial personality disorder." This disorder is characterized by chronic and continuous antisocial behavior (and is not due to severe mental retardation, schizophrenia, or manic episodes). This behavior pattern, which is more common in males than in females, generally begins before the age of 15 with such infractions as lying, stealing, fighting, truancy, vandalism, theft, drunkenness, and substance abuse. It then continues after age 18 with at least four of the following manifestations: inability to work consistently, inability to function as a responsible parent, repeated violations of the law, inability to maintain an enduring sexual relationship, frequent fights and beatings inside and outside the home, failure to repay debts and provide child support, travel from place to place without planning, repeated lying and conning, and extreme recklessness in driving and other activities.

Questions

1. After I tell them about Hernando, students frequently ask me: "Why didn't Sarah Gould escape? She seemed to have so many chances, why didn't she take advantage of them?" Because I never had an opportunity to speak with Sarah, I will never know the answers for sure, but like my students, I can't help but wonder about it.

    The sociologist Max Weber introduced sociologists to the concept of *verstehen*—that's a German term meaning "empathic understanding." According to Weber, one way to better our understanding of people's behavior is to use empathy to put ourselves in their places to determine what they were thinking and feeling about their situations. With this concept in mind, why do you think Sarah didn't try to escape from Hernando?

2. Assume that you are a sociologist who is presented with the opportunity to act as an investigator for Hernando's defense team. In that role, you have the opportunity to ask questions of everyone involved in the case—Hernando himself; his attorneys, family, friends, and psychiatrists; and Sarah Gould's family and friends. Who would you want to interview? What questions would you ask?

3. Suppose you are the mayor of Chicago and you've just read all the facts of Hernando's murder of Sarah Gould. In a memo to your chief of police, what suggestions might you make to improve the structure of the city's law enforcement to help prevent this sort of crime from happening again?

4

MEN AS SUCCESS OBJECTS AND WOMEN AS SEX OBJECTS

A Study of Personal Advertisements

Simon Davis

As the following 1990 article recounts, Simon Davis used what social scientists refer to as an "unobtrusive method" to conduct his research. Unlike obtrusive methods—surveys, experiments, participant observation—in which the researcher's presence may have an effect on the people being studied, unobtrusive measures do not. Specifically Davis studied the personal ads that people place in newspapers. The research is unobtrusive because it is done after the fact, and none of the people being studied is aware of what's going on.

To give himself (and the readers) confidence in his findings, Davis used a basic statistical test known as "chi-square" (χ^2). This test enables the researcher to determine whether it's valid to say that a relationship exists between the variables being studied. How does that work?

Suppose you are gambling with a coin. We would expect, simply by chance, that the coin would come up heads about 50 percent of the time. But what if you got heads two times in a row? Would you conclude that something was fishy? No, two heads in a row is not that different from what you would expect from chance. But what if you got heads fifty times in a row? In this case, you would rightly be suspicious that something was wrong with the coin, that something other than random chance was operating.

If two heads are okay but fifty heads make you suspicious, what about three heads? Four heads? Ten heads? At what point do you begin to suspect that the outcome is not owing to random chance? To determine where to draw the line, we would use something like a chi-square test. Doing a chi-square test allows us to determine if what we actually get is significantly different statistically from what we would expect to get by chance.

"Men as Success Objects and Women as Sex Objects: A Study of Personal Advertisements" by Simon Davis from *Sex Roles,* Vol. 23, Nos. 1/2. Copyright © 1990. Reprinted with kind permission from Springer Science and Business Media.

The bottom line is this: When researchers report that their findings are "significant" or "statistically significant," they are saying that there is most likely a real relationship between the variables, that their findings are not owing merely to random chance.

consent
not their   but doesn't   show them   being true

Previous research has indicated that, to a large extent, selection of opposite-sex partners is dictated by traditional sex stereotypes (Urberg 1979). More specifically, it has been found that men tend to emphasize sexuality and physical attractiveness in a mate to a greater extent than women (e.g., Deaux and Hanna 1984; Harrison and Saeed 1977; Nevid 1984); this distinction has been found across cultures, as in the study by Stiles and colleagues (1987) of American and Icelandic adolescents.

The relatively greater preoccupation with casual sexual encounters demonstrated by men (Hite 1987, 184) may be accounted for by the greater emotional investment that women place in sex; Basow (1986, 80) suggests that the "gender differences in this area (different meaning attached to sex) may turn out to be the strongest of all gender differences."

Women, conversely, may tend to emphasize psychological and personality characteristics (Curry and Hock 1981; Deaux and Hanna 1984), and to seek longevity and commitment in a relationship to a greater extent (Basow 1986, 213).

Women may also seek financial security more so than men (Harrison and Saeed 1977). Regarding this last point, Farrell (1986, 25) suggests that the tendency to treat men as success objects is reflected in the media, particularly in advertisements in women's magazines. On the other hand, men themselves may reinforce this stereotype in that a number of men still apparently prefer the traditional marriage with working husband and unemployed wife (Basow 1986, 210).

Men have traditionally been more dominant in intellectual matters, and this may be reinforced in the courting process: Braito (1981) found in his study that female coeds feigned intellectual inferiority with their dates on a number of occasions. In the same vein, Hite, in her 1981 survey, found that men were less likely to seek intellectual prowess in their mate (108).

The mate selection process has been characterized in at least two ways. Harrison and Saeed (1977) found evidence for a matching process, where individuals seeking particular characteristics in a partner were more likely to offer those characteristics in themselves. This is consistent with the observation that "like attracts like" and that husbands and wives tend to resemble one another in various ways (Thiessen and Gregg 1980). Additionally, an exchange process may be in operation, wherein a trade-off is made with women offering "domestic work and sex for financial support" (Basow 1986, 213).

With respect to sex stereotypes and mate selection, the trend has been for "both sexes to believe that the other sex expects them to live up to the gender stereotype" (Basow 1986, 209).

Theoretical explanations of sex stereotypes in mate selection range from the sociobiological (Symons 1987) to radical political views (Smith, 1973). Of interest in recent years has been demographic influences, that is, the lesser availability of men because of population shifts and marital patterns (Shaevitz 1987, 40). Age may differentially affect women, particularly when children are desired; this, combined with women's generally lower economic status [particularly when unmarried (Halas 1981, 124)], may mean that the need to "settle down" into a secure, committed relationship becomes relatively more crucial for women.

quality looked for
→ Did not specify to style
people out / not individualized, grouping in generalized categories
unlike myers

The present study looks at differential mate selection by men and women as reflected in newspaper companion ads. Using such a forum for the exploration of sex stereotypes is not new; for instance, in the study by Harrison and Saeed (1977) cited earlier, the authors found that in such ads women were more likely to seek financial security and men to seek attractiveness; a later study by Deaux and Hanna (1984) had similar results, along with the finding that women were more likely to seek psychological characteristics, specific personality traits, and to emphasize the quality and longevity of the relationship. The present study may be seen as a follow-up of this earlier research, although on this occasion using a Canadian setting. Of particular interest was the following: Were traditional stereotypes still in operation, that is, women being viewed as sex objects and men as success objects (the latter defined as financial and intellectual accomplishments)?

Method

Personal advertisements were taken from the *Vancouver Sun,* which is the major daily newspaper serving Vancouver, British Columbia. The *Sun* is generally perceived as a conservative, respectable journal—hence it was assumed that people advertising in it represented the "mainstream." It should be noted that people placing the ads must do so in person. For the sake of this study, gay ads were not included. A typical ad would run about 50 words, and included a brief description of the person placing it and a list of the attributes desired by the other party. Only the parts pertaining to the attributes desired in the partner were included for analysis. Attributes that pertained to hobbies or recreations were not included for the purpose of this study.

The ads were sampled as follows: Only Saturday ads were used, since in the *Sun* the convention was for Saturday to be the main day for personal ads, with 40 to 60 ads per edition—compared to only 2 to 4 ads per edition on weekdays. Within any one edition *all* the ads were included for analysis. Six editions were randomly sampled, covering the period of September 30, 1988, to September 30, 1989. The attempt to sample through the calendar year was made in an effort to avoid an unspecified seasonal effect. The size of the sample (six editions) was large enough to meet goodness-of-fit requirements for statistical tests.

The attributes listed in the ads were coded as follows:

1. *Attractive:* specified that a partner should be, for example, "pretty" or "handsome."

2. *Physique:* similar to 1; however, this focused not on the face but rather on whether the partner was "fit and trim," "muscular," or had "a good figure." If it was not clear if body or face was being emphasized, this fell into variable (1) by default.

3. *Sex:* specified that the partner should have, for instance, "high sex drive," or should be "sensuous" or "erotic," or if there was a clear message that this was an arrangement for sexual purposes ("lunch-time liaisons—discretion required").

4. *Picture:* specified that the partner should include a photo in his/her reply.

5. *Profession:* specified that the partner should be a professional.

6. *Employed:* specified that the partner should be employed, e.g., "must hold steady job" or "must have steady income."

7. *Financial:* specified that the partner should be, for instance, "financially secure" or "financially independent."

8. *Education:* specified that the partner should be, for instance, "well educated"

or "well read," or should be a "college grad."

9. *Intelligence:* specified that the partner should be "intelligent," "intellectual," or "bright."

10. *Honest:* specified, for instance, that the partner should be "honest" or have "integrity."

11. *Humor:* specified "sense of humor" or "cheerfulness."

12. *Commitment:* specified that the relationship was to be "long term" or "lead to marriage," or some other indication of stability and longevity.

13. *Emotion:* specified that the partner should be "warm," "romantic," "emotionally supportive," "emotionally expressive," "sensitive," "loving," "responsive," or similar terms indicating an opposition to being cold and aloof.

In addition to the 13 attribute variables, two other pieces of information were collected: The length of the ad (in lines) and the age of the person placing the ad. Only if age was exactly specified was it included; if age was vague (e.g., "late 40s") this was not counted.

Variables were measured in the following way: Any ad requesting one of the 13 attributes was scored once for that attribute. If not explicitly mentioned, it was not scored. The scoring was thus "all or nothing," e.g., no matter how many times a person in a particular ad stressed that looks were important it was only counted as a single score in the "attractive" column; thus, each single score represented one person. Conceivably, an individual ad could mention all, some, or none of the variables. Comparisons were then made between the sexes on the basis of the variables, using percentages and chi-squares. Chi-square values were derived by cross-tabulating gender (male/female) with attribute (asked for/not asked for). Degrees of freedom in all cases

equaled one. Finally, several of the individual variables were collapsed to get an overall sense of the relative importance of (a) physical factors, (b) employment factors, and (c) intellectual factors.

Results *broader study*

A total of 329 personal ads were contained in the six newspaper editions studied. One ad was discarded in that it specified a gay relationship, leaving a total sample of 328. Of this number, 215 of the ads were placed by men (65.5%) and 113 by women (34.5%).

The mean age of people placing ads was 40.4. One hundred and twenty-seven cases (38.7%) counted as missing data in that the age was not specified or was vague. The mean age for the two sexes was similar: 39.4 for women (with 50.4% of cases missing) and 40.7 for men (with 32.6% of cases missing).

Sex differences in desired companion attributes are summarized in Table 1. It will be seen that for 10 of the 13 variables a statistically significant difference was detected. The three largest differences were found for attractiveness, professional and financial status. To summarize the table: in the case of attractiveness, physique, sex, and picture (physical attributes) the men were more likely than the women to seek these. In the case of professional status, employment status, financial status, intelligence, commitment, and emotion (nonphysical attributes) the women were more likely to seek these. The women were also more likely to specify education, honesty and humor, however not at a statistically significant level.

The data were explored further by collapsing several of the categories: the first 4 variables were collapsed into a "physical" category, variables 5–7 were collapsed into an "employment" category, and variables 8 and 9 were collapsed into an "intellectual" category. The

Table 1 Gender Comparison for Attributes Desired in Partner

Variable	Gender		Chi-square
	Desired by Men (*n* = 215)	Desired by Women (*n* = 113)	
1. Attractive	76 (35.3%)	20 (17.7%)	11.13[a]
2. Physique	81 (37.7%)	27 (23.9%)	6.37[a]
3. Sex	25 (11.6%)	4 (3.5%)	6.03[a]
4. Picture	74 (34.4%)	24 (21.2%)	6.18[a]
5. Profession	6 (2.8%)	19 (16.8%)	20.74[a]
6. Employed	8 (3.7%)	12 (10.6%)	6.12[a]
7. Financial	7 (3.2%)	22 (19.5%)	24.26[a]
8. Education	8 (3.7%)	8 (7.1%)	1.79 (ns)
9. Intelligence	22 (10.2%)	24 (21.2%)	7.46[a]
10. Honest	20 (9.3%)	17 (15.0%)	2.44 (ns)
11. Humor	36 (16.7%)	26 (23.0%)	1.89 (ns)
12. Commitment	38 (17.6%)	31 (27.4%)	4.25[a]
13. Emotion	44 (20.5%)	35 (31.0%)	4.36[a]

[a]Significant at the .05 level.

Table 2 Gender Comparison for Physical, Employment, and Intellectual Attributes Desired in Partner

Variable	Gender		Chi-square
	Desired by Men (*n* = 215)	Desired by Women (*n* = 113)	
Physical (collapsing variables 1–4)	143 (66.5%)	50 (44.2%)	15.13[a]
Employment (collapsing variables 5–7)	17 (7.9%)	47 (41.6%)	51.36[a]
Intellectual (collapsing variables 8 and 9)	29 (13.5%)	31 (27.4%)	9.65[a]

[a]Significant at the .05 level.

assumption was that the collapsed categories were sufficiently similar (within the three new categories) to make the new larger categories conceptually meaningful; conversely, it was felt the remaining variables (10–13) could not be meaningfully collapsed any further.

Sex differences for the three collapsed categories are summarized in Table 2. Note that the Table 2 figures were not derived simply by adding the numbers in the Table 1 categories: recall that for variables 1–4 a subject could specify all, one, or none; hence simply adding the Table 1 figures would be biased by those individuals who were more effusive in specifying various physical traits. Instead, the Table 2 categories are (like Table 1) all or nothing:

whether a subject specified one or all four of the physical attributes it would only count once. Thus, each score represented one person.

In brief, Table 2 gives similar, although more exaggerated, results to Table 1. (The exaggeration is the result of only one item of several being needed to score within a collapsed category.) The men were more likely than the women to specify some physical attribute. The women were considerably more likely to specify that the companion be employed, or have a profession, or be in good financial shape. And the women were more likely to emphasize the intellectual abilities of their mate. . . .

Discussion

SEX DIFFERENCES

This study found that the attitudes of the subjects, in terms of desired companion attributes, were consistent with traditional sex role stereotypes. The men were more likely to emphasize stereotypically desirable feminine traits (appearance) and deemphasize the non-feminine traits (financial, employment, and intellectual status). One inconsistency was that emotional expressiveness is a feminine trait but was emphasized relatively less by the men. Women, on the other hand, were more likely to emphasize masculine traits such as financial, employment, and intellectual status, and valued commitment in a relationship more highly. One inconsistency detected for the women concerned the fact that although emotional expressiveness is not a masculine trait, the women in this sample asked for it, relatively more than the men, anyway. Regarding this last point, it may be relevant to refer to Basow's (1986, 210) conclusion that "women prefer relatively androgynous men, but men, especially traditional ones, prefer relatively sex-typed women."

These findings are similar to results from earlier studies, e.g., Deaux and Hanna (1984),

and indicate that at this point in time and in this setting sex role stereotyping is still in operation. . . .

METHODOLOGICAL ISSUES

Content analysis of newspaper ads has its strengths and weaknesses. By virtue of being an unobtrusive study of variables with face validity, it was felt some reliable measure of gender-related attitudes was being achieved. That the mean age of the men and women placing the ads was similar was taken as support for the assumption that the two sexes in this sample were demographically similar. Further, sex differences in desired companion attributes could not be attributed to differential verbal ability in that it was found that length of ad was similar for both sexes.

On the other hand, there were some limitations. It could be argued that people placing personal ads are not representative of the public in general. For instance, with respect to this study, it was found that the subjects were a somewhat older group—mean age of 40—than might be found in other courting situations. This raises the possibility of age being a confounding variable. Older singles may emphasize certain aspects of a relationship, regardless of sex. On the other hand, there is the possibility that age differentially affects women in the mate selection process, particularly when children are desired. The strategy of controlling for age in the analysis was felt problematic in that the numbers for analysis were fairly small, especially given the missing data, and further, that one cannot assume the missing cases were not systematically different (i.e., older) from those present.

References

Basow, S. 1986. *Gender Stereotypes: Traditions and Alternatives.* Pacific Grove, CA: Brooks/Cole.

Braito, R. 1981. "The Inferiority Game: Perceptions and Behavior." *Sex Roles* 7:65–72.

Curry, T., and R. Hock. 1981. "Sex Differences in Sex Role Ideals in Early Adolescence." *Adolescence* 16: 779–789.

Deaux, K., and R. Hanna. 1984. "Courtship in the Personals Column: The Influence of Gender and Sexual Orientation." *Sex Roles* 11: 363–375.

Farrell, W. 1986. *Why Men Are the Way They Are.* New York: Berkeley Books.

Halas, C. 1981. *Why Can't a Woman Be More Like a Man?* New York: Macmillan.

Harrison, A., and L. Saeed. 1977. "Let's Make a Deal: An Analysis of Revelations and Stipulations in Lonely Hearts Advertisements." *Journal of Personality and Social Psychology* 35: 257–264.

Hite, S. 1981. *The Hite Report on Male Sexuality.* New York: Knopf.

Nevid, J. 1984. "Sex Differences in Factors of Romantic Attraction." *Sex Roles* 11: 401–411.

Shaevitz, M. 1987. *Sexual Static.* Boston: Little, Brown.

Smith, D. 1973. "Women, the Family, and Corporate Capitalism." In M. Stephenson (ed.), *Women in Canada.* Toronto: New Press.

Stiles, D., J. Gibbon, S. Hardardottir, and J. Schnellmann. 1987. "The Ideal Man or Woman as Described by Young Adolescents in Iceland and the United States." *Sex Roles* 17: 313–320.

Symons, D. 1987. "An Evolutionary Approach." In J. Geer and W. O'Donohue (eds.), *Theories of Human Sexuality.* New York: Plenum Press.

Thiessen, D., and B. Gregg. 1980. "Human Assortive Mating and Genetic Equilibrium: An Evolutionary Perspective." *Ethology and Sociobiology* 1: 111–140.

Urberg, K. 1979. "Sex Role Conceptualization in Adolescents and Adults." *Developmental Psychology* 15: 90–92.

Questions

1. What does Davis mean by "sex objects" and "success objects"?

2. According to Davis's findings, what are the major differences between the personal ads placed by men and those placed by women?

3. In the research reported here, Davis wants to investigate whether mate selection continues to be influenced by traditional sex stereotypes. Sociologists are always concerned about whether their results can be used to make generalizations about the larger population. This works only to the degree that there are no important differences between the general population and those who place ads. Think about it—why might we hesitate before saying that the findings from this study of personal ads can inform us about the influence of sex-role stereotypes in mate selection more generally?

4. Since Davis conducted his research, have gender relations changed much? If you replicated this study today, do you think your results would be similar or different? Why?

5

SKIPPING CLASS

An Analysis of Absenteeism Among First-Year College Students

Gary Wyatt

Once I suggested to a student that more regular attendance might help her do better in my course, and she patiently explained that she does attend regularly: once every two weeks. As my students frequently remind me, my class is not necessarily the primary focus of their college experience; some of them have even suggested that attending my class isn't even in the top ten on their list of things to do on any particular day. Why do students miss class? As you will see, Professor Wyatt wasn't content with the conventional assumption that absenteeism is simply a "personal trouble."

One of the most perplexing things that I have noticed about college life is the propensity of many students to skip class. As a naive young first-year student, I was both surprised and intrigued by this behavior. Why would so many people spend so much money on tuition and then not show up to get what they paid for? Some of my fellow students attended classes sporadically at best and only on test days at worst. Some got the lecture notes from friends, read the text and hoped that was enough, or simply did not worry about it at all.

Later I realized that paying tuition gave people much more than the opportunity to enroll in and attend courses. It bestowed a status on them as well, a status that allowed them to attend football and basketball games, to participate in intramural sports, to establish social relationships, to join clubs, to use university facilities, and to have a good time. For some, tuition seemed to be little more than an expensive cover charge that allowed them entrance into an exciting social world—a world that was often apart from learning and class attendance.

As a result of my work as a sociologist, a professor, and an academic advisor, I continue to be concerned about absenteeism form class. Others share this concern. A professor quoted in a Carnegie Foundation Report stated, "If you're batting .666 on attendance, you're doing well" (cited in Boyer 1987, p. 140). That is, one-third of the students will not be in attendance on any given day. While writing this paper I spoke with a number of professors who teach at three different universities. Most told me that approximately 20 to 40 percent of

"Skipping Class: An Analysis of Absenteeism Among First-Year College Students" by Gary Wyatt from *Teaching Sociology*, Vol. 20, No. 3 (July, 1992: pp. 201–207). Reprinted by permission of the American Sociological Association and the author.

the undergraduates enrolled in their classes are absent from each class meeting.

Because skipping class affects the quality of a student's education as well as the morale of the faculty, it is important to learn more about students who skip class and their reasons for doing so. Thus the purpose of this research was to explore this subject in greater detail. Specifically I wanted to measure a number of variables and determine their relationship with first-year students' propensity to miss class. I focused on first-year students because, as Upcraft and Gardner (1989, p. 1) note, there is "overwhelming evidence that student success is largely determined during the freshman year." I agree, however, with Katchadourian and Boli (1985), who argue that first-year students differ from other students with regard to their academic attitudes and behaviors. Consequently I will not generalize my results beyond first-year students. On the basis of the literature and personal experience, I selected the following variables: (1) liking or disliking the class, (2) living arrangements, (3) time spent studying, (4) frequency of alcohol consumption, (5) time spent working at part- and full-time jobs, (6) gender, (7) age, (8) parental income, and (9) previous semester's grade point average.

I acknowledge that the subject of teaching itself my seem peripheral to most of these variables. I contend, however, that a knowledge of the relationships which exist between these variables and absenteeism will be useful to many teachers. For example, I believe that to a degree teachers may be able to minimize the effects of some of these variables. Also they may feel less demoralized if they realize that factors unrelated to teaching quality account for absences among students. Finally the amount of variance in absenteeism explained by these variables, as reported in the "results" section, makes them difficult to ignore.

I hypothesized that students would be more likely to miss classes which they disliked than those which they liked. My argument here was intuitive: people are likely to repeat experiences that they find enjoyable and rewarding (Blackman 1974). I believed this point would hold true for class attendance.

Living arrangements have a significant impact on college students (Boyer 1987). Upcraft (1989, p. 142) stated, "Freshmen who live in residence halls are more likely to succeed in college than those who live elsewhere." Clearly, first-year students who live on campus may be integrated better into campus life. They are in a better position to participate in resident hall and other campus activities, and they may have more friends on campus. I hypothesized that students who lived off campus would miss more class meetings than students who did not. Attending class regularly may be less convenient for these students. Problems such as bad weather, car trouble, and the like could be more problematic for those who live off campus.

I also examined time spent in studying. I believed that those who studied diligently would be more likely to attend class regularly. In view of the alternatives facing college students as to how to spend their time, it seemed clear to me that those who choose to study are more dedicated to academic achievement. Furthermore, the more effort a student invests in studying, the more likely a student is to find class attendance rewarding (Michaels and Miethe 1989). Finally students may view increased study as an investment of time and energy that would be undermined by excessive absenteeism. Thus I hypothesized that as time spent studying increased, the likelihood of missing class would decrease.

Alcohol consumption is associated with a variety of problems for students (Dean 1989). These problems include but are not limited to absenteeism, drowsiness, acting out, poor performance on tests, and unfinished homework assignments. I have discussed the negative effects of excessive drinking on academic performance with my academic advisees.

On the basis of this information, I hypothesized that frequency of alcohol consumption would be associated positively with missing class.

The next variable I examined was the number of hours a student works each week at a full- or part-time job. I suspected that the more hours a student worked each week, the greater would be the likelihood of conflicts with class attendance. Some students have jobs that occupy them late into the night, which may make it difficult for them to attend classes consistently. Others occasionally may find themselves scheduled to work when they should be in class. Thus it is reasonable to hypothesize that as the number of hours a student worked each week increased, the number of classes missed also would increase.

Another variable I included was gender. A significant amount of evidence suggests that the classroom is a more hostile place for females than for males (Cherry 1975). In a review of the literature, Block (1983, p. 1344) reported, "Teachers have been observed to interact more with boys, to give boys more positive feedback, and to direct more criticism towards girls." These patterns also seem to hold true at the college and university level (Feldman 1974; Hochschild 1975). If, in fact, the classroom is a more hostile place for females, they are likely to miss more classes.

I also included students' age in the study. I suspected that because older students often sacrifice more to attend college, they would miss fewer classes than younger students. I measured and included parental income because of evidence suggesting that children of upper-income families have higher levels of educational attainment and achievement (see Aitkin 1982; Astin 1964; Bank, Slavings, and Biddle 1990; McCartin and Meyer 1988). On the basis of these findings I suspected that students from upper-income families would attend more regularly than students from lower-income families.

The final variable I included was grade point average. I believed that students who had a history of earning good grades would be less likely to miss class than students who did not. Students who earn good grades like college more than students who do not (Wyatt and Melhorn 1991); therefore it seemed reasonable to assume that those who liked college would be more apt to attend class regularly than those who did not.

Despite this line of reasoning, one can argue that I have stated the case backwards. Clearly it is possible to contend that regular attendance affects grades more strongly than grades affect attendance. It is also possible, as Chambliss (1981) reported, that some students who earn good grades miss class frequently without any negative consequences. Basing my argument on Bem's (1967) perception theory, however, I suggest that an equally strong case can be made for my hypothesis. Bem stated that attitudes and behaviors are a reflection of people's perception of their competencies and of attributions based on those perceptions. Consequently people who earn good grades are likely to develop more positive attitudes towards college and to behave accordingly. To test this hypothesis, I found it necessary to measure grade point average at one point in time and number of classes missed at another. (I will discuss the entire procedure in greater detail in the "method" section.)

Method

Near the end of the spring 1989 semester, I mailed a questionnaire to 170 randomly selected second-semester, first-year students at a public university in the midwest that enrolls more than 6,000 students. I had obtained a list of such students from the registration office at the university and obtained my sample of 170 using a random numbers table. I received 110 completed questionnaires for a return rate of 65 percent.

This survey was administered toward the end of the semester and required the students to respond based on memory. Despite the potential for error due to faulty memory and the desire to give "acceptable" answers, I am convinced the data are useful. The results of this study, however, like the results of many other studies that rely on self-reported data, should be interpreted with caution.

I measured the dependent variables by asking the students to state how many times they missed the classes they liked and how many times they missed the classes they disliked during the spring semester. (I measured the number of individual class sessions missed rather than the number of days missed.) The mean for missing classes liked was 3.09, with a range from 0 to 15. The mean for missing classes disliked was 5.31, with a range from 0 to 38.

The students were asked to indicate their living arrangements. Fifty-five percent of the students lived on campus in the residence halls, 20 percent lived off campus in nearby apartments, and 15 percent lived "at home" with relatives. Ten percent of the students, all of whom were commuters, had "other" living arrangements.

I asked the students to indicate on a scale of 1 to 8, how much time they spent studying each week. A score of 1 meant that no time was spent studying, and a score of 8 represented 30 hours or more. I also asked them to report how often they consumed alcohol during a given semester. Their responses were measured on a scale of 1 to 5 (1 = never, 5 = nearly every day).

To measure work time I asked the students to state the average number of hours they worked each week at full- or part-time jobs. The students also were asked to state their gender and their age in years. I measured parental income by asking the students to indicate how much money their parents made each year on a scale of 1 to 6 (1 = $9,999 or less, 6 = $75,000 or more).

The registration office supplied the grade point average for each participating student for the semester preceding the administration of this questionnaire. Table 1 presents the means and the number of respondents for each variable discussed above, except residence and gender.

I tested the research hypotheses by analyzing the difference in means and by conducting ordinary least squares (OLS) regression analysis. Significance levels were set at the .05 level. I used one-tailed t-tests for the OLS analysis because the direction of relationships

Table 1 Means and Number of Respondents for All Variables, Except Residence and Gender

Variables	Means	N
Missing classes liked	3.09	107
Missing classes disliked	5.31	104
Frequency of alcohol consumption (scale of 1 to 5)	2.38	107
Hours spent working per week	12.68	107
Time spent studying (scale of 1 to 8)	4.32	106
Age	20.84	106
Parents' income (scale of 1 to 6)	3.72	96
Grade point average	2.70	110

Table 2 Correlations Between Missing Classes Liked and Disliked and Independent Variables

Variable	Correlation
Classes Liked	
Time studying	−.28*
Frequency of alcohol consumption	.15
Hours working	.06
Age	.09
Parents' income	.24*
Grade point average	−.25*
Classes Disliked	
Time studying	−.31*
Frequency of alcohol consumption	.25*
Hours working	.01
Age	−.21
Parents' income	.28*
Grade point average	−.33*

*Statistically significant at <.05
Note: The starred (*) coefficients were found to be "statistically significant." That means that the relationship found between two variables is not likely to be the result of chance. Here the author says that the probability (p) of the starred coefficients being the result of chance is less than (<) 5%.—Ed.

was specified. The critical value of t for this level is plus or minus 1.66.

Results

CORRELATIONS

Table 2 shows the correlation coefficients[1] for the interval and ordinal variables. Missing classes liked was associated positively with

[1]Correlation coefficients indicate the degree to which the variables are related. These coefficients can range from −1 to +1; the greater the distance of the coefficient from zero, the more the variables are related. A *positive* coefficient indicates a positive relationship between the variables; that is, as one variable increases, the other variable increases (or, as one variable decreases, the other variable does too). A *negative* coefficient means there is a negative relationship between the variables (that is, as one variable increases the other decreases, and vice versa).—Ed.

parental income and negatively with time spent studying and previous grade point average. Missing classes disliked was associated positively with frequency of alcohol consumption and parental income and negatively with time spent studying and previous grade point average.

I assessed the effect of liking or disliking a class on class absences by analyzing the means for these variables. The mean for missing classes that the students liked was 3.09; and for classes that they did not like the mean was 5.31. I tested the difference between these means with a matched-samples t-test (Kushner and De Maio 1980). The results supported my hypothesis that students are more likely to miss classes they do not like than classes they like (t = 4.06, p ≤ .01). I also tested the difference between the means of missing class for residence: the results revealed no relationship between absenteeism and living arrangements. . . .

Discussion

Student absenteeism from classes that they dislike has important implications. At a recent symposium, a student leader stated that the most common complaint she hears about teaching is that it is "so boring." Many of the professors in attendance countered with the argument that they are not performers; students should judge them on their ability to educate, not on their ability to entertain. Both arguments have legitimacy. Some professors should throw away their old, yellowed notes and come to class better prepared. Students, on the other hand, will find that with careful attention and proper motivation, most lectures are interesting.

I explored this topic further by interviewing a number of first-year students about the characteristics of classes that they liked and disliked. Students liked classes where the instructors were well prepared. In fact they expressed a great deal of frustration toward professors who were not prepared: these students felt they were wasting their time and money. Some students expressed discontent with general education courses in which they were required to enroll; they did not see the relevance of these courses. Consequently they missed meetings of these classes. This finding suggests that professors who teach general education courses (a category that includes many lower-division sociology courses) should be more concerned with demonstrating the relevance of their respective disciplines.

This research suggests that good study habits are important: students who study more miss fewer classes. It seems to me that many colleges and universities could do much more to enhance the emphasis on scholarship and study among students. Many of the first-year students whom I encounter did not know how to study when they came to the university. Others, who earned good grades in high school although they did little homework, are shocked by the amount of homework required. Many factors contribute to poor study habits, but more classroom discussion of homework expectations and proper study habits may help.

These findings also suggest that college and university officials, faculty members, and students should be aware of the effect of alcohol on missing class. Perhaps as instructors and student advisors we should become more involved in educating our students about this problem.

Surprisingly time spent working at part- and full-time jobs was not associated with missing class. An additional analysis demonstrated that the number of hours worked each week also did not affect grade point average. Apparently the students who missed class were not absent because they were working, and those students who worked did not suffer academically. These findings are reassuring: because many students must work in order to afford college, I was pleased that they do not appear to be harmed by working. Perhaps we can be less hesitant to suggest employment to needy students.

My hypothesis concerning gender was confirmed. The females in my sample reported missing more class meetings than the males, particularly for classes disliked. If I am at least partially correct in my suspicion that females report higher rates of absenteeism because the classroom is a less hospitable place for them, perhaps we should be more aware of the things that may happen in class to aggravate this situation. The literature cited earlier suggests that teachers are often unaware of the negative expectations, attitudes, and behaviors that they direct toward female students. Perhaps more sensitivity on the part of teachers and advisors will help.

As I said earlier, I believe that earning good grades will reinforce and encourage regular attendance. The results reported here support that claim for disliked classes. I suspect that students with good grades are more highly motivated to attend these classes because they want to maintain their grade point average; perhaps they have more to lose by being absent.

Many students are infected with what Rabow and Hernandez (1988) call the "grade point average perspective," whereby good grades, not wisdom and understanding, are the important considerations. Perhaps if we look for ways to make academic life more intrinsically rewarding, students with lower grades will attend more regularly.

Conclusions

Class absenteeism among first-year students is affected by several variables. Yet despite the significant explanatory power of the variables that I analyzed, other factors also should be explored. First, do rates of absenteeism differ among colleges and universities? Are students who attend state universities less likely to attend regularly than students at higher-priced private institutions? Second, because this study focused on first-year students, it would be interesting to determine whether their behavior is comparable to that of other students. Third, the issue of gender emerged in the results of this study. Future research should continue to focus on gender in an effort to understand more clearly the differences between males' and females' behavior and experiences at institutions of higher education. Fourth, what is the effect of health and personal crises on class attendance? Finally, what kinds of policies and practices will be most effective in minimizing this problem? Some professors award points for attendance; others give pop quizzes. Are these types of attempts

necessary? Are they appropriate, regardless of the effects?

By exploring these issues we will be able to improve the quality of education. We will make the academy a more coherent, more productive, and more satisfying place for both faculty and students.

References

Aitkin, Norman D. 1982. "College Student Performance, Satisfaction and Retention: Specification and Estimation of a Structural Model." *Journal of Higher Education* 53:32–50.

Astin, Alexander W. 1964. "Personal and Environmental Factors Associated with College Dropouts among High Aptitude Students." *Journal of Educational Psychology* 4:219–27.

Bank, Barbara J., Ricky L. Slavings, and Bruce J. Biddle. 1990. "Effects of Peer, Faculty, and Parental Influences on Students' Persistence." *Sociology of Education* 63:208–25.

Bem, Daryl J. 1967. "Self Perception." *Psychological Review* 74:183–200.

Blackman, Derek. 1974. *Operant Conditioning*. New York: Heltivan.

Block, Jeanne H. 1983. "Differential Premises Arising from Differential Socialization of the Sexes: Some Conjectures." *Child Development* 54:1334–54.

Boyer, Ernest L. 1987. *College: The Undergraduate Experience in America*. New York: Harper and Row.

Chambliss, William J. 1981. "The Saints and the Roughnecks." Pp. 236–47 in *Deviance: The Interactionist Perspective*, 4th ed., edited by Earl Rubington and Martin S. Weinberg. New York: Macmillan.

Cherry, Louise 1975. "The Preschool Teacher–Child Dyad: Sex Differences in Verbal Interaction." *Child Development* 46:532–35.

Dean, Orville A. 1989. *Facing Chemical Dependency in the Classroom*. Deerfield Beach, FL: Health Communications.

Feldman, Saul. 1974. *Escape from the Doll House: Women in Graduate and Professional School Education*. New York: McGraw-Hill.

Hochschild, Arlie. 1975. "Inside the Clockwork of Male Careers." Pp. 47–80 in *Women and the Power* to Change, edited by Florence Howe. New York: McGraw-Hill.

Katchadourian, Herant A. and John Boli. 1985. Careerism and Intellectualism among College Students. San Francisco: Jossey-Bass.

Kushner, Harvey W. and Gerald De Maio. 1980. Understanding Basic Statistics. San Francisco: Holden-Day.

McCartin, Rosemarie and Katrina A. Meyer. 1988. "The Adolescent, Academic Achievement, and College Plans: The Role of Family Variables." Youth and Society 19:378–94.

Michaels, James W. and Terence D. Miethe. 1989. "Academic Effort and College Grades." Social Forces 68:309–19.

Rabow, Jerome and Anthony Hernandez. 1988. "The Price of the 'GPA Perspective': An Empirical Study of 'Making the Grade.'" Youth and Society 19:363–77.

Upcraft, M. Lee. 1989. "Residence Halls and Campus Activities." Pp. 142–55 in The Freshman Year Experience, edited by M. Lee Upcraft and John N. Gardner. San Francisco: Jossey-Bass.

Upcraft, M. Lee and John N. Gardner, eds. 1989. The Freshman Year Experience. San Francisco: Jossey-Bass.

Wyatt, Gary and J. Jack Melhorn. 1991. "Liking the University: A Preliminary Study." Free Inquiry in Creative Sociology 19:51–56.

Questions

1. One of the things that researchers worry about is whether the questions they ask people can be answered accurately. Assuming everyone tries to be honest, do you think that people who attend class frequently can be more or less accurate in their answers than people who attend class infrequently? How easy would it be to give an accurate answer to questions about how often you miss class or your reasons for doing so? Why or why not?

2. This research included several independent variables ("causes") in an attempt to explain absenteeism: liking or disliking the class, living arrangements, time spent studying, frequency of alcohol consumption, time spent working, gender, age, parental income, and grade point average. What other variables might help explain why students miss class?

3. Professor Wyatt mentioned that not only does missing class have an impact on the student's education, but it affects the *professor's morale*. Assume that students were told that when they missed class it hurt the professor's feelings. Under what circumstances would this knowledge increase or decrease attendance?

6
DOING THE RIGHT THING

Ethics in Research

Lisa J. McIntyre

There is more to doing sociological research than choosing variables, picking respondents, gathering data, and doing an analysis. More than ever before, every choice the social researcher makes must be informed by considerations of ethics. At base, doing the right thing means not subjecting the people we study and (those around them) to unnecessary risk of harm. What's behind the increasing stress on ethics in research? What are the responsibilities of the ethical researcher? Above all, what is "harm"? This 1999 paper explores these questions.

Ethical guides are not simply prohibitions; they also support our positive responsibilities. For example, scientists have an obligation to advance knowledge through research. They also have a responsibility to conduct research as competently as they can and to communicate their findings accurately to other scientists.

—Diener and Crandall 1978

To begin, it is important to note that the term *ethics* has both a conventional (or everyday) meaning and a technical meaning. The fact that there are two ways to use this term causes a great deal of confusion. In the conventional or everyday sense, ethics is synonymous with morality, and doing the ethical thing simply means doing the moral thing. Conversely, unethical behavior is immoral behavior.

Ethics: Technical Meaning and Origins

In the technical sense, ethics and morals are different. Although in many cases there may be an overlap between ethical and moral behavior,

there are no guarantees that this will occur. The following two scenarios give examples of how morals and ethics may diverge.

Scenario 1
Chris confesses to a friend to having killed someone and hidden the body under a pile of garbage near an old shack at the lake. The police can't find the missing victim, nor do they know that Chris is the killer. The friend calls the police and tells them where to find Chris and the victim's body.

Has the friend done something moral or immoral? In spite of the fact that there is a widely accepted rule in society against snitching on one's friends, most people probably would say that the friend did the moral thing. It is not right to allow murderers to go free, and the victim certainly has a right to a proper burial.

Scenario 2
Chris hires an attorney and then confesses the murder and burial to that attorney. The police can't find the missing victim, nor do they know that Chris is the killer. The lawyer isn't all that sure about Chris's story and drives up to the lake to check it out. A search through the

garbage reveals the body. After taking a Polaroid of the body, the lawyer reburies it in the garbage. Returning to town, the lawyer urges Chris to go to the police but does not call the police.[1]

Because the lawyer does not turn in the murderer, he or she does not seem to be acting morally. But there is an important consideration: Whereas in scenario 1 the friend may have a moral obligation to turn Chris in to the police, the lawyer has an ethical obligation to keep the client's confidence—even when the client is a murderer! This is not a gray area, either; this ethical requirement is spelled out clearly in the legal profession's *Code of Professional Responsibility:* "The lawyer must hold in strictest confidence the disclosures made by the client in the professional relationship. The first duty of an ethical attorney is 'to keep the secrets of his clients'" (Ethical Consideration 4-1). Preserving a client's secrets is such an important ethical obligation that had the lawyer turned Chris in, that attorney could have been disbarred and never again allowed to practice law.

In the technical sense, *behavior is ethical insofar as it follows the rules that have been specifically oriented to the welfare of the larger society and not to the self-interests of the professional.* So, ethics are designed to promote the welfare of others. You might be wondering how this lawyer could be promoting the welfare of others. The short answer is this: The legal profession is committed to the idea that people are innocent until proved guilty, that everyone accused of a crime has a right to the best defense, and that this is possible only if those accused of crimes can trust their attorneys. No client would trust an attorney who did not keep his or her secrets.

To be ethical, professionals have the burden of having to do things that others might consider to be immoral. For lawyers, in addition to keeping possibly nasty secrets, being ethical involves the duty to defend what may be unpopular cases and vicious criminals.

To become a professional, one must promise to abide by the relevant professional ethical codes. This is not a matter of personal choice—if you want to be a physician, you must follow the medical rules of ethics. To act unethically is to act unprofessionally.

It is important to be precise here: What do I mean by "professional"? In conventional language, we use the term at least three different ways. Sometimes, we apply the word to a job that is well done: "You did a very professional job of building that doghouse." Other times, we label someone a professional because he or she is paid to do something, regardless of the quality of the outcome: "John was a professional baseball player—but he never could hit a curve ball."

When sociologists use the term *professional,* however, they generally mean something else. Sociologically speaking, a professional is a member of a special kind of occupational group. Originally, only three occupational groups qualified as professions: lawyers, physicians, and clergy. These three groups have several things in common that set them apart from other occupations:

1. Their practitioners study for years to acquire technical knowledge and skills.

2. The knowledge they possess involves traditions and secrets that are not shared by outsiders.

3. Their knowledge is useful to outsiders and frequently means the difference between life and death.

From the first three characteristics of the professional derives a fourth—and this is really what sets the professional apart from other workers:

4. The work of a professional cannot be judged or supervised by anyone who is not a member of the same profession.

[1]A very similar case happened several years ago in Lake Pleasant, New York.

As sociologists see it, these qualities are characteristics of doctors, lawyers, and clergy, but not of plumbers or hairstylists. Although people in any occupational group may refer to themselves as professionals ("I am a professional hairstylist" or "I am a professional plumber"), relatively few occupations really are professions.[2]

The nature of the professional's job is such that *how* it is done is as important as (if not more important than) what the outcome is. The problem is that as laypeople, we cannot judge how well the job was done. For example, if patient Q's family suspects that the surgeon wasn't competent and that this incompetence led to Q's death, they might want to sue the surgeon for malpractice. Q's family might feel righteous in claiming that if the surgeon had done the job right, Q would still be alive. But that is not necessarily true (recall the old saying, "The operation was a success, but the patient died"). The views of Q's family are legally irrelevant and will hold no water in court. According to the law, only another physician can judge whether the surgeon was truly negligent. So, Q's family will have to find another surgeon who is willing to testify that it was the poor quality of the surgeon's work that led to the patient's death.[3]

Even though they could not tell if their doctor, lawyer, priest, or rabbi was doing all that ought to be done, for a long time people trusted these professionals to do the right thing. But by the mid-nineteenth century, many people were growing increasingly suspicious of professionals and were beginning to suggest that perhaps professionals ought not to be given so much freedom and autonomy.

Professionals responded by emphasizing the fact that their actions were prompted not by self-interest, but by their concern for their clients, patients, or parishioners. According to members of the medical profession, then, doctors do not perform surgery simply to make money, but to relieve people's suffering. And according to members of the legal profession, then, lawyers do not represent clients simply for the money, but because everyone has a right to representation.

One of the ways that professionals emphasized their commitment to the public welfare over self-interest was to promulgate or announce codes of ethics. They promised that they would follow these codes of ethics and punish any member of their profession who failed to do so. As we moved into the twentieth century, however, it became increasingly clear that at least one aspect of professional work was not being regulated properly by the professionals themselves: research.

Research Atrocities

Gross abuses of professional power in research became public knowledge after World War II. When Nazi physicians were brought to trial at Nuremberg in the late 1940s, the tales of their "research" horrified the world:

> Physicians forced people [in concentration camps] to drink seawater to find out how long a man might survive without fresh water. At Dachau, Russian prisoners of war were immersed in icy waters to see how long a pilot might survive when shot down over the English Channel and to find out what kinds of protective gear or rewarming techniques were most effective. Prisoners were placed in vacuum chambers to find out how the human body responds when pilots are forced to bail out at

---

[2] I do not mean to disrespect members of any occupational group by claiming that they are not professionals. I simply mean to illustrate how sociologists use the term *professional* to highlight the qualities of certain occupational groups.

[3] There are exceptions. Some errors are so obvious that the law does not require an expert witness to testify—as when a surgeon cuts off the wrong leg or sews a surgical instrument into the wound. (The legal phrase for such exceptions is *res ipsa loquitur,* a Latin term meaning "the thing speaks for itself.")

high altitudes. . . . At Auschwitz, physicians experimented with new ways to sterilize or castrate people as part of the plan to repopulate Eastern Europe with Germans. Physicians performed limb and bone transplants (on persons with no medical need) and, in at least one instance, injected prisoners' eyes with dyes to see if eye color could be permanently changed. At Buchenwald, Gerhard Rose infected prisoners with spotted fever to test experimental vaccines against the disease; at Dachau, Ernst Grawitz infected prisoners with a broad range of pathogens to test [different cures]. . . . Hundreds of people died in these experiments; many of those who survived were forced to live with painful physical or psychological scars. (Annas and Grodin 1992, 26)

At their trials, many Nazi physicians protested that they "had only been following orders." But much evidence suggested otherwise: "Contrary to postwar apologies, doctors were never forced to perform such experiments. Physicians volunteered—and in several cases, *Nazi officials actually had to restrain overzealous physicians from pursuing even more ambitious experiments*" (Annas and Grodin 1992, 26; emphasis added).

What could have motivated these physicians, these professional healers, to misapply their professional skills so horribly? At the time, many Americans believed that there was something fundamentally wrong with the German "personality type." For one thing (or so it was thought), Germans were all too quick to follow orders without exercising independent judgment. Certainly, such things could never happen in the United States!

What many people did not know or appreciate was the long tradition among U.S. physicians of conducting questionable research. For example, in the nineteenth century, orphans, the "feeble-minded," and hospital patients frequently were made the unwilling victims of medical experiments.

> In his autobiography, physician J. Marion Sims described how, between 1845 and 1849, he kept several black female slaves at his hospital to test his discovery of a repair for vesicovaginal fistula. The fistulas, allowing urine or feces to leak through the vaginal opening, caused great discomfort and distress. . . . Sims performed dozens of operations on the women—this in the days before anesthetics—and praised their "heroism and bravery." (Lederer 1995, 115–116)

There have even been cases in which U.S. military personnel were required to participate in surgical experiments—under threat of court-martial!

In any case, outraged at the evidence they heard, the judges at Nuremberg promulgated the Nuremberg Code. The ten principles of the code were written to protect the rights of research subjects. Never again, the judges said, would humans be placed at risk of serious harm by being used as unwilling guinea pigs. But less than 30 years later, there was another research scandal. This time, the physicians were not only Americans but were employed by the United States Public Health Service! This study, known as the Tuskegee Syphilis Experiment, began in 1932 when public health workers came to Macon County, Georgia, in search of African American men who suffered from syphilis. The physicians preyed on the poverty of the men and recruited research subjects by offering to "pay" for their participation—free medical exams, transportation to and from the medical facilities where the exams would be held, and free meals on examination days. The biggest incentive was that the families of each subject would be paid $50 to help with burial expenses.

Not one of the subjects was told that he had syphilis—though each was told that he had "bad blood." And, although a cure for syphilis was widely available throughout most of the 30-year period during which the study was conducted, not one of the men was given this medication despite the fact that it would have

---

The Nuremberg Code

1. The voluntary consent of the human subject is absolutely essential. . . .

2. The research should be such as to yield fruitful results for the good of society, unprocurable by other methods or means. . . .

3. The research should be so designed . . . so that the anticipated results will justify the performance of the experiment.

4. The research should be so conducted as to avoid all unnecessary physical and mental suffering and injury.

5. No research should be conducted where there is . . . reason to believe that death or disabling injury will occur.

6. The degree of risk to be taken should never exceed that determined by the humanitarian importance of the problem to be solved by the research.

7. Proper preparations should be made . . . to protect the research subject against even remote possibilities of injury, disability, or death.

8. The research should be conducted only by scientifically qualified persons. . . .

9. During the course of the research the human subject should be at liberty to bring the research to an end if he has reached the physical or mental state where continuation of the research seems to him to be impossible.

10. During the course of the research the scientist in charge must be prepared to terminate the research at any stage, if he has probable cause to believe . . . the continuation of the research is likely to result in injury, disability, or death to the research subject.

Note: The writers of the original code emphasized the need to protect subjects in experimental research. Because social scientists use a variety of techniques, I have substituted the word "research" for "experiment."

---

saved his life.[4] You see, the researchers were intent on studying the effects of *untreated* syphilis. The study continued until 1972 when its existence became public. At that point, the research was terminated because of public outrage (Jones 1981).

---

[4]Alexander Fleming discovered the cure (penicillin) in 1928, but it would be another decade before the drug was used by medical practitioners. In the late 1930s, just in time for World War II, two British researchers, Ernst Chain and Howard Florey, discovered a process that purified penicillin and made it safe. The drug was widely used by the military in the war and in the civilian sector after the war.

The Case for Sociological Research

You might well think that members of the general public have little to fear from sociologists. After all, what harm can a bunch of geeks with clipboards do by asking questions?

There is potential for harm in any sort of research that involves human subjects. The potential harm in sociological research frequently involves not what we do or do not do to our research subjects, but what we find out about them. Sociologists and other social scientists find out information that people often would prefer to keep private.

One of the most famous examples of social science research that many believed crossed the ethical lines was Laud Humphreys' study, which he titled *Tearoom Trade* (1970).

Technically speaking, *Tearoom Trade* was a study of impersonal sexual activity between male homosexuals. Less technically speaking, Humphreys began his research (or so he later said) by trying to find an answer to a question posed by his graduate advisor: "Where does the average guy go just to get a blow job?"

As Humphreys discovered, the answer to that particular question was "a tearoom" (that is, a restroom in a public park). In these tearooms, Humphreys did observational research. More specifically, to hide the fact that he was a researcher, he took on the role of "watch queen" (a third man who serves as a lookout for those engaged in homosexual acts and obtains voyeuristic pleasure from his observations).

From his observations, Humphreys obtained a great deal of information about how men approach each other and negotiate sex. But, given the circumstances, he could not very well find out much else. Humphreys wanted to know, Who are these men? How do they spend the rest of their time?

So, in addition to making his secret observations, Humphreys recorded each participant's license plate number. He then took this list of numbers to the police, told them he was doing "market research," and obtained the names and addresses of each man.

But, then what? He could hardly show up at the men's doorsteps and announce, "Hi, I saw you engaging in homosexual sex in the park last month, and now I would like to ask you a few questions about the rest of your life." (Sometimes, the most straightforward approach simply does not work.)

Around that time, another researcher at the same university was conducting a study on issues related to health care. Humphreys persuaded this researcher to include the names of his tearoom players on the list of subjects for the health study and schedule them for interviews. Humphreys himself would interview these men. To reduce the chances that the men would recognize him, Humphreys waited a year and changed his hairstyle. Then, no doubt armed with that ubiquitous clipboard, Humphreys visited and interviewed each of the men. This way, posing as a health-care researcher, he was able to find out all about the men's socioeconomic status (mostly middle class), their educational level (pretty high), and their family life (mostly married with children). Humphreys discovered that the only nonconventional thing about these men was that they visited tearooms for anonymous sex.

What might be ethically questionable about Humphreys' research? Although some might object that the very topic of Humphreys' research was immoral, the nature of the topic is not an *ethical* concern. What is of concern ethically is the fact that Humphreys deceived his subjects—they never knew that they were participating in research, and they didn't have the opportunity to choose to participate. Moreover, Humphreys conducted his research during a time when homosexual behavior was illegal where the research was conducted. By recording their names and addresses, Humphreys was placing his research subjects in great jeopardy. After his book was published, what if the police had demanded that Humphreys turn over his list of subjects' names and addresses? There was a great risk not only of legal prosecution but of psychological and social harm as well. And, had their names been discovered, some of the men might even have been subjected to extortion.

Humphreys defended his research by pointing out that it is important for sociologists to know about such men and their activities in order to understand them. In point of fact, Humphreys' research did contradict many social myths about men who have sex in public bathrooms. Most were established members of the community with wives and children, and in practicing consensual sex, they were not hurting anyone and certainly not bothering children. Humphreys' research was published and widely cited and may well have played a role in decriminalizing some sexual acts between consenting adults.

Humphreys' research was perhaps extreme in this respect, but it is not unusual for sociologists to uncover embarrassing details. Sometimes, what we learn not only is embarrassing but may place the research subject in legal jeopardy. In such cases, we have to figure out what our duty is—do we keep the secrets only of those whom we respect as "good people"? The problem may be compounded by the fact that the people we study are often those who have little power in society: it almost seems as if sociologists are obsessed with marginalized people (the poor, the homeless, street criminals, and so on).[5]

There are few hard-and-fast rules about what is and is not ethical behavior in sociological research. As far as I am concerned, the only thing that is consistently unethical is to not think through the possible consequences of our research.

As we think through the possible consequences of our research, we need to remember that we have an obligation not only to our research subjects but to other sociologists, to the university, and to members of the community at large. Making ethical decisions involves weighing the costs and benefits of the research to all of these groups.

This takes a great deal of thought; frequently, our research may have consequences that extend beyond the obvious. For example, in the early 1960s, a woman named Kitty Genovese was raped and murdered in New York City. What set the Genovese murder apart from the many other murders that happened that year was the fact that a number of people had heard her screams for help, which lasted for many minutes, but not a single one called the police.

The Genovese murder caught the imagination of social researchers in a big way. Under what conditions would people help strangers in trouble? What followed was a multitude of so-called bystander intervention studies. Some of these were pretty benign, such as a boy on crutches dropping all of his school books to see whether anyone would stop to help. Other versions included scenes of staged violence, such as a woman yelling from the bushes, "Help, rape." Soon, people grew leery and distrustful as they walked around college campuses and nearby neighborhoods—there were so many researchers out and about that one never knew when one might become an involuntary research subject.

Then, the inevitable but still unthinkable happened:

> At the University of Washington in Seattle in 1973, a male student accosted another student on campus and shot him. Students on their way to class did not stop to aid the victim, nor did anyone follow the assailant (who was caught anyway). When the campus reporters asked some students about their lack of concern over the murder, they said they thought it was just a psychology experiment. (Diener and Crandall 1978, 87)

In this case, the harm caused by the overdoing of bystander and other sorts of research in the field did not affect only the research subjects. It contaminated the researcher's world by making people distrust researchers. And, far worse, it may have contributed to the death of a college student.

---

[5]Part of the reason for this apparent obsession is that it is much easier to gain access to people with little power. It's easier to get permission to examine, say, prison inmates than executives of Ford Motor Company.

The Nature of Informed Consent

"Informed consent is the procedure in which individuals choose whether to participate in an investigation after being informed of facts that would be likely to influence their decision. Informed consent includes several key elements: (a) subjects learn that the research is voluntary; (b) they are informed about aspects of the research that might influence their decision to participate; and (c) they exercise a continuous free choice to participate that lasts throughout the study. The greater the possibility of danger in the study and the greater the potential harm involved, or the greater the rights relinquished, the more thorough must be the procedure of obtaining informed consent" (Diener and Crandall 1978).

Institutional Review Boards: The Dawn of a New Era

These days, before any member of the university community (student, faculty, or staff) can conduct research that involves humans, they must submit a research proposal to a university officer or committee charged with ensuring that research is done ethically. If there is any question of risk to the human subjects, a committee consisting of both faculty (from a variety of disciplines) and community members will scrutinize the proposal. These committees are commonly called Institutional Review Boards (IRBs). If the members of the IRB judge that the researcher has not created sufficient safeguards to protect the rights of the research subjects and the general public, and even the researcher him- or herself, the researcher is prohibited from going on.

Like the Nuremberg Code, contemporary ethical guidelines place a great deal of emphasis on treating research subjects with respect. In many cases, researchers must obtain not merely *consent* from potential subjects but *informed consent*. As a general rule, deception must be kept to the absolute minimum. Members of IRBs are particularly skeptical of any research that places research subjects at risk of injury (physical, psychological, emotional, or legal) greater than the risk that surrounds the routine activities of everyday life.

How Heroic Must an Ethical Researcher Be?

To what extremes must the sociological researcher go to fulfill his or her ethical duty? As I noted previously, one of the reasons Laud Humphreys was criticized when he published *Tearoom Trade* was that homosexual acts were prohibited by law where he did his research. In theory, the district attorney could have subpoenaed the list of names and addresses of Humphreys' subjects and prosecuted these men.[6] Would being ethical have required Humphreys to choose jail over releasing his information? In fact, this course of action apparently was contemplated, though it never materialized.

A little over a decade later, another sociologist came even closer to being forced to decide between breaching confidentiality and

---

[6]A subpoena (sa-PEE-na) is nothing to fool around with. It is a command from a legal authority to appear and give testimony. If you refuse to comply with a subpoena, you can be charged with contempt of court and sent to jail until you change your mind (or until the judge accepts the fact that nothing is going to change your mind).

going to jail. Mario Brajuhas, a graduate student at the State University of New York at Stony Brook, was doing participant observation research as a waiter in a restaurant. When the restaurant burned down, the police suspected arson. Investigators knew of Brajuhas's research and of the fact that he had taken copious field notes; they suspected that those field notes might help identify the arsonist. The local prosecutor subpoenaed the notes, but Brajuhas refused to hand them over, even when threatened with jail. Finally (after 2 years), the major suspects in the fire died, and the prosecutor dropped the case.

In the early 1990s, Rik Scarce, a graduate student at Washington State University, took a vacation. He left an acquaintance of his, Rodney Coronado, behind as a housesitter. Scarce and Coronado had become acquainted when Scarce, prior to going to graduate school, had been researching a book on radical environmentalists entitled *Eco-Warriors: Understanding the Radical Environmental Movement* (1990). Coronado was involved with the Animal Liberation Front (ALF), which was adamantly opposed to the use of animals for research.

While Scarce was on vacation, the ALF raided a research laboratory at Washington State University. Several animals were set free, and the researchers' computers were destroyed. The university estimated the damage at about $100,000. Several months later, Scarce was subpoenaed and commanded to appear before a grand jury that had been convened to investigate the crime. Scarce did appear and answer several questions, but he declined to answer questions that, he said, required him to breach the confidentiality of his research subjects. Scarce quoted from the American Sociological Association's Code of Ethics, which states that "confidential information provided by research participants must be treated as such, even when this information enjoys no legal protection or privilege and legal force is applied." As Scarce later explained, "I told the judge that I feared for my ability to earn a living as a sociologist if I were compelled to testify. Research subjects might not be willing to speak with me, and institutions might not be willing to hire an unethical researcher" (Scarce 1994).

The judge was not moved by Scarce's explanation. Ultimately, after he continued to refuse to testify, Scarce was sent to jail as a "recalcitrant [unwilling] witness." He spent more than 5 months in jail before the judge, finally convinced that Scarce could not be compelled to testify, freed him.

The Scarce case sounded a warning bell to sociologists everywhere. According to their ethical code, they have an obligation to keep confidential information to themselves even when they have no legal right to do so. This puts sociologists in a different position than lawyers and doctors. Communication between lawyers and clients and between doctors and patients is *legally privileged*. Lawyers and physicians have not only an *ethical duty* to keep information confidential but the *legal right* to do so. Sociologists, on the other hand, have no such clear legal right, although they do have an ethical duty.

References

Annas, George J., and Michael A. Grodin. 1992. *The Nazi Doctors and the Nuremberg Code.* New York: Oxford University Press.

Diener, Edward, and Rick Crandall. 1978. *Ethics in Social and Behavioral Research.* Chicago: University of Chicago Press.

Humphreys, Laud. 1970. *Tearoom Trade: Impersonal Sex in Public Places.* Chicago: Aldine.

Jones, James H. 1981. *Bad Blood: The Tuskegee Syphilis Experiment.* New York: Free Press.

Lederer, Susan E. 1995. *Subjected to Science: Human Experimentation in America Before the Second World War.* Baltimore: Johns Hopkins University.

Scarce, Rik. 1994. "(No) Trial (But) Tribulations: When Courts and Ethnography Conflict." *Journal of Contemporary Ethnography* 23: 123–149.

Scarce, Rik, 1990. *Eco-Warriors: Understanding the Radical Environmental Movement.* Chicago: Noble Press.

Questions

1. One problem that often crops up in survey research is that many people do not fill out and return questionnaires. Researchers have learned that it helps increase the "response rate" if survey respondents are sent a reminder a week or so after they are sent the questionnaire. This doesn't sound controversial, does it? Well, consider the following situation:

   > For her senior research project, Mary is doing an anonymous survey. In other words, she has stated on the cover of each questionnaire that responses will be totally anonymous—no names will be asked for or in any way recorded.
   >
   > From reading the literature on response rates, Mary expects that only about a third of those to whom she mails the questionnaire will send it back. She knows that she can perhaps double her response rate if she sends everyone a reminder. However, she barely had enough money to send out the questionnaire in the first place, and she can't afford to send a postcard reminder to everyone. She comes up with what she thinks is a great plan. She will embed a secret symbol somewhere in each questionnaire—a different symbol for each respondent. As each survey is returned, she will locate the symbol, consult the master list, and determine the name of each respondent. That way, she will be able to check off the name of each respondent who has returned his or her questionnaire. After a week or so, Mary will send reminder cards to respondents who have not yet returned their questionnaires.

   You are Mary's thesis advisor. What ethical issues would you raise with her?

2. A sociology professor offers her students extra credit for participating in an experiment. As far as the students are concerned, the down side is the fact that participating in this particular experiment will expose them to embarrassing situations; the up side is that obtaining the extra credit will have a big impact on their grades.

   Is a student's participation really voluntary when to not participate means he or she will miss out on some valuable rewards and possibly fail the class? What might this professor do to make her plan more ethical?

3. Bob is writing his senior thesis on "The Functions of Symbols in the Secret Rituals of College Fraternities." He plans to ask his fraternity brothers to give him their views on the ceremonies of their fraternity. In addition, he plans to secretly record an upcoming fraternity initiation ritual.

   As his thesis advisor, what ethical issues would you feel compelled to raise with Bob about his research?

7

IF HITLER ASKED YOU TO ELECTROCUTE A STRANGER, WOULD YOU? PROBABLY

Philip Meyer

When he reflected back on the tales of Nazi horror that surfaced after World War II, Stanley Milgram wanted to know how ordinary people could be led to participate in such brutality. Like many others, Milgram had persuaded himself that it was something about the German character or culture that allowed the Holocaust to happen; such a horrible thing could never take place, for example, in the United States. Milgram's original plan was to go to Germany to test his hypothesis. Before he could do that, however, he needed a point of comparison. So, he tried out his experiment in New Haven and Bridgeport, Connecticut. As Philip Meyer explains in this 1970 article, Milgram never got to Germany.

In the beginning, Stanley Milgram was worried about the Nazi problem. He doesn't worry much about the Nazis anymore. He worries about you and me, and perhaps, himself a little bit too.

Stanley Milgram is a social psychologist, and when he began his career at Yale University in 1960 he had a plan to prove, scientifically, that Germans are different. The Germans-are-different hypothesis has been used by historians, such as William L. Shirer,[1] to explain the systematic destruction of the Jews by the Third Reich. One madman could decide to destroy the Jews and even create a master plan for getting it done. But to implement it on the scale that Hitler did meant that thousands of other people had to go along with the scheme and help to do the work. The Shirer thesis, which Milgram set out to test, is that Germans have a basic character flaw which explains the whole thing, and this flaw is a readiness to obey authority without question, no matter what outrageous acts the authority commands.

The appealing thing about this theory is that it makes those of us who are not Germans feel better about the whole business. Obviously, you and I are not Hitler, and it seems equally obvious that we would never do Hitler's dirty work for him. But now, because of Stanley Milgram, we are compelled to wonder. Milgram developed a laboratory experiment which provided a systematic way to measure obedience. His plan was to try it out in New Haven on Americans and then go to Germany and try it out on Germans. He was strongly motivated by scientific curiosity, but there was also some moral content in his decision to pursue this line of research, which was,

---

[1]William Lawrence Shirer began his career as a journalist. Shirer went to work for CBS in 1937, broadcasting the events of the war from both Europe and the United States. In 1940, Shirer took a job with the New York *Herald Tribune,* for which he wrote a column for a couple of years. In 1960, his book *The Rise and Fall of the Third Reich* won the National Book Award.—Ed.

53

never tested Germans — *racially unethical*

in turn, colored by his own Jewish background. If he could show that Germans are more obedient than Americans, he could then vary the conditions of the experiment and try to find out just what it is that makes some people more obedient than others. With this understanding, the world might, conceivably, be just a little bit better.

But he never took his experiment to Germany. He never took it any farther than Bridgeport. The first finding, also the most unexpected and disturbing finding, was that we Americans are an obedient people: not blindly obedient, and not blissfully obedient, just obedient. "I found so much obedience," says Milgram softly, a little sadly, "I hardly saw the need for taking the experiment to Germany."

There is something of the theatre director in Milgram, and his technique, which he learned from one of the old masters in experimental psychology, Solomon Asch, is to stage a play with every line rehearsed, every prop carefully selected, and everybody an actor except one person. That one person is the subject of the experiment. The subject, of course, does not know he is in a play. He thinks he is in real life. The value of this technique is that the experimenter, as though he were God, can change a prop here, vary a line there, and see how the subject responds. Milgram eventually had to change a lot of the script just to get people to stop obeying. They were obeying so much, the experiment wasn't working—it was like trying to measure oven temperature with a freezer thermometer.

Tell nature of experiment?

The experiment worked like this: If you were an innocent subject in Milgram's melodrama, you read an ad in the newspaper or received one in the mail asking for volunteers for an educational experiment. The job would take about an hour and pay $4.50. So you make an appointment and go to an old Romanesque stone structure on High Street with the imposing name of The Yale Interaction Laboratory. It looks something like a broadcasting studio. Inside, you meet a young, crew cut man in a laboratory coat, who says he is Jack Williams, the experimenter. There is another citizen, fiftyish, Irish face, an accountant, a little overweight, and very mild and harmless-looking. This other citizen seems nervous and plays with his hat while the two of you sit in chairs side by side and are told that the $4.50 checks are yours no matter what happens. Then you listen to Jack Williams explain the experiment.

It is about learning, says Jack Williams in a quiet, knowledgeable way. Science does not know much about the conditions under which people learn and this experiment is to find out about negative reinforcement. Negative reinforcement is getting punished when you do something wrong, as opposed to positive reinforcement which is getting rewarded when you do something right. The negative reinforcement in this case is electric shock. You notice a book on the table, titled *The Teaching-Learning Process,* and you assume that this has something to do with the experiment.

Then Jack Williams takes two pieces of paper, puts them in a hat, and shakes them up. One piece of paper is supposed to say, "Teacher" and the other, "Learner." Draw one and you will see which you will be. The mild-looking accountant draws one, holds it close to his vest like a poker player, looks at it, and says, "Learner." You look at yours. It says, "Teacher." You do not know that the drawing is rigged, and both slips say "Teacher." The experimenter beckons to the mild-mannered "learner."

"Want to step right in here and have a seat, please?" he says. "You can leave your coat on the back of that chair . . . roll up your right sleeve, please. Now what I want to do is strap down your arms to avoid excessive movement on your part during the experiment. This electrode is connected to the shock generator in the next room.

"And this electrode paste," he says, squeezing some stuff out of a plastic bottle and putting it on the man's arm, "is to provide a good contact and to avoid a blister or burn. Are there any questions now before we go into the next room?"

You don't have any, but the strapped-in "learner" does.

"I do think I should say this," says the learner. "About two years ago I was at the veterans' hospital . . . they detected a heart condition. Nothing serious, but as long as I'm having these shocks, how strong are they—how dangerous are they?"

Williams, the experimenter, shakes his head casually. "Oh, no," he says. "Although they may be painful, they're not dangerous. Anything else?"

Nothing else. And so you play the game. The game is for you to read a series of word pairs: for example, blue-girl, nice-day, fat-neck. When you finish the list, you read just the first word in each pair and then a multiple-choice list of four other words, including the second word of the pair. The learner, from his remote, strapped-in position, pushes one of four switches to indicate which of the four answers he thinks is the right one. If he gets it right, nothing happens and you go on to the next one. If he gets it wrong, you push a switch that buzzes and gives him an electric shock. And then you go to the next word. You start with 15 volts and increase the number of volts by 15 for each wrong answer. The control board goes from 15 volts on one end to 450 volts on the other. So that you know what you are doing, you get a test shock yourself, at 45 volts. It hurts. To further keep you aware of what you are doing to that man in there, the board has verbal descriptions of the shock levels, ranging from "Slight Shock" at the left-hand side, through "Intense Shock" in the middle, to "Danger: Severe Shock" toward the far right. Finally, at the very end, under 435- and 450-volt switches, there are three ambiguous X's. If, at any point, you hesitate, Mr. Williams calmly tells you to go on. If you still hesitate, he tells you again.

Except for some terrifying details, which will be explained in a moment, this is the experiment. The object is to find the shock level at which you disobey the experimenter and refuse to pull the switch.

When Stanley Milgram first wrote this script, he took it to fourteen Yale psychology majors and asked them what they thought would happen. He put it this way: Out of one hundred persons in the teacher's predicament, how would their break-off points be distributed along the 15-to-450-volt scale? They thought a few would break off very early, most would quit someplace in the middle and a few would go all the way to the end. The highest estimate of the number out of one hundred who would go all the way to the end was three. Milgram then informally polled some of his fellow scholars in the psychology department. They agreed that very few would go to the end. Milgram thought so too.

"I'll tell you quite frankly," he says, "before I began this experiment, before any shock generator was built, I thought that most people would break off at 'Strong Shock' or 'Very Strong Shock.' You would get only a very, very small proportion of people getting out to the end of the shock generator, and they would constitute a pathological fringe."

In his pilot experiments, Milgram used Yale students as subjects. Each of them pushed the shock switches, one by one, all the way to the end of the board.

So he rewrote the script to include some protests from the learner. At first, they were mild, gentlemanly, Yalie protests, but, "it didn't seem to have as much effect as I thought it would or should," Milgram recalls. "So we had more violent protestation on the part of the person getting the shock. All of the time, of course, what we were trying to do was not to create a macabre situation, but simply to generate disobedience. And that was one of the first findings. This was not only a technical deficiency of the experiment, that we didn't

Bad!!
Rode!!

get disobedience. It really was the first finding: that obedience would be much greater than we had assumed it would be and disobedience would be much more difficult than we had assumed."

As it turned out, the situation did become rather macabre. The only meaningful way to generate disobedience was to have the victim protest with great anguish, noise, and vehemence. The protests were tape-recorded so that all the teachers ordinarily would hear the same sounds and nuances, and they started with a grunt at 75 volts, proceeded through a "Hey, that really hurts," at 125 volts, got desperate with, "I can't stand the pain, don't do that," at 180 volts, reached complaints of heart trouble at 195, an agonized scream at 285, a refusal to answer at 315, and only heart-rending, ominous silence after that.

Still, sixty-five percent of the subjects, twenty- to fifty-year-old American males, everyday, ordinary people like you and me, obediently kept pushing those levers in the belief that they were shocking the mild-mannered learner, whose name was Mr. Wallace, and who was chosen for the role because of his innocent appearance, all the way up to 450 volts.

Milgram was now getting enough disobedience so that he had something he could measure. The next step was to vary the circumstances to see what would encourage or discourage obedience. There seemed very little left in the way of discouragement. The victim was already screaming at the top of his lungs and feigning a heart attack. So whatever new impediment to obedience reached the brain of the subject had to travel by some route other than the ear. Milgram thought of one.

He put the learner in the same room with the teacher. He stopped strapping the learner's hand down. He rewrote the script so that at 150 volts the learner took his hand off the shock plate and declared that he wanted out of the experiment. He rewrote the script some more so that the experimenter then told the teacher to grasp the learner's hand and physically force it down on the plate to give Mr. Wallace his unwanted electric shock.

"I had the feeling that very few people would go on at that point, if any," Milgram says. "I thought that would be the limit of obedience that you would find in the laboratory."

It wasn't.

Although seven years have now gone by, Milgram still remembers the first person to walk into the laboratory in the newly rewritten script. He was a construction worker, a very short man. "He was so small," says Milgram, "that when he sat on the chair in front of the shock generator, his feet didn't reach the floor. When the experimenter told him to push the victim's hand down and give the shock, he turned to the experimenter, and he turned to the victim, his elbow went up, he fell down on the hand of the victim, his feet kind of tugged to one side, and he said, 'Like this, boss?' ZZUMPH!"

The experiment was played out to its bitter end. Milgram tried it with forty different subjects. And thirty percent of them obeyed the experimenter and kept on obeying.

"The protests of the victim were strong and vehement, he was screaming his guts out, he refused to participate, and you had to physically struggle with him in order to get his hand down on the shock generator," Milgram remembers. But twelve out of forty did it.

Milgram took his experiment out of New Haven. Not to Germany, just twenty miles down the road to Bridgeport. Maybe, he reasoned, the people obeyed because of the prestigious setting of Yale University. If they couldn't trust a center of learning that had been there for two centuries, whom could they trust? So he moved the experiment to an untrustworthy setting.

The new setting was a suite of three rooms in a run-down office building in Bridgeport. The only identification was a sign with a fictitious name: "Research Associates of Bridgeport."

Questions about professional connections got only vague answers about "research for industry."

Obedience was less in Bridgeport. Forty-eight percent of the subjects stayed for the maximum shock, compared to sixty-five percent at Yale. But this was enough to prove that far more than Yale's prestige was behind the obedient behavior.

For more than seven years now, Stanley Milgram has been trying to figure out what makes ordinary American citizens so obedient. The most obvious answer—that people are mean, nasty, brutish and sadistic—won't do. The subjects who gave the shocks to Mr. Wallace to the end of the board did not enjoy it. They groaned, protested, fidgeted, argued, and in some cases, were seized by fits of nervous, agitated giggling.

"They even try to get out of it," says Milgram, "but they are somehow engaged in something from which they cannot liberate themselves. They are locked into a structure, and they do not have the skills or inner resources to disengage themselves."

Milgram, because he mistakenly had assumed that he would have trouble getting people to obey the orders to shock Mr. Wallace, went to a lot of trouble to create a realistic situation.

There was crew cut Jack Williams and his grey laboratory coat. Not white, which might denote a medical technician, but ambiguously authoritative grey. Then there was the book on the table, and the other appurtenances of the laboratory which emitted the silent message that things were being performed here in the name of science, and were therefore great and good.

But the nicest touch of all was the shock generator. When Milgram started out, he had only a $300 grant from the Higgins Fund of Yale University. Later he got more ample support from the National Science Foundation, but in the beginning he had to create this authentic-looking

machine with very scarce resources except for his own imagination. So he went to New York and roamed around the electronic shops until he found some little black switches at Lafayette Radio for a dollar apiece. He bought thirty of them. The generator was a metal box, about the size of a small footlocker, and he drilled the thirty holes for the thirty switches himself in a Yale machine shop. But the fine detail was left to professional industrial engravers. So he ended up with a splendid-looking control panel dominated by the row of switches, each labeled with its voltage, and each having its own red light that flashed on when the switch was pulled. Other things happened when a switch was pushed. Besides the ZZUMPHing noise, a blue light labeled "voltage energizer" went on, and a needle on a dial labeled "voltage" flicked from left to right. Relays inside the box clicked. Finally, in the upper left-hand corner of the control panel was this inscription, engraved in precise block letters:

SHOCK GENERATOR TYPE ZLB
DYSON INSTRUMENT COMPANY
WALTHAM, MASS.
OUTPUT: 15 VOLTS–450 VOLTS

One day a man from the Lehigh Valley Electronics Company of Pennsylvania was passing through the laboratory, and he stopped to admire the shock generator.

"This is a very fine shock generator," he said. "But who is this Dyson Instrument Company?" Milgram felt proud at that, since Dyson Instrument Company existed only in the recesses of his imagination.

When you consider the seeming authenticity of the situation, you can appreciate the agony some of the subjects went through. It was pure conflict. As Milgram explains to his students, "When a parent says, 'Don't strike old ladies,' you are learning two things: the content and, also, to obey authority. This experiment creates conflicts between the two elements."

Here is a partial transcription from one of the experiments. The naïve "teacher" is a heavyset, worried-looking man with prematurely grey hair. He is wearing a polo shirt. He is very polite. He has just pushed the 180-volt lever. A hidden camera is recording the performance.

LEARNER (*who, from the teacher's point of view is heard but not seen, an offstage voice*): Ow, I can't stand the pain. Don't do that. . . .

TEACHER (*pivoting around in his chair and shaking his head*): I can't stand it. I'm not going to kill that man in there. You hear him hollering?

EXPERIMENTER: As I told you before, the shocks may be painful, but—

TEACHER: But he's hollering. He can't stand it. What's going to happen to him?

EXPERIMENTER (*His voice is patient, matter-of-fact.*): The experiment requires that you continue, Teacher.

TEACHER: Aaah, but, unh, I'm not going to get that man sick in there . . . know what I mean?

EXPERIMENTER: Whether the learner likes it or not, we must go on, through all the word pairs.

TEACHER: I refuse to take the responsibility. He's in there hollering!

EXPERIMENTER: It's absolutely essential that you continue, Teacher.

TEACHER (*indicating the unused questions*): There's too many left here, I mean, Geez, if he gets them wrong, there's too many of them left. I mean who's going to take the responsibility if anything happens to that gentleman?

EXPERIMENTER: I'm responsible for anything that happens to him. Continue please.

TEACHER: All right. (*Consults list of words.*) The next one's "Slow—walk, truck, dance, music." Answer, please. (*A buzzing sound indicates the learner has signaled his answer.*) Wrong. A hundred and ninety-five volts. "Dance." (*Zzumph!*)

LEARNER: Let me out of here. My heart's bothering me! (*Teacher looks at experimenter.*)

EXPERIMENTER: Continue, please.

LEARNER (*screaming*): Let me out of here, you have no right to keep me here. Let me out of here, let me out, my heart's bothering me, let me out! (*Teacher shakes head, pats the table nervously.*)

TEACHER: You see, he's hollering. Hear that? Gee, I don't know.

EXPERIMENTER: The experiment requires. . . .

TEACHER (*interrupting*): I know it does, sir, but I mean—hunh! He don't know what he's getting in for. He's up to 195 volts! (*Experiment continues, through 210 volts, 225 volts, 240 volts, 255 volts, 270 volts, delivered to the man in the electric chair, at which point the teacher, with evident relief, runs out of word-pair questions.*)

EXPERIMENTER: You'll have to go back to the beginning of that page and go through them again until he's learned them all correctly.

TEACHER: Aw, no. I'm not going to kill that man. You mean I've got to keep going up with the scale. No sir. He's hollering in there. I'm not going to give him 450 volts.

EXPERIMENTER: The experiment requires that you go on.

TEACHER: I know it does, but that man is hollering in there, sir.

EXPERIMENTER (*same matter-of-fact tone*): As I said before, although the shocks may be painful . . .

TEACHER (*interrupting*): Awwww. He—he—he's yelling in there.

EXPERIMENTER: Start with "Blue," please, at the top of the page. Continue, please, Teacher. Just go ahead.

TEACHER (*concentrating intently on list of words in front of him, as if to shut everything else out*): "Blue—boy, girl, grass, hat." (*Buzz indicates answer.*) Correct. "Night—day, sky, job, chair." (*Buzz*) Wrong. The answer is "day." Two hundred and eighty-five volts. (*Zzumph!*)

LEARNER: *Ohhhuhhoohhh!*

EXPERIMENTER: Continue, please.

TEACHER: "Fat—man, lady, tub, neck." Answer, please. (*Buzz*) Wrong. The answer is "neck." Three hundred volts. (*Zzumph!*)

LEARNER: Ohhh. I absolutely refuse to answer any more. (*Shouting urgently, now*) Let me out of here. You can't hold me here. Get me out. Get—me—out—of—here.

EXPERIMENTER: Continue. The next word is "Green," please.

TEACHER: "Green—grass, hat, ink, apple." (*Nothing happens. No answering buzz. Just gloomy silence.*)

TEACHER: I don't think he is going to answer.

EXPERIMENTER: If the learner doesn't answer in a reasonable time, about four or five seconds, consider the answer wrong. And follow the same procedures you have been doing for wrong answers. Say "Wrong," tell him the number of volts, give him the punishment, read him the correct answer. Continue, please.

TEACHER: "Green—grass, hat, ink, apple." Answer, please. (*More silence. Teacher just sits there.*)

EXPERIMENTER: Go on with the procedure, please, Teacher.

TEACHER: Three hundred and fifteen volts. The answer is "ink." (*Zzumph!*)

LEARNER: Ohh, Ooohh.

TEACHER (*relieved to hear response*): Next one . . .

LEARNER: I absolutely refuse to answer.

TEACHER: You got to. You get a shock if you don't answer. (*Experiment continues with learner refusing to answer, and finally failing even to grunt or groan. At 375 volts, the teacher stands up. Has he had enough? Will he break off the experiment? Will he disobey?*)

TEACHER: I think something's happened to that fellow in there. I don't get no answer. He was hollering at less voltage. Can't you check in and see if he's all right, please?

EXPERIMENTER (*same detached calm*): Not once we've started. Please continue, Teacher.

TEACHER (*sits down, sighs deeply*): "Cool—day, shade, water, paint." Answer, please. Are you all right in there? Are you all right?

EXPERIMENTER: Please continue, Teacher. Continue, please. (*Teacher pushes lever. Zzumph!*)

TEACHER (*swiveling around in his chair*): Something's happened to that man in there. (*Swiveling back*) Next one. "Low—dollar, necklace, moon, paint." (*Turning around again*) Something's happened to that man in there. You better check in on him, sir. He won't answer or nothing.

EXPERIMENTER: Continue. Go on, please.

TEACHER: You accept all responsibility.

EXPERIMENTER: The responsibility is mine. Correct. Please go on. (*Teacher returns to his list, starts running through words as rapidly as he can read them, works through to 450 volts.*)

TEACHER: That's that.

EXPERIMENTER: Continue using the last switch on the board, please. The four-fifty switch for each wrong answer. Continue, please.

TEACHER: But I don't get no anything!

EXPERIMENTER: Please continue. The next word is "White."

TEACHER: Don't you think you should look in on him, please.

EXPERIMENTER: Not once we've started the experiment.

TEACHER: But what if something has happened to the man?

EXPERIMENTER: The experiment requires that you continue. Go on, please.

TEACHER: Don't the man's health mean anything?

EXPERIMENTER: Whether the learner likes it or not . . .

TEACHER: What if he's dead in there? (*Gestures toward the room with the electric chair*) I mean, he told me he can't stand the shock, sir. I don't mean to be rude, but I think you should look in on him. All you have to do is look in the door. I don't get no answer, no noise. Something might have happened to the gentleman in there, sir.

EXPERIMENTER: We must continue. Go on, please.

TEACHER: You mean keep giving him what? Four hundred fifty volts, what he's got now?

EXPERIMENTER: That's correct. Continue. The next word is "White."

TEACHER (*now at a furious pace*): "White—cloud, horse, rock, house." Answer, please. The answer is "horse." Four hundred and fifty volts. (*Zzumph!*) Next word. "Bag—paint, music, clown, girl." The answer is "paint." Four hundred and fifty volts. (*Zzumph!*) Next word is "Short—sentence, movie . . ."

EXPERIMENTER: Excuse me, Teacher. We'll have to discontinue the experiment.

(*Enter Milgram from camera's left. He has been watching from behind one-way glass.*)

MILGRAM: I'd like to ask you a few questions. (*Slowly, patiently, he dehoaxes the teacher, telling him that the shocks and screams were not real.*)

TEACHER: You mean he wasn't getting nothing? Well, I'm glad to hear that. I was getting upset there. I was getting ready to walk out. (*Finally, to make sure there are no hard feelings, friendly, harmless Mr. Wallace comes out in coat and tie. Gives jovial greeting. Friendly reconciliation takes place. Experiment ends.*)

Subjects in the experiment were not asked to give the 450-volt shock more than three times. By that time, it seemed evident that they would go on indefinitely. "No one," says Milgram, "who got within five shocks of the end ever broke off. By that point, he had resolved the conflict."

Why do so many people resolve the conflict in favor of obedience?

Milgram's theory assumes that people behave in two different operating modes as different as ice and water. He does not rely on Freud or sex or toilet-training hang-ups for this theory. All he says is that ordinarily we operate in a state of autonomy, which means we pretty much have and assert control over what we do. But in certain circumstances, we operate under what Milgram calls a state of agency (after agent, n . . . one who acts for or in the place of another by authority from him; a substitute; a deputy. —*Webster's Collegiate Dictionary*). A state of agency, to Milgram, is nothing more than a frame of mind.

"There's nothing bad about it, there's nothing good about it," he says. "It's a natural circumstance of living with other people. . . . I think of a state of agency as a real transformation of a person: if a person has different properties when he's in that state, just as water can turn to ice under certain conditions of temperature, a person can move to the state of mind that I call agency . . . the critical thing is that you see yourself as the instrument of the execution of another person's wishes. You do not see yourself as acting on your own. And there's a real transformation, a real change of properties of the person."

To achieve this change, you have to be in a situation where there seems to be a ruling authority whose commands are relevant to some legitimate purpose; the authority's power is not unlimited.

But situations can be and have been structured to make people do unusual things, and not just in Milgram's laboratory. The reason, says Milgram, is that no action, in and of itself, contains meaning.

"The meaning always depends on your definition of the situation. Take an action like killing another person. It sounds bad.

"But then we say the other person was about to destroy a hundred children, and the only way to stop him was to kill him. Well, that sounds good.

"Or, you take destroying your own life. It sounds very bad. Yet, in the Second World War, thousands of persons thought it was a good thing to destroy your own life. It was set in the proper context. You sipped some saki from a whistling cup, recited a few haiku. You said 'May my death be as clean and as quick as the shattering of crystal.' And it almost seemed like a good, noble thing to do, to crash your kamikaze plane into an aircraft carrier. But the main thing was, the definition of what a kamikaze pilot was doing had been determined by the relevant authority. Now, once you are in a state of agency, you allow the authority to determine, to define what the situation is. The meaning of your action is altered."

So, for most subjects in Milgram's laboratory experiments, the act of giving Mr. Wallace his painful shock was necessary, even though unpleasant, and besides they were doing it on behalf of somebody else and it was for science. There was still strain and conflict, of course. Most people resolved it by grimly sticking to their task and obeying. But some broke out. Milgram tried varying the conditions of the experiment to see what would help break people out of their state of agency.

"The results, as seen and felt in the laboratory," he has written, "are disturbing. They raise the possibility that human nature, or more specifically the kind of character produced in American democratic society, cannot be counted on to insulate its citizens from brutality and inhumane treatment at the direction of malevolent authority. A substantial proportion of people do what they are told to do, irrespective of the content of the act and without limitations of conscience, so long as they perceive that the command comes from a legitimate authority. If, in this study, an anonymous experimenter can successfully command adults to subdue a fifty-year-old man and force on him painful electric shocks against his protest, one can only wonder what government, with its vastly greater authority and prestige, can command of its subjects."

This is a nice statement, but it falls short of summing up the full meaning of Milgram's work. It leaves some questions still unanswered.

The first question is this: Should we really be surprised and alarmed that people obey? Wouldn't it be even more alarming if they all refused to obey? Without obedience to a relevant ruling authority there could not be a civil society. And without a civil society, as Thomas Hobbes pointed out in the seventeenth century, we would live in a condition of war, "of every man against every other man," and life would be "solitary, poor, nasty, brutish and short."

In the middle of one of Stanley Milgram's lectures at C.U.N.Y. recently, some mini-skirted undergraduates started whispering and giggling in the back of the room. He told them to cut it out. Since he was the relevant authority in that time and that place, they obeyed, and most people in the room were glad that they obeyed.

This was not, of course, a conflict situation. Nothing in the coeds' social upbringing made it a matter of conscience for them to whisper and giggle. But a case can be made that in a conflict situation it is all the more important to obey. Take the case of war, for example. Would we really want a situation in which every participant in a war, direct or indirect—from front-line soldiers to the people who sell coffee and cigarettes to employees at the Concertina barbed-wire factory in Kansas—stops and consults his conscience before each action? It is asking for an awful lot of mental strain and anguish from an awful lot of people. The value of having civil order is that one can do his duty, or whatever interests him, or whatever seems to benefit him at the moment, and leave the agonizing to others. When Francis Gary Powers was being tried by a Soviet military tribunal after his U-2 spy plane was shot down, the presiding judge asked if he had thought about the possibility that his flight might have provoked a war. Powers replied with Hobbesian clarity: "The people who sent me should think of these things. My job was to carry out orders. I do not think it was my responsibility to make such decisions."

It was not his responsibility. And it is quite possible that if everyone felt responsible for each of the ultimate consequences of his own tiny contributions to complex chains of events, then society simply would not work. Milgram, fully conscious of the moral and social implications of his research, believes that people should feel responsible for their actions. If someone else had invented the experiment, and if he had been the naïve subject, he feels certain that he would have been among the disobedient minority.

"There is no very good solution to this," he admits, thoughtfully. "To simply and categorically say that you won't obey authority may resolve your personal conflict, but it creates more problems for society which may be more serious in the long run. But I have no doubt that to disobey is the proper thing to do in this [the laboratory] situation. It is the only reasonable value judgment to make."

The conflict between the need to obey the relevant ruling authority and the need to follow your conscience becomes sharpest if you insist on living by an ethical system based on a rigid code—a code that seeks to answer all questions in advance of their being raised. Code ethics cannot solve the obedience problem. Stanley Milgram seems to be a situation ethicist, and situation ethics does offer a way out: When you feel conflict, you examine the situation and then make a choice among the competing evils. You may act with a presumption in favor of obedience, but reserve the possibility that you will disobey whenever obedience demands a flagrant and outrageous affront to conscience. This, by the way, is the philosophical position of many who resist the draft. In World War II, they would have fought. Vietnam is a different, an outrageously different, situation.

Life can be difficult for the situation ethicist, because he does not see the world in straight lines, while the social system too often assumes such a God-given, squared-off structure. If your moral code includes an injunction against all

war, you may be deferred as a conscientious objector. If you merely oppose this particular war, you may not be deferred.

Stanley Milgram has his problems, too. He believes that in the laboratory situation, he would not have shocked Mr. Wallace. His professional critics reply that in his real-life situation he has done the equivalent. He has placed innocent and naïve subjects under great emotional strain and pressure in selfish obedience to his quest for knowledge. When you raise this issue with Milgram, he has an answer ready. There is, he explains patiently, a critical difference between his naïve subjects and the man in the electric chair. The man in the electric chair (in the mind of the naïve subject) is helpless, strapped in. But the naïve subject is free to go at any time.

Immediately after he offers this distinction, Milgram anticipates the objection.

"It's quite true," he says, "that this is almost a philosophic position, because we have learned that some people are psychologically incapable of disengaging themselves. But that doesn't relieve them of the moral responsibility."

The parallel is exquisite. "The tension problem was unexpected," says Milgram in his defense. But he went on anyway. The naïve subjects didn't expect the screaming protests from the strapped-in learner. But they went on.

"I had to make a judgment," says Milgram. "I had to ask myself, was this harming the person or not? My judgment is that it was not. Even in the extreme cases, I wouldn't say that permanent damage results."

Sound familiar? "The shocks may be painful," the experimenter kept saying, "but they're not dangerous."

After the series of experiments was completed, Milgram sent a report of the results to his subjects and a questionnaire, asking whether they were glad or sorry to have been in the experiment. Eighty-three and seven-tenths percent said they were glad and only 1.3 percent were sorry; 15 percent were neither sorry nor glad. However, Milgram could not be sure at the time of the experiment that only 1.3 percent would be sorry.

Kurt Vonnegut Jr. put one paragraph in the preface to *Mother Night*, in 1966, which pretty much says it for the people with their fingers on the shock-generator switches, for you and me, and maybe even for Milgram. "If I'd been born in Germany," Vonnegut said, "I suppose I would have *been* a Nazi, bopping Jews and gypsies and Poles around, leaving boots sticking out of snowbanks, warming myself with my sweetly virtuous insides. So it goes."

Just so. One thing that happened to Milgram back in New Haven during the days of the experiment was that he kept running into people he'd watched from behind the one-way glass. It gave him a funny feeling, seeing those people going about their everyday business in New Haven and knowing what they would do to Mr. Wallace if ordered to. Now that his research results are in and you've thought about it, you can get this funny feeling too. You don't need one-way glass. A glance in your own mirror may serve just as well.

Questions

1. Ultimately, Milgram conducted this experiment with thousands of individuals from all walks of life. One series of experiments involved the use of women in the teacher role. Milgram notes that their performance was "virtually identical to the performance of men," although women experienced a higher level of conflict than men did. One variation that Milgram did not attempt was using women as "learners." What effect might this have had on, say, male teachers' performance?

2. In your judgment, if the technician ("Jack Williams") had been female, would this have changed the outcome of the experiment? Why or why not?

3. Milgram has been criticized for being unethical in conducting this research. Why? How did he respond to these criticisms? Are you more persuaded by Milgram or by his critics? Why?

4. Meyer implies that Milgram's motives were something other than purely scientific—that his decision was in part a "moral one," "colored by his own Jewish background." Did Milgram's moral convictions lead him to invalid findings? Why or why not?

5. Elsewhere, Milgram wrote this:

   > The problem of obedience, therefore, is not wholly psychological. The form and shape of society and the way it is developed have much to do with it. There was a time, perhaps, when men were able to give a fully human response to any situation because they were fully absorbed in it as human beings. But as soon as there was a division of labor among men, things changed. Beyond a certain point, the breaking up of society into people carrying out narrow and very special jobs takes away from the human quality of work and life. A person does not get to see the whole situation but only a small part of it, and is thus unable to act without some kind of over-all direction. He yields to authority but in so doing is alienated [separated] from his own actions. (Milgram, *Obedience to Authority* [New York: Harper & Row, 1975], p. 11)

   Do you agree or disagree with Milgram? Why?

8

QUEER CUSTOMS

Clyde Kluckhohn

Clyde K. M. Kluckhohn (1905–1960) was born in Iowa and studied anthropology at Princeton, Wisconsin, Vienna, and Oxford universities. In 1935, Kluckhohn accepted a position at Harvard University, where he stayed for the remainder of his career. Kluckhohn's particular area of expertise was the Navajo. The following essay is excerpted from his 1949 book *Mirror for Man*, which Kluckhohn wrote in order to explain cultural theory to the lay public.

Why do the Chinese dislike milk and milk products? Why would the Japanese die willingly in a Banzai[1] charge that seemed senseless to Americans? Why do some nations trace descent through the father, others through the mother, still others through both parents? Not because different peoples have different instincts, not because they were destined by God or Fate to different habits, not because the weather is different in China and Japan and the United States. Sometimes shrewd common sense has an answer that is close to that of the anthropologist: "because they were brought up that way." By "culture" anthropology means the total life way of a people, the social legacy the individual acquires from his group. Or culture can be regarded as that part of the environment that is the creation of man.

This technical term has a wider meaning than the "culture" of history and literature. A humble cooking pot is as much a cultural product as is a Beethoven sonata. In ordinary speech a man of culture is a man who can speak languages other than his own, who is familiar with history, literature, philosophy, or the fine arts. In some cliques that definition is still narrower. The cultured person is one who can talk about James Joyce, Scarlatti, and Picasso.[2] To the anthropologist, however, to be human is to be cultured. There is culture in general, and then there are the specific cultures such as Russian, American, British, Hottentot,[3] Inca. The general abstract notion

[1] Banzai is a Japanese war cry.—Ed.

"Queer Customs" from *Mirror for Man* by Clyde Kluckhohn, pp. 17–20, 24–27, 30–33. Copyright © 1949 George E. Taylor. Reprinted by permission of George E. Taylor.

[2] So, are you a cultured person by this definition? James Joyce (1882–1941) was an Irish author. His best-known book, *Ulysses*, was a novel about a day in Dublin (June 4, 1904). It was published in Paris in 1922 but was banned in the United States until 1937. Alessandro Scarlatti (1660–1725) was a Sicilian composer noted mostly for his operas. Pablo Picasso (1881–1973) was a prolific artist. Born in Spain (in Málaga), he spent much of his life in France. During his lifetime, he created more than 50,000 works—drawings, paintings, sculptures, and even ceramics and lithographs.—Ed.

[3] More properly called the *Khoikhoi*—a people mostly of Namibia, Africa. Nomadic and pastoral, their numbers were decimated by Dutch colonists in the seventeenth and eighteenth centuries.—Ed.

serves to remind us that we cannot explain acts solely in terms of the biological properties of the people concerned, their individual past experience, and the immediate situation. The past experience of other men in the form of culture enters into almost every event. Each specific culture constitutes a kind of blueprint for all of life's activities.

One of the interesting things about human beings is that they try to understand themselves and their own behavior. While this has been particularly true of Europeans in recent times, there is no group which has not developed a scheme or schemes to explain man's actions. To the insistent human query "why?" the most exciting illumination anthropology has to offer is that of the concept of culture. Its explanatory importance is comparable to categories such as evolution in biology, gravity in physics, disease in medicine. A good deal of human behavior can be understood, and indeed predicted, if we know a people's design for living. Many acts are neither accidental nor due to personal peculiarities nor caused by supernatural forces nor simply mysterious. Even those of us who pride ourselves on our individualism follow most of the time a pattern not of our own making. We brush our teeth on arising. We put on pants—not a loincloth or a grass skirt. We eat three meals a day—not four or five or two. We sleep in a bed—not in a hammock or on a sheep pelt. I do not have to know the individual and his life history to be able to predict these and countless other regularities, including many in the thinking process, of all Americans who are not incarcerated in jails or hospitals for the insane.

To the American woman a system of plural wives seems "instinctively" abhorrent. She cannot understand how any woman can fail to be jealous and uncomfortable if she must share her husband with other women. She feels it "unnatural" to accept such a situation. On the other hand, a Koryak woman of Siberia, for example, would find it hard to understand how a woman could be so selfish and so undesirous of feminine companionship in the home as to wish to restrict her husband to one mate.

Some years ago I met in New York City a young man who did not speak a word of English and was obviously bewildered by American ways. By "blood" he was as American as you or I, for his parents had gone from Indiana to China as missionaries. Orphaned in infancy, he was reared by a Chinese family in a remote village. All who met him found him more Chinese than American. The facts of his blue eyes and light hair were less impressive than a Chinese style of gait, Chinese arm and hand movements, Chinese facial expression, and Chinese modes of thought. The biological heritage was American, but the cultural training had been Chinese. He returned to China.

Another example of another kind: I once knew a trader's wife in Arizona who took a somewhat devilish interest in producing a cultural reaction. Guests who came her way were often served delicious sandwiches filled with a meat that seemed to be neither chicken nor tuna fish yet was reminiscent of both. To queries she gave no reply until each had eaten his fill. She then explained that what they had eaten was not chicken, not tuna fish, but the rich, white flesh of freshly killed rattlesnakes. The response was instantaneous—vomiting, often violent vomiting. A biological process is caught in a cultural web.

A highly intelligent teacher with long and successful experience in the public schools of Chicago was finishing her first year in an Indian school. When asked how her Navaho pupils compared in intelligence with Chicago youngsters, she replied, "Well, I just don't know. Sometimes the Indians seem just as bright. At other times they just act like dumb animals. The other night we had a dance in the high school. I saw a boy who is one of the best students in my English class standing off by himself. So I took him over to a pretty girl and told them to dance. But they just stood there with their heads down. They wouldn't even say anything." I inquired if she knew whether or not they were members of the same clan. "What difference would that make?"

"How would you feel about getting into bed with your brother?" The teacher walked off in a huff, but, actually, the two cases were quite comparable in principle. To the Indian the type of bodily contact involved in our social dancing has a directly sexual connotation. The incest taboos between members of the same clan are as severe as between true brothers and sisters. The shame of the Indians at the suggestion that a clan brother and sister should dance and the indignation of the white teacher at the idea that she should share a bed with an adult brother represent equally nonrational responses, culturally standardized unreason. . . .

Culture and Society

Since culture is an abstraction, it is important not to confuse culture with society. A "society" refers to a group of people who interact more with each other than they do with other individuals—who cooperate with each other for the attainment of certain ends. You can see and indeed count the individuals who make up a society. A "culture" refers to the distinctive ways of life of such a group of people. Not all social events are culturally patterned. New types of circumstances arise for which no cultural solutions have as yet been devised.

A culture constitutes a storehouse of the pooled learning of the group. A rabbit starts life with some innate responses. He can learn from his own experience and perhaps from observing other rabbits. A human infant is born with fewer instincts and greater plasticity. His main task is to learn the answers that persons he will never see, persons long dead, have worked out. Once he has learned the formulas supplied by the culture of his group, most of his behavior becomes almost as automatic and unthinking as if it were instinctive. There is a tremendous amount of intelligence behind the making of a radio, but not much is required to learn to turn it on.

The members of all human societies face some of the same unavoidable dilemmas, posed by biology and other facts of the human situation. This is why the basic categories of all cultures are so similar. Human culture without language is unthinkable. No culture fails to provide for aesthetic expression and aesthetic delight. Every culture supplies standardized orientations toward the deeper problems, such as death. Every culture is designed to perpetuate the group and its solidarity, to meet the demands of individuals for an orderly way of life and for satisfaction of biological needs.

However, the variations on these basic themes are numberless. Some languages are built up out of twenty basic sounds, others out of forty. Nose plugs were considered beautiful by the predynastic Egyptians but are not by the modern French. Puberty is a biological fact. But one culture ignores it, another prescribes informal instructions about sex but no ceremony, a third has impressive rites for girls only, a fourth for boys and girls. In this culture, the first menstruation is welcomed as a happy, natural event; in that culture the atmosphere is full of dread and supernatural threat. Each culture dissects nature according to its own system of categories. The Navaho Indians apply the same word to the color of a robin's egg and to that of grass. A psychologist once assumed that this meant a difference in the sense organs, that Navahos didn't have the physiological equipment to distinguish "green" from "blue." However, when he showed them objects of the two colors and asked them if they were exactly the same colors, they looked at him with astonishment. His dream of discovering a new type of color blindness was shattered.

Every culture must deal with the sexual instinct. Some, however, seek to deny all sexual expression before marriage, whereas a Polynesian adolescent who was not promiscuous would be distinctly abnormal. Some cultures enforce lifelong monogamy; others, like our own, tolerate serial monogamy; in still other cultures, two or more women may be joined to one man or several men to a single woman. Homosexuality has been a permitted pattern in the Greco-Roman world, in parts of Islam, and in various primitive tribes. Large portions of the population of Tibet, and of Christendom at some places and periods, have practiced complete celibacy. To us marriage is first and foremost an arrangement between two individuals. In many more societies marriage is merely one facet of a complicated set of reciprocities, economic and otherwise, between two families or two clans.

The essence of the cultural process is selectivity. The selection is only exceptionally conscious and rational. Cultures are like Topsy. They just grew.[4] Once, however, a way of handling a situation becomes institutionalized, there is ordinarily great resistance to change or deviation. When we speak of "our sacred beliefs," we mean of course that they are beyond criticism and that the person who suggests modification or abandonment must be punished. No person is emotionally indifferent to his culture. Certain cultural premises may become totally out of accord with a new factual situation. Leaders may recognize this and reject the old ways in theory. Yet their emotional loyalty continues in the face of reason because of the intimate conditionings of early childhood.

A culture is learned by individuals as the result of belonging to some particular group, and it constitutes that part of learned behavior which is shared with others. It is our social legacy, as contrasted with our organic heredity. It is one of the important factors which permits us to live together in an organized society, giving us ready-made solutions to our problems, helping us to predict the behavior of others, and permitting others to know what to expect of us.

Culture regulates our lives at every turn. From the moment we are born until we die there is, whether we are conscious of it or not, constant pressure upon us to follow certain types of behavior that other men have created for us. Some paths we follow willingly, others we follow because we know no other way, still others we deviate from or go back to most unwillingly. Mothers of small children know how unnaturally most of this comes to us—how little regard we have, until we are "culturalized," for the "proper" place, time, and manner for certain acts such as eating, excreting, sleeping, getting dirty, and making loud noises. But by more or less adhering to a system of related designs for carrying out all the acts of living, a group of men and women feel themselves linked together by a powerful chain of sentiments. Ruth Benedict gave an almost complete definition of the concept when she said, "Culture is that which binds men together." . . .

No participant in any culture knows all the details of the cultural map. The statement frequently heard that St. Thomas Aquinas was the last man to master all the knowledge of his society is intrinsically absurd. St. Thomas

---

[4]To grow like Topsy means to flourish without being purposefully tended. The roots of this odd-sounding expression are to be found in *Uncle Tom's Cabin*, by Harriet Beecher Stowe. In 1850, the Congress enacted a Fugitive Slave Act which required the return of runaway slaves who fled to states where slavery had been abolished. Beecher Stowe's novel was written in a protest against this law and slavery in general. The character Topsy was a young slave girl of about eight or nine years old. Purchased from an abusive family, Topsy is brought to New England to be raised by the pious Ophelia St. Clare. Asked by Miss Ophelia how old she is, Topsy says she has no idea: Another slave explains to Miss Ophelia that it is common practice in the South for speculators to purchase black infants and raise them for the slave market. When queried about her parents, Topsy says, "I spect I growed. Don't think nobody never made me."—Ed.

would have been hard put to make a pane of cathedral glass or to act as a midwife. In every culture there are what Ralph Linton has called "universals, alternatives, and specialties." Every Christian in the thirteenth century knew that it was necessary to attend mass, to go to confession, to ask the Mother of God to intercede with her Son. There were many other universals in the Christian culture of Western Europe. However, there were also alternative cultural patterns even in the realm of religion. Each individual had his own patron saint, and different towns developed the cults of different saints. The thirteenth-century anthropologist could have discovered the rudiments of Christian practice by questioning and observing whomever he happened to meet in Germany, France, Italy, or England. But to find out the details of the ceremonials honoring St. Hubert or St. Bridget he would have had to seek out certain individuals or special localities where these alternative patterns were practiced. Similarly, he could not learn about weaving from a professional soldier or about canon law from a farmer. Such cultural knowledge belongs in the realm of the specialties, voluntarily chosen by the individual or ascribed to him by birth. Thus, part of a culture must be learned by everyone, part may be selected from alternative patterns, part applies only to those who perform the roles in the society for which these patterns are designed.

Many aspects of a culture are explicit. The explicit culture consists in those regularities in word and deed that may be generalized straight from the evidence of the ear and the eye. The recognition of these is like the recognition of style in the art of a particular place and epoch. If we have examined twenty specimens of the wooden saints' images made in the Taos valley of New Mexico in the late eighteenth century, we can predict that any new images from the same locality and period will in most respects exhibit the same techniques of carving, about the same use of colors and choice of woods, a similar quality of artistic conception. Similarly, if, in a society of 2,000 members, we record 100 marriages at random and find that in 30 cases a man has married the sister of his brother's wife, we can anticipate that an additional sample of 100 marriages will show roughly the same number of cases of this pattern.

The above is an instance of what anthropologists call a behavioral pattern, the practices as opposed to the rules of the culture. There are also, however, regularities in what people say they do or should do. They do tend in fact to prefer to marry into a family already connected with their own by marriage, but this is not necessarily part of the official code of conduct. No disapproval whatsoever is attached to those who make another sort of marriage. On the other hand, it is explicitly forbidden to marry a member of one's own clan even though no biological relationship is traceable. This is a regulatory pattern—a Thou Shalt or a Thou Shalt Not. Such patterns may be violated often, but their existence is nevertheless important. A people's standards for conduct and belief define the socially approved aims and the acceptable means of attaining them. When the discrepancy between the theory and the practice of a culture is exceptionally great, this indicates that the culture is undergoing rapid change. It does not prove that ideals are unimportant, for ideals are but one of a number of factors determining action.

Cultures do not manifest themselves solely in observable customs and artifacts. No amount of questioning of any save the most articulate in the most self-conscious cultures will bring out some of the basic attitudes common to the members of the group. This is because these basic assumptions are taken so for granted that they normally do not enter into consciousness. This part of the cultural map must be inferred by the observer on the basis of consistencies in thought and action. Missionaries in various societies are often disturbed or puzzled because the natives do not regard "morals" and "sex code" as almost synonymous. The natives seem to feel that morals are concerned with sex just about as much as with eating—no less and no more. No society fails to have some restrictions on sexual behavior, but sex activity outside of marriage need not necessarily be furtive or attended with guilt. The Christian tradition has tended to assume that sex is inherently nasty as well as dangerous. Other cultures assume that sex in itself is not only natural but one of the good things of life, even though sex acts with certain persons under certain circumstances are forbidden. This is implicit culture, for the natives do not announce their premises. The missionaries would get further if they said, in effect, "Look, our morality starts from different assumptions. Let's talk about those assumptions," rather than ranting about "immorality." ...

In our highly self-conscious Western civilization that has recently made a business of studying itself, the number of assumptions that are literally implicit, in the sense of never having been stated or discussed by anyone, may be negligible. Yet only a trifling number of Americans could state even those implicit premises of our culture that have been brought to light by anthropologists. If one could bring to the American scene a Bushman who had been socialized in his own culture and then trained in anthropology, he would perceive all sorts of patterned regularities of which our anthropologists are completely unaware. In the case of the less sophisticated and less self-conscious societies, the unconscious assumptions characteristically made by individuals brought up under approximately the same social controls bulk even larger. But in any society, as Edward Sapir said, "Forms and significances which seem obvious to an outsider will be denied outright by those who carry out the patterns; outlines and implications that are perfectly clear to these may be absent to the eye of the onlooker." ...

Questions

1. According to Kluckhohn, what is the difference between culture and society? (Many people improperly use these terms interchangeably, but now that you know the difference you can avoid that error.)

2. What does Kluckhohn mean by the phrase "culturally standardized unreason"? Can you think of any examples of this sort of unreason from your own culture?

3. What does Kluckhohn mean by the concept of "behavioral pattern"? What is a "regulatory pattern"? Give a couple of examples from your own culture of instances in which behavioral and regulatory patterns are consistent. Then, give examples from your own culture in which behavioral and regulatory patterns are inconsistent. (Which was harder to do—to find examples of consistency or of inconsistency between behavioral patterns and regulatory patterns? Why do you think this is?)

9

BODY RITUAL AMONG THE NACIREMA

Horace Miner

The American anthropologist Horace Miner was one of the first to make public the results of anthropological research on the Nacirema. Although in the decades that followed the 1956 publication of Miner's work many more studies have been published, none more dramatically reveals the role of myth, magic, and ritual in the lives of this rather exotic group of people.

The anthropologist has become so familiar with the diversity of ways in which different peoples behave in similar situations that he is not apt to be surprised by even the most exotic customs. In fact, if all of the logically possible combinations of behavior have not been found somewhere in the world, he is apt to suspect that they must be present in some as yet undescribed tribe. This point has, in fact, been expressed with respect to clan organization by Murdock (1949, 71). In this light, the magical beliefs and practices of the Nacirema present such unusual aspects that it seems desirable to describe them as an example of the extremes to which human behavior can go.

Professor Linton first brought the ritual of the Nacirema to the attention of anthropologists [over seventy] years ago (1936, 326), but the culture of this people is still very poorly understood. They are a North American group living in the territory between the Canadian Cree, the Yaqui and Tarahumare of Mexico, and the Carib and Arawak of the Antilles. Little is known of their origin, although tradition states that they came from the east.

According to Nacirema mythology, their nation was originated by a culture hero, Notgnihsaw, who is otherwise known for two great feats of strength—the throwing of a piece of wampum across the river Po-To-Mac and the chopping down of a cherry tree in which the Spirit of Truth resided.

Nacirema culture is characterized by a highly developed market economy which has evolved in a rich natural habitat. While much of the people's time is devoted to economic pursuits, a large part of the fruits of these labors and a considerable portion of the day are spent in ritual activity. The focus of this activity is the human body, the appearance and health of which loom as a dominant concern in the ethos of the people. While such a concern is certainly not unusual, its ceremonial aspects and associated philosophy are unique.

The fundamental belief underlying the whole system appears to be that the human body is ugly and that its natural tendency is to debility and disease. Incarcerated in such a body, man's only hope is to avert these characteristics through the use of the powerful influences of ritual and ceremony. Every household has one or more shrines devoted to this purpose. The more powerful individuals in the society have several shrines in their houses and, in fact, the opulence of a house is often referred to in terms of the number of such ritual centers it possesses. Most houses are of wattle and daub construction, but the shrine rooms of the more wealthy are walled with stone. Poorer families imitate the rich by applying pottery plaques to their shrine walls.

While each family has at least one such shrine, the rituals associated with it are not family ceremonies but are private and secret. The rites are normally only discussed with children, and then only during the period when they are being initiated into these mysteries. I was able, however, to establish sufficient rapport with the natives to examine these shrines and to have the rituals described to me.

The focal point of the shrine is a box or chest which is built into the wall. In this chest are kept the many charms and magical potions without which no native believes he could live. These preparations are secured from a variety of specialized practitioners. The most powerful of these are the medicine men, whose assistance must be rewarded with substantial gifts. However, the medicine men do not provide the curative potions for their clients, but decide what the ingredients should be and they write them down in an ancient and secret language. This writing is understood only by the medicine men and by the herbalists who, for another gift, provide the required charm.

The charm is not disposed of after it has served its purpose, but is placed in the charm-box of the household shrine. As these magical materials are specific for certain ills, and the real or imagined maladies of the people are many, the charm-box is usually full to overflowing. The magical packets are so numerous that people forget what their purposes were and fear to use them again. While the natives are very vague on this point, we can only assume that the idea in retaining all the old magical materials is that their presence in the charm-box, before which the body rituals

are conducted, will in some way protect the worshipper.

Beneath the charm-box is a small font. Each day every member of the family, in succession, enters the shrine room, bows his head before the charm-box, mingles different sorts of holy water in the font, and proceeds with a brief rite of ablution. The holy waters are secured from the Water Temple of the community, where the priests conduct elaborate ceremonies to make the liquid ritually pure.

In the hierarchy of magical practitioners, and below the medicine men in prestige, are specialists whose designation is best translated "holy-mouth-men." The Nacirema have an almost pathological horror of and fascination with the mouth, the condition of which is believed to have a supernatural influence on all social relationships. Were it not for the rituals of the mouth, they believe that their teeth would fall out, their gums bleed, their jaws shrink, their friends desert them, and their lovers reject them. They also believe that a strong relationship exists between oral and moral characteristics. For example, there is a ritual ablution of the mouth for children which is supposed to improve their moral fiber.

The daily body ritual performed by everyone includes a mouth-rite. Despite the fact that these people are so punctilious about care of the mouth, this rite involves a practice which strikes the uninitiated stranger as revolting. It was reported to me that the ritual consists of inserting a small bundle of hog hairs into the mouth, along with certain magical powders, and then moving the bundle in a highly formalized series of gestures.

In addition to the private mouth-rite, the people seek out a holy-mouth-man once or twice a year. These practitioners have an impressive set of paraphernalia, consisting of a variety of augers, awls, probes, and prods. The use of these objects in the exorcism of the evils of the mouth involves almost unbelievable ritual torture of the client. The holy-mouth-man opens the client's mouth and, using the above mentioned tools, enlarges any holes which decay may have created in the teeth. Magical materials are put into these holes. If there are no naturally occurring holes in the teeth, large sections of one or more teeth are gouged out so that the supernatural substance can be applied. In the client's view, the purpose of these ministrations is to arrest decay and to draw friends. The extremely sacred and traditional character of the rite is evident in the fact that the natives return to the holy-mouth-men year after year, despite the fact that their teeth continue to decay.

It is to be hoped that, when a thorough study of the Nacirema is made, there will be careful inquiry into the personality structure of these people. One has but to watch the gleam in the eye of a holy-mouth-man, as he jabs an awl into an exposed nerve, to suspect that a certain amount of sadism is involved. If this can be established, a very interesting pattern emerges, for most of the population shows definite masochistic tendencies. It was to these that Professor Linton referred in discussing a distinctive part of the daily body ritual which is performed only by men. This part of the rite involves scraping and lacerating the surface of the face with a sharp instrument. Special women's rites are performed only four times during each lunar month, but what they lack in frequency is made up in barbarity. As part of this ceremony, women bake their heads in small ovens for about an hour. The theoretically interesting point is that what seems to be a preponderantly masochistic people have developed sadistic specialists.

The medicine men have an imposing temple, or *latipso*, in every community of any size. The more elaborate ceremonies required to treat very sick patients can only be performed at this temple. These ceremonies involve not only the thaumaturge but a permanent group of vestal maidens who move sedately about the temple chambers in distinctive costume and headdress.

The *latipso* ceremonies are so harsh that it is phenomenal that a fair proportion of the really sick natives who enter the temple ever recover. Small children whose indoctrination is still incomplete have been known to resist attempts to take them to the temple because "that is where you go to die." Despite this fact, sick adults are not only willing but eager to undergo the protracted ritual purification, if they can afford to do so. No matter how ill the supplicant or how grave the emergency, the guardians of many temples will not admit a client if he cannot give a rich gift to the custodian. Even after one has gained admission and survived the ceremonies, the guardians will not permit the neophyte to leave until he makes still another gift.

The supplicant entering the temple is first stripped of all his or her clothes. In every-day life the Nacirema avoids exposure of his body and its natural functions. Bathing and excretory acts are performed only in the secrecy of the household shrine, where they are ritualized as part of the body-rites. Psychological shock results from the fact that body secrecy is suddenly lost upon entry into the *latipso*. A man, whose own wife has never seen him in an excretory act, suddenly finds himself naked and assisted by a vestal maiden while he performs his natural functions into a sacred vessel. This sort of ceremonial treatment is necessitated by the fact that the excreta are used by a diviner to ascertain the course and nature of the client's sickness. Female clients, on the other hand, find their naked bodies are subjected to the scrutiny, manipulation and prodding of the medicine men.

Few supplicants in the temple are well enough to do anything but lie on their hard beds. The daily ceremonies, like the rites of the holy-mouth-men, involve discomfort and torture. With ritual precision, the vestals awaken their miserable charges each dawn and roll them about on their beds of pain while performing ablutions, in the formal movements of which the maidens are highly trained. At other times they insert magic wands in the supplicant's mouth or force him to eat substances which are supposed to be healing. From time to time the medicine men come to their clients and jab magically treated needles into their flesh. The fact that these temple ceremonies may not cure, and may even kill the neophyte, in no way decreases the people's faith in the medicine men.

There remains one other kind of practitioner, known as a "listener." This witchdoctor has the power to exorcise the devils that lodge in the heads of people who have been bewitched. The Nacirema believe that parents bewitch their own children. Mothers are particularly suspected of putting a curse on children while teaching them the secret body rituals. The counter-magic of the witchdoctor is unusual in its lack of ritual. The patient simply tells the "listener" all his troubles and fears, beginning with the earliest difficulties he can remember. The memory displayed by the Nacirema in these exorcism sessions is truly remarkable. It is not uncommon for the patient to bemoan the rejection he felt upon being weaned as a baby, and a few individuals even see their troubles going back to the traumatic effects of their own birth.

In conclusion, mention must be made of certain practices which have their base in native esthetics but which depend upon the pervasive aversion to the natural body and its functions. There are ritual fasts to make fat people thin and ceremonial feasts to make thin people fat. Still other rites are used to make women's breasts larger if they are small, and smaller if they are large. General dissatisfaction with breast shape is symbolized in the fact that the ideal form is virtually outside the range of human variation. A few women afflicted with almost inhuman hypermammary development are so idolized that they make a handsome living by simply going from village to village and permitting the natives to stare at them for a fee.

Reference has already been made to the fact that excretory functions are ritualized, routinized, and relegated to secrecy. Natural reproductive functions are similarly distorted. Intercourse is taboo as a topic and scheduled as an act. Efforts are made to avoid pregnancy by the use of magical materials or by limiting intercourse to certain phases of the moon. Conception is actually very infrequent. When pregnant, women dress so as to hide their condition. Parturition takes place in secret, without friends or relatives to assist, and the majority of women do not nurse their infants.

Our review of the ritual life of the Nacirema has certainly shown them to be a magic-ridden people. It is hard to understand how they have managed to exist so long under the burdens which they have imposed upon themselves. But even such exotic customs as these take on real meaning when they are viewed with the insight provided by Malinowski when he wrote (1948, 70):

Looking from far and above, from our high places of safety in the developed civilization, it is easy to see all the crudity and irrelevance of magic. But without its power and guidance early man could not have mastered his practical difficulties as he has done, nor could man have advanced to the higher stages of civilization.

References

Linton, Ralph. 1936. *The Study of Man.* New York: Appleton-Century.

Malinowski, Bronislaw. 1948. *Magic, Science, and Religion.* Glencoe, IL: Free Press.

Murdock, George P. 1949. *Social Structure.* New York: Macmillan.

Questions

1. What is a thaumaturge?

2. Why would it be ethnocentric to think of the Nacirema as weird—or even silly—for their beliefs?

3. Can you see any signs that Miner experienced "culture shock" as he investigated the Nacirema? Explain.

4. Do you think you would enjoy taking a vacation in the land of the Nacirema? Why or why not?

10

ACT YOUR AGE

Cheryl Laz

Sociologists tend to question many of the things that most people take for granted. In the process they have discovered surprising things about social life. In this article, Professor Laz manages to surprise even many sociologists when she focuses on something that even sociologists have taken for granted: age. Age, she argues, is not just something we have, it's something we perform. And how we perform it depends upon the expectations of those around us.

Introduction

Age is norm

To laypersons (and to many sociologists in their unguarded moments) it seems almost absurd to think about age as anything but a chronological fact and as something every individual simply *is*. Like race and gender, for most people most of the time, age is unproblematic. When asked "How old are you?" we offer the number of years since our birth. When someone directs us to act our age, we know what age is (the number of years since our birth), usually know what is being demanded of us, and often are prepared to account for our "misbehavior." We assume that as people get older, they will fulfill different roles in a predictable sequence. When the sequence or the timing is altered, we linguistically mark the discrepancy (teenage mothers, nontraditional students), and we want an explanation, an account, for being "off time."

As with race and gender, the apparently objective and factual nature of age make it ideal for sociological inquiry. Sociologists now understand race as a social construction rather than a biological "fact." Race is defined by and constituted within social groups (How much "blood" makes one black or Native American?), and it is accomplished by individuals (What does it mean to "pass" as one race and not another?). Moreover, a sociological understanding of race has led us to appreciate more fully the relations of power and the pervasive normative ideas that create and sustain the supposedly biological "fact" of race.

Similarly, sociologists understand gender as a social construction and individual accomplishment. Gender is defined and constituted within social groups (What does masculinity entail for a heterosexual steelworker? a gay bank manager?), and it is accomplished by individuals in interaction (How does a woman in a male-dominated job "act" feminine?). Further, normative cultural ideas traditionally have equated gender with women. We view the dominant group, in this case men, as if its members had no gender.

There is much to suggest that age, like race and gender, is anything but natural and involves much more than the number of years since one's birth. "Act your age. You're a big kid now," we say to children to encourage independence (or obedience). "Act your age. Stop being so childish," we say to other adults when we think they are being irresponsible. "Act your age; you're not as young as you used

Superior ~ do the pay

"Act Your Age" by Cheryl Laz from *Sociological Forum*, Vol. 13, No. 1 (March, 1998: pp. 85–87, 98–110). Reprinted by permission of Blackwell Publishing Ltd.

to be," we say to an old person pursuing "youthful" activities. The sanctioned actions vary, but the command "Act!" remains the same. When we say "act your age" we press for behavior that conforms to norms. However, the saying also expresses a commonsense understanding that age is not natural or fixed, and it implies that age requires work, i.e., physical or mental effort. As such, the saying encapsulates a fundamentally sociological view of age and provides us with the useful metaphor of *performance*. Age *is* an act, a performance in the sense of something requiring activity and labor, and age is normative. Whether we do it well or poorly, according to the dominant rules or not, our accomplishment of age—indeed age itself—is always collective and social. However, age is not simply *shaped* by social forces; it is *constituted* in interaction and gains its meaning in interaction and in the context of larger social forces. We all perform or enact age; we perform our own age constantly, but we also give meaning to other ages and to age in general in our actions and interactions, our beliefs and words and feelings, our social policies.

This essay develops a framework with which to understand age as *accomplished*. "Accomplish," and the closely related "perform," can refer to ongoing actions as well as to actions finished or carried through to completion. In this essay, I emphasize accomplishment not as the full or final completion of an action, but rather as ongoing action that is ultimately social and public. (Although it also may be private, the accomplishment of age is never only private.) Accomplishing age involves often routine, sometimes impressive, but always ongoing, recurring work. . . .

"Doing Gender"

In "Doing Gender," Candace West and Don Zimmerman argue that gender is an *accomplishment*: an emergent feature of social situations that is both an outcome of and a rationale for the most fundamental division of society (1987; also West and Fenstermaker, 1993:151). Rather than viewing gender as a role, identity, or individual attribute, gender is a feature of social situations. It is embedded in and constituted by everyday interaction. We do gender in the actual or virtual presence of others, even when it seems irrelevant or unrelated to interaction. Casual conversation (Henley and Freeman, 1989), making dinner (Devault, 1991), working as an engineer (McIlwee and Robinson, 1992) or a flight attendant (Hochschild, 1983) are occasions for doing gender at the same time that they are conversations, meals, and work.

This distinctively sociological view is grounded in ethnomethodology, which "proposes that the properties of social life which seem objective, factual, and transsituational, are actually managed accomplishments or achievements of local processes" (Zimmerman, 1978, cited in West and Fenstermaker, 1993:152). To see "the objective reality of social facts *as* an ongoing accomplishment," ethnomethodologists and other sociologists treat the commonplace and unproblematic as unfamiliar or "anthropologically strange" (Garfinkel, 1967:vii).

West and Zimmerman show how even the most taken-for-granted aspects of social life (like the "fact" that there are two, and only two, sexes) are actually the result of socially guided conceptual, interactional, and micropolitical processes (1987:126). That we describe, explain, rationalize, justify—account—for ourselves and our actions is central to these processes (Heritage, 1984:136). Further, we act with an eye toward accountability; that is, we anticipate how our actions may be characterized, understood or misunderstood, excused, condemned, etc., and act in ways that will minimize the need for accounting (since accounting holds the possibilities of being misunderstood, discounted, or contradicted). As a result, we often conform to dominant norms and conceptualizations, including those related to age and gender, even if we question or reject those norms.

In West and Zimmerman's view, when individuals do gender "right" (i.e., in accordance with dominant beliefs about women and men, masculinity and femininity), gender becomes invisible. As we collectively "do it right," dominant assumptions about gender become natural. Indeed, gender itself is naturalized. Moreover, "If we do gender appropriately, we simultaneously sustain, reproduce, and render legitimate the institutional arrangements that are based on sex category. . . . [Ultimately,] an understanding of how gender is produced in social situations will afford clarification of the interactional scaffolding of social structure and the social control processes that sustain it" (West and Zimmerman, 1987:146–147). West and Zimmerman are, in the end, less interested in the production of a *gendered self* than they are in the production of *gender itself*. They intend for this formulation to overcome the twin dangers of self-determination and overdetermination by pointing out the reciprocal relationship between interaction and social structure, between choice, negotiation, and constraint.

Doing Age

West and Zimmerman explain how gender is constituted in and through interaction and how its accomplishment sustains social organization and social order. Like gender, age is accomplished—not in the sense of something completed, but in the sense of something "brought to pass" or continually carried on. In accomplishing age, we create and maintain selves, roles, and identities. But we also participate in and constitute a larger shared universe in which we impart meaning to age in ways that influence but transcend us as individuals. In this section, I outline the idea of age-as-accomplished in relation to the assumptions about age described earlier.

Although age often feels like something we simply are, it feels this way because we enact age in all interactions. Since we usually act our age in predictable ways—predictable given the particular context—we make age invisible. We make age *seem* natural.

Of course, age is not always invisible; occasionally it comes to the forefront of our consciousness and we must deliberately make sense of age, often in the context of particular events or milestones (birthdays, anniversaries, deaths of parents), changes in our physical appearance or physical condition, or social roles and norms (Eisenhandler, 1991; Karp, 1991). David Karp describes between ages 50 and 60 as "a decade of reminders . . . during which people, more sharply than before, are made to feel their age. . . . Contextual events giving rise to distinctive consciousness are correlated with age, but not determined by age" (1991:67, 69). At these moments, age is momentarily denaturalized; its meaning cannot be taken for granted.

Feminists in the 1970s referred to moments when gender or sex inequality was foregrounded in individual consciousness as a "click." "Clicks" are significant because they represent the point at which one can no longer take existing knowledge, relations, and practices as "givens."

While such reminders may be more frequent and intense at later ages, younger people are not exempt. During informal conversations over the past several years, colleagues not infrequently share their "age-click" anecdotes. One colleague (now in her mid-40s) confessed that the first time she refused to tell someone her "real" (i.e., chronological) age, something clicked; she was forced to examine what age meant to her personally and to women in general in the context of her social circles and in the larger society. Another relates the following anecdote. "Fifteen or 20 years ago (that makes me 30–35) I was sitting on the front step with D— and A—, and one of the children came up asking for a conflict resolution. I was all of a sudden struck by the fact that *we* were the 'grown ups.' I was shocked."

Perhaps the click comes from realizing that we are not acting our age or from noticing how effectively and unconsciously we have been acting our age. Or maybe we realize that we are "ahead of" or "behind time" (for example, more or less advanced in our careers or family lives in comparison to other people of the same chronological age or of the same cohort; observe the multiple ways to measure age). "Clicks" often require us to offer accounts to others or to ourselves, and accountability is social and interactional. Sociologists can study disruptions of "the normal," like the "clicks" described above, to explore how normalcy is accomplished, how "the natural" *becomes* natural.

Conceptualizing age-as-accomplished does not ignore the "fact" of chronology. Rather, it enables sociologists to examine the process by which chronology is *made* "factual" and to view the consequences of our acting *as if* chronology were natural. Moreover, viewing age-as-accomplished does not require rejecting the concepts of age norms or roles. Rather, it enables us to clarify how norms and roles work in social situations. Norms and roles are resources that individuals draw on in interaction. They are among the tools we use to act our age; they do not themselves constitute age. Conceptualizing age-as-accomplished also helps bridge the self-determined/overdetermined dichotomy by making explicit the "interactional scaffolding of social structure and the social control processes that sustain it" (West and Zimmerman, 1987:146–147). The reciprocal relationship between actors acting and structural factors constraining and enabling action is central. Finally, the idea of age-as-accomplished radically transforms the notion of age as a problem. If age is accomplished, then it is not a social problem in the sense of a troublesome condition requiring solution. It is, instead, a problem in the sense of a situation that presents uncertainty or difficulty that can be managed or negotiated, at best temporarily resolved, though never permanently eliminated.

Resources for Doing Age

If age is something everyone does, then how to act one's age is a "problem" each of us faces in innumerable encounters every day. How we act our age in any given situation is the product of the interpretations and choices (often unconscious) we make among available individual, cultural, and institutional resources. What are the resources from which we may choose? How do we choose among them? What shapes our accomplishment of age?

Ann Swidler has proposed "the image of culture as a 'tool kit' of symbols, stories, rituals, and world-views, which people may use in varying configurations to solve different kinds of problems" (1986:273). When people solve problems they construct strategies of action— persistent (but not fixed or immutable) ways of ordering action through time. Culture is significant, "not in defining ends of action [i.e., providing values or goals], but in providing cultural components that are used to construct strategies of action. . . . To adopt a line of conduct, one needs an image of the kind of world in which one is trying to act, a sense that one can read reasonably accurately . . . how one is doing, and a capacity to choose among alternative lines of action" (Swidler, 1986:273, 275).

This conceptualization has the advantage of seeing individuals as active and skilled users of culture, rather than as passive "cultural dopes" (Swidler, 1986:277). It has the advantage of seeing how "action is necessarily integrated into larger assemblages [strategies of action]" (Swidler, 1986:276) rather than seeing actions as something people choose one at a time according to their values or interests. It admits the potential for using culture in new, challenging, or unpredictable ways at the same time that it explains continuities and order. And it bridges the self-determined/ overdetermined dichotomy by positing active and skilled users of culture who nonetheless construct persistent ways of ordering action.

THE TOOL KIT

Our culture provides us with multiple images of and resources for doing age. These images and resources shape our consciousness of age, our expectations about the life course and life course changes, our behavior and feelings about our experiences, and our life chances. We draw on resources of different types from the most individual and personal—our bodies and interpersonal relations—to the organizational and institutional.

Resources are not simply "out there" waiting to be used in identical ways by all. Rather, in interaction we draw on and give meaning to available resources, then use that meaning as a guide to action. Arlie Hochschild's work on the sociology of emotions helps us understand how we make use of the available resources. Hochschild argues that emotions are culturally shaped and publicly displayed; the choice of display is constrained by macro social and cultural forces and by individual concerns for impression management and self-concept. Actors do "emotion work" in deciding how to feel and act in particular situations. In addition, Hochschild (1989) argues that emotions mediate between what people believe, say, and actually do; feelings mediate between ideals, goals, values, and actions and thus are crucial for understanding "strategies of action." In short, emotions function to transform available resources for acting one's age into the actual accomplishment of age.

I visualize available "age resources" as a set of concentric circles with the inner circle(s) consisting of personal and highly individualized resources—the body and interpersonal relationships. The outer circles consist of cultural, bureaucratic, institutional, and structural factors available to larger groups of people. Since individuals draw simultaneously on more personal (and possibly idiosyncratic) resources and impersonal bureaucratic and structural resources as they actively construct strategies of action, their strategies are ultimately patterned by age without being determined by age. Sociologists can thus generalize about age categories and age-related behaviors and statuses and at the same time appreciate variation and "deviance."

At the individual level, our bodies (appearance, physical capabilities, and changes) are a source of age consciousness and a resource for doing age. We interpret "internal" messages conveyed by bodies (stiffness in the morning, decreased agility) in the context of age. In addition, we get "external" messages about bodies (people comment on the presence or absence of grey hair or wrinkles). But the resources provided by our bodies require interpretation, and the experience and interpretation of bodies in relation to age is situational. For the "aging" table dancers—most in their late teens and early twenties—studied by Carol Ronai (1992), setting and situation, more than chronological age, give meaning to "old." Studies of nursing home residents (Gubrium, 1977, 1993; Diamond, 1992) also illustrate how the body and its functions are variously interpreted and acted upon.

Interpersonal interactions provide resources for and constraints on the accomplishment of age. For example, Gubrium et al. (1994:139) show how juvenile delinquents "act their age" in encounters with the police. Officers exercise a great deal of discretion and, in interaction with juveniles, demeanor is a crucial factor shaping officer response. "Those who act their age—appearing neither overly immature nor worldly beyond their years—are generally not seen as problems" (Gubrium et al., 1994:139). In this example, not acting one's age appropriately—appearing too immature or too worldly—might very well get one taken into custody. In the field of aging, research on housing and living arrangements (e.g., Margolis, 1990), care giving (e.g., Abel, 1991), and nursing homes (Gubrium, 1977; Ross, 1977; Hazan, 1992) shows the ways that

Society informs views [handwritten margin note]

things based on norms [handwritten margin note]

formal and informal attachments within and to social organizations and networks provide the setting for interpersonal relations and interaction, influence our feelings about age, and ultimately shape how we act our age.

Our culture, in the forms of language and cognitive and conceptual categories, provides yet another resource for accomplishing age. Hockey and James (1993:10) show how metaphors of childhood (with their assumptions of dependency) provide frames of reference for everyday encounters with people in multiple age categories and lay the foundation for treating physically dependent adults as childlike. Gubrium *et al.* (1994) examine the ways that images of the life course are used by mental health and social service professionals with serious consequences (hospitalization or release, course of treatment, etc.) for individuals.

Institutions such as the media, advertising, education, medicine, and religion depend on and sustain our consciousness of age, and they provide us with additional resources. For example, from the mass media we get images of different age categories with which to compare ourselves. These messages are not always consistent, nor are they necessarily desirable or attractive, as studies of ageism and stereotyping (Butler, 1996; Scrutton 1996) have shown. Yet, we situate ourselves vis-à-vis these images and as a consequence feel guilty or proud, ashamed or delighted, at our ability to "measure up."

Our legal system uses chronological age to regulate education, sexual intercourse, marriage, and labor force participation, to name just a few examples. Law, public policy, and bureaucratic requirements provide a resource for age consciousness and for actually accomplishing age since formal requirements enable and constrain strategies of action (Buchmann, 1989). For instance, much of how kids accomplish age is shaped by the requirements of teachers and administrators, the school day,

and the academic year (and this is historically specific; see Chudacoff, 1989). In addition, their accomplishment of age outside of school also is patterned by compulsory education. For example, for kids, getting older means getting to stay up later at night. But getting older also means an earlier start to the school day. During the school week, then, a 14-year-old's ability to act "grown up" and stay awake late is circumscribed.

Trends in the economy, employment, and labor markets influence life chances and the meaning and accomplishment of age. For example, the creation and extension of Social Security and employer pension plans make it possible (though not inevitable) to think of oneself as a retiree or future retiree. Conversely, assumptions about age, the typical life course, and life course transitions (especially education, marriage, childbearing, work, and retirement), in conjunction with assumptions about class, race/ethnicity, and gender, shape labor market practices and public policies such as Social Security.

In her studies of changes in labor force participation rates and early withdrawal (through disability, unemployment, and pension systems), Guillemard (1996) has found that "the age when persons stop working has been lowered significantly" in many Western industrialized countries. "The chronological thresholds used both to determine personal identities throughout the life course and to organize the transition to old age have been torn up during the last fifteen years" (Guillemard, 1996:180).

Guillemard argues that together welfare systems and work/retirement policies have had the effect of reorganizing the life course (1996:181). Mayer and Müller (1986) argue that both the modern, bureaucratic welfare state and the contemporary life course are joint products of the same processes of societal development (rationalization, social differentiation, and social control).

CHOOSING FROM AMONG THE TOOLS

... Accomplishing age requires that individuals use and interpret available resources, have emotional reactions, and act accordingly. As a result, ideologies (beliefs about age and aging including roles and norms), "objective" factors (such as chronological age or physical condition), and macro societal policies or trends (for example, opportunities for early labor force withdrawal) provide clues but do not tell us how individuals actually will feel about and accomplish their age. Instead we can examine how, in particular contexts, individuals constitute and respond to the meaning of available resources.

It is worth observing that people do not necessarily act their age in an explicit or self-conscious manner. Rather, the accomplishment of age is mediated through characteristics we assume to be related to age categories (for example, dependence and independence, competence, maturity). These attributes, themselves social constructions, serve as proxies for age.[1] Thus, elementary school students and nursing home residents, each in their own way, act their age by demonstrating, in interaction and with the help of others, their "competence" (i.e., their ability to do the things that someone "of that age" should be able to do) (Gubrium *et al.*, 1994:118–154).

Two recent studies of old-age home residents illustrate both the complex process of "doing age" and a variety of possible outcomes. In his study of an Israeli old-age home designated for the "able bodied" aged, Haim Hazan describes residents as deliberately demonstrating "functioning" to other residents, staff, and administrators. In this case, "functioning"

serves as a proxy for age. Because of the great number of applicants, the director is compelled to remove as large a number of "nonfunctioning" aged as often as possible. And because the cost of other institutions is much greater and because residents know transfer denotes physical deterioration, residents feel compelled to demonstrate their functioning. They know that administrators look favorably on officially sanctioned group activities. Hazan's description of the Talmudic study in the synagogue group is especially telling.

> The teacher [hired specifically for this purpose] reads and interprets in Yiddish, despite the fact that some 'students' do not understand the language. No questions are asked, and if remarks are made, these are usually digressions. Some participants do not even turn the pages . . . some whisper between themselves . . . [one] hums oriental melodies quietly to himself and glances at his watch every now and then, in order to see if the time has come for the lesson to end. He also does not turn over any pages— sometimes reading aloud a line or two, irrespective of what the teacher is saying. . . . It is absolutely clear that the participants do not comprehend the content of the lessons. . . . Nevertheless, many of the congregants wanted the treasurers to organize more lessons on weekdays . . . (Hazan, 1992:129)

In addition to their participation in sanctioned group activities, residents demonstrate their functioning in the public lobby, hallways, elevators, and dining room, in the possession and circulation of photographs, and in their clothing and appearance.

The dominant sociological approach (and a mainstream gerontological approach) might view these behaviors as indicative of some actual level of functioning or as signs of the necessity for certain kinds of programs or activities. Hazan, in contrast, sees them as ways that group members organize their own world of meaning in the context of power relations in an institutional setting. Each resident takes into

---

[1]West and Zimmerman (1987) demonstrate that in "doing gender," women "do deference" and men "do dominance." In other words, we can tease out dimensions of gender (femininity, masculinity, domination, subordination) that are accomplished.

account features of the organizational setting (the authority of the director; the director's obligation to transfer nonfunctioning adults), beliefs about age, health, and physical condition (functioning is defined by the director as "able-bodied"), and her/his own physical capabilities (Can I move about unassisted? Am I physically able to eat with others in the dining room?). Each resident has an emotional reaction (fear of being transferred, determination to participate in activities, pride in abilities) and acts accordingly (attending Talmudic study group).

In contrast to the residents Hazan studies are the residents of Les Floralies, an old-age home in a Parisian suburb where anthropologist Jennie-Keith Ross lived and did field work. Les Floralies residents make very different choices about how to act like old-age home residents. Health condition is a characteristic that residents often talk about, but unlike in the Israeli home, health and "functioning" are not the dominant principles for social organization and interaction. Instead, "sex and political identification are important principles of social organization in this community" (Ross, 1977:54–55).

The residents of Les Floralies are similar in some ways to the residents Hazan studies. Both groups are of similar ages (most residents are between 70 and 79 years old) and have similar (working) class and educational backgrounds. Their context for interaction, however, is significantly different. The Israeli home is much larger than Les Floralies (400 vs. 150 residents) and, most importantly, Les Floralies does not transfer "non able-bodied" residents. These features have significant effects on the meaning and nature of interaction among and between residents, staff, administrators, and "outsiders." The juxtaposition of these two studies (and the variations within each group of residents) illustrates how people can nonetheless accomplish age very differently given the combination of, and their reaction to, available resources.

Conclusion

. . . Like gender, age is "potentially omnirelevant." This means that age is not the property of "the elderly"; it is potentially relevant to people of all (chronological) ages. One effect, then, of the view of age-as-accomplished is to shift the focus away from "the elderly" to broader social processes that affect people in multiple age categories throughout their lives.

The second implication of age as "potentially omnirelevant" is that, although we continually "act our age," age is not always or equally relevant—i.e., salient—in all situations. Qualitative research has revealed the ways that individuals notice, feel, and experience their age in varying ways in different settings and at different points in the life course (e.g., Luborsky and Rubinstein, 1987). Moreover, statistical portraits, first-person and ethnographic accounts (Ross, 1977; Hazan, 1992), and age theory (e.g., Dannefer, 1988) attest to diversity within age categories. The view of age-as-accomplished can deflect attention away from "success" in aging (so often the focus of gerontology) in order to devote more attention to diversity and the appreciation of variability.

In giving credit to actors and in granting them agency, I do not want to minimize the extent to which performances are constrained. Representations of age and the life course not only are resources but also are used as means of control (Gubrium et al., 1994). Beliefs about age and the life course permeate our mechanisms of formal control and are institutionalized in law, medicine, psychiatry, and education (Karp and Yoels, 1982; Buchmann, 1989). The familiarity of the phrase "act your age" and the frequency with which it is used to direct the actions of others (and ourselves) testifies to the pervasiveness of beliefs about age as a method of informal social control. In short, age is never accomplished outside of relations of power.

The emphases of the age-as-accomplished framework have implications for research agendas. The effort to counter the dominant assumptions may be a guide for research into age-as-accomplished. The refusal to take chronological age as fixed or determinate and a focus on group process (in contrast to individual attributes) generate a variety of research possibilities including historical studies, ethnography, and cross-national comparisons as well as research into cognitive and conceptual categories. Relatively small-scale, ethnographic, and qualitative studies will enable sociologists to investigate the nuances of acting one's age. Secondary analysis involving comparisons between and among ethnographic studies will enable sociologists to understand patterns and sources of variation in the construction and accomplishment of age. Historical, statistical, and macro level studies, because they tend to stress structural factors as opposed to meaning, interpretation, and interaction, will not be supplanted by the age-as-accomplished framework. Rather, the framework of age-as-accomplished will benefit from and complement these studies.

In sum, the metaphor of acting and the idea of age-as-accomplished can make explicit what often goes unrecognized in the sociology of age: the performative, interactive work of accomplishing age, the emotion work involved in "becoming" and "being" an age, and the strategies people develop and use as they create and display themselves as aged (that is, as being of a particular age). To understand "age" as situated, contingent, and negotiated, and as continually constituted in interaction, provides the foundation for a sociology of age.

References

Abel, Emily K. 1991. *Who Cares for the Elderly?* Philadelphia, PA: Temple University Press.

Buchmann, Marlis. 1989. *The Script of Life in Modern Society: Entry into Adulthood in a Changing World.* Chicago: University of Chicago Press.

Butler, Robert. 1996. "Dispelling ageism: The cross-cutting intervention." Pp. 131–140 in Jill Quadagno and Debra Street (eds.), *Aging for the Twenty-first Century.* New York: St. Martin's.

Chudacoff, Howard P. 1989. *How Old Are You? Age Consciousness in American Culture.* Princeton, NJ: Princeton University Press.

Dannefer, Dale. 1988. "What's in a name? An account of the neglect of variability in the study of aging." Pp. 356–364 in James E. Birren and Vern L. Bengtson (eds.), *Emergent Theories of Aging.* New York: Springer Publishing.

Devault, Marjorie. 1991. *Feeding the Family.* Chicago: University of Chicago Press.

Diamond, Timothy. 1992. *Making Gray Gold: Narratives of Nursing Home Care.* Chicago: University of Chicago Press.

Eisenhandler, Susan A. 1991. "The Asphalt Identikit: Old age and the driver's license." Pp. 107–120 in Beth Hess and Elizabeth Markson (eds.), *Growing Old in America.* New Brunswick, NJ: Transaction Publishers.

Garfinkel, Harold. 1967. *Studies in Ethnomethodology.* Englewood Cliffs, NJ: Prentice-Hall.

Gubrium, Jaber. 1977. *Living and Dying at Murray Manor.* New York: St. Martin's.

———. 1993. *Speaking of Life: Horizons of Meaning for Nursing Home Residents.* New York: Aldine de Gruyter.

Gubrium, Jaber F., James A. Holstein, and David R. Buckholdt. 1994. *Constructing the Life Course.* Dix Hills, NY: General Hall.

Guillemard, Anne-Marie. 1996. "The trend toward early labor force withdrawal and the reorganization of the life course: A cross-national analysis." Pp. 177–193 in Jill Quadagno and Debra Street (eds.), *Aging for the Twenty-first Century.* New York: St. Martin's.

Hazan, Haim. 1992. *Managing Change in Old Age: The Control of Meaning in an Institutional Setting.* Albany, NY: State University of New York Press.

Henley, Nancy and Jo Freeman. 1989. "The sexual politics of interpersonal behavior." Pp. 457–469 in Jo Freeman (ed.), *Women: A Feminist Perspective.* Mountain View, CA: Mayfield.

Heritage, John. 1984. *Garfinkel and Ethnomethodology.* New York: Polity Press.

Hochschild, Arlie. 1983. *The Managed Heart.* Berkeley: University of California.

———. 1989. *The Second Shift.* New York: Avon.

Hockey, Jenny and Allison James. 1993. *Growing Up and Growing Old.* London: Sage.

Karp, David A. 1991. "A Decade of Reminders: Changing Age Consciousness between Fifty and

Sixty Years Old." Pp. 67–92 in Beth Hess and Elizabeth Markson (eds.), *Growing Old in America*. New Brunswick, NJ: Transaction Publishers.

Karp, David A. and William C. Yoels. 1982. *Experiencing the Life Cycle: A Social Psychology of Aging*. Springfield, IL: Charles C. Thomas.

Luborsky, Mark and Robert L. Rubinstein. 1987. "Ethnicity and lifetimes: Self concepts and situational contexts of ethnic identity in late life." Pp. 35–50 in Donald E. Gelfand and Charles M. Barresi (eds.), *Ethnic Dimensions of Aging*. New York: Springer Publishing.

Margolis, Richard. 1990. *Risking Old Age in America*. Boulder, CO: Westview.

Mayer, Karl Ulrich and Walter Müller. 1986. "The state and the structure of the life course." Pp. 217–245 in Aage B. Sorensen, Franz E. Weinert, and Lonnie R. Sherrod (eds.), *Human Development and the Life Course: Multidisciplinary Perspectives*. Hillsdale, NJ: Lawrence Erlbaum.

McIlwee, Judith S. and J. Gregg Robinson. 1992. *Women in Engineering*. Albany: State University of New York Press.

Ronai, Carol Rambo. 1992. "Managing aging in young adulthood: The 'aging' table dancer." *Journal of Aging Studies* 6: 307–317.

Ross, Jennie-Keith. 1977. *Old People, New Lives: Community Creation in a Retirement Residence*. Chicago: University of Chicago Press.

Scrutton, Steve. 1996. "Ageism: The foundation of age discrimination." Pp. 141–154 in Jill Quadagno and Debra Street (eds.), *Aging for the Twenty-first Century*. New York: St. Martin's.

Swidler, Ann. 1986. "Culture in action: Symbols and strategies." *American Sociological Review* 51: 273–286.

West, Candace and Sarah Fenstermaker. 1993. "Power, inequality and the accomplishment of gender: An ethnomethodological view." Pp. 151–174 in Paula England (ed.), *Theory on Gender/Feminism on Theory*. New York: Aldine deGruyter.

West, Candace and Don H. Zimmerman. 1987. "Doing gender." *Gender & Society* 1: 125–151.

Questions

1. Obviously age is a chronological fact. Why, then, does Professor Laz insist age is a *social* construction?

2. Describe the kinds of circumstances under which someone is most likely to be told to act his or her age.

3. Is there one aspect of your life in which you don't "act your age"? If so, describe it. Is this something you hide or flaunt? If so, do you usually do it alone or in the company of others?

4. According to Laz, what are the possible consequences for not acting one's age?

11

MARITAL NAME CHANGE: PLANS AND ATTITUDES OF COLLEGE STUDENTS

Laurie Scheuble and David R. Johnson

I was a proud new reader in primary school. One day, I was looking (okay, snooping) through my mom's desk and came upon a bunch of address labels. After I stuck them all over the place, my mom asked me what I was doing! Attempting to change the subject, I asked her where her labels were. She told me those were her labels. "No," I said, "these are daddy's labels. See, it says 'David McIntyre.' Your name is 'Jean.'" Mom said, "My name is *Mrs.* David McIntyre." "Oh," I said.

Things have changed in recent decades. Now women aren't forced to change their surnames when they marry. Turns out, however, most women don't take advantage of the freedom to keep their names. Professors Scheuble and Johnson examine why that's so.

Marriage and family role expectations have experienced tremendous change in the last few decades. This change has been driven by increased educational levels and labor force participation for women, lower fertility and higher divorce rates, and the challenging of institutional structures which have devalued women. Women's identities are no longer defined solely in relation to marriage and family roles mandated by history and tradition, one aspect of which is the expectation that women will take the last name of their spouse when they marry. Changes in marital role expectations may lead to increases both in the number of women electing to keep their birth name when they marry and in more tolerance toward these practices. Given the changes that are currently taking place in marriage and family role expectations, marital name change issues clearly warrant examination, yet this topic has been virtually unexplored by social scientists. This study makes a step toward filling this void by analyzing plans for and attitudes toward marital name change in a sample of Midwestern college students.

The examination of marital naming for both prominent and ordinary women is important because it challenges society's idea of women's identities and roles. Language and the meanings and symbols attached to its use provide a basis for understanding how social relations began and how they operate in everyday situations (McDowell & Pringle, 1992). The examination of attitudes toward women's and men's marital name choices permits further insight into overall societal understanding of relationships and the meanings these relationships have for members. The cultural expectation that women are to change their birth names to that of their husbands at the time of marriage is part of the language system which underscores

"Marital Name Change" by Laurie Scheuble and David R. Johnson from *Journal of Marriage and the Family* 55 (August, 1993: pp. 747–754). Reprinted by permission of Blackwell Publishing Ltd.

85

traditional roles in a patriarchal society (Pearson, 1985). When a woman takes on the last name of her spouse, this act serves to symbolically reinforce the expectation that her identity as an individual is subsumed under her status as a wife (Weitzman, 1981). Indeed, this is best illustrated by the common practice of referring to married women by their husband's full name (e.g., Mrs. Bill Clinton).

Personal observations and information presented in the media suggest that women may be becoming more likely to keep their birth names when they marry and that society is becoming more tolerant of this change. However, there is little systematic research to support this belief, and a limited research finding which could lead to the opposite conclusion (Perry & Birnbaum, 1993). The popular press has given some attention to issues raised when women marry and keep their birth names, particularly those concerning naming of children and the bureaucratic complications of some naming choices (e.g., Cherlin, 1978; Chua-Eoan, 1989; Ferraro, 1993; Mickelsen, 1988).

Recently, the issue surfaced in the press's scrutiny of the life of Hillary Rodham Clinton, the spouse of Bill Clinton, the 42nd President of the United States. Coverage focused on her decision to keep her birth name (Rodham) when she first married Bill Clinton and her later decision to take her husband's last name following his loss of the gubernatorial election. Media reports suggested that her decision to follow the more conventional naming practice was the result of pressure from Arkansas constituents who viewed keeping her birth name as her last name as inappropriate (Fullerton & Lemons, 1992; Grove, 1992; Marx, 1990; Morrison, 1992). Apparently, residents of Arkansas were not entirely prepared to have the governor of their state married to a woman who did not take his last name. This preference may not be unique to residents of Arkansas. A Wall Street Journal/NBC nationwide news poll found that, by a large margin (56%), people preferred that the

president's spouse not use her birth name as her middle name (Perry & Birnbaum, 1993). These findings about the name choice of one prominent married woman in the United States suggest that the public has low tolerance of non-traditional marital naming choices. However, it may not be appropriate to generalize the negative reaction to the naming choices of the wife a prominent public figure to such choices by ordinary married women.

Some attention to marital naming has been given in marriage and family textbooks (e.g., Knox & Schacht, 1991; Melville, 1988; Scanzoni & Scanzoni, 1988; Turner & Helms, 1988). Textbooks emphasize the legal history of marital name change for women and a woman's decision-making process as she considers retaining her birth name when she marries. However, none provide evidence about the prevalence of nontraditional marital name choices or about public attitudes toward nontraditional naming practices.

Most of the literature on marital naming focuses on historical and legal aspects. Early in U.S. history, no law required married women to take their husband's last name. Since it was assumed that women were property of their husbands, no such law appeared necessary. It was only during the 19th century that the right of a woman to retain her birth name became an issue that needed to be clarified. By the 1930's, the standard practice was that a woman would take her husband's last name when she married. Social custom and norms assumed that a wife had no legal identity apart from her husband. During the 1970's, several states clarified the point that their state did not require women to take their husband's last name. However, during the same period, other states required women to change their last name (DiCanio, 1989; MacDougall, 1973; Mead, 1973; Schroeder, 1986). Currently, it is legal in all states for a woman to keep her birth name as a last name when she marries (NOW Legal Defense and Education Fund & Cherow-O'Leary, 1987).

However, there is little empirical evidence that this legal right is reflected in attitudes towards name change or naming practices.

The marital naming practices and attitudes towards naming in the predominately white American culture or in racial or ethnic minorities have not been explored in the research literature and are thus unknown. There is evidence that, for reasons of convenience and simplicity, married women in some cultures have opted to use their birth names on a day-to-day basis. Susan Lobo (1982), in an ethnographic study of women in the squatter settlements in Lima, Peru, found that women generally keep their birth names when they marry due to the transient nature of the marital relationship. Some women in her study were beginning to take on the middle-class name change pattern and to use the last name of their husband. While women of all socioeconomic levels in Peru might elect to use their birth name in everyday life, in legal documents the law requires that they use their husband's last name as their own. In some Latino countries, both husbands and wives keep their father's and mother's last name as their last name (Cherlin, 1978). It is not known to what extent this practice is continued by Latinos in the United States.

While it is clear that American women now have the right to retain their birth name or to select other nontraditional naming patterns, nothing is known of the prevalence of such nontraditional practices or attitudes toward such practices. People tolerating women retaining their birth names when they marry, or men changing their birth names when they marry, may represent a change in societal expectations for men and women and for the institution of marriage.

The present research examined plans for and attitudes toward marital name change in a sample of Midwestern college students. The focus of the study included comparing views of male students with those of female students on a series of statements about situations in which

husbands and wives kept or changed their birth names. Variables that may affect the likelihood of tolerance toward and expectations of marital name change were examined. These include college class, father's and mother's education, marriage plans, number of children wanted, and expected work roles after the birth of the first child. Research has shown (Kiecolt & Acock, 1988; Losh-Hesselbart, 1987; Thorton, Alwin, & Camburn, 1983) that there is a relationship between youth, labor force experience, educational attainment, and egalitarian views of women's roles. Therefore, we expected that those students who are further along in their educational career, have parents with higher levels of education, and who plan to marry late, have a small family, and continue to work after the birth of children would be more accepting of nontraditional marital name choices than their counterparts. We also expected that there would be a relationship between gender role nontraditionalism and attitudes toward marital name change. Changing one's last name at marriage, or not doing so, is a choice based on cultural expectations of appropriate behavior for males and females. Drawing on research findings that husbands tend to be more traditional and less egalitarian than wives (Thorton et al., 1983), we expected men to be more traditional and less tolerant of marital name change variations than women. The effect of community size was examined because there is evidence of greater prevalence of traditional norms among those residing in a rural area (White & Booth, 1978). We anticipated that those students growing up in more rural areas would have more conservative responses to nontraditional name change situations than would other students.

Methods

The data for this study come from personal interviews with 258 students attending a small residential Midwestern college in 1990. The sample consists of all full-time students, excluding international students and students enrolled in the course gathering the data. Each student in the course received a cluster of 15 randomly chosen students and each completed 10 personal interviews. Four students refused to be interviewed. The respondents represented approximately one-third of the student body. The interview included questions on issues dealing with marriage and family, gender roles, health, campus services, and social issues.

The demographic characteristics of the sample and the entire student body were not significantly different. Of the respondents, 61.2% were female and 38.8% were male; 32% were in their 1st year of college, 28% were in their 2nd year, 22% were in their 3rd year, and 18% were in their 4th or 5th year. Over 98% of the student body was white. Students also responded to an item about their dating and marital status; 21.3% were not dating, 35.3% reported casual dating, 37.2% were steady dating, 5% were engaged, and 1.2% were married.

Twenty-eight items were included on the questionnaire on attitudes toward changing or keeping one's birth name when one marries. The first two items asked female respondents if they planned to change their birth name or to hyphenate their birth name when they married. Three items were included to measure general approval of a woman keeping her birth name when she marries and the statement that this decision makes about the woman's commitment to the marriage. Finally, 23 items asked respondents to indicate situations where they believed it was appropriate for a woman to keep her birth name when she marries, for her to change her last name to that of her husband, and for a man to change his birth name to that of his wife.

To identify those characteristics predicting approval of marital name change, 10 variables identified as background, control, and intervening variables were examined. Background variables included the size of community in which the respondent lived in high school, measured in six categories from farm residence to residence in a city of over 500,000. Father's and mother's education were also included as background variables and were coded in six ordinal categories from less than high school to more than a college education. Sex of the interviewer (males = 1; female = 2) was included as a control. Some researchers have concluded that sex is a characteristic of the interview situation that affects answers to interview items concerning sexual behavior, political views, and feminist issues (Axinn, 1991; Hutchinson & Wegge, 1991; Landis, Sullivan, & Sheley, 1973; Lowenstein & Varma, 1970; Zehner, 1970). College class was also included as a control variable, categorized as years in school.

Five intervening variables were examined. These represent factors that might account for the relationship between the background variables and tolerance toward name change. Included were the age at which the respondent wanted to marry (coded from under 20 years of age to over 35), the number of desired children, and the desired sex of the respondent's first child (a boy, a girl, or no preference). Also included were anticipated work roles after the birth of a child, ranging from (1) the woman will not work anymore, to (4) the wife will continue to work after a short maternity leave, to (7) the husband will not work outside the home anymore but the wife will.

The final intervening variable was a four-item gender role traditionalism scale. Items in the scale were responded to on a (1) strongly agree to (5) strongly disagree format. The items were recorded in the same direction with nontraditional respondents scoring higher. The items were: (a) Most of the important decisions in the life of the family should be made by the man of the house; (b) I would feel more comfortable in a time of national crisis if the president were a man and not a woman; (c) Men and women should be paid the same amount of money if they do the same work; and (d) A husband should earn a larger salary than his wife. The gender role traditionalism scale has an alpha reliability of .76.

Findings

Table 1 presents marital name change items and the percentage of respondents agreeing with each item by sex. Most of the women (81.6%) planned to change their last name to that of their husband if they married. In addition, 7% of the female respondents indicated that they planned to hyphenate their last name with that of their future spouse.

Of the 20 items in Table 1 that compare male and female respondents' attitudes toward marital name change and situations where marital name change is acceptable, men's and women's views were significantly different on 12 items. Females were significantly more

Table 1 Percentage Selecting "Yes" as a Response to Name Change Variables

Item	Males ($n = 100$)	Females ($n = 158$)
If you marry, do you plan to change your last name to that of your spouse?		81.6
If you marry, do you plan to hyphenate your last name with your spouse's last name?		7.0
I think it is all right if a woman wants to keep her maiden name when she gets married.[a][b]	57.0	91.8*
A woman who changes to her husband's name when she gets married is more committed to the marriage than a woman who does not change her name.[a][b]	25.0	2.5*
Couples who hyphenate their last names when they marry are more committed to the relationship than other couples.[a]	6.0	1.3
Circumstances under which it is acceptable for a woman to keep her maiden name.		
If the woman is a professional.	68.0	84.8*
If the woman likes her maiden name.[b]	46.0	75.9*
If the woman is afraid she will get divorced.	11.0	13.3
If the husband is divorced and has a previous wife with his name.	44.0	42.4
If the woman does not like the husband's last name.	24.0	40.5*
If the woman is older when she gets married.	20.0	36.7*
If the woman wants to keep her family name going.[b]	66.0	87.3*
When a woman marries, under what circumstances should she take husband's last name?		
If she has, or plans to have, children.	51.0	54.4
If she does not work.	21.0	19.0
If her husband wants her to change her last name.	36.0	30.4
If her relatives think she should change her last name.	20.0	3.8*
If she wants to take her husband's last name.[b]	84.0	94.9*
A woman should always change her name to that of her husband.[b]	32.0	5.1*
When a man marries, under what circumstances should he take his wife's last name?		
If his wife wants him to take her last name.	12.0	19.0
If he wants to change his last name.[b]	70.0	84.8*
If he marries a woman who is well known in her field of work.	14.0	19.0
A man should never change his last name to that of his spouse.[b]	33.0	19.6*

[a]These questions were asked in a strongly agree, agree, uncertain, disagree, strongly disagree format. The percentage responding strongly agree or agree is reported above.
[b]Items included in the tolerance scale.
*Indicates that the differences between men's and women's responses are statistically significant.

likely than males to believe that it is acceptable for a woman to keep her maiden name when she marries. Also, females were more likely than males to agree that it is appropriate for a woman to keep her birth name if she is a professional, if she likes her maiden name, if she does not like her husband's last name, if the woman is older when she marries, and if she wants to keep her own family name going.

When asked about situations where a woman should change her last name to that of her husband, three significant gender differences were identified. Males were more likely than females to believe that a woman should take her husband's last name when she marries if her relatives think she should, and to believe that women should always change their last name to that of their husband. Women were significantly more likely than men to believe that a woman should change her last name to her husband's if she wants to take his last name.

The final set of name change items examine circumstances under which a man should take his wife's last name. Two gender differences were identified. Females were significantly more likely than males to think that a man should change his last name to that of his wife if he wants to do so, and males were more likely than females to think that a man should never change his last name to that of his wife.

Regression analysis was used to examine how other variables influence name change attitudes and plans. . . . Only two variables were significantly related to a woman saying that she planned to change her last name to that of her husband if she married. Women planning to marry at a later age and women planning more liberal work roles after the birth of children were less likely to plan a marital name change. . . .

Other Results

When the intervening variables were added to the equation, sex of interviewer and community size retained their significant effect, and three of the six intervening variables were also significant. Male respondents expressing a desire for small family size were more tolerant than males wanting a large family. The expectation of liberal work roles after the birth of the first child was positively related to tolerance, as were nontraditional gender role attitudes. . . .

The results differ somewhat for female respondents. Women from a larger community were also more likely to be tolerant of marital name change than those from a small community. Mother's education appeared to affect the degree of tolerance of the women respondents. Women with mothers having higher levels of education were more likely to be tolerant than those with mothers having lower educational levels. When the intervening variables were added to the equation, the effect of mother's education remained significant. Community size, however, was no longer significant, due to a strong correlation with gender role nontraditionalism. Of the five intervening variables, two were significant. Females who wanted their first child to be a male were less likely to be tolerant of marital name change than females who wanted their first child to be a female or had no preference. As found for the male respondents, women holding nontraditional gender role attitudes were more likely to be tolerant of marital name change than those endorsing more traditional roles for women. . . .

To determine if the differences in effects between men and women respondents were significant, a regression analysis was conducted including interactions with sex of respondent on all variables. Several differences were found to be statistically significant. Both male and female respondents were less tolerant toward marital name change if they wanted their first child to be a boy. However, the effect was greater for men than for women. The effect of the desired number of children varied significantly by gender. While both men and women who wanted large families were less tolerant than those who wanted small families, the effect was significantly stronger for the men. A similar pattern was found for work role plans. For both men and women, the less traditional the work role plans, the higher the tolerance of name change. Again, the effect was significantly stronger for men. . . .

Discussion and Conclusions

Researchers have concluded that more studies on marital name change are needed (DiCanio, 1989; Dralle & Mackiewicz, 1981). The present study adds to a sparse body of empirical research by examining attitudes toward marital name change of students at a Midwestern residential college. Overall, both college males and females are somewhat accepting of women keeping their birth names when they marry and of men changing their birth names when they marry. Clearly, women are both far more accepting of nontraditional marital name choices and more tolerant of choices made by others than are their male counterparts. However, accepting nontraditional name change options does not necessarily result in wanting a nontraditional last name option for oneself. For the women in this sample, where more than three-fourths are planning to change their last name to that of their husband if they marry, attitudes and plans regarding naming were found to be uncorrelated.

However, indirect evidence suggests that college students are more accepting of nontraditional marital name change options than is the larger population. The recent poll that found that only 6% of respondents believed Hillary Clinton should be known as Hillary Rodham Clinton (Perry & Birnbaum, 1993) suggests high intolerance of nontraditional naming. College students may have more exposure to these issues than the general population since they may have professors who have

chosen nontraditional marital naming options. Clearly, additional research needs to be done on national samples to better estimate the degree of tolerance.

As the institution of marriage and family continues to change, and as more college students graduate and marry, it is possible that an increase in the proportion of women keeping their birth name or of men changing their birth name could take place. This is clearly an important area for future research. Empirical studies are needed to determine how many women are opting to retain their birth names, hyphenate their birth name with that of their spouse, or use their birth name as their middle name. Studies also need to examine how women selecting nontraditional last name options differ from those women following the expected norm of changing their birth name to that of their spouse.

Although there has been a change in American culture in role expectations for women, it may be decades before this manifests itself in a change in marital name practices. It appears that students, particularly female students, are ready to accept women retaining their birth name and men changing their birth name to that of their spouse, and to identify circumstances where these nontraditional behaviors are appropriate. Although many accept this behavior for others, they do not plan to choose a nontraditional marital name change option for themselves. This suggests that in marital name change, attitudes are changing more quickly than behavior. Future research examining actual naming determinants and effects of nontraditional naming practices is needed to address this issue.

References

Axinn, W. G. (1991). The influence of interviewer sex on responses to sensitive questions in Nepal. *Social Science Research, 20,* 303–318.

Cherlin, A. (1978, December). Hereditary hyphens? *Psychology Today,* p. 150.

Chua-Eoan, H. G. (1989, April 17). It hyphened one night. *Time*, p. 78.

DiCanio, M. (1989). *The encyclopedia of marriage, divorce and the family.* New York: Facts on File.

Dralle, P., Asson, W., & Mackiewicz, K. (1981). Psychological impact on women's name change at marriage: Literature review and implications for further study. *The American Journal of Family Therapy, 9,* 50–55.

Ferraro, S. (1993, May 2). Name dropper. *The New York Times Magazine*, pp. 18–20.

Fullerton, J., & Lemons, T. (1992, February 16). First lady Hillary Clinton not content with playing second fiddle. *Arkansas Democrat-Gazette.*

Grove, L. (1992, March 10). Hillary Clinton, trying to have it all. *Washington Post*, p. E1.

Hutchinson, K. L., & Wegge, D. G. (1991). The effects of interviewer gender upon response in telephone survey research. *Journal of Social Behavior and Personality, 6,* 573–584.

Kiecolt, K. K., & Acock, A. C. (1988). The long-term effects of family structure on gender role attitudes. *Journal of Marriage and the Family, 50,* 707–717.

Knox, D., & Schacht, C. (1991). *Choices in relationships: An introduction to marriage and the family.* St. Paul, MN: West.

Landis, J. B., Sullivan, D., & Sheley J. (1973) Feminist attitudes as related to sex of the interviewer. *Pacific Sociological Review, 16,* 305–314.

Lobo, S. (1982). *A House of My Own: Social organization in the squatter settlements of Lima, Peru.* Tucson, AZ: University of Arizona Press.

Losh-Hesselbart, S. (1987). Development of gender roles. In M. Sussman & S. Steinmetz (Eds.), *Handbook of marriage and the family.* New York: Plenum Press.

Lowenstein, R., & Varma, A. O. (1970). Effects of interaction of interviewers and respondents in health surveys. *Public Opinion Quarterly, 34,* 472–473.

MacDougall, P. R. (1973). Married women's common law rights to their own surnames. *Women's Rights Law Reporter, 1,* 2–14.

Marx, C. E. (1990, August 12). Hillary Clinton: Lawyer, parent, political activist. *Arkansas Democrat Gazette.*

McDowell, L., & Pringle, R. (Eds.). (1992). *Defining women: Social institutions and gender divisions.* Cambridge: Polity Press.

Mead, L. J. (1973). Married women's right to her maiden name: The possibilities for change. *Buffalo Law Review, 23,* 243–262.

Melville, K. (1988). *Marriage and family today.* New York: Random House.

Mickelsen, L. (1988, May). Our marriage was equal in name and spirit until we had our baby. *Glamour*, p. 34.

Morrison, P. (1992, July 14). Time for a feminist as first lady? *Los Angeles Times*, p. Al.

NOW Legal Defense and Education Fund, & Cherow-O'Leary, R. (1987). *The state-by-state guide to women's legal rights.* New York: McGraw-Hill.

Pearson, J. (1985). *Gender and communication.* Dubuque, IA: Wm. C. Brown.

Perry, J. M., & Birnbaum, J. H. (1993, January 28). Hillary Clinton turns the first lady role into a powerful post. *The Wall Street Journal*, pp. 1, 16.

Scanzoni, L. D., & Scanzoni, J. (1988). *Men, women, and change.* New York: McGraw-Hill.

Schroeder, L. O. (1986). A rose by any other name: Post-marital right to use maiden name: 1934–1982. *Sociology and Social Research, 70,* 290–293.

Thorton, A., Alwin, D. F., & Camburn, D. (1983). Causes and consequences of sex-role attitudes and attitude change. *American Sociological Review, 48,* 211–227.

Turner, J. S., & Helms, D. B. (1988). *Marriage and family: Traditions and transitions.* San Diego; Harcourt, Brace, Jovanovich.

Weitzman, L. J. (1981). *The marriage contract: Spouses, lovers, and the law.* New York: Free Press.

White, L., & Booth, A. (1978). *Rural-urban differences in Nebraska: Debunking a myth* (Nebraska Annual Social Indicators Survey, Report No. 5). Lincoln: University of Nebraska, Bureau of Sociological Research.

Zehner, R. B. (1970). Sex effects in the interviewing of young adults. *Sociological Focus, 3,* 75–84.

Questions

1. What is your attitude about whether women should change their names when they marry? Does it reflect the findings reported in Scheuble and Johnson's article?

2. As Scheuble and Johnson found, there are many reasons why women may choose or not choose to change their names after marriage. Think about this: What is the *social meaning* attributed to the practice of women changing their names once they are married?

    What would be the *social meaning* attached to a man changing his name to his wife's name?

3. Research what one has to do in your state to change one's name. How hard is it?

12

THE CODE OF THE STREETS

Elijah Anderson

Except in the most general sense, it is wrong to speak of "American" culture as if it were a single entity. American society is not homogeneous, nor is its culture. In this 1994 article, Elijah Anderson focuses on a particular *subculture* that exists within the larger culture. In this subculture, the ubiquitous human search for respect creates what has been called a "perverse etiquette of violence," one from which it may well be impossible to escape.

Of all the problems besetting the poor inner-city black community, none is more pressing than that of interpersonal violence and aggression. It wreaks havoc daily in the lives of community residents and increasingly spills over into downtown and residential middle-class areas. Muggings, burglaries, carjackings, and drug-related shootings, all of which may leave their victims or innocent bystanders dead, are now common enough to concern all urban and many suburban residents. The inclination to violence springs from the circumstances of life among the ghetto poor—the lack of jobs that pay a living wage, the stigma of race, the fallout from rampant drug use and drug trafficking, and the resulting alienation and lack of hope for the future.

Simply living in such an environment places young people at special risk of falling victim to aggressive behavior. Although there are often forces in the community which can counteract the negative influences, by far the most powerful being a strong, loving, "decent" (as inner-city residents put it) family committed to middle-class values, the despair is pervasive enough to have spawned an oppositional culture, that of "the streets," whose norms are often consciously opposed to those of mainstream society. These two orientations—decent and street—socially organize the community, and their coexistence has important consequences for residents, particularly children growing up in the inner city. Above all, this environment means that even youngsters whose home lives reflect mainstream values—and the majority of homes in the community do—must be able to handle themselves in a street-oriented environment.

This is because the street culture has evolved what may be called a code of the streets, which amounts to a set of informal rules governing interpersonal public behavior, including violence. The rules prescribe both a proper comportment and a proper way to respond if challenged. They regulate the use of violence and so allow those who are inclined to aggression to precipitate violent encounters in an approved way. The rules have been established and are enforced mainly by the street-oriented, but on the streets the distinction between street and decent is often irrelevant; everybody knows that if the rules are violated, there are penalties. Knowledge of the code is thus largely defensive; it is literally necessary for operating in public. Therefore, even though families with a decency orientation are usually opposed to the values of the code, they often

"The Code of the Streets" by Elijah Anderson from *The Atlantic Monthly*, May 1994. Reprinted by permission of the author.

reluctantly encourage their children's familiarity with it to enable them to negotiate the inner-city environment.

At the heart of the code is the issue of respect—loosely defined as being treated "right," or granted the deference one deserves. However, in the troublesome public environment of the inner city, as people increasingly feel buffeted by forces beyond their control, what one deserves in the way of respect becomes more and more problematic and uncertain. This in turn further opens the issue of respect to sometimes intense interpersonal negotiation. In the street culture, especially among young people, respect is viewed as almost an external entity that is hard-won but easily lost, and so must constantly be guarded. The rules of the code in fact provide a framework for negotiating respect. The person whose very appearance—including his clothing, demeanor, and way of moving—deters transgressions feels that he possesses, and may be considered by others to possess, a measure of respect. With the right amount of respect, for instance, he can avoid "being bothered" in public. If he is bothered, not only may he be in physical danger but he has been disgraced or "dissed" (disrespected). Many of the forms that dissing can take might seem petty to middle-class people (maintaining eye contact for too long, for example), but to those invested in the street code, these actions become serious indications of the other person's intentions. Consequently, such people become very sensitive to advances and slights, which could well serve as warnings of imminent physical confrontation.

This hard reality can be traced to the profound sense of alienation from mainstream society and its institutions felt by many poor inner-city black people, particularly the young. The code of the streets is actually a cultural adaptation to a profound lack of faith in the police and the judicial system. The police are most often seen as representing the dominant white society and not caring to protect inner-city residents. When called, they may not respond, which is one reason many residents feel they must be prepared to take extraordinary measures to defend themselves and their loved ones against those who are inclined to aggression. Lack of police accountability has in fact been incorporated into the status system: the person who is believed capable of "taking care of himself" is accorded a certain deference, which translates into a sense of physical and psychological control. Thus the street code emerges where the influence of the police ends and personal responsibility for one's safety is felt to begin. Exacerbated by the proliferation of drugs and easy access to guns, this volatile situation results in the ability of the street-oriented minority (or those who effectively "go for bad") to dominate the public spaces.

Decent and Street Families

Although almost everyone in poor inner-city neighborhoods is struggling financially and therefore feels a certain distance from the rest of America, the decent and the street family in a real sense represent two poles of value orientation, two contrasting conceptual categories. The labels "decent" and "street," which the residents themselves use, amount to evaluative judgments that confer status on local residents. The labeling is often the result of a social contest among individuals and families of the neighborhood. Individuals of the two orientations often coexist in the same extended family. Decent residents judge themselves to be so while judging others to be of the street, and street individuals often present themselves as decent, drawing distinctions between themselves and other people. In addition, there is quite a bit of circumstantial behavior—that is, one person may at different times exhibit both decent and street orientations, depending on the circumstances. Although these designations result from so much social jockeying, there do exist concrete features that define each conceptual category.

Generally, so-called decent families tend to accept mainstream values more fully and attempt to instill them in their children. Whether married couples with children or single-parent (usually female) households, they are generally "working poor" and so tend to be better off financially than their street-oriented neighbors. They value hard work and self-reliance and are willing to sacrifice for their children. Because they have a certain amount of faith in mainstream society, they harbor hopes for a better future for their children, if not for themselves. Many of them go to church and take a strong interest in their children's schooling. Rather than dwelling on the real hardships and inequities facing them, many such decent people, particularly the increasing number of grandmothers raising grandchildren, see their difficult situation as a test from God and derive great support from their faith and from the church community.

Extremely aware of the problematic and often dangerous environment in which they reside, decent parents tend to be strict in their child-rearing practices, encouraging children to respect authority and walk a straight moral line. They have an almost obsessive concern about trouble of any kind and remind their children to be on the lookout for people and situations that might lead to it. At the same time, they are themselves polite and considerate of others, and teach their children to be the same way. At home, at work, and in church, they strive hard to maintain a positive mental attitude and a spirit of cooperation.

So-called street parents, in contrast, often show a lack of consideration for other people and have a rather superficial sense of family and community. Though they may love their children, many of them are unable to cope with the physical and emotional demands of parenthood, and find it difficult to reconcile their needs with those of their children. These families, who are more fully invested in the code of the streets than the decent people are, may aggressively socialize their children into it in a normative way. They believe in the code and judge themselves and others according to its values.

In fact the overwhelming majority of families in the inner-city community try to approximate the decent-family model, but there are many others who clearly represent the worst fears of the decent family. Not only are their financial resources extremely limited, but what little they have may easily be misused. The lives of the street-oriented are often marked by disorganization. In the most desperate circumstances people frequently have a limited understanding of priorities and consequences, and so frustrations mount over bills, food, and, at times, drink, cigarettes, and drugs. Some tend toward self-destructive behavior; many street-oriented women are crack-addicted ("on the pipe"), alcoholic, or involved in complicated relationships with men who abuse them. In addition, the seeming intractability of their situation, caused in large part by the lack of well-paying jobs and the persistence of racial discrimination, has engendered deep-seated bitterness and anger in many of the most desperate and poorest blacks, especially young people. The need both to exercise a measure of control and to lash out at somebody is often reflected in the adults' relations with their children. At the least, the frustrations of persistent poverty shorten the fuse in such people—contributing to a lack of patience with anyone, child or adult, who irritates them.

In these circumstances a woman—or a man, although men are less consistently present in children's lives—can be quite aggressive with children, yelling at and striking them for the least little infraction of the rules she has set down. Often little if any serious explanation follows the verbal and physical punishment. This response teaches children a particular lesson. They learn that to solve any kind of interpersonal problem one must quickly resort to hitting or other violent behavior. Actual peace and quiet, and also the appearance of calm, respectful children conveyed to her neighbors and friends, are often what the young mother most desires, but at times she will be very aggressive in trying to get them. Thus she may be quick to beat her children, especially if they defy her law, not because she hates them but because this is the way she knows to control them. In fact, many street-oriented women love their children dearly. Many mothers in the community subscribe to the notion that there is a "devil in the boy" that must be beaten out of him or that socially "fast girls need to be whupped." Thus much of what borders on child abuse in the view of social authorities is acceptable parental punishment in the view of these mothers.

Many street-oriented women are sporadic mothers whose children learn to fend for themselves when necessary, foraging for food and money any way they can get it. The children are sometimes employed by drug dealers or become addicted themselves. These children of the street, growing up with little supervision, are said to "come up hard." They often learn to fight at an early age, sometimes using short-tempered adults around them as role models. The street-oriented home may be fraught with anger, verbal disputes, physical aggression, and even mayhem. The children observe these goings-on, learning the lesson that might makes right. They quickly learn to hit those who cross them, and the dog-eat-dog mentality prevails. In order to survive, to protect oneself, it is necessary to marshal inner resources and be ready to deal with adversity in

a hands-on way. In these circumstances physical prowess takes on great significance.

In some of the most desperate cases, a street-oriented mother may simply leave her young children alone and unattended while she goes out. The most irresponsible women can be found at local bars and crack houses, getting high and socializing with other adults. Sometimes a troubled woman will leave very young children alone for days at a time. Reports of crack addicts abandoning their children have become common in drug-infested inner-city communities. Neighbors or relatives discover the abandoned children, often hungry and distraught over the absence of their mother. After repeated absences, a friend or relative, particularly a grandmother, will often step in to care for the young children, sometimes petitioning the authorities to send her, as guardian of the children, the mother's welfare check, if the mother gets one. By this time, however, the children may well have learned the first lesson of the streets: survival itself, let alone respect, cannot be taken for granted; you have to fight for your place in the world.

Campaigning for Respect

These realities of inner-city life are largely absorbed on the streets. At an early age, often even before they start school, children from street-oriented homes gravitate to the streets, where they "hang"—socialize with their peers. Children from these generally permissive homes have a great deal of latitude and are allowed to "rip and run" up and down the street. They often come home from school, put their books down, and go right back out the door. On school nights eight- and nine-year-olds remain out until nine or ten o'clock (and teenagers typically come in whenever they want to). On the streets they play in groups that often become the source of their primary social bonds. Children from decent homes tend to be more carefully supervised and are thus likely to have curfews and to be taught how to stay out of trouble.

When decent and street kids come together, a kind of social shuffle occurs in which children have a chance to go either way. Tension builds as a child comes to realize that he must choose an orientation. The kind of home he comes from influences but does not determine the way he will ultimately turn out—although it is unlikely that a child from a thoroughly street-oriented family will easily absorb decent values on the streets. Youths who emerge from street-oriented families but develop a decency orientation almost always learn those values in another setting—in school, in a youth group, in church. Often it is the result of their involvement with a caring "old head" (adult role model).

In the street, through their play, children pour their individual life experiences into a common knowledge pool, affirming, confirming, and elaborating on what they have observed in the home and matching their skills against those of others. And they learn to fight. Even small children test one another, pushing and shoving, and are ready to hit other children over circumstances not to their liking. In turn, they are readily hit by other children, and the child who is toughest prevails. Thus the violent resolution of disputes, the hitting and cursing, gains social reinforcement. The child in effect is initiated into a system that is really a way of campaigning for respect.

In addition, younger children witness the disputes of older children, which are often resolved through cursing and abusive talk, if not aggression or outright violence. They see that one child succumbs to the greater physical and mental abilities of the other. They are also alert and attentive witnesses to the verbal and physical fights of adults, after which they compare notes and share their interpretations of the event. In almost every case the victor is the person who physically won the altercation, and this person often enjoys the esteem and respect of onlookers. These experiences reinforce the lessons the children have learned at home: might makes right, and toughness is a virtue, while humility is not. In effect they learn the social meaning of fighting. When it is left virtually unchallenged, this understanding becomes an ever more important part of the child's working conception of the world. Over time the code of the streets becomes refined.

Those street-oriented adults with whom children come in contact—including mothers, fathers, brothers, sisters, boyfriends, cousins, neighbors, and friends—help them along in forming this understanding by verbalizing the messages they are getting through experience: "Watch your back." "Protect yourself." "Don't punk out." "If somebody messes with you, you got to pay them back." "If someone disses you, you got to straighten them out." Many parents actually impose sanctions if a child is not sufficiently aggressive. For example, if a child loses a fight and comes home upset, the parent might respond, "Don't you come in here crying that somebody beat you up; you better get back out there and whup his ass. I didn't raise no punks! Get back out there and whup his ass. If you don't whup his ass, I'll whup your ass when you come home." Thus the child obtains reinforcement for being tough and showing nerve.

While fighting, some children cry as though they are doing something they are ambivalent about. The fight may be against their wishes, yet they may feel constrained to fight or face the consequences—not just from peers but also from caretakers or parents, who may administer another beating if they back down. Some adults recall receiving such lessons from their own parents and justify repeating them to their children as a way to toughen them up. Looking capable of taking care of oneself as a form of self-defense is a dominant theme among both street-oriented and decent adults who worry about the safety of their children. There is thus at times a convergence in their child-rearing practices, although the rationales behind them may differ.

Self-Image Based on "Juice"

By the time they are teenagers, most youths have either internalized the code of the streets or at least learned the need to comport themselves in accordance with its rules, which chiefly have to do with interpersonal communication. The code revolves around the presentation of self. Its basic requirement is the display of a certain predisposition to violence. Accordingly, one's bearing must send the unmistakable if sometimes subtle message to "the next person" in public that one is capable of violence and mayhem when the situation requires it, that one can take care of oneself. The nature of this communication is largely determined by the demands of the circumstances but can include facial expressions, gait, and verbal expressions—all of which are geared mainly to deterring aggression. Physical appearance, including clothes, jewelry, and grooming, also plays an important part in how a person is viewed; to be respected, it is important to have the right look.

Even so, there are no guarantees against challenges, because there are always people around looking for a fight to increase their share of respect—or "juice," as it is sometimes called on the street. Moreover, if a person is assaulted, it is important, not only in the eyes of his opponent but also in the eyes of his "running buddies," for him to avenge himself. Otherwise he risks being "tried" (challenged) or "moved on" by any number of others. To maintain his honor he must show he is not someone to be "messed with" or "dissed." In general, the person must "keep himself straight" by managing his position of respect among others; this involves in part his self-image, which is shaped by what he thinks others are thinking of him in relation to his peers.

Objects play an important and complicated role in establishing self-image. Jackets, sneakers, gold jewelry, reflect not just a person's taste, which tends to be tightly regulated among adolescents of all social classes, but also a willingness to possess things that may require defending. A boy wearing a fashionable, expensive jacket, for example, is vulnerable to attack by another who covets the jacket and either cannot afford to buy one or wants the added satisfaction of depriving someone else of his. However, if the boy forgoes the desirable jacket and wears one that isn't "hip," he runs the risk of being teased and possibly even assaulted as an unworthy person. To be allowed to hang with certain prestigious crowds, a boy must wear a different set of expensive clothes—sneakers and athletic suit—every day. Not to be able to do so might make him appear socially deficient. The youth comes to covet such items—especially when he sees easy prey wearing them.

In acquiring valued things, therefore, a person shores up his identity—but since it is an identity based on having things, it is highly precarious. This very precariousness gives a heightened sense of urgency to staying even with peers, with whom the person is actually competing. Young men and women who are able to command respect through their presentation of self—by allowing their possessions and their body language to speak for them—may not have to campaign for regard but may, rather, gain it by the force of their manner. Those who are unable to command respect in this way must actively campaign for it—and are thus particularly alive to slights.

One way of campaigning for status is by taking the possessions of others. In this context, seemingly ordinary objects can become trophies imbued with symbolic value that far exceeds their monetary worth. Possession of the trophy can symbolize the ability to violate somebody—to "get in his face," to take something of value from him, to "dis" him, and thus to enhance one's own worth by stealing someone else's. The trophy does not have to be something material. It can be another person's sense of honor, snatched away with a derogatory remark. It can be the outcome of a fight. It can be the imposition of a certain standard, such as a girl's getting herself recognized as the most beautiful. Material things, however, fit easily into the pattern. Sneakers, a pistol, even somebody else's girlfriend, can become a trophy. When a person can take something from another and then flaunt it, he gains a certain regard by being the owner, or the controller, of that thing. But this display of ownership can then provoke other people to challenge him. This game of who controls what is thus constantly being played out on inner-city streets, and the trophy—extrinsic or intrinsic, tangible or intangible—identifies the current winner.

An important aspect of this often violent give-and-take is its zero-sum quality. That is, the extent to which one person can raise himself up depends on his ability to put another person down. This underscores the alienation that permeates the inner-city ghetto community. There is a generalized sense that very little respect is to be had, and therefore everyone competes to get what affirmation he can of the little that is available. The craving for respect that results gives people thin skins. Shows of deference by others can be highly soothing, contributing to a sense of security, comfort, self-confidence, and self-respect. Transgressions by others which go unanswered diminish these feelings and are believed to encourage further transgressions. Hence one must be ever vigilant against the transgressions of others or even *appearing* as if transgressions will be tolerated. Among young people, whose sense of self-esteem is particularly vulnerable, there is an especially heightened concern with being disrespected. Many inner-city young men in particular crave respect to such a degree that they will risk their lives to attain and maintain it.

The issue of respect is thus closely tied to whether a person has an inclination to be violent, even as a victim. In the wider society people may not feel required to retaliate physically after an attack, even though they are aware that they have been degraded or taken advantage of. They may feel a great need to defend themselves *during* an attack, or to behave in such a way as to deter aggression (middle-class people certainly can and do become victims of street-oriented youths), but they are much more likely than street-oriented people to feel that they can walk away from a possible altercation with their self-esteem intact. Some people may even have the strength of character to flee, without any thought that their self-respect or esteem will be diminished.

In impoverished inner-city black communities, however, particularly among young males and perhaps increasingly among females, such flight would be extremely difficult. To run away would likely leave one's self-esteem in tatters. Hence people often feel constrained not only to stand up and at least attempt to resist during an assault but also to "pay back"—to seek revenge—after a successful assault on their person. This may include going to get a weapon or even getting relatives involved. Their very identity and self-respect, their honor, is often intricately tied up with the way they perform on the streets during and after such encounters. This outlook reflects the circumscribed opportunities of the inner-city poor. Generally people outside the ghetto have other ways of gaining status and regard, and thus do not feel so dependent on such physical displays. . . .

"Going for Bad"

In the most fearsome youths such a cavalier attitude toward death grows out of a very limited view of life. Many are uncertain about how long they are going to live and believe they could die violently at any time. They accept this fate; they live on the edge. Their manner conveys the message that nothing intimidates them; whatever turn the encounter takes, they maintain their attack—rather like a pit bull, whose spirit many such boys admire. The demonstration of such tenacity "shows heart" and earns their respect.

This fearlessness has implications for law enforcement. Many street-oriented boys are much more concerned about the threat of "justice" at the hands of a peer than at the hands of the police. Moreover, many feel not only that they have little to lose by going to prison but that they have something to gain. The toughening-up one experiences in prison can actually enhance one's reputation on the streets. Hence the system loses influence over the hard core who are without jobs, with little perceptible stake in the system. If mainstream society has done nothing *for* them, they counter by making sure it can do nothing *to* them.

At the same time, however, a competing view maintains that true nerve consists in backing down, walking away from a fight, and going on with one's business. One fights only in self-defense. This view emerges from the decent philosophy that life is precious, and it is an important part of the socialization process common in decent homes. It discourages violence as the primary means of resolving disputes and encourages youngsters to accept nonviolence and talk as confrontational strategies. But "if the deal goes down," self-defense is greatly encouraged. When there is enough positive support for this orientation, either in the home or among one's peers, then nonviolence has a chance to prevail. But it prevails at the cost of relinquishing a claim to being bad and tough, and therefore sets a young person up as at the very least alienated from street-oriented peers and quite possibly a target of derision or even violence.

Although the nonviolent orientation rarely overcomes the impulse to strike back in an encounter, it does introduce a certain confusion and so can prompt a measure of soul-searching, or even profound ambivalence. Did the person back down with his respect intact or did he back down only to be judged a "punk"—a person lacking manhood? Should he or she have acted? Should he or she have hit the other person in the mouth? These questions beset many young men and women during public confrontations. What is the "right" thing to do? In the quest for honor, respect, and local status—which few young people are uninterested in—common sense most often prevails, which leads many to opt for the tough approach, enacting their own particular versions of the display of nerve. The presentation of oneself as rough and tough is very often quite acceptable until one is tested. And then that presentation may help the person pass the test, because it will cause fewer questions to be asked about what he did and why. It is hard for a person to explain why he lost the fight or why he backed down. Hence many will strive to appear to "go for bad," while hoping they will never be tested. But when they are tested, the outcome of the situation may quickly be out of their hands, as they become wrapped up in the circumstances of the moment.

An Oppositional Culture

The attitudes of the wider society are deeply implicated in the code of the streets. Most people in inner-city communities are not totally invested in the code. But the significant minority of hard-core street youths who are have to maintain the code in order to establish reputations because they have—or feel they have—few other ways to assert themselves. For these young people the standards of the street code are the only game in town. The extent to which some children—particularly those who through upbringing have become most alienated and those lacking in strong and conventional social support—experience, feel, and internalize racist rejection and contempt from mainstream society may strongly encourage them to express contempt for the more conventional society in turn. In dealing with this contempt and rejection, some youngsters will consciously invest themselves and their considerable mental resources in what amounts to an oppositional culture to preserve themselves and their self-respect. Once they do, any respect they might be able to garner in the wider system pales in comparison with the respect available in the local system; thus they often lose interest in even attempting to negotiate the mainstream system.

At the same time, many less alienated young blacks have assumed a street-oriented demeanor as a way of expressing their blackness while really embracing a much more moderate way of life; they, too, want a nonviolent setting in which to live and raise a family. These decent people are trying hard to be part of the mainstream culture, but the racism, real and perceived, that they encounter helps to legitimate the oppositional culture. And so on occasion they adopt street behavior. In fact, depending on the demands of the situation, many people in the community slip back and forth between decent and street behavior.

A vicious cycle has thus been formed. The hopelessness and alienation many young inner-city black men and women feel, largely as a result of endemic joblessness and persistent racism, fuels the violence they engage in. This violence serves to confirm the negative feelings many whites and some middle-class blacks harbor toward the ghetto poor, further legitimating the oppositional culture and the code of the streets in the eyes of many poor young blacks. Unless the cycle is broken, attitudes on both sides will become increasingly entrenched, and the violence, which claims victims black and white, poor and affluent, will only escalate.

Questions

1. How would you define each of the following terms (used by Anderson in his article)?
   a. mayhem
   b. oppositional culture
   c. zero-sum

2. What factors of life on the street make it difficult for people to be "decent"?

3. In your judgment, are young men from more "middle-class" cultural settings at all preoccupied with earning respect? How do young men in middle-class culture earn the respect of others and prove themselves to be properly "manly"?

13

ROCK IN A HARD PLACE: GRASSROOTS CULTURAL PRODUCTION IN THE POST-ELVIS ERA

William T. Bielby

Fifty years ago, Elvis Presley was big news—but not necessarily in a good way. Many adults were appalled by Presley's "bodily contortions" and "sexual gyrations" and worried that rock and roll would "overstimulate" American teenagers. In this article, Professor Bielby discusses how Elvis helped give rise to a "new cultural form": the rock and roll band. But, as Bielby explains, the development of rock and roll was shaped by existing culture norms and expectations as much as it was by music icons.

He used to carry his guitar in a gunny sack
Go sit beneath the tree by the railroad track
....
Maybe someday your name will be in lights
Saying Johnny B. Goode tonight.

Lyrics by Chuck Berry, 1958,
"Johnny B. Goode"

Joe, who was raised in a working-class industrial suburb south of Chicago, gave the following account about his first guitar:

> It was probably about my freshman year in high school [1958], that I decided to play guitar. And my parents went out, I'll never forget it. The old song, Johnny B. Goode? Used to carry his guitar in a gunny sack? I actually carried my guitar in a gunny sack. They went out to a pawnshop and bought me a white, arch-topped guitar with the f-holes. And the top was cracked, I remember that, and I said well, now I

"Rock in a Hard Place: Grassroots Cultural Production in the Post-Elvis Era: 2003 Presidential Address" by William T. Bielby from *American Sociological Review,* Vol. 69, No. 1 (February, 2004: pp. 1–13). Reprinted by permission of the American Sociological Association and the author.

> got to learn how to play this thing. And every time I learned it, I put my guitar in my sack and go over to all my friends house, and every time I learned a new song, "hey, want to hear the song I learned?"

In 1958, Joe was not a professional musician. Not even close. But his story account describes his very first efforts at participating in the performance of rock and roll music. Joe's experience, participating in the making of music at the local level, in "grassroots cultural production," is rarely studied by cultural sociologists.

Of course, popular music has not escaped the attention of cultural sociologists, although rarely has scholarship on rock and roll in particular or popular music in general appeared in our discipline's mainstream journals. A search of sociology abstracts in JSTOR for the terms "rock and roll," "rock music," "music industry," and "popular music" yields just nine articles published over a span of a quarter of a century; just three since 1990. These nine articles are listed in Table 1. With only a few exceptions, this scholarship is mostly about

Table 1 Sociology Articles Containing the Phrases "Rock and Roll," "Rock Music," "Music Industry," or "Popular Music," 1957–1999

1. "When Women Play the Bass: Instrument Specialization and Gender Interpretation in Alternative Rock Music." Mary Ann Clawson. *Gender and Society* (April, 1999)

2. "Innovation and Diversity in the Popular Music Industry, 1969 to 1990." Paul D. Lopes. *American Sociological Review* (February, 1992)

3. "Just Me and the Boys? Women in Local-Level Rock and Roll." Stephen B. Groce; Margaret Cooper. *Gender and Society* (June, 1990)

4. "Music as Social Circumstance." Judith R. Blau. *Social Forces* (June, 1988)

5. "The Mass Society and Group Action Theories of Cultural Production: The Case of Stylistic Innovation in Jazz." Lars Bjorn. *Social Forces* (December, 1981)

6. "Cycles in Symbol Production: The Case of Popular Music." Richard A. Peterson; David G. Berger. *American Sociological Review* (April, 1975)

7. "Entrepreneurship in Organizations: Evidence from the Popular Music Industry." Richard A. Peterson; David G. Berger. *Administrative Science Quarterly* (March, 1971)

8. "Changing Courtship Patterns in the Popular Song." James T. Carey. *American Journal of Sociology* (May, 1969)

9. "Youth and Popular Music: A Study in the Sociology of Taste." John Johnstone; Elihu Katz. *American Journal of Sociology* (May, 1957)

Data source: JSTOR.

commercially produced music and the music industry, not about grassroots performance. For example, there is the small number of important studies by Richard Peterson and others on how the industrial and organizational structure of the music industry affects the proliferation of musical styles (Table 1). There is also old work found in the communication studies traditions on consumption behavior and the content of popular songs. Just two studies deal with the social organization of rock music performance at the local level, notably, both published in *Gender & Society*.

But what is sociologically interesting about grassroots cultural production? I maintain that it is sociologically significant at three levels. The first is as a status attainment process. Participation in the grassroots music scene is likely to have effects, for better or worse, on school experiences, on the transition to adulthood, and on the adult experiences of those who performed in the bands. Drawing on the work of Paul DiMaggio (1982; DiMaggio and Mohr 1985), experience in a teenage band can

be thought of as an issue of how acquisition of lowbrow cultural capital and participation in socially devalued status cultures affect adult attainment (Hagan 1991). The second is as an issue about organizations and institutions, namely, what shapes the emergence of a new and perhaps distinctive organizational form of cultural production—in this case the teen rock and roll band. The third, which I address only briefly, is that music (including commercially produced rock music) is a cultural commodity that is consumed, appropriated, and reinterpreted in a way that provides meaning in people's lives, including the many individuals who participate in making rock and roll music at a grassroots level.

In this article, I draw on eighteen months of interviews and historical work done on the first generation of grassroots rock and roll performers to come out of the mostly working-class south suburbs of Chicago. I chose this site for three reasons. First, I was interested in how the mostly white teen performers did and did not relate to the music performed by and marketed to African Americans. The Chicago south suburbs is a racially mixed but extremely segregated set of communities, just a few miles from Chicago's Black Belt, the birthplace of modern urban blues. Many of the teenagers—especially the musicians—from that part of metropolitan Chicago, who were deeply into the rock and roll scene, had their musical tastes shaped in part by the rhythm & blues and the urban blues music coming from Chicago's African American radio stations broadcasting to the south side.

At the same time, this region is *not* known for racial tolerance, especially in the late 1950s, when these suburbs experienced explosive growth as working-class white ethnics fled Chicago's changing neighborhoods (Tauber and Tauber 1965; Massey and Denton 1993; Rosen 1998). It is a region where most teens went either to mostly white or to mostly African American grade schools. For most of them, high school was the locus of their first substantive social interaction with age peers of a different race. And even then, in the high schools, interracial interaction was minimal during classroom hours. Thus, popular music may have provided an opportunity for black-white interaction among those engaged as performers in the local music scene; however, racism and racial exclusion, especially segregation of performance venues, may have precluded all but the most superficial interaction between white and African American teen musicians.

Second, I chose a working-class milieu far from the major recording centers of New York and Los Angeles to understand what personal and cultural resources could be marshaled by aspiring teen musicians with no family, personal, or business connections to the music industry. My working hypothesis is that the first wave of truly homegrown rock and roll teenage performance groups came largely from such modest backgrounds. In future work, I plan to test this hypothesis by contrasting the rate at which bands formed and dis-

solved in this area compared to the rate in the more affluent and predominately white suburbs north and west of the city.

Finally, I chose this area because it is a region for which there is systematic data about teenage musical tastes and practices in the immediate post-Elvis era. This data is from the survey and interview research done by James Coleman and his colleagues in nine Illinois high schools in 1957 and published in his book, *The Adolescent Society* (Coleman 1961). Coleman's data is the only systematic survey data available on teenage engagement with popular music during the early rock and roll era.

I define a teenage band as any local teenage rock and roll performance group that had a drummer, at least one electric guitarist, a band name, and a business card. With this definition, I have identified most if not all of the local bands of this region from the post-Elvis, pre-Beatles era (1958 through 1963). I have been interviewing the people who performed in those bands as well as the people who ran the venues where the bands performed, who sold the instruments the teen musicians played, who worked in the record stores where teenagers shopped and hung out, and who regularly frequented the performances.

Grassroots Performance and Status Attainment

Much of my scholarship over the past twenty-five years has addressed how structures and processes within and among organizations shape an individual's career. My collaborator Denise Bielby and I made the "cultural turn" by applying this approach to understand the dynamics of age, gender, and racial stratification of film and television writers and to analyze how mediating institutions like talent agencies broker labor markets and shape careers in Hollywood (Bielby and Bielby 2002). Similar substantive concerns led me to approach teenage musical performance as embedded in a status attainment process stratified by gender, race, and age.

The emergence of the local, grassroots rock and roll band phenomenon among teenagers in the late 1950s is especially interesting from the perspective of organizations and stratification. First, it is profoundly stratified by gender, race, and age. Teenage girls were, with only rare exception, excluded from the local bands of that era. The music had roots in African American traditions but was performed primarily by white teens for white audiences. And, of course, the music was marketed to a specific age group, and, some scholars claim, a very specific kind of youth subculture developed around it. Second, those first-generation grassroots bands were organized more or less autonomously from schools, workplaces, and other formal institutions. Therefore, it is unlikely that the highly structured patterns of gender, race, and age stratification can be linked directly to specific policies and practices within organizations. Understanding how stratified cultural practices emerge through informal and semiautonomous social interaction among ordinary people presents a unique challenge to cultural sociologists interested in social inequality.

The Teen Band's Emergence as a Male-Dominated Cultural Form

The teen rock and roll band that emerged in the late 1950s quickly became institutionalized as a male-dominated form of subcultural involvement in musical performance. Why? Consider Joe's story again. He acquired his guitar, and he taught himself how to play it. It is a distinctive feature of the grassroots rock world, one highlighted by Ruth Finnegan (1989) in her fascinating study, *The Hidden Musicians,* that these musicians are largely self-taught and have launched their careers as

grassroots performers largely outside of formal organizations. In this way, their world is closer to that of grassroots folk music than that of either the orchestral or jazz musician. And the first generation of grassroots rock and rollers were making up the cultural form of the homegrown band as they went along.

Today, a teenager with Joe's musical interests would have no problem finding like-minded individuals to make music collectively. In the local arts and entertainment weekly or on the Internet, she or he can readily find notices of music-making opportunities like those listed in Table 2. Indeed, these examples provide a sense of the rich, highly differentiated institutional field an aspiring grassroots musician would encounter. Consider, for example, the subgenres identified here—"cover band" with Petty, Little Feat influences, "Voodoo" influenced by Johnny Cash, Bauhaus, X, and so on. Interestingly, while a number of these advertisements make reference to age, none mention gender, either explicitly or implicitly (perhaps because of the paper's antidiscrimination policies).

In contrast, in Joe's era, the late 1950s, these subgenre categories and the model for starting a band did not exist. Indeed, the term "garage band," which is often assumed to have originated in the early rock and roll era, did not gain currency until more than a decade later, after the phenomenon of the teen band had become well established and taken for granted. So what about the immediate post-Elvis era? I started thinking about it this way when I began my project:

- See Elvis on TV
- Decide you want to be Elvis
- Ask Mom & Dad to get you a guitar
- Discover you are not Elvis
- Now what to do with that guitar? Learn how to play
- Start a band? But how?

Table 2 Musician Help-Wanted Advertisements, Summer 2003

BASS PLAYER wanted young, well equipped, pro., rock/pop, aggressive, success minded, JDL xxx–xxxx

BLUES/HARP PLAYER seeks acoustic blues guitar player to jam with 1–2 times a week. Call Dan xxx–xxxx

DRUMMER WANTED: The Hollywood Horrors seek young, pro, well-equipped, rock drummer. JDL xxx–xxxx

EXPERIENCED LEAD Singer wanted for established SB band, age 20–30. Call Ryan xxx–xxxx

ISO GUITARIST w/Vocal for Cover Band. Infl: Petty, Band, Little Feat. Call Cy, xxx–xxxx

ISO RHYTHM guitar for Voodoobilly band. Infl:Johnny Cash- Danzig- Bauhaus & X. Have gigs/CDs xxx–xxxx

Advertisements from "Music Callboard," *Santa Barbara Independent.*

So, perhaps there is a simple reason why women were excluded. Teenage boys saw Elvis impress the girls, so they got their friends, other teenage boys, to start bands with them. Girls need not apply. However, my research indicates that there is much more to the story, involving the relationship between rock and roll and high school culture in the post-Elvis era.

Today, it is taken for granted that the teen rock band is, and always has been, a male domain. However, a large body of scholarship demonstrates that it is always possible to make attributions after the fact to explain why a line of work is dominated by men or by women, even when the objective circumstances at the time a field is emerging do not dictate that outcome (Reskin 1988, Tuchman 1989, Reskin and Roos 1990). A closer look at the teen popular music scene in the immediate post-Elvis era suggests that it was no exception. First, in the mid-1950s, before the explosive expansion of rock and roll music on AM radio, popular music was not particularly male dominated. According to Groce and Cooper (1990), women accounted for a third of the artists on the singles charts in 1955. High school yearbook photos from that era clearly show that the gender balance was relatively mixed among participants in organized school music programs. . . .

The data collected by Coleman and his colleagues and published in *The Adolescent Society* show that high school age girls listened to music as a leisure activity nearly three times as much as boys (Coleman 1961:13; Figure 1).

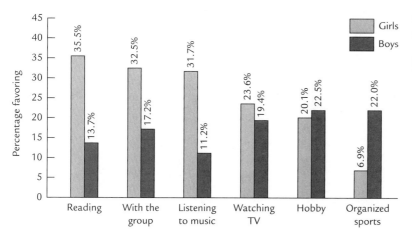

Figure 1 *Leisure Activities of High School Boys and Girls, 1957*

Note: Data adapted from Coleman 1961 (Table 5, p. 13).

Coleman's data also show that girls were more attentive to popular music than boys were, at least as reflected in their purchasing habits. Although the difference was modest, the percentage of teenage girls buying records was higher than it was for boys, and among those purchasing records, girls were purchasing more on average than were boys (Coleman 1961, Figure 2.2, p. 20). Other data collected by Coleman (1961:14) indicate that, in the post-Elvis era, girls were generally more attuned to popular culture than boys were. Compared to boys, the same-sex friendship activities of girls were more likely to be organized around going to dances and movies (Figure 2). Also, the Coleman data as well as other studies indicate that, in the 1950s and 1960s, female high school students were more oriented towards success in social realms than were boys (Eder 1985; Eder and Parker 1987). All these factors suggest that, compared to boys, girls would be as inclined, if not more inclined, to engage in popular music, not just as listeners, but as performers.

Given the participation of teenage girls in other forms of musical performance and engagement with popular music, what explains their absence from the bandstand? One explanation draws on the mythology that 1950s rock and roll was the anthem of male teenage rebellion and male sexuality, which was portrayed in films like *Blackboard Jungle, Rebel Without a Cause*, and the *Wild One* and personified in Elvis's early television performances. Martin and Segrave (1993) describe the emergence of rock and roll from 1953 to 1962 in *Anti-Rock: The Opposition to Rock 'n' Roll.* They provide the following account of early rock and roll as teen rebellion:

> Adults resisted teen culture in order to regain their authority over the young. The battle took place in many areas; but nowhere was the conflict more intense than in the music. Rock was particularly threatening because young people often wrote, played, and performed it themselves. . . . From the beginning rock and roll was viewed by the adult world as the clarion call to teenagers to rise up and defy their elders, to flaunt morality, to mock their ideals, to break away from adult control, to reject the adult world. The adult world was determined to undermine rock and roll. . . . (Martin and Segrave 1993:14)

While this account is exaggerated to say the least, sociologists writing in respectable venues

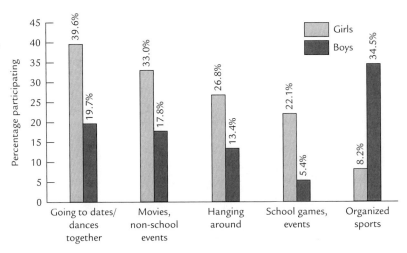

Figure 2 *Activities and Interests That Friends Have in Common: High School Boys and Girls, 1957*
Note: Data adapted from Coleman 1961 (Table 6, p. 14).

Girls
Boys

Percentage participating

Going to dates/ dances together — 39.6% / 19.7%
Movies, non-school events — 33.0% / 17.8%
Hanging around — 26.8% / 13.4%
School games, events — 22.1% / 5.4%
Organized sports — 8.2% / 34.5%

have reproduced a version of this account (Dotter 1987, 1995), sometimes dressed up in the "moral panic" jargon of the social problems literature (Cohen 2002). And, of course, the male teen rebel has been immortalized in rock and roll songs, as in the Phil Spector-produced hit by the Crystals:

He's a rebel and he'll never ever be any good.
He is a rebel and he'll never ever be understood.
And just because he doesn't do what everybody else does,
That's no reason why I can't give him all my love
Lyrics by Gene Pitney, "He's A Rebel"

In sum, the "teen rebel" explanation of rock and roll as a male domain goes as follows: Rebellious teenager boys of the era were drawn to "authentic" rock and roll, with its African American roots and charged sexuality. The boys picked up their electric guitars and turned up the volume on their amplifiers as acts of defiance against parents and teachers, a theme that runs through scores of rock and roll songs from the 1950s to the present. In contrast, teenage girls of the era were more engaged with popular culture, but they were less rebellious. They were drawn to softer, more highly produced music, to songs with orchestral

accompaniment and narratives of romance, not the kind of music that lends itself to grassroots performance. This is a coherent account, consistent with cultural scripts about rock and roll, but it does not fit the data from the post-Elvis era. In 1957, Coleman and his team found that rock and roll music was the favorite musical style for about half of the high school boys as well as for about half of the high school girls they surveyed (1961:23). At the height of Elvis Presley's popularity, when Coleman and his team surveyed these teens about their favorite artists, they found that, for *both* boys and girls, by far the most popular artist was not Elvis Presley, the authentic rock and roller, but Pat Boone, whose early success was based on bland "cover" versions of songs originally recorded by African American artists (Figure 3).

Missing from the "teen rebel" account is any serious consideration of the social organization of schools and how that intersects with teenager subcultural involvements. In fact, there is a significant body of sociological scholarship that I believe provides the basis for a more complete account of why the teen band phenomenon emerged as an almost exclusively male domain. As can be seen in the

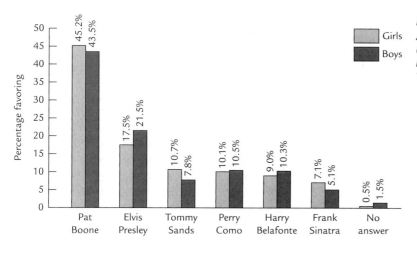

Figure 3 *Favorite Recording Artist: High School Boys and Girls, 1957*
Note: Data adapted from Coleman 1961 (Table 8, p. 22).

Coleman data in Figure 2, the most significant subcultural pursuit for teenage boys in 1957 was organized sports. Even today, organized sports is the main cultural event of high school life, and that was even more true in the late 1950s and early 1960s (Rehberg and Schafer 1968; Spreitzer and Pugh 1973; Otto and Alwin 1977). For boys, it provided what DiMaggio has called, in a somewhat different context, a "status culture" (DiMaggio 1982). In their 1985 article on high school cultural participation and adult attainment, DiMaggio and Mohr wrote the following:

> The ability to participate in a status culture is a cultural resource that permits actors to get ahead by managing impressions, developing positive local reputations, impressing gatekeepers, and constructing social networks that may be useful in educational, marital, and occupational attainment. . . . [It] enables individuals . . . to sustain relationships with those in control of the allocation of rewards that constitutes the stratification process. (1985:1235).

While they were writing about teen participation in elite culture (literature, the arts, classical music), a large body of sociological scholarship demonstrates rather conclusively that for boys, organized sports works in just this way (Eitzen 1975; Kessler et al. 1985, Eder and Parker 1987).

The central role of sports in high school peer cultures was first documented systematically by Coleman (1961) in *The Adolescent Society,* and elegantly revisited and revised by Donna Eder and Stephen Parker in an article that appeared in *Sociology of Education* in 1987. Three important insights from their work are relevant to understanding rock and roll performance versus organized sports as teen subcultural pursuits. The first is that high school sports is a *formally organized school-sponsored activity* that exposes participants—mostly boys, even to this day, but especially so in the post-Elvis era—to a value system that emphasizes not just teamwork but also unequal status and

rewards, hierarchy, and competition. The second is that this value system is then incorporated, in modified form, into the teens' own informal peer groups and status hierarchies. The third is that as a result, contrary to the claims of Coleman in the early 1960s and the British cultural studies scholars after that (e.g., Willis 1977; Hebdige 1984), the peer group value system that emerges is one that is formed and sustained largely in accord with, rather than in opposition to, the dominant value system.

How do organized sports activities contrast with involvement in rock and roll performance? A theme that comes up in almost all of my interviews with the former teen musicians, consistent with what DiMaggio (1982) and others (e.g., Bourdieu 1977) have written about elite culture and social standing, is a narrative about status as culturally enacted. For teenage boys entering high school in the 1950s, more so than today, there were few alternative paths to peer status outside of organized sports. But for boys lacking the physical strength and skill, success in organized sports was not an option. To teens of Joe's era, demonstrating competence in rock and roll performance was seen as a potential means of gaining the same kind of peer acceptance as one does from being athletically competent—and again, and in my interviews, it is typically articulated in just that way.

For a culturally aware teenage boy with a guitar, inventing a rock and roll identity is relatively straightforward and requires little in the way of material resources. For example, white bucks, rolled up jeans or polished cotton pants with a buckle on the back, sleeves rolled up two turns on a short-sleeved shirt, and a skinny belt buckled on the side would make a teenage boy immediately recognizable as part of teen music subculture in Chicago's south suburbs in the late 1950s. Moreover, it is easy for such a boy to acquire the cultural codes that define the appropriate presentation of self by observing peer culture and by exposure to mass media via television, radio, and teen magazines.[1]

While participation in rock and roll performance was an alternative route to status for some teenage boys, it was not its functional equivalent. On the one hand, for the athletically challenged teen boy of this era, successfully enacting this rock and roll image could provide a status similar to the male athlete. In the socially and culturally segregated milieu of the late 1950s, this role could give him standing not just with his male peers, but with girls too. On the other hand, there are some very important differences in the social organization of the two status cultures—organized sports and rock and roll performance. Most importantly, the latter had absolutely no standing in the schools of the immediate post-Elvis era, and that remained true in most schools into the late 1960s. Though not actively suppressed as some accounts maintain, being in a rock and roll band was in no way an official school extracurricular activity. School venues were largely off limits to local rock and roll bands until around the Beatles era. Putting together and participating in a band was completely autonomous from teachers, counselors, formal curricula, informal curricula, and, to a large extent, parental authority. While the initial motivation was often to enhance one's standing in the school's status hierarchy, if anything, participation in an even modestly successful band drew teens away from the "extracurriculum" and provided some distance between their music world and the school value system.

In fact, participation in this kind of status culture has more in common with what sociologists have described as deviant subcultural involvements. John Hagan (1991), borrowing the concept of "subcultural drift" from David Matza's early work in control theory (Matza 1964), developed a model of the consequences of participation in deviant subcultures for adult attainments. In his work, Hagan criticized conventional status attainment models for being overly deterministic and for giving inadequate attention to the contingent ways movement in and out of various adolescent subcultural involvements—located between deviance and conformity—can alter life-course trajectories. Hagan also recognized that DiMaggio's cultural stratification approach could be applied productively to study the consequences of engagement with "lowbrow" culture and devalued status cultures. Literally, Hagan wanted to put "the fun and thrill-seeking side of teenage culture" back into status attainment and cultural stratification research, noting that certain kinds of mildly deviant subcultural involvements might have positive effects on later attainments (Hagan 1991:570). And, again, drawing from control theory, Hagan's model addresses how the level of parental direction and control influences subcultural involvements.

Hagan's effort to use control theory to bring subcultural participation into status attainment models also tempers the strategic, prospectively rational imagery that I invoked above. Indeed, the former teen rock and rollers I interviewed can now, as adults, tell a story about making a choice to engage the performance subculture of rock and roll music to enact an identity that had currency in their high school status culture. And there is more contemporary qualitative research done in high schools that does not rely on retrospective accounts, which also suggests such strategic

---

[1]However, even with the appropriate clothes, haircut, language, pose, and $25 mail-order guitar, the young man still faces the dilemma that confronted Joe and other teen musicians. In 1957, even after learning how to play the guitar reasonably well, there are no established models or pathways for seeking out and assembling like-minded teens to perform rock and roll. How teens from working-class families invented and institutionalized the "rock combo" as a cultural form is the subject of my ongoing research on teenage grassroots cultural production.

behavior is common. One of the better studies is the provocatively titled article, "From Nerds to Normals: The Recovery of Identity among Adolescents from Middle School to High School" by David Kinney (1993). Kinney's research shows how some students labeled as "nerds" in middle school deliberately choose to engage in specific high school activities to successfully enact a new, higher status personal identity.

However, teens also drift into participation in the grassroots rock performance subculture, and indeed—given its autonomy from adult institutions—they may simply take to it because it is fun and fulfilling. Regardless of the motivating factors, Hagan's elaboration of the cultural stratification approach and his quantitative research suggest that such participation can have, and is likely to have, consequences for school experiences and outcomes, the transition to adulthood, and adult attainments.

While the qualitative work I have completed does not provide definitive empirical support for the idea of subcultural engagement in rock and roll performance as a status-enhancing process, Hagan's research, based on panel data on teens in Toronto in the late 1970s, has some intriguing findings that resonate with some of what I found in my interviews. His work also suggests why it is sociologically interesting to study grassroots cultural production from a status attainment perspective. Besides more serious forms of deviance, Hagan analyzed "party subculture" (parties, concerts, drinking, dating) as an intervening variable. He found that a parental control measure reduced girls' engagement with party subculture, but that was not the case for boys (Hagan 1991:575–6). Several of my interviews suggest that this was a factor keeping girls out of the band scene in the immediate post-Elvis era as well. Specifically, some parents were willing to tolerate their sons devoting school nights to band practice and weekends to performances throughout

the greater Chicago area, but allowing their daughters to do the same was inconceivable.

Another intriguing finding in Hagan's study is that, for men of non-working-class origins, identification with party subculture, as expected, is associated with lower educational attainment; however, the net effect of that is positive. That is, among middle class men with comparable schooling, those who identified with the party subculture when they were teens eventually had higher occupational attainments (Hagan 1991:576–80). Hagan speculated that this kind of subcultural involvement socializes young men into leisure pursuits that become the basis for social bonds and for gendered social networks as adults. Therefore, participating in a subculture—like the rock music performance scene—could have an effect similar to, for example, college fraternity life (e.g., the "frat band") and careers where after-hours socializing (or on-the-job socializing) is an important part of workplace culture.

In sum, in the early days of rock and roll, grassroots performance was an "empty field" (Tuchman 1989) not yet dominated by males or by females. In terms of tastes and talent, teenage girls were as engaged with the music as were teenage boys. The absence of girls from the performance scene cannot be explained by skills or preferences, nor is it plausible to attribute their exclusion to gendered responses to musical narratives about rebellion and romance. Instead, their near total exclusion from grassroots performance is more plausibly explained by the distinctive way in which rock and roll performance created an opening for enactment of status roles autonomous from and in response to the school-sanctioned and gendered status hierarchy of organized sports. Because rock and roll performance was sustained outside the high school extracurriculum, the act of assembling a band, practicing, and, especially, performing meant that teen musicians would be participating mostly away from home and away from direct adult supervision. That aspect of the subculture likely made most parents much more reluctant to allow their daughters, rather than their sons, to participate in the performance of rock and roll music at the grassroots level. Finally, research on the adult consequences of mildly deviant subcultural involvements suggests that the teenage boys who performed in bands early in the rock and roll era may have acquired a kind of lowbrow cultural capital that had a positive effect on status attainment in male-dominated occupational settings.

By the mid-1960s, the grassroots rock and roll band had been fully institutionalized as a male-dominated cultural form. For decades, the women who had participated in bands had done so primarily in gendered roles, such as vocalists. They were rarely accepted by either fellow musicians or audiences as instrumentalists, especially as guitarists or drummers. Also, women typically had been marginalized in the band's decision-making processes (Groce and Cooper 1995). As Mary Ann Clawson (1999) has shown, the one area women have made inroads more recently is as bassists in alternative rock bands. But even there, Clawson demonstrates, the gains have come about through a mechanism that is typical of other work roles that become feminized: the skill becomes devalued as men's work, leading to male flight, and women enter as new feminized cultural scripts developed to rationalize the task as "women's work."

Rock and Roll Never Dies? Retrospective Accounts of the Decision to Leave the Performance Scene

We know from research on the careers of artists in contemporary society that sustaining any kind of artistic career into and through adulthood is extremely difficult (e.g., Becker 1951 on jazz musicians; Baker and Faulkner 1991 on careers in the motion picture industry; Bielby and Bielby 2002 on film and television writers), and the first generation of homegrown rock and roll musicians is no exception. Nevertheless, in my interviews, I was surprised by how many of the former teen musicians did sustain musical careers through at least part of their adult lives, approximately half of those I have contacted. The transition to adulthood and the intersection of professional and family life course trajectories is a central concern of status attainment scholars, but their approach rarely has been applied to participation in grassroots cultural pursuits.

The life course transitions of grassroots musicians whose careers started in the post-Elvis era provide an interesting contrast to the dominant pattern of the time. Describing the trend of the last century, Glen Elder wrote the following:

> The range of choice and action in the lives of late-nineteenth-century youth has been replaced by a more tightly organized schedule of contingent transitions to adult status. Early life transitions are more compressed and contingent because they are more constrained by the scheduling of formal institutions. Control over these transitions has shifted from the family of origin, which allowed a wide measure of flexibility, to young people themselves and the generalized requirements of school and workplace. (1980:33)

For the first cohort of grassroots rock and roll musicians who earned any sort of living from their craft, the transitions were far from being tightly organized or strongly shaped by the requirements of formal institutions. The life cycle transitions of a musician attempting to sustain a career in a struggling, never famous, or "almost famous" rock group through the 1960s, 1970s, and beyond is almost always out of synch with those of family members and peers whose professional lives are not in the realms of music and art.

For most people who decided to stay with the band after leaving school, the initial decision to attempt to sustain a musical career was motivated less by considerations of fame and fortune than by a passion for the music and performance, an "art for art's sake" orientation to their craft (Caves 2000), even if they were just performing "covers" of top 40 songs. As Joe put it, in the period following high school graduation in 1962, "it wasn't about the money":

> Like I said, back then it wasn't about the money anyway. We would play if we didn't get a nickel. [Were you living at home at this time?] I was still at home, yeah. [Did you have a day job?] Not at that time, No. All I did was music. Uh, and like I said, it was just fun. It was what we wanted to do. I mean, we were basically, still young. Obviously you had these dreams that you are going to become famous. Well to us, a great day was we'd go on a Sunday afternoon. Jim Lounsbury used to do a lot of dances at the Chicagoland Music Hall, 32 West Randolph, down the street from the Greyhound station. They'd have a lot of military guys on leave. We'd do a gig there in the afternoon, he'd pay us fifteen bucks a man, we'd go to Michigan. Fifteen bucks a man. We'd pack up the gig there, then we'd head out to Elgin and do the Blue Moon Ballroom in Elgin that night for fifteen dollars. And we made thirty dollars that night and thought we were rich!

From my interviews, consistent with other scholarship (e.g., Finnegan 1989, Ch. 19), I found that the effects on marriage and family life are exactly what is expected given the nature of the job, the timing of those other life-course transitions, and the nature of the times. This is the first generation of rock musicians trying to "go pro" just before and into the era when young people's lives were profoundly affected by the military draft, urban unrest, social movements, drug cultures, etc. Almost all of my interviewees tell a story about hanging on, waiting to make it, despite economic hardship and turmoil, and then eventually confronting the fact that the big break just was not

going to happen. The stories all have a similar structure, regardless of whether the people were in their twenties, thirties, forties, or even older when the "stay or leave" decision became unavoidable. The story invariably involves a narrative along the lines of "even though I did not make it, it was worth it." But as they relate these stories, it becomes apparent that they are trying to convince *themselves* as much as they are trying to convince the interviewer. For Joe, the decision to give it up came shortly after he turned 30. Despite tours to Europe and Japan and modest success in Las Vegas with a racially integrated soul band, he realized that a musical career was no longer viable:

> We just got fed up with that; bookings were getting harder to come by, we thought we could get back into Vegas. But, the country was in somewhat of a recession at that time. And the gigs at the lounges and hotels, where the 'up-and-coming' groups could get them, now, big stars—that aren't as big as they once were—were taking those gigs. The guys trying to come up, [they were] squeezing them out. So we never could get back into Vegas.
>
> And I remember Bill Fix had gotten an audition for us with the producer from the Rolling Stones. And the guitar player was two hours late for the audition. He had gotten us a country club to do this audition. I can remember walking around on the tennis court, I think I was like 26 or 27 years old at the time. And I had like 50 bucks to my name. And I had a long talk with myself. I said, you know what? That's not even two dollars a year for every year you've lived on this earth. I know I can do better. And my parents had been after me to quit. I had gone through . . . well, I was not divorced then, but all but. And I had told everybody, when it is time to quit, I won't need anybody to tell me. I'll know. And I told myself right then and there, you know what, it's time to go. . . . And that was just the final straw to me. I said, You know what, my livelihood is depending on all of us pulling that rope the same way. If you got two or three guys pulling in a different direction, it

isn't going to work. I mean I gave it my best shot, it must not have been intended to be, it's time for me to go home and do something else with my life. So that's when I made up my mind that I was out of it. And I came home.

Kal, the most successful of my interviewees, made the transition from a regional touring bar band to a major recording contract in the 1970s, recorded some critically acclaimed but only modestly successful albums over the years, and sustained a career with session work and gigging with several incarnations of a highly regarded blues band. At the time of our interview, he was still performing at his blues club in Palm Springs, but he had just put the club up for sale. As Kal is turning 60, his words echo Joe's story. He faces a similar dilemma regarding his commitment to music and the challenges of surviving financially:

> I'm not sure, as far as my next chapter. "In the life of," you know. I'm not really sure where it is going to take me. But, uh, I can't really see me without a guitar in my hand. Although, uh, I read the writing on the wall. I mean, the record business is kind of no more. I mean, there's millions of dollars being made by somebody. I don't see it in the future for me. Like, to break into the record business now would be pretty impossible. But, uh, I will find a next thing, you know, and there's going to be music in there somewhere, so, that's where I'm goin'.

Towards a Sociology of Grassroots Cultural Production

Cultural sociologists who have studied popular music have focused almost exclusively on the production, distribution, and consumption of music created commercially for a mass market. Very few sociologists have studied the way ordinary people become involved in the creation and performance of popular music, and hardly any scholarship addresses the emergence of new cultural forms of grassroots performance, such as the teen rock and roll band. A small but growing body of social science scholarship examines gender and racial stratification of careers in culture industries, but little of that research focuses on grassroots participation. While it is no surprise that the grassroots rock and roll performance scene was distinctively structured by gender and race even before the teen band became institutionalized as a cultural form, there has been little serious scholarship on why this was the case, given the similarities in musical talents and tastes by gender and the origins of rock and roll in African American musical genres. I argue here that the young people who formed the first bands did so outside of the structured environment of the schools and mostly independent of adult supervision. Nevertheless, the social structure and status system of the schools and segregated community institutions most likely contributed substantially, albeit indirectly, to the emergence of the teen band as an almost exclusively white male cultural form.

Although it has been mostly ignored by cultural sociologists, participation in grassroots rock and roll musical performance was both meaningful and consequential in the lives of those who entered that world. This effect is especially true during their school age years and almost certainly into young adulthood. It may also hold during later adulthood, as some benefit from returns to "popular cultural capital." Whether those who entered that world did so strategically as part of the management of personal identity or drifted into it in a search for fun and excitement is an open question. There is much to learn about what sustains them in creative pursuits into adulthood. The answers to these research questions have implications for how young people are drawn into creative subcultural involvements outside of formal institutional structures and the circumstances under which grassroots performance as an adolescent becomes a viable work option as an adult, despite the almost inevitable social and economic hardships of an artistic career. Moreover, retrospective accounts of the musical careers of former teen performers show how these people find personal meaning in experiences that almost always fell far short of early aspirations. Such accounts also show how they justify to themselves and others that the choices they made during the course of chaotic careers were valid ones. Sociologists who study popular culture are only beginning to study its aesthetic content (Bielby and Bielby 2004), and the personal accounts of my interviewees suggest that there is much to be learned by engaging issues of interpretation as they apply to the meaning creative performers find in their work. Finally, I have attempted to demonstrate here that theories and models from "mainstream" areas—such as status attainment, life course, and deviance paradigms—can be as useful to advancing knowledge about grassroots cultural engagements as are the most fashionable interpretive approaches from around the bend of the "cultural turn."

References

Baker, Wayne E. and Robert R. Faulkner. 1991. "Role as Resource in the Hollywood Film Industry." *American Journal of Sociology* 97:279–309.

Becker, Howard S. 1951. "The Professional Dance Musician and His Audience." *American Journal of Sociology* 57:136–44.

Bourdieu, Pierre. 1977. "Cultural Reproduction and Social Reproduction." Pp. 487–511 in *Power and Ideology in Education*, edited by Jerome Karabel and A. H. Halsey. New York: Oxford.

Bielby, Denise D. and William T. Bielby. 2004. "Audience Aesthetics and Popular Culture." Forthcoming in *Matters of Culture: Cultural Sociology in Practice*, edited by Roger Friedland and John Mohr. New York: Cambridge University Press.

———. 2002. "Hollywood Dreams, Hard Realities: Writing for Film and Television." *Contexts* 1:21–7.

Caves, Richard E. 2000. *Creative Industries: Contracts Between Art and Commerce.* Cambridge, MA: Harvard University Press.

Clawson, Mary Ann. 1999. "When Women Play the Bass: Instrument Specialization and Gender Interpretation in Alternative Rock Music." *Gender & Society* 13:193–210.

Cohen, Stanley. 2002. *Folk Devils and Moral Panics: The Creation of the Mods and the Rockers.* London: Routledge.

Coleman, James S. 1961. *The Adolescent Society: The Social Life of the Teenager and Its Impact on Education.* New York: Free Press.

DiMaggio, Paul. 1982. "Cultural Capital and School Success: The Impact of Status Culture Participation on the Grades of U.S. High School Students." *American Sociological Review* 47:189–201.

DiMaggio, Paul and John Mohr. 1985. "Cultural Capital, Educational Attainment and Marital Selection." *American Sociological Review* 90:1231–61.

Dotter, Daniel. 1987. "Growing Up Is Hard to Do: Rock and Roll Performers as Cultural Heroes." *Sociological Spectrum* 7:25–44.

———. 1995. "Rock and Roll Is Here to Stay: Youth Subculture, Deviance, and Social Typing in Rock's Early Years." Pp. 87–114 in *Adolescents and Their Music: If It's Too Loud, You're Too Old*, edited by Jonathan S. Epstein. New York: Garland.

Eder, Donna. 1985. "The Cycle of Popularity: Interpersonal Relations Among Female Adolescents." *Sociology of Education* 58:154–65.

Eder, Donna and Stephen Parker. 1987. "The Cultural Production and Reproduction of Gender: The Effects of Extracurricular Activities on Peer-Group Culture." *Sociology of Education* 60:200–13.

Eitzen, Stanley D. 1975. "Athletics in the Status System of Male Adolescents: A Replication of Coleman's 'The Adolescent Society'." *Adolescence* 10:267–76.

Elder, Glen. 1980. "Adolescence in Historical Perspective." Pp. 3–46 in *Handbook of Adolescent Psychology*, edited by J. Andelson. New York: Wiley.

Finnegan, Ruth. 1989. *The Hidden Musicians: Music-making in an English Town.* New York: Cambridge.

Groce, Stephen B. and Margaret Cooper. 1990. "Just Me and the Boys: Women in Local-Level Rock and Roll." *Gender & Society* 4:220–9.

Hagan, John. 1991. "Destiny and Drift: Subcultural Preferences, Status Attainments, and The Risks and Rewards of Youth." *American Sociological Review* 56:567–82.

Hebdige, Dick. 1984. *Subculture: The Meaning of Style.* London: Methuen.

Kessler, Sandra, Dean Ashenden, Robert W. Connell, and Gary Dowsett. 1985. "Gender Relations in Secondary Schooling." *Sociology of Education* 58:34–47.

Kinney, David A. 1993. "From Nerds to Normals: The Recovery of Identity among Adolescents from Middle School to High School." *Sociology of Education* 66:21–40.

Martin, Linda and Kerry Segrave. 1993. *Anti-Rock: The Opposition to Rock 'n' Roll.* Cambridge, MA: Da Capo Press.

Massey, Douglas S. and Nancy A. Denton. 1993. *American Apartheid: Segregation and the Making of the Underclass.* Cambridge, MA: Harvard.

Matza, David. 1964. *Delinquency and Drift.* New York: Wiley.

Otto, Luther and Duane Alwin. 1977. "Athletics, Aspirations and Attainments. *Sociology of Education* 42: 102–13.

Rehberg, Richard A. and Walter E. Schafer. 1968. "Participation in Interscholastic Athletics and College Expectations." *American Journal of Sociology* 73:732–40.

Reskin, Barbara F. 1988. "Bringing Men Back In: Sex Differentiation and the Devaluation of Women's Work." *Gender & Society* 2:58–81.

Reskin, Barbara F. and Patricia A. Roos. 1990. *Job Queues, Gender Queues: Explaining Women's Inroads into Male Occupations.* Philadelphia: Temple University Press.

Rosen, Louis. 1998. *The South Side: The Racial Transformation of an American Neighborhood.* Chicago: Ivan R. Dee.

Spreitzer, Elmer and Meredith Pugh. 1973. "Interscholastic Athletics and Educational Expectations." *Sociology of Education* 46:171–82.

Tauber, Karl E. and Alma F. Tauber. 1965. *Negroes in Cities: Residential Segregation and Neighborhood Change.* Chicago: Aldine.

Tuchman, Gaye. 1989. *Edging Women Out: Victorian Novelists, Publishers, and Social Change.* New Haven: Yale University Press.

Willis, Paul. 1977. *Learning to Labour.* London: Saxon House.

Questions

1. According to the article, rock and roll bands were almost exclusively male. Why were females excluded?

2. Consider contemporary *bands*—are they still mostly male? If so, why?

3. Why are women more likely to make it as solo artists than as band members?

4. According to Bielby, the primary way for boys to attain status in the 1950s was to participate in sports and participation in rock and roll came to be an alternative path to status. How about today? What are the ways in which high school boys can achieve high status? What are the major paths to high status for girls?

14

THE PRESENTATION OF SELF IN EVERYDAY LIFE

Erving Goffman

In this 1959 reading, Erving Goffman introduces what has come to be called the *dramaturgical* approach to the study of social interaction (so called because, in effect, it views social life as theater). Goffman's focus is on what happens when people are in the presence of others, on how they play their roles. As you will see, from Goffman's point of view, routine social interaction is a cooperative effort between the social actor and his or her audience. The actor may play a role, but frequently he or she must be helped along by the complicity of the audience.

When an individual enters the presence of others, they commonly seek to acquire information about him or to bring into play information about him already possessed. They will be interested in his general socio-economic status, his conception of self, his attitude toward them, his competence, his trustworthiness, etc. Although some of this information seems to be sought almost as an end in itself, there are usually quite practical reasons for acquiring it. Information about the individual helps to define the situation, enabling others to know in advance what he will expect of them and what they may expect of him. Informed in these ways, the others will know how best to act in order to call forth a desired response from him.

For those present, many sources of information become accessible and many carriers (or "sign-vehicles") become available for conveying this information. If unacquainted with the individual, observers can glean clues from his conduct and appearance which allow them to apply their previous experience with individuals roughly similar to the one before them or, more important, to apply untested stereotypes to him. They can also assume from past experience that only individuals of a particular kind are likely to be found in a given social setting. They can rely on what the individual says about himself or on documentary evidence he provides as to who and what he is. If they know, or know of, the individual by virtue of experience prior to the interaction, they can rely on assumptions as to the persistence and generality of psychological traits as a means of predicting his present and future behavior.

However, during the period in which the individual is in the immediate presence of the others, few events may occur which directly provide the others with the conclusive information they will need if they are to direct wisely their own activity. Many crucial facts lie beyond the time and place of interaction or lie concealed with it. For example, the "true" or "real" attitudes, beliefs, and emotions of the individual can be ascertained only indirectly, through his avowals or through what appears to be involuntary expressive behavior. Similarly, if the individual offers the others a product or service, they will often find that during the interaction there will be no time and place immediately available for eating the pudding that the proof can be found in. They will be forced to accept some events as conventional or natural signs of something not directly available to the senses. In other terms, the individual will have to act so that he intentionally or unintentionally *expresses* himself, and the others will in turn have to be *impressed* in some way by him (Ichheiser 1949, 6–7).

The expressiveness of the individual (and therefore his capacity to give impressions) appears to involve two radically different kinds of sign activity: the expression that he *gives*, and the expression that he *gives off*. The first involves verbal symbols or their substitutes which he uses admittedly and solely to convey the information that he and the others are known to attach to these symbols. This is communication in the traditional and narrow sense. The second involves a wide range of action that others can treat as symptomatic of the actor, the expectation being that the action was performed for reasons other than the information conveyed in this way. As we shall have to see, this distinction has only an initial validity. The individual does of course intentionally convey misinformation by means of both of these types of communication, the first involving deceit, the second feigning.

Taking communication in both its narrow and broad sense, one finds that when the individual is in the immediate presence of others, his activity will have a promissory character. The others are likely to find that they must accept the individual on faith, offering him a just return while he is present before them in exchange for something whose true value will not be established until after he has left their presence. (Of course, the others also live by inference in their dealings with the physical world, but it is only in the world of social interaction that the objects about which they make inferences will purposely facilitate and hinder this inferential process.) The security that they justifiably feel in making inferences about the individual will vary, of course, depending on such factors as the amount of information they already possess about him, but no amount of such past evidence can entirely obviate the necessity of acting on the basis of inferences. As William I. Thomas suggested:

> It is also highly important for us to realize that we do not as a matter of fact lead our lives, make our decisions, and reach our goals in everyday life either statistically or scientifically. We live in inference. I am, let us say, your guest. You do not know, you cannot determine scientifically, that I will not steal your money or your spoons. But inferentially I will not, and inferentially you have me as a guest. (quoted in Volkart 1951, 5)

Let us now turn from the others to the point of view of the individual who presents himself before them. He may wish them to think highly of him, or to think that he thinks highly of them, or to perceive how in fact he feels toward them, or to obtain no clear-cut impression; he may wish to ensure sufficient harmony so that the interaction can be sustained, or to defraud, get rid of, confuse, mislead, antagonize, or insult them. Regardless of the particular objective which the individual has in mind and of his motive for having this objective, it will be in his interests to control the conduct of the others, especially their responsive treatment of him. This control is achieved largely by influencing the definition of the situation which the others come to formulate, and he can influence this definition by expressing himself in such a way as to give them the kind of impression that will lead them to act voluntarily in accordance with his own plan. Thus, when an individual appears in the presence of others, there will usually be some reason for him to mobilize his activity so that it will convey an impression to others which it is in his interests to convey. Since a girl's dormitory mates will glean evidence of her popularity from the calls she receives on the phone, we can suspect that some girls will arrange for calls to be made, and Willard Waller's (n.d., 730) finding can be anticipated.

> It has been reported by many observers that a girl who is called to the telephone in the dormitories will often allow herself to be called several times, in order to give all the other girls ample opportunity to hear her paged.

Of the two kinds of communication—expressions given and expressions given off—this report will be primarily concerned with the latter, with the more theatrical and contextual kind, the non-verbal, presumably unintentional kind, whether this communication be purposely engineered or not. As an example of what we must try to examine, I would like to cite at length a novelistic incident in which Preedy, a vacationing Englishman, makes his first appearance on the beach of his summer hotel in Spain:

> But in any case he took care to avoid catching anyone's eye. First of all, he had to make it clear to those potential companions of his holiday that they were of no concern to him whatsoever. He stared through them, round them, over them—eyes lost in space. The beach might have been empty. If by chance a ball was thrown his way, he looked surprised; then let a smile of amusement lighten his face (Kindly Preedy), looked round dazed to see that there *were* people on the beach, tossed it back with a smile to himself and not a smile *at* the people, and then resumed carelessly his nonchalant survey of space.

But it was time to institute a little parade, the parade of the Ideal Preedy. By devious handlings he gave any who wanted to look a chance to see the title of his book—a Spanish translation of Homer, classic thus, but not daring, cosmopolitan too—and then gathered together his beach-wrap and bag into a neat sand-resistant pile (Methodical and Sensible Preedy), rose slowly to stretch at ease his huge frame (Big-Cat Preedy), and tossed aside his sandals (Carefree Preedy, after all).

> The marriage of Preedy and the sea! There were alternative rituals. The first involved the stroll that turns into a run and a dive straight into the water, thereafter smoothing into a strong splashless crawl towards the horizon. But of course not really to the horizon. Quite suddenly he would turn on to his back and thrash great white splashes with his legs, somehow thus showing that he could have swum further had he wanted to, and then would stand up a quarter out of water for all to see who it was.

> The alternative course was simpler, it avoided the cold-water shock and it avoided the risk of appearing too high-spirited. The point was to appear to be so used to the sea, the Mediterranean, and this particular beach, that one might as well be in the sea as out of it. It involved a slow stroll down and into the edge of the water—not even noticing his toes were wet, land and water all the same to *him!*—with his eyes up at the sky gravely surveying portents, invisible to others, of the weather (Local Fisherman Preedy). (Sansom 1956, 230–232)

The novelist means us to see that Preedy is improperly concerned with the extensive impressions he feels his sheer bodily action is giving off to those around him. We can malign Preedy further by assuming that he has acted merely in order to give a particular impression, that this is a false impression, and that the others present receive either no impression at all, or, worse still, the impression that Preedy is affectedly trying to cause them to receive this particular impression. But the important point for us here is that the kind of impression Preedy thinks he is making is in fact the kind of impression that others correctly and incorrectly glean from someone in their midst.

I have said that when an individual appears before others his actions will influence the definition of the situation which they come to have. Sometimes the individual will act in a thoroughly calculating manner, expressing himself in a given way solely in order to give the kind of impression to others that is likely to evoke from them a specific response he is concerned to obtain. Sometimes the individual will be calculating in his activity but be relatively unaware that this is the case. Sometimes he will intentionally and consciously express himself in a particular way, but chiefly because the tradition of his group or social status requires this kind of expression and not because of any particular response (other than vague acceptance or approval) that is likely to be evoked from those impressed by the expression. Sometimes the traditions of an individual's role will lead him to give a well-designed impression of a particular kind and yet he may be neither consciously nor unconsciously disposed to create such an impression. The others, in their turn, may be suitably impressed by the individual's efforts to convey something, or may misunderstand the situation and come to conclusions that are warranted neither by the individual's intent nor by the facts. In any case, in so far as the others act *as if* the individual had conveyed a particular impression, we may take a functional or pragmatic view and say that the individual has "effectively" projected a given definition of the situation and "effectively" fostered the understanding that a given state of affairs obtains.

There is one aspect of the others' response that bears special comment here. Knowing that the individual is likely to present himself in a light that is favorable to him, the others may divide what they witness into two parts: a part that is relatively easy for the individual to manipulate at will, being chiefly his verbal assertions, and a part in regard to which he seems to have little concern or control, being chiefly derived from the expressions he gives off. The others may then use what are considered to be the ungovernable aspects of his expressive behavior as a check upon the validity of what is conveyed by the governable aspects. In this a fundamental asymmetry is demonstrated in the communication process, the individual presumably being aware of only one stream of his communication, the witnesses of this stream and one other. For example, in Shetland Isle one crofter's wife, in serving native dishes to a visitor from the mainland of Britain, would listen with a polite smile to his polite claims of liking what he is eating; at the same time she would take note of the rapidity with which the visitor lifted his fork or spoon to his mouth, the eagerness with which he passed food into his mouth, and the gusto expressed in chewing the food, using these signs as a check on the stated feelings of the eater. The same woman, in order to discover what one acquaintance (A) "actually" thought of another acquaintance (B), would wait until B was in the presence of A but engaged in conversation with still another person (C). She would then covertly examine the facial expressions of A as he regarded B in conversation with C. Not being in conversation with B, and not being directly observed by him, A would sometimes relax usual constraints and tactful deceptions, and freely express what he was "actually" feeling about B. This Shetlander, in short, would observe the unobserved observer.

Now given the fact that others are likely to check up on the more controllable aspects of behavior by means of the less controllable, one can expect that sometimes the individual will try to exploit this very possibility, guiding the impression he makes through behavior felt to be reliably informing. For example, in gaining admission to a tight social circle, the participant observer may not only wear an accepting look while listening to an informant, but may also be careful to wear the same look when observing the informant talking to others; observers of the observer will then not as easily discover where he actually stands. A specific illustration may be cited from Shetland Isle. When a neighbor dropped in to have a cup of tea, he would ordinarily wear at least a hint of an expectant warm smile as he passed through the door into the cottage. Since lack of physical obstructions outside the cottage and lack of light within it usually made it possible to observe the visitor unobserved as he approached the house, islanders sometimes took pleasure in watching the visitor drop whatever expression he was manifesting and replace it with a sociable one just before reaching the door. However, some visitors, in appreciating that this examination was occurring, would blindly adopt a social face a long distance from the house, thus ensuring the projection of a constant image.

This kind of control upon the part of the individual reinstates the symmetry of the communication process, and sets the stage for a kind of information game—a potentially infinite cycle of concealment, discovery, false revelation, and rediscovery. It should be added that since the others are likely to be relatively unsuspicious of the presumably unguided aspect of the individual's conduct, he can gain much by controlling it. The others of course may sense that the individual is manipulating the presumably spontaneous aspects of his behavior, and seek in this very act of manipulation some shading of conduct that the individual has not managed to control. This again provides a check upon the individual's behavior, this time his presumably uncalculated behavior, thus re-establishing the asymmetry of the communication process. Here I would like only to add the suggestion that the arts of piercing an individual's effort at calculated unintentionality seem better developed than our capacity to manipulate our own behavior, so that regardless of how many steps have occurred in the information game, the witness

is likely to have the advantage over the actor, and the initial asymmetry of the communication process is likely to be retained.

When we allow that the individual projects a definition of the situation when he appears before others, we must also see that the others, however passive their role may seem to be, will themselves effectively project a definition of the situation by virtue of their response to the individual and by virtue of any lines of action they initiate to him. Ordinarily the definitions of the situation projected by the several different participants are sufficiently attuned to one another so that open contradiction will not occur. I do not mean that there will be the kind of consensus that arises when each individual present candidly expresses what he really feels and honestly agrees with the expressed feelings of the others present. This kind of harmony is an optimistic ideal and in any case not necessary for the smooth working of society. Rather, each participant is expected to suppress his immediate heartfelt feelings, conveying a view of the situation which he feels the others will be able to find at least temporarily acceptable. The maintenance of this surface of agreement, this veneer of consensus, is facilitated by each participant concealing his own wants behind statements which assert values to which everyone present feels obliged to give lip service. Further, there is usually a kind of division of definitional labor. Each participant is allowed to establish the tentative official ruling regarding matters which are vital to him but not immediately important to others, e.g., the rationalizations and justifications by which he accounts for his past activity. In exchange for this courtesy he remains silent or noncommittal on matters important to others but not immediately important to him. We have then a kind of interactional *modus vivendi*.[1]

---

[1]*Modus vivendi* is Latin and can be literally translated as "a way of living." But generally it refers to "a way of acting" so that people who might not feel positively toward one another can nonetheless get along.—Ed.

Together the participants contribute to a single over-all definition of the situation which involves not so much a real agreement as to what exists but rather a real agreement as to whose claims concerning what issues will be temporarily honored. Real agreement will also exist concerning the desirability of avoiding an open conflict of definitions of the situation.[2] I will refer to this level of agreement as a "working consensus." It is to be understood that the working consensus established in one interaction setting will be quite different in content from the working consensus established in a different type of setting. Thus, between two friends at lunch, a reciprocal show of affection, respect, and concern for the other is maintained. In service occupations, on the other hand, the specialist often maintains an image of disinterested involvement in the problem of the client, while the client responds with a show of respect for the competence and integrity of the specialist. Regardless of such differences in content, however, the general form of these working arrangements is the same.

In noting the tendency for a participant to accept the definitional claims made by the others present, we can appreciate the crucial importance of the information that the individual *initially* possesses or acquires concerning his fellow participants, for it is on the basis of this initial information that the individual starts to define the situation and starts to build up lines of responsive action. The individual's initial projection commits him to what he is proposing to be and requires him to drop all pretenses of being other things. As the interaction among the participants progresses, additions and modifications in this initial informational state will of course occur, but it is essential that these later developments be related without contradiction to, and even built up from, the initial positions taken by several participants. It would seem that an individual can more easily make a choice as to what line of treatment to demand from and extend to the others present at the beginning of an encounter than he can alter the line of treatment that is being pursued once the interaction is underway.

In everyday life, of course, there is a clear understanding that first impressions are important. Thus, the work adjustment of those in service occupations will often hinge upon a capacity to seize and hold the initiative in the service relation, a capacity that will require subtle aggressiveness on the part of the server when he is of lower socio-economic status than his client. W. F. Whyte (1946, 132–133) suggests the waitress as an example:

> The first point that stands out is that the waitress who bears up under pressure does not simply respond to her customers. She acts with some skill to control their behavior. The first question to ask when we look at the customer relationship is, "Does the waitress get the jump on the customers, or does the customer get the jump on the waitress?" The skilled waitress realizes the crucial nature of this question. . . .
>
> The skilled waitress tackles the customer with confidence and without hesitation. For example, she may find that a new customer has seated himself before she could clear off the dirty dishes and change the cloth. He is now leaning on the table studying the menu. She greets him, says, "May I change the cover, please?" and, without waiting for an answer, takes his menu away from him so that he moves back from the table, and she goes about her work. The relationship is handled politely but firmly, and there is never any question as to who is in charge.

[2]An interaction can be purposely set up as a time and place for voicing differences in opinion, but in such cases participants must be careful to agree not to disagree on the proper tone of voice, vocabulary, and degree of seriousness in which all arguments are to be phrased, and upon the mutual respect which disagreeing participants must carefully continue to express toward one another. This debaters' or academic definition of the situation may also be invoked suddenly and judiciously as a way of translating a serious conflict of views into one that can be handled within a framework acceptable to all present.

When the interaction that is initiated by "first impressions" is itself merely the initial interaction in an extended series of interactions involving the same participants, we speak of "getting off on the right foot" and feel that it is crucial that we do so. Thus, one learns that some teachers take the following view:

> "You can't ever let them get the upper hand on you or you're through. So I start out tough. The first day I get a new class in, I let them know who's boss. . . . You've got to start off tough, then you can ease up as you go along. If you start out easy-going, when you try to get tough, they'll just look at you and laugh." (quoted in Becker n.d., 459)

Similarly, attendants in mental institutions may feel that if the new patient is sharply put in his place the first day on the ward and made to see who is boss, much future difficulty will be prevented (Taxel 1953).

Given the fact that the individual effectively projects a definition of the situation when he enters the presence of others, we can assume that events may occur within the interaction which contradict, discredit, or otherwise throw doubt upon this projection. When these disruptive events occur, the interaction itself may come to a confused and embarrassed halt. Some of the assumptions upon which the responses of the participants had been predicated become untenable, and the participants find themselves lodged in an interaction for which the situation has been wrongly defined and is now no longer defined. At such moments the individual whose presentation has been discredited may feel ashamed while the others present may feel hostile, and all the participants may come to feel ill at ease, nonplussed, out of countenance, embarrassed, experiencing the kind of anomy that is generated when the minute social system of face-to-face interaction breaks down.

In stressing the fact that the initial definition of the situation projected by an individual tends to provide a plan for the cooperative activity that follows—in stressing this action point of view—we must not overlook the crucial fact that any projected definition of the situation also has a distinctive moral character. It is this moral character of projections that will chiefly concern us in this report. Society is organized on the principle that any individual who possesses certain social characteristics has a moral right to expect that others will value and treat him in an appropriate way. Connected with this principle is a second, namely that an individual who implicitly or explicitly signifies that he has certain social characteristics ought in fact to be what he claims he is. In consequence, when an individual projects a definition of the situation and thereby makes an implicit or explicit claim to be a person of a particular kind, he automatically exerts a moral demand upon the others, obliging them to value and treat him in the manner that persons of his kind have a right to expect. He also implicitly forgoes all claims to be things he does not appear to be and hence forgoes the treatment that would be appropriate for such individuals. The others find, then, that the individual has informed them as to what is and as to what they *ought* to see as the "is."

One cannot judge the importance of definitional disruptions by the frequency with which they occur, for apparently they would occur more frequently were not constant precautions taken. We find that preventive practices are constantly employed to avoid these embarrassments and that corrective practices are constantly employed to compensate for discrediting occurrences that have not been successfully avoided. When the individual employs these strategies and tactics to protect his own projections, we may refer to them as "defensive practices"; when a participant employs them to save the definition of the situation projected by another, we speak of "protective practices" or "tact." Together, defensive and protective practices comprise the techniques employed to safeguard the impression fostered by an individual during his presence before others. It should be added that while we may be ready to see that no fostered impression would survive if defensive practices were not employed, we are less ready perhaps to see that few impressions could survive if those who received the impression did not exert tact in their reception of it.

In addition to the fact that precautions are taken to prevent disruption of projected definitions, we may also note that an intense interest in these disruptions comes to play a significant role in the social life of the group. Practical jokes and social games are played in which embarrassments which are to be taken unseriously are purposely engineered. Fantasies are created in which devastating exposures occur. Anecdotes from the past—real, embroidered, or fictitious—are told and retold, detailing disruptions which occurred, almost occurred, or occurred and were admirably resolved. There seems to be no grouping which does not have a ready supply of these games, reveries, and cautionary tales, to be used as a source of humor, a catharsis for anxieties, and a sanction for inducing individuals to be modest in their claims and reasonable in their projected expectations. The individual may tell himself through dreams of getting into impossible positions. Families tell of the time a guest got his dates mixed and arrived when neither the house nor anyone in it was ready for him. Journalists tell of times when an all-too-meaningful misprint occurred, and the paper's assumption of objectivity or decorum was humorously discredited. Public servants tell of times a client ridiculously misunderstood form instructions, giving answers which implied an unanticipated and bizarre definition of the situation (Blau n.d., 127–129). Seamen, whose home away from home is rigorously he-man, tell stories of coming back home and inadvertently asking mother to "pass the fucking butter" (Beattie 1950, 35). Diplomats tell of the time a near-sighted queen asked a republican ambassador about the health of his king (Ponsonby 1952, 46). . . .

It will be convenient to end this introduction with some definitions that are implied in what has gone before and required for what is to follow. For the purpose of this report, interaction (that is, face-to-face interaction) may be roughly defined as the reciprocal influence of individuals upon one another's actions when in one another's immediate physical presence. An interaction may be defined as all the interaction which occurs throughout any one occasion when a given set of individuals are in one another's continuous presence; the term "an encounter" would do as well. A "performance" may be defined as all the activity of a given participant on a given occasion which serves to influence in any way any of the other participants. Taking a particular participant and his performance as a basic point of reference, we may refer to those who contribute the other performances as the audience, observers, or co-participants. The pre-established pattern of action which is unfolded during a performance and which may be presented or played through on other occasions may be called a "part" or "routine." These situational terms can easily be related to conventional structural ones. When an individual or performer plays the same part to the same audience on different occasions, a social relationship is likely to arise. Defining social role as the enactment of rights and duties attached to a given status, we can say that a social role will involve one or more parts and that each of these different parts may be presented by the performer on a series of occasions to the same kinds of audience or to an audience of the same persons.

References

Beattie, Walter M., Jr. 1950. "The Merchant Seaman." Unpublished M. A. report, Department of Sociology, University of Chicago.

Becker, Howard S. n.d. "Social Class Variations in the Teacher–Pupil Relationship." *Journal of Educational Sociology* 25.

Blau, Peter. n.d. "Dynamics of Bureaucracy." Ph.D. dissertation, Department of Sociology, Columbia University.

Ichheiser, Gustav. 1949. "Misunderstandings in Human Relations." Supplement to *The American Journal of Sociology* 55 (September).

Ponsonby, Sir Frederick. 1952. *Recollections of Three Reigns.* New York: Dutton.

Sansom, William. 1956. *A Contest of Ladies.* London: Hogarth.

Taxel, Harold. 1953. "Authority Structure in a Mental Hospital Ward." Unpublished M.A. thesis, Department of Sociology, University of Chicago.

Volkart, E. H. (ed.). 1951. "Contributions of W. I. Thomas to Theory and Social Research." In *Social Behavior and Personality.* New York: Social Science Research Council.

Waller, Willard. n.d. "The Rating and Dating Complex." *American Sociological Review* 2.

Whyte, W. F. 1946. "When Workers and Customers Meet." Chap. 7 in W. F. Whyte (ed.), *Industry and Society.* New York: McGraw-Hill.

Questions

1. What is Goffman's distinction between expressions that one gives and expressions that one gives off?

2. Suppose you are about to visit your professor to ask a question about the upcoming exam. Besides information gathering, you would like to influence your professor's definition of the situation such that he or she infers that you are a smart student. How might you do this (in terms of both expressions you give and expressions you give off)?

    Now suppose you are preparing for a date that you've been looking forward to for several days. Your goal this time is to have fun and to influence your date's definition of the situation so that he or she infers that you are a cool person. How might you do this?

    Is there a difference between how you would act in each situation? Which is the "real" you?

3. Think of a time in which you exercised "tact." Using that situation as an example, how did you (as Goffman would say) employ this projective technique in order to save the definition of the situation projected by another?

15

THE NOT-SO-LONELY CROWD

Friendship Groups in Collective Behavior

Adrian F. Aveni

In my introductory sociology class, I define a *group* as "one or more individuals with whom we share some sense of identity or common goals and with whom we interact within a specific social structure." I contrast a group to a social *aggregate*, or a "collectivity of people who happen to be in the same place at the same time."

Crowds are somewhere between groups and aggregates, but have been something of a puzzle to social thinkers. More specifically, sociologists and others thought that crowds are comprised of individuals who, in the midst of many, feel free to act out because of their anonymity. In this research, Professor Aveni takes us down a different path and suggests that crowds are perhaps better understood as collections of individuals and *groups*.

Most of the literature in collective behavior has dealt with crowds in individualistic terms. Crowds are typically seen as spatially proximate collections of individuals (cf. Milgram and Toch, 1969) who are undergoing some common experience. While group-level phenomena have not been entirely overlooked by social analysts, such phenomena have played a relatively small part in the conceptualization and empirical description of crowds.

Three writers who have laid much of the groundwork for contemporary thought about crowd behavior are LeBon, Park, and Blumer. Among these theorists, two related patterns can be observed. The first concerns the way in which the term "crowd" is conceptualized.

Common to all three theorists is the use of the individual as the referent in the conceptualization. Crowds, according to these writers, are simply composed of individuals. When crowds are formed, or when transformations occur, the changes are seen as involving the behavior of individual members of the collectivity. This approach is illustrated by the following passage on the psychological crowd:

> Whoever be the individuals that compose it, however like or unlike their mode of life, their occupations, their intelligence, the fact that they have transformed into a crowd puts them in possession of a sort of collective mind which makes them feel, think, and act in a manner quite different from that in which each individual of them would . . ./ordinarily behave/. . . (LeBon, 1969:22–23).

Similar passages, in which the individual is used as the sole referent for crowd behavior,

"The Not-So-Lonely Crowd: Friendship Groups in Collective Behavior" by Adrian F. Aveni from *Sociometry*, Vol. 40, No. 1, (March, 1977: pp. 96–99). Reprinted by permission of the American Sociological Association and the author.

can be identified in the writings of Park (1972:15, 18 and 19) and Blumer (1946:179–180).

The second pattern common to LeBon, Park and Blumer is that crowd behavior is largely *understood* by examining individual behaviors within the crowd. For example, Blumer (1946:181) states that crowd behavior can be better understood if certain aspects of the individual member are assessed, including ". . . his loss of self-concern and critical judgment, the surging forth of impulses and feelings, . . . his sense of expansion and greatness, and his suggestibility to his fellows." Similarly, in discussing causes of crowd characteristics, LeBon (1969:25) notes that ". . . the individual forming part of a crowd acquires, solely from numerical considerations, a sentiment of invincible power. . . ." As a final example, Park (1972:50) describes crowds as controlled by a common drive that is evoked by the mechanism of "reciprocal interaction" among the members. Thus, crowd behavior is examined in the context of the behavior of individuals.

That theorists have not entirely discussed crowd behavior from an individualistic perspective can be illustrated by the works of Smelser, and of Turner and Killian. Smelser's (1962) *Theory of Collective Behavior,* for example, employs both structural and psychological factors. Turner and Killian's (1972:21–25; 39; and 114–118) approach to crowds both directly and indirectly identifies the importance of groups in crowd behavior. Yet, while these writers include group or structural factors in their treatment of crowds, their discussions of these subjects tend to be brief or to play a minor part in their overall theoretical frameworks.

Significantly, one of the most recent approaches to crowd behavior reaffirms the emphasis upon the individual actor in the crowd. Crowds are examined almost totally in terms of the individual participants. The approach interprets crowd behavior through the use of decision-making models in which crowd members are assumed to maximize their rewards and minimize costs. Part of the original impetus for this approach can be attributed to Olson's (1968) analysis of collectivities in economic markets. Berk (1974a, 1974b) is perhaps the most easily identifiable of those who have directly applied the decision-making model to crowd analysis.

The Appropriateness of the Individual-Level Approach

Given the literature's focus on individual behavior, it is worthwhile to consider the extent to which people actually do act as individuals in crowd situations. If people do behave as individuals, acting relatively independently of other influences, then the individual-level of analysis is indeed appropriate and should be consciously continued. Alternatively, if people do not act as individuals *per se*, but instead as group members or even as parts of formal organizations, then there is some question of the appropriateness of the individual level in crowd analysis, especially to the exclusion of other levels.

One way of evaluating the appropriateness of the focus on individual behavior in crowd analysis is to consider past observations of crowd behavior. This researcher's observations of crowds of students, during anti-war and university-reform demonstrations, suggest that a sizeable number of persons were with friends. People moved together in groups, yelled or shouted obscenities in groups, and disbanded in groups. Regarding civil disturbances in the black ghettos during the 1960's, Quarantelli and Dynes (1970) noted the existence of many television and movie films showing looters working in pairs or small groups. While no observations have been found regarding the prison riots of the 1970's, it would appear likely that many of the participants in these activities were also acting as members of primary or secondary groups.

While observational data on crowd behavior provides a basis for believing that a significant amount of behavior occurs in a group context the data are inadequate in some respects. The observations are not quantified and, in some instances, rely on interpretations of behavior (e.g., that persons walking in close proximity are in fact friends). Hence, alternative sources of data are desirable.

An Empirical Study

The Ohio State University has sustained a football rivalry with the University of Michigan for decades. In recent years the teams have played one another for the Big Ten football championship and the honor of going to the Rose Bowl. Ohio State victories over its rival have provided the occasion for crowds of celebrating fans to carry their enthusiasm to the streets of Columbus, Ohio, blocking traffic and in some instances throwing projectiles, breaking windows and skirmishing with the police. Such an episode occurred in 1970. No crowd developed in 1972, probably because of two deterrents: bad weather, and the presence of a very large number of riot-equipped police. The present study was conducted in Columbus on the evening following the 1974 game between Ohio State and its rival.

During the evening we estimate that there were between two and three thousand persons milling about in the 10-block stretch which constitutes the "university area." However, the greatest amount of pedestrian traffic on this and other evenings following university football events occurs at the intersection of 15th and High Streets. This intersection is located in the middle of the "university area," with bars, shops, sources of live music and restaurants located along High Street on both sides of the 15th Street intersection. While persons stroll along this stretch during most Friday and Saturday nights of the year, traffic is especially dense on evenings following a football game, and this is the area in which most crowds assembled.

Interviewers for the study were stationed near the intersection of 15th and High Streets. Eight interviewing locations were used,[1] each approximately fifty yards from the intersection. Two field workers stood at each location, one conducting the interview while the other recorded responses. After each interview was completed the interviewer allowed ten persons to pass towards the intersection and then asked the next person to participate in the study. A total of 204 interviews were obtained between 6:00 and 9:45. The percentage of refusals was 29%.[2]

The persons gathered near or passing through the 15th and High intersection never actually constituted a crowd. While there was considerable excitement in the air, with large numbers of persons milling about, no common focus of attention emerged among those who had assembled during the time period of the study.[3] (The lack of a common focus might be attributed to the overwhelming presence of riot-equipped police who kept people continuously moving.) Thus, the data that were collected were not of members of a crowd *per se* but of an assembly which had the potential of becoming a crowd. Such an assembly might be

---

[1]From 6:00 to 8:00 P.M. all eight locations were used. Two of the locations were closed at 8:00 P.M. Three more were closed at 9:15. The remainder were closed at 9:45 P.M.

[2]A comparison of the characteristics of respondents with those who refused does not reveal any great differences: respondents' mean age was 21.0 while the average of the respectively estimated ages of refusers was 21.5; 68% of the respondents were male vs. 70% for refusers; 74% of the respondents were with friends while 66% of refusers appeared to be with friends.

[3]Immediately following the football game people assembled, at the 15th and High Street intersection and proceeded to march in the street with sections of the field goal posts for 10 or 15 minutes. This did constitute an episode of crowd behavior.

called a "pre-crowd." This may present a limitation of the data. On the other hand, it seems unlikely that the composition of those assembled in the High Street area would have substantially changed if a common focus of attention had developed.

The findings of this study indicate that only a small portion (26%) of the total number of persons who were interviewed were by themselves. The majority (74%) were with one or more friends. The friends consisted of boy or girl friends, roommates, friends from living units or just simply "friends." Among those who were with friends, 54% said they were with one other person, 18% were with two others, 16% were with three others and 12% reported that they were with four or more persons. Thus a large number of those assembled along the sidewalks were members of groups.

Also of significance is the fact that 64% of those interviewed said they saw or met others they recognized or knew. Included among the persons who were identified by the respondents were relatives, friends from work, classes or living quarters and home town friends. Among those who had seen or met others in the assembly, the median number of persons so identified was 4.6. Again, the findings indicate that persons in the assembly were not isolated, anonymous individuals.

Summary and Discussion

The fact that a large number of those participating in the celebrations were found to be either with friends or to have seen friends has implications for the conceptualization of crowd behavior. As mentioned at the outset the traditional and contemporary literature on crowd behavior focuses heavily upon individual behavior. The data of the present study suggest that crowds consist both of isolated individuals as well as persons in groups. This means that two inter-related levels of analysis will have to be applied to crowd behavior in order to interpret it completely: the individual level and the group level. Also implied by this conceptualization is that models of crowd behavior may have to be made more complex to take into account both the behavior of unattached individuals as well as that of group members. A related point is that even the behavior of unattached individuals may be modified if such persons are cognizant of the existence of others in the crowd who know them. In other words, the extent of anonymity in crowds should be treated as a *variable* rather than a constant.

References

Berk, Richard A. 1974a. *Collective Behavior*. Dubuque, Iowa: Wm. C. Brown Company.

———. 1974b. "Crowd behavior." *American Sociological Review* 39:355–373.

Blumer, Herbert. 1946. "Elementary collective groupings." Pp. 178–198 in Alfred McClung Lee (ed.), *Principles of Sociology*. Barnes & Noble.

LeBon, Gustave. 1969. *The Crowd*. New York: Ballantine Books.

Milgram, Stanley and Hans Toch. 1969. "Collective behavior: Crowds and social movements." Pp. 507–610 in Gardner Lindzey and Elliot Aronson (eds.), *The Handbook of Social Psychology*. Vol. 4. Reading, MA: Addison-Wesley.

Olson, Mancur. 1965. *The Logic of Collective Action*. Cambridge, MA: Harvard University Press.

Park, Robert E. 1972. *The Crowd and the Public*. Chicago: The University of Chicago Press.

Quarantelli, E. L. and Russell R. Dynes. 1970. "Property norms and looting, their patterns in community crises." *Phylon* 31:168–182.

Smelser, Neil J. 1962. *Theory of Collective Behavior*. New York: The Free Press.

Turner, Ralph H. and Lewis M. Killian. 1972. *Collective Behavior*. (2nd ed.) Englewood Cliffs, NJ: Prentice-Hall.

Questions

1. Based on what you read in this article, what is the difference between a crowd and an aggregate of people? (Aggregate was defined in the introduction to the article.)

2. This research focused on crowd behavior following an important college football game. How might the conditions that arise under this sort of circumstance differ from the conditions that give rise to other sorts of crowds (e.g., shoppers waiting for stores to open their doors at 6:00 A.M. on the morning after Thanksgiving)?

3. Conventional wisdom suggests that even the most upright citizens might be led to do bad things when they are in a crowd because they can act anonymously. Aveni suggests, however, that most of the people in a crowd are not truly anonymous because they are parts of groups. So, if people do bad things when in a group that's part of a crowd, what, in your judgment, is going on?

16
THE PATHOLOGY OF IMPRISONMENT

Philip G. Zimbardo

When I was a kid in school, I was very shy. I rarely volunteered answers to questions posed by my teachers, and I cringed whenever I was asked to do an arithmetic problem on the chalkboard. That wasn't the best way to fulfill my role as a student, but it was an acceptable way. Now I am a professor, and I am the one who not only asks questions but makes scholarly pronouncements that I expect everyone in the room to write down. My first-grade teacher, who regarded my shyness with despair, would be shocked to see that I actually seem to do these professorial things comfortably. Has my personality changed? Not really. I'm still shy. But the role expectations of a professor evoke a different side of me, one that's "outgoing" and even extroverted. As you will read in this 1972 article by Philip Zimbardo, roles—the social scripts that are attached to the statuses people occupy—are powerfully evocative. They can bring out parts of someone's "personality" that the individual never knew existed.

I was recently released from solitary confinement after being held therein for 37 months [months!]. A silent system was imposed upon me and to even whisper to the man in the next cell resulted in being beaten by guards, sprayed with chemical mace, blackjacked, stomped and thrown into a strip-cell naked to sleep on a concrete floor without bedding, covering, wash basin or even a toilet. The floor served as toilet and bed, and even there the silent system was enforced. To let a moan escape your lips because of the pain and discomfort . . . resulted in another beating. I spent not days, but months there during my 37 months in solitary. . . . I have filed every writ possible against the administrative acts of brutality. The state courts have all denied the petitions. Because of my refusal to let the things die down and forget all

that happened during my 37 months in solitary . . . I am the most hated prisoner in [this] penitentiary, and called a "hard-core incorrigible."

Maybe I am an incorrigible, but if true, it's because I would rather die than to accept being treated as less than a human being. I have never complained of my prison sentence as being unjustified except through legal means of appeals. I have never put a knife on a guard's throat and demanded my release. I know that thieves must be punished and I don't justify stealing, even though I am a thief myself. But now I don't think I will be a thief when I am released. No, I'm not rehabilitated. It's just that I no longer think of becoming wealthy by stealing. I now only think of killing—killing those who have beaten me and treated me as if I were a dog. I hope and pray for the sake of my own soul and future life of freedom that I am able to overcome the bitterness and hatred which eats daily at my soul, but I know to overcome it will not be easy.

This eloquent plea for prison reform—for humane treatment of human beings, for the basic dignity that is the right of every American—came to me secretly in a letter from a prisoner who cannot be identified because he is still in a state correctional institution. He sent it to me because he read of an experiment I recently conducted at Stanford University. In an attempt to understand just what it means psychologically to be a prisoner or a prison guard, Craig Haney, Curt Banks, Dave Jaffe and I created our own prison. We carefully screened over 70 volunteers who answered an ad in a Palo Alto city newspaper and ended up with about two dozen young men who were selected to be part of this study. They were mature, emotionally stable, normal, intelligent college students from middle-class homes throughout the United States and Canada. They appeared to represent the cream of the crop of this generation. None had any criminal record and all were relatively homogeneous on many dimensions initially.

Half were arbitrarily designated as prisoners by a flip of a coin, the others as guards. These were the roles they were to play in our simulated prison. The guards were made aware of the potential seriousness and danger of the situation and their own vulnerability. They made up their own formal rules for maintaining law, order and respect, and were generally free to improvise new ones during their eight-hour, three-man shifts. The prisoners were unexpectedly picked up at their homes by a city policeman in a squad car, searched, handcuffed, fingerprinted, booked at the Palo Alto station house and taken blindfolded to our jail. There they were stripped, deloused, put into a uniform, given a number and put into a cell with two other prisoners where they expected to live for the next two weeks. The pay was good ($15 a day) and their motivation was to make money.

We observed and recorded on videotape the events that occurred in the prison, and we interviewed and tested the prisoners and guards at various points throughout the study. Some of the videotapes of the actual encounters between the prisoners and guards were seen on the NBC News feature "Chronolog" on November 26, 1971.

At the end of only six days we had to close down our mock prison because what we saw was frightening. It was no longer apparent to most of the subjects (or to us) where reality ended and their roles began. The majority had indeed become prisoners or guards, no longer able to clearly differentiate between role playing and self. There were dramatic changes in virtually every aspect of their behavior, thinking and feeling. In less than a week the experience of imprisonment undid (temporarily) a lifetime of learning; human values were suspended, self-concepts were challenged and the ugliest, most base, pathological side of human nature surfaced. We were horrified because we saw some boys (guards) treat others as if they were despicable animals, taking pleasure in cruelty, while other boys (prisoners) became servile, dehumanized robots who thought only of escape, of their own individual survival and of their mounting hatred for the guards.

We had to release three prisoners in the first four days because they had such acute situational traumatic reactions as hysterical crying, confusion in thinking and severe depression. Others begged to be paroled, and all but three were willing to forfeit all the money they had earned if they could be paroled. By then (the fifth day) they had been so programmed to think of themselves as prisoners that when their request for parole was denied, they returned docilely to their cells. Now, had they been thinking as college students acting in an oppressive experiment, they would have quit once they no longer wanted the $15 a day we used as our only incentive. However, the reality was not quitting an experiment but "being paroled by the parole board from the Stanford County Jail." By the last days, the earlier solidarity among the prisoners (systematically broken by the guards) dissolved into "each man for himself." Finally, when one of their fellows was put in solitary confinement (a small closet) for refusing to eat, the prisoners were given a choice by one of the guards: give up their blankets and the incorrigible prisoner would be let out, or keep their blankets and he would be kept in all night. They voted to keep their blankets and to abandon their brother.

About a third of the guards became tyrannical in their arbitrary use of power, in enjoying their control over other people. They were corrupted by the power of their roles and became quite inventive in their techniques of breaking the spirit of the prisoners and making them feel they were worthless. Some of the guards merely did their jobs as tough but fair correctional officers, and several were good guards from the prisoners' point of view since they did them small favors and were friendly. However, no good guard ever interfered with a command by any of the bad guards; they never intervened on the side of the prisoners, they never told the others to ease off because it was only an experiment, and they never even came to me as prison superintendent or experimenter in charge to complain. In part, they were good because the others were bad; they needed the others to help establish their own egos in a positive light. In a sense, the good guards perpetuated the prison more than the other guards because their own needs to be liked prevented them from disobeying or violating the implicit guards' code. At the same time, the act of befriending the prisoners created a social reality which made the prisoners less likely to rebel.

By the end of the week the experiment had become a reality, as if it were a Pirandello[1] play directed by Kafka[2] that just keeps going after the audience has left. The consultant for our prison, Carlo Prescott, an ex-convict with 16 years of imprisonment in California's jails, would get so depressed and furious each time he visited our prison, because of its psychological similarity to his experiences, that he would have to leave. A Catholic priest who was a former prison chaplain in Washington, D.C., talked to our prisoners after four days and said they were just like the other firsttimers he had seen.

But in the end, I called off the experiment not because of the horror I saw out there in the prison yard, but because of the horror of realizing that I could have easily traded places with the most brutal guard or become the weakest prisoner full of hatred at being so powerless that I could not eat, sleep or go to the toilet without permission of the authorities. *I* could have become Calley at My Lai, George Jackson at San Quentin, one of the men at Attica or the prisoner quoted at the beginning of this article.

Individual behavior is largely under the control of social forces and environmental contingencies rather than personality traits, character, will power or other empirically unvalidated constructs. Thus we create an illusion of freedom by attributing more internal control to

---

[1]Luigi Pirandello (1867–1936) was a Sicilian author. He won the 1934 Nobel Prize for literature. His fame is primarily owing to his grimly humorous plays dealing with the confusions of illusions and reality (for example, *Six Characters in Search of an Author*).—Ed.

[2]The writer Franz Kafka (1883–1924) was born in Prague of Jewish parents. In his novels and short stories, Kafka painted a world that was steeped in illusion and contradiction. His characters suffered from feelings of guilt, anxiety, and despair and an overwhelming sense of futility as they struggled to cope with rigid bureaucracies and totalitarian regimes. Today, similarly tortured visions of society are often referred to as "Kafkaesque."—Ed.

ourselves, to the individual, than actually exists. We thus underestimate the power and pervasiveness of situational controls over behavior because (a) they are often non-obvious and subtle, (b) we can often avoid entering situations where we might be so controlled, (c) we label as "weak" or "deviant" people in those situations who do behave differently from how we believe we would.

Each of us carries around in our heads a favorable self-image in which we are essentially just, fair, humane and understanding. For example, we could not imagine inflicting pain on others without much provocation or hurting people who had done nothing to us, who in fact were even liked by us. However, there is a growing body of social psychological research which underscores the conclusion derived from this prison study. Many people, perhaps the majority, can be made to do almost anything when put into psychologically compelling situations—regardless of their morals, ethics, values, attitudes, beliefs or personal convictions. My colleague, Stanley Milgram, has shown that more than 60 percent of the population will deliver what they think is a series of painful electric shocks to another person even after the victim cries for mercy, begs them to stop and then apparently passes out. The subjects complained that they did not want to inflict more pain but blindly obeyed the command of the authority figure (the experimenter) who said that they must go on. In my own research on violence, I have seen mild-mannered coeds repeatedly give shocks (which they thought were causing pain) to another girl, a stranger whom they had rated very favorably, simply by being made to feel anonymous and put in a situation where they were expected to engage in this activity.

Observers of these and similar experimental situations never predict their outcomes and estimate that it is unlikely that they themselves would behave similarly. They can be so confident only when they are outside the situation. However, since the majority of people in these studies do act in non-rational, non-obvious ways, it follows that the majority of observers would also succumb to the social psychological forces in the situation.

With regard to prisons, we can state that the mere act of assigning labels to people and putting them into a situation where those labels acquire validity and meaning is sufficient to elicit pathological behavior. This pathology is not predictable from any available diagnostic indicators we have in the social sciences, and is extreme enough to modify in very significant ways fundamental attitudes and behavior. The prison situation, as presently arranged, is guaranteed to generate severe enough pathological reactions in both guards and prisoners as to debase their humanity, lower their feelings of self-worth and make it difficult for them to be part of a society outside of their prison. . . .

Questions

1. What are the similarities between Zimbardo's findings and Milgram's (see reading 7)?

2. Zimbardo's experiment cemented sociologists' conviction that the roles people play have a lot of power to elicit particular behaviors from them. Sociologists refer to the process by which people take on socially constructed roles and carry them out as "role-taking." The men chosen to be prisoners and to be guards were, for all intents and purposes, the same until they took on their respective

roles; it was taking on and playing the roles that "changed" them (or elicited new behaviors from them).

Role-taking is a part of everyday life. When an individual reaches adulthood (or possibly sooner!), he or she may take the status and role of married person—husband or wife. As many women and men have found in recent decades, it is hard to change those roles to fit new understandings of, for example, gender roles. But sociologists are aware that all people, in all cases, do not simply take on conventional roles, that people do not simply do role-taking. In some cases, people adapt the roles to themselves rather than the other way around. Sociologists call that "role-making." It isn't easy; when you do not act the way people expect you to act, you can expect some sort of response—often, informal negative sanctions. Think of the young man who wishes, for example, to study ballet rather than football. He wants to make the role of young man fit his own proclivities.

Consider how you play the role of student. What things do you do that an observer would judge to be role-taking? What do you do that an observer would judge to be role-making?

17
"GETTING" AND "MAKING" A TIP

Greta Foff Paules

In this 1991 article, Greta Foff Paules, who received a Ph.D in cultural anthropology from Princeton University, takes us into the world of the waitress. If you've never waited on tables, you might naturally assume that waitresses (and waiters, for that matter) are there to serve the customers. But as Paules discovered through participant observation, there is a lot more to the customer–waitress relationship than meets the eye. You decide who has what kind of power in this relationship.

The waitress can't help feeling a sense of personal failure and public censure when she is "stiffed."

—William F. Whyte,
"When Workers and Customers Meet"

They're rude, they're ignorant, they're obnoxious, they're inconsiderate. . . . Half of these people don't deserve to come out and eat, let alone try and tip a waitress.

—Route waitress

Making a Tip at Route

A common feature of past research is that the worker's control over the tipping system is evaluated in terms of her efforts to con, coerce, compel, or otherwise manipulate a customer into relinquishing a bigger tip. Because these efforts have for the most part proven futile, the worker has been seen as having little defense against the financial vicissitudes of the tipping system. What these studies have overlooked is that an employee can increase her tip income by controlling the number as well as the size of tips she receives. This oversight has arisen from the tendency of researchers to concentrate narrowly on the relationship between server and served, while failing to take into account the broader organizational context in which this relationship takes place.

Like service workers observed in earlier studies, waitresses at Route strive to boost the amount of individual gratuities by rendering special services and being especially friendly. As one waitress put it, "I'll sell you the world if you're in my station." In general though, waitresses at Route Restaurant seek to boost their tip income, not by increasing the amount of individual gratuities, but by increasing the number of customers they serve. They accomplish this (a) by securing the largest or busiest stations and working the most lucrative shifts; (b) by "turning" their tables quickly; and (c) by controlling the flow of customers within the restaurant.

Technically, stations at Route are assigned on a rotating basis so that all waitresses, including rookies, work fast and slow stations equally. Station assignments are listed on the work schedule that is posted in the office window where it can be examined by all workers on all shifts, precluding the possibility of blatant favoritism or discrimination. Yet

"'Getting' and 'Making' a Tip" from *Dishing It Out: Power and Resistance among Waitresses in a New Jersey Restaurant* by Greta Foff Paules. Reprinted by permission of Temple University Press. Copyright © 1991 by Temple University. All Rights Reserved.

a number of methods exist whereby experienced waitresses are able to circumvent the formal rotation system and secure the more lucrative stations for themselves. A waitress can trade assignments with a rookie who is uncertain of her ability to handle a fast station; she can volunteer to take over a large station when a *call-out*[1] necessitates reorganization of station assignments; or she can establish herself as the only waitress capable of handling a particularly large or chaotic station. Changes in station assignments tend not to be formally recorded, so inconsistencies in the rotation system often do not show up on the schedule. Waitresses on the same shift may notice of course that a co-worker has managed to avoid an especially slow station for many days, or has somehow ended up in the busiest station two weekends in a row, but the waitresses' code of noninterference . . . inhibits them from openly objecting to such irregularities.

A waitress can also increase her tip income by working the more lucrative shifts. Because day is the busiest and therefore most profitable shift at Route, it attracts experienced, professional waitresses who are most concerned and best able to maximize their tip earnings. There are exceptions: some competent, senior-ranking waitresses are unable to work during the day due to time constraints of family or second jobs. Others choose not to work during the day despite the potential monetary rewards, because they are unwilling to endure the intensely competitive atmosphere for which day shift is infamous.

The acutely competitive environment that characterizes day shift arises from the aggregate striving of each waitress to maximize her tip income by serving the greatest possible number of customers. Two strategies are enlisted to this end. First, each waitress attempts to turn her tables as quickly as possible. Briefly stated, this means she takes the order, delivers the food, clears and resets a table, and begins serving the next party as rapidly as customer lingering and the speed of the kitchen allow. A seven-year veteran of Route describes the strategy and its rewards:

> What I do is I prebus my tables. When the people get up and go all I got is glasses and cups, pull off, wipe, set, and I do the table turnover. But see that's from day shift. See the girls on graveyard . . . don't understand the more times you turn that table the more money you make. You could have three tables and still make a hundred dollars. If you turn them tables.

As the waitress indicates, a large part of turning tables involves getting the table cleared and set for the next customer. During a rush, swing and grave waitresses tend to leave dirty tables standing, partly because they are less experienced and therefore less efficient, partly to avoid being given parties, or *sat*, when they are already behind. In contrast, day waitresses assign high priority to keeping their tables cleared and ready for customers. The difference in method reflects increased skill and growing awareness of and concern with money-making strategies.

A waitress can further increase her customer count by controlling the flow of customers within the restaurant. Ideally the hostess or manager running the front house rotates customers among stations, just as stations are rotated among waitresses. Each waitress is given, or *sat*, one party at a time in turn so that all waitresses have comparable customer counts at the close of a shift. When no hostess is on duty, or both she and the manager are detained and customers are waiting to be seated, waitresses will typically seat incoming parties.

Whether or not a formal hostess is on duty, day waitresses are notorious for bypassing the

---

[1] A call-out (which more logically might be termed a "call-in") occurs when an employee calls in sick or with some other reason why he or she can't make it to work that day.—Ed.

instead of to other waitresses' tables

rotation system by racing to the door and directing incoming customers to their own tables. A sense of the urgency with which this strategy is pursued is conveyed in the comment of one five-year veteran, "They'll run you down to get that person at the door, to seat them in their station." The competition for customers is so intense during the day that some waitresses claim they cannot afford to leave the floor (even to use the restroom) lest they return to find a co-worker's station filled at their expense. "In the daytime, honey," remarks an eight-year Route waitress, "in the daytime it's like pulling teeth. You got to stay on the floor to survive. To survive." It is in part because they do not want to lose customers and tips to their co-workers that waitresses do not take formal breaks. Instead, they rest and eat between waiting tables or during lulls in business, returning to the floor intermittently to check on parties in progress and seat customers in their stations.

The fast pace and chaotic nature of restaurant work provide a cover for the waitress's aggressive pursuit of customers, since it is difficult for other servers to monitor closely the allocation of parties in the bustle and confusion of a rush. Still, it is not uncommon for waitresses to grumble to management and co-workers if they notice an obvious imbalance in customer distribution. Here again, the waitress refrains from directly criticizing her fellow servers, voicing her displeasure by commenting on the paucity of customers in her own station, rather than the overabundance of customers in the stations of certain co-waitresses. In response to these grumblings, other waitresses may moderate somewhat their efforts to appropriate new parties, and management may make a special effort to seat the disgruntled server favorably.

A waitress can also exert pressure on the manager or hostess to keep her station filled. She may, for instance, threaten to leave if she is not seated enough customers.

I said, "Innes [a manager], I'm in [station] one and two. If one and two is not filled at all times from now until three, I'm getting my coat, my pocketbook, and I'm leaving." And one and two was filled, and I made ninety-five dollars.

Alternatively, she can make it more convenient for the manager or hostess to seat her rather than her co-workers, either by keeping her tables open (as described), or by taking extra tables. If customers are waiting to be seated, a waitress may offer to pick up parties in a station that is closed or, occasionally, to pick up parties in another waitress's station. In attempting either strategy, but especially the latter, the waitress must be adept not only at waiting tables, but in interpersonal restaurant politics. Autonomy and possession are of central concern to waitresses, and a waitress who offers to pick up tables outside her station must select her words carefully if she is to avoid being accused of invading her co-workers' territory. Accordingly, she may choose to present her bid for extra parties as an offer to help—the manager, another waitress, the restaurant, customers—rather than as a request.

The waitress who seeks to increase her tip income by maximizing the number of customers she serves may endeavor to cut her losses by refusing to serve parties that have stiffed her in the past. If she is a low-ranking waitress, her refusal is likely to be overturned by the manager. If she is an experienced and valuable waitress, the manager may ask someone else to take the party, assure the waitress he will take care of her (that is, pad the bill and give her the difference), or even pick up the party himself. Though the practice is far from common, a waitress may go so far as to demand a tip from a customer who has been known to stiff in the past.

This party of two guys come in and they order thirty to forty dollars worth of food . . . and they stiff us. Every time. So Kaddie told them, "If you don't tip us, we're not going to wait

performance may benefit you

on you." They said, "We'll tip you." So Kaddie waited on them, and they tipped her. The next night they came in, I waited on them and they didn't tip me. The third time they came in [the manager] put them in my station and I told [the manager] straight up, "I'm not waiting on them. . . ." So he made Hailey pick them up. And they stiffed Hailey. So when they came in the next night . . . [they] said, "Are you going to give us a table?" I said, "You going to tip? I'm not going to wait on you. You got all that money, you sell all that crack on the streets and you come here and you can't even leave me a couple of bucks?" . . . So they left me a dollar. So when they come in Tuesday night, I'm telling them a dollar ain't enough.

The tactics employed by waitresses, and particularly day-shift waitresses, to increase their customer count and thereby boost their tip earnings have earned them a resounding notoriety among their less competitive co-workers. Day (and some swing) waitresses are described as "money hungry," "sneaky little bitches," "self-centered," "aggressive," "back-stabbing bitches," and "cutthroats over tables." The following remarks of two Route waitresses, however, indicate that those who employ these tactics see them as defensive, not aggressive measures. A sense of the waitress's preoccupation with autonomy and with protecting what is hers also emerges from these comments.

> You have to be like that. Because if you don't be like that, people step on you. You know, like as far as getting customers. I mean, you know, I'm sorry everybody says I'm greedy. I guess that's why I've survived this long at Route. Cause I am greedy. . . . *I want what's mine,* and if it comes down to me cleaning your table or my table, I'm going to clean my table. Because see I went through all that stage where I would do your table. To be fair. And you would walk home with seventy dollars, and I'd have twenty-five, cause I was being fair all night. (emphasis added)

> If the customer comes in the door and I'm there getting that door, don't expect me to cover your backside while you in the back smoking a cigarette and I'm here working for myself. You're not out there working for me. . . . When I go to the door and get the customers, when I keep my tables clean and your tables are dirty, and you wonder why you only got one person . . . then that's just tough shit. . . . You're damn right my station is filled. *I'm not here for you.* (emphasis added)

Whether the waitress who keeps her station filled with customers is acting aggressively or defensively, her tactics are effective. It is commonly accepted that determined day waitresses make better money than less competitive co-workers even when working swing or grave. Moreover Nera, the waitress most infamous for her relentless use of "money-hungry tactics," is at the same time most famous for her consistently high daily takes. While other waitresses jingle change in their aprons, Nera is forced to store wads of bills in her shoes and in paper bags to prevent tips from overflowing her pockets. She claims to make a minimum of five hundred dollars a week in tip earnings; her record for one day's work exceeds two hundred dollars and is undoubtedly the record for the restaurant.

Inverting the Symbolism of Tipping

It may already be apparent that the waitress views the customer—not as a master to pamper and appease—but as a substance to be processed as quickly and in as large a quantity as possible. The difference in perspective is expressed in the objectifying terminology of waitresses: a customer or party is referred to as a *table,* or by table number, as *table five* or simply *five;* serving successive parties at a table is referred to as *turning the table;* taking an order is also known as *picking up a table;* and to serve water, coffee, or other beverages is to *water, coffee,* or *beverage* a table, number, or customer. Even personal acquaintances assume the status of inanimate matter, or tip-bearing plants, in the language of the server:

> I got my fifth-grade teacher [as a customer] one time. . . . I kept her coffeed. I kept her boyfriend coked all night. Sodaed. . . . And I kept them filled up.

If the customer is perceived as material that is processed, the goal of this processing is the production or extraction of a finished product: the tip. This image too is conveyed in the language of the floor. A waitress may comment that she "got a good tip" or "gets good tips," but she is more likely to say that she "made" or "makes good tips." She may also say that she "got five bucks out of" a customer, or complain that some customers "don't want to give up on" their money. She may accuse a waitress who stays over into her shift of "tapping on" her money, or warn an aspiring waitress against family restaurants on the grounds that "there's no money in there." In all these comments (and all are actual), the waitress might as easily be talking about mining for coal or drilling for oil as serving customers.

Predictably, the waitress's view of the customer as substance to be processed influences her perception of the meaning of tips, and especially substandard tips. At Route, low tips and stiffs are not interpreted as a negative reflection on the waitress's personal qualities or social status. Rather, they are felt to reveal the refractory nature or poor quality of the raw material from which the tip is extracted, produced, or fashioned. In less metaphorical terms, a low tip or stiff is thought to reflect the negative qualities and low status of the customer who is too cheap, too poor, too ignorant, or too coarse to leave an appropriate gratuity. In this context, it is interesting to note that *stiff,* the term used in restaurants to refer to incidents of nontipping or to someone who does not tip, has also been used to refer to a wastrel or penniless man, a hobo, tramp, vagabond, deadbeat, and a moocher (Wentworth and Flexner 1975).

Evidence that waitresses assign blame for poor tips to the tipper is found in their reaction to being undertipped or stiffed. Rather than breaking down in tears and lamenting her "personal failure," the Route waitress responds to a stiff by announcing the event to her co-workers and managers in a tone of angry disbelief. Co-workers and managers echo the waitress's indignation and typically ask her to identify the party (by table number and physical description), or if she has already done so, to be more specific. This identification is crucial for it allows sympathizers to join the waitress in analyzing the cause of the stiff, which is assumed a priori[2] to arise from some shortcoming of the party, not the waitress. The waitress and her co-workers may conclude that the customers in question were rude, troublemakers, or bums, or they may explain their behavior by identifying them as members of a particular category of customers. It might be revealed, for instance, that the offending party was a church group: church groups are invariably tightfisted. It might be resolved that the offenders were senior citizens, Southerners, or businesspeople: all well-known cheapskates. If the customers were European, the stiff will be attributed to ignorance of the American tipping system; if they were young, to immaturity; if they had children, to lack of funds.

These classifications and their attendant explanations are neither fixed nor trustworthy. New categories are invented to explain otherwise puzzling incidents, and all categories are subject to exception. Though undependable as predictive devices, customer typologies serve a crucial function: they divert blame for stiffs and low tips from the waitress to the characteristics of the customer. It is for this reason

not personal failure

---

[2]*A priori* is Latin for "from what comes before," or reasoning from what is already known.—Ed.

that it is "important" for workers to distinguish between different categories of customers, despite the fact that such distinctions are based on "unreliable verbal and appearance clues." In fact, it is precisely the unreliability, or more appropriately the flexibility, of customer typologies that makes them valuable to waitresses. When categories can be constructed and dissolved on demand, there is no danger that an incident will fall outside the existing system of classification and hence be inexplicable.

While waitresses view the customer as something to be processed and the tip as the product of this processing, they are aware that the public does not share their understanding of the waitress–diner–tip relationship. Waitresses at Route recognize that many customers perceive them as needy creatures willing to commit great feats of service and absorb high doses of abuse in their anxiety to secure a favorable gratuity or protect their jobs. They are also aware that some customers leave small tips with the intent to insult the server and that others undertip on the assumption that for a Route waitress even fifty cents will be appreciated. One waitress indicated that prior to being employed in a restaurant, she herself subscribed to the stereotype of the down-and-out waitress "because you see stuff on television, you see these wives or single ladies who waitress and they live in slummy apartments or slummy houses and they dress in rags." It is these images of neediness and desperation, which run so strongly against the waitress's perception of herself and her position, that she attacks when strained relations erupt into open conflict.

> Five rowdy black guys walked in the door and they went to seat themselves at table seven. I said, "Excuse me. You all got to wait to be seated." "We ain't got to do *shit*. We here to eat. . . ." So they went and sat down. And I turned around and just looked at them. And they said, "Well, I hope you ain't our waitress, cause you blew your tip. Cause you ain't

getting nothing from us." And I turned around and I said, "You need it more than I do, baby."

This waitress's desire to confront the customer's assumption of her destitution is widely shared among service workers whose status as tipped employees marks them as needy in the eyes of their customers. Davis (1959, 162–163) reports that among cabdrivers "a forever repeated story is of the annoyed driver, who, after a grueling trip with a Lady Shopper, hands the coin back, telling her, 'Lady, keep your lousy dime. You need it more than I do.'" Mars and Nicod (1984, 75) report a hotel waitress's claim that "if she had served a large family with children for one or two weeks, and then was given a 10p piece,[3] she would give the money back, saying, 'It's all right, thank you, I've got enough change for my bus fare home.'" In an incident I observed (not at Route), a waitress followed two male customers out of a restaurant calling, "Excuse me! You forgot this!" and holding up the coins they had left as a tip. The customers appeared embarrassed, motioned for her to keep the money, and continued down the sidewalk. The waitress, now standing in the outdoor seating area of the restaurant and observed by curious diners, threw the money after the retreating men and returned to her work. Episodes such as these allow the worker to repudiate openly the evaluation of her financial status that is implied in an offensively small gratuity, and permit her to articulate her own understanding of what a small tip says and about whom. If customers can only afford to leave a dime, or feel a 10p piece is adequate compensation for two weeks' service, they must be very hard up or very ignorant indeed.

In the following incident the waitress interjects a denial of her neediness into an altercation

---

[3]Until it converts to the Eurodollar, the British monetary unit is the pound sterling (£). One pound is worth about $1.65 in U.S. currency. There are 100 pence to the pound. So, 10p (pronounced "10 pea") is worth about 17 cents.—Ed.

that is not related to tipping, demonstrating that the customer's perception of her financial status is a prominent and persistent concern for her.

> She [a customer] wanted a California Burger with mayonnaise. And when I got the mayonnaise, the mayonnaise had a little brown on it. . . . So this girl said to me, she said, "What the fuck is this you giving me?" And I turned around, I thought, "Maybe she's talking to somebody else in the booth with her." And I turned around and I said, "Excuse me?" She said, "You hear what I said. I said, 'What the fuck are you giving me?'" And I turned around, I said, "I don't know if you're referring your information to *me*," I said, "but if you're referring your information to *me*," I said, "I don't *need* your bullshit." I said, "I'm not going to even take it. . . . Furthermore, I could care less if you eat or *don't* eat. . . . And you see this?" And I took her check and I ripped it apart. . . . And I took the California Burger and I says, "You don't have a problem anymore now, right?" She went up to the manager. And she says, "That black waitress"—I says, "Oh. By the way, what is my name? I don't have a name, [using the words] 'that black waitress'. . . . My name happens to be Nera. . . . That's N-E-R-A. . . . And I don't need your bullshit, sweetheart. . . . People like you I can walk on, because you don't know how to talk to human beings." And I said, "I don't need you. I don't need your quarters. I don't need your nickels. I don't need your dimes. So if you want service, be my guest.

> Don't you *ever* sit in my station, cause I won't wait on you." The manager said, "Nera, please. Would you wait in the back?" I said, "No. I don't take back seats no more for nobody."

In each of these cases, the waitress challenges the customer's definition of the relationship in which tipping occurs. By speaking out, by confronting the customer, she demonstrates that she is not subservient or in fear of losing her job; that she is not compelled by financial need or a sense of social hierarchy to accept abuse from customers; that she does not, in Nera's words, "take back seats no more for nobody." At the same time, she reverses the symbolic force of the low tip, converting a statement on her social status or work skills into a statement on the tipper's cheapness or lack of savoir faire.[4] . . .

References

Davis, Fred. 1959. "The Cabdriver and His Fare: Facets of a Fleeting Relationship." *American Journal of Sociology* 65(2): 158–165.

Mars, Gerald, and Michael Nicod. 1984. *The World of Waiters*. London: Allen & Unwin.

Wentworth, Harold, and Stuart Berg Flexner (eds. and comps.). 1975. *Dictionary of American Slang*. 2nd supplemental ed. New York: Crowell.

---

[4]*Savoir faire* is French and means literally "knowing how to do." Generally the phrase is used to mean "a knowledge of how to get around in the world," or simply, tact.—Ed.

Questions

1. You've just been out to dinner at a nice restaurant. Your waitress presented you with a tab for $72.50. Assuming the service was fine, how much did you tip her? How much do you think she might have expected? Where did you learn the appropriate amount to tip?

2. Have you ever tried to send a "message" to a waitperson by leaving no tip or a very small one? What was that message? Whether you've ever sent such a message, based on what you've read in Paules's article, do you think the message was received?

3. One of the techniques for understanding how people interact within a social structure is to look at "role sets"—that is, the set of statuses with which one interacts in carrying out one's role. In the accompanying diagram, I've sketched my role set as a professor. Try your hand at this by sketching the role set of the waitress.

   Generally, people within a particular role set have a similar understanding of one another's role—that is, their rights and duties as incumbents in a particular status. As Paules tells it, however, the customer has a different understanding of the waitress's role than the waitress does. To what sorts of complications might this lead? What would be the effect on the relationship if both customer and waitress understood the waitress's role from the waitress's point of view? From the customer's point of view?

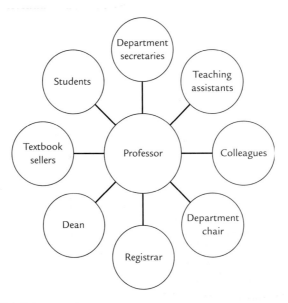

Professor's Role Set

18

COMMANDING THE ROOM IN SHORT SKIRTS

Cheering as the Embodiment of Ideal Girlhood

Natalie Adams and Pamela Bettis

Cheerleading isn't what it used to be. A generation ago, no one thought of cheerleading as a sport; the idea of cheerleader conjured up images of pompoms, short
skirts, and pep. Today, it's different; cheerleading requires an athleticism that
rivals that displayed by the players on the field. But, as Professor Adams and
Bettis discover, cheerleaders have it tougher than other athletes—they have to
smile when they get hurt and they aren't allowed to burp or fart.

---

live up to?

In the United States, the cheerleader is a
cultural icon, on one hand, symbolizing
"youthful prestige, wholesome attractiveness,
peer leadership and popularity," while simultaneously representing "mindless enthusiasm,
shallow boosterism, objectified sexuality, and
promiscuous availability" (Hanson 1995, 2). A
staple of American life and popular culture,
the cheerleader has received little scholarly
attention. When discussed at all in academic
research, as illustrated in the following
quote, cheerleading is typically presented as
an activity that exploits and demeans girls:
"The function of the cheerleader is to encourage the worship of the men—the prettiest,
nicest and most lively are selected to show and
encourage adoration" (Weis 1997, 83).

In this article, we challenge such trivializa-
tion of cheerleading in academic research and
argue that a feminist poststructuralist reading

of cheerleading offers a unique opportunity to
theorize this role in ways that honor the
concrete realities of girls' lives. We follow
Walkerdine's (1993, 15) suggestion to prob-
lematize traditional approaches to studying
girls, as found in developmental psychology
and socialization theories, by carrying out
research that

> understand[s] the social world as constituted
> materially and discursively and replete with
> fantasies and fictions which shore up power in
> all its many guises. To understand the consti-
> tution of girls within this means that we
> understand girlhood as constituted in and
> through the discursive practices that make up
> the social world.

Drawing on an ethnographic study of a Midwestern middle school, we discuss cheerleading as a socially sanctioned space for a few
girls to create multiple gendered subject positions that accommodate the shifting and often
contradictory meanings of normative adolescent femininity. Our intent is to offer an examination of cheerleading that acknowledges
the multiple meanings embedded in this cultural institution. We argue that cheerleading

"Commanding the Room in Short Skirts" by Natalie Adams
and Pamela Bettis from *Gender & Society*, 2003, Vol. 17. No. 1
(February: pp. 73–91). Copyright © 2003 by Sociologists for
Women in Society. Reprinted by permission of Sage
Publications, Inc.

represents a liberating shift in normative femininity while simultaneously perpetuating a norm that does not threaten dominant social values and expectations about the role of girls and women. . . .

The Changing Face of Cheerleading: A Historical Overview

Originally, cheerleading was an exclusively male activity representing normative masculinity. During the mid- to late 1800s and the early 1900s, cheerleading was an idealized activity for privileged males and was seen as both an athletic and an aesthetic endeavor, as reported by the editors of *The Nation* (Organized cheering 1911, 6), who argued that organized cheering was a noble activity for undergraduates (i.e., males), and

> the reputation of having been a valiant "cheerleader" is one of the most valuable things a boy can take away from college. As a title to promotion in professional or public life, it ranks hardly second to that of having been a quarterback.

Girls began entering collegiate organized cheering in small numbers in the late 1920s and early 1930s, but as late as the 1930s, cheerleading was still considered to be a male activity, associated with masculine characteristics of athleticism and leadership (Hanson 1995).

By the 1940s, more than 30,000 American high schools and colleges had cheerleaders, many of whom were girls. The trend to include girls in this previously masculine activity was precipitated in part by World War II. As young men fought in the war, girls were offered entrance into spaces once relegated solely for males. Cheerleading was one of those spaces (Hanson 1995). However, as men returned from the war, they sought to reclaim their place in the public spheres, including cheerleading squads. Thus, by the 1950s, several colleges (e.g., the University of Tennessee) and high schools began to ban girls from the cheering squad (Gonzales 1956).

Despite the ban on women cheerleaders in some squads and the number of men still participating in cheerleading at the collegiate level, by the 1950s, cheerleading was becoming more and more feminized, as illuminated in a 1955 published list of desirable traits for high school cheerleaders. Gymnastics ability was not included; rather, the important traits were manners, cheerfulness, and good disposition—traits traditionally associated with women and girls (Kutz 1955, 310). Noting the transformation of cheerleading by the 1960s from a masculine activity to a highly feminized activity, McElroy (1999, 15) asserted,

> Cheerleading in the sixties consisted of pompoms, cutesy chants, big smiles and revealing uniforms. There were no gymnastic tumbling runs. No complicated stunting. Never any injuries. About the most athletic thing sixties cheerleaders did was a cartwheel followed by the splits.

However, in the aftermath of the second wave of feminist activism and theorizing in the 1960s, and the passage of title IX in 1972, the cultural scripts for ideal femininity began to change. The new ideal woman was one who did not relegate her needs to the needs of men. She sought to enter spheres once reserved only for men (e.g., occupations, sports). As the signifier of normative femininity began to change, so too did notions of the ideal girl, who, of course, had to be prepared for taking on a new role in adult society. As gendered identity began to be rethought, cheerleading began to be shaped by different discursive practices with different aims than before.

Recognizing the potential of losing profits due to an outdated image of cheerleading, national cheerleading organizations actively sought to reshape this activity as congruent with the newer ideals of normative femininity

(Woodmansee 1993). As Argetsinger (1999, A-3) asserted, "in post–Title IX, cheerleading might have vanished but it harnessed the spirit of the time, evolving into a melange of highflying acrobatics and show-biz flair that required more athleticism than before." Tight athletic motions, difficult jumps, and pyramid building began to be emphasized in the hundreds of cheerleading camps offered throughout the country. These new cheerleading techniques required girls who not only were strong but also were agile, were well-coordinated, and possessed athletic prowess.

Part of the transformation of cheerleading centered on the introduction of national, state, and regional competitions. Cheerleaders suddenly moved from the sidelines where they were motivational spectators to become the competitors themselves. In 1981, the first national high school cheerleading competition was held, and in 1983, ESPN televised the event (Hanson 1995). With the introduction and proliferation of national competitions, demands on cheerleading squads increased, with many squads practicing 12 months a year, often two or three times a day. Special coaches were often hired to teach squads difficult and often dangerous routines for competition (Argetsinger 1999).

By the 1990s, competitive cheerleading squads (called All-Star) were being formed throughout the United States. These competitive cheerleading squads were not affiliated with schools or any sports teams but competed for themselves (Argetsinger 1999; Brenner 1999; McElroy 1999). According to the National Federation of State High Schools, in the 1997–1998 school year, approximately 59,000 girls participated in competitive cheerleading—an increase of approximately 25,000 since 1995–1996 (Deardorff 1999).

As illuminated in this brief overview of the evolution of cheerleading, the discursive practices of this activity have changed to accommodate the changing nature of gender roles and normative gendered behavior in our society. From the late 1800s to the 1930s, cheerleading squads comprised primarily men, and cheerleading signified ideal masculinity. However, by the mid-1950s, cheerleading had changed significantly from an activity representing normative masculinity to one representing ideal femininity. In discussing the shift from a masculine activity to a naturalized feminine activity during this time period, Davis (1990, 155) pointed out that cheerleaders came to symbolize "dominant ideology about how females should look and act in our society." That is, women/cheerleaders were to be pretty, were to possess appealing figures, were to play a secondary role to males, and were not to be taken too seriously. In the aftermath of title IX and the second wave of women's rights, notions of the appropriate role and behavior of women in society began to shift; thus, cheerleading had to change to reflect new ideals about normative femininity and ideal girlhood. This study illuminates those changes.

Data Collection

In August 1998, along with two other researchers,[1] we began a study focusing on girls and leadership at Powhaton Middle School, a sixth- and seventh-grade school located in a Midwestern town of 26,000.[2] The racial composition of the student body was 75 percent white, 14 percent Native American, 8.3 percent Hispanic, 4.5 percent African American, and 0.8 percent Asian. During the initial interviews with 61 seventh-grade girls, and throughout our field notes, cheerleaders were frequently mentioned as leaders in the school. Therefore, beginning in January 1999, we began five

---

[1]Drs. Deb Jordan and Diane Montgomery, along with the authors, collected the data for the larger study on girls and leadership.

[2]Pseudonyms are used for all people and places in this study.

months of weekly observations of two cheerleading classes the school had instituted to prepare girls for the March cheerleading tryouts. The details leading to the creation of this class are complicated and are discussed elsewhere (Adams and Bettis in press). However, for the purposes of this article, it is sufficient to explain that the Powhaton school district implemented a cheerleading preparation class at two schools as one way to meet the demands of the Office of Civil Rights after a grievance was filed against the district in 1994. These cheerleading preparation classes were intended to level the playing field by offering any girl the opportunity to enroll in the class as a physical education elective. The purpose of the class, according to the school board's minutes, was to "provide an elective physical education class to teach skills needed in cheerleading and drill teams to grades 7–9." At Powhaton Middle School, this class was referred to as the cheer prep class.

The two cheer prep classes were scheduled back to back to meet the schedule of the part-time instructor who was the cheerleader sponsor for the junior varsity cheerleading squad at the local high school. Typically, we situated ourselves along the gym wall and took copious field notes while the girls participated in the various activities Louise Stone, the teacher, planned for helping them prepare for tryouts.[3] We also observed the cheerleading clinic held after school to teach the girls the tryout routines, the mock tryouts (held the night before the real tryouts, which were closed to the public), and a cheerleading camp for those

who were selected for the team during the following summer. We conducted initial interviews before the tryouts with 22 of the 64 girls enrolled in the class. These 22 girls were all part of the larger study on girls and leadership and had been previously interviewed about their perceptions of leadership. A second round of interviews with 18 of the 22 was conducted following tryouts.

Of the 20 girls ultimately chosen for the squad, 19 were white, and 1 was Native American.[4] The racial composition of the girls we initially interviewed consisted of 14 whites, 5 Native Americans, and 3 African Americans: 13 of the 20 girls chosen for the squad were among those we interviewed. In addition, 9 other girls who did not make the squad or who decided not to try out, but who were in the cheer preparation class, were interviewed. The two formal interviews were semistructured and conducted in a variety of locations during the cheer preparation class while informal interviews took place at lunch and before and after classes. The cheer preparation teacher, Ms. Stone, was also interviewed. Documents pertinent to the study, including handouts disseminated to students and parents about tryouts, local newspaper articles featuring the cheerleaders, and Powhaton School Board minutes, were also studied. . . .

---

[3]In our larger study of cheerleading (Adams and Bettis in press), we found that a majority of cheerleading sponsors are former cheerleaders, and they have great passion for the activity. In this sense, Ms. Stone, as a former high school and junior college cheerleader, represents a fairly typical cheerleading sponsor. She is somewhat atypical in that there is a high turnover rate among cheerleader sponsors, but Ms. Stone has been a cheerleader sponsor in this school district for more than 10 years.

---

[4]As we discuss elsewhere (Adams and Bettis in press), despite the Office of Civil Rights's involvement, five years later, the cheerleading squads continued to be white and middle class. The school board policies were not fully implemented. Social class continued to be a major factor in who made the squad. Only those girls who could afford the hefty fees at private gyms learned advanced tumbling skills, which greatly enhanced one's chances of being selected. More important, many of the working-class white, Native American, and African American girls contested certain facets of normative femininity found in the cheerleading identity of this middle school while many of the middle-class white girls who were also members of a dominant group called the preps embraced the requirements of achieving this identity.

Data: Cheerleading and the Ideal Girl

I am not arrogant.
I am confident.
I am not a daredevil.
I am daring.
I am not a beauty queen.
I am an athlete.
I am not a stereotype.
I am my own person.
I am not interested in the past.
I am living for the future.
I am not afraid of success.
I am afraid of nothing.
I am not another face in the crowd.
I am the ones others wish they could be.
I am not just any cheerleader.
I am the one in the Varsity uniform.
                    —Varsity Spirit Corporation (1999, 1)

As is evident in the above poem from the 1999 Varsity Cheerleading catalog, the cheerleader has been reconstructed to represent new ideals of normative femininity, which include confidence, rationality, risk taking, athleticism, independence, and fearlessness. In this section, we demonstrate how the girls in our study take up these signifiers of ideal girlhood to create their own version of femininity, one that allows them to dabble with the traditional markers of masculinity without having to give up those feminine characteristics they deem enjoyable and desirable. We argue that while they are playing an active role in constituting their own gendered identity within the discursive practice of cheerleading, they are also "constrained by larger material practices, structures and discourses that shape and coerce as well as potentiate individual action" (Davies 1989, xi). By doing so, we hope to demonstrate how girls are both productions of and producers of their own gendered subjectivities.

MASCULINITY AND THE CHEERLEADER ATHLETE: DISCIPLINE, RISK TAKING, AND POWER IN THE PHYSICAL

In the cheerleading preparation classes we observed at Powhaton Middle School, cheerleading as an athletic endeavor was emphasized repeatedly. In preparation for trying out in front of three judges, the cheerleader sponsor continuously instructed the girls to show off their muscular bodies: "All right, girls, make your muscles tight so the judges can see them. Tight across the shoulders. Tomorrow you should hurt. Legs are tight. This is a great time to show off your muscles." In addition to having a muscular, fit body, the ability to tumble and maintain tight motion technique—rigid body movements that some would characterize as almost militaristic in style—were also critical to making the squad. Lisa, a petite blonde who scored the highest number of points at tryouts, explained the importance of being tight:

> Like when you cheer, your arms have to be tight, and your emotions are like aggressive, not like to where you're going to punch someone, just like when they're tight. Like when I get up there, I'm like [hard snapping noise] push my arms down and slap them.

This aggressive attitude was encouraged by Ms. Stone, whose language during practices was replete with militaristic jargon. "Command the room" was a phrase she frequently used to motivate the girls into maintaining an aggressive attitude toward the judges and audience. In teaching proper motion techniques, she would instruct them, "Punch forward—don't swing your arms. Keep everything close to your body. Think close. Tight, tight, tight." Much like a drill sergeant, while working with the girls on motion technique, Ms. Stone would yell,

> Chins up, shoulders back, smiles. Hit the motion. Hit. Hit. Hit. 1, 2, 3, hit. 1, 2, 3, hit. When I say Hit, do a V. When I say, Hit, do a down V. Hit L; Hit V; Hit Down V.

At one point, she advised the girls, "Don't be afraid to push through the floor. Smash—power off your toes." At another time, she told the girls, "Attack those jumps even if you don't like the side we're doing." In addition to the girls' using robotic, tight motions, cheers were to be yelled in a deep, masculine voice.

Disciplining the body is an integral part of cheerleading. Preparation for cheerleading at Powhaton means that one must work long hours to master the movements, techniques, and tumbling required to be a serious contender for the cheerleading squad. Two of the criteria judges use at Powhaton to select the girls for the junior high squad are jumps (e.g., herkies, toe touches) and tumbling (back handsprings, back tucks), both of which require practice, perseverance, and athletic prowess. Every girl we interviewed who eventually was selected cheerleader either participated in tumbling classes at one of the local gyms or paid money to individuals to help them in mastering the requisite cheerleading skills. Although Ms. Stone would often tell the girls that tumbling was not an absolute requirement for making the squad, the reality was, as Patti, eventually selected cocaptain of the squad, noted, "all of us can do a back handspring."

Part of disciplining the cheerleader body entailed assuming a stance of invulnerability to pain. Embodying the image of the fierce athlete who is able to overcome pain to emerge the triumphant victor, Lisa recounted the harrowing events of tryouts, which eventually led to her obtaining the number 1 spot on the cheerleading squad:

> On the day of tryouts, I had 104 degrees fever; I had pneumonia. I had been sick for days and lost six pounds before tryouts. At tryouts, I fell on my head during my back handspring. It was like my wrists just collapsed. But I scored number 1. I couldn't even come to school the next day because I was so sick. My dad said he was proud of me because I showed determination.

During the cheer prep class, Leslie tore a ligament and had to be sent to the emergency room. Michelle suffered a severe sprain and was on crutches for two weeks. Neither saw these injuries as a deterrent to their trying out.

In describing the typical cheerleader, Julie, who was selected to be an eighth-grade cheerleader, said, "They are really peppy and hyper and just jump all over the place all the time." Sharon, also selected cheerleader, stated that she wanted to be a cheerleader because she was "always hyper." The reality is that cheering is not a spontaneous emotional activity. Rather, cheerleaders are to practice rationality and discipline. Indeed, unbridled emotion and spontaneity is appropriate only on the sidelines of sports events and only in certain contexts (e.g., a football player intercepts the ball and runs for a 60-yard touchdown). At all other times, cheerleading is a very controlled, organized, and disciplined activity. Cheers are orchestrated with complex tumbling moves, pyramid building, and partner stunts; dances are choreographed with precision; and chants often sound like military yells. There is little room for individual creativity in cheerleading at Powhaton.

Part of controlling one's emotion means the girls were to act in a way that on the surface seemed inauthentic. As preparation for tryouts, Ms. Stone repeatedly told the girls, "Pretend that you are having the time of your life. Show it in your faces, in your smiles." The ability to assume an inauthentic stance was most readily visible in the edicts to the girls to always have a smile on their face. More than any other quality, the ability to smile at all times seemed to be the most prized cheerleading attribute. Yet smiling in this context is not a spontaneous emotional response; rather, the ability to plaster a smile on one's face at a moment's notice was a very disciplined activity requiring a particular mind-set and lots of practice, as illustrated in the following comments:

You have to have a cheerleading personality, you know, smile all the time. Like Ms. Stone told me, "I don't care if it's a fake smile or not, just smile." (Terry, selected cheerleader)

You have to smile to look good, so everyone will think you're having a wonderful time. (Allison, selected cheerleader)

When you see a cheerleader, she's always smiling. But I can't smile if I don't feel like smiling. (Tamara, member of the cheer prep class, did not try out)

You've got to have fake smiles all the time. You know, cheesey. It takes practice to smile without it looking fake. I practice all the time in front of my mirror. It's hard work. (Lisa, selected cheerleader)

You have to be a prep to become a cheerleader because they got that fake happy look about them. I can't get that. I have to really be happy to look happy. (Daneka, member of cheer prep class, did not try out)

The ability to execute tight movements and complicated jumps and tumbling feats was a source of confidence for the girls selected cheerleader, as explained by Lisa—"It just gives you confidence, makes you feel good when you know you can make your body do these really hard things"—and Allison—"the prep girls will make it because they have confidence; they can jump, tumble, and do tight motions. They have it all." Karla, who tried out but was not selected, probably because of her lack of tumbling ability, noted,

> When you can tumble, the judges think of you as more flexible. Life you can do things better than everybody else. It gives them confidence. If they mess up, they don't just sit there. They get back up and do it again.

Clearly, for some girls, cheerleading offers a space for them to gain confidence in their bodies and themselves.

The desired female body is continuously rethought and reshaped through disciplining and normalizing practices that reflect both contemporary and historical understandings

of what constitutes ideal femininity. Unlike the ideal female body of yesteryear that was prized because of its inertness, delicacy, and helplessness, the revered female body today is that of the hard-muscled, sleek athlete, and girls today are being taught that it is not only appropriate but desirable to run, jump, tumble, act boldly, and move daringly (Bordo 1993). Cheerleading offers a safe space for girls to do just this, that is, to revel and delight in the physicality of their bodies. This is one of the main reasons why cheerleading, despite feminist critiques, continues to grow and attract large numbers of girls. With the assumption of many of the discursive practices once associated primarily with men and sports (e.g., musculature, strength, athletic prowess, fear of danger, and risk taking), cheerleading offers a space for some girls to embody the masculine look of the athlete and the concomitant values of self-discipline, aggressiveness, and self-mastery, thus entering a sphere once relegated to only boys and men.

FEMININITY AND GIRLIE GIRLS DIVERTING THE GAZE: PLEASURE AND SEXUALIZED SUBJECTIVITY IN CHEERLEADING

> Most of us want to be cheerleaders because we are more into being a girlie girl. (Lisa)

The girls selected cheerleader at Powhaton embraced the public nature of cheerleading, which allowed them to demonstrate to the world that they were confident, assertive, competitive, and athletic. However, the appeal of cheerleading went beyond simply the opportunity to prove they were athletes. In fact, the majority of the girls selected cheerleader were already known at their school as accomplished athletes; many of them had to juggle track and basketball practice with the mandatory cheerleading preparation clinic. This number is in line with recent data from a poll of 2,500 cheerleaders conducted by the Universal Cheerleaders

Association, which found that more than 50 percent of girls who cheer also participate in other athletic activities at their school (Roenigk 2002). Cheerleading was appealing to these girls because it also offered them a space to revel in what they called being a girlie girl. Unlike other athletes, these girls are participating in an activity that remains firmly entrenched within a feminine discourse; thus, they do not have to veil their masculinity nor worry, like other athletes, about being stigmatized as too masculine or as lesbians. These girls embrace cheerleading as a way to have it all—to flirt with the masculine without ever questioning or having someone else question their femininity or their sexual identity.

Traditionally, cheerleading has been constructed as an activity that valorizes stereotypical feminine virtues such as nurturance, selflessness, subservience, and loyalty. Cheerleading as a stereotypical feminine discourse was certainly evident at Powhaton, particularly as enacted in the values and beliefs of Ms. Stone, who explains the purpose of cheerleading as follows:

> My school spirit comes from the heart, and these young women need to learn how to be loyal. They need to learn how to take the eyes off of themselves. We're there for other people; we're not there for ourselves. . . . If it weren't for the athletes in the building, there would be no reason for us; we're to give of ourselves; we are serving our athletes.

The Powhaton Cheerleading Constitution, which all cheerleaders must sign, clearly situates cheerleaders in a supportive role: "The primary purpose of cheerleading is to promote unity, sportsmanship, and school spirit at school and school events. . . . The primary function of a cheerleading program is to support interscholastic athletics."

Interestingly, none of the girls interviewed indicated that the purpose of cheerleading was to demonstrate loyalty to their school.

Most of them, like Nan, wanted to be a cheerleader "because all my friends are doing it and you get to cheer in front of people and have lots of fun." The cheerleaders in this study do not view themselves as passive girls on the sidelines, and they certainly do not intend, as Ms. Stone suggested, to take the "eyes off of themselves," as explained by Lisa, Julie, and Patti:

> I thought cheerleading's just neat 'cause you get to tumble and you get to be some of the stars of the game. . . . It's just you want to be one of the main focuses of the game instead of the players. And you want to get people's attention. (Lisa)

> I like getting up in front of people and, like, being the one in charge. I like showing off and being with the guys. (Julie)

> Most of us are loud, and we like to cheer because we like to draw attention to ourselves. (Patti)

For the girls in this study, one of the primary joys of being a cheerleader derived from the knowledge that cheerleaders are the object of everyone's gaze—not just males. Most of the girls who were selected cheerleader told stories of how they, as early as four years old, envied and wanted to emulate the cheerleaders they saw from their view in the stands. Lisa explained,

> There are so many people who aren't into basketball or football and all they do is watch the cheerleaders and say, "Wow! I want to do that!" And they think of them as a role model, like, Yeah, mom there's a cheerleader. I want to be that when I grow up. That's what I did.

Being the center of attention, being the one "others wish they could be," offered these girls a form of power and pleasure not experienced in other activities, such as playing basketball or being in the school orchestra. Milea, the only Native American chosen for the squad, explained the difference between cheerleading and other sports: "Cheerleading is a sport you can have fun at. Sports were invented so that people could have fun, but most sports have turned into work, not fun. But not cheerleading. It's just fun!" The cheerleaders in this study saw themselves as central to the sporting event being observed and believed they had the power to control how the crowd and the players respond to the game on the field or the court, as illuminated in the following quotes:

> Cheerleaders are supposed to cheer the players on so they feel like they're doing good even when everyone knows they stink. (Allison)
>
> Cheerleaders are supposed to, like, even if your team's not that good, show them that, like, to try hard and motivate them. (Suzi)
>
> During a game, you'd be out there and you'd be leading a cheer, like to help the team players, you know, make them feel confident that they can do it. (Terry)
>
> Cheerleaders are leaders because if the team is losing, they'll get those big old smiles on and get all perky and they're able to get everybody back into the game. (Sharon)

In conveying her implicit understanding of the ideal woman as one who is heterosexual, a wife, and a mother, Ms. Stone explicated how cheerleading prepares girls for adult womanhood:

> Cheerleaders are still very feminine, and we work on those characteristics. We have rules, no burping, no farting. You are young ladies. But we build, we jump, we try to get a balance because cheerleading does prepare them for later on in life. They've got to be strong. They've got to bear pain to have children. . . . They've got to be able to stand on their feet and make decisions when it may be mom, or dad, or husband, who's laid out there and you've got to do what is the right thing to do. You've got to support. You've got to lift up. That's the whole role of being an adult woman.

Undoubtedly, cheerleading can still be read as a discourse that affirms heterosexualized femininity in which a woman's most basic desire is to be affiliated with a man. Although none of the girls expressed the sentiment that cheerleading was excellent preparation for being a wife and mother, many of the girls trying out for cheerleader at Powhaton expressed the belief that cheerleading made one more popular, thus increasing one's likelihood of gaining a boyfriend, a high-status marker for adolescent girls at this school. For example, Milea pointed out, "Boys like cheerleaders so that makes you popular. I want more boys to like me." Shanna, who was in the cheer prep class but did not try out, explained, "Some girls think the boys will like you if you're a cheerleader 'cause boys like the cheeriest people." Daneka, who did not try out for cheerleader although she participated in the cheer prep class, stated that "girls want to be cheerleaders because they believe that guys will like them more—they will see them as cute women in short skirts."

Daneka's use of "girls" and "women" in the same sentence reflects a primary attraction of cheerleading for many girls: It allows girls to try on a womanly (i.e., sexualized) identity in a school-sanctioned space. Walkerdine (1993) argued that in most accounts about girls' experiences in schools, the schoolgirl typified is the one who follows rules and is deferential, is loyal, is quiet, and works hard. This image of the schoolgirl, Walkerdine (1993, 20) asserted, has been constructed as a "defence against being the object of male fantasies. The erotic is displaced [in school accounts] as too dangerous. But it re-enters, it enters in the spaces that are outlawed in the primary school: popular culture." Cheerleading does allow the erotic to enter into school spaces; in fact, cheerleading at Powhaton Middle School offered the only school-sanctioned space for girls simultaneously to play with or to try on the identity of the all-American nice girl next door and the sexually provocative woman. Cheerleaders are allowed to wear short skirts and tight-fitting vests, which violate school dress codes, while performing sexually provocative dance moves (e.g., pelvic thrusts) on the school stage to popular music typically not allowed elsewhere in school. For many of the girls, such as Julie, this opportunity to play with a sexualized identity was a primary reason cheerleading was so appealing. She explained, "I'm in it for the short skirts, the guys, getting in front of everybody, and making a total fool of myself."

Yet at the same time, cheerleaders at Powhaton were viewed as leaders who serve the interests of the school and community, symbolizing values and traditions deemed positive in American culture (Eckert 1989). As mentioned earlier, cheerleaders were cited as school leaders by almost all of the 61 girls interviewed in the larger study. The girls selected to be cheerleaders took this role seriously and recognized that being a cheerleader meant they would be role models for others. Suzi offered this explanation of the responsibility of cheerleading:

> It's not like it used to be, like popularity and stuff. Now you have to like have what it takes to be a cheerleader. You can't just like get up there and just smile. You have to have tight motions. You have to know what you're supposed to be doing, and you have big responsibility now. You have to be at cheerleading practice on time. If you have to have the tape for the dance, you have to remember to bring it. You have to be responsible. You're going to have a lot of people looking up to you, and so you're going to have lots of responsibility to do right things.

Undeniably, the sexualized nature of cheerleading, which situates girls as objects of desire—clad in short skirts and tight-fitting vests—was part of the discourse of cheerleading at Powhaton. While performing tight, militaristic movements and using a deep voice, the girls were also instructed to look at the judges in a sexy way. "When you make that turn," instructed Ms. Stone, "give the judges a sexy look." She further instructed them, "You should

be oozing out cheerleading stuff. Dazzle me, smile, give me goosebumps. I want to be dazzled." The last advice Ms. Stone gave the girls before the day of tryouts was to "put Vaseline on your teeth and put on a little extra makeup, but not too much. Don't come looking like someone who could stand on the street."

Conclusion

Operating at the juncture of all-American good looks, traditional femininity, and sports-like athleticism, contemporary cheerleading provides a culturally sanctioned space for performing the requisite traits of the ideal girl in the new millennium. Quite literally, cheerleading is a performative act—one that has been traditionally understood as girls performing for the pleasure of others, particularly men. Many would argue, as in the film *American Beauty*, that this performance situates the girl body as the object of the masculine gaze and male fantasy. As Kurman (1986, 58) noted, "the cheerleader is a disturbing erotic icon. . . . She incarnates, in a word, a basic male-voyeuristic fantasy." Yet Kenway et al. (1994, 205), in discussing their work with adolescent girls and gender reform in Australia, offered a different reading of the performance metaphor:

> The performance metaphor allows the girls to feel a sense of control over different performance genres, to pick up, discard, play and take risks within them, and even to go beyond them through improvisation, collage, and carnival. Femininity can then become a source of power and pleasure rather than a source of control.

We found ample evidence in our study to suggest that cheerleading offers a critical space for certain girls to take risks, to try on different personas, to delight in the physicality of their bodies, and to control and revel in their own power and desire. In other words, cheerleading offers some girls the opportunity to perform ideal girlhood without being located in a disabling discourse of femininity that equates femininity with exploitation and oppression. In many ways, these girls have embraced cheerleading as a way of accommodating the contradictions of constructing oneself as a feminine subject. Thus, any reading of cheerleading and the new girl order must acknowledge that girls themselves play an active role in reconstituting ideal femininity as they resist, rethink, and re-envision for themselves who they want to be as gendered individuals.

Although the girls in this study took up multiple gendered subjectivities within the discursive practices of cheerleading, they are not free to construct any gender identity they desire. As feminist poststructuralists (Davies 1989; Walkerdine 1993; Weedon 1987) have pointed out, constructing a gendered identity is always constrained by larger material practices, structures, and discourses. This study shows how these shape and influence the ways in which girls negotiate a gendered identity within a patriarchal society that continues to define ideal girlhood very narrowly. Hence, we are reminded how powerful certain discourses are despite the changing landscape for normative masculinity and femininity. As several researchers of girl culture have pointed out (Brumberg 1997; Inness 1998; Johnson, Roberts, and Worell 1999), growing up female is not an easy task, particularly in a time when the signifiers of masculinity and femininity seem to be always in flux. As ideal femininity has shifted, girls in the twenty-first century are faced with the problem of how far they can go in displaying femininity and masculinity, in what contexts such displays are appropriate, and to what degree. This study reveals how these contradictions play out in the discursive practices associated with contemporary cheerleading and sports. For example, cheerleaders dressed in short skirts and tight vests often cheer for female basketball players dressed in baggy shorts and shirts. Through their uniforms, the cheerleaders accentuate their femininity while the basketball players hide theirs. The cheerleaders try to play up their masculinity, not through their clothing but through their stunts and tumbling, while the female basketball players often play up their femininity off court to become the "heterosexy" athlete (Griffin 1992), thus gaining acceptance and avoiding the lesbian label.[5]

Obviously, cheerleading is but one avenue for girls to contest stereotypical images of the docile, unathletic female body. Girls now have opportunities, although much more limited, to engage in ice hockey, football, boxing, and bodybuilding. However, as Inness (1999) and Lowe (1998) pointed out, despite the gains women have made in many areas once relegated solely for men, in the twenty-first century, we still do not exactly know what to do with women who box, women bodybuilders, and women who want to play professional football and ice hockey. When women enter a masculine discourse and assume masculine signifiers, mainstream society is threatened, and when a woman steps over the boundaries of acceptable feminine behavior, she is typically viewed as gender deviant (Adams 1999; Inness 1999). Similar to the All-American Girls Baseball League begun in the 1940s and disbanded in the 1950s, cheerleaders, as personifications of the ideal girl, merely flirt with the masculine. As Candice Berry, coach of the Greenup County High cheerleading squad in Kentucky, one of the top cheerleading squads in the country, stated, "cheerleading offers budding young women something that girls' basketball, track, soccer, softball can't offer: lessons in how to be a *lady*, how to be tough without imitating men" (McElroy 1999, 119). Cheerleaders, for all their athleticism, toughness, and risk taking, do not disrupt twenty-first-century, taken-for-granted notions of

---

[5]We would like to thank one of the reviewers for this helpful insight.

normative femininity and masculinity. In other words, they ultimately do not challenge the status quo by transgressing gendered boundaries.

References

Adams, Natalie. 1999. Fighting to be somebody: The discursive practices of adolescent girls fighting. *Educational Studies* 30:115–39.

Adams, Natalie, and Pamela Bettis. In press. *Spirit! Let's hear it! The making and remaking of the American cheerleader.* New York: Palgrave Press.

Argetsinger, Amy. 1999. When cheerleaders are the main event: For private teams, victory is their own. *Washington Post,* 10 July, A1.

Bordo, Susan. 1993. Unbearable weight: Feminism, Western culture, and the body. Berkeley: University of California Press.

Brenner, Elsa. 1999. Cheerleading changes as boys join sidelines: Stereotypes slip away, attitudes shift and a sport calls for more acrobatics. *New York Times,* 2 May, Section 14, 1, 4–5.

Brumberg, Joan. 1997. *The body project: An intimate history of American girls.* New York: Random House.

Davies, Bronwyn. 1989. *Frogs and snails and feminist tales.* Sydney, Australia: Allen and Unwin.

———. 1993. *Shards of glass: Children reading and writing beyond gendered identity.* Cresskill, NJ: Hampton Press.

Davis, L. 1990. Male cheerleaders and the naturalization of gender. In *Sports, men and the gender order,* edited by Michael Messner and Don Sabo. Champaign, IL: Human Kinetics Books.

Deardorff, Julie. 1999. Cheerleaders want R-E-S-P-E-C-T: Competitions take pep squads beyond old sis-boom bah. *Chicago Tribune,* 30 May, 1, 3.

Eckert, Penelope. 1989. *Jocks and burnouts.* New York: Teachers College Press.

Gonzales, Arturo. 1956. The first college cheer. *American Mercury* 83:100–104.

Griffin, Pat. 1992. Changing the game: Homophobia, sexism, and lesbians in sport. *Quest* 44:251–65.

Hanson, Mary Ellen. 1995. *Go! Fight! Win! Cheerleading in American culture.* Bowling Green, OH: Bowling Green University Press.

Inness, Sherrie. 1998. *Millennium girls: Today's girls around the world.* Lanham, MD: Rowman & Littlefield.

———. 1999. *Tough girls: Women warriors and wonder women in popular culture.* Philadelphia: University of Pennsylvania Press.

Johnson, Norine, Michael Roberts, and Judith Worell. 1999. *Beyond appearance: A new look at adolescent girls.* Washington, DC: American Psychological Association.

Kenway, Jane, Sue Willis, Jill Blackmore, and Leonia Rennie. 1994. Making "hope practical" rather than "despair convincing": Feminist poststructuralism, gender reform and educational change. *British Journal of Sociology of Education* 15:187–210.

Kurman, George. 1986. What does girls' cheerleading communicate? *Journal of Popular Culture* 20:57–64.

Kutz, F. B. 1955. Cheerleading rules, desirable traits and qualifications. *School Activities* 26:310.

Lowe, Maria. 1998. *Women of steel: Female body builders and the struggle for self-definition.* New York: New York University Press.

McElroy, James. 1999. *We've got spirit: The life and times of America's greatest cheerleading team.* New York: Simon & Schuster.

Organized cheering. 1911. *Nation* 92:5–6.

Roenigk, Alyssa. 2002. Cheer safety: Setting the record straight. *American Cheerleader* 8:46–48.

Varsity Spirit Corporation. 1999. *Varsity.* Memphis, TN: Varsity Spirit Corporation.

Walkerdine, Valerie. 1990. *Schoolgirl fictions.* London: Verso.

———. 1993. Girlhood through the looking glass. In *Girls, girlhood and girls' studies in transition,* edited by Marion de Ras and Mieke Lunenberg. Amsterdam: Het Spinhuis.

Weedon, Chris. 1987. *Feminism practice and poststructuralist theory.* Oxford, UK: Basil Books.

Weis, Lois. 1997. Gender and the reports: The case of the missing piece. In *Feminist critical policy analysis: A perspective from primary and secondary schooling,* edited by Catherine Marshall. London: Falmer.

Woodmansee, Ken. 1993. Cheers! Jeff Webb's multicolored world wide spirit machine. *Memphis Business* 3:14–19.

Questions

1. The authors of this article assert that cheerleading operates "at the juncture . . . of traditional femininity and sports-like athleticism." How does the modern cheerleader combine these traits?

2. Female athletes are frequently regarded with suspicion in American society—for example, many athletic women may be suspected of being lesbians. How is it that female cheerleaders manage to avoid this sort of suspicion?

3. At Powhaton Middle School, any girl was allowed to take classes to learn the skills needed to be a cheerleader. As it turns out, however, other skills (e.g., tumbling) are needed to be selected as a cheerleader. How do the girls acquire these additional skills? What are the implications of this for the composition of the cheerleading squad—does everyone have an equal chance?

4. Historically, cheerleading was a male domain and, according to one commentator cited in the article,

   the reputation of having been a valiant "cheer-leader" is one of the most valuable things a boy can take away from college. As a title to promotion in professional or public ranks, it ranks hardly second to that of having been a quarterback.

   There still are male cheerleaders, of course, but does the fact of having been a valiant cheer-leader still have the same positive impact on a man's career? Why or why not? What is its impact on a woman's career?

19

THE REST ROOM
AND EQUAL OPPORTUNITY*

Harvey Molotch

On the face of it, this article is about the degree to which Western society provides men and women with equal opportunities to pee. Now, while few would argue that having a place to pee is a trivial matter, this would hardly seem to be a topic worthy of inclusion in a book of sociological readings. If you read this article carefully, however, you will discover that Professor Molotch is making a larger point: Structure affects behavior as well as opportunities. Yes, people make choices, but their choices are influenced by pre-existing social arrangements. And, given all of the relevant facts, structures that seem equal may not be.

At the risk of appearing disrespectful, let me say that the best way to understand equal opportunity is to use the public toilet. Sometimes a gross approach can best clarify a subtle issue. Through the example of how society is organized to provide men and women with the capacity to relieve themselves, we can understand what it takes, as a more general matter, to provide members of different social groups with authentic equal opportunity.

In many public buildings, the amount of floor area dedicated for the men's room and the women's room is the same. The prevailing public bathroom doctrine in the U.S. is one of segregation among the genders, but with equality the guiding ideology. In some jurisdictions, this square footage equality is enshrined in law. Such an arrangement follows the dictum that equality can be achieved only by policies that are "gender-blind" (or "color-blind" or "ethnic-blind") in the allocation of a public resource. To give less to women (or blacks or Hispanics) would be discrimination; to give more would be "reverse discrimination." Women and men have the same proportion of a building to use as rest rooms. Presumably this should provide members of both genders with equal opportunity for dealing with their bodily needs in a timely and convenient way.

The trouble with this sort of equality is that, being blind, it fails to recognize differences between men as a group and women as a group. These differences are not amenable to easy change. Part of women's demand for bathrooms cannot exist for men because only women menstruate. Women make trips to the rest room to secure hygienic and socially appropriate adaptations to this physical fact. And because men's physiology suits them for the use of urinals, a large number of men can be serviced by a relatively small physical space. Women in our society use toilets to urinate, and toilets require a larger area than urinals. By creating men's and women's rooms of the same size, society guarantees that

"The Rest Room and Equal Opportunity." by Harvey Molotch from *Sociological Forum*, Vol. 3, No. 1 (Winter, 1988: pp. 128–132). Copyright © 1988. Reprinted by permission of Blackwell Publishing Ltd.

*Encouragement and assistance was provided by Howard Becker, Gayle Binion, and Beth Schneider.

individual women will be worse off than individual men. By distributing a resource equally, an unequal result is structurally guaranteed.

The consequences are easily visible at intermission time whenever men and women congregate in theater lobbies. When the house is full, the women form a waiting line in front of the bathroom while the men do their business without delay. Women experience discomfort and are excluded from conversations that occur under more salutary conditions elsewhere in the lobby. If toward the rear of the line, women may experience anxiety that they will miss the curtain rise. Indeed, they may arrive too late to be seated for the opening scene, dance routine, or orchestral movement. Their late arrival is easily taken by others (particularly men) as evidence of characterological slowness or preoccupation with primping and powder room gossip. All these difficulties are built into the structure of the situation. Equality of square feet to the genders delivers women special burdens of physical discomfort, social disadvantage, psychological anxiety, compromised access to the full product (the performance), and public ridicule.

An obvious solution, one I'll call the "liberal" policy, is to make women's rooms larger than men's. Women's bathrooms need to be big enough to get women in and out as quickly as men's bathrooms get men in and out. No more and no less. A little applied sociological research in various types of settings would establish the appropriate ratios needed to accomplish such gender equality.

An alternative solution, one I'll call "conservative," would be for women to change the way they do things, rather than for society to change the structuring of rest room space. There is no need to overturn the principle of equality of square footage among the genders. Instead, women need to use their allotted square footage more efficiently. If women truly want to relieve themselves as efficiently as men, they can take some initiative. Options do

exist short of biological alteration. While women may not be capable of adapting to urinals, they could relieve themselves by squatting over a common trough. This would save some space—perhaps enough to achieve efficiency parity with men. Women are not physically bound to use up so many square feet. It is a cultural issue, and in this case the problem derives from a faulty element of women's culture. It is not physiologically given that each woman should have her own cubicle, much less her own toilet, or that she should sit rather than squat.

This joins the issue well. Should women be forced to change or should the burden be placed on men who may have to give up some of their own square footage so that women might have more? The response from the liberal camp is that even if women's spatial needs are cultural, these needs should be recognized and indulged. Cultural notions of privacy and modes of using toilets were not arrived at by women in isolation from men. Men's conceptions of "decency"—at least as much as women's—encourage women to be physically modest and demure. Men's recurring violence toward women encourages bathroom segregation in the first instance because segregation makes it easier for potential assailants to be spotted as "out of place." Providing women with latched cubicles provides a further bit of security in a world made less secure by men. Thus, prescriptions of dignity and protections from assault come from the common culture produced by women and men. Whatever their origins, these cultural imperatives have become a real force and are sustained by continuing pressures on women's lives. Until this common culture is itself transformed, U.S. women cannot become as efficient as Tiwi women in their capacity to urinate in public settings, regardless of the efficiency advantages. On the other hand, altering the spatial allocations for men's and women's bathrooms is relatively simple and inexpensive.

It becomes harder to be a liberal as the weight of cultural imperative seems to lighten. Suppose, for example, that *a part* of the reason for the line in front of the ladies' room is, in fact, a tendency for women to primp longer than men or to gossip among one another at the sinks (although the lines in front of *toilet stalls* would belie such an assumption). Should vanity and sociability be subsidized at the expense of the larger community? But here again, the culture that men and women have produced in common becomes relevant. Perhaps women "take a powder" to escape the oppression of men, using the rest room as a refuge from social conditions imposed by the dominant gender? Perhaps the need to look lovely, every moment and in every way, is created by men's need to display a public companion whose make-up is flawless, whose head has every hair in place, and whose body is perfectly scented. Women are driven to decorate themselves as men's commodities and the consequence is bathroom demand. Should men pay for this "service" through sacrificing their own square footage or should women adjust by waiting in line and climbing all over one another for a patch of the vanity mirror?

Again it turns on who should change what. The conservative answer might be for women to give up primping, but that would fly in the face of the demand (also championed by conservatives) that women's cultural role is to be beautiful for their men. Although not because they wished to increase rest room efficiency, radical feminists have argued that women should ease up on their beauty treatments, precisely because it ratifies their subservience to men and deflects them from success in occupational and other realms. But again the liberal view holds appeal: at least until the transition to feminism, the existing *cultural arrangement* necessitates an asymmetric distribution of space to provide equality of opportunity among the genders.

As the issues become subtle, reasonable people come to disagree on who should do what and what community expense should be incurred to achieve parity. Such controversy stems from the effort to provide equal opportunity for individuals by taking into account differences among groups. The same problem arises no matter what the issue and no matter what the group. If people commonly get their job leads by word-of-mouth through friends and neighbors, then black people—excluded from the neighborhoods of employers and of those employed in expanding job sectors—will be at a labor market disadvantage. Black people's chronically higher unemployment rate stands as evidence of disadvantage: their longer queue for jobs is analogous to the longer line in front of the women's rest room. Blacks can be told to work harder, to use their meager resources more efficiently, to rearrange their lives and cultures to better their job qualifications. Alternatively, their present plight can be understood as *structural*—stemming from a history of enslavement, Jim Crow segregation, and white prejudice that now results in concrete arrangements that hinder individual life changes. One must be color-sighted, rather than color-blind, to deal with these differences. But this is no reverse racism: it rests on perception of social structural locations, not upon inherent inferiority attributed to group membership. Such government mandated policies as open job-searches, ethnic hiring targets, and preference for minority vendors and subcontractors can counteract structural biases that hold down opportunities of women, blacks, and other minorities. Affirmative action programs should be conceived as compensatory efforts to overcome such structured disadvantage (although the legal interpretation of the statutes is usually drawn more narrowly).

Equality is not a matter of arithmetic division, but of social accounting. Figuring out what is equal treatment necessitates—in every instance—a sociological analysis of exactly how it is that structures operate on people's lives. Besides rejecting the conservatives' penchant for blaming the victim, liberal policies need a concrete analytic basis that goes beyond good-hearted sympathy for the downtrodden. As in the rest room case, we need to specify how current patterns of "equal" treatment of groups yield unequal opportunities to individuals. We then should determine exactly what it would take (e.g., square feet to gender ratios) to redress the inequality.

Besides careful analysis, equality also involves a decision as to who is going to change and in what way. These decisions will often take from some and give to others. Thus we have the two-pronged essence of action on behalf of equal opportunity: sociological analysis and political struggle.

Questions

1. Briefly summarize the author's point: Under what circumstances does equality of space to pee not mean equality of opportunity to pee? Do you agree or disagree with his analysis?

2. At one point, Professor Molotch offers two possibilities for creating more equality between men and women. One of these options he labels as "liberal"; the other he labels as "conservative." Summarize (briefly) each option. Which option seems (to you) to be more fair? Why?

3. Here's a difficult question: Why does the author use the labels "liberal" and "conservative" to describe the options for change?

20

SOCIALIZATION MESSAGES IN PRIMARY SCHOOLS: AN ORGANIZATIONAL ANALYSIS

Steven Brint, Mary F. Contreras, and Michael T. Matthews

"College Students Think They Are So Special," or so reads a recent newspaper headline. The article under the headline cited research that found that college students today are more self-centered and narcissistic than ever before. The researchers speculated that today's college student's sense of entitlement originates in the messages that these students received as they were growing up—messages which encouraged them to think they were so special.

American students may be more self-centered now than ever before, but just what are the messages they hear in their younger years? Are those messages all about building "self-esteem"?

Brint, Contreras, and Matthews took a multifaceted approach to their study of the messages sent to primary school students; they examined (1) classroom interactions with the teachers, (2) the curriculum, (3) routine classroom practices, (4) schoolwide programs, and (5) the use of public space.

Social commentators and politicians have also had much to say about the schools' role in socialization. Cultural conservatives, such as former Secretary of Education William Bennett, have urged a return to curricula emphasizing "moral virtues," such as honesty, fairness, perseverance, compassion, and courage. In the introduction to his best-selling *The Book of Virtues,* Bennett (1993:11) wrote: "Where do we go to find the material that will help our children in [the] task [of developing moral literacy]? The simple answer is we ... have a wealth of material to draw on—materials that virtually all schools and homes and churches once taught to students for the sake of shaping character. That many no longer do is something this book hopes to change."

In the 1990s many cultural conservatives declared that a "culture war" was flaring in the schools between those who advocated multicultural curricula and the importance of modern values of self-expression and those who hoped to maintain an emphasis on Western history and literature and to reintroduce character training in the classroom (see, e.g.,

"Socialization Messages in Primary Schools: An Organizational Analysis" by Steven Brint, Mary F. Contreras and Michael T. Matthews from *Sociology of Education*, Vol. 74, No. 3 (July, 2001): pp. 157–180). Reprinted by permission of the American Sociological Association and the authors.

Bernstein 1994; Cheney 1987, 1990; N. Glazer 1997; Healey 1996; Hunter 1991, 1994). The concerns of conservative critics helped to spark interest in "character education" curricula, which were adopted by hundreds of school districts during the 1990s (Healy 1996).

But do we really know that socialization messages in the public schools no longer focus on virtues like honesty, fairness, reliability, and responsibility or that they now emphasize the values of cultural diversity, self-esteem, and self-expression? Journalists and politicians may be unreliable guides to answering questions like these because they can be tempted in the nature of their work to rely on anecdotal materials, selectively chosen and presented for dramatic effect. The few recent studies by social scientists have looked at only a limited set of indicators of the schools' role in socialization. Some have concentrated on representations of American heroes in textbooks or on teachers' answers to questions about values they consider important to teach (see, e.g., Farkas and Johnson 1996; Fitzgerald 1979; Frisch 1989; Sharp and Wood 1992; Wong 1991). . . .

The School Socialization Study

Our analysis grew out of a study conducted in 64 classrooms in southern California during the spring and fall of 1998. Follow-up surveys on the use of classroom time were conducted in late 1999 and early 2000. . . . We collected data using three methods: classroom observations, interviews with teachers and principals, and reading of curricular and program materials. . . .

CLASSROOM INTERACTION

Socialization messages are conveyed most directly through interaction in the classroom. Framing this interaction are rules that are intended to identify behavior that is permissible and desirable from behavior that is impermissible or undesirable as defined by the teachers. Our observations of classroom interaction indicate that the great majority of teacher-initiated socialization messages have to do with *orderliness and effort*—in other words, with the operational foundations of work performance.

We coded an average of more than 18 teacher-initiated interaction messages per hour of observation. Approximately three out of four of these messages were related to orderliness in the classroom (see Table 1). These messages reflected the teachers' efforts to quiet the students, to keep them from answering questions without recognition, or to redirect their straying attention to the task at hand. In these classrooms, the teachers frequently quieted students and controlled their movements with observations, such as "you can't be talking and working at the same time."

The next most frequent messages—approximately one out of seven—had to do with work effort. They included teachers' mentions of the students' need to stay on task, finish on time, work faster, and the like. Specific students and entire classes were repeatedly told that they "should be busy." The teachers frequently noted, "I don't see [student's name] working." In two-fifths of the classrooms, the *only* messages we coded during our hour of observation had to do with orderliness and work effort. No other behaviors or values began to approach these two in frequency. These findings support the conclusions of sociologists who have argued that schools as performance-oriented bureaucracies have fundamental interests in order and effort (see, e.g., Cusick 1992; Lortie 1975; Waller 1932). Schools are the first performance-oriented bureaucracies that children encounter, and the great emphasis on orderliness follows directly from their interest in coaxing effort out of "immature workers" in settings where opportunities for distraction are great.

Table 1 Behavior and Value References in One-Hour Observations of 64 Primary School Classrooms

Reference Category	Percentage of Total	N
Basic Organizational Controls		
Orderliness	71	839
Industriousness, hard work	13	147
Regulation of Self and Self's Relation to Others		
Respect, considerateness	3	38
Participation	3	38
Self-direction, autonomy	3	29
Cooperation	2	21
Traditional Moral Virtues		
Fairness, justice	1	15
Responsibility	1	12
Self-control	1	11
Courage	.9	10
Honesty	.6	7
Modern Values		
Individual uniqueness	.4	4
Choice, variety	.3	3
Respect for group differences	.3	3
Respect for own group culture	.2	2

Note: Total references = 1,179; references per observation period = 18.4.

The next most common messages concerned the *regulation of the self and the self's relation to others*. In this category, we included messages related to respect for others, participation, cooperation, self-control, and self-direction. These messages have to do with how others are to be treated and the conditions that require the self to engage others as opposed to acting in its own right. Teachers are interested in helping students control their impulses in ways that allow them to work well with others and, at the same time, to learn to make choices for themselves about how to use their time and solve problems.

A few teachers paid special attention to these issues. Thus, in one second-grade classroom in District A, the teacher encouraged particular students to participate in the discussion by asking them to describe a character in the story the class was reading and emphasized the need for self-direction in managing time and completing work. "You can either keep going or you can stop. You choose," she said to one student. To another student, she said, "You can either draw checks or circles. It's your choice." Other teachers praised students for solving problems by themselves without asking for help and asked students to help others if they had finished their own work. Each of the values related to the regulation of the self and the self's relation to others accounted for approximately 2–3 percent of all the socialization messages that were coded. These messages are comparatively common in primary school classrooms because many children are inclined to follow their personal predilections and need cues about the conditions under which they are expected to act with others and to act alone.

The third most common messages concerned *traditional moral virtues,* including messages about fairness, responsibility, perseverance, courage, and honesty. Each of these values accounted for approximately 1 percent of all the socialization messages that were coded. The teachers were particularly interested in encouraging the students to take responsibility for their actions and to persevere even in the face of difficult work. They were also interested in helping students to take responsibility for solving issues that came up in the classroom—for example, to help resolve conflicts in the classroom. One teacher in District A observed, "Even these second graders need to learn to be responsible for bringing in their homework and for the consequences of their actions." One teacher in District B said, "Fifth graders learn a lot of new concepts, and it can be difficult for students who have learned easily up until then, so it's important to . . . persevere, but don't be too hard on yourself. Don't give up." Issues of honesty and fairness rarely emerged during our classroom observations because discussions about honesty and fairness tend to be provoked by specific events, and these events do not occur every day. In the interviews, the teachers said that incidents related to stealing, cheating, or conflict over perceived favoritism came up periodically during the year and were addressed when they arose.

The least frequent messages had to do with *modern values,* including the values of individual uniqueness and special talent, cultural diversity, choice, and variety. These modern values accounted for well under 1 percent of all the socialization messages that we coded. The values of individual uniqueness and cultural diversity were more likely to come up during specific occasions in the school year than during an ordinary day. If the students were studying about immigration in social studies, for instance, this topic naturally gave rise to discussions about the contributions of different ethnic groups. Stories about exceptional persons often encouraged the teachers to mention the importance of individual uniqueness. In one class, for example, students were reading about the jazz trumpeter Wynton Marsalis, and this story elicited several remarks from the teacher about the special talents of individuals. The teachers were certainly not opposed in principle to modern values, but they had little occasion to bring them up during an ordinary classroom instruction period.

We observed only a few instances—fewer than six in the 64 classrooms—in which the teachers broke away from their instructional focus to discuss moral or behavioral issues. One such discussion had to do with a cheating incident and another with an altercation on the soccer field. Instead, most of the socialization messages were delivered as a running commentary in the context of instructional activities. Thus, the general flavor of classroom life is similar to that of a coaching session in which the coach peppers in comments on the level of individual and group attention and effort as she or he provides instruction on a specific skill. In classrooms, as in coaching, these comments contribute to the pacing of the class, as well as to its moral tone. Many comments about values consisted of brief slogans, such as "Be the captain of your own ship!" and "Go the extra mile!"

Socialization messages tended to be delivered in a neutral manner of mentioning or directing, rather than of criticizing or praising particular students. Mentions of and directions

Table 2 Context of Socialization Messages in 64 California Primary School Classrooms

Context	Percentage of Total Marks ($N = 1,179$)	Percentage of Total Marks Excluding Marks for "Orderliness" ($N = 340$)
Teacher mentions	56	50
Teacher criticizes	18	14
Teacher praises	15	21
Classroom ritual	8	4
Classroom discussion of issues	2	6
Discussion of stories, lessons	2	4

concerning behavior and values were three times more common than either criticism or praise (see Table 2). Many teachers told us that criticism and praise were not necessary because "students know the rules." However, it seems likely that in the inclusive environment of the school, praise may also be avoided for its tendency to create resentment among the nonfavored majority against the favored few, while criticism may be avoided for its tendency to encourage alienation among the nonconforming few against the conforming majority.

The written rules framing interaction in the classroom also emphasized operational fundamentals related to orderliness and work performance. Every teacher had a set of rules that he or she used to set behavioral guidelines. Most teachers posted these rules on their classroom walls, along with lists of the rewards for good behavior and the consequences for misbehavior. The two domains of classroom life that were the most likely to be covered by these rules were "respect for other students" and "following directions." Rules in these domains were found in approximately two-thirds of the classrooms. The next most common rule domain, found in one-third of the classrooms, concerned work effort. Rules

in this domain included "do your work on time," "do all your homework," and "do your best work." In addition, approximately one-quarter of the classrooms had rules requiring students to "respect school property," "respect teachers and principals," or "work quietly." Thus, the six areas most commonly addressed by classroom rules all had to do with operational fundamentals as seen from the perspective of the school authorities: order, work effort, and compliance with school authorities.

THE SUBJECT-MATTER CURRICULUM

The subject-matter curriculum is a second organizational level of schooling in which socialization messages are embedded. Not all curricular materials are strongly inscribed with socialization messages; even in language arts and social studies, many materials are directed less to teaching values than to providing information or awakening a sense of curiosity about the world. Thus, stories may give information about interesting and unusual occupations, such as movie director or environmentalist. They may seek to create a sense of wonder and interest in learning about outer space or unusual animals, for example. Or they may help students understand the world by, for instance, discussing how people find their way around a city.

At the same time, it is clear that many value-related messages *are* incorporated into the language arts and social studies curricula. Our content analysis of the language arts and social studies texts used in the two districts indicated that approximately three-quarters of the stories and lessons included value-relevant messages. It is here that both traditional virtues, such as persistence and responsibility, and modern values, such as appreciating cultural diversity, come most explicitly into play in the life of the classroom.

The value messages found in the language arts and social studies curricula were a blend of the new and the old. All the second-grade texts included many messages that encouraged the students to recognize that people have different special talents, that the country is made up of people from many different backgrounds, that it is important to understand and to appreciate these different cultures, and that we all depend on other people and should learn to work together in a cooperative spirit. In addition to emphasizing these modern values, the second-grade literature texts also included many messages connected to such traditional virtues as the rewards of hard work, persistence, and courage in the face of hardships. These messages were frequently found in adventure stories, such as *Survival at Sea*. The same mixed set of values appeared as dominant themes in the fifth-grade literature text adopted by both public school districts.

In contrast, the fifth-grade social studies text adopted by both districts provided a relatively conventional treatment of American history from the period before European settlement through the Civil War. Themes related to diversity and tolerance, the ways of life of different peoples, and the importance of interpretation from multiple points of view were certainly apparent in sections of this text. Yet

these themes received less attention than did technological changes, trading relations, social customs, and defining historical events that are presumed to be important to all Americans. In the chapters on colonial America, for example, the text included such standard topics as witchcraft in Salem, trade in New England, the Stamp Act, and the ratification of the Constitution.

The appreciation of cultural diversity also came up at times in classroom projects and holiday celebrations. Most teachers in the sample, at a minimum, assigned a project requiring students to trace and discuss their ancestry. Many posted maps with pins representing the ancestral homes of students in their classrooms. Holidays have become an important vehicle for celebrating cultural diversity. Martin Luther King's birthday and Cinco de Mayo serve as opportunities to discuss the achievements of African Americans and Mexican Americans. Most schools now celebrate cultural diversity during the Christmas season as well; the old sentiments of "peace on earth and goodwill to men" have become an entry way to a new outlook, "goodwill to cultures." At Halloween, some teachers ask students to bring in ghost stories from their families' countries of origin. Several of the schools celebrated a separate "International Day" in which ethnic dress and food were featured.

Teachers have many reasons for wanting to encourage students to appreciate their own cultures and those of their classmates. One fifth-grade teacher in District B observed, "I've had some Hispanic students [who] would denigrate their own culture ... who saw Mexican culture as something they want to escape from and not understand." Another said: "It is important to show students not to be afraid of difference. When I taught sixth grade, each student did a report on a different country and prepared some food from that country. They may have thought the food from other countries was strange at first, but trying different things led them to appreciate them more."

Multiculturalism has become so dominant an aspiration in these classrooms that the term is often applied to stories and lessons with traditional themes simply because the main characters are girls or members of minority groups. Some teachers in our sample, for instance, described as "multicultural" both a story about an African American girl who perseveres, in the face of the resistance of her peers and teacher, to play Peter Pan in the class play and a standard assimilation story about a Chinese girl who feels the tension between her Chinese culture and her new American life. This mislabeling suggests that the multicultural orientation of contemporary primary schools is indistinguishable in many ways from the schools' long-standing commitments to achievement and assimilation. Traditional themes remain important, even if they are sometimes mislabeled by teachers as reflecting commitments to cultural diversity.

ROUTINE CLASSROOM PRACTICES

In discussions of classroom socialization, the term *the hidden curriculum* has been used to describe the routine, embedded practices of classroom life that shape children's orientations in ways that are consistent with the demands of adult life. These practices are a third organizational level in which socialization messages are embedded. This curriculum is said to be hidden because, unlike the subject-matter curriculum, it directs students' attention through invisible means, rather than through overt and explicit instruction. Because they are not explicitly stated, the value orientations encouraged by the hidden curriculum must be inferred. Yet there can be little doubt that orientations to the world are shaped as much or more by daily repetition as by didactic practices and exhortation (see, e.g., Bourdieu 1979).

The elements of the hidden curriculum emphasized in classic studies by Dreeben (1968) and Jackson (1968) continue to be important features of schooling. Children still learn the values of individualism and achievement in their daily assignments and frequent evaluations. Children still learn patience from waiting in line for lunch and recess or to drink from a water fountain, and they still learn to cope with evaluation by the constant testing they encounter in the classroom. At the same time, our observations and discussions with teachers suggest that the hidden curriculum of schooling has expanded. In this section, we call attention to three increasingly important routine features of schooling: (1) token economies, (2) group projects, and (3) activity centers and rotations.

Token Economies. The classrooms we studied no longer rely exclusively on obedience to the teachers' authority to gain compliance. Instead, they also rely on symbolic rewards that are convertible into material goods, distributed through a token economy, to encourage approved forms of character and conduct. Strikingly, every teacher in our sample but one used such incentive systems, based on token economies, to motivate desired behavior. In exchange for doing their work on time, keeping out of trouble, and following class rules, individual students and table groups were given points, marbles, stickers, or other tokens that they could eventually trade in for candy, pizza, or class parties. Teachers say that these rewards help them to recognize every student in their classroom "for something" at least several times a month.

Although these token economies directly reflect the importance of behavioral psychology as a control strategy, we believe they ultimately reflect the significance of material rewards and the market economy in American society. Several schools made the connection explicit, by handing out "Greenbucks" or

"Scholar Dollars" that could be accumulated and exchanged later for merchandise. Some teachers explicitly set up a game environment in which the students were "paid" for performing well and "paid" the teacher if they broke a rule. At the end of the week, the totals were counted, and if anyone reached a certain level, the teacher brought in ice cream and candy for all. Rewards, said one second-grade teacher, "are something they get excited about and [are] something they can share with their family."

Group Projects.   Group projects, activity centers, and rotations reflect another new condition of classroom life: The isolated learner in a regimented classroom is no longer the most common presence in school. Group activities played a significant role in the majority of the classrooms we visited. During a school week, table groups of four to six students may discuss their journal entries together, help each other with a difficult exercise, or design and execute a science or social studies project together. For the average teacher in our sample, group learning activities accounted for nearly 20 percent of the instructional time during a typical school week, higher than the amount of time spent on individual seat work. Indeed, only whole-class instruction (accounting for 25–30 percent of the weekly instructional time for the average teacher in our sample) ranked higher in use as an instructional strategy.

Group activities encourage some students to receive the support they need from peers, rather than authorities, and allow other students to develop leadership skills. Many teachers see the need to work cooperatively as being explicitly linked to the work that students will be doing in later life, and some see collateral advantages as well. One fifth-grade teacher in District B said, "I tell them they will have to do this in the future . . . work with all different kinds of people. . . . I ask them: 'How do you think adults are able to work with their peers?' " Another fifth-grade teacher observed, "A lot of other things are interrelated [with group work], including developing integrity and appreciation of individual differences."

Activity Centers.   These teachers also adopted instructional strategies that increased variety and choice during the school week and associated increased variety with higher levels of student engagement. "You have to keep things moving," said one fifth-grade teacher in District A, "or you are going to lose many of them." Activity centers played a role in three-quarters of the classrooms we studied. These centers are places in the classroom that students can choose to go when they have finished their assigned work or through which they can rotate as part of the normal instructional day. The computer may be one activity center; the art table another. A third activity center may be set up to ask students to solve a challenging logical puzzle. In the classrooms that used activity centers, the teachers reported that an average of just over 10 percent of the instructional time during the week was spent in these centers.

Rotations.   Some schools also introduced variety into the classroom through rotations. During rotations, students from one classroom move to the classroom of another teacher who is the school's expert on a particular subject matter—often science, art, or music in which specialized talents are at a premium. In our sample, approximately half the teachers said that their students participated in rotations, usually for only a small part of the instructional week. Even this limited use of rotations is high when compared to the one-teacher-per-class norms of the past.

Nor were these the only ways in which these schools communicated the values of variety and change. To provide students with varied instructional settings, nearly every teacher in our sample also incorporated work in the library and/or computer lab into his or her weekly schedule. In their reading assignments, the teachers also tended to move quickly between genres as a means of increasing variety. Language arts textbooks included a highly varied set of materials, all in relatively short snippets. Units might include a short poem, a news story, a short story, a folk tale, or a scene from a play to perform, but lengthy works were not in evidence.

Like the routines emphasized by early investigators of the hidden curriculum, these new routine practices—token economies, group projects, activity centers, and rotations— encourage distinct orientations to the world and are consistent with the demands of contemporary adult society. Token economies encourage utilitarian motivations and reflect the increasing importance of material incentives as a form of social control. Group projects encourage comfort with collaboration and reflect the increasing collaborative character of work in many middle-class occupations. Activity centers and rotations encourage outlooks favorable to variety and choice and the capacity to move easily between many fast-changing activities. These outlooks are consistent with the fast-paced, multiple task environments that many middle-class adults face in their jobs and with the symbolic environment of mass entertainment and marketing.

SCHOOLWIDE PROGRAMS

Schoolwide programs are a fourth level of school organization in which socialization messages are embedded. The values associated with the schools' efforts in this area reflect a management philosophy that encourages every student to feel a sense of identification with the school and at the same time attempts to maintain order and minimize conflict among students.

The schools used a number of means to encourage a sense of inclusiveness through identification with the behavioral ideals of the school. All the schools provided gift certificates (usually at local supermarkets or restaurants) for students who were nominated by their teachers for exemplary conduct. These certificates were distributed at school assemblies. Six of the eight public school principals said that every student in the school would be recognized "for something" at some time during the year. All the principals emphasized the importance of public recognition for building the self-esteem of students, but it seems likely that creating a sense of identification with the school is even more important as a means of promoting the academic goals of the school and as a way of reducing the number of potentially alienated students. Half the schools provided additional rewards for students who were "caught doing good" by a staff member at any time during the day. These rewards included first-in-line-for-lunch passes, tickets redeemable for prizes, and "caught-doing-good" pencils. A variety of colorful names have been adopted for school programs that reward heroes and heroines of conduct: "Tiger-rifics," "Lion's Pride," 'Thumb's Up," and the like.

If the ideals of participation, respect, and self-esteem were promoted by programs aimed at maximizing students' involvement with the schools' behavioral ideals, other formal programs were used to minimize trouble. All the schools we studied controlled behavior outside the classroom with sanctions as well as rewards. These sanctions were based on a formal set of schoolwide rules barring taunting, physical violence, and the presence of dangerous substances and weapons on school grounds. All but one of the public schools had adopted a formal conflict resolution program, such as "Peace Path," "Peacebuilders," or "Resolving Conflict Creatively." In addition, all the schools participated in a state-sponsored drug education program, known as DARE (Drug Abuse Resistance Education), and all the schools offered "pull-out" counseling programs for students who were identified as being troubled by family, social adjustment, or behavioral problems. The importance of these programs to the schools can be measured by their costs. Each of these programs required extensive teacher training, and each cost the schools several dollars per student.

The principals said that they felt compelled to offer inclusiveness programs and conflict resolution programs because many students were perceived to be unprepared to interact peacefully in the ordered environment of the school. One principal in District A said: "We do have a problem. Children respect each other less and less, and parents are too busy to get involved. When they are asked to intervene, they say, 'I don't have time.' We've had to pick up the pieces. . . . [The parents] work all day. They're tired, and they don't want to have to deal with discipline." Another principal said: "Look at some of the parents we have. They come home at night and say, 'I can't be responsible to feed or take care of children because I'm too stressed.' The neglect of parents like these [is] hindering their children. . . . It's a huge frustration for the schools and . . . sad for all of us." Conflict resolution programs are directly related to the basic organizational interest of the schools in maintaining an orderly environment. From the principals' perspective, other available programs (such as character education curricula) can appear, by contrast, to be unnecessary "frills."

USES OF PUBLIC SPACE

Socialization messages can also be embedded in the uses of public space through visual displays or oral rituals. In the schools we studied, these means were used only infrequently. This low level of use may reflect the desire of schools to avoid public displays of value commitments that may offend parents or taxpayers who are interested primarily in academics or that may encourage cynicism among students.

Apart from the widespread practice of posting classroom rules, few walls were adorned with images and messages that were concerned with values. A small number of classrooms featured pictures of famous Americans who were women or members of minority groups. One room included pictures of athletes and words associated with the values of sports, such as *determination, sportsmanship, courage,* and *resilience.* In addition, principals at two of the schools said they occasionally hung banners on the school grounds that focused on values, such as responsibility and respect, which were illuminated with familiar cartoon characters. Only one school included value messages on the pencils, pins, cups, and T-shirts it sold to students and parents for fund-raising purposes. This school decorated pins with "PRIDE Paws," with "PRIDE" standing for "personal responsibility in daily efforts." This slogan was the school's emblem; it appeared on the school's awards and was, according to the principal, "talked about all the time." Two other principals said that they had included such messages in the past. Instead of attempting to instill adult values, some of the schools appealed to peer values. T-shirts for one school, for instance, were decorated with the motto "Where the cool go to school."

The few oral and verbal rituals connected to socialization tended to encourage deference to authority more than any other behavior or value. Students at all the schools were required, for example, to be quiet during daily announcements by the principals over the public address system. Students stood at attention for daily flag pledges, and many teachers used ritual means of maintaining quiet, such as sounding a bell or raising an index finger. One fifth-grade teacher in District A called out the word "Salami" (short for

"Stop and Look at Me") when he wanted students to pay attention to him. Only a few classrooms and schools engaged in active efforts to build a value consensus through verbal rituals. Two schools used a chant that the students were asked to repeat on occasion in classes and assemblies. One of these chants was called the "Jag Code" (for the school's jaguar mascot): "I am respectful, I am prepared to learn, I take responsibility." The other was, "You can do it if you put your mind to it."

The schools' relative restraint in using public space to promote values may encourage the sense among some critics that schools are doing little in the area of socialization. Uses of public space, after all, are highly visible to outsiders. But this view overlooks the volume and range of socialization messages that are found in every other arena of classroom and school life.

Influences on School Socialization Messages

In this section, we present an analysis of the sources of the socialization messages we found in these 64 classrooms. This analysis emphasizes three themes. The first theme concerns the centrality of the underlying organizational interests of schools. The second theme concerns the ways in which social forces can influence the schools' repertoire of socialization messages. In particular, our analysis suggests two ways in which societal values may enter the school: through social movement activism institutionalized by the state or through the changing expectations of students and their parents based on changes in the organization of adult middle-class lives. The third theme concerns the organizational shaping of these environmental influences. When new values enter the school, they are, we believe, in every case refracted through the prism of the schools' underlying organizational interests.

THE CENTRALITY OF THE SCHOOLS' ORGANIZATIONAL INTERESTS

The organizational interests of schools are shaped by their purposes and the major challenges that schools face. Schools are production-oriented bureaucracies whose clientele are not yet mature and who represent a mix of backgrounds and personality types. These immature and heterogeneous students must work in group settings where distractions loom large. The schools have had long-standing interests in maintaining order and minimizing trouble, derived both from their production orientation and from the immaturity of their clientele. The schools' emphasis on energetic and persistent hard work follows from the underlying purpose of schooling—the transmission of school knowledge in a fashion as efficient and effective as these conditions of instruction allow.

In recent years, schools have developed new interests. Clearly, schools were not always interested in celebrating the contributions of every single student to the classroom and school community. Indeed, in the past, disinterested and marginal students were actively discouraged from continuing with their schooling (Tyack 1974; Tyack and Hansot 1982). In all likelihood, as students spend more years in school, schools experience greater incentives to encourage the commitment of all students. In addition, the philosophy of progressive education (which arose, not incidentally, at a time when secondary schooling was becoming the norm) helped to convince educators that the interest of students must be captured, rather than commandeered. This philosophy has led to an increasing emphasis on finding ways to avoid boredom in the classroom. Schools also developed interests, over the course of recent generations, in creating a sense of identification between all students and the school community. In part, such identifications help to reduce alienation and therefore the potential for trouble. In part, they may also be valued as a means of improving the achievement orientation of socially or academically marginal students.

Many of the socialization messages expressed most frequently in our study reflect this set of historically developed organizational interests. The classroom interaction data are well explained by the schools' long-standing priorities on the maximization of order and industriousness. Schoolwide conflict resolution programs reinforce these values while responding to a perceived decrease in parental discipline. The emphases on variety and choice we found in classroom practices reflect the newer priorities of schools in capturing the interest of all students. The emphases in schoolwide programs on respect for others, participation, and building self-esteem reflect the schools' interest in encouraging identifications between students and the school community.

SOURCES OF SOCIETAL INFLUENCE

Not all the findings of the study, however, can be accounted for by an emphasis on the centrality of the schools' underlying organizational priorities. This is particularly true of many of the behavioral priorities and values we found in both the subject-matter curriculum and the "new hidden curriculum" of the schools we studied. To explain these findings, it is necessary to turn attention away from the organizational interests of the schools to examine the ways in which values originating outside the schools are incorporated by the schools.

Our analysis suggests that new values enter the schools in one of two ways: (1) through the successful advocacy of social-movement and educational activists supported by governmental officials and (2) through the changing experiences and expectations of middle-class citizens as mediated by the popularity of new pedagogical philosophies. The values associated with multiculturalism are a good example of the first means by which new values enter the schools. Many of the values associated with the newer elements of the hidden curriculum, such as the use of token economies and group projects, are good examples of the second. We use these examples to illustrate the two processes through which we hypothesize that new values and behavioral priorities are incorporated into the schools.

Process 1: Educational Activism Institutionalized with State Support. The background forces encouraging multiculturalism in the 1970s and 1980s are clear. One important factor is that the non-Hispanic white proportion of the population dropped from 90 percent to 75 percent between 1950 and 1990. In many urban centers, people of color now make up the majority or the near-majority of the population. Another important factor is globalization. East Asian, European, and North American firms are tied together through complex networks of joint ownership, joint capitalization, and franchising and licensing agreements. Financial markets have become fully internationalized among the wealthier countries, with changes in one stock exchange affecting the other major exchanges. Travel and tourism continue to grow as part of the global economy, and other forms of International exchange—from scholarly conferences to international peacekeeping forces—have also become commonplace. Continued global integration means the growth of trade and exchange in other regions of the world (see, e.g., Brint 1998).

These forces of demographic change and globalization created conditions favorable to multicultural, rather than monocultural, outlooks. However, to be successful, social movements must mobilize and become institutionalized. Multiculturalism was, in its early days, very much the child of the civil rights and feminist movements. Traditions of activism and generational conflict, which were carried over into the educational arena, played a critical role in its rise. As Gates (1992:19), the literary scholar and a participant in these conflicts, wrote: "Ours was the generation that took over buildings in the late 1960s and demanded black and women's studies programs and now . . . has come back to challenge the traditional [curriculum]."

It is important to emphasize that educational movements are rarely successful unless they eventually receive the support of the state. In the case of multiculturalism, institutionalization occurred both informally and under the aegis of the state. By the late 1980s, many U.S. states (beginning with California in 1987) added principles in their curricular guidelines that required multicultural and gender-fair perspectives. By the mid-1990s, a near-majority of states had adopted such guidelines (Rosenfelt 1994).

Multiculturalism is not the only recent social movement to become incorporated into classroom socialization practices. The "character education" movement, although much less successful than the multicultural movement, has similarly been promoted by educational activists—indeed, partly as a reaction to the schools' emphasis on diversity—and it, too, has relied on governmental support in those states in which it has been most successful (S. Glazer 1996).

Process 2: New Practices Reflecting Changes in Middle-Class Lives.   If we take as a premise that in relation to values training, schools are essentially middle-class institutions, we can see how new features of the hidden curriculum may be connected to changes in the organization of middle-class adults' lives. Whereas the classic elements of the hidden curriculum prepared students for adult lives of individualist achievement and bureaucratic regulation, the new elements prepare students for a "dual society" that is organized along market and bureaucratic lines in its work

activities and along entertainment and consumerist lines in its leisure activities. Classroom token economies are clearly connected to the dominant incentives offered by the surrounding market economy. Group projects are connected to the collaborative nature of much contemporary work, particularly in professional and managerial occupations. And, of course, the enjoyment of variety and choice are important features of the consumer economy.

We hypothesize that new routine practices typically enter the schools in the following way: As society changes, children and their parents develop new expectations. The schools find it advantageous to address these expectations in order to maintain commitment. Pedagogical practices that resonate with these expectations, therefore, have a greater chance of gaining a foothold in the schools than those that do not. Thus, broad social changes in the organization of middle-class lives are typically carried into classrooms through the popularity of pedagogical movements with which they show a close affinity. From this perspective, token economies may ultimately reflect the importance of market rewards in American life, but they are encouraged more immediately by the influence of behavioral psychology in contemporary educational philosophies. Similarly, the rise of joint and collaborative activities in adult work lives may be the ultimate condition from which new expectations of the importance of teamwork arise, but the popularity of "cooperative learning" philosophies is the immediate source of the schools' recent emphasis on group learning opportunities.

THE ORGANIZATIONAL FILTER

New ideas and values have a chance to become popular only if they fit or, at least, do not significantly threaten the organizational priorities of schools. Conflict resolution programs address issues that are close to the fundamental interests of schools in minimizing trouble, and they have consequently become more popular than many other programs that are potentially available to schools. Similarly, an emphasis on building self-esteem can help to make every student feel a part of the school community, another fundamental organizational interest in today's public schools. By contrast, the emphasis of conservative reformers on traditional values strikes a less resonant chord from the perspective of the schools' main organizational interests because this emphasis does not necessarily lead to the improvement of order, the minimization of trouble, or a more inclusive level of identification with the school community.

Schools also tend to moderate the force of social activism in line with their interests in orderliness and getting all students to identify with the school. If one considers the range of ways in which multiculturalism could have been embedded in the schools, it is clear that it has been institutionalized only in a limited form. An extensive form of institutionalization may involve using multicultural material in all aspects of the curriculum. It may involve advocacy of the doctrine of cultural relativism or even of the doctrine of European whites as oppressors. (For a study of challenges based on such alternative forms, see Binder 2000.) It may also involve programs to address differences in the learning styles of members of different groups. In the classrooms we visited, it has meant none of these things. Instead, support for multiculturalism (and the underlying value of cultural diversity) has been expressed in one or two class projects a year about ethnic origins and minority achievers, a handful of stories and lessons about minority cultures or nonwhite characters, and cross-cultural holiday celebrations.

In the limited form in which it has been institutionalized, multiculturalism is far from a divisive influence in the schools. Instead, it encourages an outlook of inclusiveness that fits well with the schools' desire to encourage all students to identify with the school community. Through multiculturalism, the ethnic and

national-origin differences among students can be both acknowledged and reconciled with two other principles that are frequently expressed in contemporary school discourse—"everyone is special in his or her own way" and "underneath our differences, we share many things."

Under these circumstances, it would be surprising if a significant conflict existed in the schools between advocates of multicultural education and advocates of traditional values. And, in fact, we found virtually no evidence of such a "culture war" in our sample population. When we divided the 64 teachers into three groups—"traditional-values conservatives," "multicultural liberals," and "combiners"—on the basis of their responses to all our interview questions, we found slightly more traditional-values conservatives than multicultural liberals, but 80 percent of the teachers fell into the group who were comfortable combining the two emphases.

Discussion

In this concluding section, we evaluate the images of school socialization messages held by cultural conservatives and critical social theorists. We then describe a new way of thinking about school socialization messages that emphasizes not the conflict between traditional virtues and modern values, but the modification and blending of the two. We also discuss a problem we observed in the way values are communicated in the schools. This problem has to do with redefinitions of value concepts along lines suggested by the schools' organizational interests.

THE BLENDING OF OLD AND NEW MESSAGES

Our analysis suggests that the advocacy of many traditional values has not been lost in today's schools. Such traditional virtues as hard work and responsibility continue to be at least as important as modern values of diversity, teamwork, variety, and choice. When we asked the teachers in our sample how they would rank the importance of seven frequently mentioned purposes of schooling, for example, they ranked "developing character traits like responsibility and hard work" higher on a 10-point scale than *any other* activity of schools, including "developing skills and knowledge in curriculum areas" (see Table 3). Moreover, demands for orderliness and work effort clearly continue to dominate teacher-initiated interaction with students in classroom instruction.

At the same time, it is fair to say that not all traditional virtues remain equally important in today's schools. Those who have lamented the decline in the teaching of values in American schools have usually been concerned with three sets of values that once found a prominent place in school readers and everyday instruction in the schools: (1) Judeo-Christian

ethical values, which included honesty, fairness, kindness, considerateness, and concern for the less fortunate; (2) civic values, which included patriotism, bravery, law-abidingness, and participation in community and civic life; and (3) entrepreneurial values, which included industriousness, the wise use of time and resources, reliability, planning for the future, responsibility, and the capacity for self-directed activity. This cluster of values has been described as reflecting the significance of Protestant, republican, and entrepreneurial influences in the nation-building efforts of elites in 19th-century America (Meyer, Tyack, Nagel, and Gordon 1979; Tyack and Hansot 1982).

Assuming that this characterization is correct, the findings of this study suggest that certain virtues that have been historically associated with the entrepreneurial ethos—hard work, responsibility, reliability, self-control, individualism, and self-direction—remain important in today's schools, but that Judeo-Christian ethical virtues and republican civic virtues have declined in importance. These

Table 3 Teachers' Ratings of Selected School Priorities, by Level of Importance, on a 10-Point Scale (percentage; $N = 64$)

Characteristic	Rating		
	10 (High)	8–9	7 or Below (Low)
Developing character traits like hard work and responsibility	77	18	5
Developing knowledge and skills in curricular areas	63	31	6
Developing children's self-esteem	59	33	8
Helping children to learn to appreciate other people's cultures	50	31	19
Helping children to express themselves well in written work	44	50	6
Helping children to express themselves orally	36	52	12
Developing children's interests in nonacademic curricular and extracurricular activities	11	47	42

trends may reflect, as some have argued, the declining influence of the dominant status group of Protestant-republican nation builders on the ideas of school administrators and the rising influence of bureaucratic authority (Tyack and Hansot 1982). The decline of republican civic virtues may also reflect, to some degree, the movement from a "heroic" to a "prosaic" stage of nationalism in the United States and other advanced societies (Kamens 1992).

Although it is clear that teachers are active in maintaining order and work discipline in their classrooms, we are nevertheless skeptical of the portraits of the classroom "disciplinary regime" offered by some critical social theorists who have been influenced by the work of Foucault (1965, 1977). By concentrating exclusively on classroom restrictions and work demands, these critics miss both the indulgent qualities of today's classrooms and the range of other values conveyed in the schools. In the classrooms we studied, teachers maintained control with a light touch more often than not, and they were extremely sensitive to the role that schooling can play in damaging students' self-esteem. The modern primary school classroom, with its many activities, group projects, constant change, and frequent celebrations, can be described as a regimented space only by rigorously limiting attention to one part of the whole story.

What, then, would be a more accurate characterization? In the minds of most teachers, new values do not replace or compete with older values. For this reason, the dominant socialization ideology of the schools should be characterized neither as "traditional" nor as "modern" but, rather, as a blend of the two. It can be accurately described as "pluralist neotraditionalism"—pluralist because it embraces cultural differences, traditionalist because it endorses a number of traditional virtues, but neotraditionalist because some traditional virtues have lost prominence (see Table 4).

The routine practices of classrooms similarly show a blending of the old and the new. The old world of bureaucratic organization and individual achievement clearly finds a place in these classrooms—universalistic standards, specialized competencies, and individual achievement are as important as ever. Yet new emphases on material rewards for conformity, group work, choice, and variety are also evident.

Our analysis shows further that different socialization messages are conveyed at different levels of classroom and school organization. Messages originating in the organizational priorities of the school are expressed primarily through teacher-initiated interactions, through the classroom rules framing these interactions, and through schoolwide programs. These messages emphasize orderliness, hard work, respect for others, and active participation. They reflect organizational priorities that have to do with the maintenance of order, the minimization of trouble, the encouragement of work effort, and the promotion of a sense of identification with the school by all students. Overlaid on these organizational priorities are value messages originating in the broader society that are expressed primarily through the subject-matter curriculum and through the routine practices of everyday classroom life. These messages combine emphases on some traditional virtues, such as persistence in the face of adversity and personal responsibility, with such modern values as appreciation of cultural diversity and delight in variety and choice. For new societal values to be accepted by the schools, they must be consistent with the fundamental organizational priorities of the schools. Curricular emphases on cultural diversity are, for example, only one way to promote the schools' interest in inclusiveness, but they are consistent with these interests and can therefore be incorporated, provided that they do not threaten other fundamental priorities.

Table 4 Elements of "Pluralist Neo-Traditionalism"

Pluralism	Neo-	Traditionalism
New interest in cultural awareness in a diverse society	*Diminished Values* Judeo-Christian ethics	Continued emphasis on orderliness
New emphasis on the ability to "get along with" people unlike oneself	Civic-nationalist values	Continued emphasis on hard work, industriousness
	Transmuted Values	
New emphasis on ability to cooperate with others on joint projects	Respect: from kindness, politeness to zones of noninterference	Continued emphasis on responsibility
		Continued emphasis on the wise use of time and resources
	Self-esteem: from based primarily on accomplishments to based primarily on support from adults	Continued emphasis on self-discipline, self-control
	New Means of Control Cognitive direction, rather than praise and criticism	
	Token economy systems as supplements to personal control by teachers	

THE ORGANIZATIONAL REDEFINITION OF VALUE CONCEPTS

If there are problems with the socialization messages conveyed in contemporary schooling, these problems have little to do, we believe, with the decline of traditional moral messages or with a contest between traditional virtues and modern values. Instead, we would highlight an entirely different problem, one that is consistent with the organizational analysis we have proposed here. Because schools address behavior and values in ways that are strongly influenced by their organizational priorities, many distortions are possible in their interpretation and use of value concepts. In our study, we saw a number of examples of such distortions. Among the most significant examples were the schools' uses of the concepts of citizenship, self-esteem, and respect. We believe that societal understandings of these concepts have been influenced—not always positively—by the redefinitions given to them in the school environment. Using the concepts of citizenship, self-esteem, and respect, we present illustrations of what we mean by the schools' redefinition of value concepts and indicate why we think it is a problem.

Virtually every teacher we interviewed said that schools should be teaching good citizenship. When we pressed the teachers to discuss the meaning of citizenship, however, fewer than 15 percent mentioned the active side of citizenship—voicing views on public issues and participating in political life. Many more teachers gave school-based definitions of citizenship that emphasized "acting responsibly" and "getting along with others." Other frequent definitions of citizenship referred to "working hard" and "showing respect for others." Thus, the definitions of citizenship that most of the teachers gave were closely related to the schools' interests in maintaining order and work effort and minimizing trouble. Several teachers made this connection explicit: "It's important for public schools to develop respectful . . . hardworking citizens," said one fifth-grade teacher in District A." [At this school], students who are good . . . respectful citizens are given 'Good Bear' tickets." More troubling still were the 11 teachers who emphasized the most passive forms of citizenship: following rules; respecting authority; and believing in the laws, the government, and the Constitution. Thus, one second-grade teacher in District A said, "Yes, it's important for schools to help students become good citizens. Schools need to teach rules and that you have to follow the rules. . . . Schools [follow] guidelines. Students need to follow guidelines."

The most common school definitions of citizenship contrast sharply—and, in our view, inappropriately—with accepted definitions of citizenship in democratic political theory. These latter definitions emphasize attentiveness to public affairs and active participation in community and political life, including protest, when necessary, in addition to the specific obligations citizens owe to the state.

The great majority of teachers we interviewed thought that the development of children's self-esteem was an essential purpose of schooling (see also Meyer 1987). It is clear that most teachers no longer believe that self-esteem comes exclusively from meeting the challenges of the external environment. Nor, however, do they fully adopt the therapeutic model of self-esteem so often ridiculed by cultural conservatives—the view that self-esteem develops solely from regular attention to children's feelings, combined with strong and

uncritical support from adults. Instead, teachers indicate some confusion about the relative importance of validating accomplishments; many think that meeting challenges is important to self-esteem but less important than feeling the support of others. Thus, at an extreme, a fifth-grade teacher in District B said, "When I concentrate on doing math, I don't get as far as when I concentrate on doing self-esteem and then doing math."

Again, we believe that the schools' interests have led to a subtle redefinition of an important concept. Schools have an interest in developing commitment among their students. As one consequence of this interest, many teachers now attempt to recognize every student "for something" at least a few times a month, and many principals attempt to recognize every student "for something" at least once during the year. Confidence-building activities and recognition "for something" may help to build a sense of commitment to the classroom community and the school, but they are less likely to help students build a durable sense of self-confidence than a mix of support and the successful accomplishment of challenging tasks.

Perhaps more than any other concept, respect has become the dominant ethical touchstone in contemporary schooling. It is used constantly by school authorities to describe how students are expected to behave toward one another. Only a few teachers, however, continue to emphasize considerateness, the just appreciation of the qualities of others or other ceremonial aspects of respect. One second-grade teacher in District B who did said, "I would like them to act kindly to one another, and I remind them what are appropriate things to say to a person, like 'please' and 'thank you.'. . . Consideration is very important, and it is one of the easiest traits to model."

Instead, for most teachers respect is the expectation that students will not taunt or bother others, will keep their hands to themselves, and will defer to authority. In this sense, the meaning of respect has also been redefined by the schools' organizational priorities; it has become another means of minimizing trouble and maintaining order. A second-grade teacher in District B told us, for example, that "the issue of respect comes up continuously" in her class: "Students will be physical with each other, touching, kicking, hitting, taking up others' personal space." Because the term *respect* suggests qualities of considerateness and the just appreciation of others, its use allows the schools to attach an aura of thoughtful regard to their underlying interest in avoiding conflict. Terms like *civilly minimal attention, zones of noninterference,* and *deference to authority* would be more accurate than *respect* to describe the actual ethical expectations of many of today's schools.

References

Bennett, William J. 1993. *The Book of Virtues.* New York: Simon & Schuster.

Bernstein, Richard. 1994. *Dictatorship of Virtue: Multiculturalism and the Battle for America's Future.* New York: Alfred A. Knopf.

Binder, Amy. 2000. "Why Do Some Curricular Challenges Work While Others Do Not? The Case of Three Afrocentric Challenges." *Sociology of Education* 73:69–91.

Bourdieu, Pierre. 1979. *Outline of a Theory of Practice.* Cambridge, England: Cambridge University Press.

Brint, Steven. 1998. *Schools and Societies.* Thousand Oaks, CA: Pine Forge Press.

Cheney, Lynne V. 1987. *American Memory: A Report on the Humanities in the Nation's Public Schools.* Washington, DC: National Endowment for the Humanities.

———. 1990. *Tyrannical Machines: A Report on Educational Policies Gone Wrong and Our Best Hopes for Setting Them Right.* Washington, DC: National Endowment for the Humanities.

Cusick, Philip. 1992. *The Educational System: Its Nature and Logic.* New York: McGraw-Hill.

Dreeben, Robert. 1968. *On What Is Learned in School.* Reading, MA: Addison-Wesley.

Farkas, Steve, and Jean Johnson. 1996. *Given the Circumstances: Teachers Talk about Public Education Today.* New York: Public Agenda.

Fitzgerald, Frances. 1979. *America Revised: History Textbooks in the 20th Century.* Boston: Little-Brown.

Foucault, Michel. 1965. *Madness and Civilization: A History of Insanity in the Age of Reason,* New York: Pantheon Books.

———. 1977. *Discipline and Punish.* New York: Pantheon Books.

Frisch, Michael. 1989. "American History and the Structures of Collective Memory: A Modest Exercise in Empirical Iconography." *Journal of American History* 75:1142–55.

Gates, Henry Louis, Jr. 1992. *Loose Canons: Notes on the Culture Wars.* New York: Oxford University Press.

Glazer, Nathan. 1997. *We Are All Multiculturalists Now.* Cambridge, MA: Harvard University Press.

Glazer, Sarah. 1996. "Teaching Values." Pp. 531–47 in *CQ Researcher 1996.* Washington, DC: Congressional Quarterly.

Healey, Melissa. 1996, May 28. "Concerned Parents Push Character Movement." *Los Angeles Times,* Pp. A1 ff.

Hunter, James Davison. 1991. *Culture Wars.* New York: Basic Books.

———. 1994. *Before the Shooting Begins: Searching for Democracy in America's Culture War.* New York: Free Press.

Jackson, Philip W. 1968. *Life in Schools.* Troy, MO: Holt, Rinehart & Winston.

Kamens, David. 1992. "Variant Forms: Cases of Countries with Distinct Curricula." Pp. 74–83 in *School Knowledge for the Masses,* edited by John W. Meyer, David H. Kamens, and Aaron Benavot. London: Falmer Press.

Lortie, Dan. 1975. *Schoolteacher.* Chicago: University of Chicago Press.

Meyer, John W. 1987. "Self and the Life Course: Institutionalization and Its Effects." Pp. 242–60 in *Institutional Structure: Constituting State, Society and the Individual,* edited by George M. Thomas, John W. Meyer, Francisco O. Ramirez, and John Boli. Newbury Park, CA: Sage.

Meyer, John W., David Tyack, Joanne Nagel, and Audri Gordon. 1979. "Public Education as Nation-Building in America, 1870–1930." *American Journal of Sociology* 85:591–613.

Rosenfelt, Deborah S. 1994. "'Definitive' Issues: Women's Studies, Multicultural Education and Curriculum Transformation in Policy and Practice in the United States." *Women's Studies Quarterly* 22:26–41.

Sharp, Patricia, and Randy M. Wood. 1992. "Moral Values: A Study of Selected Third and Fifth Grade Reading and Social Studies Textbooks." *Religion and Public Education* 19:143–53.

Tyack, David B. 1974. *The One Best System.* Cambridge, MA: Harvard University Press.

Tyack, David B., and Elizabeth Hansot. 1982. *Managers of Virtue: Public School Leadership in America, 1820–1980.* New York: Basic Books.

Waller, Willard. 1932. *The Sociology of Teaching.* New York: John Wiley & Sons.

Willis, Paul. 1979. *Learning to Labour: How Working-Class Kids Get Working-Class Jobs.* Westmead, England: Saxon House.

Wong, Sandra. 1991. "Evaluating the Context of Textbooks: Public Interest and Professional Authority." *Sociology of Education* 64:11–18.

Questions

1. In the introduction to this article, I mentioned recent research which suggests that the contemporary emphasis of self-esteem training has led to college students being more self-centered than previous generations of students. Based on what you read in this article, are students' experiences in primary school partly responsible for college students' self-centeredness?

2. Some critics have asserted that today's schools spend too much time on such things as "cultural diversity" and not enough on such traditional values as honesty, fairness and respect for others. Based on what you read in this article, do you agree or disagree with these critics?

3. What is the "hidden agenda" of the primary schools studied by Brint and his colleagues?

21

"HOW CAN YOU DO IT?"

Dirty Work and the Challenge of Constructing a Positive Identity

Blake E. Ashford and Glen E. Kreiner

One of the first questions that adults ask of people they meet is, "So, what do you do for a living?" It's a crucial question because one's occupation, in big part, determines how much respect and deference one is owed. We may want to think that we treat everyone equally, but most people will treat a judge differently than they treat a truck driver.

Dirty work is work that others regard as "disgusting or degrading." As you read this article, think about the ways in which people who do dirty work cope with the stigma of their occupations.

I have this question lots of times: "How can I take it?" They ask if I'm calm when I bury people. If you stop and think, a funeral is one of the natural things in the world . . . I enjoy it very much, especially in summer (a gravedigger, quoted in Terkel, 1975: 661).

Oil field trash and damn proud of it (from a T-shirt worn by workers on an oil rig, courtesy of Roger Mayer, personal communication).

Everett Hughes (1951) invoked the term *dirty work* to refer to tasks and occupations that are likely to be perceived as disgusting or degrading. Hughes (1962) observed that society delegates dirty work to groups who act as agents on society's behalf, and that society then stigmatizes these groups, effectively disowning and disavowing the work it has mandated. As we

will argue, group members are seen to personify the dirty work such that they become, literally, "dirty workers."

This phenomenon raises a provocative issue for organizational behavior. As we discuss later, identity research indicates that people typically seek to see themselves in a positive light, and this positive sense of self is largely grounded in socially important and salient roles—including occupations—and how those roles are perceived by others. Thus, given the stigma of dirty work, it seems likely that dirty workers would have a very difficult time constructing a positive sense of self, at least in the workplace. However, abundant qualitative research from a wide variety of occupations indicates that people performing dirty work tend to retain relatively *high* occupational esteem and pride (e.g., Emerson & Pollner, 1976; Gold, 1964; Heinsler, Kleinman, & Stenross, 1990; Hong & Duff, 1977; McIntyre, 1987; Meara, 1974; Perry, 1978; Simpson & Simpson, 1959; Thompson, 1991; Wacquant, 1995). This creates a puzzling research question that we attempt to answer:

> How do members of dirty work occupations seek and secure social affirmation for what they do when society tends to deny them affirmation?

Unfortunately, just as dirty work has been marginalized in society, so too has it been neglected in the organizational literature. But the study of dirty work and how dirty workers attempt to resolve the identity puzzle has much to teach organizational scholars about the negotiation of meaning in the workplace. As Hughes concludes in a retrospective commentary on occupational research, "If a certain problem turned up in one occupation, it was nearly certain to turn up in all" (1970: 149). It is precisely because the need for edifying meaning and identity is often so raw in stigmatized occupations that we can learn a great deal about the social construction of meaning from the experiences of dirty workers.

Our discussion focuses primarily on the occupation or workgroup level of analysis rather than the individual or organization level, because the stigma of dirty work is typically a group-level issue. We examine how members of dirty work occupations (particularly of low prestige) collectively attempt to secure positive meaning in the face of pervasive stigmas. Thus, we focus on mechanisms that appear to be shared by members of a given occupation rather than on idiosyncratic mechanisms. We argue that the stigma of dirtiness often fosters relatively "strong" occupational and work-group cultures—that is, widely shared and deeply held systems of values, beliefs, and norms (Trice & Beyer, 1993)—with attendant ideologies and "social weighting practices" (i.e., selective social comparisons and differential weighting of outsiders' views). These ideologies and practices serve to protect the occupation/workgroup members from the identity

threat that the stigma represents; thus, we can view them as a collective resource that members draw upon, enact, and affirm through their daily actions to enhance the meaningfulness of their work (Beyer, 1981).[1] We argue that the outcome of this process is work role identification, where the dirty workers define themselves at least partly in terms of the occupation. . . .

The Nature of Dirty Work

In this section we explore the meaning and social significance of dirty work.

DEFINING DIRTY WORK

Physical, Social, and Moral Taint. In Hughes' original formulation, work could be "dirty" in one of several ways:

> It may be simply physically disgusting. It may be a symbol of degradation, something that wounds one's dignity. Finally, it may be dirty work in that it in some way goes counter to the more heroic of our moral conceptions. (1951: 319)

Hughes subsequently defined dirty work more succinctly as tasks that are "physically, socially or morally" (1958:122) tainted but did not elaborate upon these terms. Later researchers who invoked the dirty work concept seldom defined it explicitly, but their applications generally were consistent with this seminal notion of physical, social, or moral taint.

Consistent with Hughes and with subsequent research on dirty work, we assume that

---

[1]However, it is important to note that meaningful work is not necessarily satisfying work, although the two tend to be correlated (Hackman & Oldham, 1980). Dirty workers may come to view their work as inherently significant and honorable and yet remain dissatisfied with various job facets. Indeed, as we will argue, the attribution of meaningfulness may at times *depend* on perceiving aspects of work as unpleasant (e.g., doing dirty work indicates toughness and self-sacrifice).

the physical, social, and moral dimensions exhaust the domain of sources of taint. However, to enhance the conceptual rigor of Hughes' classification of dirty work, we offer two criteria for each of the three forms of taint. We derived these criteria inductively from our reading of a diverse array of research on dirty work and occupational stereotypes.

Physical taint occurs where an occupation is either directly associated with garbage, death, effluent, and so on (e.g., butcher, janitor, chimney sweep, exterminator, funeral director, proctologist) or is thought to be performed under particularly noxious or dangerous conditions (e.g., miner, soldier, farmhand, sweatshop worker, firefighter, dentist). Social taint occurs where an occupation involves regular contact with people or groups that are themselves regarded as stigmatized (what Page [1984] refers to as a "courtesy stigma"; e.g., prison guard, AIDS worker, police detective, psychiatric ward attendant, public defender, social worker) or where the worker appears to have a servile relationship to others (e.g., shoe shiner, customer complaints clerk, butler, maid). Moral taint occurs where an occupation is generally regarded as somewhat sinful or of dubious virtue (e.g., exotic dancer, pawnbroker, tattoo artist, psychic, casino manager) or where the worker is thought to employ methods that are deceptive, intrusive, confrontational, or that otherwise defy norms of civility (e.g., bill collector, tabloid reporter, telemarketer, private investigator, police interrogator).

Of course, the boundaries between the physical, social, and moral dimensions are inherently fuzzy, and many occupations appear to be tainted on multiple dimensions. Examples include hospice workers (physical and social), prostitutes (physical and moral), bounty hunters (social and moral), and executioners (physical, social, and moral).

There are two important provisos to this typology. First, "dirtiness" is a social construction: it is not inherent in the work itself or the

workers but is imputed by people, based on necessarily subjective standards of cleanliness and purity (cf., Ball, 1970). We reserve the terms *taint, dirtiness, stigma,* and so forth for widespread (i.e., societal) social constructions. Second, the common denominator among tainted jobs is not so much their specific attributes but the visceral repugnance of people to them. Indeed, it is precisely because the occupations of, say, butcher and funeral director or prison guard and social worker evoke the same reaction—despite their obvious differences in job design and context—that the construct of dirty work is so intriguing. People ask funeral directors, "How can you do it?" just as surely as they do butchers.

Occupational Prestige. While most people's implicit schema of occupations would not combine butchers and funeral directors or prison guards and social workers, a dimension that cuts across the three forms of taint and draws on common schemas is that of *occupational prestige.* This concept has a long history in the sociological literature as a composite of status, power, quality of work, education, and income (Treiman, 1977). Prestige scores capture societal perceptions of the differential evaluations or rankings of occupations (Dunkerley, 1975) and have been found to be highly reliable across respondents, locales, and time (Fossum & Moore, 1975; Sawinski & Domanski, 1991). This perceptual basis makes occupational prestige particularly appropriate for our classification scheme, in that it represents enduring and deeply embedded social perceptions of various types of work and, thereby, likely affects the social construction of occupations.

Crossing the three forms of taint with two levels of occupational prestige (relatively low and relatively high) produces the 3 × 2 classification scheme of dirty work occupations in Table 1. Of course, because taint reduces prestige, these dimensions are not independent, and most dirty work occupations have relatively

Table 1 Classifying Dirty Work Occupations[a]

Primary Taint	Occupational Prestige	
	Relatively Low	Relatively High
Physical		
—Garbage, death, effluent, etc.	• Butcher (32)	• Funeral director (52)
—Noxious conditions	• Miner (26)	• Dentist (70)
Social		
—Regular contact with stigmatized others	• Prison guard (guard) (22)	• Social worker (52)
—Servile relationship	• Shoe shiner (bootblack) (9)	• NA[b]
Moral		
—Sinful or dubious virtue	• Exotic dancer (NA)	• Casino manager (NA)
—Deceptive, intrusive, confrontational, etc., methods	• Bill collector (26)	• Police interrogator (police) (48)

[a]Cell entries are illustrative—not exhaustive. Occupational prestige scores are derived from the National Opinion Research Center (NORC, 1989). Scores range from a low of 9 (bootblack) to a high of 82 (physician). The occupational names shown in parentheses are the actual names used by NORC.

[b]A servile relationship is likely to severely reduce the status element of prestige.

low prestige. Although those in both high- and low-prestige occupations are faced with the challenge of constructing an esteem-enhancing identity, our analysis will focus primarily on relatively low-prestige occupations; their lack of a "status shield" (Stenross & Kleinman, 1989) to buffer incumbents from the social assaults of others makes the challenge doubly difficult. Further, because we are attempting to construct a general model of how dirty workers respond to stigma, we emphasize similarities rather than differences between responses to the three forms of taint. We believe, however, that the 3 × 2 classification scheme provides a useful means of outlining the wide scope and variety of dirty work occupations. Later, we briefly consider differences in identity dynamics among the three forms of taint.

THE SOCIAL SIGNIFICANCE OF DIRT

Douglas's (1966) conceptual work on purity and pollution helps explain the sociological significance of physical, social, and moral taint.

Based on a review of ethnographic research on the cultures of a variety of industrialized and nonindustrialized nations, Douglas argues that societies equate cleanliness with goodness and dirtiness with badness, such that cleanliness and dirtiness assume moral overtones. In this respect, physical and social taint also carry some of the stigma of moral taint. Because dirt threatens the sanctity of cleanliness, it is cast as taboo, and societies strive to separate what is clean from what is dirty.

Consequently, people who must deal with pollution—who perform dirty work—tend to become "stigmatized"—that is, society projects the negative qualities associated with dirt onto them so that they are seen as dirty workers. Hughes (1962) argues further that it is precisely because dirty workers handle the distasteful tasks that are necessary for the effective functioning of society that others can continue to regard themselves as clean and, therefore, superior. Attributing dirtiness to others effectively devalues them and enables one to ignore a necessary and otherwise unavoidable aspect of one's role set (Ashforth & Humphrey, 1995).

We emphasize that dirty work frequently is *not* viewed by societies as unimportant or trivial. The stigma comes from the view of the work as distasteful if not disgusting, as necessary but polluting—thus, according to Douglas (1966), as threatening to the moral order. Although people may applaud certain dirty work as noble (e.g., counseling the terminally ill), they generally remain psychologically and behaviorally distanced from that work and those who do it, glad that it is someone else. In short, the taint affects people's relationship with the dirty workers, even while they may applaud the workers.[2]

The Challenge of Constructing an Esteem-Enhancing Identity

In this section we argue that people seek esteem-enhancing or positive self-definitions, including occupational identity, but that the stigma of dirty work renders this goal problematic for dirty workers. Nonetheless, research suggests that dirty workers do not tend to suffer from low occupational esteem, creating a puzzle that we attempt to answer later.

SELF-DEFINITION AND SOCIAL VALIDATION

Research on identity indicates that individuals need a relatively secure and stable sense of self-definition—of who they are—within a

given situation to function effectively (Erez & Earley, 1993; Schwalbe & Mason-Schrock, 1996). According to social identity theory, self-definitions are an amalgam of the idiosyncratic attributes (e.g., assertive, ambitious) and social identities (e.g., gender, occupation) that are most relevant (Tajfel & Turner, 1986). Self-definitions are important because they help *situate* individuals in the context and, thereby, suggest what to do, think, and even feel (Ashforth & Mael, 1996; Wiley & Alexander, 1987). A fundamental tenet of social identity theory that is critical to this article is that individuals seek to enhance their self-esteem through their social identities (Tajfel & Turner, 1986; cf., Hogg & Abrams, 1990). Individuals, in short, have a strong desire to view their self-definitions in positive terms.

Identity theorists further argue that self-definitions and their inherent value are at least partly grounded in the perceptions of others (Felson, 1992; Weigert, Teitge, & Teitge, 1986). Through social interaction and the internalization of collective values, meanings, and standards, individuals come to see themselves somewhat through the eyes of others and construct more or less stable self-definitions and a sense of self-esteem. Thus, social validation sharpens and strengthens self-definitions and self-esteem.

OCCUPATIONAL IDENTITY AND THE STIGMA OF DIRTY WORK

A major component of self-definition is the occupational identity—that is, the set of central, distinctive, and enduring characteristics that typify the line of work (Van Maanen & Barley, 1984; cf., Albert & Whetten, 1985). Because organizations tend to be structured around occupational specialties, organization members are largely known by their occupations and come to situate themselves in terms of their occupations (Trice, 1993; Van Maanen & Barley, 1984). Pipefitters for Exxon likely will have a much different perspective of the workplace and

---

[2]Some scholars have applied the term *dirty work* to a variety of socially undesirable activities, including unethical or substandard performance (e.g., Stannard, 1973); to tasks that appear to be trivial, tedious, or unnecessary (e.g., Henson, 1996); and to tasks that seem to be unrewarded, unappreciated, or beneath one's claimed status (e.g., Davis, 1982). However, these applications do not preserve the seminal notion that dirty work is both *necessary* and *polluting* and, thereby, that the work threatens to brand the workers themselves as polluted.

their role within it than will PR managers, and they likely will be regarded by others in much different ways. Outside the organization, ice-breaking rituals often institutionalize the exchange of occupational information: in meeting a stranger, we often ask what she or he does, and we expect to be asked the same question. Thus, job titles serve as prominent identity badges. The robustness of occupational prestige rankings attests to the salience and importance that society ascribes to occupational identities.

With regard to dirty work occupations, the stigma attached to such occupations makes social validation highly problematic. First, dirty workers, prior to entering their occupations, are exposed to the same socializing influences as other members of society (e.g., disparaging remarks about dirty workers, negative depictions of dirty work in movies and sitcoms). Thus, absent any interpersonal influences to the contrary, dirty workers may have internalized the same stereotypes of their eventual line of work. Once in the occupation, they can exercise some control over what media they are exposed to, but the influence of popular culture remains essentially ubiquitous and inescapable (Cullen, 1996).

Second, like any occupation, their work tends to bring them into regular contact with others, particularly coworkers and clients. In the absence of clear and concerted attempts by management and other power holders to negate common stereotypes of dirty work, coworkers are likely to import those stereotypes and act accordingly. As noted, the perceived taint of the dirty work is apt to be projected onto the workers so that they are seen to personify dirt. The stigma may be communicated directly through putdowns, reduced deference and respect, and demeaning questions ("How can you do it?") and more subtly through discrimination and avoidance. Sudnow (1967) describes how hospital employees viewed the morgue attendant as symbolizing death and so tended to avoid him;

when they did interact, these employees often asked intrusive questions about the morgue attendant's work so that he was constantly reminded of his association with death.

Similar dynamics may occur outside the organization since dirty workers often have little power over clients or members of the public. Moreover, workers lacking a status shield to hide behind must cope with implicit assaults on their character and worth. Henslin (1974) describes how taxicab passengers sometimes act as though the cabbie were not present (e.g., by having an intimate conversation).

Thus, it is not surprising that a great deal of qualitative research indicates that people performing dirty work tend to be acutely aware of the stigma that attends their work (Davis, 1984; Gold, 1964; Levin & Arluke, 1987; McIntyre, 1987; Ouellet, 1994; Palmer, 1978; Perry, 1978; Petrillo, 1989–90; Rollins, 1985; Stephens, 1974; Thompson, 1991; Thompson & Harred, 1992). Given the importance of social validation to a positive sense of self, it seems likely that the salience or conspicuousness of social perceptions of dirtiness would undermine individuals' attempts to identify with their work role—that is, to willingly define themselves at least partly on the basis of the occupational identity. Thus, our first proposition is as follows:

> Proposition 1: The greater the salience of social perceptions of dirtiness to the dirty workers, the weaker the identification of dirty workers with their work role will be.

A Puzzle

Proposition 1 suggests that dirty workers should have a difficult time securing an esteem-enhancing self-definition in the workplace. However, as noted earlier, abundant qualitative research indicates that such workers tend to have relatively high occupational esteem. They generally do not appear to suffer from existential doubt, anomie, or angst (although, as we argue later, they may remain somewhat ambivalent). For example, Jacobs (1981) found that two-thirds of his sample of prison guards strongly agreed or agreed with the statement that "people are more sympathetic to inmates than to correctional officers," and yet when asked how they felt about telling people what their occupation was, almost half described themselves as very proud or somewhat proud, and only 5 percent reported being "embarrassed." Returning to the research question from the introduction, the real issue for dirty workers, then, is not so much "How can they do the work?" but "How do they retain a positive self-definition in the face of social assaults on the work they do?" Or, to paraphrase Davis (1984), how are they able to see themselves as good people *doing dirty* work or, better yet, good people *doing good* work?

Dirty Work and Strong Cultures

In this section we argue that the dirty work stigma facilitates the development of strong occupational or workgroup cultures; in the next we describe how strong cultures, in turn, facilitate esteem-enhancing social identities.

THE CENTRAL ROLE OF OCCUPATIONAL AND WORKGROUP CULTURES

Because a stigma can severely damage workers' status and, thus, their credibility and performance (Ashforth & Humphrey, 1995; Katz, 1981), management and other power-holders are more likely to attempt to negate common stereotypes of dirty work the more central or critical that work is to the organization's identity and mission. However, given the well-known difficulty of changing entrenched beliefs, and given that managers—as people—are likely to subscribe to those same beliefs, the perceived need to "resocialize" organizational members is apt to drop rapidly the more

peripheral the dirty work is thought to be. Indeed, management and other organizational members may actively deny their dependence on dirty workers.

Thus, we contend that the answer to the question of how dirty workers retain positive self-definitions is to be found less often at the organizational or individual level of analysis than at the occupational or workgroup level. Typically, although not always, attributions of dirtiness arise not because of the organizational membership or personal characteristics of individuals but because of their occupational membership. Thus, it is the occupational group that is directly threatened, and it is *as* a group that the members typically respond (Schwalbe & Mason-Schrock, 1996).

EMERGENCE OF STRONG CULTURES

It is precisely because of the salience of the dirty work stigma that strong cultures tend to coalesce around the occupation as a whole and/or individual workgroups. First, the occupational title and the negative attributions that people attach to it make the occupation, per se, salient. The putdowns, intrusive questions, and so on are predicated on perceptions of what the occupation entails, thereby cuing the occupational identity. Thus, the negative interactions are lodged not merely at the interpersonal level (between individuals) but at the *intergroup* level (between role occupants, with the individual personifying the occupation; Ashforth & Humphrey, 1995).

Second, as noted, the stigma of dirty work frustrates the desire for social validation, therefore constituting a threat to the desire for self-esteem. As research on group formation indicates, the perception of a shared threat helps foster cohesion (Cohen, 1970; Forsyth, 1990), particularly when the threat has an antagonistic quality, as in the case of such dirty workers as repossessors and abortion workers (Korn, 1996). People sharing a common social category and social pressures come to regard themselves as "in the same boat"—as sharing a common fate.

Third, as the individuals begin to coalesce into a group, they come to view the world in terms of "us versus them" (Freud, 1951). They begin to articulate their occupational or work-group identity: the attributes that differentiate "us" from "them" (Pratt, 1998). In short, group members draw a psychological boundary around the group, thus exacerbating the sense of difference and separation—if not isolation—from others. Arluke (1991) discusses how the rise of the animal rights movement induced animal researchers to articulate the rationales for their research, thereby making their occupation more salient to themselves and underscoring the boundary that divided them from outsiders.

This process through which subcultures (i.e., distinctive and localized occupational/workgroup cultures embedded within the overall organizational culture; Trice & Beyer, 1993) are formed is more likely to be realized under certain conditions identified in the group formation and culture literatures. These conditions include the use of collective socialization, high task interdependencies and physical proximity between individuals, clear physical boundaries and isolation, and group longevity. For example, workers isolated in logging camps and oil fields and miners based in company towns are noted for the strength, if not the militancy, of their subcultures (Lynch, 1987; Moodie & Ndatshe, 1994), and neophyte construction workers undergo active hazing as a means of simultaneously exalting the conditions that make their work dirty (e.g., poor weather, rats) and testing their ability to surmount those conditions (Riemer, 1979).

Other factors more specific to certain types of dirty work may further promote subcultures. Inherent danger (e.g., soldier, prison guard) adds to the sense of threat and separateness; unconventional work hours or habits (e.g., firefighters' night shifts, the frequent travel of exotic dancers) inhibit the development of relationships outside work; a reliance on kin-based recruitment (as in funeral directing and commercial fishing) increases the insularity of the occupational community; and demographic clustering (e.g., female maids, young bouncers, minority farmhands) facilitates interaction (Trice, 1993; Van Maanen & Barley, 1984).

Indeed, subcultures and the sense of distance from the rest of society may be so strong that individuals come to socialize largely with co-workers (Trice, 1993). For example, Mulcahy (1995) notes how police internal affairs officers, mandated to investigate allegations of police misconduct, are reviled by other officers for their perceived breach of the solidarity norm. Internal affairs officers respond, in part, by withdrawing from the social life of their departments.

In summary, while the stigma of dirty work undermines the status of certain occupations, it simultaneously facilitates the development of strong occupational cultures.

EXCEPTIONS TO THE RULE

Given the strong social pressures for group formation in dirty work occupations, a weak subculture is likely to exist only if one or more factors actively inhibit group formation. The most prevalent inhibitors in dirty work are likely to be physical isolation, high turnover, and interpersonal competition for rewards. First, organizations may hire only one member of an occupation or may distribute members geographically or temporally such that they lack ongoing contact with their peers (e.g., janitor, security guard, hospital morgue attendant), members may work more or less independently (e.g., parole officer, private investigator, domestic worker), or they may be self-employed (e.g., funeral director, prostitute, tattoo artist). Even in these circumstances, however, occupational remembers often seek out other members for both instrumental and expressive social support (e.g., Cohen, 1991; Delacoste & Alexander, 1987). A funeral director states:

> A lot of people ask us how we can stand to be in this business. . . . They act like we must be strange or something. When we go to the conventions and meet with all of the other people there who are just like us . . . I feel *normal* again. (Thompson, 1991: 420)

As Trice notes, various "communication interlocks" (e.g., conferences, newsletters, and media reports) transcend the need for frequent personal contact (1993: 143).

Second, given the relatively low prestige of most dirty work occupations, turnover may be high, thus inhibiting group formation. Turnover is likely to be particularly high in occupations that have minimal barriers to entry, such as education and experience, and that are viewed as lacking in upward mobility and intrinsic or extrinsic rewards (e.g., exterminator, bill collector, dogcatcher).

Third, the occupational reward structure (e.g., pay, promotions) may pit members against one another, thus undermining their trust and cohesion (e.g., used car salesperson, manual laborer, taxi driver). For example, Gold (1964) describes how the possibility of "building stealing" kept apartment janitors from fully trusting each other. Once again, however, even in these various circumstances, occupational members often succeed in forging strong subcultures (e.g., Hayano, 1977; Henslin, 1974), although their attitudes toward their peers may remain ambivalent.

This discussion suggests the following proposition:

> Proposition 2a: The greater the salience of social perceptions of dirtiness, the stronger the culture of the relevant occupation or workgroup will be.

> Proposition 2b: However, the culture of the relevant occupation or workgroup may be weakened to the extent that individuals are physically isolated, turnover is high, and the reward structure encourages competition between individuals.

Securing and Sustaining a Positive Social Identity: The Meaning of Dirt

In this section we argue that individuals often recast their dirty work in more positive terms, through occupational ideologies that confer esteem-enhancing meaning and, as we argue in the next section, through practices that moderate the impact of stigma. Because these collective defense mechanisms must counter widespread social perceptions of dirtiness, they are more likely to emerge from strong occupational or workgroup cultures. Put differently, strong subcultures provide the social resources needed to counteract the influence of the wider culture in which the occupation or workgroup is embedded (Beyer, 1981; Trice, 1993).

OCCUPATIONAL IDEOLOGIES

Organizational life is often equivocal—that is, open to multiple and perhaps conflicting interpretations (Weick, 1995). Through the actions and interpretations of individuals, systems of belief or *ideologies* emerge to help make sense of—or impose order on—this equivocality. Dressel and Petersen define an *occupational* ideology as "a coherent perspective . . . that details the nature of the relationship between the occupation and its members with other types of work as well as with the larger society" (1982: 401). Occupational ideologies, then, are systems of beliefs that provide a means for interpreting and understanding what the occupation does and why it matters.

However, given members' desire for self-esteem, ideologies tend to be at least somewhat self-serving. Nonetheless, as a particular ideology is enacted, it becomes shared among members, thus fostering confidence in its validity.

Consensus, in short, creates conviction (Hardin & Higgins, 1996). The result is that *groups often can sustain beliefs that individuals cannot.*

Accordingly, groups often amplify the tendency of individuals to construct self-serving beliefs (e.g., McClure, 1991). Whereas an ideology that implicitly disparages the group ("We perform dirty work because we have limited job options") provides a very tenuous basis for identification, an ideology that edifies the group ("We perform dirty work because we're tough") provides a rallying point. In this way dirty work ideologies attempt to *justify* the work in the sense meant by Scott and Lyman: they "assert its positive value in the face of a claim to the contrary" (1968: 51). The collective desire to think well of the group appears to provide a kind of social license to foster edifying justifications that outsiders would tend to question.

The common purpose of the three ideological techniques discussed below—reframing, recalibrating, and refocusing—is to transform the meaning of the stigmatized work by simultaneously negating or devaluing negative attributions and creating or revaluing positive ones. In so doing, the techniques may justify the occupation and render it more palatable and perhaps even attractive to insiders and outsiders alike, helping persuade dirty workers to identify with their work role. However, almost by definition, the lower the prestige of an occupation, the less likely that its ideology (or ideologies) will be known and accepted by outsiders (Berger, 1964). Thus, one can generally view dirty work ideologies as beliefs that dirty workers primarily tell each other and receptive outsiders (e.g., family and friends) and, thus, that have their greatest impact on *internal* rather than *external* legitimacy.

Reframing. This technique involves transforming the meaning attached to a stigmatized occupation. There are at least two forms of reframing. The first is *infusing,* where the stigma is imbued with positive value, thus transforming it into a badge of honor. Perhaps the most common justification for dirty work is to describe the occupational mission—the espoused purpose for which the work was created—in value-laden terms. Public defenders assert they are protecting the constitutional rights of all citizens to a fair trial—not helping rapists and drug dealers beat the system (McIntyre, 1987); exotic dancers and prostitutes claim they are providing a therapeutic and educational service, rather than selling their bodies (Miller, 1978; Thompson & Harred, 1992); and funeral directors state they are helping relatives and friends of the deceased deal with grief, rather than processing dead bodies and profiting from their work (Thompson, 1991). The "dirty particulars" are wrapped in more abstract and uplifting values associated with the larger purpose. Indeed, there is *no* occupation that cannot be described in fairly grand, value-laden terms. Note that, given the equivocality of meaning, both the value-laden and the sullied constructions in the above examples are defensible (e.g., funeral directors *do* help people deal with grief and *do* profit from their work), and each construction is preferred by some segment of society.

A related form of infusing is to couch the occupational tasks in edifying ways. If the mission refers to occupational ends, the tasks refer to occupational means. Construction workers interpret their manual labor as reflecting traditional notions of masculinity (Riemer, 1979), boxers liken their work to that of craftsmen and performing artists (Wacquant, 1995), and supermarket meatcutters take pride in their dexterity with knives and their ability to tolerate cold rooms (Meara, 1974). Given that ends are less immediate and proximal than means, it is often difficult for the ends of work to remain *continuously* salient. Thus, the more distal the ends, the more prevalent the reframing of means.

The second form of reframing is *neutralizing,* where the negative value of the stigma is negated. The literature on deviance includes various "neutralization techniques" (e.g., Hong & Duff, 1977; Levi, 1981; Sykes & Matza, 1957), three of which are most relevant here. In "denial of responsibility," occupational members assert that they are simply doing their job—that someone or something else is responsible or that no one is responsible (i.e., system imperatives demand that the role be performed). Thus, bill collectors rationalize that angry debtors are upset at their plight—not at the particular collector (Sutton, 1991)—and meatpackers assert that they are merely fulfilling society's demand for meat (Lesy, 1987).

Two other techniques—"denial of injury" and "denial of victim"—are most relevant where work is morally tainted by perceived exploitation. In denial of injury, occupational members maintain that no harm was actually done. Hong and Duff describe the guilt felt by a novice taxi-dancer at leading her customers on by playing along with their romantic interests. A veteran taxi-dancer told her, "They [the customers] know about it. They are not that foolish" (1977: 334)—that is, the customers were also playing along as part of the "game." In denial of victim, members argue that the "exploited" either desire or deserve their fate. Tabloid reporters maintain that celebrities want publicity and their claims to the contrary are often a calculated means of heightening the public's curiosity about them and, thus, *encouraging* publicity (Levin & Arluke, 1987), and pimps believe that women seek security, are willing to exchange their bodies for that security, and desire and need to be protected and controlled by men (Ritzer & Walczak, 1986).

Neutralizing and infusing are complementary in that a given stigma can be both negated and transformed. Indeed, because an ideology, like any theory, attempts to resolve equivocality and simplify complexity in a manner that people can accept, multiple ideologies are often necessary to address multiple questions and multiple individuals. Thus, strong occupational and workgroup cultures often contain multiple and somewhat loosely coupled, if not contradictory, justifications (Fine, 1996; Ritzer & Walczak, 1986).

Recalibrating. This technique refers to adjusting the implicit standards that are invoked to assess the magnitude (how much) and/or valence (how good) of a given dirty work attribute. Adjusting the perceptual and evaluative standards can make an undesired and ostensibly large aspect seem smaller and less significant and a desired but small aspect seem larger and more significant. If less is expected, more is found.

Palmer (1978) describes how dogcatchers took tasks that would appear to an outsider to be universally dirty and arrayed them in a value hierarchy. For example, calls regarding possible rabies and bites were valued more positively, whereas calls regarding strays were valued negatively. The differentiation created value. Moreover, dirty workers are inclined to retell and relive positively valued experiences, thus giving periodic boosts to their occupational esteem (e.g., Kinkade & Katovich, 1997; Santino, 1990). Accordingly, dirty workers may sincerely perceive positive attributes and derive personal fulfillment from tasks that many others consider repugnant.

Similarly, in what one may phrase the "for want of a nail" argument,[3] seemingly minor activities that are unappreciated in the organization may be seen by dirty workers as highly significant. Hospital orderlies remark that key medical procedures could not be performed if the orderlies did not transport patients

---

[3]"For the want of a nail the shoe was lost, for the want of a shoe the horse was lost, for the want of a horse the man was lost, for the want of a man the battle was lost" (from "The Horseshoe Nail," *Grimm's Fairy Tales*).

around the hospital (Reed, 1989); racetrack "backstretch" workers maintain that horses would not be fit to race if not for the workers' menial tasks (Rosecrance, 1985); and hospital cleaning staff note the importance of their role, particularly in preventing patients from getting sicker: "If it wasn't for us, this hospital wouldn't be open. They [doctors and nurses] don't realize that" (Dutton, Debebe, & Wrzesniewski, 1996: 40).

Recalibrations acquire the status of an occupational ideology to the extent that dirty workers share their views on the "appropriate" ways of gauging the merits of their work. Social information processing theory indicates that job incumbents often derive their standards for assessing the attributes and satisfactoriness of work from their coworkers (e.g., Griffin, 1987). The inherent equivocality of organizations requires that the meaning of working conditions be mediated by subjective and usually social processes.

Refocusing. In refocusing, the center of attention is shifted from the stigmatized features of the work to the nonstigmatized features. Whereas reframing actively transforms the stigmatized properties of dirty work and recalibrating magnifies their redeeming qualities, refocusing actively overlooks the stigmatized properties. Occupational members willfully disattend to the features of work that are socially problematic. McIntyre (1987) reports that public defenders do not want to know if their clients are guilty and focus instead on winning by exploiting weaknesses in the prosecution's case. By investing their attention and emotion in winning versus losing, rather than guilt versus innocence, the public defenders are less likely to feel conflict and more likely to feel in control.

Because refocusing involves a shift in attention from stigmatized to nonstigmatized features, the greater the proportion of core attributes that are stigmatized, the more likely attention will refocus on features that are extrinsic to the work itself. Thus, garbage collectors draw satisfaction from their pay and flexible hours (Walsh, 1975), longshoremen take pride in their social solidarity (Pilcher, 1972), and gravediggers enjoy being outdoors (Petrillo, 1989–90). Similarly, many dirty workers attempt to minimize the immediacy of the stigmatized work by regarding their efforts as instrumental to longer-term or extraorganizational goals. Male strippers may share the hope that their showmanship skills will be discovered, leading to a career as an entertainer (Dressel & Petersen, 1982), and domestic workers may derive self-respect from their ability to support their families (Rollins, 1985).

Like the other techniques, refocusing rationales attain the status of an occupational ideology to the extent that dirty workers actively construct and exchange them. However, like the "sad tales" exchanged between the patients of a psychiatric hospital, studied by Goffman (1961), some aspirations have a wistful and fanciful quality and seem unlikely to be realized. Nonetheless, a hopeful tomorrow may render a bleak today more tolerable. Thus, as Goffman found, norms are likely to emerge that constrain direct challenges to espoused dreams.

However, just as ends are less immediate and proximal than means, the extrinsic features of work are less proximal than the work itself. A fat paycheck may excuse an undesired job, but it is difficult to actively think about the paycheck 8 hours a day, 5 days a week. Thus, in the absence of reframing or recalibrating, extrinsic rewards and good hygiene factors may provide sufficient "external justification" (Staw, 1980) in the sense that they compensate incumbents for the stigmatized work, but they do not recast the intrinsic qualities of the work itself. Indeed, high extrinsic rewards may even *undermine* attempts to find intrinsic rewards.

CONTRASTING THE IDEOLOGICAL TECHNIQUES

Reframing, recalibrating, and refocusing are not mutually exclusive, and evidence of all three can be found in many dirty work occupations. Because of its power to transform the very meaning of the work itself, we argue that reframing has the greatest potential to combat attributions of dirtiness and will be more strongly associated with work role identification than will recalibrating or refocusing. However, because it is difficult for a single worker to transform the meaning of work in the face of a pervasive stigma, reframing requires a stronger occupational or workgroup culture than do recalibrating and refocusing.

Recalibrating does not transform meaning per se, but it modifies the significance of whatever meaning can be found. Thus, while recalibrating can be used to augment reframing, its largest impact occurs in circumstances where the occupational or workgroup culture is not sufficiently strong to support reframing. Finally, because refocusing is a compensatory technique, it is not likely to be as strongly associated with identification as either reframing or recalibrating, and it has its largest impact when neither of these ideological techniques are tenable. However, refocusing can also augment these techniques by shifting attention away from residual stigmata that have not been reframed or recalibrated effectively.

This discussion suggests the following summary propositions:

Proposition 3: The stronger the culture of the dirty work occupation or workgroup, the greater the use of ideological reframing, recalibrating, and refocusing will be.

Proposition 4a: The greater the use of ideological reframing, recalibrating, and refocusing, the stronger the identification of dirty workers with their work role will be.

Proposition 4b: Reframing will be most strongly associated with identification, followed by recalibrating and then refocusing.

Securing and Sustaining a Positive Social Identity: The Social Salience of Dirt

In this section we focus on practices that moderate the impact of the salience of social perceptions of dirtiness on work role identification. These practices typically complement the ideological techniques discussed above and, like the ideological techniques, are fostered by strong occupational and workgroup cultures.

SOCIAL WEIGHTING

Because dirtiness is socially constructed, "outsiders" (e.g., other organizational members, clients, family, neighbors) constitute an ongoing threat to the oppositional identity work inherent in dirty work subcultures. Whereas dirty workers may have internalized their occupation's ideologies, outsiders, preoccupied with stereotypes of dirt, usually have not. Thus, dirty workers often are concerned about their relationships with outsiders, and these relationships are often a major theme of dirty work subcultures (Ghidina, 1992).

Differentiation of Outsiders: Condemning the Condemners.   Given the desire for social affirmation, dirty workers need to reconcile outsiders' derogatory perceptions with their own desire for self-esteem. One way is to "condemn the condemners" (Sykes & Matza, 1957), to impugn the motives, character, knowledge, or authority—in short, the *legitimacy*—of critical outsiders as moral arbiters. Condemning the condemners thus enables dirty workers to dismiss the condemners' perceptions. Gold (1964) found that janitors labeled particularly "bad" tenants as ignorant, nutty, or nervous and therefore did not get concerned with negative interactions; Rollins (1985) found that domestic workers often believed that their more affluent employers were lonely and unfulfilled and, therefore, worse off than the domestics and in no position to pass judgment. Thompson and Harred quote a topless dancer:

> They will come in here on Saturday nights, get drunk, and play "grab ass," and then go to church on Sunday and condemn what we do. In general, I think we're a whole lot more honest than they are. (1992: 306)

In the absence of obvious taint, members of nonstigmatized occupations likely *assume* respect. But for dirty workers, particularly those from low-prestige occupations, respect—and, thus, social validity—typically are problematic, fostering a heightened sensitivity to potential signs of disrespect. Thus, dirty workers tend to be wary in their dealings with outsiders and may perceive slights where none were intended (e.g., Dutton et al., 1996; Rollins, 1985). This sensitivity predisposes dirty workers to condemn outsiders so that relations between dirty workers and outsiders often polarize over time.

Differentiation of Outsiders: Supporting the Supporters.

Just as dirty workers often come to condemn their condemners, they come to place more credence in those outsiders (if any) who provide a positive view of their work. Indeed, Heinsler et al. (1990) found that police detectives preferred to interact with criminals rather than victims, because a criminal could appreciate the detectives' legwork in apprehending him or her, and the very presence of a criminal validated the detectives' espoused identity as a crime-fighter. However, it seems likely that dirty workers would, if possible, gravitate toward supportive outsiders of high status as well as high salience (e.g., through regular interaction or personal relationships) because they offer the greatest promise of social validation (e.g., Trice, 1993).

In the absence of supportive outsiders, dirty workers are likely to psychologically and socially withdraw to the safer confines of their occupational cohort and to look more exclusively to it for affirmation. However, in further disconnecting with society, the cohort becomes more likely to adopt values and beliefs that are out of step with, or that deliberately defy, those of the society that "rejected" them (Lemert, 1967). Thus, a group of male construction workers may flaunt norms of civility and verbally harass female passersby, precisely because the workers believe they are held in contempt by outsiders. In turn, the negative responses of the passersby complete the circle.

Selective Social Comparisons.

Social comparison theory indicates that the desires for self-esteem and self-knowledge are fulfilled partly by subjectively assessing ambiguous attributes through comparisons with similar and salient others (Wood, 1989). Downward social comparisons are associated with self-esteem, providing protection for a vulnerable ego (Gibbons & Gerrard, 1991), whereas upward social comparisons are associated with self-knowledge, providing benchmarks for motivational or aspirational purposes (Major, Testa, & Bylsma, 1991). Social comparison theory indicates that downward comparisons are likely when the focal actors are experiencing threat (Forsyth, 1990; Gibbons & Gerrard, 1991). Given the ongoing threat of a pervasive stigma, dirty workers, therefore, are likely to favor downward comparisons (Crocker & Major, 1989).

Social comparisons occur between and within groups. Between groups, members of dirty work occupations are motivated to draw comparisons against salient occupational groups that they consider to be somewhat similar in prestige but disadvantaged in some way. Such groups are sufficiently similar that the comparison is informative, yet sufficiently "inferior" to gratify the desire for self-esteem. However, given the low prestige of many dirty work occupations, it might appear difficult to locate salient groups that are downwind. Nonetheless, research on the "social creativity postulate" (Tajfel & Turner, 1986) indicates that groups are quite facile at "finding or creating new comparison dimensions on which they are superior to [an] out-group, or reinterpreting extant comparisons in a manner more flattering to the in-group" (Hinkle & Brown, 1990: 54; e.g., Jackson, Sullivan, Harnish, & Hodge, 1996). Thus, dirty workers often resort to reference groups and comparison criteria that would appear to outsiders to be specious or trivial. Ouellet (1994) describes how truckers tend to disparage the regimented tasks of factory workers, despite the truckers being closely monitored by tachographs (and, more recently, satellite tracking) and subjected to numerous regulations, as well as the mechanical parameters of their vehicles.

Between-group comparisons are typically supplemented by within-group comparisons, including subgroup and interpersonal comparisons (Ellemers & Van Rijswijk, 1997). Given our group-level focus, we restrict our attention to subgroup comparisons. Subgroup comparisons tend to be popular among members of dirty work occupations because they hold the stigma constant, thereby facilitating contrasts on other, more socially valued, attributes (perhaps allowing their subgroup to become "a big fish in a little pond"). Just as intergroup comparisons tend to focus on referents that are similar and preferably somewhat socially inferior, so too do subgroup comparisons. Thus, call girls feel superior to streetwalkers (Bryan, 1965), veteran fishers disparage newcomers (Bourassa & Ashforth, 1998), and slaves who did household chores felt superior to ones who did fieldwork (Mellon, 1990). However, the more salient the subgroup differences, the more likely that the occupational or workgroup culture will fragment and diverge along subgroup lines.

We view the three forms of social weighting—condemning condemners, supporting supporters, and selective social comparing—as complementary. Indeed, there may be interactive synergies among these mechanisms. For example, research on identity and intergroup dynamics suggests that having supporters (an ingroup) facilitates the labeling and condemnation of condemners (the outgroup) and that selective social comparisons may further polarize views of supporters and condemners (Oakes, Haslam, & Turner, 1994; Tajfel & Turner, 1986).

In sum, a strong occupational or workgroup culture provides the social resources needed to selectively attend to outsiders and to selectively engage in social comparisons. Selective attention and comparisons enable dirty workers to place more weight on social referents that affirm the workers' value and less weight on referents that do not, thereby moderating the impact of the social salience of dirtiness on work role identification, as well as directly enhancing identification. This discussion suggests the following propositions:

Proposition 5: The stronger the culture of the dirty work occupation or workgroup, the greater the use of social weighting will be (via differentiation of outsiders through condemning condemners and supporting supporters, and via selective social comparisons).

Proposition 6: Social weighting moderates the association between the salience of social perceptions of dirtiness and work role identification, such that the association is weakened by the use of social weighting.

Proposition 7: Social weighting is directly and positively associated with work role identification (by focusing on favorable social referents and comparisons).

IDEOLOGIES AND SOCIAL WEIGHTING

Finally, the ideological techniques of reframing, recalibrating, and refocusing are likely to both reinforce and be reinforced by social weighting. Dirty work ideologies typically externalize or attribute the dirty work stigma to the ignorance or malevolence of outsiders and foster stereotypic characterizations of both detractors and supporters. Note, then, that an individual dirty worker may not need to have personal or direct experience with given outsiders to condemn/support them. Similarly, by placing less credence in the views of condemners and more in the views of supporters, social weighting serves to bolster dirty work ideologies. A frequent result of this reciprocal relationship between ideology and social weighting is that dirty workers may become more detached from mainstream society and, thus, further marginalized. In sum:

> Proposition 8: There is a reciprocal, positive relationship between the use of the ideological techniques and social weighting.[4]

The Meaning and Salience of Dirty Work Over Time

In this section we briefly examine the dynamics from the previous two sections regarding the meaning and salience of dirty work in the broader temporal context of work adjustment. We speculate that, despite concerted attempts to secure a positive social identity, many dirty workers ultimately adopt a somewhat ambivalent stance toward their work.

SOCIALIZATION TO DIRTY WORK

The socialization literature indicates that the act of entering any new work setting is inherently upending, as newcomers are confronted with novelty, ambiguity, and perhaps disconfirmed expectations (Louis, 1980). These discontinuities provoke sensemaking, as the newcomers endeavor to understand their jobs and work context and to form positive social identities.

This need for sensemaking is particularly acute for newcomers to dirty work occupations, because they must confront and reconcile themselves to the disparaged aspects of the work (Levi, 1981). As members of society, newcomers likely import stereotypic expectations but lack the subcultural armor to cope with the stereotypes and the dirty particulars of the work. Novice exterminators must actively search for cockroaches, mice, and other pests they would ordinarily avoid; new dentists must become comfortable with routinely inflicting pain and discomfort on others; and bill collectors must learn to actively intimidate people over the telephone. In addition, newcomers must also contend with the negative views that others hold toward the occupation and its practitioners. Although social weighting helps moderate the impact of stigma over time, occupational ideologies are needed to provide esteem-enhancing interpretations of the stigma.

A good example of the socialization of newcomers can be found in Hong and Duff's (1977) study of taxi-dancers. Job interviews conveyed the impression to prospective dancers that the work was easy and fun. However, novice taxi-dancers soon learned that the job involved fending off unwanted sexual advances and that many customers were older and of different ethnic backgrounds. Veteran hostesses and management attempted to actively neutralize the negative connotations and infuse the work with value (e.g., taxi-dancers are helping lonely men). By the end of the third week, newcomers were able to offer these same justifications (likely self-consciously) when responding to questions about their work. As the newcomers gradually accepted the ideology, they became less likely to verbalize it when talking about their work and more likely to say simply that they liked the job and that it was, indeed, easy and fun.

Thus, ideology serves as an important bridge for the transition from outsider to

---

[4]However, for a given incident involving an identity threat (e.g., an insult from a client), the ideological techniques and social weighting may be used in a more compensatory manner. That is, the threat may be adequately countered by a single tactic (e.g., disparaging the client).

insider, providing alternative and edifying interpretations for the problematic features of work. This bridging is facilitated by the well-known tools of symbolic management (Trice, 1993; Van Maanen & Barley, 1984). Occupational stories—many apocryphal—convey the "appropriate" attitude and behavior toward clients, management, and other salient outsiders. For example, Pullman porters exchange stories about rude passengers that help clarify the bounds of deference (Santino, 1990). Rites of passage signal acceptance into a special fraternity. Newcomers in fishing and high-steel iron work are assigned derogatory nicknames and low-status tasks, and they are verbally and perhaps physically harassed until they have proven their mettle to the veterans (Bourassa & Ashforth, 1998; Haas, 1972). Uniforms, titles, physical artifacts, and jargon signify and cue occupational identities. Reed (1989) describes how the presence of a catheter kit and his hospital orderly uniform helped define the act of handling a patient's penis as a medical rather than erotic act. However, such occupational trappings may be adopted with some ambivalence, because they also cue the derogatory stereotypes retained by outsiders. Finally, euphemisms, rituals, and taboos help regulate emotion and facilitate smooth performance. Funeral directors lessen the salience of death by referring to corpses as "the loved one" or by name, viewing rooms as the "sunset room" or "eternal slumber room," and cemeteries as "final resting places" (Pine, 1975; Thompson, 1991). Prostitutes offer various sexual services but regard lip kissing as taboo because it connotes emotional involvement (Trice, 1993).

Once an occupational ideology is fully internalized and the impact of stigma salience is moderated through social weighting, dirty workers may more or less mindlessly enact their roles (Ashforth & Fried, 1988). At that point, it is likely that only occasional discontinuities will precipitate a need for further identity repair. A particularly abusive client, a newcomer who is not yet comfortable in the role and makes awkward comments, a sudden job opportunity, or a neighbor who asks intrusive questions may trigger new rounds of sensemaking and cause occupational members to question their involvement in the role.

WORK ROLE IDENTIFICATION AND AMBIVALENCE

As we have argued, a compelling occupational ideology (particularly one based on reframing [infusing] and recalibrating), coupled with social weighting, can recast dirty work in more ennobling terms and bestow a positive identity on those who perform it. Accordingly, dirty workers are more likely to identify with the work role. Further, the greater the proportion of members that identify with the work role, the more the ideology becomes socially affirmed, thus fostering a virtuous circle.

Indeed, dirty work occupations may actually elicit *higher* identification and collective esteem than many other occupations, precisely because the stigma may foster a strong culture with robust protective techniques for warding off the social threat and enhancing self-image. Further, the strong culture may reify the stigma as a salient external cause for whatever personal misfortunes are encountered by members ("People don't like me because I work in a slaughterhouse"), thus exonerating members from personal blame (Crocker & Major, 1989). The culture may effectively "inoculate" members against the slings and arrows of misfortune.

However, we do not wish to overstate the strength of identification across the membership of any given dirty work occupation. Given Proposition 1, it seems likely that most members will retain some ambivalence about their jobs, because they remain part of the larger culture with its stigmatizing views and they have ongoing contact with people outside their occupation. The opposing poles of ambivalence—approach and avoidance—are likely to be most evident at different times.

The distinction in the stress literature between chronic and acute stressors provides a useful analogy (Eden, 1990). A chronic stressor is a source of stress that is constantly present (e.g., a manager's responsibility for the welfare of others), whereas an acute stressor is a source that temporarily flares into prominence (e.g., an impending deadline). Similarly, social perceptions of dirtiness are chronically salient—as noted, qualitative research consistently indicates that dirty workers are very aware of their occupation's stigma—creating an ongoing threat to work role identification (Proposition 1). The occupational or work-group defense mechanisms (i.e., ideological techniques and social weighting) arise to help keep this threat at bay (Propositions 2–8). However, specific incidents or circumstances may render social perceptions acutely salient, temporarily overwhelming the defense mechanisms. For example, ideological reframing and social weighting may help public defenders cope with the chronic stigma of assisting people charged with felonies, yet hostile comments and invasive questions at a party may cause them to feel temporarily embarrassed and ashamed. Thus, depending on the mix of chronic and acute threats from social perceptions of dirtiness, and on the utilization and efficacy of defense mechanisms, dirty workers are apt to fluctuate somewhat in the degree of work role identification they feel.

Thus, our final proposition is as follows:

> Proposition 9: Given the negative association posited in Proposition 1 (between salience and identification) and the sequence of positive associations posited in Propositions 2–8 (involving culture, ideology, social weighting, and identification), most dirty workers will be somewhat ambivalent about their work role; specifically, at those times when social perceptions are acutely salient, work role

identification will be lower (via Proposition 1), and when social perceptions are not acutely salient identification will be higher (via Propositions 2–8).

Discussion

Work is said to be dirty if society perceives it to be physically, socially, or morally tainted (Hughes, 1951, 1958). The construct of dirt has tremendous social significance because society draws a sharp distinction between purity and pollution, viewing people who perform dirty work as dirty or polluted themselves (Douglas, 1966). This stigma creates a challenge for dirty workers because they, like all people, rely somewhat on others for validation but are likely to be denied that validation by society. This is particularly true of dirty workers from relatively low-prestige occupations. Nonetheless, dirty workers often appear able to create and maintain a positive work role identity.

The reason, we have argued, is that the dirty work stigma makes the work role per se salient, and the threat embodied in the stigma fosters strong cohesion and the emergence of an occupational or workgroup culture to help counter the threat. The stronger the threat, the stronger the culture, and the more the perceptions of "us versus them" are reinforced. A strong culture provides the social resources to reframe, recalibrate, and refocus the meaning of dirty work—that is, to foster ennobling ideologies.

Dirty work ideologies often glorify precisely those aspects of the work that are most stigmatized: less onerous work would have required lesser people. The transformation of meaning is often supplemented with practices that moderate the impact of the salience of dirtiness by altering the relative social weights placed on detractors and supporters and by enabling selective social comparisons. Through these mechanisms, dirty workers, thus, are more likely to embrace the work role, although most retain some ambivalence and may fluctuate between higher and lower identification as social perceptions of dirtiness become more or less salient.

References

Albert, S., & Whetten, D. A. 1985. Organizational identity. In L. L. Cummings & B. M. Staw (Eds.), *Research in organizational behavior,* vol. 7: 263–295. Greenwich, CT: JAI Press.

Arluke, A. 1991. Going into the closet with science: Information control among animal experimenters. *Journal of Contemporary Ethnography,* 20: 306–330.

Ashforth, B. E., & Fried, Y. 1988. The mindlessness of organizational behaviors. *Human Relations,* 41: 305–329.

Ashforth, B. E., & Humphrey, R. H. 1995. Labeling processes in the organization: Constructing the individual. In L. L. Cummings & B. M. Staw (Eds.), *Research in organizational behavior,* vol. 17: 413–461. Greenwich, CT: JAI Press.

Ashforth, B. E., & Mael, F. A. 1996. Organizational identity and strategy as a context for the individual. In J. A. C. Baum & J. E. Dutton (Eds.), *Advances in strategic management,* vol. 13: 19–64. Greenwich, CT: JAI Press.

Ball, D. W. 1970. The problematics of respectability. In J. D. Douglas (Ed.), *Deviance & respectability: The social construction of moral meanings:* 326–371. New York: Basic Books.

Berger, P. L. 1964. Some general observations on the problem of work. In P. L. Berger (Ed.), *The human shape of work: Studies in the sociology of occupations:* 211–241. New York: Macmillan.

Beyer, J. M. 1981. Ideologies, values, and decision making in organizations. In P. C. Nystrom & W. H. Starbuck (Eds.), *Handbook of organizational design,* vol. 2: 166–202. Oxford, England: Oxford University Press.

Bourassa, L., & Ashforth, B. E. 1998. You are about to party *Defiant* style: Socialization and identity onboard an Alaskan fishing boat. *Journal of Contemporary Ethnography,* 27: 171–196.

Bryan, J. H. 1965. Apprenticeships in prostitution. *Social Problems,* 12: 287–297.

Cohen, A. K. 1970. A general theory of subcultures. In D. O. Arnold (Ed.), *The sociology of subcultures:* 96–111. Santa Barbara, CA: Glendessary Press.

Cohen, R. 1991. Women of color in white households: Coping strategies of live-in domestic workers. *Qualitative Sociology,* 14: 197–215.

Crocker, J., & Major, B. 1989. Social stigma and self-esteem: The self-protective properties of stigma. *Psychological Review,* 98.

Cullen, J. 1996. *The art of democracy: A concise history of popular culture in the United States.* New York: Monthly Review Press.

Davis, D. S. 1984. Good people doing dirty work: A study of social isolation. *Symbolic Interaction,* 7: 233–247.

Davis, P. W. 1982. *Labor infra dignitatem:* The dimensions and conditions of occupational "diary work" [sic] for the police patrol officer. *International Journal of Contemporary Sociology,* 19: 205–220.

Delacoste, F., & Alexander, P. (Eds.). 1987. *Sex work: Writings by women in the sex industry.* Pittsburgh, PA: Cleis Press.

Douglas, M. 1966. *Purity and danger: An analysis of concepts of pollution and taboo.* London: Routledge and Kegan Paul.

Dressel, P. L., & Petersen, D. M. 1982. Becoming a male stripper: Recruitment, socialization, and ideological development. *Work and Occupations,* 9: 387–406.

Dunkerley, D. 1975. *Occupations and society.* London: Routledge and Kegan Paul.

Dutton, J. E., Debebe, G., & Wrzesniewski, A. 1996. *The revaluing of de-valued work: The importance of relationships for hospital cleaning staff.* Paper presented at the annual meeting of the Academy of Management, Cincinnati, OH.

Eden, D. 1990. Acute and chronic job stress, strain, and vacation relief. *Organizational Behavior and Human Decision Processes,* 45: 175–193.

Ellemers, N., & Van Rijswijk, W. 1997. Identity needs versus social opportunities: The use of group-level and individual-level identity management strategies. *Social Psychology Quarterly,* 60: 52–65.

Emerson, R. M., & Pollner, M. 1976. Dirty work designations: Their features and consequences in a psychiatric setting. *Social Problems,* 23: 243–254.

Erez, M., & Earley, P. C. 1993. *Culture, self-identity, and work.* New York: Oxford University Press.

Felson, R. B. 1992. Coming to see ourselves: Social sources of self-appraisals. In E. J. Lawler,

B. Markovsky, C. Ridgeway, & H. A. Walker (Eds.), *Advances in group processes,* vol. 9: 185–205. Greenwich, CT: JAI Press.

Fine, G. A. 1996. Justifying work: Occupational rhetorics as resources in restaurant kitchens. *Administrative Science Quarterly,* 41: 90–115.

Forsyth, D. R. 1990. *Group dynamics* (2nd ed.). Pacific Grove, CA: Brooks/Cole Publishing.

Fossum, J. A., & Moore, M. L. 1975. The stability of longitudinal and cross-sectional occupational prestige rankings. *Journal of Vocational Behavior,* 7: 305–311.

Freud, S. 1951. *Group psychology and the analysis of the ego.* (First published in 1922.) New York: Liveright.

Ghidina, M. J. 1992. Social relations and the definition of work: Identity management in a low-status occupation. *Qualitative Sociology,* 15: 73–85.

Gibbons, F. X., & Gerrard, M. 1991. Downward comparison and coping with threat. In J. Suls & T. A. Wills (Eds.), *Social comparison: Contemporary theory and research:* 317–345. Hillsdale, NJ: Lawrence Erlbaum Associates.

Goffman, E. 1961. *Asylums: Essays on the social situation of mental patients and other inmates.* Garden City, NY: Doubleday.

Gold, R. L. 1964. In the basement—the apartment-building janitor. In P. L. Berger (Ed.), *The human shape of work: Studies in the sociology of occupations:* 1–49. New York: Macmillan.

Griffin, R. W. 1987. Toward an integrated theory of task design. In L. L. Cummings & B. M. Staw (Eds.), *Research in organizational behavior,* vol. 9: 79–120. Greenwich, CT: JAI Press.

Haas, J. 1972. Binging: Educational control among high steel iron workers. *American Behavioral Scientist,* 16: 27–34.

Hackman, J. R., & Oldham, G. R. 1980. *Work redesign.* Reading, MA: Addison-Wesley.

Hardin, C. D., & Higgins, E. T. 1996. Shared reality: How social verification makes the subjective objective. In R. M. Sorrentino & E. T. Higgins (Eds.), *Handbook of motivation and cognition,* vol. 3: 28–84. New York: Guilford Press.

Hayano, D. M. 1977. The professional poker player: Career identification and the problem of respectability. *Social Problems,* 24: 556–564.

Heinsler, J. M., Kleinman, S., & Stenross, B. 1990. Making work matter: Satisfied detectives and dissatisfied campus police. *Qualitative Sociology,* 13: 235–250.

Henslin, J. M. 1974. The underlife of cabdriving: A study in exploitation and punishment. In P. L. Stewart & M. G. Cantor (Eds.), *Varieties of work experience: The social control of occupational groups and roles:* 67–79. New York: Wiley.

Henson, K. D. 1996. *Just a temp.* Philadelphia: Temple University Press.

Hinkle, S., & Brown, R. 1990. Intergroup comparisons and social identity: Some links and lacunae. In D. Abrams & M. A. Hogg (Eds.), *Social identity theory: Constructive and critical advances:* 48–70. New York: Springer-Verlag.

Hogg, M. A., & Abrams, D. 1990. Social motivation, self-esteem and social identity. In D. Abrams & M. A. Hogg (Eds.), *Social identity theory: Constructive and critical advances:* 28–47. New York: Springer-Verlag.

Hong, L. K., & Duff, R. W. 1977. Becoming a taxi-dancer: The significance of neutralization in a semi-deviant occupation. *Sociology of Work and Occupations,* 4: 327–342.

Hughes, E. C. 1951. Work and the self. In J. H. Rohrer & M. Sherif (Eds.), *Social psychology at the cross-roads:* 313–323. New York: Harper & Brothers.

Hughes, E. C. 1958. *Men and their work.* Glencoe, IL: Free Press.

Hughes, E. C. 1962. Good people and dirty work. *Social Problems,* 10: 3–11.

Hughes, E. C. 1970. The humble and the proud: The comparative study of occupations. *Sociological Quarterly,* 11: 147–156.

Jackson, L. A., Sullivan, L. A., Harnish, R., & Hodge, C. N. 1996. Achieving positive social identity: Social mobility, social creativity, and permeability of group boundaries. *Journal of Personality and Social Psychology,* 70: 241–254.

Jacobs, J. B. 1981. What prison guards think: A profile of the Illinois force. In R. R. Ross (Ed.), *Prison guard/correctional officer: The use and abuse of the human resources of prisons:* 41–53. Toronto: Butterworths.

Katz, I. 1981. *Stigma: A social psychological analysis.* Hillsdale, NJ: Lawrence Erlbaum Associates.

Kinkade, P. T., & Katovich, M. A. 1997. The driver: Adaptations and identities in the urban worlds of pizza delivery employees. *Journal of Contemporary Ethnography,* 25: 421–448.

Korn, P. 1996. *Lovejoy: A year in the life of an abortion clinic.* New York: Atlantic Monthly Press.

Lemert, E. M. 1967. *Human deviance, social problems, and social control.* Englewood Cliffs, NJ: Prentice-Hall.

Lesy, M. 1987. *The forbidden zone.* New York: Farrar, Straus & Giroux.

Levi, K. 1981. Becoming a hit man: Neutralization in a very deviant career. *Urban Life,* 10: 47–63.

Levin, J., & Arluke, A. 1987. *Gossip: The inside scoop.* New York: Plenum.

Louis, M. R. 1980. Surprise and sense making: What newcomers experience in entering unfamiliar organizational settings. *Administrative Science Quarterly,* 25: 226–251.

Lynch, G. 1987. *Roughnecks, drillers, and tool pushers: Thirty-three years in the oil fields.* Austin: University of Texas Press.

Major, B., Testa, M., & Bylsma, W. H. 1991. Responses to upward and downward social comparisons: The impact of esteem-relevance and perceived control. In J. Suls & T. A. Wills (Eds.), *Social comparison: Contemporary theory and research:* 237–260. Hillsdale, NJ: Lawrence Erlbaum Associates.

McClure, J. 1991. *Explanations, accounts, and illusions: A critical analysis.* Cambridge, England: Cambridge University Press.

McIntyre, L. J. 1987. *The public defender: The practice of law in the shadows of repute.* Chicago: University of Chicago Press.

Meara, H. 1974. Honor in dirty work: The case of American meat cutters and Turkish butchers. *Sociology of Work and Occupations,* 1: 259–283.

Mellon, J. (Ed.). 1990. *Bullwhip days: The slaves remember: An oral history.* New York: Avon.

Miller, G. 1978. *Odd jobs: The world of deviant work.* Englewood Cliffs, NJ: Prentice-Hall.

Moodie, T. D., & Ndatshe, V. 1994. *Going for gold: Men, mines, and migration.* Berkeley, CA: University of California Press.

Mulcahy, A. 1995. "Headhunter" or "real cop"? Identity in the world of internal affairs officers. *Journal of Contemporary Ethnography,* 24: 99–130.

National Opinion Research Center (NORC). 1989. *General social surveys, 1972–1989: Cumulative codebook.* Chicago: University of Chicago.

Oakes, P. J., Haslam, S. A., & Turner, J. C. 1994. *Stereotyping and social reality.* Oxford, England: Blackwell.

Ouellet, L. J. 1994. *Pedal to the metal: The work lives of truckers,* Philadelphia: Temple University Press.

Page, R. M. 1984. *Stigma.* London: Routledge and Kegan Paul.

Palmer, C. E. 1978. Dog catchers: A descriptive study. *Qualitative Sociology,* 1: 79–107.

Perry, S. E. 1978. *San Francisco scavengers: Dirty work and the pride of ownership.* Berkeley, CA: University of California Press.

Petrillo, G. 1989–90. The distant mourner: An examination of the American gravedigger. *Omega,* 20: 139–148.

Pilcher, W. W. 1972. *The Portland longshoremen.* New York: Henry Holt.

Pine, V. R. 1975. *Caretaker of the dead: The American funeral director.* New York: Irvington.

Pratt, M. G. 1998. To be or not to be? Central questions in organizational identification. In D. A. Whetten & P. C. Godfrey (Eds.), *Identity in organizations: Building theory through conversations:* 171–207. Thousand Oaks, CA: Sage.

Reed, D. A. 1989. An *orderly world: The social construction of reality within an occupation.* Unpublished doctoral dissertation, Indiana University, Bloomington.

Reid, D. 1991. *Paris sewers and sewermen: Realities and representations.* Cambridge, MA: Harvard University Press.

Riemer, J. W. 1979. *Hard hats: The work world of construction workers.* Beverly Hills, CA: Sage.

Ritzer, G., & Walczak, D. 1986. *Working: Conflict and change* (3rd ed.). Englewood Cliffs, NJ: Prentice-Hall.

Rollins, J. 1985. *Between women: Domestics and their employers.* Philadelphia: Temple University Press.

Rosecrance, J. 1985. The invisible horsemen: The social world of the backstretch. *Qualitative Sociology,* 8: 248–265.

Santino, J. 1990. The outlaw emotions: Narrative expressions on the rules and roles of occupational identity. *American Behavioral Scientist,* 33: 318–329.

Sawinski, Z., & Domanski, H. 1991. Stability of prestige hierarchies in the face of social changes: Poland, 1958–1987. *International Sociology,* 6: 227–241.

Schwalbe, M. L., & Mason-Schrock, D. 1996. Identity work as group process. In B. Markovsky, M. J. Lovaglia, & R. Simon (Eds.), *Advances in group processes,* vol. 13: 113–147. Greenwich, CT: JAI Press.

Scott, M. B., & Lyman, S. M. 1968. Accounts. *American Sociological Review,* 33: 46–62.

Simpson, R. L., & Simpson, I. H. 1959. The psychiatric attendant: Development of an occupational self-image in a low-status occupation. *American Sociological Review,* 24: 389–392.

Stannard, C. I. 1973. Old folks and dirty work: The social conditions for patient abuse in a nursing home. *Social Problems,* 20: 329–342.

Staw, B. M. 1980. Rationality and justification in organizational life. In B. M. Staw & L. L. Cummings (Eds.), *Research in organizational behavior,* vol. 2: 45–80, Greenwich, CT: JAI Press.

Stenross, B., & Kleinman, S. 1989. The highs and lows of emotional labor: Detectives' encounters with criminals and victims. *Journal of Contemporary Ethnography,* 17: 435–452.

Stephens, J. 1974. Carnies and marks: The sociology of elderly street peddlers. *Sociological Symposium,* No. 11: 25–41.

Sudnow, D. 1967. *Passing on: The social organization of dying.* Englewood Cliffs, NJ: Prentice-Hall.

Sutton, R. I. 1991. Maintaining norms about expressed emotions: The case of bill collectors. *Administrative Science Quarterly,* 36: 245–268.

Sykes, G. M., & Matza, D. 1957. Techniques of neutralization: A theory of delinquency. *American Sociological Review,* 22: 664–670.

Tajfel, H., & Turner, J. C. 1986. The social identity theory of intergroup behavior. In S. Worchel & W. G. Austin (Eds.), *Psychology of intergroup relations* (2nd ed.): 7–24. Chicago: Nelson-Hall Publishers.

Terkel, S. 1975. *Working.* New York: Avon.

Thompson, W. E. 1991. Handling the stigma of handling the dead: Morticians and funeral directors. *Deviant Behavior,* 12: 403–429.

Thompson, W. E., & Harred, J. L. 1992. Topless dancers: Managing stigma in a deviant occupation. *Deviant Behavior,* 13: 291–311.

Treiman, D. J. 1977. *Occupational prestige in comparative perspective.* New York: Academic Press.

Trice, H. M. 1993. *Occupational subcultures in the workplace.* Ithaca, NY: ILR Press.

Trice, H. M., & Beyer, J. M. 1993. *The cultures of work organizations.* Englewood Cliffs, NJ: Prentice-Hall.

Van Maanen, J., & Barley, S. R. 1984. Occupational communities: Culture and control in organizations. In B. M. Staw & L. L. Cummings (Eds.), *Research in organizational behavior,* vol. 6: 287–365. Greenwich, CT: JAI Press.

Wacquant, L. J. D. 1995. The pugilistic point of view: How boxers think and feel about their trade. *Theory and Society,* 24: 489–535.

Walsh, E. J. 1975. *Dirty work, race and self-esteem.* Ann Arbor: Institute of Labor Relations, University of Michigan.

Weick, K. E. 1995. *Sensemaking in organizations.* Thousand Oaks, CA: Sage.

Weigert, A., Teitge, J. S., & Teitge, D. W. 1986. *Society and identity: Toward a sociological psychology.* New York: Cambridge University Press.

Wiley, M. G., & Alexander, C. N., Jr. 1987. From situated activity to self attribution: The impact of social structural schemata. In K. Yardley & T. Honess (Eds.), *Self and identity: Psychosocial perspectives:* 105–117. Chichester, England: Wiley.

Wood, J. V. 1989. Theory and research concerning social comparisons of personal attributes. *Psychological Bulletin,* 106: 231–248.

Questions

1. What makes work dirty?

2. The authors of this article said that they focused their analysis on the "occupation or workgroup level of analysis rather than the individual or organization level, because the stigma of dirty work is typically a group-level issue." Explain what they meant.

BLAKE E. ASHFORD AND GLEN E. KREINER

3. Professors Ashforth and Kreiner suggest that "while the stigma of dirty work undermines the status of certain occupations, it simultaneously facilitates the development of strong occupational cultures." What do they mean by this?

4. The hospital orderly who cleans up the blood and guts from the floor of the operating room is doing dirty work, but the surgeon who made the mess in the first place isn't. Why is that?

5. The authors of this article quote Everett Hughes (arguably the founder of sociological studies of occupations) who said that "If a certain problem turned up in one occupation, it was nearly certain to turn up in all." What can an understanding of how workers cope with dirty work tell us about workers in non-dirty occupations?

22

ANYBODY'S SON WILL DO

Gwynne Dyer

Ordinary people would be loathe to do the sorts of things that soldiers may be called upon to do—but societies seem to need soldiers. As Dyer explains in this chapter excerpted from his 1985 book *War*, the means of socializing men out of the civilian role and into the soldier/killer role has become institutionalized as a result of centuries of experience.

. . . All soldiers belong to the same profession, no matter what country they serve, and it makes them different from everybody else. They have to be different, for their job is ultimately about killing and dying, and those things are not a natural vocation for any human being. Yet all soldiers are born civilians. The method for turning young men into soldiers—people who kill other people and expose themselves to death—is basic training. It's essentially the same all over the world, and it always has been, because young men everywhere are pretty much alike.

Human beings are fairly malleable, especially when they are young, and in every young man there are attitudes for any army to work with: the inherited values and postures, more or less dimly recalled, of the tribal warriors who were once the model for every young boy to emulate. Civilization did not involve a sudden clean break in the way people behave, but merely the progressive distortion and redirection of all the ways in which people in the old tribal societies used to behave, and modern definitions of maleness still contain a great deal of the old warrior ethic. The anarchic machismo of the primitive warrior is not what modern armies really need in their soldiers, but it does provide them with promising raw material for the transformation they must work in their recruits.

Just how this transformation is wrought varies from time to time and from country to country. In totally militarized societies—ancient Sparta, the samurai class of medieval Japan, the areas controlled by organizations like the Eritrean People's Liberation Front today[1]—it begins at puberty or before, when the young boy is immersed in a disciplined society in which only the military values are allowed to penetrate. In more sophisticated modern societies, the process is briefer and more concentrated, and the way it works is much more visible. It is, essentially, a conversion process in an almost religious sense—and as in all conversion phenomena, the emotions are far more important than the specific ideas. . . .

> When I was going to school, we used to have to recite the Pledge of Allegiance every day. They don't do that now. You know, we've got kids that come in here now, when they first get here, they don't know the Pledge of Allegiance to the

---

[1]Eritrea, an Italian colony from 1885 to 1941, was annexed by Ethiopia in 1962. After a 30-year civil war, Eritrea gained its independence in 1992.—Ed.

flag. And that's something—that's like a cardinal sin. . . . My daughter will know that stuff by the time she's three; she's two now and she's working on it. . . . You know, you've got to have your basics, the groundwork where you can start to build a child's brain from. . . .

—USMC drill instructors,
Parris Island recruit training depot, 1981

That is what the rhetoric of military patriotism sounds like, in every country and at every level—and it is virtually irrelevant so far as the actual job of soldiering is concerned. Soldiers are not just robots; they are ordinary human beings with national and personal loyalties, and many of them do feel the need for some patriotic or ideological justification for what they do. But which nation, which ideology, does not matter: men will fight as well and die as bravely for the Khmer Rouge as for "God, King, and Country." Soldiers are the instruments of politicians and priests, ideologues and strategists, who may have high national or moral purposes in mind, but the men down in the trenches fight for more basic motives. The closer you get to the front line, the fewer abstract nouns you hear.

Armies know this. It is their business to get men to fight, and they have had a long time to work out the best way of doing it. All of them pay lip service to the symbols and slogans of their political masters, though the amount of time they must devote to this activity varies from country to country. It is less in the United States than in the Soviet Union, and it is still less in a country like Israel, which actually fights frequent wars. Nor should it be thought that the armies are hypocritical—most of their members really do believe in their particular national symbols and slogans. But their secret is that they know these are not the things that sustain men in combat.

What really enables men to fight is their own self-respect, and a special kind of love that has nothing to do with sex or idealism. Very few men have died in battle, when the moment actually arrived, for the United States of America or for the sacred cause of Communism, or even for their homes and families; if they had any choice in the matter at all, they chose to die for each other and for their own vision of themselves. . . .

The way armies produce this sense of brotherhood in a peacetime environment is basic training: a feat of psychological manipulation on the grand scale which has been so consistently successful and so universal that we fail to notice it as remarkable. In countries where the army must extract its recruits in their late teens, whether voluntarily or by conscription, from a civilian environment that does not share the military values, basic training involves a brief but intense period of indoctrination whose purpose is not really to teach the recruits basic military skills, but rather to change their values and their loyalties. "I guess you could say we brainwash them a little bit," admitted a U.S. Marine drill instructor, "but you know they're good people." . . .

It's easier if you catch them young. You can train older men to be soldiers; it's done in every major war. But you can never get them to believe that they like it, which is the major reason armies try to get their recruits before they are twenty. There are other reasons too, of course, like the physical fitness, lack of dependents, and economic dispensability of teenagers, that make armies prefer them, but the most important qualities teenagers bring to basic training are enthusiasm and naiveté. Many of them actively want the discipline and the closely structured environment that the armed forces will provide, so there is no need for the recruiters to deceive the kids about what will happen to them after they join.

There is discipline. There is drill. . . . When you are relying on your mates and they are relying on you, there's no room for slackness or sloppiness. If you're not prepared to accept the rules, you're better off where you are.

—British army recruiting advertisement, 1976

People are not born soldiers, they become soldiers. . . . And it should not begin at the moment when a new recruit is enlisted into the ranks, but rather much earlier, at the time of the first signs of maturity, during the time of adolescent dreams.

—*Red Star* (Soviet army newspaper), 1973

Young civilians who have volunteered and have been accepted by the Marine Corps[2] arrive at Parris Island, the Corps's East Coast facility for basic training, in a state of considerable excitement and apprehension: most are aware that they are about to undergo an extraordinary and very difficult experience. But they do not make their own way to the base; rather, they trickle in to Charleston airport on various flights throughout the day on which their training platoon is due to form, and are held there, in a state of suppressed but mounting nervous tension, until late in the evening. When the buses finally come to carry them the seventy-six miles to Parris Island, it is often after midnight—and this is not an administrative oversight. The shock treatment they are about to receive will work most efficiently if they are worn out and somewhat disoriented when they arrive.

The basic training organization is a machine, processing several thousand young men every month, and every facet and gear of it has been designed with the sole purpose of turning civilians into Marines as efficiently as possible. Provided it can have total control over their bodies and their environment for approximately three months, it can practically guarantee converts. Parris Island provides that controlled environment, and the recruits do not set foot outside it again until they graduate as Marine privates eleven weeks later.

They're allowed to call home, so long as it doesn't get out of hand—every three weeks or so they can call home and make sure everything's all right, if they haven't gotten a letter or there's a particular set of circumstances. If it's a case of an emergency call coming in, then they're allowed to accept that call; if not, one of my staff will take the message. . . .

In some cases I'll get calls from parents who haven't quite gotten adjusted to the idea that their son had cut the strings—and in a lot of cases that's what they're doing. The military provides them with an opportunity to leave home but they're still in a rather secure environment.

—Captain Brassington, USMC

For the young recruits, basic training is the closest thing their society can offer to a formal rite of passage,[3] and the institution probably stands in an unbroken line of descent from the lengthy ordeals by which young males in pre-civilized groups were initiated into the adult community of warriors. But in civilized societies it is a highly functional institution whose product is not anarchic warriors, but trained soldiers.

Basic training is not really about teaching people skills; it's about changing them, so that they can do things they wouldn't have dreamt of otherwise. It works by applying enormous physical and mental pressure to men who have been isolated from their normal civilian environment and placed in one where the only right way to think and behave is the way the Marine Corps wants them to. The key word the men who run the machine use to describe this process is *motivation*.

I can motivate a recruit and in third phase, if I tell him to jump off the third deck, he'll jump off the third deck. Like I said before, it's a captive audience and I can train that guy; I can get him to do anything I want him to do. . . . They're good kids and they're out to do the

---

[2]Something you might not know if you have no military experience and don't watch war movies or attend the ballet is that the word *corps* is pronounced "core" (from the Latin *corpus,* meaning "body").—Ed.

[3]The concept of rite of passage (or *rites de passage*) is discussed in *The Practical Skeptic,* chapter 10.—Ed.

right thing. We get some bad kids, but you know, we weed those out. But as far as motivation—here, we can motivate them to do anything you want, in recruit training.

—USMC drill instructor, Parris Island

The first three days the raw recruits spend at Parris Island are actually relatively easy, though they are hustled and shouted at continuously. It is during this time that they are documented and inoculated, receive uniforms, and learn the basic orders of drill that will enable young Americans (who are not very accustomed to this aspect of life) to do everything simultaneously in large groups. But the most important thing that happens in "forming" is the surrender of the recruits' own clothes, their hair—all the physical evidence of their individual civilian identities.

During a period of only seventy-two hours, in which they are allowed little sleep, the recruits lay aside their former lives in a series of hasty rituals (like being shaven to the scalp) whose symbolic significance is quite clear to them even though they are quite deliberately given absolutely no time for reflection, or any hint that they might have the option of turning back from their commitment. The men in charge of them know how delicate a tightrope they are walking, though, because at this stage the recruits are still newly caught civilians who have not yet made their ultimate inward submission to the discipline of the Corps.

> Forming Day One makes me nervous. You've got a whole new mob of recruits, you know, sixty or seventy depending, and they don't know anything. You don't know what kind of a reaction you're going to get from the stress you're going to lay on them, and it just worries me the first day.
>
> Things could happen, I'm not going to lie to you. Something might happen. A recruit might decide he doesn't want any part of this stuff and maybe take a poke at you or something like that. In a situation like that it's going to be a spur-of-the-moment thing and that worries me.
>
> —USMC drill instructor

But it rarely happens. The frantic bustle of forming is designed to give the recruit no time to think about resisting what is happening to him. And so the recruits emerge from their initiation into the system, stripped of their civilian clothes, shorn of their hair, and deprived of whatever confidence in their own identity they may previously have had as eighteen-year-olds, like so many blanks ready to have the Marine identity impressed upon them.

The first stage in any conversion process is the destruction of an individual's former beliefs and confidence, and his reduction to a position of helplessness and need. It isn't really as drastic as all that, of course, for three days cannot cancel out eighteen years; the inner thoughts and the basic character are not erased. But the recruits have already learned that the only acceptable behavior is to repress any unorthodox thoughts and to mimic the character the Marine Corps wants. Nor are they, on the whole, reluctant to do so, for they *want* to be Marines. From the moment they arrive at Parris Island, the vague notion that has been passed down for a thousand generations that masculinity means being a warrior becomes an explicit article of faith, relentlessly preached: to be a man means to be a Marine.

There are very few eighteen-year-old boys who do not have highly romanticized ideas of what it means to be a man, so the Marine Corps has plenty of buttons to push. And it starts pushing them on the first day of real training: the officer in charge of the formation appears before them for the first time, in full dress uniform with medals, and tells them how to become men.

> The United States Marine Corps has 205 years of illustrious history to speak for itself. You have made the most important decision in your life . . . by signing your name, your life, your pledge to the Government of the United States, and even more importantly, to the United States Marine Corps—a brotherhood, an elite unit. In 10.3 weeks you are going to become a member

of that history, those traditions, this organization—if you have what it takes.

All of you want to do that by virtue of your signing your name as a man. The Marine Corps says that we build men. Well, I'll go a little bit further. We develop the tools that you have— and everybody has those tools to a certain extent right now. We're going to give you the blueprints, and we are going to show you how to build a Marine. *You've* got to build a Marine—you understand?
—Captain Pingree, USMC

The recruits, gazing at him with awe and adoration, shout in unison, "Yes sir!" just as they have been taught. They do it willingly, because they are volunteers—but even conscripts tend to have the romantic fervor of volunteers if they are only eighteen years old. Basic training, whatever its hardships, is a quick way to become a man among men, with an undeniable status, and beyond the initial consent to undergo it, it doesn't even require any decisions.

> I had just dropped out of high school and I wasn't doing much on the street except hanging out, as most teenagers would be doing. So they gave me an opportunity—a recruiter picked me up, gave me a good line, and said that I could make it in the Marines, that I have a future ahead of me. And since I was living with my parents, I figured that I could start my own life here and grow up a little.
> —USMC recruit, 1982

> I like the hand-to-hand combat and . . . things like that. It's a little rough going on me, and since I have a small frame I would like to become deadly, as I would put it. I like to have them words, especially the way they've been teaching me here.
> —USMC recruit (from Brooklyn),
> Parris Island, 1982

The training, when it starts, seems impossibly demanding physically for most of the recruits—and then it gets harder week by week. There is a constant barrage of abuse and insults aimed at the recruits, with the deliberate

purpose of breaking down their pride and so destroying their ability to resist the transformation of values and attitudes that the Corps intends them to undergo. At the same time the demands for constant alertness and for instant obedience are continuously stepped up, and the standards by which the dress and behavior of the recruits are judged become steadily more unforgiving. But it is all carefully calculated by the men who run the machine, who think and talk in terms of the stress they are placing on the recruits: "We take so many c.c.'s of stress and we administer it to each man— they should be a little bit scared and they should be unsure, but they're adjusting." The aim is to keep the training arduous but just within most of the recruits' capability to withstand. One of the most striking achievements of the drill instructors is to create and maintain the illusion that basic training is an extraordinary challenge, one that will set those who graduate apart from others, when in fact almost everyone can succeed.

There has been some preliminary weeding out of potential recruits even before they begin training, to eliminate the obviously unsuitable minority, and some people do "fail" basic training and get sent home, at least in peacetime. The standards of acceptable performance in the U.S. armed forces, for example, tend to rise and fall in inverse proportion to the number and quality of recruits available to fill the forces to the authorized manpower levels. (In 1980, about 15 percent of Marine recruits did not graduate from basic training.) But there are very few young men who cannot be turned into passable soldiers if the forces are willing to invest enough effort in it.

Not even physical violence is necessary to effect the transformation, though it has been used by most armies at most times.

> It's not what it was fifteen years ago down here. The Marine Corps still occupies the position of a tool which the society uses when it feels like that is a resort that they have to fall to. Our

society changes as all societies do, and our society felt that through enlightened training methods we could still produce the same product—and when you examine it, they're right. . . . Our 100 c.c.'s of stress is really all we need, not two gallons of it, which is what used to be.[4] . . . In some cases with some of the younger drill instructors it was more an initiation than it was an acute test, and so we introduced extra officers and we select our drill instructors to "fine-tune" it.

—Captain Brassington, USMC

There is, indeed, a good deal of fine-tuning in the roles that the men in charge of training any specific group of recruits assume. At the simplest level, there is a sort of "good cop–bad cop" manipulation of the recruits' attitudes toward those applying the stress. The three younger drill instructors with a particular serial are quite close to them in age and unremittingly harsh in their demands for ever higher performance, but the senior drill instructor, a man almost old enough to be their father, plays a more benevolent and understanding part and is available for individual counseling. And generally offstage, but always looming in the background, is the company commander, an impossibly austere and almost godlike personage.

At least these are the images conveyed to the recruits, although of course all these men cooperate closely with an identical goal in view. It works: in the end they become not just role models and authority figures, but the focus of the recruits' developing loyalty to the organization.

I imagine there's some fear, especially in the beginning, because they don't know what to expect. . . . I think they hate you at first, at least for a week or two, but it turns to respect. . . . They're seeking discipline, they're seeking someone to take charge, 'cause at home they never got it. . . . They're looking to be told what to do and then someone is standing there enforcing what they tell them to do, and it's kind of like the father-and-son game, all the way through. They form a fatherly image of the DI[5] whether they want to or not.

—Sergeant Carrington, USMC

Just the sheer physical exercise, administered in massive doses, soon has the recruits feeling stronger and more competent than ever before. Inspections, often several times daily, quickly build up their ability to wear the uniform and carry themselves like real Marines, which is a considerable source of pride. The inspections also help to set up the pattern in the recruits of unquestioning submission to military authority: standing stock-still, staring straight ahead, while somebody else examines you closely for faults is about as extreme a ritual act of submission as you can make with your clothes on.

But they are not submitting themselves merely to the abusive sergeant making unpleasant remarks about the hair in their nostrils. All around them are deliberate reminders—the flags and insignia displayed on parade, the military music, the marching formations and drill instructors' cadenced calls—of the idealized organization, the "brotherhood" to which they will be admitted as full members if they submit and conform. Nowhere in the armed forces are the military courtesies so elaborately observed, the staffs' uniforms so immaculate (some DIs change several times a day), and the ritual aspects of military life so highly visible as on a basic training establishment.

Even the seeming inanity of close-order drill has a practical role in the conversion process. It has been over a century since mass formations of men were of any use on the battlefield, but every army in the world still drills its troops, especially during basic training, because marching

---

[4]As a point of information, there are 4 c.c.'s in a teaspoon.—Ed.

[5]Drill instructor.—Ed.

in formation, with every man moving his body in the same way at the same moment, is a direct physical way of learning two things a soldier must believe: that orders have to be obeyed automatically and instantly, and that you are no longer an individual, but part of a group.

The recruits' total identification with the other members of their unit is the most important lesson of all, and everything possible is done to foster it. They spend almost every waking moment together—a recruit alone is an anomaly to be looked into at once—and during most of that time they are enduring shared hardships. They also undergo collective punishments, often for the misdeed or omission of a single individual (talking in the ranks, a bed not swept under during barracks inspection), which is a highly effective way of suppressing any tendencies toward individualism. And, of course, the DIs place relentless emphasis on competition with other "serials" in training: there may be something infinitely pathetic to outsiders about a marching group of anonymous recruits chanting, "Lift your heads and hold them high, 3313 is a-passin' by," but it doesn't seem like that to the men in the ranks.

Nothing is quite so effective in building up a group's morale and solidarity, though, as a steady diet of small triumphs. Quite early in basic training, the recruits begin to do things that seem, at first sight, quite dangerous: descend by ropes from fifty-foot towers, cross yawning gaps hand-over-hand on high wires (known as the Slide for Life, of course), and the like. The common denominator is that these activities are daunting but not really dangerous: the ropes will prevent anyone from falling to his death off the rappelling tower, and there is a pond of just the right depth—deep enough to cushion a falling man, but not deep enough that he is likely to drown—under the Slide for Life. The goal is not to kill recruits, but to build up their confidence as individuals and as a group by allowing them to overcome apparently frightening obstacles.

You have an enemy here at Parris Island. The enemy that you're going to have at Parris Island is in every one of us. It's in the form of cowardice. The most rewarding experience you're going to have in recruit training is standing on line every evening, and you'll be able to look into each other's eyes, and you'll be able to say to each other with your eyes: "By God, we've made it one more day! We've defeated the coward."

—Captain Pingree, USMC

Number on deck, sir, forty-five . . . highly motivated, truly dedicated, rompin', stompin', bloodthirsty, kill-crazy United States Marine Corps recruits, SIR!

—Marine chant, Parris Island, 1982

If somebody does fail a particular test, he tends to be alone, for the hurdles are deliberately set low enough that most recruits can clear them if they try. In any large group of people there is usually a goat: someone whose intelligence or manner or lack of physical stamina marks him for failure and contempt. The competent drill instructor, without deliberately setting up this unfortunate individual for disgrace, will use his failure to strengthen the solidarity and confidence of the rest. When one hapless young man fell off the Slide for Life into the pond, for example, his drill instructor shouted the usual invective—"Well, get out of the water. Don't contaminate it all day"—and then delivered the payoff line: "Go back and change your clothes. You're useless to your unit now."

"Useless to your unit" is the key phrase, and all the recruits know that what it means is "useless *in battle.*" The Marine drill instructors at Parris Island know exactly what they are doing to the recruits, and why. They are not rear-echelon people filling comfortable jobs, but the most dedicated and intelligent NCOs[6] the Marine Corps can find: even now, many of them have combat experience. The Corps has a

---

[6]Noncommissioned officers.—Ed.

clear-eyed understanding of precisely what it is training its recruits for—combat—and it ensures that those who do the training keep that objective constantly in sight.

The DIs "stress" the recruits, feed them their daily ration of synthetic triumphs over apparent obstacles, and bear in mind all the time that the goal is to instill the foundations for the instinctive, selfless reactions and the fierce group loyalty that is what the recruits will need if they ever see combat. They are arch-manipulators, fully conscious of it, and utterly unashamed. These kids have signed up as Marines, and they could well see combat; this is the way they have to think if they want to live. . . .

Combat is the ultimate reality that Marines—or any other soldiers, under any flag—have to deal with. Physical fitness, weapons training, battle drills, are all indispensable elements of basic training, and it is absolutely essential that the recruits learn the attitudes of group loyalty and interdependency which will be their sole hope of survival and success in combat. The training inculcates or fosters all of those things, and even by the halfway point in the eleven-week course, the recruits are generally responding with enthusiasm to their tasks.

But there is nothing in all this (except the weapons drill) that would not be found in the training camp of a professional football team. What sets soldiers apart is their willingness to kill. But it is not a willingness that comes easily to most men—even young men who have been provided with uniforms, guns, and official approval to kill those whom their government has designated as enemies. They will, it is true, fall very readily into the stereotypes of the tribal warrior group. Indeed, most of them have had at least a glancing acquaintance in their early teens with gangs (more or less violent, depending on, among other things, the neighborhood), the modern relic of that ancient institution.

And in many ways what basic training produces is the uniformed equivalent of a modern street gang: a bunch of tough, confident kids full of bloodthirsty talk. But gangs don't actually kill each other in large numbers. If they behaved the way armies do, you'd need trucks to clean the bodies off the streets every morning. They're held back by the civilian belief—the normal human belief—that killing another person is an awesome act with huge consequences.

There is aggression in all of us—men, women, children, babies. Armies don't have to create it, and they can't even increase it. But most of us learn to put limits on our aggression, especially physical aggression, as we grow up. . . .

There is such a thing as a "natural soldier": the kind of man who derives his greatest satisfaction from male companionship, from excitement, and from the conquering of physical and psychological obstacles. He doesn't necessarily want to kill people as such, but he will have no objections if it occurs within a moral framework that gives him a justification—like war—and if it is the price of gaining admission to the kind of environment he craves. Whether such men are born or made, I do not know, but most of them end up in armies (and many move on again to become mercenaries, because regular army life in peacetime is too routine and boring).

But armies are not full of such men. They are so rare that they form only a modest fraction even of small professional armies, mostly congregating in the commando-type special forces. In large conscript armies they virtually disappear beneath the weight of numbers of more ordinary men. And it is these ordinary men, who do not like combat at all, that the armies must persuade to kill. Until only a generation ago, they did not even realize how bad a job they were doing.

Armies had always assumed that, given the proper rifle training, the average man would kill in combat with no further incentive than the knowledge that it was the only way to defend his own life. After all, there are no historical records of Roman legionnaires refusing to use their swords, or Marlborough's infantrymen[7] refusing to fire their muskets against the enemy. But then dispersion hit the battlefield, removing each rifleman from the direct observation of his companions—and when U.S. Army Colonel S. L. A. Marshall finally took the trouble to inquire into what they were doing in 1943–45, he found that on average only 15 percent of trained combat riflemen fired their weapons at all in battle. The rest did not flee, but they would not kill—even when their own position was under attack and their lives were in immediate danger.

> The thing is simply this, that out of an average one hundred men along the line of fire during the period of an encounter, only fifteen men on average would take any part with the weapons. This was true whether the action was spread over a day, or two days or three. . . . In the most aggressive infantry companies, under the most intense local pressure, the figure rarely rose above 25% of total strength from the opening to the close of an action.
>
> —Col. S. L. A. Marshall

Marshall conducted both individual interviews and mass interviews with over four hundred infantry companies, both in Europe and in the Central Pacific, immediately after they had been in close combat with German or Japanese troops, and the results were the same each time. They were, moreover, as astonishing to the company officers and the troops themselves as they were to Marshall; each man who hadn't fired his rifle thought he had been alone in his defection from duty.

Even more indicative of what was going on was the fact that almost all the crew-served weapons had been fired. Every man had been trained to kill and knew it was his duty to kill, and so long as he was in the presence of other

soldiers who could see his actions, he went ahead and did it. But the great majority of the riflemen, each unobserved by the others in his individual foxhole, had chosen not to kill, even though it increased the likelihood of his own death. . . .

But the question naturally arises: if the great majority of men are not instinctive killers, and if most military killing these days is in any case done by weapons operating from a distance at which the question of killing scarcely troubles the operators—then why is combat an exclusively male occupation? The great majority of women, everyone would agree, are not instinctive killers either, but so what? If the remote circumstances in which the killing is done or the deliberate conditioning supplied by the military enable most men to kill, why should it be any different for women?

My own guess would be that it probably wouldn't be different; it just hasn't been tried very extensively. But it is an important question, because it has to do with the causes and possible cure of war. If men fight wars because that is an intrinsic part of the male character, then nothing can abolish the institution of warfare short of abolishing the male half of the human race (or at least, as one feminist suggested, disfranchising it for a hundred years).

If, on the other hand, wars are a means of allocating power between civilized human groups, in which the actual soldiers have always been male simply because men were more suited to it by their greater physical strength and their freedom from the burden of childbearing, then what we are discussing is not Original Sin, but simply a mode of social behavior. The fact that almost every living male for thousands of generations has imbibed some of the warrior mystique is no proof of a genetic predisposition to be warlike. The cultural continuity is quite enough to transmit such attitudes, and men were specialized in the hunting and warrior functions for the same physical reasons long before civilized war was invented.

---

[7]John Churchill (1650–1722), first Duke of Marlborough, British general, supreme commander of the British forces in the War of the Spanish Succession.—Ed.

It was undoubtedly men, the "hunting" specialists, who invented civilized war, just as it was probably women, specializing in the "gathering" part of the primitive economy, who invented agriculture. That has no necessary relevance today: we all eat vegetables, and we can all die in war. It is a more serious allegation against males to say that all existing forms of political power have been shaped predominantly by men, so that even if wars are about power and not about the darker side of the masculine psyche, war is still a male problem. That has unquestionably been true through all of history (although it remains to be proven that women exercising power respond very differently to its temptations and obsessions). But there is no need to settle that argument: if war and masculinity are not inseparable, then we have already moved onto negotiable ground. For the forms of political power, unlike psyches, are always negotiable.

Unfortunately there is little direct support for this optimistic hypothesis in the prevailing current of opinion among soldiers generally, where war and maleness are indeed seen as inseparable. To say that the combat branches of the armed forces are sexist is like remarking that gravity generally pulls downward, and nowhere is the contempt for women greater than at a recruit training base like Parris Island. The DIs are quite ruthless in exploiting every prejudice and pushing every button that will persuade the recruits to accept the value system they are selling, and one of those buttons (quite a large one) is the conviction of young males—or at least the desire to be convinced—that they are superior to young females. (After all, even recruits want to feel superior to somebody, and it certainly isn't going to be anybody in their immediate vicinity at Parris Island.)

When it's all boys together, especially among the younger men, Marine Corps slang for any woman who isn't the wife, mother, or daughter of anyone present is "Suzie." It is short for "Suzie Rottencrotch"—and Suzie crops up a lot in basic training. Even when the topic of instruction is hand and arm signals in combat.

> Privates, if you don't have a little Suzie now, maybe you're going to find one when you get home. You bet. You'll find the first cheap slut you can get back home. What do you mean, "No"? You're a Marine, you're going to do it.
>
> If we get home with little Suzie . . . we're in a nice companionship with little Suzie and here you are getting hot and heavy and then you're getting ready to go down there and make that dive, privates, and Suzie says . . . Suzie says it's the wrong time of the month. Privates, if you don't want to get back home and indulge in this little adventure, you can show your girlfriend the hand and arm signal for "close it up."
>
> And you want her to close up those nasty little thighs of hers, do you not, privates? The hand and arm signal: the arms are laterally shoulder height, the fingers are extended, and the palms are facing toward the front. This is the starting position for "close it up" [tighten up the formation]: just like closing it up, bring the arms together just like that.
>
> Privates, in addition, I want you to dedicate all this training to one very special person. Can anyone tell me who that is, privates?
>
> (Voice) The Senior Drill Instructor, sir?
>
> No, not your Senior Drill Instructor. You're going to dedicate all this training, privates, to your enemy . . . to your enemy. To your enemy: the reason being, so *he* can die for *his* country. So who are we going to dedicate all this training to, privates?
>
> —lecture on hand and arm signals, Parris Island, 1982

And they shouted enthusiastically: "The enemy, sir! The enemy, sir!" It would not be instantly clear to the disinterested observer from Mars, however, why these spotty-faced male eighteen-year-olds are uniquely qualified to kill the enemy, while their equally spotty-faced female counterparts get to admire them from afar (or so the supposition goes), and get called Suzie Rottencrotch for their trouble.

Interestingly, it isn't entirely clear either to the senior military and civilian officials whose responsibility it is to keep the organization filled up with warm bodies capable of doing the job. Women are not employed in combat roles in the regular armed forces of any country (though increasing numbers of women have been admitted to the noncombat military jobs in the course of this century). But in the last decade the final barrier has come under serious consideration. It was, unsurprisingly, in the United States, where the problems of getting enough recruits for the all-volunteer armed forces converged with the changes of attitude flowing from the women's liberation movement, that the first serious proposals to send women into combat were entertained, during the latter years of the Carter administration.

> There is no question but that women could do a lot of things in the military. So could men in wheelchairs. But you couldn't expect the services to want a whole company of people in wheelchairs.
>
> —Gen. Lewis B. Hershey,
> former director, Selective Service System, 1978

> If for no other reason than because women are the bearers of children, they should not be in combat. Imagine your daughter as a ground soldier sleeping in the fields and expected to do all the things that soldiers do. It represents to me an absolute horror.
>
> —Gen. Jacqueline Cochran, U.S. Air Force

Despite the anguished cries of military conservatives, both male and female, the reaction of younger officers in the combat branches (all male, of course) was cautious but not entirely negative. The more intelligent ones dismissed at once arguments about strength and stamina—the average American woman, one pointed out, is bigger than the average Vietnamese man—and were as little impressed by the alleged special problems arising from the fact that female soldiers may become pregnant. In the noncombat branches, the army loses less time from its women soldiers due to pregnancy than it loses from desertion, drug abuse, and alcoholism in its male soldiers.

More important, few of the male officers involved in the experimental programs giving combat training to women recruits in the late 1970s had any doubt that the women would function effectively in combat. Neither did the women themselves. Despite their lack of the traditional male notions about the warrior stereotype, the training did its job. As one female trainee remarked: "I don't like the idea of killing anything . . . [and] I may not at this moment go into combat. But knowing that I can fire as well as I can fire now, knowing that today, I'd go in. I believe in my country . . . I'd fight to keep it."

The one major reservation the male officers training the "infantrywomen" had was about how the presence of women in combat would affect the men. The basic combat unit, a small group of men bound together by strong male ties of loyalty and trust, was a time-tested system that worked, and they were reluctant to tamper with it by adding an additional, unknown factor to the equation.

In the end a more conservative administration canceled the idea of introducing women to American combat units, and it may be some years yet before there are female soldiers in the infantry of any regular army. But it is manifestly sheer social conservatism that is retarding this development. Hundreds of thousands, if not millions, of women have fought in combat as irregular infantry in the past half-century, from the Yugoslav and Soviet partisans of World War II to Nicaragua in 1978–79. They performed quite satisfactorily, and so did the mixed units of which they were members. There are numerous differences of detail between guerrilla and regular army units, but none of them is of the sort to suggest that women would not fight just as well in a regular infantry battalion, or that the battalion would function less well if women were present.

The point of all this is not that women should be allowed (or indeed compelled) to take their fair share of the risks in combat. It is rather that war has moved a very long way from its undeniably warrior male origins, and that human behavior, male or female, is extremely malleable. Combat of the sort we know today, even at the infantryman's level—let alone the fighter pilot's—simply could not occur unless military organizations put immense effort into reshaping the behavior of individuals to fit their unusual and exacting requirements. The military institution, for all its imposing presence, is a highly artificial structure that is maintained only by constant endeavor. And if ordinary people's behavior is malleable in the direction the armed forces require, it is equally open to change in other directions. . . .

Questions

1. Why did Dyer title his article "*Anybody's* Son Will Do"?

2. "To be a man means to be a Marine"—or so recruits are taught. In what ways does the success of basic training seem to rely on the additional idea that if one cannot perform as a Marine, one is no better than a woman? How might the presence of female Marines in boot camp complicate the job of socializing males into their soldier role?

3. Erving Goffman, in *Asylums* (1961), defined "total institution" as "a place of residence and work where a large number of like-situated individuals, cut off from the wider society for an appreciable period of time, together lead an enclosed, formally administered round of life." Imagine that you've been put in charge of creating a total institution that has the goal of radically changing people's behavior. Military boot camp is one of the most successful types of total institutions. Based on what you've learned from Dyer's description of the way this total institution resocializes men, what sorts of procedures would you institute in your total institution to help ensure its success? For example, what sorts of things would you do to your "recruits" when they first arrive at your total institution?

23

SUSPENDED IDENTITY

Identity Transformation in a Maximum Security Prison

Thomas J. Schmid and Richard S. Jones

Schmid and Jones look closely at the resocialization process that new prison inmates undergo—but from the point of view of the prisoner and his concerns about his identity. As you read this 1991 article, consider how experiences in this sort of total institution differ from those undergone by men in boot camp.

A prison sentence constitutes a "massive assault" on the identity of those imprisoned (Berger 1963, 100–101). This assault is especially severe on first-time inmates, and we might expect radical identity changes to ensue from their imprisonment. At the same time, a prisoner's awareness of the challenge to his identity affords some measure of protection against it. As part of an ethnographic analysis of the prison experiences of first-time, short-term inmates, this article presents an identity transformation model that differs both from the gradual transformation processes that characterize most adult identity changes and from such radical transformation processes as brainwashing or conversion.

Data for the study are derived principally from ten months of participant observation at a maximum security prison for men in the upper midwest of the United States. One of the authors was an inmate serving a felony sentence for one year and one day, while the other

participated in the study as an outside observer. Relying on traditional ethnographic data collection and analysis techniques, this approach offered us general observations of hundreds of prisoners, and extensive field-notes that were based on repeated, often daily, contacts with about fifty inmates, as well as on personal relationships established with a smaller number of inmates. We subsequently returned to the prison to conduct focused interviews with other prisoners; using information provided by prison officials, we were able to identify and interview twenty additional first-time inmates who were serving sentences of two years or less. See Schmid and Jones (1987) for further description of this study.

Three interrelated research questions guided our analysis: How do first-time, short-term inmates define the prison world, and how do their definitions change during their prison careers? How do these inmates adapt to the prison world, and how do their adaptation strategies change during their prison careers? How do their self-definitions change during their prison careers? Our analyses of the first two questions are presented in detail elsewhere (Schmid and Jones 1987, 1990); an abbreviated outline of these analyses, to which we will

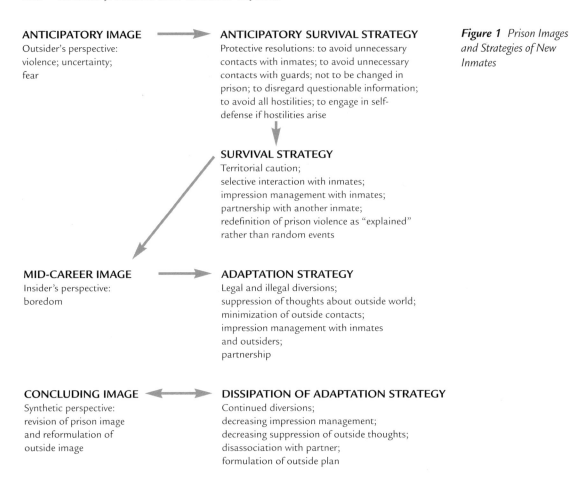

ANTICIPATORY IMAGE
Outsider's perspective:
violence; uncertainty;
fear

ANTICIPATORY SURVIVAL STRATEGY
Protective resolutions: to avoid unnecessary
contacts with inmates; to avoid unnecessary
contacts with guards; not to be changed in
prison; to disregard questionable information;
to avoid all hostilities; to engage in self-
defense if hostilities arise

SURVIVAL STRATEGY
Territorial caution;
selective interaction with inmates;
impression management with inmates;
partnership with another inmate;
redefinition of prison violence as "explained"
rather than random events

MID-CAREER IMAGE
Insider's perspective:
boredom

ADAPTATION STRATEGY
Legal and illegal diversions;
suppression of thoughts about outside world;
minimization of outside contacts;
impression management with inmates
and outsiders;
partnership

CONCLUDING IMAGE
Synthetic perspective:
revision of prison image
and reformulation of
outside image

DISSIPATION OF ADAPTATION STRATEGY
Continued diversions;
decreasing impression management;
decreasing suppression of outside thoughts;
disassociation with partner;
formulation of outside plan

Figure 1 *Prison Images and Strategies of New Inmates*

allude throughout this article, is presented in Figure 1. The identity transformation model presented here, based on our analysis of the third question, is outlined in Figure 2.

Preprison Identity

Our data suggest that the inmates we studied have little in common before their arrival at prison, except their conventionality. Although convicted of felonies, most do not possess "criminal" identities (cf. Irwin 1970, 29–34). They begin their sentences with only a vague, incomplete image (Boulding 1961) of what prison is like, but an image that nonetheless stands in contrast to how they view their own social worlds. Their prison image is dominated by the theme of violence: they see prison inmates as violent, hostile, alien human beings, with whom they have nothing in common. They have several specific fears about what will happen to them in prison, including fears of assault, rape, and death. They are also concerned about their identities, fearing that—if they survive prison at all—they are in danger of changing in prison, either through the intentional efforts of rehabilitation personnel or through the unavoidable hardening effects of the prison environment. Acting on this imagery (Blumer 1969)—or, more precisely, on the inconsonance of their self-images with this

Figure 2 Suspended
Identity Dialectic

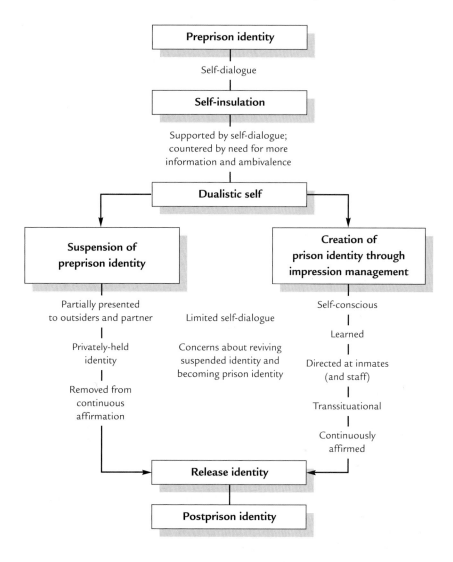

prison image—they develop an anticipatory survival strategy (see Figure 1) that consists primarily of protective resolutions: a resolve to avoid all hostilities; a resolve to avoid all nonessential contacts with inmates and guards; a resolve to defend themselves in any way possible; and a resolve not to change, or to be changed, in prison.

A felon's image and strategy are formulated through a running self-dialogue, a heightened state of reflexive awareness (Lewis 1979)

through which he ruminates about his past behavior and motives, and imaginatively projects himself into the prison world. This self-dialogue begins shortly after his arrest, continues intermittently during his trial or court hearings, and becomes especially intense at the time of his transfer to prison.

You start taking a review—it's almost like your life is passing before your eyes. You wonder how in the heck you got to this point and, you know, what are—what's your family gonna think about it—your friends, all the talk, and how are you going to deal with that—and the kids, you know, how are they gonna react to it? . . . All those things run through your head. . . . The total loss of control—the first time in my life that some other people were controlling my life.

• • •

My first night in the joint was spent mainly on kicking myself in the butt for putting myself in the joint. It was a very emotional evening. I thought a lot about all my friends and family, the good-byes, the things we did the last couple of months, how good they had been to me, sticking by me. I also thought about my fears: Am I going to go crazy? Will I end up fighting for my life? How am I going to survive in here for a year? Will I change? Will things be the same when I get out?

His self-dialogue is also typically the most extensive self-assessment he has ever conducted; thus, at the same time that he is resolving not to change, he is also initiating the kind of introspective analysis that is essential to any identity transformation process.

Self-Insulation

A felon's self-dialogue continues during the initial weeks and months of his sentence, and it remains a solitary activity, each inmate struggling to come to grips with the inconsonance of his established (preprison) identity and his present predicament. Despite the differences in their preprison identities, however, inmates now share a common situation that affects their identities. With few exceptions, their self-dialogues involve feelings of vulnerability, discontinuity, and differentiation from other inmates, emotions that reflect both the degradations and deprivations of institutional life (cf. Garfinkel 1956; Goffman 1961; and Sykes 1958) and their continuing outsiders' perspective on the prison world. These feelings are obviously the result of everything that has happened to the inmates, but they are some-

thing else as well: they are the conditions in which every first-time, short-term inmate finds himself. They might even be called the common attributes of the inmates' selves-in-prison, for the irrelevance of their preprison identities within the prison world reduces their self-definitions, temporarily, to the level of pure emotion. These feelings, and a consequent emphasis on the "physical self" (Zurcher 1977, 176), also constitute the essential motivation for the inmates' self-insulation strategies.[1]

An inmate cannot remain wholly insulated within the prison world, for a number of reasons. He simply spends too much of his time in the presence of others to avoid all interaction with them. He also recognizes that his prison image is based on incomplete and inadequate information, and that he must interact with others in order to acquire first-hand information about the prison world. His behavior in prison, moreover, is guided not only by his prison image but by a fundamental ambivalence he feels about his situation, resulting from his marginality between the prison and outside social worlds (Schmid and Jones 1987). His ambivalence has several manifestations throughout his prison career, but the most important is his conflicting desires for self-insulation and for human communication.

Managing a Dualistic Self

An inmate is able to express both directions of his ambivalence (and to address his need for

---

[1]There are four principal components to the survival strategies of the inmates we studied, in the early months of their prison sentences. "Selective interaction" and "territorial caution" are essentially precautionary guidelines that allow inmates to increase their understanding of the prison world while minimizing danger to themselves. "Partnership" is a special friendship bond between two inmates, typically based on common backgrounds and interests (including a shared uncertainty about prison life) and strengthened by the inmates' mutual exploration of a hostile prison world. The fourth component of their strategies, impression management, is discussed in subsequent sections of this article.

more information about the prison) by drawing a distinction between his "true" identity (i.e., his outside, preprison identity) and a "false" identity he creates for the prison world. For most of a new inmate's prison career, his preprison identity remains a "subjective" or "personal" identity while his prison identity serves as his "objective" or "social" basis for interaction in prison (see Goffman 1963; Weigert 1986). This bifurcation of his self (Figure 2) is not a conscious decision made at a single point in time, but it does represent two conscious and interdependent identity-preservation tactics, formulated through self-dialogue and refined through tentative interaction with others.

First, after coming to believe that he cannot "be himself" in prison because he would be too vulnerable, he decides to "suspend" his preprison identity for the duration of his sentence. He retains his resolve not to let prison change him, protecting himself by choosing not to reveal himself (his "true" self) to others. Expressions of a suspension of identity emerged repeatedly and consistently in both the fieldwork and interview phases of our research through such statements as

> I was reserved. . . . I wouldn't be very communicative, you know. I'd try to keep conversation to a minimum. . . . I wasn't interested in getting close to anybody . . . or asking a lot of questions. You know, try to cut the conversation short . . . go my own way back to my cell or go to the library or do something.
>
> • • •
>
> I didn't want nobody to know too much about me. That was part of the act.

An inmate's decision to suspend his preprison identity emanates directly from his feelings of vulnerability, discontinuity and differentiation from other inmates. These emotions foster something like a "proto-sociological attitude" (Weigert, 1986, 173; see also Zurcher 1977), in which new inmates find it necessary to step outside their taken-for-granted preprison

identities. Rather than viewing these identities and the everyday life experience in which they are grounded as social constructions, however, inmates see the *prison* world as an artificial construction, and judge their "naturally occurring" preprison identities to be out of place within this construction. By attempting to suspend his preprison identity for the time that he spends in prison, an inmate believes that he will again "be his old self" after his release.

While he is in confinement, an inmate's decision to suspend his identity leaves him with little or no basis for interaction. His second identity tactic, then, is the creation of an identity that allows him to interact, however cautiously, with others. This tactic consists of his increasingly sophisticated impression management skills (Goffman 1959;[2] Schlenker 1980), which are initially designed simply to hide his vulnerability, but which gradually evolve into an alternative identity felt to be more suitable to the prison world. The character of the presented identity is remarkably similar from inmate to inmate:

> Well, I learned that you can't act like—you can't get the attitude where you are better than they are. Even where you might be better than them, you can't strut around like you are. Basically, you can't stick out. You don't stare at people and things like that. I knew a lot of these things from talking to people and I figured them out by myself. I sat down and figured out just what kind of attitude I'm going to have to take.
>
> • • •
>
> Most people out here learn to be tough, whether they can back it up or not. If you don't learn to be tough, you will definitely pay for it. This toughness can be demonstrated through a mean look, tough language, or an extremely big build. . . . One important thing is never to let your guard down.

---

[2]Recall from reading 14 Goffman's concepts of expressions given and expressions given off—these are important components of impression management.—Ed.

An inmate's prison identity, as an inauthentic presentation of self, is not in itself a form of identity transformation but is rather a form of identity construction. His prison identity is simply who he must pretend to be while he is in prison. It is a false identity created for survival in an artificial world. But this identity nonetheless emerges in the same manner as any other identity: it is learned from others, and it must be presented to, negotiated with, and validated by others. A new inmate arrives at prison with a general image of what prisoners are like, and he begins to flesh out this image from the day of his arrival, warily observing others just as they are observing him. Through watching others, through eavesdropping, through cautious conversation and selective interaction, a new inmate refines his understanding of what maximum security prisoners look like, how they talk, how they move, how they act. Despite his belief that he is different from these other prisoners, he knows that he cannot appear to be too different from them, if he is to hide his vulnerability. His initial image of other prisoners, his early observations, and his concern over how he appears to others thus provide a foundation for the identity he gradually creates through impression management.

Impression management skills, of course, are not exclusive to the prison world; a new inmate, like anyone else, has had experience in presenting a "front" to others, and he draws upon his experience in the creation of his prison identity. He has undoubtedly even had experience in projecting the very attributes—strength, stoicism, aplomb—required by his prison identity. Impression management in prison differs, however, in the totality with which it governs interactions and in the perceived costs of failure: humiliation, assault, or death. For these reasons the entire impression management process becomes a more highly conscious endeavor. When presenting himself before others, a new inmate pays close attention to such minute details of his front as eye contact, posture, and manner of walking:

> I finally got out of orientation. I was going out with the main population, going down to get my meals and things. The main thing is not to stare at a bunch of people, you know. I tried to just look ahead, you know, not stare at people. 'Cause I didn't really know; I just had to learn a little at a time.
>
> • • •
>
> The way you look seems to be very important. The feeling is you shouldn't smile, that a frown is much more appropriate. The eyes are very important. You should never look away; it is considered a sign of weakness. Either stare straight ahead, look around, or look the person dead in the eyes. The way you walk is important. You shouldn't walk too fast; they might think you were scared and in a hurry to get away.

To create an appropriate embodiment (Stone 1962; Weigert 1986) of their prison identities, some new inmates devote long hours to weightlifting or other body-building exercises, and virtually all of them relinquish their civilian clothes—which might express their preprison identities—in favor of the standard issue clothing that most inmates wear. Whenever a new inmate is open to the view of other inmates, in fact, he is likely to relinquish most overt symbols of his individuality, in favor of a standard issue "prison inmate" appearance.

By acting self-consciously, of course, a new inmate runs the risk of exposing the fact that he *is* acting. But he sees no alternative to playing his part better; he cannot "not act" because that too would expose the vulnerability of his "true" identity. He thus sees every new prison experience, every new territory that he is allowed to explore, as a test of his impression management skills. Every nonconfrontive encounter with another inmate symbolizes his success at these skills, but it is also a social validation of his prison identity. Eventually he comes to see that many, perhaps most, inmates are engaging in the same kind of inauthentic presentations of self (cf. Glaser and Strauss 1964). Their identities are as "false" as his, and their validations of his identity may be equally false. But he realizes that he is powerless to change this state of affairs, and that he must continue to present his prison identity for as long as he remains in prison.

A first-time inmate enters prison as an outsider, and it is from an outsider's perspective that he initially creates his prison identity. In contrast to this suspended preprison identity, his prison identity is a *shared* identity, because it is modeled on his observations of other inmates. Like those of more experienced prisoners, his prison identity is tied directly to the social role of "prison inmate" (cf. Scheff 1970; Solomon 1970); because he is an outsider, however, his prison identity is also severely limited by his narrow understanding of that role. It is based on an outsider's stereotype of who a maximum security inmate is and what he acts like. It is, nonetheless, a *structural* identity (Weigert 1968), created to address his outsider's institutional problems of social isolation and inadequate information about the prison world.

By the middle of his sentence, a new inmate comes to adopt what is essentially an insider's perspective on the prison world. His prison image has evolved to the point where it is dominated by the theme of boredom rather than violence. (The possibility of violence is still acknowledged and feared, but those violent incidents that do occur have been redefined as the consequences of prison norm violations rather than as random predatory acts; see Schmid and Jones 1990.) His survival strategy, although still extant, has been supplemented by such general adaptation techniques as legal and illegal diversionary activities and conscious efforts to suppress his thoughts about the outside world (Figure 1). His impression management

tactics have become second nature rather than self-conscious, as he routinely interacts with others in terms of his prison identity.

An inmate's suspension of his preprison identity, of course, is never absolute, and the separation between his suspended identity and his prison identity is never complete. He continues to interact with his visitors at least partially in terms of his preprison identity, and he is likely to have acquired at least one inmate "partner" with whom he interacts in terms of his preprison as well as his prison identity. During times of introspection, however—which take place less frequently but do not disappear—he generally continues to think of himself as being the same person he was before he came to prison. But it is also during these periods of self-dialogue that he begins to have doubts about his ability to revive his suspended identity.

> That's what I worry about a lot. Because I didn't want to change. . . . I'm still fighting it, 'cause from what I understood, before, I wasn't that bad—I wasn't even violent. But I have people say stuff to me now, before I used to say "O.k., o.k."—but now it seems like I got to eye them back, you know.

• • •

> I don't know, but I may be losing touch with the outside. I am feeling real strange during visits, very uncomfortable. I just can't seem to be myself, although I am not really sure what myself is all about. My mind really seems to be glued to the inside of these walls. I can't even really comprehend the outside. I haven't even been here three months, and I feel like I'm starting to lose it. Maybe I'm just paranoid. But during these visits I really feel like I'm acting. I'm groping for the right words, always trying to keep the conversation going. Maybe I'm just trying to present a picture that will relieve the minds of my visitors, I just don't know.

• • •

> I realized that strength is going to be an important factor whether I'm going to turn into a cold person or whether I'm going to keep my

humanitarian point of view. I know it is going to be an internal war. It's going to take a lot of energy to do that. . . . I just keep telling myself that you gotta do it and sometimes you get to the point where you don't care anymore. You just kinda lose it and you get so full of hate, so full of frustration, it gets wound up in your head a lot.

At this point, both the inmate's suspended preprison identity and his created prison identity are part of his "performance consciousness" (Schechner 1985), although they are not given equal value. His preprison identity is grounded primarily in the memory of his biography (Weigert 1986) rather than in self-performance. His concern, during the middle of his sentence, is that he has become so accustomed to dealing with others in terms of his prison identity—that he has been presenting and receiving affirmation of this identity for so long—that it is becoming his "true" identity.[3]

An inmate's fear that he is becoming the character he has been presenting is not unfounded. All of his interactions within the prison world indicate the strong likelihood of a "role-person merger" (Turner 1978). An inmate views his presentation of his prison identity as a necessary expression of his inmate status. Unlike situational identities presented through impression management in the outside world, performance of the inmate role is transsituational and continuous. For a new inmate, prison consists almost exclusively of front regions, in which he must remain in character. As long as he is in the maximum security institution, he remains in at least partial view of the audience for which his prison identity is intended: other prison inmates. Moreover, because the stakes of his performance are so high, there is little room for self-mockery or other forms of role distance (Coser 1966; Ungar 1984) from his prison identity, and there is little possibility that an inmate's performance will be "punctured" (Adler and Adler 1989) by his partner or other prison acquaintances. And because his presentation of his prison identity is continuous, he also receives continuous affirmation of his identity from others—affirmation that becomes more significant in light of the fact that he also remains removed from day-to-day reaffirmation of his preprison identity by his associates in the outside world. The inauthenticity of the process is beside the point: Stone's (1962, 93) observation that "one's identity is established when others *place* him as a social object by assigning him the same words of identity that he appropriates for himself or *announces*" remains sound even when both the announcements and the placements are recognized as false.

Standing against these various forms of support for an inmate's prison identity are the inmate's resolve not to be changed in prison, the fact that his sentence is relatively brief (though many new inmates lose sight of this brevity during the middle of their careers) and the limited reaffirmation of his preprison identity that he receives from outsiders and from his partner. These are not insubstantial resources, but nor do they guarantee an inmate's future ability to discard his prison identity and revive the one he has suspended.

Identity Dialectic

When an inmate's concerns about his identity first emerge, there is little that he can do about them. He recognizes that he has no choice but

---

[3]Clemmer (1958, 299) has defined "prisonization" as the "taking on in greater or less degree of the folkways, mores, customs, and general culture of the penitentiary." Yet new inmates begin to "take on" these things almost immediately, as part of the impression they are attempting to present to other inmates. Thus, we would argue instead that prisonization (meaning assimilation to the prison world) begins to occur for these inmates when their prison identities become second nature—when their expressions of prison norms and customs are no longer based on self-conscious acting. A new inmate's identity concerns, during the middle of his sentence, are essentially a recognition of this assimilation.

to present his prison identity so, following the insider's perspective he has now adopted, he consciously attempts to suppress his concerns. Eventually, however, he must begin to consider seriously his capacity to revive his suspended identity: his identity concerns, and his belief that he must deal with them, become particularly acute if he is transferred to the minimum security unit of the prison for the final months of his sentence.[4] At the conclusion of his prison career, an inmate shifts back toward an outsider's perspective on the prison world (see Figure 1); this shift involves the dissipation of his maximum security adaptation strategy, further revision of his prison image, reconstruction of an image of the outside world, and the initial development of an outside plan.[5] The inmate's efforts to revive his suspended identity are part of his shift in perspectives.

It is primarily through a renewed self-dialogue that the inmate struggles to revive his suspended identity—a struggle that amounts to a dialectic between his suspended identity and his prison identity. Through self-dialogue he recognizes, and tries to confront, the extent to which these two identities really do differ. He again tries to differentiate himself from maximum security inmates.

> There seems to be a concern with the inmates here to be able to distinguish . . . themselves from the other inmates. That is—they feel they are above the others. . . . Although they may associate with each other, it still seems important to degrade the majority here.

And he does have some success in freeing himself from his prison identity.

> Well, I think I am starting to soften up a little bit. I believe the identity I picked up in the prison is starting to leave me now that I have left the world of the [maximum security] joint. I find myself becoming more and more involved with the happenings of the outside world. I am even getting anxious to go out and see the sights, just to get away from this place.

But he recognizes that he *has* changed in prison, and that these changes run deeper than the mask he has been presenting to others. He has not returned to his "old self" simply because his impression management skills are used less frequently in minimum security. He raises the question—though he cannot answer it—of how permanent these changes are. He wonders how much his family and friends will see him as having changed. As stated by one of our interview respondents:

> I know I've changed a little bit. I just want to realize how the people I know are going to see it, because they [will] be able to see it more than I can see it. . . . Sometimes I just want to go somewhere and hide.

He speculates about how much the outside world—especially his own network of outside relationships—has changed in his absence. (It is his life, not those of his family and friends, that has been suspended during his prison sentence; he knows that changes have occurred in the outside world, and he suspects that some of these changes may have been withheld from him, intentionally or otherwise.) He has questions, if not serious doubts, about his ability to "make it" on the outside, especially concerning his relationships with others; he knows, in any case, that he cannot

---

[4]Not all prisoners participate in this unit; inmates must apply for transfer to the unit, and their acceptance depends both on the crimes for which they were sentenced and staff evaluation of their potential for success in the unit. Our analysis focuses on those inmates who are transferred.

[5]There are three features of the minimum security unit that facilitate this shift in perspectives: a more open physical and social environment; the fact that the unit lies just outside the prison wall (so that an inmate who is transferred is also physically removed from the maximum security prison); and greater opportunity for direct contact with the outside world, through greater access to telephones, an unrestricted visitor list, unrestricted visiting hours and, eventually, weekend furloughs.

simply return to the outside world as if nothing has happened. Above all, he repeatedly confronts the question of who he is, and who he will be in the outside world.

An inmate's struggle with these questions, like his self-dialogue at the beginning of his prison career, is necessarily a solitary activity. The identity he claims at the time of his release, in contrast to his prison identity, cannot be learned from other inmates. Also like his earlier periods of self-dialogue, the questions he considers are not approached in a rational systematic manner. The process is more one of rumination—of pondering one question until another replaces it, and then contemplating the new question until it is replaced by still another, or suppressed from his thoughts. There is, then, no final resolution to any of the inmate's identity questions. Each inmate confronts these questions in his own way, and each arrives at his own understanding of who he is, based on this unfinished, unresolved self-dialogue. In every case, however, an inmate's release identity is a synthesis of his suspended preprison identity and his prison identity.[6]

Postprison Identity

Because each inmate's release identity is the outcome of his own identity dialectic, we cannot provide a profile of the "typical" release identity. But our data do allow us to specify some of the conditions that affect this outcome. Reaffirmations of his preprison identity by outsiders—visits and furloughs during which others interact with him as if he has not changed—provide powerful support for his efforts to revive his suspended identity. These

efforts are also promoted by an inmate's recollection of his preprison identity (i.e., his attempts, through self-dialogue, to assess who he was before he came to prison), by his desire to abandon his prison identity, and by his general shift back toward an outsider's perspective. But there are also several factors that favor his prison identity, including his continued use of diversionary activities; his continued periodic efforts to suppress thoughts about the outside world; his continued ability to use prison impression management skills; and his continuing sense of injustice about the treatment he has received. Strained or cautious interactions with outsiders, or unfulfilled furlough expectations, inhibit the revival of his preprison identity. And he faces direct, experiential evidence that he has changed: when a minimum security resident recognizes that he is now completely unaffected by reports of violent incidents in maximum security, he acknowledges that he is no longer the same person that he was when he entered prison. Turner (1978, 1) has suggested three criteria for role-person merger: "failure of role compartmentalization, resistance to abandoning a role in the face of advantageous alternative roles, and the acquisition of role-appropriate attitudes"; at the time of their release from prison, the inmates we studied had already accrued some experience with each of these criteria.

Just as we cannot define a typical release identity, we cannot predict these inmates' future, postprison identities, not only because we have restricted our analysis to their prison experiences but because each inmate's future identity is inherently unpredictable. What effect an ex-inmate's prison experience has on his identity depends on how he, in interaction with others, defines this experience. Some of the men we have studied will be returned to prison in the future; others will not. But all will have been changed by their prison experiences. They entered the prison world fearing for their lives; they depart with the knowledge that they have survived. On the one hand, these men are

---

[6]This is an important parallel with our analysis of the inmate's changing prison definitions: his concluding prison image is a synthesis of the image he formulates before coming to prison and the image he holds at the middle of his prison career; see Schmid and Jones, 1990.

undoubtedly stronger persons by virtue of this accomplishment. On the other hand, the same tactics that enabled them to survive the prison world can be called upon, appropriately or not, in difficult situations in the outside world. To the extent that these men draw upon their prison survival tactics to cope with the hardships of the outside world—to the extent that their prison behavior becomes a meaningful part of their "role repertoire" (Turner 1978) in their everyday lives—their prison identities will have become inseparable from their "true" identities. . . .

References

Adler, Patricia A., and Peter Adler. 1989. "The Gloried Self: The Aggrandizement and the Construction of Self." *Social Psychology Quarterly* 52: 299–310.

Berger, Peter L. 1963. *Invitation to Sociology: A Humanistic Perspective.* Garden City, NY: Doubleday Anchor Books.

Blumer, Herbert. 1972. "Action vs. Interaction: Review of *Relations in Public* by Erving Goffman." *Transaction* 9: 50–53.

———. Blumer, Herbert. 1969. *Symbolic Interactionism: Perspective and Method.* Englewood Cliffs, NJ: Prentice-Hall.

Boulding, Kenneth. 1961. *The Image.* Ann Arbor: University of Michigan Press.

Clemmer, Donald. 1958. *The Prison Community.* New York: Holt, Rinehart & Winston.

Coser, R. 1966. "Role Distance, Sociological Ambivalence and Traditional Status Systems." *American Journal of Sociology* 72: 173–187.

Garfinkel, Harold. 1956. "Conditions of Successful Degradation Ceremonies." *American Journal of Sociology* 61: 420–424.

Glaser, Barney, and Anselm Strauss. 1964. "Awareness Contexts and Social Interaction." *American Sociological Review* 29: 669–679.

Goffman, Erving. 1961. *Asylums.* Garden City, NY: Doubleday Anchor Books.

———. 1959. *The Presentation of Self in Everyday Life.* Garden City, NY: Doubleday Anchor Books.

———. 1963. *Stigma: Notes on the Management of Spoiled Identity.* Englewood Cliffs, NJ: Prentice-Hall.

Irwin, John. 1970. *The Felon.* Englewood Cliffs, NJ: Prentice-Hall.

Lewis, David J. 1979. "A Social Behaviorist Interpretation of the Median I." *American Journal of Sociology* 84: 261–287.

Schechner, Richard. 1985. *Between Theater and Anthropology.* Philadelphia: University of Pennsylvania Press.

Scheff, Thomas. 1970. "On the Concepts of Identity and Social Relationships." Pp. 193–207 in T. Shibutani (ed.), *Human Nature and Collective Behavior.* Englewood Cliffs, NJ: Prentice-Hall.

Schlenker, B. 1980. *Impression Management: The Self Concept, Social Identity and Interpersonal Relations.* Belmont, CA: Wadsworth.

Schmid, Thomas, and Richard Jones. 1987. "Ambivalent Actions: Prison Adaptation Strategies of New Inmates." American Society of Criminology, annual meetings, Montreal, Quebec.

Schmid, Thomas, and Richard Jones. 1990. "Experiential Orientations to the Prison Experience: The Case of First-Time, Short-Term Inmates." Pp. 189–210 in Gale Miller and James A. Holstein (eds.), *Perspectives on Social Problems.* Greenwich, CT: JAI Press.

Solomon, David N. 1970. "Role and Self-Conception: Adaptation and Change in Occupations." Pp. 286–300 in T. Shibutani (ed.), *Human Nature and Collective Behavior.* Englewood Cliffs, NJ: Prentice-Hall.

Stone, Gregory P. 1962. "Appearance and the Self." Pp. 86–118 in Arnold Rose (ed.), *Human Behavior and Social Processes.* Boston: Houghton Mifflin.

Sykes, Gresham. 1958. *The Society of Captives: A Study of a Maximum Security Prison.* Princeton, NJ: Princeton University Press.

Turner, Ralph H. 1978. "The Role and the Person." *American Journal of Sociology* 84: 1–23.

Ungar, Sheldon. 1984. "Self-Mockery: An Alternative Form of Self-Presentation." *Symbolic Interaction* 7: 121–133.

Weigert, Andrew J. 1986. "The Social Production of Identity: Metatheoretical Foundations." *Sociological Quarterly* 27: 165–183.

Zurcher, Louis A. 1977. *The Mutable Self.* Beverly Hills, CA: Sage.

Questions

1. Define the following terms, as used by Schmid and Jones in the article.
   a. rumination
   b. inauthentic presentation of self
   c. performance consciousness
   d. identity dialectic
   e. proto-sociological attitude

2. How do Schmid and Jones distinguish between "identity transformation" and "identity construction"?

3. In what ways, if any, do you think prison might have a different effect on women's identity than on men's identity? Explain.

4. Identify the parallels between identity transformation in prison and the implicit identity transformation undergone by kids as they are introduced to street culture (as described by Anderson in reading 12).

24

HOW WOMEN RESHAPE
THE PRISON GUARD ROLE

Lynn Zimmer

As Professor Zimmer observes, sociologists have traditionally assumed that personal behavior is very much shaped by the social arrangements in which an individual finds him- or herself. For example, as you read in reading 16, college men altered their behavior when put into the role of prison guard.

Yet what happens when one set of social arrangements (i.e., socially prescribed gender rules) come face to face with another (i.e., the socially prescribed role of prison guard)? Professor Zimmer finds that in such cases, becoming a prison guard isn't just "role-taking"; it requires innovating and "role-making."

Today, few people would question the ability of women to perform successfully in most occupations in which the workers are predominantly men; however, a number of jobs, such as soldier, police officer, and prison guard, retain their male identification, and a decade or more of women's presence in these jobs has not eliminated speculation regarding women's ability to perform them. Both during and after conducting research on women guards who work in men's prisons (Zimmer 1986), the question constantly asked of me was, "Can women really do the job?" Since the job requirements of prison guards seem to be in direct contrast to the traditional norms for women's behavior, the question is not surprising. Expectations for women have changed over the past two decades, to be sure, but not so much that women's ability to perform in jobs traditionally held by men

goes unquestioned, especially if the job entails the exercise of power and authority.

What is generally meant when people ask whether women can perform as prison guards is whether their performance is similar to that of their male counterparts. It is assumed that jobs, especially those at the lower ranks, exist as predetermined slots waiting to be filled by workers. Weber (1964) suggests that the efficient bureaucracy breeds conformity and that individual workers become dispensable, replaceable, and interchangeable. More recently, Hall (1977) has claimed that because the same occupational role constraints operate on each worker, organizational behavior is not dependent on the characteristics of individuals:

> When a new member enters the organization, he is confronted with a social structure . . . and a set of expectations for . . . behavior. It does not matter who the particular individual is; the organization has established a system of norms and expectations to be followed regardless of who its personnel happen to be. (p. 26)

Nieva and Gutek (1981) similarly suggest that when women workers enter jobs traditionally

"How Women Reshape the Prison Guard Role" by Lynn Zimmer from *Gender & Society,* Vol. 1, No. 4 (December 1987: pp. 415–431). Copyright © 1987 by Sociologists for Women in Society. Reprinted by permission of Sage Publications, Inc.

held by men, they will generally not be able to alter work roles so as to reduce the conflict between occupational norms and gender-role norms. Instead, they will have to alter their own behavior:

> Although individuals will always retain some latitude in deciding how to act, social structures heavily shape the options and tools available to them. Individual behaviors adapt to their environment. (p. 132)

Rosabeth Kanter (1977) agrees: "To a very large degree, organizations make their workers into who they are. Adults change to fit the system" (p. 263).

If occupational role restraints are strong in all work organizations, they might be expected to be particularly strong in highly structured, paramilitary organizations like prisons. E. Johnson (1981) describes the rigidity of the guard's job:

> The prison guard must follow the rules and their interpretations made by his superiors; the guard is not free to act toward inmates—either sentimentally or punitively—as he would personally prefer. (p. 82)

Research by Haney et al. (1973), in which student subjects assigned as guards in a mock prison quickly assumed fairly typical guard behaviors, further suggests that the guard's role requirements overshadow any individual characteristics or predispositions.

The work behavior of women prison guards calls these assumptions regarding the rigidity of work roles into question. Based on unstructured interviews with 70 women guards working in men's prisons in New York and Rhode Island, as well as with a high-level personnel in the central administrative offices, midlevel supervisors at the prisons, men guards, and men prisoners,[1] this study explores the ways women have reshaped the guard role and how their presence has an impact on the prisons and the job of guarding. The data indicate that workers, even in highly regulated environments like prisons, can develop innovative and successful ways to perform the job when they find established work roles inadequate or find they are blocked from achieving success using predetermined definitions of appropriate work behavior. Employment roles, like other social roles, offer opportunity for role making as well as role taking (Turner 1962), and women working as guards in men's prisons have, out of both choice and necessity, acted upon this opportunity, creating new ways to do an old job. This pattern of role making may be typical of women in other traditionally male occupations as well. To find out, researchers need to examine more closely the various ways women perform jobs and evaluate their performance on its own terms rather than how closely it resembles that of men.

The Job of Prison Guard

The prison guard is, according to Hawkins (1976), "the key figure in the penal equation, the man on whom the whole edifice of the penitentiary system depends" (p. 105). Because prisons are, in effect, separate societies, guards must perform a wide range of diverse tasks to keep the prison operating, but the most important ones center around their custody and control functions—keeping prisoners inside the walls and following the rules and regulations for inmate behavior that have been established by prison administrators.

The primary mechanism through which guards maintain control in prisons is the constant regulation of inmate movement. On a normal day, most prisoners are released from their cells for meals, work detail, school, medical care, recreation, and visits, but they will constantly be monitored by guards who are stationed throughout the prison. Many guards spend their day checking inmate passes, frisking

---

[1] For a more detailed description of the research methodology used in this analysis, see Appendix in Zimmer (1986).

inmates as they move from one area to another, and unlocking and then relocking gates as inmates pass through. Several times a day, all prisoners are ordered to their cells, allowing guards to take "the count" and make sure no prisoners have escaped.

Guards are also responsible for enforcing the extensive rules that govern inmate behavior. In addition to rules similar to the laws outside of prison—rules that forbid assault, rape, theft, and the like, there are many rules specific to prison life that, for example, prohibit profanity and gambling, regulate smoking, establish grooming and clothing standards, and dictate the items considered contraband. There may also be very general rules for inmate conduct, requiring them to obey direct orders of guards and treat guards with appropriate respect. Not all of the rules are equally important to the maintenance of internal order, and many guards are willing to overlook violation of some petty rules, but for both the guards' own safety and the security of the institution, it is important that most inmates obey most of the rules most of the time. Given the low guard-to-inmate ratio in prisons, there is always the potential for mass violence. Because guards have limited ability to control inmate behavior during a riot or takeover, they must prevent such situations from occurring by controlling inmate movement and obtaining inmate compliance to the most critical rules.

One way guards may obtain inmate compliance with prison rules is through the threat of institutionalized punishment: segregation, loss of privileges (such as commissary, recreation, visitation), and loss of good-time credits. Guards generally cannot implement these punishments themselves, but can write reports to be reviewed by a special disciplinary committee, which may then order appropriate penalties. This threat of formal punishment is an important management tool, and guards use it frequently. However, since this process is time consuming and removes punishment from the immediate situation, guards often

supplement the formal system with an informal system of rewards and punishments over which they have more direct control.

Prisoners are dependent on guards to provide a wide range of services for them, and although Crouch (1980a) points out that inmate dependency has been reduced by the recent increase in prisoners' legal rights, guards still have the potential to increase substantially the "pains of imprisonment" (Sykes 1958) that accompany incarceration. For example, the inmate who too frequently disobeys the rules may find that he or she is always the last to receive mail or that a written request to make a phone call has been "lost" in the pile of paperwork that cell-block guards accumulate. Guards can also manipulate rewards, and the compliant inmate may be able to obtain a favorable work assignment, a roomier cell, or more freedom of movement. Even small privileges are important to prisoners and, knowing this, guards can grant or withhold privileges as a way of encouraging compliant behavior.

Guards may also obtain inmate cooperation with regard to important rules by agreeing to ignore prisoners' minor infractions, in what Sykes (1956) calls "corruptions of the guard's authority." Such arrangements are potentially dangerous because prisoners may try to "up the ante," asking for even greater concessions from guards for the same amount of compliance. In spite of this danger, most guards do find it advantageous to engage in such mutual accommodations with prisoners; as long as they are used only to supplement and not replace other techniques of control, such "corruption" seems to present no serious threat to prison security.

Finally, guards may use the threat of physical force to control prison behavior; being unarmed and outnumbered, guards cannot use force to control the prison population on a regular basis, but force may be used to punish particular unruly or disrespectful inmates and serve as an example to others (Marquart 1986).

There are many techniques of control, then, that have become part of the guard role as it has traditionally been performed by men. Individual guards may differ in the degree to which they stress some techniques over others, but the overriding strategy is to remain in a position of control vis-à-vis inmates. Concessions and accommodations may be granted, but only if they add to rather than compromise the guards' position of superiority. Crouch (1980b), a noted authority on the guard role, compares guard-inmate interaction to a contest in which the two parties remain in constant competition, each trying to establish dominance. To emerge victorious, the guard must project an image of personal, physical dominance:

> All officers, to maintain some respect and authority, must project some degree of physical competence. Regardless of duty assignment, the man who cannot muster some version of this masculine image before both inmates and peers is in for trouble. For example, one rather obese young man I worked with . . . had never been able to gain respect from either [inmates or other officers]. . . . His appearance and behavior did not fit with the informal expectations of this masculine world. (p. 219)

Physical strength, but more important, an image of masculinity and dominance, are crucial characteristics of the traditional guard role. They are characteristics that women entering this profession do not generally possess. To survive on this job, then, it has been necessary for women to redefine the guard role in a way that eliminates the competitive atmosphere and instead utilizes the skills, characteristics, and patterns of interaction that women are likely to bring to the job.

Women in the Guard Role

Most of the women who work as guards in men's prisons have neither the desire nor the capacity to perform the job as it has been traditionally performed by men. Perhaps many of the women have experienced the type of role conflict that Hughes (1944, 1958) suggests occurs when sexual status and occupational status are incongruent. If they have, women guards have not resolved that conflict by embracing one set of role expectations over the other, as researchers have found of women in other occupations (Kanter 1977; Martin, 1980; Nieva and Gutek 1981; Rustad 1982). Instead, women guards, like the women police officers studied by Hunt (1986), have integrated certain aspects of the traditional female gender role into a traditional male occupational role to create new ways of performing the job. Jurik's (1985a) research shows that women and men guards do not differ substantially in their attitudes toward crime and punishment, but my research shows that men and women do behave differently on the job. Not all women guards perform the job alike, but they do, by and large, use strategies different from those used by men.[2]

Women guards who work in direct contact with prisoners[3] use many of the control techniques that are part of the traditional guard role; they maintain control through regulation of inmate movement and use of the formal system of punishment for rule violation. Women guards can also implement informal rewards and punishments, but because they lack the

---

[2]There are some women guards who try to perform the job "by the book," but even this is different from the way men generally perform the job. These women have adopted what I call the "institutional role" (Zimmer 1986), hoping that a strict adherence to the rules will provide solutions to all job-related problems and insulate them from any criticism by male coworkers and supervisors. Male guards are much more likely to "bend the rules" when the formal rules seem to them to be inappropriate.

[3]There are a number of women guards who do not regularly work in direct contact with men prisoners because they have managed to receive a job assignment in an area of the prison where such contact is minimal (e.g., administrative offices, mailroom, visiting room). These women perform a "modified role" in the prison and, because they have so little contact with inmates, have not developed a style of guarding consistent with that outlined in this article (see Zimmer 1986).

support and cooperation of most of the men guards in the prison (Fox 1982; Peterson 1982; Zimmer 1986), such efforts may be undermined. Women guards have complained, for example, that male coworkers sometimes reverse their decisions, taking away privileges they had granted to inmates or punishing inmates for actions they had approved.

Like the men, women guards can also engage in mutual accommodations with inmates, ignoring some rules in return for inmate compliance to others, a control technique that women find particularly useful. Although not all women guards can be counted on to ignore minor rule violations, inmates often report that the women who guard them are more willing than the men to overlook what inmates consider the petty rules related to clothing and grooming. In return, prisoners agree to comply with the rules that are more critical to prison security.

While utilizing many traditional guard techniques, women guards also use a strategy that is seldom used by men: the development of friendly, pleasant relationships with prisoners as a way of generating prisoners' voluntary compliance. Some women play a mothering, nurturing role vis-à-vis inmates, a role that is in direct contrast to the macho, competitive role typical of men guards. Women guards are also more likely to have a social worker's orientation toward the job and to spend a great deal of time listening to inmate problems, discussing their family relationships, assisting them in letter writing, and helping them make plans for their release. Prison administrators are uneasy about the development of friendly bonds between inmates and guards, especially women guards, fearing that the guard's allegiance could shift from the prison to the prisoner and jeopardize security. Many prisons, in fact, have specific rules that prohibit undue familiarity between guards and inmates (May 1981); Toch's (1981) research suggests that when men guards violate these rules, they risk the disapproval not only of administrators but also of their colleagues, many of whom define prisoners as the enemy (Duffee 1974). Because women seldom have the approval of men guards to begin with, they may be freer to use friendship-oriented strategies for gaining inmate compliance with prison rules.

Men prisoners, for the most part, respond positively to women's style of guarding. They follow the daily routine under women's supervision and comply with women's direct orders. Moreover, prisoners tend to behave better in women's presence by, for example, refraining from extensive use of vulgar language. Some men prisoners try to help the women by taking responsibility for control of the more troublesome inmates; in a few instances, men prisoners have even protected women against physical attack.

This style of guarding successfully incorporates aspects of women's traditional behavior into the guard role; as one woman guard put it, "to survive on this job, women have to do what they know best." At the same time, of course, this strategy is successful only because many men prisoners are willing to accept and contribute to the development of friendly, cooperative relationships with the women who guard them. Their motivations in doing so may be complex, and almost certainly contain a large component of self-interest, but it is also the case that men prisoners come into the prison with their own traditional patterns of interacting differently with women and men. No matter how women guards perform the job, most men prisoners will respond to them in gender-specific ways. Many of the women who succeed in this job have found ways of using male responses to their advantage.

Guarding techniques typical of the women, like those of the men, are far from foolproof, and inmate rule violation, sometimes of a serious nature, is common in prisons. Nonetheless, the women's techniques do represent a viable strategy that has allowed many women to remain on a job that they would find difficult to perform in a more traditional, male-defined way. Like the women who broke into the professions at the turn of the century, women guards have used "every creative strategy that could serve their larger purposes of building meaningful careers" (Glazer and Slater 1987).

There are a number of explanations for why most women do not perform the job of prison guard as it is generally performed by men. For one thing, women often fail to receive adequate socialization during the on-the-job training phase of their employment; their trainers are generally men guards, most of whom do not want the women there. They may actively undermine women's ability to succeed on the job by denying them information about both formal and informal techniques for handling inmates. The training assignments of men and women may also differ, so that at the end of their probationary period, many women have had only limited experience in dealing directly with inmates, especially in emergencies. As women continue on the job, they face persistent opposition and sexual harassment from male guards; many women remain skeptical about men's willingness to assist them if needed. In short, women do not receive the kind of support from coworkers that is important to success on any job (Feldman 1976; Terborg et al. 1982; Van Maanen and Schein 1979); without that support, many women find it useful to develop alliances with inmates who will then voluntarily comply with women's orders and even offer to protect women when potentially dangerous situations erupt.

While it is true that women face many obstacles in performing the job like men, it is not at all clear that these obstacles alone are the cause of women's occupational behavior or that the removal of those obstacles would lead women to choose a job performance strategy identical to that of men. There are, of course, many individual differences among women guards and the kind of skills and abilities they bring to the job, but it is important to remember that the women who become guards today have been socialized in a society in which expectations for women are only gradually changing. Women guards therefore tend to bring to this job a set of experiences and, to some extent, a mind-set quite different from men. For most men, growing up in this society has prepared them for confrontational situations; most men who work as prison guards have had considerable experience in competitive exchanges with other men, and they are used to vying for control. Most women who work as prison guards have not had these kinds of experiences and, even if they have, find it difficult to replicate them in the prison, where their ability to compete physically with inmates for control is questionable. So instead, women rely on the qualities and characteristics that have served them well in their relationships outside of prison: skills of communication and persuasion and the ability to generate voluntary cooperation from others.

Finally, it is important to see women guards' job behavior as, in some ways, reflective of male-female interactive patterns outside of prison. If women's style of guarding were based solely on what they bring to the job with them—skills and abilities somewhat different from men—then we would expect women guards to behave the same whether working among men or women prisoners. They do not. Pollock's (1986) research indicates that both women and men change their style of guarding as the sex of the inmate population changes and that each of the four combinations (male guard–male inmate; male guard–female inmate; female guard–female inmate; female guard–male inmate) produces different strategies for managing inmates. Some of the strategies used by women who guard men incorporate role behaviors more typical of women interacting with men than of guards interacting with prisoners (e.g., being friendly, understanding, and supportive). This works for women because most prisoners are willing, in turn, to respond with typically male role behaviors (e.g., being protective). These interactive patterns do not replace those of guard and inmate but are interwoven into them in a way that allows women guards to perform the basic requirements of the job and allows men prisoners to feel comfortable having women in official positions of authority over them.[4]

Impact of Women in Prisons and on the Job of Guarding

Women have shown their ability to perform the job of guarding on a day-to-day basis while remaining less intimidating, less competitive, and less physical than most men guards, but there are some occasions in the prison when intimidation, confrontation, and physical force are needed. In even the best-run prison, fights between inmates are common, inmate attacks against guards occur, and there is always the potential for mass violence should a riot take place; it is guards who must bring these situations under control and, in doing so, may find it necessary to use force and violence themselves. Male administrators and male guards feel that the women working as guards are extremely reluctant to respond to situations in which physical force may be necessary and that they are inadequately prepared to perform this aspect of the job. In their eyes, the presence of women presents a danger to prison security.

In actuality, there has been no reported decrease in prison security or internal order in the decade or more since women began working in men's prisons. Women, of course, do remain a small proportion of the staff in men's prisons, and it is impossible to predict the impact of many more women guards, but current levels do not appear to pose a security risk. An even greater proportion of women might be easily accommodated if prison administrators followed the suggestions of a 1981 American Correctional Association report that special tactical teams be trained and made available in all prisons for response to emergency situations. Rank-and-file men guards may, in fact, act too aggressively in such situations and produce an escalation of violence by those they are trying to control (Attica 1972; Stotland 1976; Toch 1977). The presence of women at the site of erupting violence might do more to reduce aggression by all parties than would any actual physical intervention by them. Several researchers have reported that women workers have a calming effect on men prisoners (Becker 1975; Biemer 1977; Cormier 1975; Flynn 1982; Graham 1981), perhaps because women are less likely to engage in competitive relationships with inmates and do not encourage the "ego-showdowns" that may, themselves, set the stage for violence between inmates and guards.

At some point, the presence of women guards who use different strategies for handling inmates may have an impact on the occupational role itself. Already some men guards use strategies that stress relationship building with prisoners (R. Johnson 1977; Toch 1981), but certainly not to the extent advocated over the years by prison reformers (Bennett 1976; Glaser 1964; Hawkins 1976; Morris and Morris 1980; Schrag 1961). Most men guards have vehemently rejected these suggestions and have, instead, insisted that they need more direct control over inmates to perform the job effectively (Fox 1982). Women's ability to perform the job without reliance on coercive control lends support to reformers' suggestions that the job of guarding itself can be

---

[4]Different methods for handling a situation in which gender status is inconsistent with occupational role requirements are outlined by Whyte (1946). He found that the physical environment in the restaurant could be altered to soften the effect of male-female interactions that conflicted with the norm.

transformed. There is, perhaps, much to be learned from women's adaptations to this job; the guard role may not be as rigid as men guards or some researchers (Haney et al. 1973) have maintained. And as the job is redesigned by women's presence, women entering prison work in the future may find it easier to adjust to the job and to gain the acceptance of their coworkers.

Women in Traditional Men's Jobs

As women have moved into traditional men's jobs, they have usually been evaluated on the basis of how closely their performance approximates that of men. These job roles were originally designed and shaped by men, presumably to fit their own particular skills and abilities, but once created, they have been assumed to be neutral positions that qualified women as well as men should be able to fill. When women have not succeeded (i.e., they have not reproduced men's occupational behavior), coworkers and supervisors, usually men, have felt justified in calling for their removal. Researchers, on the other hand, have often pointed to the structural obstacles in their way, implying that when such barriers are removed, women's work behavior will be more similar to that of men (Jurik 1985b; Kanter 1977; Martin 1980; Rustad 1982). Others have focused on how gender-role socialization has left women unprepared for "men's work" (Hennig and Jardim 1977) and suggest that women themselves need to change—to act, talk, dress, and think like men (Carr-Ruffino 1982; Harley and Koff 1980; Mirides and Cote 1980; Smith and Grenier 1982) or learn to play "the games mother never taught you" (Harrigan 1978).

This study of women guards suggests that there is more than discrimination and structural barriers to prevent most women from performing jobs like men. These factors are important determinants of women's occupational behavior and need to be given serious attention, but also important is the different approach that many women themselves bring to the job. This study also indicates that women need not change themselves nor copy men's behavior to perform traditional men's jobs successfully.

Other research on women working in male-dominated occupations leads to the same conclusion. Loden (1985) claims that a "feminine leadership style," typical of many (but not all) women managers, is just as successful in managing subordinates as is the traditional masculine style and may be more productive under some circumstances. Ramey (1981) finds that women, in general, approach scientific problems differently from men and maintains that the approaches of women scientists should be valued for their difference, because the more varied approaches brought to scientific problems, the more likely it is solutions will be found. Goffee and Scase's (1985) research on women entrepreneurs identifies their successful adaptations to business, some of which successfully incorporate traditional gender roles.

Research on women in policing, an occupation—like guarding—identified with men, has been equivocal. Gross (1981) and Berg and Budnick (1986) have found "defeminized" women officers, displaying "pseudo-masculinity," to be more successful on the job and more accepted by their peers. But others have found women officers with less aggressive personalities to be more successful in defusing potentially violent situations and decreasing the chance of injury to all participants (Bell 1982; Block and Anderson 1974; Remmington 1981; Sherman 1975).

The main reason for such disparity in the evaluation of women police officers is the lack of clear criteria for what constitutes good job performance. Public sector, service-oriented occupations present special difficulties in establishing evaluation criteria (Wholey et al.

1986), and policing, an occupation in which professionals themselves argue over the most important role requirements (Whitaker et al. 1982), is particularly problematic. Morash and Greene (1986) show that most evaluation studies of the police stress the attributes and tasks that are biased toward men and do little more than measure officers' conformity to stereotypical men's behavior. This is true of evaluations of prison guards as well, and such gender-typed evaluations probably occur to some degree in all occupations in which the workers are predominantly men or women.

The evaluation of women (and men) workers, then, by their peers, supervisors, and even outside researchers, continues to contain a great deal of gender bias. When women are evaluated according to occupational standards created for men, many women fail to make the grade. When women do perform like men, they are still not evaluated positively (West 1982). Nor do women receive positive evaluations when they find ways to produce results without duplicating typical men's strategies. Auster (1987) shows that occupational gender bias is particularly prevalent when tasks are unpredictable, complex, or difficult to measure; in the prisons, where accomplishments like reducing tension, de-escalating conflict, and averting riots cannot be quantified, or even observed, the opportunity for bias against women guards is enormous.

Conclusions

This article has focused on the subtle but insidious form of bias against women in the devaluation of their different approaches to their work. This bias occurs in many different social contexts—when women think, act, or approach problems differently from men, the women's approach tends to be undercut and devalued (French 1985; Gilligan 1982; Keller 1985; Oakley 1981).

This article argues that it would be beneficial to women's efforts to achieve equality, and ultimately beneficial to the organizations in which women work, if the different approaches used by women were valued precisely because they are different. If, at some point in the future, there is less distinction between what it means to be a man and what it means to be a woman, some of the differences in how women and men perform jobs may disappear. In the meantime, gender equality may best be achieved through an equal valuing of current differences, both in and out of the workplace. A truly nonsexist society is not only one in which structural barriers and gender discrimination are removed but also one in which women and men have the opportunity to change and reshape the roles they fill.

References

American Correctional Association. 1981. *Riots and Disturbances in Correctional Institutions.* College Park, MD: American Correctional Association.

Attica. 1972. *Official Report of the New York State Commission on Attica.* New York: Bantam Books.

Auster, Ellen. 1987. "Task Characteristics as a Bridge Between Macro and Micro Research on Male-Female Wage Differences." Paper presented at Academy of Management Meetings, New Orleans, LA.

Becker, Arlene. 1975. "Women in Corrections: A Process of Change." *Resolutions* 1:19–21.

Bell, Daniel J. 1982. "Policewomen: Myths and Reality." *Journal of Police Science and Administration* 10:112–20.

Bennett, Lawrence. 1976. "A Study of Violence in California Prisons: A Review with Policy Implications." Pp. 149–68 in *Prison Violence,* edited by A. Cohen et al. Lexington, MA: Lexington Books.

Berg, Bruce and Kimberly Budnick. 1986. "Defeminization of Women in Law Enforcement: A New Twist on the Traditional Police Personality." *Journal of Police Science and Administration* 14:314–19.

Biemer, Carol. 1977. "The Role of the Female Mental Health Professional in a Male Correctional Setting." *Journal of Sociology and Social Welfare* 4:882–87.

Block, Peter and Deborah Anderson. 1974. *Police-women on Patrol: Final Report.* Washington, DC: Police Foundation.

Carr-Ruffino, Norma. 1982. *The Promotable Woman.* New York: Van Nostrand.

Cormier, Bruno. 1975. *The Watcher and the Watched.* Plattsburgh, NY: Tundra Books.

Crouch, Ben M. 1980a. "The Guard in a Changing Prison World." Pp. 5–45 in *The Keepers,* edited by B. Crouch. Springfield, IL: Charles C Thomas.

———. 1980b. "The Book vs. the Boot: Two Styles of Guarding in a Southern Prison." Pp. 207–23 in *The Keepers,* edited by B. Crouch. Springfield, IL: Charles C Thomas.

Duffee, David. 1974. "The Correction Officer Subculture and Organizational Change." *Journal of Research in Crime and Delinquency* 11:155–72.

Feldman, D. C. 1976. "A Contingency Theory of Socialization." *Administrative Science Quarterly* 21:433–52.

Flynn, Edith Elisabeth. 1982. "Women as Criminal Justice Professionals: A Challenge to Change Tradition." Pp. 305–40 in *Judge, Lawyer, Victim, Thief,* edited by N. Rafter and E. Stanko. Boston: Northeastern University Press.

Fox, James. 1982. *Organizational and Racial Conflict in Maximum-Security Prisons.* Lexington, MA: Lexington Books.

French, Marilyn. 1985. *Beyond Power: On Women, Men, and Morals.* New York: Ballantine Books.

Gilligan, Carol. 1982. *In a Different Voice.* Cambridge, MA: Harvard University Press.

Glaser, Daniel. 1964. *The Effectiveness of a Prison and Parole System.* New York: Bobbs-Merrill.

Glazer, Penina and Miriam Slater. 1987. *Unequal Colleagues: The Entrance of Women into the Professions, 1890–1940.* New Brunswick, NJ: Rutgers University Press.

Goffee, Robert and Richard Scase. 1985. *The Experiences of Female Entrepreneurs.* London: George Allen and Unwin.

Graham, Camille. 1981. "Women Are Succeeding in Male Institutions." *American Correctional Association Monographs* 1:27–36.

Gross, S. 1981. "Socialization in Law Enforcement: The Female Police Recruit." Final Report for the Southeast Institute of Criminal Justice, Miami, FL.

Hall, Richard. 1977. *Organizations: Structure and Process* (revised edition). Englewood Cliffs, NJ: Prentice-Hall.

Haney, Craig et al. 1973. "Interpersonal Dynamics in a Simulated Prison." *International Journal of Criminology* 1:69–97.

Harley, Joan and Lois Koff. 1980. "Prepare Women for Tomorrow's Managerial Challenge." *The Personnel Administrator* 25:41–42.

Harrigan, Betty. 1978. *Games Mother Never Taught You.* New York: Warner Books.

Hawkins, Gordon. 1976. *The Prison—Policy and Practice.* Chicago: University of Chicago Press.

Hennig, Margaret and Ann Jardim. 1977. *The Managerial Woman.* New York: Doubleday.

Hughes, Everett. 1944. "Dilemmas and Contradictions of Status." *American Journal of Sociology* 50:353–59.

———. 1958. *Men and Their Work.* Glencoe, IL: Fret Press.

Hunt, Jennifer. 1986. "The Logic of Sexism Among Police." Paper presented at American Sociological Association Annual Meeting, New York, NY.

Johnson, Elmer. 1981. "Changing World of the Correctional Officer." Pp. 77–85 in *Prison Guard/Correctional Officer,* edited by R. Ross. Toronto: Butterworths.

Johnson, Robert. 1977. "Ameliorating Prison Stress: Some Helping Roles for Custodial Personnel." *International Journal of Criminology and Penology* 5:263–73.

Jurik, Nancy. 1985a. "Individual and Organizational Determinants of Correctional Officer Attitudes Toward Inmates." *Criminology* 23:523–40.

———. 1985b. "An Officer and a Lady: Organizational Barriers to Women Working as Correctional Officers in Men's Prisons." *Social Problems* 32:373–88.

Kanter, Rosabeth. 1977. *Men and Women of the Corporation.* New York: Basic Books.

Keller, Evelyn Fox. 1985. *Reflections on Gender and Science.* New Haven, CT: Yale University Press.

Loden, Marilyn. 1985. *Feminine Leadership.* New York: Time Books.

Marquart, James. 1986. "Prison Guards and the Use of Physical Coercion as a Mechanism of Prisoner Control." *Criminology* 24:347–66.

Martin, Susan. 1980. *Breaking and Entering: Police-women on Patrol.* Berkeley: University of California Press.

May, Edgar. 1981. "Prison Guards in America—The Inside Story." Pp. 19–40 in *Prison Guard/Correctional Officer,* edited by R. Ross. Toronto: Butterworths.

Mirides, Ellyn and Andre Cote. 1980. "Women in Management: The Obstacles and Opportunities They Face." *Personnel Administrator* 25: 25–28, 48.

Morash, Merry and Jack Greene. 1986. "Evaluating Women on Patrol: A Critique of Contemporary Wisdom." *Evaluation Review* 10:230–55.

Morris, Terrance and Pauline Morris. 1980. "Where Staff and Prisoners Meet." Pp. 247–68 in *The Keepers: Prison Guards and Contemporary Corrections,* edited by B. Crouch. Springfield, IL: Charles C Thomas.

Nieva, Veronica and Barbara Gutek. 1981. *Women and Work: A Psychological Perspective.* New York: Praeger.

Oakley, Ann. 1981. *Subject Women.* New York: Pantheon Books.

Peterson, Cheryl Bowser. 1982. "Doing Time with the Boys: An Analysis of Women Correctional Officers in All-Male Facilities." Pp. 437–60 in *The Criminal Justice System and Women,* edited by B. Price and N. Sokoloff. New York: Clark Boardman.

Pollock, Joycelyn. 1986. *Sex and Supervision: Guarding Male and Female Inmates.* New York: Greenwood Press.

Ramey, Estelle (in interview with Barbara Goldman). 1981. "Different Is Not Lesser: Women in Science." Pp. 42–54 in *Outsiders on the Inside,* edited by B. Forisha and B. Goldman. Englewood Cliffs, NJ: Prentice-Hall.

Remmington, Patricia. 1981. *Policing: The Occupation and the Introduction of Female Officers.* Washington, DC: University Press of America.

Rustad, Michael. 1982. *Women in Khaki.* New York: Praeger.

Schrag, Clarence. 1961. "Some Foundations for a Theory of Correction." Pp. 309–57 in *The Prison: Studies in Institutional Organization and Change,* edited by D. Cressey. New York: Holt, Rinehart, & Winston.

Sherman, Lawrence. 1975. "Evaluation of Police-women on Patrol in a Suburban Police Department." *Journal of Police Science and Administration* 3:434–38.

Smith, Howard L. and Mary Grenier. 1982. "Sources of Organizational Power for Women: Overcoming Structural Obstacles." *Sex Roles* 8:733–46.

Stotland, Ezra. 1976. "Self-Esteem and Violence by Guards and State Troopers at Attica." *Criminal Justice and Behavior* 3:85–96.

Sykes, Gresham. 1956. "The Corruption of Authority and Rehabilitation." *Social Forces* 34:157–62.

———. 1958. *The Society of Captives.* Princeton, NJ: Princeton University Press.

Terborg, James et al. 1982. "Socialization Experiences of Women and Men Graduate Students in Male Sex-Typed Career Fields." Pp. 124–55 in *Women in the Workforce,* edited by H. J. Bernardin. New York: Praeger.

Toch, Hans. 1977. *Police, Prisons, and the Problem of Violence.* Washington, DC: U.S. Government Printing Office.

———. 1981. "Is a 'Correctional Officer' by Any Other Name, a 'Screw?'" Pp. 87–104 in *Prison Guard/Correctional Officer,* edited by R. Ross. Toronto: Butterworths.

Turner, Ralph. 1962. "Role Taking: Process Versus Conformity." Pp. 20–40 in *Human Behavior and Social Processes,* edited by A. Rose. Boston: Houghton Mifflin.

Van Maanen, John and E. H. Schein. 1979. "Towards a Theory of Organizational Socialization." *Research in Organizational Behavior* 1:209–64.

Weber, Max (translated by A. M. Henderson and T. Parsons). 1964. *The Theory of Social and Economic Organization.* New York: Free Press.

West, Candace. 1982. "Why Can't a Woman Be More Like a Man?" *Work and Occupations* 9:5–29.

Whitaker, G. P. et al. 1982. *Basic Issues in Police Performance.* Washington, DC: National Institute of Justice.

Wholey, Joseph et al. 1986. *Performance and Credibility: Developing Excellence in Public and Nonprofit Organizations.* Lexington, MA: Lexington Books.

Whyte, William Foote. 1946. *Industry and Society.* New York: McGraw-Hill.

Zimmer, Lynn. 1986. *Women Guarding Men.* Chicago: University of Chicago Press.

Questions

1. Zimmer (and others) have suggested that women don't fare well when the quality of a woman's performance is judged on the basis of whether she does her job the same way her male colleagues do. Yet, how else should people's job performances be evaluated in traditionally male-dominated occupations?

2. According to Zimmer's research, who responds best to the strategies used by women guards: male guards or male prisoners?

3. Imagine that Zimbardo and his colleagues (reading 16) had used women students to guard male prisoners in the Stanford Prison Experiment. Based on what Zimmer discovered, how would the behavior of female guards have differed from the behavior of the male guards studied by Zimbardo?

25

NOT JUST BODIES: STRATEGIES FOR DESEXUALIZING THE PHYSICAL EXAMINATION OF PATIENTS

Patti A. Giuffre and Christine L. Williams

The role of a health care practitioner requires one to maintain what sociologist Talcott Parsons called "affective neutrality": one must keep a tight grip on one's affect (emotions). At no time is the need for affective neutrality more important than during the physical exam. Patients are comforted by their belief that the sight of a naked body is routine to physicians and nurses; they trust that not only will their health care practitioner not comment on the size or shape of their body parts, but that he or she does not even notice them except in medically relevant ways. As Giuffre and Williams point out, however, affective neutrality does not come easily to practitioners.

Physicians and nurses routinely examine naked bodies and discuss intimate, sexual issues with their patients. Yet, these health care professionals are expected to avoid or deny personal sexual feelings and ignore the expression of any sexual desire from their patients. How do they do it? That is, how do they desexualize the physical exam?

Health care professionals are guided in this task in several ways. First, formal organizational policies and professional ethics govern

"Not Just Bodies: Strategies for Desexualizing the Physical Examination of Patients" by Patti A. Giuffre and Christine L. Williams from *Gender & Society*, Vol. 14, No. 4 (June 2000: pp. 457–482) Copyright © 2000 Sociologists for Women in Society. Reprinted by permission of Sage Publications, Inc.

AUTHORS' NOTE: *We would like to thank Kirsten Dellinger, Dana Britton, Martin Button, Ellen Slaten, Edith Elwood, Beth Schneider, and the reviewers for comments on this article. We would also like to thank Teresa Sullivan, Ronald Angel, Charles Bonjean, Sue Hoppe, and Janice Beyer, who supervised the original research.*

doctors' and nurses' interactions with patients. Health care providers are usually prohibited from engaging in sexual relationships with patients, particularly when patients are under their direct care. Second, the medical school curriculum socializes students to desexualize the human body. Medical students are trained to hide their feelings and avoid emotional involvement with their patients. Students are taught to use scientific, biomedical language for the human body, rather than colloquial terms, which may encourage students to approach the human body in a less personal, more abstract way. Medical students often devise their own strategies for managing inappropriate feelings, for example, engaging in sick humor with other students and mentally transforming their patients into inanimate objects.

Interaction rituals also may help to desexualize the physical examination of patients. For example, some physicians engage in casual conversation with the fully clothed patient prior to the actual exam, leave the room and allow the nurse to enter and instruct the patient about the exam, insist on the presence of a nurse to chaperone the exam, or use draping sheets to expose only specific parts of the body. By adhering closely to scripted performances such as these, physicians may be better able to control the interaction and repress the arousal of sexual feelings and interpretations.

Because social definitions of appropriate—and inappropriate—sexual behavior are linked to gender, it is likely that men and women use different desexualization strategies, but researchers have yet to examine this possibility. In this article, we address the following questions: Do male and female health care professionals rely on different strategies for desexualizing the physical exam? Are male and female patients subjected to different strategies? Are there differences in how doctors and nurses examine the bodies of male and female patients?

To address these questions, we conducted in-depth interviews with nurses and physicians who routinely conduct physical examinations of patients. Our overall goal is to investigate how the enactment of the physical examination is based on, and reproduces assumptions about, gender differences. We do not make claims about the average or typical behavior of men and women (an impossible goal in a qualitative study such as this). Rather, we describe and analyze the gendered meanings in the logic used by men and women health care providers who are trying to desexualize the physical examination of their patients. How does the gender of the doctor or nurse, and the gender of their patients, figure into their choices of which strategies to use? We are less interested in the effectiveness of these strategies and more interested in understanding what logic compels male and female health care providers to use different strategies. We also seek to understand why nurses and physicians might choose different strategies for desexualizing the physical exam of male and female patients.

Method

Semistructured in-depth interviews were conducted with 36 nurses (licensed vocational nurses and registered nurses) and 34 doctors, most of whom were employed in one teaching hospital. To protect the anonymity of the respondents and to generate a more racially diverse sample, doctors and nurses from two surrounding cities who did not work in this teaching hospital were also interviewed. Four of the nurses were faculty members at the nursing school; the others were hospital staff nurses. The sample of doctors includes men and women from a variety of clinical specialties, including family practice, several surgical specialties, and internal medicine. Excluded were specialties that did not require physical examinations of patients while they are partially or fully unclothed, such as psychiatry and ophthalmology.

Only one respondent (a physician) said during the interview that he was gay. Several nurses and physicians noted that it was difficult for their gay and lesbian coworkers to be "out" in the hospital with patients and among colleagues.

The sample was generated by using "snowball" techniques. An original list of contacts was obtained from colleagues in the teaching hospital and through personal acquaintances. This group were sent letters describing the study and inviting their participation. At the close of each interview, respondents were asked for names of other doctors or nurses who might be willing to be interviewed, who were also sent letters. In total, 81 letters were sent. Fifty-four of the 81 people who received letters agreed to do the interview. (Two people refused to participate, and 27 never responded to the letter.) An additional 16 respondents were contacted by telephone or in person, and all agreed to participate, making the total response rate 72 percent.

Findings

With few exceptions, the men and women in this study reported that they were uncomfortable performing physical examinations in the early part of their training but that they became more comfortable as they progressed through their careers. Several physicians and nurses noted that they "see 20 patients a day and everybody looks the same" and that they "have been doing this for so long" that they never get uncomfortable. All of the respondents, however, had developed strategies to desexualize the physical exam so that their patients would not interpret the interaction as sexual and to repress any feelings of sexual attraction that they might have toward their patients.

Three of the strategies mentioned were general ones, used by both men and women health care providers, regardless of the patient's characteristics. To make patients feel more comfortable, some doctors and nurses engaged them in casual conversation or nonsexual joking ("Try on our designer gown"). Some physicians insisted on meeting their patients fully clothed prior to the exam to decrease patients' feelings of vulnerability. Finally, two physicians mentioned using medical terms instead of colloquial terms, which helped to define the interaction as a scientific, diagnostic encounter instead of a sexual and personal one.

However, six strategies were used more selectively. The respondent either indicated that there was a special condition for the use of these strategies or the strategy emerged from the analysis as one that was mentioned primarily by men or women. In the discussion that follows, we describe each of these "gendered strategies" and explore the organizational logic and individual interests that underlie them.

USING A CHAPERONE

Nineteen physicians (13 men and 6 women) and two nurses (both men) insisted on the presence of a chaperone during physical exams. Two of the women used chaperones for both male and female patients, but all of the others who mentioned this strategy used chaperones only for their female patients. And with only one exception, the chaperone was always a woman.

The men and women who mentioned this strategy used it for a variety of reasons. Some believed that having a chaperone present helped to comfort their female patients:

> I always use chaperones for gynecological examinations and breast examinations. Part of it is a medical-legal issue, and part of it is that it's a big comfort to the patient. There's been a situation where I've only had a male nurse, and I won't or I guess I can't use a male nurse for chaperones with female patients . . . I don't think women would be comfortable with two men in the room. A female needs to be physically present. (Latino family practitioner)

Why are only female patients offered the comfort of a female chaperone? When directly asked, most physicians could not explain why they did not use chaperones for male patients, noting that they "have just never thought about it." One of the four male physicians who did not use chaperones explained that his reason was because all of his patients were men, and "male patients are comfortable with a male physician." Another doctor explained why she did not use chaperones with men:

> I can't have a woman in the room with me when I'm examining a man. Plus I think it would be worse to have another guy in there for the guy . . . I just think it's embarrassing enough for him already. I think it would be even more embarrassing if there was another guy in there. . . . I have male help, so theoretically I could have someone else in there with me but it would be embarrassing for them. (white female physician in internal medicine)

This physician believes that her physical presence during the exam is "embarrassing enough" to male patients; adding a chaperone to the scene potentially would worsen his embarrassment.

Thus, female patients are protected by chaperones, but men must be protected from chaperones. Men's vulnerability during the physical exam is defined differently from women's. Perhaps, as Cassell (1998) argues, the comfort provided by a female surgeon's body elicits feelings of childish dependency. While such feelings may be considered acceptable in female patients, they may be considered emasculating in male patients. A woman physically examining a man may be "embarrassing enough" because this is an affront to a man's sense of mastery and self-control. The presence of a witness to this emasculation—either a man or a woman—could exacerbate his feelings of powerlessness.

A second interpretation of this asymmetry is that in our society women are more readily defined as victims than men are; thus, female patients are considered to be in greater need of a chaperone to comfort and protect them. In a male doctor/female patient situation, the female chaperone equalizes the female power of the weaker member of the encounter (the female patient). The presence of the second man as a chaperone would be more threatening and could lead to suggestions of multiple men abusing a woman. In contrast, a man is assumed to have sufficient resources to protect himself, and this appears to be true even when he is a patient in a doctor-patient encounter. The presence of a chaperone would tip the scales in favor of the physician's power and thus make the male patient a potential "victim." Using any chaperone might also imply that any given man is unable to protect himself, which could be interpreted as an affront to his masculinity. Thus, the gender differences in the use of chaperones reflect assumptions about the relative power and powerlessness of men and women in social interactions.

Some health care providers claim that they use chaperones for *their* protection and not their patients. Respondents mentioned three ways that chaperones protected them. First, chaperones provide legal protection in cases where patients falsely accuse doctors of sexual misconduct. One male physician referred to chaperones as "cheap insurance" against such charges. This rationale for using chaperones was given by both male and female physicians, as well as by two male nurses. Because "sexual allegations usually come from women," as one female doctor put it, most believed they only needed this legal protection from female patients.

The women who used chaperones did not articulate any fears about false accusations from lesbian patients in particular, but this may have been a contributing factor in their practice. A nurse claimed that a complaint of sexual misconduct from a lesbian patient about a female physician prompted some women in the teaching hospital to start using chaperones for their female patients. On the other hand, female physicians may feel the need to protect themselves from accusations that they harbor lesbian desires toward their patients. Although none of these female doctors articulated this concern, it is commonly assumed that women in nontraditional occupations are lesbian, and granted the intimate nature of their work, some may feel especially vulnerable to such charges.

A second form of protection provided by chaperones is protection from sexual advances by patients. This rationale was mentioned by one female doctor, a urologist, which is a specialty composed of only 2 percent women (Randolph, Seidman, and Pasko 1996). She claimed that many men, especially her Hispanic patients, are often embarrassed to be treated by her because they are "really macho" and uneasy with women "in a position of authority." She discussed a variety of strategies she uses to make her male patients feel comfortable during invasive procedures such as the rectal exam, but she did not mention chaperones until she was asked (in a follow-up question), "Has a male patient ever tried to fondle you or anything?" In direct response, she said, "I have a chaperone in the room with me any time I examine a patient. Male or female. I have a male chaperone with men, and a female with women." The context of the interview suggests that her purpose for using a chaperone is physical protection from sexual harassment or assault.

Several other female health care providers we interviewed experienced sexual harassment by patients, but they did not use chaperones to protect themselves. This urologist was unique in using this strategy. Instead, as we will discuss later, female doctors and nurses typically relied on more informal strategies for dealing with the problem of sexual harassment and assault from patients.

The third form of protection that chaperones offer, according to the respondents, is protection from the doctor's own sexual feelings. Four men in this study gave this rationale for using a chaperone. A surgeon explained,

> One time I had a patient . . . [and] there were times I couldn't even examine her. I don't know if she and I were flirting with each other. It really unsettled me. She was gorgeous. I knew then that if I ever got in that situation again, I needed to use a chaperone. A chaperone not for her comfort but for mine. (white male orthopedic surgeon)

For this physician the presence of a chaperone helps him control his own sexual desires.

Some female health care professionals admitted that they sometimes experienced unwanted sexual feelings when examining an attractive man, but they never used chaperones to control themselves or diffuse this sexual tension. The women who were interviewed

seemed more concerned about controlling their male patients' sexual desire. Several respondents perceive that men are expected to act on their sexual desires and women are not. One nurse suggested that this social expectation limits the roles of male nurses:

> Younger teenage girls, I would rather just female nurses take care of them. I think we kind of discourage male nurses from taking care of teenage girls. You don't want anybody to get the wrong idea. Teenage boys are very uncomfortable with me, so I try to distract them, talk to them, try to make them more comfortable. (Latina nurse)

Although this nurse admits that teenage boys may be uncomfortable with her, she does not believe that a man should be called in to replace her because this discomfort is unlikely to result in the "wrong idea," that is, that the nurse is not in control of her sexual feelings and might sexually assault the boys. However, this is the assumption made of male nurses, and it is compelling enough for her to dissuade men from administering care to teenage girls. Again, this asymmetry reflects certain hegemonic beliefs regarding gender and sexuality. Just as women are more likely to be cast in the role of "victim," so are men likely to be seen as sexual aggressors. These beliefs are internalized by some health care providers and institutionalized in the patterns of chaperone use.

Nurses typically do not have the organizational authority to call in a chaperone, but as the above example illustrates, on occasion a male or a female nurse may be specifically requested to administer certain invasive procedures. One nurse recalled that in her training, women were not allowed to catheterize male patients. Today this rule is no longer in place, but occasionally male patients will request a male nurse for this procedure. This practice seems intended to lessen the discomfort and embarrassment of the patient, more than to protect them from sexual assault by female nurses. She said, "If a male patient wants a male, that's fine. Some male patients are hesitant about anyone catheterizing them. They feel their pride. They feel embarrassed. They usually feel okay if men do it" (white female nurse). On the other hand, some male patients prefer female nurses to perform such intimate procedures because they are uncomfortable with men. One nurse claimed that "some men are homophobic. They think their male nurses are homosexual" and thus prefer female nurses. Again, the unstated assumption is that men will act on their sexual desires; women will not.

Using a chaperone is a complex gendered strategy for desexualizing the physical exam. According to the organization's logic, female patients are comforted by the presence of a female chaperone, but male patients are likely to be embarrassed by one. Some doctors and nurses consider chaperones necessary when examining female patients to protect them from false accusations of sexual misconduct, but they assume that male patients will not falsely accuse them: Male patients are perceived to be better able to protect themselves from such misconduct. One doctor uses a chaperone to protect her from sexual harassment or assault from her patients. Some male doctors use chaperones to help them control their sexual feelings toward their female patients. Male nurses are almost never chosen as chaperones; in fact, some male nurses are expected to use chaperones (or to refrain from performing certain procedures altogether) for the same reasons that male physicians use chaperones. It is critical in most instances that the chaperone is a woman: A man in this role might make female patients feel even more victimized and vulnerable, and might be emasculating for male patients.

This complex strategy to desexualize the physical exam is grounded on assumptions about men's and women's sexuality. Men are sexually powerful; women are sexually vulnerable. Women's bodies are comforting and soothing, but they also elicit feelings of childish vulnerability, which is an acceptable feeling in women but not in men. Men act on their sexual desires; women do not. These gender and sex stereotypes are bolstered through the organizational practice of using chaperones to desexualize the physical exam.

OBJECTIFYING THE PATIENT

Eight of the physicians and nurses reported that viewing their patients as something other than a person helped them to cope with the sexual nature of their work. This finding is consistent with previous research indicating that medical students and residents deal with uncomfortable feelings about patient nudity and examinations by objectifying their patients' bodies. Smith and Kleinman (1989) noted that students referred to examining patients as analogous to "looking under the hood of a car." The medical curriculum encourages students to dehumanize their patients' bodies because it focuses on the biological disease process and its cure ("lung in room 5") (Todd 1989). In contrast, the nursing school curriculum with its focus on "caring" and not "curing" emphasizes a more humane and holistic approach to treating patients. Fisher (1995) suggests that the nursing profession's focus on empathy discourages nurses from dehumanizing their patients in an extreme manner.

We found that both men and women objectify patients, but we noticed that the men and women interviewed used different metaphors in the process. The four women who mentioned using this strategy referred to their patients as "just another body" and did so for male and female patients. The four men who mentioned using this strategy referred to their patient as something other than a human being, usually a car. Moreover, these men only used this strategy with female patients.

A white female nurse described her training:

[The nursing faculty] tried to tell us like, "Don't think about it. Treat it like just another body." Usually, you've already messed with cadavers by the time you get to the hospital. So it's just another body. The hardest thing is trying to convince your patients of that . . . that it doesn't bother you.

Because she dissected cadavers in nursing school, this nurse was better able to view her patients as "just another body" and thus desexualize her own view of the patient. And according to a physician:

I'm never uncomfortable now. . . . You forget that students get uncomfortable. It's almost humorous, when you see how uncomfortable they are and you remember how uncomfortable it was at first. I tell them that it is just a body. If you get embarrassed, then your patient is going to be embarrassed. . . . If you're a professional, then they'll think it's a matter of course. (white female neurologist)

Many women provide care for their children and other relatives. If women routinely manage bodies in their personal lives, they may be more comfortable than men examining naked bodies in their professional lives, without thinking of them in a sexual way. One nurse explained that she thought of her patients as family members to make herself more comfortable with the physical exam:

I've never been nervous. My husband sometimes asks me about it. I tell him, "I can't even tell you what size a man was. I don't look at their bodies in that way." . . . You focus on a certain part of their body, and it's just a body. Nothing else. They stressed in school that we should preserve dignity and privacy. Treat the patient like they were one of your family members. Put yourself in their place. (African American female nurse)

While this nurse refers to her patients as "just a body," she also empathizes with them, thinking of them as family members. Referring to

patients as bodies does not seem to imply that these women lose compassion or empathy for their patients as human beings.

In contrast, the four male practitioners who claimed to dehumanize their patients as a strategy to desexualize the physical exam compared them to machines, and they did so only for their female patients. For example, a nurse said that examining female patients was no different from "checking the oil." Similarly, a physician described examining female patients:

When you're doing an examination, the genital examination, it's so routine and mundane. . . . You're looking at the body and trying to identify other things that are going on, like a pathology. . . . Sometimes I use the analogy of the car. . . . What you're focusing on is under the hood. You step back and say, "This is a nice car." But I'm not looking at the car. I'm checking the spark plugs. . . . It's part of my job. They are there because their car is misfiring. . . . You're not looking at it on a personal level or a sexual excitement level . . . it's not a turn on. (Latino physician in family practice)

This physician is not uncomfortable examining female patients because he is not looking at their bodies for his own personal sexual enjoyment. From his point of view, examining a patient "on a personal level" might provoke "sexual excitement." Thinking of his female patients as inanimate objects enables him to desexualize the exam.

Some physicians report they are most uncomfortable examining people they know. Having a personal relationship with someone clouds professional judgment according to one physician: "It's harder to take care of patients you know very well, and they're in a dangerous situation. I still treat them, but I'm more nervous about it compared to patients who I've just met" (white male cardiologist).

In the operating room, the patient may be more anonymous, and even unconscious, making the encounter less personal and unsettling for this physician. Having a personal relationship with a patient who is being examined is more difficult for him. This contrasts with the nurse, quoted above, who attributed family status to her patients to ensure the top quality of care.

Similarly, some physicians said they managed to maintain their composure around nude patients when the patient is passively lying down on an examination table, but they are more vulnerable to embarrassment if the patient is not so passive:

> I can walk into an exam room and see a lady in the wide-open-legs position, and examine her, and do a breast exam and pelvic exam, and that doesn't bother me at all. That's so clinical. But if I walk in, and you're getting dressed or undressed, I lose it. I get flabbergasted. I turn red and I have to walk out. That's the weird thing. I can see you totally buck naked and it doesn't bother me, but if you're getting dressed or undressed, that's it. . . . It's like when you're undressed and you have a gown on, and you're on the table, you're an auto engine. You're not really, but . . . I'm here to do a job, to make a diagnosis and do a treatment, and there are certain things I have to look for so it becomes mechanical. (white male urologist)

This physician is less able to dehumanize his patients like "an auto engine" when he sees female patients in a stage of dressing. Witnessing the transition between the clothed and the unclothed states disturbs his fantasy that the human being is an inanimate machine. Three other male physicians and nurses reported that they were only uncomfortable during physical exams if they saw a female patient dressing or undressing. None of the women reported that this made them uncomfortable.

The men who were interviewed only mentioned this strategy when describing exams of female patients. They did not describe dehumanizing their male patients in this way, perhaps because these heterosexual men only fear sexual arousal with their female patients. They may not have to dehumanize their male

patients as cars because they perceive no danger of sexual attraction.

Dehumanization seems to help these health care professionals deal with the sexual nature of their work. This strategy sheds new light on complaints that doctors do not care enough about their patients. Health care professionals are taught that they should have some level of detachment to deal rationally with their patients' problems. For some physicians and nurses, objectifying their patients might also help them to cope with the sexual nature of their work. Our interviews suggest further that this may be a gendered strategy, with men more likely than women to feel the need to distance themselves from their female patients to provide a high level of care.

EMPATHIZING WITH THE PATIENT AND PROTECTING PRIVACY

Some health care providers used the opposite strategy to objectification: to diffuse sexual tension and to make their patients feel more comfortable during the physical exam, they said they empathized with them. Some said that this empathy was combined with their efforts to protect the patient's privacy, by draping or covering the patient, exposing only the small area in need of attention, or drawing privacy curtains around the patient's bed. We combined empathy and protecting privacy in tallying up the strategies since the rationale given by the respondents was similar in both cases. In sum, 6 men and 27 women reported using one or both of these strategies to desexualize the physical exam.

For example, to make her patients feel more comfortable during the exam, one nurse follows these guidelines:

> First, explain what's going to happen and that privacy will be maintained as much as possible. The door will be shut and the curtains will be drawn or whatever. Let them know that you understand how uncomfortable it can be. Empathize. (white female nurse)

This practice of empathizing with the patient, and protecting their privacy, seems more characteristic of nursing than medicine. Seven of the physicians and 15 of the nurses said that they always covered their patients.

Whereas several nurses explained that they were taught in nursing school to empathize with their patients' needs for privacy, the opposite lesson was stressed in the medical training of some of the physicians who were interviewed. One doctor reported that a former professor required students to physically examine him in front of the class:

> He tried to show that there's nothing to be uncomfortable about during the exam. Every year it escalated, and it got to the point where he completely disrobed and insisted that all parts of the exam be performed on him in front of this huge group of people. I don't know how effective it was. I thought it was embarrassing. (white male internist)

Students even administered a rectal exam on this professor in front of the class. In contrast to nursing education, which stresses patient dignity and privacy, the goal here seems to be to desensitize medical students and to disregard the personal and physical boundaries of patients.

Other physicians mentioned aspects of their education that seem intended to violate their own physical integrity and sense of personal boundaries. One medical student intern described a former professor who forced some of the male students to be physically examined in front of the class, an experience he described as sexual harassment. Female students were not called upon to submit to these public examinations; the organization almost certainly would have considered that an illegal and harmful practice. At the medical school where most of this study was conducted, students had been required to conduct full examinations of each other, but when the students collectively rebelled against this practice, the school changed to its current practice of employing people from the community to help students practice their exam skills.

Nurses also are required to examine each other in training and even to give each other bed baths, but unlike these examples from medical schools, nursing students are explicitly taught how to conduct these invasive procedures while maintaining personal boundaries. One nurse recalled how she was taught to "be gentle and handle conversation carefully":

> Conversation shouldn't be about what you see on their body. It should be about the weather or the game that was on last night, or finding something in common with your patient. You should be able to converse with all people, from the retired professional to the laborer who can't read. I feel like we were trained well. (white female nurse)

In this way, sensitivity to the patients' needs for privacy and dignity is emphasized as part of the standard nursing curriculum.

In contrast, some doctors are subjected to insensitivity training. One doctor recalled being shown "desensitization tapes" as preparation for dealing with patients' sexuality:

> You're not supposed to be judgmental [as a doctor]. They showed us a bunch of tapes, like on sexual counseling. It's supposed to desensitize us to sexual things and to help us acknowledge our own sexual feelings and deal with them. They were generally kind of like gross porno-like films. Not porno films, but everybody made a lot of fun of them. In medical school, some people were offended by them, by the nudity in them. So they began showing them at night. Of course, the students were still uncomfortable. There were still jokes, but everybody was uncomfortable watching naked people and sexual acts. This was stuff we had never seen outside of porno films. (white female gynecologist)

Empathy and modesty, which are values built into nursing education, appear to be actively suppressed in physician education. This difference reflects a gendered organizational logic: Since most nursing students are women, and until recently, women have been vastly underrepresented among medical students, the expectations of appropriate professional behavior that are embedded in physician and nurse education reflect and reinforce gender stereotypes. To be a good nurse/woman means to be empathetic and modest; to be a good physician/man means to be unflappable, detached, and powerful. The hidden curriculum of health care education is thus a gendered and, to some extent, sexualized curriculum.

JOKING ABOUT SEX

Joking about sex might seem incongruent with attempts to desexualize interactions with patients, but eight men and women engaged in sexual banter with their patients as a strategy to make themselves or the patient more comfortable with intimate topics, such as the sexual history. The interviews indicate, however, that this strategy was used selectively: With a few exceptions, the men and women interviewed only joked with opposite-sex patients or older patients.

A male urologist said he occasionally jokes about sex with his female patients:

> There is innuendo. Like yesterday there was a 23-year-old girl in, who had recurrent urinary tract infections. . . . It seemed to be with her new partner that she got a lot of infections . . . I said, "Well, what you're going to need to do is take an antibiotic tablet after you have intercourse . . . every time after you have intercourse. For some women, that means you have to take one everyday." She looked at me and said, "Everyday?" I said, "There was a time in my life where I would have had to take one everyday. It didn't last very long but. . . ." So that's about as risqué as it gets. . . . Men are more uncomfortable being messed with, with their bodies than women. Women pretty much recognize that they have to go get a pap smear, and when they've

had babies, everyone is sticking their fingers up there. So women, from an early age are pretty much, for lack of a better word, resigned to it. Men . . . don't like it. You know, we see a lot of men for impotence. . . . That's . . . getting into intimate details, broaching subjects that . . . many men find very difficult to talk about . . . there's not that much joking with the men. . . . When they're talking about difficulty getting an erection, I don't think they want a locker room discussion. (white male urologist)

While he is cautious about engaging in sexual banter with women, he assumes that women are more comfortable joking about these personal matters. He perceives men's exams and histories as more sensitive than women's. He therefore avoids sexual joking with men; he does not think the examining room is the proper context for a "locker room discussion." Because the joking that does take place in locker rooms and other all-male contexts typically involves the ritual exchange of sexual insults—about sexual practices, the women they date, and the size of a man's penis (Lyman 1987)—it is inappropriate in the examining room, where the unclothed patient is in an especially passive and vulnerable position, unable to return the banter or to maintain his composure. Moreover, in the context of the exam, any sexual innuendo made to another man might be interpreted as sexual harassment.

The other physicians who mentioned this strategy engaged in joking with patients of the opposite sex to make patients more comfortable. A female general surgeon describes how she occasionally jokes about sex:

> I remember one time . . . this guy had a hernia. . . . His wife was with him. He had been coming to see us for several weeks, once a week, so we kind of had a relationship going. I walked in the room and said, "Drop your pants." He said, "Oh, I love it when women talk dirty." We all stood around laughing. It's not something you would do with everybody, but I

felt comfortable in this situation. I think most patients respond well to humor, when they know it's humor. (white female surgeon)

Joking about sex with this patient seems to diffuse any hint of sexual interest. Their sexual banter plays on the absurdity of sexual interest between a female doctor and a male patient, thus dispelling any concerns the patient's wife might have.

This function of sexual humor was most apparent when some of the men and women discussed ways to avoid false allegations. A female nurse described how she avoided false allegations from patients:

> Well, really I don't worry because I use a lot of joking and kidding and get to know my patients a little bit before I have to do anything to them. I have a patient now, and the first thing this guy said was, "You just want to peek at me, don't you? You just want to take a look at me?" I said, "Sure, that's going to be the thrill of my day. I've seen 9 million of these things honey." (white female nurse)

This nurse uses joking to assure her male patient that this exam is not intended to have sexual overtones, even though he initiates the banter. These interviews suggest that joking about sex is a way to let the patient know that the physician or nurse is not sexually attracted to them, and that any hint of sexual attraction is both outrageous and taboo. As Fine (1976, 135) observes, sexual joking often functions this way: "By describing behavior considered sexually improper (and thus comical), [sexual humor] reveals by implication the correct forms of sexual interaction."

Men and women also engaged in sexual joking with older patients. A male nurse described how he made older patients more comfortable during physical exams:

> I joke about sex with some of the male patients. Once in a while I might say something to a female. . . . One woman that we're rendering care to right now is 93 years old. When you go to

visit her, the first thing she wants to know is why hasn't she died. . . . One day I said, "I think it's because you need to find a man. You haven't done that yet." She laughed, but I don't think I would go more than that. With male patients, we joke pretty openly. Like a diabetic patient in his middle seventies, who also had a little bit of cancer of the prostate, asked me if he should be involved in sex. . . . He wanted to know about protection with respect to AIDS. . . . Well, I seriously doubt he was going to get any, pardon my language (laughs). . . . With younger males, it's easy. I even joke with homosexuals a little bit, but not about homosexuals. I tell homosexuals heterosexual jokes. They know I'm straight pretty soon. (white male nurse)

This nurse engages in sexual joking with older patients and some young men as a way to set them at ease. But significantly, the strategy is used very selectively. He makes the ageist assumption that joking with older patients is safe because these individuals are neither active sexually nor do they have sexual interests. This reaffirms the hegemonic belief that only young people are sexual. His joking with young men appears to be a strategy designed to let them know that he is straight. Male nurses often face stereotypes that they are gay (Williams 1995), and this may be one way to dispel this suspicion among his patients.

Sexual banter with patients is a strategy that might fail if the patient is gay or lesbian, and the physician or nurse is heterosexual. Stevens (1996) conducted a study of lesbians' experiences with physicians during physical exams and found that physicians engaged in sexual innuendo with the respondents. The respondents noted that physicians seemed uncomfortable and unsure how to proceed if they "came out" during the physical examination. For example, one woman noted that her physician "didn't seem to know how to make conversation with a female client except through heterosexual jokes" (Stevens 1996, 34). Stevens' research suggests that joking about sex was based on the assumption of heterosexuality of the doctor and patient, and it might be used more often in heterosocial encounters in the intimate context of the physical exam.

Joking reaffirms the legitimacy and normalcy of some sexual behaviors, and the taboo nature of others. But it does this by inverting the normal and the taboo. Often what makes a joke funny is the absurdity and impossibility of the situations it describes. Thus, some of the health care workers who were interviewed felt comfortable joking about sex with opposite-sex patients and elderly patients. By pointing out what is absurd, it affirms what is normal and expected. Sexual joking is also a means through which men establish intimacy, although typically this involves challenging each other's masculinity and sexual prowess. Male joking of this type requires that participants appear invulnerable to these attacks (Lyman 1987), a situation impossible to maintain in the context of a medical examination. Consequently, this type of joking is absent from the accounts of our respondents, except in the case of the male nurse who uses joking to demonstrate his heterosexuality to his male patients. Finally, joking can decrease the social distance between patients and their health care providers, and hence it can be used to help comfort and empathize with patients. Even so, it is used selectively, often only with elderly patients, reflecting the ageist assumption that old people are asexual. Several health care providers did acknowledge that sexual joking is potentially dangerous in heterosocial encounters in the examining room because of its sexualized overtones: Consequently, most of the doctors and nurses interviewed said they assiduously avoid any such joking because they fear it will be misconstrued as a sexual interest.

THREATENING THE PATIENT

Four female physicians and nurses encountered problems desexualizing the physical examination of their patients because they experienced unwanted sexual advances from male patients. To control such patients, they threatened to physically or verbally punish them. Some men also reported sexual harassment from patients, but they never threatened them to control their behaviors. Seven physicians (5 of them were women) and 11 nurses (9 of them women) said they experienced sexual harassment from patients, ranging from male patients who attempted to fondle or grab them, to engage in sexual innuendo, and/or to expose themselves. Some of these behaviors were experienced as threatening; others were seen as "nothing to get upset about" and "a part of the job."

Recent studies indicate that sexual harassment affects many women in the health care industry. Phillips and Schneider (1993) found that 75 percent of female doctors surveyed reported sexual harassment from patients, most of whom were male. Grieco (1987) found that 76 percent of nurses surveyed experienced sexual harassment from both physicians and patients. Foner's (1994) study of a nursing home indicates that some female health care workers actually may be required to tolerate these behaviors as part of their jobs.

A nurse described her experience of sexual harassment:

> I had a patient try to pull me into bed with him. I hit him. . . . I reached down to take his pulse, and he yanked my hand. I had a foreigner grab my hand and shove it down his pants. . . . At first I thought, "Well, he's just a foreigner. He can't speak English. He's used to having women serve all of his needs." He wasn't speaking so I assumed that he didn't speak English. He was pretty dark. I thought he was Middle Eastern. He took my hand like he was trying to tell me something. So I was saying, "What's the matter? What are you trying to tell me?" He grabbed my hand, pulled it down his pants and he had a hard-on. That was very scary . . . I got very angry. I yelled at him, "I don't care if you speak English or not! You don't do that again! I'll tie you to the bed!" I went back and got mad at the other nurses for

not telling me about him. They were like, "Whoops. We forgot he did that to young women." I said, "He's done this before?!" They said, "You can give him up if you want to." I said, "No. I can handle it." He would say, "Will you help me?" I said, "Nope. Don't you touch me." I was rude. (white female nurse)

The fact that her coworkers "forgot" to tell her that this patient sexually harassed other women suggests that sexual harassment is a routine and expected part of their job, which is managed through informal "warnings" about patients who instigate unwanted sexual advances. To desexualize the exam and control this patient, she gets "rude" and threatens to tie his hands.

None of the physicians or nurses interviewed had received formal or informal training about handling unwanted sexual advances from patients. The women who were interviewed had to devise their own strategies to control behaviors of male patients. According to one nurse:

Oh yeah. [Sexual harassment from male patients] happens all the time. Oh yeah (laughs). . . . Last week, this one guy exposed himself to me every time I walked in the room, or he'd grab himself and leer at me. I've had them proposition me, grab my boobs, my butt. It's been a wild time (laughs). . . . The guy who was exposing himself and grabbing himself just had an infected left hand. There was nothing wrong up here [points to her forehead] . . . I said to him, "Are you having trouble keeping your gown down, buddy?" I talk to them real stern. With my size, they tend to do what I say. . . . I've had to report a couple of guys who wouldn't keep their hands to themselves. I went to their doctor. The doctors are always real supportive about that. I tell them, "I'm having trouble with this guy," and the doctor goes in and says, "That's not acceptable. You leave the nurses alone." (white female nurse)

Even though she feels protected because of her size (she is more than six feet tall), ultimately this nurse must call on physicians to control

the unacceptable sexual behavior of some of her patients. Three other nurses noted that they threaten to call the police if male patients "got out of hand." This strategy thus perpetuates gendered beliefs about women (nurses) as victims and men (police/doctors) as protectors.

One female physician changed specialties from internal medicine to obstetrics-gynecology to avoid sexual harassment by male patients:

When I was in internal medicine—I remember one guy in the ER had a heart attack. I was listening to his heart beating and he reaches around and grabs my butt. I said, "I don't think you understand. You have had a heart attack. I'm your doctor. If I were you, I don't think I'd piss me off." He was drunk as a skunk. Out dancing with a woman who wasn't his wife. I said, "Would you like for me to call your wife and explain the situation to your family? Okay. We understand each other." . . . I was [in] internal medicine for about four months. I found [the male patients] unpleasant and went into ob-gyn. (white female physician in obstetrics-gynecology)

In order to control the sexual behavior of her patient, this physician had to assert her professional status and threaten to expose his sexual infidelity to his family. After she changed specialties to obstetrics-gynecology, she treated only female patients. In this way, sexual harassment may contribute to internal occupational segregation in the health care professions. In fact, research shows that women in professional, nontraditional occupations suffer high rates of sexual harassment, often the "hostile work environment" type that punishes women for entering traditionally male environments (DiTomaso 1989); Konrad and Gutek 1986; Schultz 1998).

Physicians are often criticized today for their domineering and controlling attitudes toward patients. Our study suggests that for at least some female physicians, asserting power may be a means to overcome sexual harassment. According to Phillips and Schneider (1993, 1939),

At a time when physicians are criticized for magnifying the inevitable differences in power that separate them from their patients, it is ironic that female doctors see the reinforcement of a physician's power as a means of protection. Despite this power, female doctors are treated primarily as women, not as physicians, by many of their male patients. The vulnerability inherent in their sex seems in many cases to override their power as doctors, leaving female physicians open to sexual harassment.

Female physicians and nurses may be forced to draw on their institutional power and authority to desexualize the physical exam, in response to unwanted sexual advances from their male patients.

LOOKING PROFESSIONAL

Four female nurses and doctors in this study attempted to control the sexual desires of their patients and diffuse the sexual meanings of the physical exam by emphasizing their professionalism. This was usually accomplished by dressing in a particular way:

> The way you dress is important. I think it's really important for women. I don't go to work with tight pants or short skirts. I wear business attire so the patient gets the idea that you're there to take care of them and nothing else. It's also important how the other people in the clinic dress. We have the nurses dress in scrubs or uniforms, and the secretaries also don't dress like they're going out to the disco (laughs). (Latina internist)

The importance of dressing to suppress sexual feelings was also emphasized by this physician:

> Some female physicians have their hair all made up, and lots of makeup and they look like a Barbie doll. I like to dress nicely but I don't wear excessive jewelry. I don't wear excessive makeup. I'm not too ornate. I don't try to look like a Barbie doll because I can see where it would be difficult for the patient to keep in mind that you're their physician, you know? (Asian American female in general medicine)

The conventional markers of femininity (styled hair, makeup, jewelry) are incompatible with "looking professional" because they sexualize the female health care provider and thus potentially arouse sexual feelings in patients. It is telling that none of the male health care providers mentioned the importance of dress for controlling patients' sexuality. Men may have an easier time than women looking the part of a professional. According to Dellinger and Williams (1997), the fact that men do not have to strategize their appearance reinforces the idea that women are the ones who bring "gender" and "sexuality" to the workplace.

Certain institutional practices exacerbate the problems women face "looking professional." Three of the female surgeons who occasionally worked at the same hospital mentioned that they were unhappy with the uniforms made available to them there. Two types of scrub suits were worn in the operating room: the typical green scrubs, which they preferred, and flowery scrubs with longer sleeves and tops intended to be worn by the female nurses. These physicians did not like the flowery scrubs because they claimed it was harder to do surgery in them, and because they did not want to be mistaken for nurses, yet they were typically the only type available in the women's changing room (which was shared by doctors and nurses). The administration ignored their complaints that the flowery scrubs undermined their efforts to look professional and garner the respect they felt they deserved. One said she often had to go into the doctors' dressing room (which was used by men only) to retrieve a set of green scrubs to wear:

> In some hospitals that don't have separate female surgeons' dressing rooms, there are no male scrubs available. So I just knock on the door to the male dressing room, and I walk in and get some scrubs. If there's men in there and they're naked, I don't care. I just walk in. I say, "If you don't like me doing this, then complain to so-and-so, and get us a female physicians' dressing room." But they don't care. The men don't care.

It's kind of a joke. They kind of laugh about it. It's another form of insidious discrimination . . . to not provide female physicians with the same clothes that they provide the male physicians. (white female urologist)

In addition to having the right clothes, having the right body shape also helps to "look professional," according to another physician. When asked if she had ever been sexually harassed, she said,

Younger guys have said something suggestive over the years but it's never been a big problem [for me]. Again, I think it helps that I am tall with dark hair. I think there are ways of being friendly, yet clearly professional, and that's hard to teach. I know some women have had more of a problem. I'm not very buxom either, and I think that makes a difference. I really think these things are things that women have no control over, but they make a huge difference. There are also clothes I wouldn't wear to see patients, like no short skirts. I dress conservatively. It shouldn't make a difference, but it does. (white female internist)

Women's bodies arouse sexual feelings, according to this physician, making it more difficult for women to achieve professional recognition. Some women's bodies may be especially incompatible with professional status. This is another example of how organizations are gendered and sexualized: The image of professionalism in the hospital is a masculine one. Women's bodies must be desexualized to achieve the same level of respect that men are accorded automatically. Having the wrong kind of body can be a formidable impediment to success.

Conclusion

Health care professionals are expected to manage their personal feelings during the physical examination of patients. This article describes how physicians and nurses control their own sexual feelings and the sexual behaviors of their patients. The men and women interviewed devised strategies to desexualize the exam, several of which were used selectively, depending on the gender and other characteristics of the patient and the health care worker. The interviews with doctors and nurses indicate that the choice to use certain strategies is shaped by, and reinforces, stereotypes about gender and sexuality.

The findings in this article are based on a small, nonrandom sample; hence, it is difficult to generalize to the entire population of doctors and nurses. Health care practitioners in other settings, such as private practices, may manage sexuality differently, compared with the physicians and nurses in teaching hospitals. The management of sexuality may also be specialty specific. Surgeons, pediatricians, urologists, and family practitioners may desexualize the exam differently.

This study suggests that desexualizing the exam is a gendered process. Men and women confront different obstacles to desexualizing the physical examination of patients. Male physicians and nurses are subject to assumptions that they are out of control of their sexuality. The use of female chaperones during their examination of female patients is based, in part, on this belief. Some men actually do fear sexual arousal, especially in their gynecological examinations of young, attractive women. Some men are also uncomfortable when they examine women they know or when they witness female patients undressing. Having a personal relationship with women is conflated with sexual meanings for some. Some endeavor to dehumanize their patient as a car to help them control their physical attraction.

In contrast, the women who were interviewed were less concerned about controlling their own sexual desire and more concerned about controlling the sexual desire of their male patients. Many of the female physicians and nurses in this study reported that sexual harassment from patients was "a part of their job." To protect themselves from sexual harassment, the female health care providers changed specialties, threatened their male patients, and dressed in ways to minimize their femininity and sexual attractiveness.

It is interesting how stereotypes about male and female patients' behavior provoke different institutional responses. Some doctors (both men and women) and male nurses fear that female patients will falsely accuse them of sexual assault, so they take measures to protect their reputations, including the institutionalized use of female chaperones. On the other hand, some female health care providers (both doctors and nurses) fear that they will be sexually harassed or assaulted by their male patients. But chaperones typically are not used to prevent these behaviors because chaperones might "embarrass" the male patient. Consequently, female health care providers must devise personal solutions to this problem without institutionalized support.

The professions of medicine and nursing, like many occupations, are profoundly gendered. Doctors are assumed to possess characteristics conventionally associated with masculinity (mastery, control, objectivity), while nurses are expected to display putatively feminine characteristics (empathy, modesty). The different training they receive in professional schools bolsters these expectations, with physicians focused on "curing" the disease and nurses learning to "care" for the whole patient. These gendered expectations are reflected in the strategies that men/doctors and women/nurses use to desexualize the exam. Women/nurses manage the relationship (empathize/protect privacy) between the provider and the patient, reflecting women's widely emphasized interactional and communication skills. The men/doctors do not stress managing the relationship; they just bring in another person (the chaperone) to control and to monitor the situation. Because female doctors and male nurses have to negotiate

conflicting sets of gender expectations, they use some strategies not common to their professional colleagues of the opposite sex. Thus, female doctors stress the importance of looking professional, and male nurses sometimes call in chaperones.

This study of desexualization strategies reveals how gender is embedded in the informal organization and daily interactions with patients in the hospital. It is difficult to imagine how an embodied procedure such as a physical exam could ever escape gendered meanings. But recognizing how cultural assumptions about gender and sexuality shape this experience is a critical first step toward eventually reconfiguring those expectations in more just and liberating ways.

References

Cassell, J. 1998. *The Woman in the Surgeon's Body.* Cambridge, MA: Harvard University Press.

Dellinger, K. A., and C. L. Williams, 1997. "Makeup at Work: Negotiating Appearance Rules in the Workplace." *Gender & Society* 11:151–77.

DiTomaso, N. 1989. "Sexuality in the Workplace: Discrimination and Harassment." In *The Sexuality of Organization,* edited by J. Hearn, D. L. Sheppard, P. Tancred-Sheriff, and G. Burrell. London: Sage.

Fine, G. A. 1976. "Obscene Joking Across Cultures." *Journal of Communication* 26:134–40.

Fisher, S. 1995. *Nursing Wounds: Nurse Practitioners/ Doctors/Women Patients/and the Negotiation of Meaning.* New Brunswick, NJ: Rutgers University Press.

Foner, N. 1994. *The Caregiving Dilemma: Work in an American Nursing Home.* Berkeley: University of California Press.

Grieco, A. 1987. "Scope and Nature of Sexual Harassment in Nursing." *Journal of Sex Research* 23:261–66.

Konrad, A. M., and B. A. Gutek. 1986. "Impact of Work Experiences on Attitudes Toward Sexual Harassment." *Administrative Science Quarterly* 31:422–38.

Lyman, P. 1987. "The Fraternal Bond as a Joking Relationship: A Case Study of the Role of Sexist Jokes in Male Group Bonding." In *Changing Men:*

New Directions in Research on Men and Masculinity, ed., M. S. Kimmel. Newbury Park, CA: Sage.

Phillips, S. P., and M. S. Schneider. 1993. "Sexual Harassment of Doctors by Patients." *New England Journal of Medicine* 329: 1936–39.

Randolph, L., B. Seidman, and T. Pasko. 1996. *Physician Characteristics and Distribution in the U.S.* Chicago: American Medical Association.

Schultz, V. 1998. "Reconceptualizing Sexual Harassment." *Yale Law Journal* 107: 1683–1805.

Smith, A. C., and S. Kleinman. 1989. "Managing Emotions in Medical School: Students' Contact with the Living and the Dead." *Social Psychology Quarterly* 52: 56–69.

Stevens, P. E. 1996. "Lesbians and doctors: Experiences of solidarity and domination in health care settings." *Gender & Society* 10:24–41.

Todd, A. D. 1989. *Intimate Adversaries: Cultural Conflict Between Doctors and Women Patients.* Philadelphia: University of Pennsylvania Press.

Williams, C. L. 1995. *Still a Man's World: Men Who Do "Women's Work."* Berkeley: University of California Press.

Questions

1. What do the authors mean when they say that the physical exam must be "desexualized"?

2. According to professors Giuffre and Williams, desexualizing physical exams is done in a gendered way. What strategies are primarily employed by women practitioners? What strategies are primarily employed by male practitioners?

3. The authors argue that "female patients are protected by chaperones, but men must be protected from chaperones." What do they mean?

4. This article focuses mostly on what practitioners do to desexualize physical exams. In your experience, what role does the patient play in desexualizing physical exams? Is the patient's response gendered? (That is, do men play their role as patients during the physical exam differently than women do?)

26

THE NORMALITY OF CRIME

Émile Durkheim

The following excerpt is from Émile Durkheim's 1895 essay *Rules of the Sociological Method*. The excerpt is brief but (like much of what people wrote in the nineteenth century) fairly complex. Durkheim begins by pointing out that crime—or acts that offend the collective conscience—is normal in every society. In other words, every society can expect some of its members occasionally to do things that offend that society's shared values and beliefs. According to Durkheim's analysis, the only way to completely do away with murder, for example, would be for every single person in the society to develop intense respect for all other members. If that happened, Durkheim points out, then the crime of murder might disappear, but previously minor offenses would then seem more serious. In a society of saints, he says, the crime of murder would not be a problem, but perhaps the "crime" of insulting others would be.

Here we are, then, in the presence of a conclusion in appearance quite paradoxical. Let us make no mistake. To classify crime among the phenomena of normal sociology is not to say merely that it is an inevitable, although regrettable phenomenon, due to the incorrigible wickedness of men; it is to affirm that it is a factor in public health, an integral part of all healthy societies. This result is, at first glance, surprising enough to have puzzled even ourselves for a long time. Once this first surprise has been overcome, however, it is not difficult to find reasons explaining this normality and at the same time confirming it.

In the first place crime is normal because a society exempt from it is utterly impossible. Crime, we have shown elsewhere, consists of an act that offends certain very strong collective sentiments. In a society in which criminal acts are no longer committed, the sentiments they offend would have to be found without exception in all individual consciousnesses, and they must be found to exist with the same degree as sentiments contrary to them. Assuming that this condition could actually be realized, crime would not thereby disappear; it would only change its form, for the very cause which would thus dry up the sources of criminality would immediately open up new ones.

society must have deviance

Indeed, for the collective sentiments which are protected by the penal law[1] of a people at a specific moment of its history to take possession of the public conscience or for them to acquire a stronger hold where they have an insufficient grip, they must acquire an intensity greater than that which they had hitherto had. The community as a whole must experience them more vividly, for it can acquire from no other source the greater force necessary to control these individuals who formerly were the most refractory. For murderers to disappear, the horror of bloodshed must become greater in those social strata from which murderers are recruited; but, first it must become greater throughout the entire society. Moreover, the very absence of crime would directly contribute to produce this horror; because any sentiment seems much more respectable when it is always and uniformly respected.

One easily overlooks the consideration that these strong states of the common consciousness cannot be thus reinforced without reinforcing at the same time the more feeble states, whose violation previously gave birth to mere infraction of convention—since the weaker ones are only the prolongation, the attenuated form, of the stronger. Thus robbery and simple bad taste injure the same single altruistic sentiment, the respect for that which is another's. However, this same sentiment is less grievously offended by bad taste than by robbery; and since, in addition, the average consciousness has not sufficient intensity to react keenly to the bad taste, it is treated with greater tolerance.

That is why the person guilty of bad taste is merely blamed, whereas the thief is punished. But, if this sentiment grows stronger, to the point of silencing in all consciousnesses the inclination which disposes man to steal, he will become more sensitive to the offenses which, until then, touched him but lightly. He will react against them, then, with more energy; they will be the object of greater opprobrium, which will transform certain of them from the simple moral faults that they were and give them the quality of crimes. For example, improper contracts, or contracts improperly executed, which only incur public blame or civil damages, will become offenses in law.

Imagine a society of saints, a perfect cloister of exemplary individuals. Crimes, properly so called, will there be unknown; but faults which appear venial to the layman will create there the same scandal that the ordinary offense does in ordinary consciousnesses. If, then, this society has the power to judge and punish, it will define these acts as criminal and will treat them as such. For the same reason, the perfect and upright man judges his smallest failings with a severity that the majority reserve for acts more truly in the nature of an offense. Formerly, acts of violence against persons were more frequent than they are today, because respect for individual dignity was less strong. As this has increased, these crimes have become more rare; and also, many acts violating this sentiment have been introduced into the penal law which were not included there in primitive times. . . .

Questions

1. Durkheim argues that crime is "normal." What does he mean by this?

2. Does Durkheim believe that it is either possible or desirable for a society to exist in which there is no crime? Why or why not?

---

[1]Penal law is criminal law.—Ed.

27

THE SAINTS AND THE ROUGHNECKS

William J. Chambliss

Robert K. Merton was inspired by the "Thomas theorem"—the notion (from W. I. Thomas) that if people "define situations as real, they are real in their consequences." Merton observed that Thomas was pointing out that people "not only respond to the objective features of a situation" but to the "meaning this situation has for them." One implication of the Thomas theorem was something that Merton called the "self-fulfilling prophecy": "The self-fulfilling prophecy is, in the beginning, a *false* definition of the situation evoking a new behavior which makes the originally false conception come *true*." For example, if a rumor circulates that the town bank is about to fail, that rumor, even if initially false, can come true simply because it's there. That is, the rumor may worry people sufficiently that they hurry to the bank and withdraw their funds. Ultimately, the bank *does* fail. Then, the rumormonger can say, "See, I told you the bank was going to fail."[1]

The following 1972 article by William Chambliss explores some of the ways in which public definitions of a situation come into being with respect to two small groups of high school kids. As you read this article, look for examples of how the ways in which people define the situation have real consequences for the people involved.

Eight promising young men—children of good, stable, white upper-middle-class families, active in school affairs, good pre-college students—were some of the most delinquent boys at Hanibal High School. While community residents and parents knew that these boys occasionally sowed a few wild oats, they were totally unaware that sowing wild oats completely occupied the daily routine of these young men. The Saints were constantly occupied with truancy, drinking, wild driving, petty theft and vandalism. Yet not one was officially arrested for any misdeed during the two years I observed them.

This record was particularly surprising in light of my observations during the same two years of another gang of Hanibal High School students, six lower-class white boys known as the Roughnecks. The Roughnecks were constantly in trouble with police and community even though their rate of delinquency was about equal with that of the Saints. What was the cause of this disparity? the result? The following consideration of the activities, social class and community perceptions of both gangs may provide some answers.

[1]From Robert Merton, *Social Theory and Social Structure* (New York: Free Press, 1968), p. 477.—Ed.

The Saints from Monday to Friday

The Saints' principal daily concern was with getting out of school as early as possible. The boys managed to get out of school with minimum danger that they would be accused of playing hookey through an elaborate procedure for obtaining "legitimate" release from class. The most common procedure was for one boy to obtain the release of another by fabricating a meeting of some committee, program or recognized club. Charles might raise his hand in his 9:00 chemistry class and ask to be excused—a euphemism for going to the bathroom. Charles would go to Ed's math class and inform the teacher that Ed was needed for a 9:30 rehearsal of the drama club play. The math teacher would recognize Ed and Charles as "good students" involved in numerous school activities and would permit Ed to leave at 9:30. Charles would return to his class, and Ed would go to Tom's English class to obtain his release. Tom would engineer Charles' escape. The strategy would continue until as many of the Saints as possible were freed. After a stealthy trip to the car (which had been parked in a strategic spot), the boys were off for a day of fun.

Over the two years I observed the Saints, this pattern was repeated nearly every day. There were variations on the theme, but in one form or another, the boys used this procedure for getting out of class and then off the school grounds. Rarely did all eight of the Saints manage to leave school at the same time. The average number avoiding school on the days I observed them was five.

Having escaped from the concrete corridors the boys usually went either to a pool hall on the other (lower-class) side of town or to a cafe in the suburbs. Both places were out of the way of people the boys were likely to know (family or school officials), and both provided a source of entertainment. The pool hall entertainment was the generally rough atmosphere, the occasional hustler, the sometimes drunk proprietor and, of course, the game of pool. The cafe's entertainment was provided by the owner. The boys would "accidentally" knock a glass on the floor or spill cola on the counter—not all the time, but enough to be sporting. They would also bend spoons, put salt in sugar bowls and generally tease whoever was working in the cafe. The owner had opened the cafe recently and was dependent on the boys' business which was, in fact, substantial since between the horsing around and the teasing they bought food and drinks.

The Saints on Weekends

On weekends the automobile was even more critical than during the week, for on weekends the Saints went to Big Town—a large city with a population of over a million 25 miles from Hanibal. Every Friday and Saturday night most of the Saints would meet between 8:00 and 8:30 and would go into Big Town. Big Town activities included drinking heavily in taverns or nightclubs, driving drunkenly through the streets, and committing acts of vandalism and playing pranks.

By midnight on Fridays and Saturdays the Saints were usually thoroughly high, and one or two of them were often so drunk they had to be carried to the cars. Then the boys drove around town, calling obscenities to women and girls; occasionally trying (unsuccessfully so far as I could tell) to pick girls up; and driving recklessly through red lights and at high speeds with their lights out. Occasionally they played "chicken." One boy would climb out the back window of the car and across the roof to the driver's side of the car while the car was moving at high speed (between 40 and 50 miles an hour); then the driver would move over and the boy who had just crawled across the car roof would take the driver's seat.

Searching for "fair game" for a prank was the boys' principal activity after they left the tavern. The boys would drive alongside a foot patrolman and ask directions to some street. If the policeman leaned on the car in the course of answering the question, the driver would speed away, causing him to lose his balance. The Saints were careful to play this prank only in an area where they were not going to spend much time and where they could quickly disappear around a corner to avoid having their license plate number taken.

Construction sites and road repair areas were the special province of the Saints' mischief. A soon-to-be-repaired hole in the road inevitably invited the Saints to remove lanterns and wooden barricades and put them in the car, leaving the hole unprotected. The boys would find a safe vantage point and wait for an unsuspecting motorist to drive into the hole. Often, though not always, the boys would go up to the motorist and commiserate with him about the dreadful way the city protected its citizenry.

Leaving the scene of the open hole and the motorist, the boys would then go searching for an appropriate place to erect the stolen barricade. An "appropriate place" was often a spot on a highway near a curve in the road where the barricade would not be seen by an oncoming motorist. The boys would wait to watch an unsuspecting motorist attempt to stop and (usually) crash into the wooden barricade. With saintly bearing the boys might offer help and understanding.

A stolen lantern might well find its way onto the back of a police car or hang from a street lamp. Once a lantern served as a prop for a reenactment of the "midnight ride of Paul Revere" until the "play," which was taking place at 2:00 A.M. in the center of a main street of Big Town, was interrupted by a police car several blocks away. The boys ran, leaving the lanterns on the street, and managed to avoid being apprehended.

Abandoned houses, especially if they were located in out-of-the-way places, were fair game for destruction and spontaneous vandalism. The boys would break windows, remove furniture to the yard and tear it apart, urinate on the walls and scrawl obscenities inside.

Through all the pranks, drinking and reckless driving the boys managed miraculously to avoid being stopped by police. Only twice in two years was I aware that they had been stopped by a Big City policeman. Once was for speeding (which they did every time they drove whether they were drunk or sober), and the driver managed to convince the policeman that it was simply an error. The second time they were stopped they had just left a nightclub and were walking through an alley. Aaron stopped to urinate and the boys began making obscene remarks. A foot patrolman came into the alley, lectured the boys and sent them home. Before the boys got to the car one began talking in a loud voice again. The policeman, who had followed them down the alley, arrested this boy for disturbing the peace and took him to the police station where the other Saints gathered. After paying a $5.00 fine, and with the assurance that there would be no permanent record of the arrest, the boy was released.

The boys had a spirit of frivolity and fun about their escapades. They did not view what they were engaged in as "delinquency," though it surely was by any reasonable definition of that word. They simply viewed themselves as having a little fun and who, they would ask, was really hurt by it? The answer had to be no one, although this fact remains one of the most difficult things to explain about the gang's behavior. Unlikely though it seems, in two years of drinking, driving, carousing and vandalism no one was seriously injured as a result of the Saints' activities.

The Saints in School

The Saints were highly successful in school. The average grade for the group was "B," with two of the boys having close to a straight "A" average. Almost all of the boys were popular and many of them held offices in the school. One of the boys was vice president of the student body one year. Six of the boys played on athletic teams.

At the end of their senior year, the student body selected ten seniors for special recognition as the "school wheels"; four of the ten were Saints. Teachers and school officials saw no problem with any of these boys and anticipated that they would all "make something of themselves."

How the boys managed to maintain this impression is surprising in view of their actual behavior while in school. Their technique for covering truancy was so successful that teachers did not even realize that the boys were absent from school much of the time. Occasionally, of course, the system would backfire and then the boy was on his own. A boy who was caught would be most contrite, would plead guilty and ask for mercy. He inevitably got the mercy he sought.

Cheating on examinations was rampant, even to the point of orally communicating answers to exams as well as looking at one another's papers. Since none of the group studied, and since they were primarily dependent on one another for help, it is surprising that grades were so high. Teachers contributed to the deception in their admitted inclination to give these boys (and presumably others like them) the benefit of the doubt. When asked how the boys did in school, and when pressed on specific examinations, teachers might admit that they were disappointed in John's performance, but would quickly add that they "knew that he was capable of doing better," so John was given a higher grade than he had actually earned. How often

this happened is impossible to know. During the time that I observed the group, I never saw any of the boys take homework home. Teachers may have been "understanding" very regularly.

One exception to the gang's generally good performance was Jerry, who had a "C" average in his junior year, experienced disaster the next year and failed to graduate. Jerry had always been a little more nonchalant than the others about the liberties he took in school. Rather than wait for someone to come get him from class, he would offer his own excuse and leave. Although he probably did not miss any more classes than most of the others in the group, he did not take the requisite pains to cover his absences. Jerry was the only Saint whom I ever heard talk back to a teacher. Although teachers often called him a "cut up" or a "smart kid," they never referred to him as a troublemaker or as a kid headed for trouble. It seems likely, then, that Jerry's failure his senior year and his mediocre performance his junior year were consequences of his not playing the game the proper way (possibly because he was disturbed by his parents' divorce). His teachers regarded him as "immature" and not quite ready to get out of high school.

The Police and the Saints

The local police saw the Saints as good boys who were among the leaders of the youth in the community. Rarely, the boys might be stopped in town for speeding or for running a stop sign. When this happened the boys were always polite, contrite and pled for mercy. As in school, they received the mercy they asked for. None ever received a ticket or was taken into the precinct by the local police.

The situation in Big City, where the boys engaged in most of their delinquency, was only slightly different. The police there did not know the boys at all, although occasionally the boys were stopped by a patrolman. Once they were caught taking a lantern from a construction site. Another time they were stopped for running a stop sign, and on several occasions they were stopped for speeding. Their behavior was as before: contrite, polite and penitent. The urban police, like the local police, accepted their demeanor as sincere. More important, the urban police were convinced that these were good boys just out for a lark.

The Roughnecks

Hanibal townspeople never perceived the Saints' high level of delinquency. The Saints were good boys who just went in for an occasional prank. After all, they were well dressed, well mannered and had nice cars. The Roughnecks were a different story. Although the two gangs of boys were the same age, and both groups engaged in an equal amount of wild-oat sowing, everyone agreed that the not-so-well-dressed, not-so-well-mannered, not-so-rich boys were heading for trouble. Townspeople would say, "You can see the gang members at the drugstore, night after night, leaning against the storefront (sometimes drunk) or slouching around inside buying cokes, reading magazines, and probably stealing old Mr. Wall blind. When they are outside and girls walk by, even respectable girls, these boys make suggestive remarks. Sometimes their remarks are downright lewd."

From the community's viewpoint, the real indication that these kids were in for trouble was that they were constantly involved with the police. Some of them had been picked up for stealing, mostly small stuff, of course, "but still it's stealing small stuff that leads to big time crimes." "Too bad," people said. "Too bad that these boys couldn't behave like the other kids in town; stay out of trouble, be polite to adults, and look to their future."

The community's impression of the degree to which this group of six boys (ranging in age from 16 to 19) engaged in delinquency was somewhat distorted. In some ways the gang was more delinquent than the community thought; in other ways they were less.

The fighting activities of the group were fairly readily and accurately perceived by almost everyone. At least once a month, the boys would get into some sort of fight, although most fights were scraps between members of the group or involved only one member of the group and some peripheral hanger-on. Only three times in the period of observation did the group fight together: once against a gang from across town, once against two blacks and once against a group of boys from another school. For the first two fights the group went out "looking for trouble"—and they found it both times. The third fight followed a football game and began spontaneously with an argument on the football field between one of the Roughnecks and a member of the opposition's football team.

Jack had a particular propensity for fighting and was involved in most of the brawls. He was a prime mover of the escalation of arguments into fights.

More serious than fighting, had the community been aware of it, was theft. Although almost everyone was aware that the boys occasionally stole things, they did not realize the extent of the activity. Petty stealing was a frequent event for the Roughnecks. Sometimes they stole as a group and coordinated their efforts; other times they stole in pairs. Rarely did they steal alone.

The thefts ranged from very small things like paperback books, comics and ballpoint pens to expensive items like watches. The nature of the thefts varied from time to time. The gang would go through a period of systematically shoplifting items from automobiles or school lockers. Types of thievery varied with the whim of the gang. Some forms of thievery were more profitable than others, but all thefts were for profit, not just thrills.

Roughnecks siphoned gasoline from cars as often as they had access to an automobile, which was not very often. Unlike the Saints, who owned their own cars, the Roughnecks would have to borrow their parents' cars, an event which occurred only eight or nine times a year. The boys claimed to have stolen cars for joy rides from time to time.

Ron committed the most serious of the group's offenses. With an unidentified associate the boy attempted to burglarize a gasoline station. Although this station had been robbed twice previously in the same month, Ron denied any involvement in either of the other thefts. When Ron and his accomplice approached the station, the owner was hiding in the bushes beside the station. He fired both barrels of a double-barreled shotgun at the boys. Ron was severely injured; the other boy ran away and was never caught. Though he remained in critical condition for several months, Ron finally recovered and served six months of the following year in reform school. Upon release from reform school, Ron was put back a grade in school, and began running around with a different gang of boys. The Roughnecks considered the new gang less delinquent than themselves, and during the following year Ron had no more trouble with the police.

The Roughnecks, then, engaged mainly in three types of delinquency: theft, drinking and fighting. Although community members perceived that this gang of kids was delinquent, they mistakenly believed that their illegal activities were primarily drinking, fighting and being a nuisance to passersby. Drinking was limited among the gang members, although it did occur, and theft was much more prevalent than anyone realized.

Drinking would doubtless have been more prevalent had the boys had ready access to liquor. Since they rarely had automobiles at their disposal, they could not travel very far, and the bars in town would not serve them. Most of the boys had little money, and this, too, inhibited their purchase of alcohol. Their major source of liquor was a local drunk who would buy them a fifth if they would give him enough extra to buy himself a pint of whiskey or a bottle of wine.

The community's perception of drinking as prevalent stemmed from the fact that it was the most obvious delinquency the boys engaged in. When one of the boys had been drinking, even a casual observer seeing him on the corner would suspect that he was high.

There was a high level of mutual distrust and dislike between the Roughnecks and the police. The boys felt very strongly that the police were unfair and corrupt. Some evidence existed that the boys were correct in their perception.

The main source of the boys' dislike for the police undoubtedly stemmed from the fact that the police would sporadically harass the group. From the standpoint of the boys, these acts of occasional enforcement of the law were whimsical and uncalled for. It made no sense to them, for example, that the police would come to the corner occasionally and threaten them with arrest for loitering when the night before the boys had been out siphoning gasoline from cars and the police had been nowhere in sight. To the boys, the police were stupid on the one hand, for not being where they should have been and catching the boys in a serious offense, and unfair on the other hand, for trumping up "loitering" charges against them.

From the viewpoint of the police, the situation was quite different. They knew, with all the confidence necessary to be a policeman, that these boys were engaged in criminal activities. They knew this partly from occasionally catching them, mostly from circumstantial evidence ("the boys were around when those tires were slashed"), and partly because the police shared the view of the community in general that this was a bad bunch of boys. The best the police could hope to do was to be sensitive to the fact that these boys were engaged in illegal acts and arrest them whenever there was some evidence that they had been involved. Whether or not the boys had in fact committed a particular act in a particular way was not especially important. The police had a broader view: their job was to stamp out these kids' crimes; the tactics were not as important as the end result.

Over the period that the group was under observation, each member was arrested at least once. Several of the boys were arrested a number of times and spent at least one night in jail. While most were never taken to court, two of the boys were sentenced to six months' incarceration in boys' schools.

The Roughnecks in School

The Roughnecks' behavior in school was not particularly disruptive. During school hours they did not all hang around together, but tended instead to spend most of their time with one or two other members of the gang who were their special buddies. Although every member of the gang attempted to avoid school as much as possible, they were not particularly successful and most of them attended school with surprising regularity. They considered school a burden—something to be gotten through with a minimum of conflict. If they were "bugged" by a particular teacher, it could lead to trouble. One of the boys, Al, once threatened to beat up a teacher and, according to the other boys, the teacher hid under a desk to escape him.

Teachers saw the boys the way the general community did, as heading for trouble, as being uninterested in making something of themselves. Some were also seen as being incapable of meeting the academic standards of the school. Most of the teachers expressed concern for this group of boys and were willing to pass them despite poor performance, in the belief that failing them would only aggravate the problem.

The group of boys had a grade point average just slightly above "C." No one in the group failed either grade, and no one had better than a "C" average. They were consistent in their achievement or, at least, the teachers were consistent in their perception of the boys' achievement.

Two of the boys were good football players. Herb was acknowledged to be the best player in the school and Jack was almost as good. Both boys were criticized for their failure to abide by training rules, for refusing to come to practice as often as they should, and for not playing their best during practice. What they lacked in sportsmanship they made up for in skill, apparently, and played every game no matter how poorly they had performed in practice or how many practice sessions they had missed.

Two Questions

Why did the community, the school and the police react to the Saints as though they were good, upstanding, nondelinquent youths with bright futures but to the Roughnecks as though they were tough, young criminals who were headed for trouble? Why did the Roughnecks and the Saints in fact have quite different careers after high school—careers which, by and large, lived up to the expectations of the community?

The most obvious explanation for the differences in the community's and law enforcement agencies' reactions to the two gangs is that one group of boys was "more delinquent" than the other. Which group *was* more delinquent? The answer to this question will determine in part how we explain the differential responses to these groups by the members of the community and, particularly, by law enforcement and school officials.

In sheer number of illegal acts, the Saints were the more delinquent. They were truant from school for at least part of the day almost every day of the week. In addition, their drinking and vandalism occurred with surprising regularity. The Roughnecks, in contrast, engaged sporadically in delinquent episodes. While these episodes were frequent, they certainly did not occur on a daily or even a weekly basis.

The difference in frequency of offenses was probably caused by the Roughnecks' inability to obtain liquor and to manipulate legitimate excuses from school. Since the Roughnecks had less money than the Saints, and teachers carefully supervised their school activities, the Roughnecks' hearts may have been as black as the Saints', but their misdeeds were not nearly as frequent.

There are really no clear-cut criteria by which to measure qualitative differences in antisocial behavior. The most important dimension of the difference is generally referred to as the "seriousness" of the offenses.

If seriousness encompasses the relative economic costs of delinquent acts, then some assessment can be made. The Roughnecks probably stole an average of about $5.00 worth of goods a week. Some weeks the figure was considerably higher, but these times must be balanced against long periods when almost nothing was stolen.

The Saints were more continuously engaged in delinquency but their acts were not for the most part costly to property. Only their vandalism and occasional theft of gasoline would so qualify. Perhaps once or twice a month they would siphon a tankful of gas. The other costly items were street signs, construction lanterns and the like. All of these acts combined probably did not quite average $5.00 a week, partly because much of the stolen equipment was abandoned and presumably could be recovered. The difference in cost of stolen property between the two groups was trivial, but the Roughnecks probably had a slightly more expensive set of activities than did the Saints.

Another meaning of seriousness is the potential threat of physical harm to members of the community and to the boys themselves. The Roughnecks were more prone to physical violence; they not only welcomed an opportunity to fight; they went seeking it. In addition, they fought among themselves frequently. Although the fighting never included deadly weapons, it was still a menace, however minor, to the physical safety of those involved.

The Saints never fought. They avoided physical conflict both inside and outside the group. At the same time, though, the Saints frequently endangered their own and other people's lives. They did so almost every time they drove a car, especially if they had been drinking. Sober, their driving was risky; under the influence of alcohol it was horrendous. In addition, the Saints endangered the lives of others with their pranks. Street excavations left unmarked were a very serious hazard.

Evaluating the relative seriousness of the two gangs' activities is difficult. The community reacted as though the behavior of the Roughnecks was a problem, and they reacted as though the behavior of the Saints was not. But the members of the community were ignorant of the array of delinquent acts that characterized the Saints' behavior. Although concerned citizens were unaware of much of the Roughnecks' behavior as well, they were much better informed about the Roughnecks' involvement in delinquency than they were about the Saints'.

Visibility

Differential treatment of the two gangs results in part because one gang was infinitely more visible than the other. This differential visibility was a direct function of the economic standing of the families. The Saints had access to automobiles and were able to remove themselves from the sight of the community. In as routine a decision as to where to go to have a milkshake after school, the Saints stayed away from the mainstream of community life. Lacking transportation, the Roughnecks could not make it to the edge of town. The center of town was the only practical place for them to meet since their homes were scattered throughout the town and any noncentral meeting place put an undue hardship on some members. Through necessity the Roughnecks congregated in a crowded area where everyone in the community passed frequently, including teachers and law enforcement officers. They could easily see the Roughnecks hanging around the drugstore.

The Roughnecks, of course, made themselves even more visible by making remarks to passersby and by occasionally getting into fights on the corner. Meanwhile, just as regularly, the Saints were either at the cafe on one edge of town or in the pool hall at the other edge of town. Without any particular realization that they were making themselves inconspicuous, the Saints were able to hide their time-wasting. Not only were they removed from the mainstream of traffic, but they were almost always inside a building.

On their escapades the Saints were also relatively invisible, since they left Hanibal and travelled to Big City. Here, too, they were mobile, roaming the city, rarely going to the same area twice.

Demeanor

To the notion of visibility must be added the difference in the responses of group members to outside intervention with their activities. If one of the Saints was confronted with an accusing policeman, even if he felt he was truly innocent of a wrongdoing, his demeanor was apologetic and penitent. A Roughneck's attitude was almost the polar opposite. When confronted with a threatening adult authority, even one who tried to be pleasant, the Roughneck's hostility and disdain were clearly observable. Sometimes he might attempt to put up a veneer of respect, but it was thin and was not accepted as sincere by the authority.

School was no different from the community at large. The Saints could manipulate the system by feigning compliance with the school norms. The availability of cars at school meant that once free from the immediate sight of the teacher, the boys could disappear rapidly. And this escape was well enough planned that no administrator or teacher was nearby when the boys left. A Roughneck who wished to escape for a few hours was in a bind. If it were possible to get free from class, downtown was still a mile away, and even if he arrived there, he was still very visible. Truancy for the Roughnecks meant almost certain detection, while the Saints enjoyed almost complete immunity from sanctions.

Bias

Community members were not aware of the transgressions of the Saints. Even if the Saints had been less discreet, their favorite delinquencies would have been perceived as less serious than those of the Roughnecks.

In the eyes of the police and school officials, a boy who drinks in an alley and stands intoxicated on the street corner is committing a more serious offense than is a boy who drinks to inebriation in a nightclub or a tavern and drives around afterwards in a car. Similarly, a boy who steals a wallet from a store will be viewed as having committed a more serious offense than a boy who steals a lantern from a construction site.

Perceptual bias also operates with respect to the demeanor of the boys in the two groups when they are confronted by adults. It is not simply that adults dislike the posture affected by boys of the Roughneck ilk; more important is the conviction that the posture adopted by the Roughnecks is an indication of their devotion and commitment to deviance as a way of life. The posture becomes a cue, just as the type of the offense is a cue, to the degree to which the known transgressions are indicators of the youths' potential for other problems.

Visibility, demeanor and bias are surface variables which explain the day-to-day operations of the police. Why do these surface variables operate as they do? Why did the police choose to disregard the Saints' delinquencies while breathing down the backs of the Roughnecks?

The answer lies in the class structure of American society and the control of legal institutions by those at the top of the class structure. Obviously, no representative of the upper class drew up the operational chart for the police which led them to look in the ghettoes and on streetcorners—which led them to see the demeanor of lower-class youth as troublesome and that of upper-middle-class youth as tolerable. Rather, the procedures simply developed from experience—experience with irate and influential upper-middle-class parents insisting that their son's vandalism was simply a prank and his drunkenness only a momentary "sowing of wild oats"—experience with cooperative or indifferent, powerless, lower-class parents who acquiesced to the law's definition of their son's behavior.

Adult Careers of the Saints and the Roughnecks

The community's confidence in the potential of the Saints and the Roughnecks apparently was justified. If anything, the community members underestimated the degree to which these youngsters would turn out "good" or "bad."

Seven of the eight members of the Saints went on to college immediately after high school. Five of the boys graduated from college in four years. The sixth one finished college after two years in the army, and the seventh spent fours years in the air force before returning to college and receiving a B.A. degree. Of these seven college graduates, three went on for advanced degrees. One finished law school and is now active in state politics, one finished medical school and is practicing near Hanibal, and one boy is now working for a Ph.D. The other four college graduates entered submanagerial, managerial or executive training positions with larger firms.

The only Saint who did not complete college was Jerry. Jerry had failed to graduate from high school with the other Saints. During his second senior year, after the other Saints had gone on to college, Jerry began to hang around with what several teachers described as a "rough crowd"—the gang that was heir apparent to the Roughnecks. At the end of his second senior year, when he did graduate from high school, Jerry took a job as a used-car salesman, got married and quickly had a child. Although he made several abortive attempts to go to college by attending night school, when I last saw him (ten years after high school) Jerry was unemployed and had been living on unemployment for almost a year. His wife worked as a waitress.

Some of the Roughnecks have lived up to community expectations. A number of them were headed for trouble. A few were not.

Jack and Herb were the athletes among the Roughnecks and their athletic prowess paid off handsomely. Both boys received unsolicited athletic scholarships to college. After Herb received his scholarship (near the end of his senior year), he apparently did an about-face. His demeanor became very similar to that of the Saints. Although he remained a member in good standing of the Roughnecks, he stopped participating in most activities and did not hang on the corner as often.

Jack did not change. If anything, he became more prone to fighting. He even made excuses for accepting the scholarship. He told the gang members that the school had guaranteed him a "C" average if he would come to play football—an idea that seems far-fetched, even in this day of highly competitive recruiting.

During the summer after graduation from high school, Jack attempted suicide by jumping from a tall building. The jump would certainly have killed most people trying it, but Jack survived. He entered college in the fall and played four years of football. He and Herb graduated in four years, and both are teaching and coaching in high schools. They are married and have stable families. If anything, Jack appears to have a more prestigious position in the community than does Herb, though both are well respected and secure in their positions.

Two of the boys never finished high school. Tommy left at the end of his junior year and went to another state. That summer he was arrested and placed on probation on a manslaughter charge. Three years later he was arrested for murder; he pleaded guilty to second degree murder and is serving a 30-year sentence in the state penitentiary.

Al, the other boy who did not finish high school, also left the state in his senior year. He is serving a life sentence in a state penitentiary for first degree murder.

Wes is a small-time gambler. He finished high school and "bummed around." After several years he made contact with a bookmaker who employed him as runner. Later he acquired his own area and has been working it ever since. His position among the bookmakers is almost identical to the position he had in the gang; he is always around but no one is really aware of him. He makes no trouble and he does not get into any. Steady, reliable, capable of keeping his mouth closed, he plays the game by the rules, even though the game is an illegal one.

That leaves only Ron. Some of his former friends reported that they had heard he was "driving a truck up north," but no one could provide any concrete information.

Reinforcement

The community responded to the Roughnecks as boys in trouble, and the boys agreed with that perception. Their pattern of deviancy was reinforced, and breaking away from it became increasingly unlikely. Once the boys acquired an image of themselves as deviants, they selected new friends who affirmed that self-image. As that self-conception became more firmly entrenched, they also became willing to try new and more extreme deviances. With their growing alienation came freer expression of disrespect and hostility for representatives of the legitimate society. This disrespect increased the community's negativism, perpetuating the entire process of commitment to deviance. Lack of a commitment to deviance works the same way. In either case, the process will perpetuate itself unless some event (like a scholarship to college or a sudden failure) external to the established relationship intervenes. For two of the Roughnecks (Herb and Jack), receiving college athletic scholarships created new relations and culminated in a break with the established pattern of deviance. In the case of one of the Saints (Jerry), his parents' divorce and his failing to graduate from high school changed some of his other relations. Being held back in school for a year and losing his place among the Saints had sufficient impact on Jerry to alter his self-image and virtually to assure that he would not go on to college as his peers did. Although the experiments of life can rarely be reversed, it seems likely in view of the behavior of the other boys who did not enjoy this special treatment by the school that Jerry, too, would have "become something" had he graduated as anticipated. For Herb and Jack outside intervention worked to their advantage; for Jerry it was his undoing.

Selective perception and labelling—finding, processing and punishing some kinds of criminality and not others—means that visible, poor, nonmobile, outspoken, undiplomatic "tough" kids will be noticed, whether their actions are seriously delinquent or not. Other kids, who have established a reputation for being bright (even though underachieving), disciplined and involved in respectable activities, who are mobile and monied, will be invisible when they deviate from sanctioned activities. They'll sow their wild oats—perhaps even wider and thicker than their lower-class cohorts—but they won't be noticed. When it's time to leave adolescence most will follow the expected path, settling into the ways of the middle class, remembering fondly the delinquent but unnoticed fling of their youth. The Roughnecks and others like them may turn around, too. It is more likely that their noticeable deviance will have been so reinforced by police and community that their lives will be effectively channelled into careers consistent with their adolescent background.

Questions

1. Why were the Saints seen as good boys and the Roughnecks seen as bad boys?

2. The conventional wisdom is that criminals are different from noncriminals, that bad things are done by bad people. To what extent does the information presented in Chambliss's article contradict the conventional wisdom?

3. In what specific way did differences in social class (for example, economic resources and cultural capital) contribute to the community's different treatment of and regard for the Saints and the Roughnecks?

4. What evidence do you find in this article that supports Merton's ideas about the self-fulfilling prophecy? What evidence seems to contradict it?

28

ON BEING SANE IN INSANE PLACES

D. L. Rosenhan

Although the following selection was written by a professor of psychology and law at Stanford University, it seems that everyone who publishes a reader for introductory sociology students includes this 1973 article (obviously, including me). There's a reason. Rosenhan's exploration of what happens to sane people in mental hospitals contains some important lessons about the impact of people's definition of the situation—especially the impact of the definitions of people in authority.

If sanity and insanity exist, how shall we know them?

The question is neither capricious nor itself insane. However much we may be personally convinced that we can tell the normal from the abnormal, the evidence is simply not compelling. It is commonplace, for example, to read about murder trials wherein eminent psychiatrists for the defense are contradicted by equally eminent psychiatrists for the prosecution on the matter of the defendant's sanity. More generally, there are a great deal of conflicting data on the reliability, utility, and meaning of such terms as "sanity," "insanity," "mental illness," and "schizophrenia." Finally, as early as 1934, Benedict suggested that normality and abnormality are not universal. What is viewed as normal in one culture may be seen as quite aberrant in another. Thus, notions of normality and abnormality may not be quite as accurate as people believe they are.

To raise questions regarding normality and abnormality is in no way to question the fact that some behaviors are deviant or odd.

Murder is deviant. So, too, are hallucinations. Nor does raising such questions deny the existence of the personal anguish that is often associated with "mental illness." Anxiety and depression exist. Psychological suffering exists. But normality and abnormality, sanity and insanity, and the diagnoses that flow from them may be less substantive than many believe them to be.

At its heart, the question of whether the sane can be distinguished from the insane (and whether degrees of insanity can be distinguished from each other) is a simple matter: do the salient characteristics that lead to diagnoses reside in the patients themselves or in the environments and contexts in which observers find them? From Bleuler[1] through the

[1]Paul Eugen Bleuler (1857–1939) was a Swiss psychiatrist who, in 1911, introduced the term *schizophrenia* (from the Greek *shizo*, "split or cleave," and *phren*, "mind") to refer to a form of dementia (madness). Today, schizophrenia refers to a general pathology characterized by disturbance of thinking, mood, and behavior (including inappropriate emotional responses and lack of empathy), and sometimes hallucinations and delusions. It is thought to afflict more than 2 million Americans, and "about half of the available hospital beds for the mentally ill (or about one-quarter of available beds in all U.S. hospitals) are occupied by patients diagnosed as schizophrenic" (Philip M. Groves and George V. Rebec, *Introduction to Biological Psychology*. [Dubuque, IA: Brown, 1988], p. 479).—Ed.

formulators of the recently revised *Diagnostic and Statistical Manual* of the American Psychiatric Association, the belief has been strong that patients present symptoms, that those symptoms can be categorized, and, implicitly, that the sane are distinguishable from the insane. More recently, however, this belief has been questioned. Based in part on theoretical and anthropological considerations, but also on philosophical, legal, and therapeutic ones, the view has grown that psychological categorization of mental illness is useless at best and downright harmful, misleading, and pejorative at worst. Psychiatric diagnoses, in this view, are in the minds of the observers and are not valid summaries of characteristics displayed by the observed.

Gains can be made in deciding which of these is more nearly accurate by getting normal people (that is, people who do not have, and have never suffered, symptoms of serious psychiatric disorders) admitted to psychiatric hospitals and then determining whether they were discovered to be sane and, if so, how. If the sanity of such pseudopatients were always detected, there would be prima facie[2] evidence that a sane individual can be distinguished from the insane context in which he is found. Normality (and presumably abnormality) is distinct enough that it can be recognized wherever it occurs, for it is carried within the person. If, on the other hand, the sanity of the pseudopatients were never discovered, serious difficulties would arise for those who support traditional modes of psychiatric diagnosis. Given that the hospital staff was not incompetent, that the pseudopatient had been behaving as sanely as he had been outside of the hospital, and that it had never been previously suggested that he belonged in a psychiatric hospital, such an unlikely outcome would support the view that psychiatric diagnosis betrays little about the patient but much about the environment in which an observer finds him.

This article describes such an experiment. Eight sane people gained secret admission to 12 different hospitals. . . .

Pseudopatients and Their Settings

The eight pseudopatients were a varied group. One was a psychology graduate student in his 20's. The remaining seven were older and "established." Among them were three psychologists, a pediatrician, a psychiatrist, a painter, and a housewife. Three pseudopatients were women, five were men. All of them employed pseudonyms, lest their alleged diagnoses embarrass them later. Those who were in mental health professions alleged another occupation in order to avoid the special attentions that might be accorded by staff, as a matter of courtesy or caution, to ailing colleagues. With the exception of myself (I was the first pseudopatient and my presence was known to the hospital administrator and chief psychologist and, so far as I can tell, to them alone), the presence of pseudopatients and the nature of the research program was not known to the hospital staffs.

The settings were similarly varied. In order to generalize the findings, admission into a variety of hospitals was sought. The 12 hospitals in the sample were located in five different states on the East and West coasts. Some were old and shabby, some were quite new. Some were research-oriented, others not. Some had good staff–patient ratios, others were quite understaffed. Only one was a strictly private hospital. All of the others were supported by state or federal funds or, in one instance, by university funds.

After calling the hospital for an appointment, the pseudopatient arrived at the admissions office complaining that he had been

---

[2]*Prima facie*, from the Latin, means "at first sight." Prima facie evidence of something is regarded as apparently valid evidence.—Ed.

hearing voices. Asked what the voices said, he replied that they were often unclear, but as far as he could tell they said "empty," "hollow," and "thud." The voices were unfamiliar and were of the same sex as the pseudopatient. The choice of these symptoms was occasioned by their apparent similarity to existential symptoms. Such symptoms are alleged to arise from painful concerns about the perceived meaninglessness of one's life. It is as if the hallucinating person were saying, "My life is empty and hollow." The choice of these symptoms was also determined by the *absence* of a single report of existential psychoses in the literature.

Beyond alleging the symptoms and falsifying name, vocation, and employment, no further alterations of person, history, or circumstances were made. The significant events of the pseudopatient's life history were presented as they had actually occurred. Relationships with parents and siblings, with spouse and children, with people at work and in school, consistent with the aforementioned exceptions, were described as they were or had been. Frustrations and upsets were described along with joys and satisfactions. These facts are important to remember. If anything, they strongly biased the subsequent results in favor of detecting sanity, since none of their histories or current behaviors were seriously pathological in any way.

Immediately upon admission to the psychiatric ward, the pseudopatient ceased simulating *any* symptoms of abnormality. In some cases, there was a brief period of mild nervousness and anxiety, since none of the pseudopatients really believed that they would be admitted so easily. Indeed, their shared fear was that they would be immediately exposed as frauds and greatly embarrassed. Moreover, many of them had never visited a psychiatric ward; even those who had, nevertheless had some genuine fears about what might happen to them. Their nervousness, then, was quite

appropriate to the novelty of the hospital setting, and it abated rapidly.

Apart from that short-lived nervousness, the pseudopatient behaved on the ward as he "normally" behaved. The pseudopatient spoke to patients and staff as he might ordinarily. Because there is uncommonly little to do on a psychiatric ward, he attempted to engage others in conversation. When asked by staff how he was feeling, he indicated that he was fine, that he no longer experienced symptoms. He responded to instructions from attendants, to calls for medication (which was not swallowed),[3] and to dining-hall instructions. Beyond such activities as were available to him on the admissions ward, he spent his time writing down his observations about the ward, its patients, and the staff. Initially these notes were written "secretly," but as it soon became clear that no one much cared, they were subsequently written on standard tablets of paper in such public places as the dayroom. No secret was made of these activities.

The pseudopatient, very much as a true psychiatric patient, entered a hospital with no foreknowledge of when he would be discharged. Each was told that he would have to get out by his own devices, essentially by convincing the staff that he was sane. The psychological stresses associated with hospitalization were

---

[3]In part of the article not included in this excerpt, Rosenhan notes that over the course of their hospitalization, "the pseudopatients were administered nearly 2100 pills, including Elavil, Stelazine, Compazine, and Thorazine, to name a few. (That such a variety of medications should have been administered to patients presenting identical symptoms is itself worthy of note.) Only two were swallowed. The rest were either pocketed or deposited in the toilet. The pseudopatients were not alone in this. Although I have no precise records on how many patients rejected their medications, the pseudopatients frequently found the medications of other patients in the toilets before they deposited their own. As long as they were cooperative, their behavior and the pseudopatients' own in this matter, as in other important matters, went unnoticed throughout."—Ed.

considerable, and all but one of the pseudopatients desired to be discharged almost immediately after being admitted. They were,
therefore, motivated not only to behave sanely,
but to be paragons of cooperation. That their
behavior was in no way disruptive is confirmed by nursing reports, which have been
obtained on most of the patients. These reports
uniformly indicate that the patients were
"friendly," "cooperative," and "exhibited no
abnormal indications."

The Normal Are Not Detectably Sane

Despite their public "show" of sanity, the
pseudopatients were never detected. Admitted, except in one case, with a diagnosis of
schizophrenia, each was discharged with a
diagnosis of schizophrenia "in remission." The
label "in remission" should in no way be dismissed as a formality, for at no time during
any hospitalization had any question been
raised about any pseudopatient's simulation.
Nor are there any indications in the hospital
records that the pseudopatient's status was
suspect. Rather, the evidence is strong that,
once labeled schizophrenic, the pseudopatient
was stuck with that label. If the pseudopatient
was to be discharged, he must naturally be "in
remission"; but he was not sane, nor, in the
institution's view, had he ever been sane.

The uniform failure to recognize sanity cannot be attributed to the quality of the hospitals,
for, although there were considerable variations
among them, several are considered excellent.
Nor can it be alleged that there was simply not
enough time to observe the pseudopatients.
Length of hospitalization ranged from 7 to 52
days, with an average of 19 days. The pseudopatients were not, in fact, carefully observed,
but this failure clearly speaks more to traditions within psychiatric hospitals than to lack
of opportunity.

Finally, it cannot be said that the failure to
recognize the pseudopatients' sanity was due
to the fact that they were not behaving sanely.
While there was clearly some tension present in
all of them, their daily visitors could detect no
serious behavioral consequences—nor, indeed,
could other patients. It was quite common for
the patients to "detect" the pseudopatients'
sanity. During the first three hospitalizations,
when accurate counts were kept, 35 of a total
of 118 patients on the admissions ward voiced
their suspicions, some vigorously. "You're
not crazy. You're a journalist, or a professor
[referring to the continual note-taking]. You're
checking up on the hospital." While most of the
patients were reassured by the pseudopatient's
insistence that he had been sick before he came
in but was fine now, some continued to believe
that the pseudopatient was sane throughout
his hospitalization. The fact that the patients
often recognized normality when staff did not
raises important questions.

Failure to detect sanity during the course of
hospitalization may be due to the fact that
physicians . . . are more inclined to call a healthy
person sick (a false positive) than a sick person
healthy (a false negative). The reasons for this
are not hard to find: it is clearly more dangerous
to misdiagnose illness than health. Better to err
on the side of caution, to suspect illness even
among the healthy.

But what holds for medicine does not hold
equally well for psychiatry. Medical illnesses,
while unfortunate, are not commonly pejorative. Psychiatric diagnoses, on the contrary,
carry with them personal, legal, and social
stigmas. It was therefore important to see
whether the tendency toward diagnosing the
sane insane could be reversed. The following
experiment was arranged at a research and
teaching hospital whose staff had heard these
findings but doubted that such an error could
occur in their hospital. The staff was informed that at some time during the following

3 months, one or more pseudopatients would attempt to be admitted into the psychiatric hospital. Each staff member was asked to rate each patient who presented himself at admissions or on the ward according to the likelihood that the patient was a pseudopatient. A 10-point scale was used, with a 1 and 2 reflecting high confidence that the patient was a pseudopatient.

Judgments were obtained on 193 patients who were admitted for psychiatric treatment. All staff who had had sustained contact with or primary responsibility for the patient—attendants, nurses, psychiatrists, physicians, and psychologists—were asked to make judgments. Forty-one patients were alleged, with high confidence, to be pseudopatients by at least one member of the staff. Twenty-three were considered suspect by at least one psychiatrist. Nineteen were suspected by one psychiatrist *and* one other staff member. Actually, no genuine pseudopatient (at least from my group) presented himself during this period.

The experiment is instructive. It indicates that the tendency to designate sane people as insane can be reversed when the stakes (in this case, prestige and diagnostic acumen) are high. But what can be said of the 19 people who were suspected of being "sane" by one psychiatrist and another staff member? Were these people truly "sane," or was it rather the case that in the course of avoiding the false positive error the staff tended to make more errors of the false negative sort—calling the crazy "sane"? There is no way of knowing. But one thing is certain: any diagnostic process that lends itself so readily to massive errors of this sort cannot be a very reliable one.

The Stickiness of Psychodiagnostic Labels

Beyond the tendency to call the healthy sick—a tendency that accounts better for diagnostic behavior on admission than it does for such behavior after a lengthy period of exposure—the data speak to the massive role of labeling in psychiatric assessment. Having once been labeled schizophrenic, there is nothing the pseudopatient can do to overcome the tag. The tag profoundly colors others' perceptions of him and his behavior.

From one viewpoint, these data are hardly surprising, for it has long been known that elements are given meaning by the context in which they occur. Gestalt psychology made this point vigorously, and Asch demonstrated that there are "central" personality traits (such as "warm" versus "cold") which are so powerful that they markedly color the meaning of other information in forming an impression of a given personality. "Insane," "schizophrenic," "manic-depressive," and "crazy" are probably among the most powerful of such central traits. Once a person is designated abnormal, all of his other behaviors and characteristics are colored by that label. Indeed, that label is so powerful that many of the pseudopatients' normal behaviors were overlooked entirely or profoundly misinterpreted. Some examples may clarify this issue.

Earlier I indicated that there were no changes in the pseudopatient's personal history and current status beyond those of name, employment, and, where necessary, vocation. Otherwise, a veridical description of personal history and circumstances was offered. Those circumstances were not psychotic. How were they made consonant with the diagnosis of psychosis? Or were those diagnoses modified in such a way as to bring them into accord with the circumstances of the pseudopatient's life, as described by him?

As far as I can determine, diagnoses were in no way affected by the relative health of the circumstances of a pseudopatient's life. Rather, the reverse occurred: the perception of his circumstances was shaped entirely by the diagnosis. A clear example of such translation is found in the case of a pseudopatient who had had a close relationship with his mother but was rather remote from his father during his early childhood. During adolescence and beyond, however, his father became a close friend, while his relationship with his mother cooled. His present relationship with his wife was characteristically close and warm. Apart from occasional angry exchanges, friction was minimal. The children had rarely been spanked. Surely there is nothing especially pathological about such a history. Indeed, many readers may see a similar pattern in their own experiences with no markedly deleterious consequences. Observe, however, how such a history was translated in the psychopathological context, this from the case summary prepared after the patient was discharged.

> This white 39-year-old male . . . manifests a long history of considerable ambivalence in close relationships, which begins in early childhood. A warm relationship with his mother cools during his adolescence. A distant relationship to his father is described as becoming very intense. Affective[4] stability is absent. His attempts to control emotionality with his wife and children are punctuated by angry outbursts and, in the case of the children, spankings. And while he says that he has several good friends, one senses considerable ambivalence embedded in those relationships also. . . .

The facts of the case were unintentionally distorted by the staff to achieve consistency with a popular theory of the dynamics of a schizophrenic reaction. Nothing of an ambivalent nature had been described in relations with parents, spouse, or friends. To the extent that ambivalence could be inferred, it was probably not greater than is found in all human relationships. It is true the pseudopatient's relationships with his parents changed over time, but in the ordinary context that would hardly be remarkable—indeed, it might very well be

expected. Clearly, the meaning ascribed to his verbalizations (that is, ambivalence, affective instability) was determined by the diagnosis: schizophrenia. An entirely different meaning would have been ascribed if it were known that the man was "normal."

All pseudopatients took extensive notes publicly. Under ordinary circumstances, such behavior would have raised questions in the minds of observers, as, in fact, it did among patients. Indeed, it seemed so certain that the notes would elicit suspicion that elaborate precautions were taken to remove them from the ward each day. But the precautions proved needless. The closest any staff member came to questioning these notes occurred when one pseudopatient asked his physician what kind of medication he was receiving and began to write down the response. "You needn't write it," he was told gently. "If you have trouble remembering, just ask me again."

If no questions were asked of the pseudopatients, how was their writing interpreted? Nursing records for three patients indicate that the writing was seen as an aspect of their pathological behavior. "Patient engages in writing behavior" was the daily nursing comment on one of the pseudopatients who was never questioned about his writing. Given that the patient is in the hospital, he must be psychologically disturbed. And given that he is disturbed, continuous writing must be a behavioral manifestation of that disturbance, perhaps a subset of the compulsive behaviors that are sometimes correlated with schizophrenia.

One tacit characteristic of psychiatric diagnosis is that it locates the sources of aberration within the individual and only rarely within the complex of stimuli that surrounds him. Consequently, behaviors that are stimulated by the environment are commonly misattributed to the patient's disorder. For example, one kindly nurse found a pseudopatient pacing the long hospital corridors. "Nervous, Mr. X?" she asked. "No, bored," he said.

---

[4]*Affective* means "emotional."—Ed.

The notes kept by pseudopatients are full of patient behaviors that were misinterpreted by well-intentioned staff. Often enough, a patient would go "berserk" because he had, wittingly or unwittingly, been mistreated by, say, an attendant. A nurse coming upon the scene would rarely inquire even cursorily into the environmental stimuli of the patient's behavior. Rather, she assumed that his upset derived from his pathology, not from his present interactions with other staff members. Occasionally, the staff might assume that the patient's family (especially when they had recently visited) or other patients had stimulated the outburst. But never were the staff found to assume that one of themselves or the structure of the hospital had anything to do with a patient's behavior. One psychiatrist pointed to a group of patients who were sitting outside the cafeteria entrance half an hour before lunchtime. To a group of young residents he indicated that such behavior was characteristic of the oral-acquisitive nature of the syndrome. It seemed not to occur to him that there were very few things to anticipate in a psychiatric hospital besides eating.

A psychiatric label has a life and an influence of its own. Once the impression has been formed that the patient is schizophrenic, the expectation is that he will continue to be schizophrenic. When a sufficient amount of time has passed, during which the patient has done nothing bizarre, he is considered to be in remission and available for discharge. But the label endures beyond discharge, with the unconfirmed expectation that he will behave as a schizophrenic again. Such labels, conferred by mental health professionals, are as influential on the patient as they are on his relatives and friends, and it should not surprise anyone that the diagnosis acts on all of them as a self-fulfilling prophecy.[5] Eventually, the patient himself accepts the diagnosis, with all of its surplus meanings and expectations, and behaves accordingly.

The inferences to be made from these matters are quite simple. Much as Zigler and Phillips have demonstrated that there is enormous overlap in the symptoms presented by patients who have been variously diagnosed, so there is enormous overlap in the behaviors of the sane and the insane. The sane are not "sane" all of the time. We lose our tempers "for no good reason." We are occasionally depressed or anxious, again for no good reason. And we may find it difficult to get along with one or another person—again for no reason that we can specify. Similarly, the insane are not always insane. Indeed, it was the impression of the pseudopatients while living with them that they were sane for long periods of time—that the bizarre behaviors upon which their diagnoses were allegedly predicated constituted only a small fraction of their total behavior. . . .

The Consequences of Labeling and Depersonalization

Whenever the ratio of what is known to what needs to be known approaches zero, we tend to invent "knowledge" and assume that we understand more than we actually do. We seem unable to acknowledge that we simply don't know. The needs for diagnosis and remediation of behavioral and emotional problems are enormous. But rather than acknowledge that we are just embarking on understanding, we continue to label patients "schizophrenic," "manic-depressive," and "insane," as if in those words we had captured the essence of understanding. The facts of the matter are that we have known for a long time that diagnoses are often not useful or reliable, but we have nevertheless continued to use them. We now

---

[5]See the introductory notes to reading 27, "The Saints and the Roughnecks," for an explanation of this concept.—Ed.

know that we cannot distinguish insanity from sanity. It is depressing to consider how that information will be used.

Not merely depressing, but frightening. How many people, one wonders, are sane but not recognized as such in our psychiatric institutions? How many have been needlessly stripped of their privileges of citizenship, from the right to vote and drive to that of handling their own accounts? How many have feigned insanity in order to avoid the criminal consequences of their behavior, and, conversely, how many would rather stand trial than live interminably in a psychiatric hospital—but are wrongly thought to be mentally ill? How many have been stigmatized by well-intentioned, but nevertheless erroneous, diagnoses? On the last point, recall again that a false positive error in psychiatric diagnosis does not have the same consequences it does in medical diagnosis. A diagnosis of cancer that has been found to be in error is cause for celebration. But psychiatric diagnoses are rarely found to be in error. The label sticks, a mark of inadequacy forever. . . .

Questions

1. With which of the following statements would Rosenhan agree, and why?
    a. In this study, the symptoms observed by the psychiatric staff led to the diagnosis.
    b. In this study, the diagnosis led to the symptoms observed by the psychiatric staff.

2. What might be the significance of the fact that many *patients* managed to detect pseudopatients while none of the staff did?

3. Why does a false diagnosis of mental illness generally have more serious repercussions than a false diagnosis of physical illness?

29

FRATERNITIES AND COLLEGIATE RAPE CULTURE

Why Are Some Fraternities More Dangerous Places for Women?

A. Ayres Boswell and Joan Z. Spade

In the mid-1980s, social scientific researchers began to identify college fraternities as places where women were in special jeopardy of being raped. In 1985, for example, Julie Ehrhart and Bernice Sandler published a study titled "Campus Gang Rape: Party Games?" (in the Association of American Colleges, *Project on the Status and Education of Women*). In 1989, Patricia Martin and Robert Hummer published their study, "Fraternities and Rape on Campus," in which they concluded that "the organization and membership of fraternities contribute heavily to coercive and often violent sex.... Brotherhood norms require 'sticking together' regardless of right or wrong; thus rape episodes are unlikely to be stopped or reported to outsiders, even when witnesses disapprove" (*Gender and Society,* December). In 1990, anthropologist Peggy Reeves Sanday published *Fraternity Gang Rape: Sex, Brotherhood, and Privilege on Campus,* in which she described her research finding that in many fraternities, gang rape was practiced as a "male bonding ritual."

The conclusion was building that fraternities were places in which a "rape culture" prevailed. In their 1996 study, A. Ayres Boswell and Joan Spade report that although fraternities can be dangerous places for women, some are more dangerous than others. Their findings bolster the sociological theory that it is not the members of the fraternity, but rather the social structure of the fraternity, that makes the difference.

Date rape and acquaintance rape on college campuses are topics of concern to both researchers and college administrators. Some

estimate that 60 to 80 percent of rapes are date or acquaintance rape (Koss et al. 1988). Further, 1 out of 4 college women say they were raped or experienced an attempted rape, and 1 out of 12 college men say they forced a woman to have sexual intercourse against her will (Koss, Gidycz, and Wisniewski 1985).

Although considerable attention focuses on the incidence of rape, we know relatively little about the context or the *rape culture* surrounding date and acquaintance rape. Rape culture is a set of values and beliefs that provide an environment conducive to rape (Buchwald, Fletcher, and Roth 1993; Herman 1984). The term applies to a generic culture surrounding and promoting rape, not the specific settings in which rape is likely to occur. We believe that the specific settings also are important in defining relationships between men and women.

Some have argued that fraternities are places where rape is likely to occur on college campuses (Martin and Hummer 1989; O'Sullivan 1993; Sanday 1990) and that the students most likely to accept rape myths and be more sexually aggressive are more likely to live in fraternities and sororities, consume higher doses of alcohol and drugs, and place a higher value on social life at college (Gwartney-Gibbs and Stockard 1989; Kalof and Cargill 1991). Others suggest that sexual aggression is learned in settings such as fraternities and is not part of predispositions or preexisting attitudes (Boeringer, Shehan, and Akers 1991). To prevent further incidences of rape on college campuses, we need to understand what it is about fraternities in particular and college life in general that may contribute to the maintenance of a rape culture on college campuses.

Our approach is to identify the social contexts that link fraternities to campus rape and promote a rape culture. Instead of assuming that all fraternities provide an environment conducive to rape, we compare the interactions of men and women at fraternities identified on campus as being especially *dangerous* places for women, where the likelihood of rape is high, to those seen as *safer* places, where the perceived probability of rape occurring is lower. Prior to collecting data for our study, we found that most women students identified some fraternities as having more sexually aggressive members and a higher probability of rape. These women also considered other fraternities as relatively safe houses, where a woman could go and get drunk if she wanted to and feel secure that the fraternity men would not take advantage of her. We compared parties at houses identified as high-risk and low-risk houses as well as at two local bars frequented by college students. Our analysis provides an opportunity to examine situations and contexts that hinder or facilitate positive social relations between undergraduate men and women.

The abusive attitudes toward women that some fraternities perpetuate exist within a general culture where rape is intertwined in traditional gender scripts. Men are viewed as initiators of sex and women as either passive partners or active resisters, preventing men from touching their bodies (LaPlante, McCormick, and Brannigan 1980). Rape culture is based on the assumptions that men are aggressive and dominant whereas women are passive and acquiescent (Buchwald et al. 1993; Herman 1984). What occurs on college campuses is an extension of the portrayal of domination and aggression of men over women that exemplifies the double standard of sexual behavior in U.S. society (Barthel 1988; Kimmel 1993).

Sexually active men are positively reinforced by being referred to as "studs," whereas women who are sexually active or report enjoying sex are derogatorily labeled as "sluts" (Herman 1984; O'Sullivan 1993). These gender scripts are embodied in rape myths and stereotypes such as "She really wanted it; she just said no because she didn't want me to think she was a bad girl" (Burke, Stets, and Pirog-Good 1989; Jenkins and Dambrot 1987; Lisak and Roth 1988; Malamuth 1986; Muehlenhard and Linton 1987; Peterson and Franzese 1987). Because men's sexuality is seen as more natural, acceptable, and uncontrollable than women's sexuality, many men and women excuse acquaintance rape by affirming that men cannot control their natural urges (Miller and Marshall 1987).

Whereas some researchers explain these attitudes toward sexuality and rape using an individual or a psychological interpretation, we argue that rape has a social basis, one in which both men and women create and re-create masculine and feminine identities and relations. Based on the assumption that rape is part of the social construction of gender, we examine how men and women "do gender" on a college campus (West and Zimmerman 1987). We focus on fraternities because they have been identified as settings that encourage rape (Sanday 1990). By comparing fraternities that are viewed by women as places where there is a high risk of rape to those where women believe there is a low risk of rape as well as two local commercial bars, we seek to identify characteristics that make some social settings more likely places for the occurrence of rape.

Method

We observed social interactions between men and women at a private coeducational school in which a high percentage (49.4 percent) of students affiliate with Greek organizations. The university has an undergraduate population of approximately 4,500 students, just more than one third of whom are women; the students are primarily from upper-middle-class families. The school, which admitted only men until 1971, is highly competitive academically.

We used a variety of data collection approaches: observations of interactions between men and women at fraternity parties and bars, formal interviews, and informal conversations. The first author, a former undergraduate at this school and a graduate student at the time of the study, collected the data. She knew about the social life at the school and had established rapport and trust between herself and undergraduate students as a teaching assistant in a human sexuality course.

The process of identifying high- and low-risk fraternity houses followed Hunter's (1953) reputational approach. In our study, 40 women students identified fraternities that they considered to be high risk, or to have more sexually aggressive members and higher incidence of rape, as well as fraternities that they considered to be safe houses. The women represented all four years of undergraduate college and different living groups (sororities, residence halls, and off-campus housing). Observations focused on the four fraternities named most often by these women as high-risk houses and the four identified as low-risk houses.

Throughout the spring semester, the first author observed at two fraternity parties each weekend at two different houses (fraternities could have parties only on weekends at this campus). She also observed students' interactions in two popular university bars on weeknights to provide a comparison of students' behavior in non-Greek settings. The first local bar at which she observed was popular with seniors and older students; the second bar was popular with first-, second-, and third-year undergraduates because the management did not strictly enforce drinking age laws in this bar.

The observer focused on the social context as well as interaction among participants at each setting. In terms of social context, she observed the following: ratio of men to women, physical setting such as the party decor and theme, use and control of alcohol and level of intoxication, and explicit and implicit norms. She noted interactions between men and women (i.e., physical contact, conversational style, use of jokes) and the relations among men (i.e., their treatment of pledges and other men at fraternity parties). Other than the observer, no one knew the identity of the high- or low-risk fraternities. Although this may have introduced bias into the data collection, students on this campus who read this article before it was submitted for publication commented on how accurately the social scene is described.

In addition, 50 individuals were interviewed including men from the selected fraternities, women who attended those parties, men not affiliated with fraternities, and self-identified rape victims known to the first author. The first author approached men and women by telephone or on campus and asked them to participate in interviews. The interviews included open-ended questions about gender relations on campus, attitudes about date rape, and their own experiences on campus.

To assess whether self-selection was a factor in determining the classification of the fraternity, we compared high-risk houses to low-risk houses on several characteristics. In terms of status on campus, the high- and low-risk houses we studied attracted about the same number of pledges; however, many of the high-risk houses had more members. There was no difference in grade point averages for the two types of houses. In fact, the highest and lowest grade point averages were found in the high-risk category. Although both high- and low-risk fraternities participated in sports, brothers in the low-risk houses tended to play intramural sports whereas brothers in the high-risk houses were more likely to be varsity athletes. The high-risk houses may be more aggressive, as they had a slightly larger number of disciplinary incidents and their reports were more severe, often with physical harm to others and damage to property. Further, in year-end reports, there was more property damage in the high-risk houses. Last, more of the low-risk houses participated in a campus rape-prevention program. In summary, both high- and low-risk fraternities seem to be equally attractive to freshmen men on this campus, and differences between the eight fraternities we studied were not great; however, the high-risk houses had a slightly larger number of reports of aggression and physical

destruction in the houses and the low-risk houses were more likely to participate in a rape-prevention program.

Results

THE SETTINGS

Fraternity Parties.   We observed several differences in the quality of the interaction of men and women at parties at high-risk fraternities compared to those at low-risk houses. A typical party at a low-risk house included an equal number of women and men. The social atmosphere was friendly, with considerable interaction between women and men. Men and women danced in groups and in couples, with many of the couples kissing and displaying affection toward each other. Brothers explained that, because many of the men in these houses had girlfriends, it was normal to see couples kissing on the dance floor. Coed groups engaged in conversations at many of these houses, with women and men engaging in friendly exchanges, giving the impression that they knew each other well. Almost no cursing and yelling was observed at parties in low-risk houses; when pushing occurred, the participants apologized. Respect for women extended to the women's bathrooms, which were clean and well supplied.

At high-risk houses, parties typically had skewed gender ratios, sometimes involving more men and other times involving more women. Gender segregation also was evident at these parties, with the men on one side of a room or in the bar drinking while women gathered in another area. Men treated women differently in the high-risk houses. The women's bathrooms in the high-risk houses were filthy, including clogged toilets and vomit in the sinks. When a brother was told of the mess in the bathroom at a high-risk house, he replied, "Good, maybe some of these beer wenches will leave so there will be more beer for us."

Men attending parties at high-risk houses treated women less respectfully, engaging in jokes, conversations, and behaviors that degraded women. Men made a display of assessing women's bodies and rated them with thumbs up or thumbs down for the other men in the sight of the women. One man attending a party at a high-risk fraternity said to another, "Did you know that this week is Women's Awareness Week? I guess that means we get to abuse them more this week." Men behaved more crudely at parties at high-risk houses. At one party, a brother dropped his pants, including his underwear, while dancing in front of several women. Another brother slid across the dance floor completely naked.

The atmosphere at parties in high-risk fraternities was less friendly overall. With the exception of greetings, men and women rarely smiled or laughed and spoke to each other less often than was the case at parties in low-risk houses. The few one-on-one conversations between women and men appeared to be strictly flirtatious (lots of eye contact, touching, and very close talking). It was rare to see a group of men and women together talking. Men were openly hostile, which made the high-risk parties seem almost threatening at times. For example, there was a lot of touching, pushing, profanity, and name calling, some done by women.

Students at parties at the high-risk houses seemed self-conscious and aware of the presence of members of the opposite sex, an awareness that was sexually charged. Dancing early in the evening was usually between women. Close to midnight, the sex ratio began to balance out with the arrival of more men or more women. Couples began to dance together but in a sexual way (close dancing with lots of pelvic thrusts). Men tried to pick up women using lines such as "Want to see my fish tank?" and "Let's go upstairs so that we can talk; I can't hear what you're saying in here."

Although many of the same people who attended high-risk parties also attended low-risk parties, their behavior changed as they moved from setting to setting. Group norms differed across contexts as well. At a party that was held jointly at a low-risk house with a high-risk fraternity, the ambience was that of a party at a high-risk fraternity with heavier drinking, less dancing, and fewer conversations between women and men. The men from both high- and low-risk fraternities were very aggressive; a fight broke out, and there was pushing and shoving on the dance floor and in general.

As others have found, fraternity brothers at high-risk houses on this campus told about routinely discussing their sexual exploits at breakfast the morning after parties and sometimes at house meetings (cf. Martin and Hummer 1989; O'Sullivan 1993; Sanday 1990). During these sessions, the brothers we interviewed said that men bragged about what they did the night before with stories of sexual conquests often told by the same men, usually sophomores. The women involved in these exploits were women they did not know or knew but did not respect, or *faceless victims*. Men usually treated girlfriends with respect and did not talk about them in these storytelling sessions. Men from low-risk houses, however, did not describe similar sessions in their houses.

The Bar Scene. The bar atmosphere and social context differed from those of fraternity parties. The music was not as loud, and both bars had places to sit and have conversations. At all fraternity parties, it was difficult to maintain conversations with loud music playing and no place to sit. The volume of music at parties at high-risk fraternities was even louder than it was at low-risk houses, making it virtually impossible to have conversations.

In general, students in the local bars behaved in the same way that students did at parties in low-risk houses with conversations typical, most occurring between men and women.

The first bar, frequented by older students, had live entertainment every night of the week. Some nights were more crowded than others, and the atmosphere was friendly, relaxed, and conducive to conversation. People laughed and smiled and behaved politely toward each other. The ratio of men to women was fairly equal, with students congregating in mostly coed groups. Conversation flowed freely and people listened to each other.

Although the women and men at the first bar also were at parties at low- and high-risk fraternities, their behavior at the bar included none of the blatant sexual or intoxicated behaviors observed at some of these parties. As the evenings wore on, the number of one-on-one conversations between men and women increased and conversations shifted from small talk to topics such as war and AIDS. Conversations did not revolve around picking up another person, and most people left the bar with same-sex friends or in coed groups.

The second bar was less popular with older students. Younger students, often under the legal drinking age, went there to drink, sometimes after leaving campus parties. This bar was much smaller and usually not as crowded as the first bar. The atmosphere was more mellow and relaxed than it was at the fraternity parties. People went there to hang out and talk to each other.

On a couple of occasions, however, the atmosphere at the second bar became similar to that of a party at a high-risk fraternity. As the number of people in the bar increased, they removed chairs and tables, leaving no place to sit and talk. The music also was turned up louder, drowning out conversation. With no place to dance or sit, most people stood around but could not maintain conversations because of the noise and crowds. Interactions between women and men consisted mostly of flirting. Alcohol consumption also was greater than it was on the less crowded nights, and the number of visibly drunk people increased. The more people drank, the more conversation and socializing broke down. The only differences between this setting and that of a party at a high-risk house were that brothers no longer controlled the territory and bedrooms were not available upstairs.

GENDER RELATIONS

Relations between women and men are shaped by the contexts in which they meet and interact. As is the case on other college campuses, *hooking up* has replaced dating on this campus, and fraternities are places where many students hook up. Hooking up is a loosely applied term on college campuses that had different meaning for men and women on this campus.

Most men defined hooking up similarly. One man said it was something that happens

> when you are really drunk and meet up with a woman you sort of know, or possibly don't know at all and don't care about. You go home with her with the intention of getting as much sexual, physical pleasure as she'll give you, which can range anywhere from kissing to intercourse, without any strings attached.

The exception to this rule is when men hook up with women they admire. Men said they are less likely to press for sexual activity with someone they know and like because they want the relationship to continue and be based on respect.

Women's version of hooking up differed. Women said they hook up only with men they cared about and described hooking up as kissing and petting but not sexual intercourse. Many women said that hooking up was disappointing because they wanted longer-term relationships. First-year women students realized quickly that hook-ups were usually one-night stands with no strings attached, but many continued to hook up because they had few opportunities to develop relationships with men on campus. One first-year woman said that "70 percent of hook-ups never talk again and try to avoid one another; 26 percent may actually hear from them or talk to them again, and 4 percent may actually go on a date, which can lead to a relationship." Another first-year woman said, "It was fun in the beginning. You get a lot of attention and kiss a lot of boys and think this is what college is about, but it gets tiresome fast."

Whereas first-year women get tired of the hook-up scene early on, many men do not become bored with it until their junior or senior year. As one upperclassman said, "The whole game of hooking up became really meaningless and tiresome for me during my second semester of my sophomore year, but most of my friends didn't get bored with it until the following year."

In contrast to hooking up, students also described monogamous relationships with steady partners. Some type of commitment was expected, but most people did not anticipate marriage. The term *seeing each other* was applied when people were sexually involved but free to date other people. This type of relationship involved less commitment than did one of boyfriend/girlfriend but was not considered to be a hook-up.

The general consensus of women and men interviewed on this campus was that the Greek system, called "the hill," set the scene for gender relations. The predominance of Greek membership and subsequent living arrangements segregated men and women. During the week, little interaction occurred between women and men after their first year in college because students in fraternities or sororities live and dine in separate quarters. In addition, may non-Greek upper-class students move off campus into apartments. Therefore,

students see each other in classes or in the library, but there is no place where students can just hang out together.

Both men and women said that fraternities dominate campus social life, a situation that everyone felt limited opportunities for meaningful interactions. One senior Greek man said,

> This environment is horrible and so unhealthy for good male and female relationships and interactions to occur. It is so segregated and male dominated. . . . It is our party, with our rules and our beer. We are allowing these women and other men to come to our party. Men can feel superior in their domain.

Comments from a senior woman reinforced his views: "Men are dominant; they are the kings of the campus. It is their environment that they allow us to enter; therefore, we have to abide by their rules." A junior woman described fraternity parties as

> good for meeting acquaintances but almost impossible to really get to know anyone. The environment is so superficial, probably because there are so many social cliques due to the Greek system. Also, the music is too loud and the people are too drunk to attempt to have a real conversation anyway.

Some students claim that fraternities even control the dating relationships of their members. One senior woman said, "Guys dictate how dating occurs on this campus, whether it's cool, who it's with, how much time can be spent with the girlfriend and with the brothers." Couples either left campus for an evening or hung out separately with their own same-gender friends at fraternity parties, finally getting together with each other at about 2 A.M. Couples rarely went together to fraternity parties. Some men felt that a girlfriend was just a replacement for a hook-up. According to one junior man, "Basically a girlfriend is someone you go to at 2 A.M. after you've hung out with the guys. She is the sexual outlet that the guys can't provide you with."

Some fraternity brothers pressure each other to limit their time with and commitment to their girlfriends. One senior man said, "The hill [fraternities] and girlfriends don't mix." A brother described a constant battle between girlfriends and brothers over who the guy is going out with for the night, with the brothers usually winning. Brothers teased men with girlfriends with remarks such as "whipped" or "where's the ball and chain?" A brother from a high-risk house said that few brothers at his house had girlfriends; some did, but it was uncommon. One man said that from the minute he was a pledge he knew he would probably never have a girlfriend on this campus because "it was just not the norm in my house. No one has girlfriends; the guys have too much fun with [each other]."

The pressure on men to limit their commitment to girlfriends, however, was not true of all fraternities or of all men on campus. Couples attended low-risk fraternity parties together, and men in the low-risk houses went out on dates more often. A man in one low-risk house said that about 70 percent of the members of his house were involved in relationships with women, including the pledges (who were sophomores).

TREATMENT OF WOMEN

Not all men held negative attitudes toward women that are typical of a rape culture, and not all social contexts promoted the negative treatment of women. When men were asked whether they treated the women on campus with respect, the most common response was "On an individual basis, yes, but when you have a group of men together, no." Men said that, when together in groups with other men, they sensed a pressure to be disrespectful toward women. A first-year man's perception of the treatment of women was that "they are treated with more respect to their faces, but behind closed doors, with a group of men present, respect for women is not an issue." One senior man stated, "In general, college-aged men don't treat women their age with respect because 90 percent of them think of women as merely a means to sex." Women reinforced this perception. A first-year woman stated, "Men here are more interested in hooking up and drinking beer than they are in getting to know women as real people." Another woman said, "Men here use and abuse women."

Characteristic of rape culture, a double standard of sexual behavior for men versus women was prevalent on this campus. As one Greek senior man stated, "Women who sleep around are sluts and get bad reputations; men who do are champions and get a pat on the back from their brothers." Women also supported a double standard for sexual behavior by criticizing sexually active women. A first-year woman spoke out against women who are sexually active: "I think some girls here make it difficult for the men to respect women as a whole."

One concrete example of demeaning sexually active women on this campus is the "walk of shame." Fraternity brothers come out on the porches of their houses the night after parties and heckle women walking by. It is assumed that these women spent the night at fraternity houses and that the men they were with did not care enough about them to drive them home. Although sororities now reside in former fraternity houses, this practice continues and sometimes the victims of hecklings are sorority women on their way to study in the library.

A junior man in a high-risk fraternity described another ritual of disrespect toward women called "chatter." When an unknown woman sleeps over at the house, the brothers yell degrading remarks out the window at her as she leaves the next morning such as "Fuck that bitch" and "Who is that slut?" He said that sometimes brothers harass the brothers whose girlfriends stay over instead of heckling those women.

Fraternity men most often mistreated women they did not know personally. Men and women alike reported incidents in which brothers observed other brothers having sex with unknown women or women they knew only casually. A sophomore woman's experience exemplifies this anonymous state: "I don't mind if 10 guys were watching or it was videotaped. That's expected on this campus. It's the fact that he didn't apologize or even offer to drive me home that really upset me." Descriptions of sexual encounters involved the satisfaction of men by nameless women. A brother in a high-risk fraternity described a similar occurrence:

> A brother of mine was hooking up upstairs with an unattractive woman who had been pursuing him all night. He told some brothers to go outside the window and watch. Well, one thing led to another and they were almost completely naked when the woman noticed the brothers outside. She was then unwilling to go any further, so the brother went outside and yelled at the other brothers and then closed the shades. I don't know if he scored or not, because the woman was pretty upset. But he did win the award for hooking up with the ugliest chick that weekend.

ATTITUDES TOWARD RAPE

The sexually charged environment of college campuses raises many questions about cultures that facilitate the rape of women. How women and men define their sexual behavior is important legally as well as interpersonally. We asked students how they defined rape and had them compare it to the following legal definition: the perpetration of an act of sexual intercourse with a female against her will and consent, whether her will is overcome by force or fear resulting from the threat of force, or by drugs or intoxicants; or when, because of mental deficiency, she is incapable of exercising rational judgment. (Brownmiller 1975, 368)

When presented with this legal definition, most women interviewed recognized it as well as the complexities involved in applying it. A first-year woman said, "If a girl is drunk and the guy knows it and the girl says, 'Yes, I want to have sex,' and they do, that is still rape because the girl can't make a conscious, rational decision under the influence of alcohol." Some women disagreed. Another first-year woman stated, "I don't think it is fair that the guy gets blamed when both people involved are drunk."

The typical definition men gave for rape was "when a guy jumps out of the bushes and forces himself sexually onto a girl." When asked what date rape was, the most common answer was "when one person has sex with another person who did not consent." Many men said, however, that "date rape is when a woman wakes up the next morning and regrets having sex." Some men said that date rape was too gray an area to define. "Consent is a fine line," said a Greek senior man student. For the most part, the men we spoke with argued that rape did not occur on this campus. One Greek sophomore man said, "I think it is ridiculous that someone here would rape someone." A first-year man stated, "I have a problem with the word rape. It sounds so criminal, and we are not criminals; we are sane people."

Whether aware of the legal definitions of rape, most men resisted the idea that a woman who is intoxicated is unable to consent to sex. A Greek junior man said, "Men should not be responsible for women's drunkenness." One first-year man said, "If that is the legal definition of rape, then it happens all the time on this campus." A senior man said, "I don't care whether alcohol is involved or not; that is not rape. Rapists are people that have something seriously wrong with them." A first-year man even claimed that when women get drunk, they invite sex. He said, "Girls get so drunk here and then come on to us. What are we supposed to do? We are only human."

Discussion and Conclusion

These findings describe the physical and normative aspects of one college campus as they relate to attitudes about and relations between men and women. Our findings suggest that an explanation emphasizing rape culture also must focus on those characteristics of the social setting that play a role in defining heterosexual relationships on college campuses (Kalof and Cargill 1991). The degradation of women as portrayed in rape culture was not found in all fraternities on this campus. Both group norms and individual behavior changed as students went from one place to another. Although individual men are the ones who rape, we found that some settings are more likely places for rape than are others. Our findings suggest that rape cannot be seen only as an isolated act and blamed on individual behavior and proclivities, whether it be alcohol consumption or attitudes. We also must consider characteristics of the settings that promote the behaviors that reinforce a rape culture.

Relations between women and men at parties in low-risk fraternities varied considerably from those in high-risk houses. Peer pressure and situational norms influenced women as well as men. Although many men in high- and low-risk houses shared similar views and attitudes about the Greek system, women on this campus, and date rape, their behaviors at fraternity parties were quite different.

Women who are at highest risk of rape are women whom fraternity brothers did not know. These women are faceless victims, nameless acquaintances—not friends. Men said their responsibility to such persons and the level of guilt they feel later if the hook-ups end in sexual intercourse are much lower if they hook up with women they do not know. In high-risk houses, brothers treated women as subordinates and kept them at a distance. Men in high-risk houses actively discouraged ongoing heterosexual relationships, routinely degraded women, and participated more fully in the hook-up scene; thus, the probability that women would become faceless victims was higher in these houses. The flirtatious nature of the parties indicated that women go to these parties looking for available men, but finding boyfriends or relationships was difficult at parties in high-risk houses. However, in the low-risk houses, where more men had long-term relationships, the women were not strangers and were less likely to become faceless victims.

The social scene on this campus, and on most others, offers women and men few other options to socialize. Although there may be no such thing as a completely safe fraternity party for women, parties at low-risk houses and commercial bars encouraged men and women to get to know each other better and decreased the probability that women would become faceless victims. Although both men and women found the social scene on this campus demeaning, neither demanded different settings for socializing, and attendance at fraternity parties is a common form of entertainment.

These findings suggest that a more conducive environment for conversation can promote more positive interactions between men and women. Simple changes would provide the opportunity for men and women to interact in meaningful ways, such as adding places to sit and lowering the volume of music at fraternity parties or having parties in neutral locations, where men are not in control. The typical party room in fraternity houses includes a place to dance but not to sit and talk. The music often is loud, making it difficult, if not impossible, to carry on conversations; however, there were more conversations at the low-risk parties, where there also was more respect shown toward women. Although the number of brothers who had steady girl-friends in the low-risk houses as compared to those in the high-risk houses may explain the differences, we found that commercial bars also provided a context for interaction between men and women. At the bars, students sat and talked and conversations between men and women flowed freely, resulting in deep discussion and fewer hook-ups.

Alcohol consumption was a major focus of social events here and intensified attitudes and orientations of a rape culture. Although pressure to drink was evident at all fraternity parties and at both bars, drinking dominated high-risk fraternity parties, at which nonalcoholic beverages usually were not available and people chugged beers and became visibly drunk. A rape culture is strengthened by rules that permit alcohol only at fraternity parties. Under this system, men control the parties and dominate the men as well as the women who attend. As college administrators crack down on fraternities and alcohol on campus, however, the same behaviors and norms may transfer to other places such as parties in apartments or private homes where administrators have much less control. At commercial bars, interaction and socialization with others were as important as drinking, with the exception of the nights when the bar frequented by under-class students became crowded. Although one solution is to offer nonalcoholic social activities, such events receive little support on this campus. Either these alternative events lacked the prestige of the fraternity parties or the alcohol was seen as necessary to unwind, or both.

In many ways, the fraternities on this campus determined the settings in which men and women interacted. As others before us have found, pressures for conformity to the norms and values exist at both high-risk and low-risk houses (Kalof and Cargill 1991; Martin and Hummer 1989; Sanday 1990). The desire to be accepted is not unique to this campus or the Greek system (Holland and Eisenhart 1990; Horowitz 1988; Moffat 1989). The degree of conformity required by Greeks may be greater than that required in most social groups, with considerable pressure to adopt and maintain the image of their houses. The fraternity system intensifies the "groupthink syndrome" (Janis 1972) by solidifying the identity of the in-group and creating an us/them atmosphere. Within the fraternity culture, brothers are highly regarded and women are viewed as outsiders. For men in high-risk fraternities, women threatened their brotherhood; therefore, brothers discouraged relationships and harassed those who treated women as equals or with respect. The pressure to be one of the guys and hang out with the guys strengthens a rape culture on college campus by demeaning women and encouraging the segregation of men and women.

Students on this campus were aware of the contexts in which they operated and the choices available to them. They recognized that, in their interactions, they created differences between men and women that are not natural, essential, or biological (West and Zimmerman 1987). Not all men and women accepted the demeaning treatment of women, but they continued to participate in behaviors that supported aspects of a rape culture. Many women participated in the hook-up scene even after they had been humiliated and hurt because they had few other means of initiating contact with men on campus. Men and women alike played out this scene, recognizing its injustices in many cases but being unable to change the course of their behaviors.

Although this research provides some clues to gender relations on college campuses, it raises many questions. Why do men and women participate in activities that support a rape culture when they see its injustices? What would happen if alcohol were not controlled by groups of men who admit that they disrespect women when they get together? What can be done to give men and women on college campuses more opportunities to interact responsibly and get to know each other better? These questions should be studied on other campuses with a focus on the social settings in which the incidence of rape and the attitudes that support a rape culture exist. Fraternities are social contexts that may or may not foster a rape culture.

Our findings indicate that a rape culture exists in some fraternities, especially those we identified as high-risk houses. College administrators are responding to this situation by providing counseling and educational programs that increase awareness of date rape including campaigns such as "No means no." These strategies are important in changing attitudes, values, and behaviors; however, changing individuals is not enough. The structure of campus life and the impact of that structure on gender relations on campus are highly determinative. To eliminate campus rape culture, student leaders and administrators must examine the situations in which women and men meet and restructure these settings to provide opportunities for respectful interaction. Change may not require abolishing fraternities; rather, it may require promoting settings that facilitate positive gender relations.

References

Barthel, D. 1988. *Putting on Appearances: Gender and Advertising.* Philadelphia: Temple University Press.

Boeringer, S. B., C. L. Shehan, and R. L. Akers. 1991. "Social Contexts and Social Learning in Sexual Coercion and Aggression: Assessing the Contribution of Fraternity Membership." *Family Relations* 40: 58–64.

Brownmiller, S. 1975. *Against Our Will: Men, Women and Rape.* New York: Simon & Schuster.

Buchwald, E., P. R. Fletcher, and M. Roth (eds.). 1993. *Transforming a Rape Culture.* Minneapolis, MN: Milkweed Editions.

Burke, P., J. E. Stets, and M. A. Pirog-Good. 1989. "Gender Identity, Self-Esteem, Physical Abuse and Sexual Abuse in Dating Relationships." In M. A. Pirog-Good and J. E. Stets (eds.), *Violence in Dating Relationships: Emerging Social Issues.* New York: Praeger.

Gwartney-Gibbs, P., and J. Stockard. 1989. "Courtship Aggression and Mixed-Sex Peer Groups." In M. A. Pirog-Good and J. E. Stets (eds.), *Violence in Dating Relationships: Emerging Social Issues.* New York: Praeger.

Herman, D. 1984. "The Rape Culture." In J. Freeman (ed.), *Women: A Feminist Perspective.* Mountain View, CA: Mayfield.

Holland, D. C., and M. A. Eisenhart. 1990. *Educated in Romance: Women, Achievement, and College Culture.* Chicago: University of Chicago Press.

Horowitz, H. L. 1988. *Campus Life; Undergraduate Cultures from the End of the 18th Century to the Present.* Chicago: University of Chicago Press.

Hunter, F. 1953. *Community Power Structure.* Chapel Hill: University of North Carolina Press.

Janis, I. L. 1972. *Victims of Groupthink.* Boston: Houghton Mifflin.

Jenkins, M. J., and F. H. Dambrot. 1987. "The Attribution of Date Rape: Observer's Attitudes and Sexual Experiences and the Dating Situation." *Journal of Applied Social Psychology* 17: 875–895.

Kalof, L., and T. Cargill. 1991. "Fraternity and Sorority Membership and Gender Dominance Attitudes." *Sex Roles* 25: 417–423.

Kimmel, M. S. 1993. "Clarence, William, Iron Mike, Tailhook, Senator Packwood, Spur Posse, Magic . . . and Us." In E. Buchwald, P. R. Fletcher, and M. Roth (eds.), *Transforming a Rape Culture.* Minneapolis, MN: Milkweed Editions.

Koss, M. P., T. E. Dinero, C. A. Seibel, and S. L. Cox. 1988. "Stranger and Acquaintance Rape: Are There Differences in the Victim's Experience?" *Psychology of Women Quarterly* 12: 1–24.

Koss, M. P., C. A. Gidycz, and N. Wisniewski. 1985. "The Scope of Rape: Incidence and Prevalence of Sexual Aggression and Victimization in a National Sample of Higher Education Students." Journal of *Consulting and Clinical Psychology* 55: 162–170.

LaPlante, M. N., N. McCormick, and G. G. Brannigan. 1980. "Living the Sexual Script: College Students' Views of Influence in Sexual Encounters." *Journal of Sex Research* 16: 338–355.

Lisak, D., and S. Roth. 1988. "Motivational Factors in Nonincarcerated Sexually Aggressive Men." *Journal of Personality and Social Psychology* 55: 795–802.

Malamuth, N. 1986. "Predictors of Naturalistic Sexual Aggression." *Journal of Personality and Social Psychology* 50: 953–962.

Martin, P. Y., and R. Hummer. 1989. "Fraternities and Rape on Campus." *Gender and Society* 3: 457–473.

Miller, B., and J. C. Marshall. 1987. "Coercive Sex on the University Campus." *Journal of College Student Personnel* 28: 38–47.

Moffat, M. 1989. *Coming of Age in New Jersey: College Life in American Culture.* New Brunswick, NJ: Rutgers University Press.

Muehlenhard, C. L., and M. A. Linton. 1987. "Date Rape and Sexual Aggression in Dating Situations: Incidence and Risk Factors." *Journal of Counseling Psychology* 34: 186–196.

O'Sullivan, C. 1993. "Fraternities and the Rape Culture." In E. Buchwald, P. R. Fletcher, and M. Roth (eds.), *Transforming a Rape Culture.* Minneapolis, MN: Milkweed Editions.

Peterson, S. A., and B. Franzese. 1987. "Correlates of College Men's Sexual Abuse of Women." *Journal of College Student Personnel* 28: 223–228.

Sanday, P. R. 1990. *Fraternity Gang Rape: Sex, Brotherhood, and Privilege on Campus.* New York: New York University Press.

West, C., and D. Zimmerman. 1987. "Doing Gender." *Gender and Society* 1: 125–151.

Questions

1. In your judgment, what sorts of questions would allow a researcher to obtain reliable and valid information about people's (men's and women's) attitudes toward acquaintance rape?

2. What are the elements of a rape culture?

3. On the campus that Boswell and Spade studied, students distinguished between different types of relationships: "hooking up," "seeing each other," and "committed." (And men and women defined hooking up differently.) Are similar distinctions made on the campuses with which you are familiar?

4. When Boswell and Spade asked men whether they treated the women on campus with respect, the most common response was "on an individual basis, yes, but when you have a group of men together, no." In your judgment, what might account for the difference?

5. Boswell and Spade conclude that "some settings are more likely places for rape than are others." How do the types of settings that are more likely places for rape differ from those that are less likely places for rape? Explain.

6. Most researchers focus their analysis on the negative impact of rape cultures on women. What are the possible negative consequences of a rape culture on men?

7. Imagine that you've been asked to write a booklet for young college women titled "How to Be Safe from Rape on This Campus." What would you include in the booklet?

30
SITUATIONAL ETHICS AND COLLEGE STUDENT CHEATING

Emily E. LaBeff, Robert E. Clark, Valerie J. Haines,
and George M. Diekhoff

In this 1990 article Professor LaBeff and her colleagues explore the ways in which
students who have cheated avoid guilt by finding excuses for their wrongdoing.
In other words, the authors explore how students "neutralize" their actions.

Introduction

Studies have shown that cheating in college is
epidemic, and some analysts of this problem
estimate that fifty percent of college students
may engage in such behavior. . . . Such studies
have examined demographic and social characteristics of students such as age, sex, academic
standing, major, classification, extracurricular
activity, level of test anxiety, degree of sanctioned threat, and internal social control. Each
of these factors has been found to be related,
to some extent, to cheating although the relationship of these factors varies considerably
from study to study. . . .

In our freshman classes, we often informally ask students to discuss whether they
have cheated in college and, if so, how. Some
students have almost bragged about which of
their methods have proven most effective including writing notes on shoes and caps and
on the backs of calculators. Rolling up a tiny
cheat sheet into a pen cap was mentioned. And
one student said he had "incredibly gifted

eyes" which allowed him to see the answers of
a smart student four rows in front of him. One
female student talked about rummaging
through the dumpsters at night close to final
examination time looking for test dittos. She
did find at least one examination. A sorority
member informed us that two of her term
papers in her freshman year were sent from a
sister chapter of the sorority at another university, retyped and submitted to the course professor. Further, many of these students saw
nothing wrong with what they were doing, although they verbally agreed with the statement
that cheating was unethical.

It appears that students hold qualified
guidelines for behavior which are situationally
determined. As such, the concept of situational
ethics might well describe this college cheating
in that rules for behavior may not be considered rigid but depend on the circumstances involved (Norris and Dodder 1979, 545). Joseph
Fletcher, in his well-known philosophical trea-
tise, *Situation Ethics: The New Morality* (1966),
argues that this position is based on the notion
that any action may be considered good or bad
depending on the social circumstances. In other
words, what is wrong in most situations might
be considered right or acceptable if the end
is defined as appropriate. This concept focuses
on contextual appropriateness, not necessarily

what is good or right, but what is viewed as fitting, given the circumstances. Central to this process is the idea that situations alter cases, thus altering the rules and principles guiding behavior (Edwards 1967).

Of particular relevance to the present study is the work of Gresham Sykes and David Matza (1957) who first developed the concept of neutralization to explain delinquent behavior. Neutralization theory in the study of delinquency expresses the process of situationally defining deviant behavior. In this view, deviance is based upon ". . . an unrecognized extension of defenses to crimes, in the form of justifications . . . seen as valid by the delinquent but not by . . . society at large" (Sykes and Matza 1957, 666). Through neutralization individuals justify violation of accepted behavior. This provides protection ". . . from self blame and the blame of others . . ." (Sykes and Matza 1957, 666). They do this before, during, and after the act. Such techniques of neutralization are separated into five categories: denial of responsibility, condemnation of condemners, appeal to higher loyalties, denial of victim, and denial of injury. In each case, individuals profess a conviction about a particular law but argue that special circumstances exist which cause them to violate the rules in a particular instance. However, in recent research, only Liska (1978) and Haines et al. (1986) found neutralization to be an important factor in college student cheating.

Methodology

The present analysis is based on a larger project conducted during the 1983–1984 academic year when a 49-item questionnaire about cheating was administered to students at a small southwestern university. The student body (N = 4950) was evenly distributed throughout the university's programs with a disproportionate number (27%) majoring in business administration. In order to achieve a representative sample from a cross-section of the university student body, the questionnaire was administered to students enrolled in courses classified as a part of the university's core curriculum. Freshmen and sophomores were overrepresented (84% of the sample versus 60% of the university population). Females were also overrepresented (62% of the sample versus 55% of the university population).

There are obvious disadvantages associated with the use of self-administered questionnaires for data-gathering purposes. One such problem is the acceptance of student responses without benefit of contest. To maximize the return rate, questionnaires were administered during regularly scheduled class periods. Participation was on a voluntary basis. In order to establish the validity of responses, students were guaranteed anonymity. Students were also instructed to limit their responses regarding whether they had cheated to the current academic year.

. . . The present analysis is intended to assess the narrative responses to the incidence of cheating in three forms, namely on major examinations, quizzes, and class assignments, as well as the perceptions of and attitudes held by students toward cheating and the effectiveness of deterrents to cheating. Students recorded their experiences in their own words. Most students (87%) responded to the open-ended portion of the questionnaire.

Results

Of the 380 undergraduate students who participated in the spring survey, 54% indicated they had cheated during the previous six-month period. Students were requested to indicate whether cheating involved examination, weekly quizzes, and/or homework assignments. Much cheating took the form of looking on someone else's paper, copying homework, and either buying term papers or getting friends to write papers for them. Only five of the 205 students who admitted cheating reported being caught by the professor. However, 7% (n = 27) of the students reported cheating more than five times during the preceding six-month period. Twenty percent (n = 76) indicated that most students openly approved of cheating. Only seventeen students reported they would inform the instructor if they saw another student cheating. Many students, especially older students, indicated they felt resentment toward cheaters, but most also noted that they would not do anything about it (i.e., inform the instructor).

To more fully explore the ways in which students neutralize their behavior, narrative data from admitted student cheaters were examined (n = 149). The narrative responses were easily classified into three of the five techniques described by Sykes and Matza (1957).

DENIAL OF RESPONSIBILITY

Denial of responsibility was the most often identified response. This technique involves a declaration by the offenders that, in light of circumstances beyond their control, they cannot be held accountable for their actions. Rather than identifying the behavior as "accidental," they attribute wrongdoing to the influence of outside forces. In some instances, students expressed an inability to withstand peer pressure to cheat. Responses show a recognition of cheating as an unacceptable behavior, implying that under different circumstances cheating would not have occurred. One student commented:

> I was working forty plus hours a week and we had a lot to read for that day. I just couldn't get it all in. . . . I'm not saying cheating is okay, sometimes you just have to.

Another student explained her behavior in the following statement:

> . . . I had the flu the week before . . . had to miss several classes so I had no way of knowing what was going to be on the exam. My grades

were good up to that point and I hadn't cheated. . . . I just couldn't risk it.

It is noteworthy that these statements indicate the recognition that cheating is wrong under normal circumstances.

Other responses demonstrate the attempt by students to succeed through legitimate means (e.g., taking notes and studying) only to experience failure. Accordingly, they were left with no alternative but to cheat. One student commented:

> . . . even though I've studied in the past, I've failed the exam so I cheated on my last test hoping to bring a better grade.

Another student explained his behavior in the following manner:

> I studied for the exam and I studied hard but the material on the test was different from what I expected. . . . I had to make a good grade.

In some accounts, students present a unique approach to the denial of responsibility. Upon entering the examination setting, these students had no intention of cheating, but the opportunity presented itself. The following statement by one student provides a clear illustration of this point:

> . . . I was taking the test and someone in another part of the room was telling someone else an answer. I heard it and just couldn't not write it down.

Although viewing such behavior as dishonest, the blame for any wrongdoing is quickly transferred to those who provide the answers. Another student justified her action in the following manner:

> . . . I didn't mean to cheat but once you get the right answer it's hard, no impossible, not to. How could you ignore an answer that you knew was right?

In addition, some students reported accidentally seeing other students' test papers. In such instances, the cheaters chastised classmates for not covering up their answer sheets. As one student wrote, such temptation simply cannot be overcome:

> I studied hard for the exam and needed an A. I just happened to look up and there was my neighbor's paper uncovered. I found myself checking my answers against his through the whole test.

APPEAL TO HIGHER LOYALTIES

Conflict also arises between peer group expectations and the normative expectations of the larger society. When this occurs, the individual may choose to sacrifice responsibility, thereby maintaining the interest of peers. Such allegiance allows these individuals to supersede moral obligations when special circumstances arise.

Students who invoke this technique of neutralization frequently described their behavior as an attempt to help another. One student stated:

> I only cheated because my friend had been sick and she needed help. . . . It (cheating) wouldn't have happened any other time.

Another student denied any wrongdoing on her part as the following statement illustrates:

> I personally have never cheated. I've had friends who asked for help so I let them see my test. Maybe some would consider that to be cheating.

These students recognize the act of cheating is wrong. However, their statements also suggest that in some situations cheating can be overlooked. Loyalty to a friend in need takes precedence over honesty in the classroom. Another student described his situation in the following manner:

> I was tutoring this girl but she just couldn't understand the material. . . . I felt I had to help her on the test.

CONDEMNATION OF CONDEMNERS

Cheaters using this technique of neutralization attempt to shift attention from their own actions to the actions of others, most often authority figures. By criticizing those in authority as being unfair or unethical, the behavior of the offender seems less consequential by comparison. Therefore, dishonest behavior occurs in reaction to the perceived dishonesty of the authority figure. Students who utilize this technique wrote about uncaring, unprofessional instructors with negative attitudes who were negligent in their behavior. These incidents were said to be a precursor to their cheating behavior. The following response illustrates this view:

> The teachers here are boring and I dislike this school. The majority of teachers here don't care about the students and are rude when you ask them for help.

In other instances, students cite unfair teaching practices which they perceive to be the reason for their behavior. One student stated:

> Major exams are very important to your grade and it seems that the majority of instructors make up the exams to try and trick you instead of testing your knowledge.

In this case, the instructor is thought to engage in a deliberate attempt to fail the students by making the examinations difficult. Also within this category were student accounts which frequently express a complaint of being overworked. As one student wrote:

> One instructor assigns more work than anyone could possibly handle . . . at least I know I can't, so sometimes cheating is the answer.

Another student described his situation as follows:

> Sometimes it seems like these instructors get together and plan to make it difficult. . . . I had three major tests in one day and very little time to study. . . .

Although less frequently mentioned, perceived parental pressure also serves as a neutralizing factor for dishonesty. One student stated:

> During my early years at school my parents constantly pressured me for good grades. . . . They would have withheld money if grades were bad.

Another student blamed the larger society for his cheating:

> In America, we're taught that results aren't achieved through beneficial means, but through the easiest means.

Another stated:

> Ted Kennedy has been a modeling example for many of us. . . . This society teaches us to survive, to rationalize. . . . It is built on injustice and expediency.

This student went on to say that he cheated throughout a difficult science course so he could spend more time studying for major courses which he enjoyed.

DENIAL OF INJURY AND DENIAL OF THE VICTIM

Denial of injury and denial of the victim do not appear in the student accounts of their cheating. In denial of injury, the wrongdoer states that no one was harmed or implies that accusations of injury are grossly exaggerated. In the second case, denial of the victim, those who violate norms often portray their targets as legitimate. Due to certain factors such as the societal role, personal characteristics, or lifestyle of the victim, the wrongdoer felt the victim "had it coming."

It is unlikely that students will either deny injury or deny the victim since there are no real targets in cheating. However, attempts to deny injury are possible when the one who is cheating argues that cheating is a personal matter rather than a public one. It is also possible that some students are cognizant of the effect their cheating activities have upon the educational system as a whole and, therefore, choose to neutralize their behavior in ways which allow them to focus on the act rather than the consequences of cheating. By observing their actions from a myopic viewpoint, such students avoid the larger issues of morality.

Conclusion

The purpose of this report was to analyze student responses to cheating in their college coursework. Using Sykes and Matza's model of techniques of neutralization, we found that students rationalized their cheating behavior and do so without challenging the norm of honesty. Student responses fit three of the five techniques of neutralization. The most common technique is a denial of responsibility. Second, students tend to "condemn the condemners," blaming faculty and testing procedures. Finally, students "appeal to higher loyalties" by arguing that it is more important to help a friend than to avoid cheating. The use of these techniques of neutralization conveys the message that students recognize and accept cheating as an undesirable behavior which, nonetheless, can be excused under certain circumstances. Such findings reflect the prevalence of situational ethics.

The situation appears to be one in which students are not caught and disciplined by instructors. Additionally, students who cheat do not concern themselves with overt negative sanctions from other students. In some groups, cheating is planned, expected, and often rewarded in that students may receive better grades. That leaves a student's ethical, internalized control as a barrier to cheating. However, the neutralizing attitude allows students to sidestep issues of ethics and guilt by placing the blame for their behavior elsewhere. Neutralization allows them to state their belief that in general cheating is wrong, but in some special circumstances cheating is acceptable, even necessary.

Given such widespread acceptance of cheating in the university setting, it may be useful to further test the salience of neutralization and other such factors in more diverse university environments. This study is limited to a small state university. It is important also to extend the research to a wider range of institutions including prestigious private colleges, large state universities, and church-related schools.

Cross-cultural studies of cheating may also prove useful for identifying broader social and cultural forces which underlie situational ethics and cheating behavior. In this regard, the process involved in learning neutralizing attitudes could be integrated with work in the field of deviance in order to expand our understanding of the rule breakers along a continuum of minor to major forms of deviance.

References

Edwards, Paul. 1967. *The Encyclopedia of Philosophy*, Vol. 3, edited by Paul Edwards. New York: Macmillan Company and Free Press.

Fletcher, Joseph. 1966. *Situation Ethics: The New Morality*. Philadelphia: The Westminster Press.

Haines, Valerie J., George Diekhoff, Emily LaBeff, and Robert Clark. 1986. "College Cheating: Immaturity, Lack of Commitment, and the Neutralizing Attitude." *Research in Higher Education* 25: 342–354.

Liska, Allen. 1978. "Deviant Involvement, Associations, and Attitudes: Specifying the Underlying Causal Structures." *Sociology and Social Research* 63: 73–88.

Norris, Terry D., and Richard A. Dodder. 1979. "A Behavioral Continuum Synthesizing Neutralization Theory, Situational Ethics and Juvenile Delinquency." *Adolescence* 55: 545–555.

Sykes, Gresham, and David Matza. 1957. "Techniques of Neutralization: A Theory of Delinquency." *American Sociological Review* 22: 664–670.

Questions

1. Explain what the authors mean by "neutralization."

2. List the five major categories of neutralization techniques. According to LaBeff and her colleagues, what do these techniques have in common?

3. Review the kinds of excuses given by student cheaters in this study. Then, assume that you are a college professor who has just caught some students cheating. Which kinds of excuses would seem the most compelling to you? Would any of these lead you to treat the students' behavior as acceptable (i.e., not take any action against them for cheating)? Which kinds of excuses would seem the most lame to you? Why?

31

DENYING THE GUILTY MIND

Accounting for Involvement in a White-Collar Crime

Michael L. Benson

In this 1985 article, Michael Benson reports on the results of conversations he had with thirty men convicted of white-collar crime. The term *white-collar crime* was coined by criminologist Edwin Sutherland in 1949 to refer to any "crime committed by a person of respectability and high social status in the course of his occupation."

Benson encouraged each convict to talk about how he felt about his involvement with the justice system. One interesting finding: None of the men said he felt he was a "criminal."

Denying the Guilty Mind

Adjudication as a criminal is, to use Garfinkel's (1956) classic term, a degradation ceremony.[1] The focus of this article is on how offenders attempt to defeat the success of this ceremony and deny their own criminality through the use of accounts. However, in the interest of showing in as much detail as possible all sides of the experience undergone by these offenders, it is necessary to treat first the guilt and inner anguish that is felt by many white-collar offenders even though they deny being criminals. This is best accomplished by beginning

with a description of a unique feature of the prosecution of white-collar crimes.

In white-collar criminal cases, the issue is likely to be *why* something was done, rather than *who* did it (Edelhertz 1970, 47). There is often relatively little disagreement as to what happened. In the words of one Assistant U.S. Attorney interviewed for the study:

> If you actually had a movie playing, neither side would dispute that a person moved in this way and handled this piece of paper, etc. What it comes down to is, did they have the criminal intent?

If the prosecution is to proceed past the investigatory stages, the prosecutor must infer from the pattern of events that conscious criminal intent was present and believe that sufficient evidence exists to convince a jury of this interpretation of the situation. As Katz (1979, 445–446) has noted, making this inference can be difficult because of the way in which white-collar illegalities are integrated into ordinary

---

[1] A degradation ceremony is a public ritual in which the individual is stripped of his or her identity as a member of respectable society and formally labeled as an outsider or even as something less than human.—Ed.

"Denying the Guilty Mind: Accounting for Involvement in a White-Collar Crime" by Michael L. Benson from *Criminology*, Vol. 23, No. 4 (1985: pp. 590–599). Reprinted by permission of the American Society of Criminology.

occupational routines. Thus, prosecutors in conducting trials, grand jury hearings, or plea negotiations spend a great deal of effort establishing that the defendant did indeed have the necessary criminal intent. By concentrating on the offender's motives, the prosecutor attacks the very essence of the white-collar offender's public and personal image as an upstanding member of the community. The offender is portrayed as someone with a guilty mind.

Not surprisingly, therefore, the most consistent and recurrent pattern in the interviews, though not present in all of them, was denial of criminal intent, as opposed to the outright denial of any criminal behavior whatsoever. Most offenders acknowledged that their behavior probably could be construed as falling within the conduct proscribed by statute, but they uniformly denied that their actions were motivated by a guilty mind. This is not to say, however, that offenders *felt* no guilt or shame as a result of conviction. On the contrary, indictment, prosecution, and conviction provoke a variety of emotions among offenders.

The enormous reality of the offender's lived emotion (Denzin 1984) in admitting guilt is perhaps best illustrated by one offender's description of his feelings during the hearing at which he pled guilty.

> You know (the plea's) what really hurt. I didn't even know I had feet. I felt numb. My head was just floating. There was no feeling, except a state of suspended animation. . . . For a brief moment, I almost hesitated. I almost said not guilty. If I had been alone, I would have fought, but my family. . . .

The traumatic nature of this moment lies, in part, in the offender's feeling that only one aspect of his life is being considered. From the offender's point of view his crime represents only one small part of his life. It does not typify his inner self, and to judge him solely on the basis of this one event seems an atrocious injustice to the offender.

For some the memory of the event is so painful that they want to obliterate it entirely, as the two following quotations illustrate.

> I want quiet. I want to forget. I want to cut with the past.

> I've already divorced myself from the problem. I don't even want to hear the names of certain people ever again. It brings me pain.

For others, rage rather than embarrassment seemed to be the dominant emotion.

> I never really felt any embarrassment over the whole thing. I felt rage and it wasn't false or self-serving. It was really (something) to see this thing in action and recognize what the whole legal system has come to through its development, and the abuse of the grand jury system and the abuse of the indictment system. . . .

The role of the news media in the process of punishment and stigmatization should not be overlooked. All offenders whose cases were reported on by the news media were either embarrassed or embittered or both by the public exposure.

> The only one I am bitter at is the newspapers, as many people are. They are unfair because you can't get even. They can say things that are untrue, and let me say this to you. They wrote an article on me that was so blasphemous, that was so horrible. They painted me as an insidious miserable creature, wringing out the last penny. . . .

Offenders whose cases were not reported on by the news media expressed relief at having avoided that kind of embarrassment, sometimes saying that greater publicity would have been worse than any sentence they could have received.

In court, defense lawyers are fond of presenting white-collar offenders as having suffered enough by virtue of the humiliation of public adjudication as criminals. On the other hand, prosecutors present them as cavalier individuals who arrogantly ignore the law and brush off its weak efforts to stigmatize them as criminals. Neither of these stereotypes is entirely accurate. The subjective effects of conviction on white-collar offenders are varied and complex. One suspects that this is true of all offenders, not only white-collar offenders.

The emotional responses of offenders to conviction have not been the subject of extensive research. However, insofar as an individual's emotional response to adjudication may influence the deterrent or crime-reinforcing impact of punishment on him or her, further study might reveal why some offenders stop their criminal behavior while others go on to careers in crime (Casper 1978, 80).

Although the offenders displayed a variety of different emotions with respect to their experiences, they were nearly unanimous in denying basic criminality. To see how white-collar offenders justify and excuse their crimes, we turn to their accounts. The small number of cases rules out the use of any elaborate classification techniques. Nonetheless, it is useful to group offenders by offense when presenting their interpretations.

ANTITRUST VIOLATORS[2]

Four of the offenders have been convicted of antitrust violations, all in the same case involving the building and contracting industry. Four major themes characterized their accounts. First, antitrust offenders focused on the everyday character and historical continuity of their offenses.

> It was a way of doing business before we even got into the business. So it was like why do you brush your teeth in the morning or something. . . . It was part of the everyday. . . . It was a method of survival.

---

[2]Antitrust laws date back to the end of the nineteenth century. They are intended to promote fair business practices. For example, it is a violation of antitrust laws for business leaders to get together (or "collude") to fix consumer prices at artificially high levels.—Ed.

The offenders argued that they were merely following established and necessary industry practices. These practices were presented as being necessary for the well-being of the industry as a whole, not to mention their own companies. Further, they argued that cooperation among competitors was either allowed or actively promoted by the government in other industries and professions.

The second theme emphasized by the offenders was the characterization of their actions as blameless. They admitted talking to competitors and admitted submitting intentionally noncompetitive bids. However, they presented these practices as being done not for the purpose of rigging prices nor to make exorbitant profits. Rather, the everyday practices of the industry required them to occasionally submit bids on projects they really did not want to have. To avoid the effort and expense of preparing full-fledged bids, they would call a competitor to get a price to use. Such a situation might arise, for example, when a company already had enough work for the time being, but was asked by a valued customer to submit a bid anyway.

> All you want to do is show a bid, so that in some cases it was for as small a reason as getting your deposit back on the plans and specs. So you just simply have no interest in getting the job and just call to see if you can find someone to give you a price to use, so that you didn't have to go through the expense of an entire bid preparation. Now that is looked on very unfavorably, and it is a technical violation, but it was strictly an opportunity to keep your name in front of a desired customer. Or you may find yourself in a situation where somebody is doing work for a customer, has done work for many, many years and is totally acceptable, totally fair. There is no problem. But suddenly they (the customer) get an idea that they ought to have a few tentative figures, and you're called in, and you are in a moral dilemma. There's really no reason for you to attempt to compete in that circumstance. And so there was a way to back out.

Managed in this way, an action that appears on the surface to be a straightforward and conscious violation of antitrust regulations becomes merely a harmless business practice that happens to be a "technical violation." The offender can then refer to his personal history to verify his claim that, despite technical violations, he is in reality a law-abiding person. In the words of one offender, "Having been in the business for 33 years, you don't just automatically become a criminal overnight."

Third, offenders were very critical of the motives and tactics of prosecutors. Prosecutors were accused of being motivated solely by the opportunity for personal advancement presented by winning a big case. Further, they were accused of employing prosecution selectively and using tactics that allowed the most culpable offenders to go free. The Department of Justice was painted as using antitrust prosecutions for political purposes.

The fourth theme emphasized by the antitrust offenders involved a comparison between their crimes and the crimes of street criminals. Antitrust offenses differ in their mechanics from street crimes in that they are not committed in one place and at one time. Rather, they are spatially and temporally diffuse and are intermingled with legitimate behavior. In addition, the victims of antitrust offenses tend not to be identifiable individuals, as is the case with most street crimes. These characteristics are used by antitrust violators to contrast their own behavior with that of common stereotypes of criminality. Real crimes are pictured as discrete events that have beginnings and ends and involve individuals who directly and purposely victimize someone else in a particular place and at a particular time.

> It certainly wasn't a premeditated type of thing in our cases as far as I can see. . . . To me it's different than—and I sitting down and we plan, well, we're going to rob this bank tomorrow and premeditatedly go in there. . . . That wasn't the case at all. . . . It wasn't like sitting down and planning I'm going to rob this bank type of thing. . . . It was just a common everyday way of doing business and surviving.

A consistent thread running through all of the interviews was the necessity for antitrust-like practices, given the realities of the business world. Offenders seemed to define the situation in such a manner that two sets of rules could be seen to apply. On the one hand, there are the legislatively determined rules—laws—which govern how one is to conduct one's business affairs. On the other hand, there is a higher set of rules based on the concepts of profit and survival, which are taken to define what it means to be in business in a capitalistic society. These rules do not just regulate behavior; rather, they constitute or create the behavior in question. If one is not trying to make a profit or trying to keep one's business going, then one is not really "in business." Following Searle (1969, 33–41), the former type of rule can be called a regulative rule and the latter type a constitutive rule. In certain situations, one may have to violate a regulative rule in order to conform to the more basic constitutive rule of the activity in which one is engaged.

This point can best be illustrated through the use of an analogy involving competitive games. Trying to win is a constitutive rule of competitive games in the sense that if one is not trying to win, one is not really playing the game. In competitive games, situations may arise where a player deliberately breaks the rules even though he knows or expects he will be caught. In the game of basketball, for example, a player may deliberately foul an opponent to prevent him from making a sure basket. In this instance, one would understand that the fouler was trying to win by gambling that the opponent would not make the free throws. The player violates the rule against fouling in order to follow the higher rule of trying to win.

Trying to make a profit or survive in business can be thought of as a constitutive rule of capitalist economies. The laws that govern *how* one is allowed to make a profit are regulative rules, which can understandably be subordinated to the rules of trying to survive and profit. From the offender's point of view, he is doing what businessmen in our society are supposed to do—that is, stay in business and make a profit. Thus, an individual who violates society's laws or regulations in certain situations may actually conceive of himself as thereby acting more in accord with the central ethos of his society than if he had been a strict observer of its law. One might suggest, following Denzin (1977), that for businessmen in the building and contracting industry, an informal structure exists below the articulated legal structure, one which frequently supersedes the legal structure. The informal structure may define as moral and "legal" certain actions that the formal legal structure defines as immoral and "illegal."

TAX VIOLATORS

Six of the offenders interviewed were convicted of income tax violations. Like antitrust violators, tax violators can rely upon the complexity of the tax laws and an historical tradition in which cheating on taxes is not really criminal. Tax offenders would claim that everybody cheats somehow on their taxes and present themselves as victims of an unlucky break, because they got caught.

> Everybody cheats on their income tax, 95% of the people. Even if it's for ten dollars it's the same principle. I didn't cheat. I just didn't know how to report it.

The widespread belief that cheating on taxes is endemic helps to lend credence to the offender's claim to have been singled out and to be no more guilty than most people.

Tax offenders were more likely to have acted as individuals rather than as part of a group and, as a result, were more prone to account for their offenses by referring to them as either mistakes or the product of special circumstances. Violations were presented as simple errors which resulted from ignorance and poor recordkeeping. Deliberate intention to steal from the government for personal benefit was denied.

> I didn't take the money. I have no bank account to show for all this money, where all this money is at that I was supposed to have. They never found the money, ever. There is no Swiss bank account, believe me.

> My records were strictly one big mess. That's all it was. If only I had an accountant, this wouldn't even of happened. No way in God's creation would this ever have happened.

Other offenders would justify their actions by admitting that they were wrong while painting their motives as altruistic rather than criminal. Criminality was denied because they did not set out to deliberately cheat the government for their own personal gain. Like the antitrust offenders discussed above, one tax violator distinguished between his own crime and the crimes of real criminals.

> I'm not a criminal. That is, I'm not a criminal from the standpoint of taking a gun and doing this and that. I'm a criminal from the standpoint of making a mistake, a serious mistake. . . . The thing that really got me involved in it is my feeling for the employees here, certain employees that are my right hand. In order to save them a certain amount of taxes and things like that, I'd extend money to them in cash, and the money came from these sources that I took it from. You know, cash sales and things of that nature, but practically all of it was turned over to the employees, because of my feeling for them.

All of the tax violators pointed out that they had no intention of deliberately victimizing the government. None of them denied the legitimacy of the tax laws, nor did they claim that they cheated because the government is not representative of the people (Conklin 1977, 99). Rather, as a result of ignorance or for altruistic reasons, they made decisions which turned out to be criminal when viewed from the perspective of the law. While they acknowledged the technical criminality of their actions, they tried to show that what they did was not criminally motivated.

VIOLATIONS OF FINANCIAL TRUST

Four offenders were involved in violations of financial trust. Three were banking officers who embezzled or misapplied funds, and the fourth was a union official who embezzled from a union pension fund.[3] Perhaps because embezzlement is one crime in this sample that can be considered *mala in se,* these offenders were much more forthright about their crimes. Like the other offenders, the embezzlers would not go so far as to say "I am a criminal," but they did say "What I did was wrong, was criminal, and I knew it was." Thus, the embezzlers were unusual in that they explicitly admitted responsibility for their crimes. . . .

Unlike tax evasion, which can be excused by reference to the complex nature of tax regulations or antitrust violations, which can be justified as for the good of the organization as a whole, embezzlement requires deliberate action on the part of the offender and is almost inevitably committed for personal reasons. The crime of embezzlement, therefore, cannot be accounted for by using the same techniques that tax violators or antitrust violators do. The act itself can only be explained by showing that one was under extraordinary circumstances which explain one's uncharacteristic behavior. Three of the offenders referred explicitly to extraordinary circumstances and

presented the offense as an aberration in their life history. For example, one offender described his situation in this manner:

> As a kid, I never even—you know kids will sometimes shoplift from the dime store— I never even did that. I had never stolen a thing in my life and that was what was so unbelievable about the whole thing, but there were some psychological and personal questions that I wasn't dealing with very well. I wasn't terribly happily married. I was married to a very strong-willed woman and it just wasn't working out.

The offender in this instance goes on to explain how, in an effort to impress his wife, he lived beyond his means and fell into debt.

A structural characteristic of embezzlement also helps the offender demonstrate his essential lack of criminality. Embezzlement is integrated into ordinary occupational routines. The illegal action does not stand out clearly against the surrounding set of legal actions. Rather, there is a high degree of surface correspondence, the offender must exercise some restraint when committing his crime. The embezzler must be discreet in his stealing; he cannot take all of the money available to him without at the same time revealing crime. Once exposed, the offender can point to this restraint on his part as evidence that he is not really a criminal. That is, he can compare what happened with what could have happened in order to show how much more serious the offense could have been if he was really a criminal at heart.

> What I could have done if I had truly had a devious criminal mind and perhaps if I had been a little smarter—and I am not saying that with any degree of pride or any degree of modesty whatever, [as] it's being smarter in a bad, an evil way—I could have pulled this off on a grander scale and I might still be doing it.

Even though the offender is forthright about admitting his guilt, he makes a distinction

---

[3]Embezzlement is not just theft. Embezzlement is theft from someone who has entrusted his or her money or property to you.—Ed.

between himself and someone with a truly "devious criminal mind."

Contrary to Cressey's (1953, 57–66) findings, none of the embezzlers claimed that their offenses were justified because they were underpaid or badly treated by their employers. Rather, attention was focused on the unusual circumstances surrounding the offense and its atypical character when compared to the rest of the offender's life. This strategy is for the most part determined by the mechanics and organizational format of the offense itself. Embezzlement occurs within the organization but not for the organization. It cannot be committed accidentally or out of ignorance. It can be accounted for only by showing that the actor "was not himself" at the time of the offense or was under such extraordinary circumstances that embezzlement was an understandable response to an unfortunate situation. This may explain the finding that embezzlers tend to produce accounts that are viewed as more sufficient by the justice system than those produced by other offenders (Rothman and Gandossy 1982). The only plausible option open to a convicted embezzler trying to explain his offense is to admit responsibility while justifying the action, an approach that apparently strikes a responsive chord with judges.

FRAUD AND FALSE STATEMENTS

Ten offenders were convicted of some form of fraud or false statements charge. Unlike embezzlers, tax violators, or antitrust violators, these offenders were much more likely to deny committing any crime at all. Seven of the ten claimed that they, personally, were innocent of any crime, although each admitted that fraud had occurred. Typically, they claimed to have been set up by associates and to have been wrongfully convicted by the U.S. Attorney handling the case. One might call this the scapegoat strategy. Rather than admitting technical wrongdoing and then justifying or excusing it, the offender attempts to paint himself as a victim by shifting the blame entirely to another party. Prosecutors were presented as being either ignorant or politically motivated.

The outright denial of any crime whatsoever is unusual compared to the other types of offenders studied here. It may result from the nature of the crime of fraud. By definition, fraud involves a conscious attempt on the part of one or more persons to mislead others. While it is theoretically possible to accidentally violate the antitrust and tax laws, or to violate them for altruistic reasons, it is difficult to imagine how one could accidentally mislead someone else for his or her own good. Furthermore, in many instances, fraud is an aggressively acquisitive crime. The offender develops a scheme to bilk other people out of money or property, and does this not because of some personal problem but because the scheme is an easy way to get rich. Stock swindles, fraudulent loan scams, and so on are often so large and complicated that they cannot possibly be excused as foolish and desperate solutions to personal problems. Thus, those involved in large-scale frauds do not have the option open to most embezzlers of presenting themselves as persons responding defensively to difficult personal circumstances.

Furthermore, because fraud involves a deliberate attempt to mislead another, the offender who fails to remove himself from the scheme runs the risk of being shown to have a guilty mind. That is, he is shown to possess the most essential element of modern conceptions of criminality: an intent to harm another. His inner self would in this case be exposed as something other than what it has been presented as, and all of his previous actions would be subject to reinterpretation in light of his new perspective. For this reason, defrauders are most prone to denying any crime at all. The cooperative and conspiratorial nature of many fraudulent schemes makes it possible to put the blame on someone else and to present oneself as a scapegoat. Typically, this is done by claiming to have been duped by others.

Two illustrations of this strategy are presented below.

> I figured I wasn't guilty, so it wouldn't be that hard to disprove it, until, as I say, I went to court and all of a sudden they start bringing in these guys out of the woodwork implicating me that I never saw. Lot of it could be proved that I never saw.

> Inwardly, I personally felt that the only crime that I committed was not telling on these guys. Not that I deliberately, intentionally committed a crime against the system. My only crime was that I should have had the guts to tell on these guys, what they were doing, rather than putting up with it and then trying to gradually get out of the system without hurting them or without them thinking I was going to snitch on them.

Of the three offenders who admitted committing crimes, two acted alone and the third acted with only one other person. Their accounts were similar to the others presented earlier and tended to focus on either the harmless nature of their violations or on the unusual circumstances that drove them to commit their crimes. One claimed that his violations were only technical and that no one besides himself had been harmed.

> First of all, no money was stolen or anything of that nature. The bank didn't lose any money. . . . What I did was a technical violation. I made a mistake. There's no question about that, but the bank lost no money.

Another offender who directly admitted his guilt was involved in a check-kiting scheme. In a manner similar to embezzlers, he argued that his actions were motivated by exceptional circumstances.

> I was faced with the choice of all of a sudden, and I mean now, closing the doors or doing something else to keep that business open. . . . I'm not going to tell you that this wouldn't have

happened if I'd had time to think it over, because I think it probably would have. You're sitting there with a dying patient. You are going to try to keep him alive.

In the other fraud cases more individuals were involved, and it was possible and perhaps necessary for each offender to claim that he was not really the culprit.

Discussion: Offenses, Accounts, and Degradation Ceremonies

The investigation, prosecution, and conviction of a white-collar offender involves him in a very undesirable status passage (Glaser and Strauss 1971). The entire process can be viewed as a long and drawn-out degradation ceremony with the prosecutor as the chief denouncer and the offender's family and friends as the chief witnesses. The offender is moved from the status of law-abiding citizen to that of convicted felon. Accounts are developed to defeat the process of identity transformation that is the object of a degradation ceremony. They represent the offender's attempt to diminish the effect of his legal transformation and to prevent its becoming a publicly validated label. It can be suggested that the accounts developed by white-collar offenders take the forms that they do for two reasons: (1) the forms are required to defeat the success of the degradation ceremony, and (2) the specific forms used are the ones available given the mechanics, history, and organizational context of the offenses.

Three general patterns in accounting strategies stand out in the data. Each can be characterized by the subject matter on which it focuses: the event (offense), the perpetrator (offender), or the denouncer (prosecutor). These are the natural subjects of accounts in that to be successful, a degradation ceremony requires each of these elements to be presented in a particular manner (Garfinkel 1956). If an account giver can undermine the presentation of one or more of the elements, then the effect of the ceremony can be reduced. Although there are overlaps in the accounting strategies used by the various types of offenders, and while any given offender may use more than one strategy, it appears that accounting strategies and offenses correlate. . . .

References

Casper, Jonathan D. 1978. *Criminal Courts: The Defendant's Perspective.* Washington, DC: U.S. Department of Justice.

Conklin, John E. 1977. *Illegal But Not Criminal: Business Crime in America.* Englewood Cliffs, NJ: Prentice-Hall.

Cressey, Donald. 1953. *Other People's Money.* New York: Free Press.

Denzin, Norman K. 1977. "Notes on the Criminogenic Hypothesis: A Case Study of the American Liquor Industry." *American Sociological Review* 42: 905–920.

Denzin, Norman K. 1984. *On Understanding Emotion.* San Francisco: Jossey-Bass.

Edelhertz, Herbert. 1970. *The Nature, Impact, and Prosecution of White Collar Crime.* Washington, DC: U.S. Government Printing Office.

Garfinkel, Harold. 1956. "Conditions of Successful Degradation Ceremonies." *American Journal of Sociology* 61: 420–424.

Glaser, Barney G., and Anselm L. Strauss. 1971. *Status Passage.* Chicago: Aldine.

Katz, Jack. 1979. "Legality and Equality: Plea Bargaining in the Prosecution of White-Collar Crimes." *Law and Society Review* 13: 431–460.

Rothman, Martin, and Robert F. Gandossy. 1982. "Sad Tales: The Accounts of White-Collar Defendants and the Decision to Sanction." *Pacific Sociological Review* 4: 449–473.

Searle, John R. 1969. *Speech Acts.* Cambridge: Cambridge University Press.

Questions

1. Look back at the list of "techniques of neutralization" that you made in response to the first question following reading 30 about student cheating. Which of the explanations offered by white-collar criminals interviewed by Benson used any of the techniques of neutralization?

2. A single white-collar criminal may steal as much money as a whole host of burglars. Why, then, do white-collar offenders deny that they are as bad as street criminals? In your judgment, who is more criminal—the thief who steals $50 from a convenience store or the thief who steals $100,000 from an insurance company?

3. Consider the student cheater who says that "cheating is the only way to get through all the ridiculous demands that teachers place on us" and the insurance executive who says that "breaking the law is the only way to do business in this country." What, if anything, do they have in common?

32

THE LAND OF OPPORTUNITY

James Loewen

Many of us who teach sociology in U.S. colleges are frequently puzzled and even stunned by students' reactions to the subject of social inequality. If we blithely explain the extent and consequences of social inequality in the United States, we find our students regarding us as if we are sadly misinformed or (less charitably) have simply gone mad: "What do you mean America is not the land of equal opportunity?" Sometimes students' responses are downright hostile.

Still, if there is one thing sociologists know, it is that there is a great deal of inequality in the United States. The question is: Why does this fact come as such a big surprise to students? Perhaps James Loewen has the answer. He says that students graduate from high school as "terrible sociologists." As you will read in this 1995 piece, he puts part of the blame for this situation on the content of those social studies and history texts to which students were subjected in elementary, middle, and high school. Loewen is confident that he is right. He explains:

> For several years I have been lugging around twelve [history] textbooks, taking them seriously as works of history and ideology, studying what they say and don't say, and trying to figure out why. I chose the twelve as representing the range of textbooks available for history courses. . . . These twelve textbooks have been my window into the world of what high school students carry home, read, memorize, and forget. In addition, I have spent many hours observing high school history classes in Mississippi, Vermont, and the Washington, DC, metropolitan area, and more hours interviewing high school history teachers.

High school students have eyes, ears, and television sets (all too many have their own TV sets), so they know a lot about relative privilege in America. They measure their family's social position against that of other families, and their community's position against other communities. Middle-class students, especially, know little about how the American class structure works, however, and nothing at all about how it has changed over time. These students do not leave high school merely ignorant of the workings of the class structure; they come out as terrible sociologists. "Why are people poor?" I have asked first-year college students.

Or, if their own class position is one of relative privilege, "Why is your family well off?" The answers I've received, to characterize them charitably, are half-formed and naive. The students blame the poor for not being successful. They have no understanding of the ways that opportunity is not equal in America and no notion that social structure pushes people around, influencing the ideas they hold and the lives they fashion.

High school history textbooks can take some of the credit for this state of affairs. Some textbooks cover certain high points of labor history, such as the 1894 Pullman strike near Chicago that President Cleveland broke with federal troops,[1] or the 1911 Triangle Shirtwaist fire that killed 146 women in New York City,[2] but the most recent event mentioned in most books is the Taft-Hartley Act of fifty years ago.[3] No book mentions the Hormel meat-packers' strike in the mid-1980s or the air traffic controllers' strike broken by President Reagan. Nor do textbooks describe any continuing issues facing labor, such as the growth of multinational corporations and their exporting of jobs overseas. With such omissions, textbook authors can construe labor history as

something that happened long ago, like slavery, and that, like slavery, was corrected long ago. It logically follows that unions appear anachronistic. The idea that they might be necessary in order for workers to have a voice in the workplace goes unstated.

Textbooks' treatments of events in labor history are never anchored in any analysis of social class. This amounts to delivering the footnotes instead of the lecture! Six of the dozen high school American history textbooks I examined contain no index listing at all for "social class," "social stratification," "class structure," "income distribution," "inequality," or any conceivably related topic. Not one book lists "upper class," "working class," or "lower class." Two of the textbooks list "middle class," but only to assure students that America is a middle-class country. "Except for slaves, most of the colonists were members of the 'middling ranks,'" says *Land of Promise,* and nails home the point that we are a middle-class country by asking students to "Describe three 'middle-class' values that united free Americans of all classes." Several of the textbooks note the explosion of middle-class suburbs after World War II. Talking about the middle class is hardly equivalent to discussing social stratification, however; in fact, as Gregory Mantsios (1988) has pointed out, "such references appear to be acceptable precisely because they mute class differences."

Stressing how middle-class we all are is particularly problematic today, because the proportion of households earning between 75 percent and 125 percent of the median income has fallen steadily since 1967. The Reagan-Bush administrations accelerated this shrinkage of the middle class, and most families who left its ranks fell rather than rose. This is the kind of historical trend one would think history books would take as appropriate subject matter, but only four of the twelve books in my sample provide any analysis of social stratification in the United States. Even these fragmentary analyses are set

---

[1]The trouble started when George M. Pullman, owner of the Pullman Palace Car Company, refused even to discuss his employees' grievances (for example, deep wage cuts) with them. The workers' cause was taken up by the American Railway Union, which started a boycott against all Pullman train cars. Because Pullman cars were used on nearly every train running, the boycott brought the entire U.S. rail system to a standstill. President Cleveland called in federal troops to break the strike (Cleveland justified his intervention by claiming that the boycott was interfering with the U.S. mail).—Ed.

[2]The fire broke out on Saturday, March 25. Smoke was first seen on the eighth floor of the building where some 500 people—mostly female—were working. Escape was nearly impossible because the owners of the factory had locked the doors in order to keep their employees at work. Many women and girls jumped to their deaths from the windows of the building rather than face death in fire.—Ed.

[3]The Taft-Hartley Act of 1947 placed serious restrictions on union activities, including the requirement that union leaders swear under oath that they weren't communists.—Ed.

mostly in colonial America. *Land of Promise* lives up to its reassuring title by heading its discussion of social class "Social Mobility." "One great difference between colonial and European society was that the colonists had more social mobility," echoes *The American Tradition.* "In contrast with contemporary Europe, eighteenth-century America was a shining land of equality and opportunity—with the notorious exception of slavery," chimes in *The American Pageant.* Although *The Challenge of Freedom* identifies three social classes—upper, middle, and lower—among whites in colonial society, compared to Europe "there was greater *social mobility.*"

Never mind that the most violent class conflicts in American history—Bacon's Rebellion and Shays's Rebellion[4]—took place in and just after colonial times. Textbooks still say that colonial society was relatively classless and marked by upward mobility. And things have gotten rosier since. "By 1815," *The Challenge of Freedom* assures us, two classes had withered away and "America was a country of middle class people and of middle class goals." This book returns repeatedly, at intervals of every fifty years or so, to the theme of how open opportunity is in America. "In the years after 1945, *social mobility*—movement from one social class to another—became more widespread in America," *Challenge* concludes. "This meant that people had a better chance to move upward in society." The stress on upward mobility is striking. There is almost nothing in any of these textbooks about class inequalities or barriers of any kind to social mobility. "What conditions made it possible for poor white immigrants to become richer in the colonies?" *Land of Promise* asks. "What

conditions made/make it difficult?" goes unasked. Textbook authors thus present an America in which, as preachers were fond of saying in the nineteenth century, men start from "humble origins" and attain "the most elevated positions."

Social class is probably the single most important variable in society. From womb to tomb, it correlates with almost all other social characteristics of people that we can measure. Affluent expectant mothers are more likely to get prenatal care, receive current medical advice, and enjoy general health, fitness, and nutrition. Many poor and working-class mothers-to-be first contact the medical profession in the last month, sometimes the last hours, of their pregnancies. Rich babies come out healthier and weighing more than poor babies. The infants go home to very different situations. Poor babies are more likely to have high levels of poisonous lead in their environments and their bodies. Rich babies get more time and verbal interaction with their parents and higher quality day care when not with their parents. When they enter kindergarten, and through the twelve years that follow, rich children benefit from suburban schools that spend two to three times as much money per student as schools in inner cities or impoverished rural areas. Poor children are taught in classes that are often 50 percent larger than the classes of affluent children. Differences such as these help account for the higher school-dropout rate among poor children.

Even when poor children are fortunate enough to attend the same school as rich children, they encounter teachers who expect only children of affluent families to know the right answers. Social science research shows that teachers are often surprised and even distressed when poor children excel. Teachers and counselors believe they can predict who is "college material." Since many working-class children give off the wrong signals, even in first grade, they end up in the "general education" track in high school. "If you are the child of low-income

---

[4]Bacon's Rebellion (1676) involved a bloody dispute between settlers and colonial authorities. The settlers' complaints included the fact that the authorities were not providing protection against hostile Native Americans. Shays's Rebellion (1786–1787) resulted from the refusal of Massachusetts legislators to assist debt-ridden farmers who were facing foreclosures.—Ed.

parents, the chances are good that you will receive limited and often careless attention from adults in your high school," in the words of Theodore Sizer's best-selling study of American high schools, *Horace's Compromise.* "If you are the child of upper-middle-income parents, the chances are good that you will receive substantial and careful attention" (quoted in Karp 1985, 73). Researcher Reba Page (1987) has provided vivid accounts of how high school American history courses use rote learning to turn off lower-class students. Thus schools have put into practice Woodrow Wilson's recommendation: "We want one class of persons to have a liberal education, and we want another class of persons, a very much larger class of necessity in every society, to forgo the privilege of a liberal education[5] and fit themselves to perform specific difficult manual tasks" (quoted in Lapham 1991).

As if this unequal home and school life were not enough, rich teenagers then enroll in the Princeton Review or other coaching sessions for the Scholastic Aptitude Test. Even without coaching, affluent children are advantaged because their background is similar to that of the test-makers, so they are comfortable with the vocabulary and subtle subcultural assumptions of the test. To no one's surprise, social class correlates strongly with SAT scores.

All these are among the reasons why social class predicts the rate of college attendance and the type of college chosen more effectively than does any other factor, including intellectual ability, however measured. After college, most affluent children get white-collar jobs, most working-class children get blue-collar jobs, and the class differences continue. As adults, rich people are more likely to have hired an attorney and to be a member of formal organizations that increase their civic power.

Poor people are more likely to watch TV. Because affluent families can save some money while poor families must spend what they make, wealth differences are ten times larger than income differences. Therefore most poor and working-class families cannot accumulate the down payment required to buy a house, which in turn shuts them out from our most important tax shelter, the writeoff of home mortgage interest. Working-class parents cannot afford to live in elite subdivisions or hire high-quality day care, so the process of educational inequality replicates itself in the next generation. Finally, affluent Americans also have longer life expectancies than lower- and working-class people, the largest single cause of which is better access to health care. Echoing the results of Helen Keller's study of blindness, research has determined that poor health is not distributed randomly about the social structure but is concentrated in the lower class. Social Security then becomes a huge transfer system, using monies contributed by all Americans to pay benefits disproportionately to longer-lived affluent Americans.

Ultimately, social class determines how people think about social class. When asked if poverty in America is the fault of the poor or the fault of the system, 57 percent of business leaders blamed the poor; just 9 percent blamed the system. Labor leaders showed sharply reversed choices: only 15 percent said the poor were at fault while 56 percent blamed the system. (Some replied "don't know" or chose a middle position.) The largest single difference between our two main political parties lies in how their members think about social class: 55 percent of Republicans blamed the poor for their poverty, while only 13 percent blamed the system for it; 68 percent of Democrats, on the other hand, blamed the system, while only 5 percent blamed the poor (Verba and Orren 1985, 72–75).

Few of these statements are news, I know, which is why I have not documented most of them, but the majority of high school students

---

[5]"Liberal education," by definition, is education suited for the free (or liberated) citizen. The contrasting form of education is not "conservative education," but "vocational training."—Ed.

do not know or understand these ideas. Moreover, the processes have changed over time, for the class structure in America today is not the same as it was in 1890, let alone in colonial America. Yet in *Land of Promise,* for example, social class goes unmentioned after 1670.

Many teachers compound the problem by avoiding talking about social class. Recent interviews with teachers "revealed that they had a much broader knowledge of the economy, both academically and experientially, than they admitted in class." Teachers "expressed fear that students might find out about the injustices and inadequacies of their economic and political institutions" (McNeil 1983, 116). . . .

Historically, social class is intertwined with all kinds of events and processes in our past. Our governing system was established by rich men, following theories that emphasized government as a bulwark of the propertied class. Although rich himself, James Madison worried about social inequality and wrote *The Federalist* #10 to explain how the proposed government would not succumb to the influence of the affluent. Madison did not fully succeed, according to Edward Pessen, who examined the social-class backgrounds of all American presidents through Reagan. Pessen found that more than 40 percent hailed from the upper class, mostly from the upper fringes of that elite group, and another 15 percent originated in families located between the upper and upper-middle classes. More than 25 percent came from a solid upper-middle-class background, leaving just six presidents, or 15 percent, to come from the middle and lower-middle classes and just one, Andrew Johnson, representing any part of the lower class. For good reason, Pessen (1984) titled his book *The Log Cabin Myth.* While it was sad when the great ship *Titanic* went down, as the old song refrain goes, it was saddest for the lower classes: among women, only 4 of 143 first-class passengers were lost, while 15 of 93 second-class passengers drowned, along with 81 of 179 third-class women and girls. The crew ordered third-class passengers to remain below deck, holding some of them there at gunpoint (Hollingshead and Redlich 1958). More recently, social class played a major role in determining who fought in the Vietnam War: sons of the affluent won educational and medical deferments through most of the conflict (Baskir and Strauss 1986). Textbooks and teachers ignore all this.

Teachers may avoid social class out of a laudable desire not to embarrass their charges. If so, their concern is misguided. When my students from nonaffluent backgrounds learn about the class system, they find the experience liberating. Once they see the social processes that have helped keep their families poor, they can let go of their negative self-image about being poor. If to understand is to pardon, for working-class children to understand how stratification works is to pardon *themselves* and their families. Knowledge of the social-class system also reduces the tendency of Americans from other social classes to blame the victim for being poor. Pedagogically, stratification provides a gripping learning experience. Students are fascinated to discover how the upper class wields disproportionate power relating to everything from energy bills in Congress to zoning decisions in small towns.

Consider a white ninth-grade student taking American history in a predominantly middle-class town in Vermont. Her father tapes Sheetrock, earning an income that in slow construction seasons leaves the family quite poor. Her mother helps out by driving a school bus part-time, in addition to taking care of her two younger siblings. The girl lives with her family in a small house, a winterized former summer cabin, while most of her classmates live in large suburban homes. How is this girl to understand her poverty? Since history textbooks present the American past as 390 years of progress and portray our society as a land of opportunity in which folks get what they deserve and deserve what they get, the failures of working-class Americans to transcend their class origin inevitably get laid at their own doorsteps.

Within the white working-class community the girl will probably find few resources—teachers, church parishioners, family members—who can tell her of heroes or struggles among people of her background, for, except in pockets of continuing class conflict, the working class usually forgets its own history. More than any other group, white working-class students believe that they deserve their low status. A subculture of shame results. This negative self-image is foremost among what Richard Sennett and Jonathan Cobb have called "the hidden injuries of class" (1972). Several years ago, two students of mine provided a demonstration: they drove around Burlington, Vermont, in a big, nearly new, shiny black American car (probably a Lexus would be more appropriate today) and then in a battered ten-year-old subcompact. In each vehicle, when they reached a stoplight and it turned green, they waited until they were honked at before driving on. Motorists averaged less than seven seconds to honk at them in the subcompact, but in the luxury car the students enjoyed 13.2 seconds before anyone honked. Besides providing a good reason to buy a luxury car, this experiment shows how Americans unconsciously grant respect to the educated and successful. Since motorists of all social stations honked at the subcompact more readily, working-class drivers were in a sense disrespecting themselves while deferring to their betters. The biting quip "If you're so smart, why aren't you rich?" conveys the injury done to the self-image of the poor when the idea that America is a meritocracy goes unchallenged in school.

Part of the problem is that American history textbooks describe American education itself as meritocratic. A huge body of research confirms that education is dominated by the class structure and operates to replicate that structure in the next generation. Meanwhile, history textbooks blithely tell of such federal largesse to education as the Elementary and Secondary Education Act, passed under President Lyndon Johnson. Not one textbook offers any data on or analysis of inequality within educational institutions. None mentions how school districts in low-income areas labor under financial constraints so shocking that Jonathan Kozol (1991) calls them "savage inequalities." No textbook ever suggests that students might research the history of their own school and the population it serves. The only two textbooks that relate education to the class system at all see it as a remedy! Schooling "was a key to upward mobility in postwar America," in the words of *The Challenge of Freedom*.

The tendency of teachers and textbooks to avoid social class as if it were a dirty little secret only reinforces the reluctance of working-class families to talk about it. Paul Cowan has told of interviewing the children of Italian immigrant workers involved in the famous 1912 Lawrence, Massachusetts, mill strike. He spoke with the daughter of one of the Lawrence workers who testified at a Washington congressional hearing investigating the strike. The worker, Camella Teoli, then thirteen years old, had been scalped by a cotton-twisting machine just before the strike and had been hospitalized for several months. Her testimony "became front-page news all over America." But Teoli's daughter, interviewed in 1976 after her mother's death, could not help Cowan. Her mother had told her nothing of the incident, nothing of her trip to Washington, nothing about her impact on America's conscience—even though almost every day, the daughter "had combed her mother's hair into a bun that disguised the bald spot" (Gutman 1987, 386–390). A professional of working-class origin told me a similar story about being ashamed of her uncle "for being a steelworker." A certain defensiveness is built into working-class culture; even its successful acts of working-class resistance, like the

Lawrence strike, necessarily presuppose lower status and income, hence connote a certain inferiority. If the larger community is so good, as textbooks tell us it is, then celebrating or even passing on the memory of conflict with it seems somehow disloyal.

Textbooks do present immigrant history. Around the turn of the century immigrants dominated the American urban working class, even in cities as distant from seacoasts as Des Moines and Louisville. When more than 70 percent of the white population was native stock, less than 10 percent of the urban working class was (Gutman 1987, 386–390). But when textbooks tell the immigrant story, they emphasize Joseph Pulitzer, Andrew Carnegie, and their ilk—immigrants who made supergood. Several textbooks apply the phrases *rags to riches* or *land of opportunity* to the immigrant experience. Such legendary successes were achieved, to be sure, but they were the exceptions, not the rule. Ninety-five percent of the executives and financiers in America around the turn of the century came from upper-class or upper-middle-class backgrounds. Fewer than 3 percent started as poor immigrants or farm children. Throughout the nineteenth century, just 2 percent of American industrialists came from working-class origins (Miller 1962, 326–328). By concentrating on the inspiring exceptions, textbooks present immigrant history as another heartening confirmation of America as the land of unparalleled opportunity.

Again and again, textbooks emphasize how America has differed from Europe in having less class stratification and more economic and social mobility. This is another aspect of the archetype of American exceptionalism: our society has been uniquely fair. It would never occur to historians in, say, France or Australia, to claim that their society was exceptionally equalitarian. Does this treatment of the United States prepare students for reality? It certainly does not accurately describe our country today. Social scientists have on many occasions compared the degree of economic equality in the

United States with that in other industrial nations. Depending on the measure used, the United States has ranked sixth of six, seventh of seven, ninth of twelve, or fourteenth of fourteen (Verba and Orren 1985, 10). In the United States the richest fifth of the population earns eleven times as much income as the poorest fifth, one of the highest ratios in the industrialized world; in Great Britain the ratio is seven to one, in Japan just four to one (Mantsios 1988, 59). In Japan the average chief executive officer in an automobile-manufacturing firm makes 20 times as much as the average worker in an automobile assembly plant; in the United States he (and it is not she) makes 192 times as much (*Harper's* 1990, 19). The Jeffersonian conceit of a nation of independent farmers and merchants is also long gone: only one working American in thirteen is self-employed, compared to one in eight in Western Europe (*Harper's* 1993, 19). Thus not only do we have far fewer independent entrepreneurs compared to two hundred years ago, we have fewer compared to Europe today.

Since textbooks claim that colonial America was radically less stratified than Europe, they should tell their readers when inequality set in. It surely was not a recent development. By 1910 the top 1 percent of the United States population received more than a third of all personal income, while the bottom fifth got less than one-eighth (Tyack and Hansot 1981). This level of inequality was on a par with that in Germany or Great Britain (Williamson and Lindert 1980). If textbooks acknowledged inequality, then they could describe the changes in our class structure over time, which would introduce their students to fascinating historical debate.

For example, some historians argue that wealth in colonial society was more equally distributed than it is today and that economic inequality increased during the presidency of Andrew Jackson—a period known, ironically, as the age of the common man. Others believe that the flowering of the large corporation in the late nineteenth century made the class structure more rigid. Walter Dean Burnham has argued that the Republican presidential victory in 1896 (McKinley over Bryan) brought about a sweeping political realignment that changed "a fairly democratic regime into a rather broadly based oligarchy,"[6] so by the 1920s business controlled public policy (1965, 23–25). Clearly the gap between rich and poor, like the distance between blacks and whites, was greater at the end of the Progressive Era in 1920 than at its beginning around 1890 (Schwartz 1991, 94). The story is not all one of increasing stratification, for between the depression and the end of World War II income and wealth in America gradually became more equal. Distributions of income then remained reasonably constant until President Reagan took office in 1981, when inequality began to grow. Still other scholars think that little change has occurred since the Revolution. Lee Soltow (1989), for example, finds "surprising inequality of wealth and income" in America in 1798. At least for Boston, Stephan Thernstrom (1973) concludes that inequalities in life chances owing to social class show an eerie continuity. All this is part of American history. But it is not part of American history as taught in high school.

To social scientists, the level of inequality is a portentous thing to know about a society. When we rank countries by this variable, we find Scandinavian nations at the top, the most equal, and agricultural societies like Colombia and India near the bottom. The policies of the Reagan and Bush administrations, which openly favored the rich, abetted a trend already in motion, causing inequality to increase measurably between 1981 and 1992. For the United States to move perceptibly toward Colombia in social inequality is a development of no small import (Danziger and Gottschalf 1993; Kohn 1990; Macrobert 1984). Surely high school students would be interested to learn that in 1950 physicians made two and a half times what unionized industrial workers made but now make six times as much. Surely they need to understand that top managers of clothing firms, who used to earn fifty times what their American employees made, now make 1,500 times what their Malaysian workers earn. Surely it is wrong for our history textbooks and teachers to withhold the historical information that might prompt and inform discussion of these trends.

Why might they commit such a blunder? First and foremost, publisher censorship of textbook authors. "You always run the risk, if you talk about social class, of being labeled Marxist," the editor for social studies and history at one of the biggest publishing houses told me. This editor communicates the taboo, formally or subtly, to every writer she works with, and she implied that most other editors do too.

Publisher pressure derives in part from textbook adoption boards and committees in states and school districts. These are subject in turn to pressure from organized groups and individuals who appear before them. Perhaps the most robust such lobby is Educational Research Analysts, led by Mel Gabler of Texas. Gabler's stable of right-wing critics regards even alleging that a textbook contains some class analysis as a devastating criticism. As one writer has put it, "Formulating issues in terms of class is unacceptable, perhaps even un-American" (Mantsios 1988). Fear of not winning adoption in Texas is a prime source of publisher angst, and might help explain why *Life and Liberty* limits its social-class analysis to colonial times in *England!* By contrast, "the colonies were places of great opportunity," even back then. Some Texans cannot easily be placated, however. Deborah L. Brezina, a Gabler ally, complained to the Texas textbook board that *Life and Liberty* describes America "as an unjust society," unfair to lower economic groups, and therefore should not be approved. Such pressure is hardly new. Harold Rugg's *Introduction to Problems of American Culture* and his popular history textbook,

---

[6]*Oligarchy* means "rule by a few"—as opposed to *aristocracy,* which means, technically, "rule by the best few."—Ed.

written during the depression, included some class analysis. In the early 1940s, according to Frances FitzGerald, the National Association of Manufacturers attacked Rugg's books, partly for this feature, and "brought to an end" social and economic analysis in American history textbooks (1979).

More often the influence of the upper class is less direct. The most potent rationale for class privilege in American history has been Social Darwinism,[7] an archetype that still has great power in American culture. The notion that people rise and fall in a survival of the fittest may not conform to the data on intergenerational mobility in the United States, but that has hardly caused the archetype to fade away from American education, particularly from American history classes (Tyack and Hansot 1981). Facts that do not fit with the archetype, such as the entire literature of social stratification, simply get left out. . . .

But isn't it nice simply to believe that America is equal? Maybe the "land of opportunity" archetype is an empowering myth— maybe believing in it might even help make it come true. For if students *think* the sky is the limit, they may reach for the sky, while if they don't, they won't.

The analogy of gender points to the problem with this line of thought. How could high school girls understand their place in American history if their textbooks told them that, from colonial America to the present, women have had equal opportunity for upward mobility and political participation? How could they then explain why no woman has been president? Girls would have to infer, perhaps unconsciously, that it has been their own gender's fault, a conclusion that is hardly empowering.

Textbooks do tell how women were denied the right to vote in many states until 1920 and faced other barriers to upward mobility. Textbooks also tell of barriers confronting racial minorities. The final question *Land of Promise* asks students following its "Social Mobility" section is "What social barriers prevented blacks, Indians, and women from competing on an equal basis with white male colonists?" After its passage extolling upward mobility, *The Challenge of Freedom* notes, "Not all people, however, enjoyed equal rights or an equal chance to improve their way of life," and goes on to address the issues of sexism and racism. But neither here nor anywhere else do *Promise* or *Challenge* (or most other textbooks) hint that opportunity might not be equal today for white Americans of the lower and working classes. Perhaps as a result, even business leaders and Republicans, the respondents statistically most likely to engage in what sociologists call "blaming the victim," blame the social system rather than African Americans for black poverty and blame the system rather than women for the latter's unequal achievement in the workplace. In sum, affluent Americans, like their textbooks, are willing to credit racial discrimination as the cause of poverty among blacks and Indians and sex discrimination as the cause of women's inequality but don't see class discrimination as the cause of poverty in general (Verba and Orren 1985, 72–75).

More than math or science, more even than American literature, courses in American history hold the promise of telling high school students how they and their parents, their communities, and their society came to be as they are. One way things are is unequal by social class. Although poor and working-class children usually cannot identify the cause of their alienation, history often turns them off because it justifies rather than explains the present. When these students react by dropping out, intellectually if not physically, their poor school performance helps convince them as well as their peers in the faster tracks that the system is meritocratic and that they themselves lack

---

[7]For a discussion of this concept, see chapter 1 in *The Practical Skeptic: Core Concepts in Sociology.*—Ed.

merit. In the end, the absence of social-class analysis in American history courses amounts to one more way that education in America is rigged against the working class.

References

Baskir, L., and W. Strauss. 1986. *Chance and Circumstance.* New York: Random House.

Bowles, S., and H. Gintis. 1976. *Schooling in Capitalist America.* New York: Basic Books.

Brezina, D. L. 1993. "Critique of *Life and Liberty*," distributed by Mel Gabler's Educational Research Analysts.

Burnham, W. D. 1965. "The Changing Shape of the American Political University." *American Political Science Review* 59: 23–25.

Danziger, S., and P. Gottschalf. 1993. *Uneven Tides.* New York: Sage.

FitzGerald, F. 1979. *America Revised.* New York: Vintage Books.

Gutman, H. 1987. *Power and Culture.* New York: Pantheon Books.

Harper's. 1990. "Index" (citing data from the United Automobile Workers; Chrysler Corp; "Notice of Annual Meeting of Stockholders"). April 1.

Harper's. 1993. "Index" (citing the Organization for Economic Cooperation and Development). January 19.

Hollingshead, A., and F. C. Redlich. 1958. *Social Class and Mental Illness.* New York: Wiley.

Karp, Walter. 1985. "Why Johnny Can't Think." *Harper's,* June, p. 73.

Kohn, A. 1990. *You Know What They Say. . . .* New York: HarperCollins.

Kozol, J. 1991. *Savage Inequalities.* New York: Crown.

Lapham, Lewis. 1991. "Notebook." *Harper's,* July, p. 10.

Macrobert, A. 1984. "The Unfairness of It All." *Vermont Vanguard Press,* September 30, pp. 12–13.

Mantsios, Gregory. 1988. "Class in America: Myths and Realities." In Paula S. Rothenberg (ed.), *Racism and Sexism: An Integrated Study.* New York: St. Martin's Press.

McNeil, Linda. 1983. "Teaching and Classroom Control." In M. W. Apple and L. Weis (eds.), *Ideology and Practice in Schooling.* Philadelphia: Temple University Press.

Miller, W. 1962. "American Historians and the Business Elite." In W. Miller (ed.), *Men in Business.* New York: Harper & Row.

Page, Reba. 1987. *The Lower-track Students' View of Curriculum.* Washington, DC: American Education Research Association.

Pessen, E. 1984. *The Log Cabin Myth.* New Haven, CT: Yale University Press.

Schwartz, B. 1991. "The Reconstruction of Abraham Lincoln," in D. Middleton and D. Edwards (eds.), *Collective Remembering.* London: Sage.

Sennett, R., and J. Cobb. 1972. *The Hidden Injuries of Class.* New York: Knopf.

Soltow, L. 1989. *Distribution of Wealth and Income in the United States in 1798.* Pittsburgh: University of Pittsburgh Press.

Thernstrom, S. 1973. *The Other Bostonians.* Cambridge, MA: Harvard University Press.

Tyack, D., and E. Hansot. 1981. "Conflict and Consensus in American Public Education." *Daedalus* 110: 11–12.

Verba, S., and G. Orren. 1985. *Equality in America.* Cambridge, MA: Harvard University Press.

Williamson and Lindert. 1980. *American Inequality: A Macroeconomic History.* New York: Academic Press.

Questions

1. Loewen asserts that high school students graduate as "terrible sociologists." To what extent do you agree or disagree with this assessment? Why?

2. Assuming that Loewen is correct about the "mythical" quality of the information given in high school history textbooks, what might be the function of these myths in American society? What might be the dysfunctions?

33

NICKEL AND DIMED

On (Not) Getting By in America

Barbara Ehrenreich

This article, published in 1999, eventually became the first chapter in Ehrenreich's book by the same title; it's an interesting but thoroughly depressing account of what it takes to survive on the proceeds of a minimum-wage job. In the introduction to her book, Ehrenreich stresses the fact that her experience represented the *best* case scenario: "A person with every advantage that ethnicity and education, health and motivation can confer attempting, in a time of exuberant prosperity, to survive in the economy's lowest depths."

At the beginning of June 1998 I leave behind everything that normally soothes the ego and sustains the body—home, career, companion, reputation, ATM card—for a plunge into the low-wage workforce. There, I become another, occupationally much diminished "Barbara Ehrenreich"—depicted on job-application forms as a divorced homemaker whose sole work experience consists of housekeeping in a few private homes. I am terrified, at the beginning, of being unmasked for what I am: a middle-class journalist setting out to explore the world that welfare mothers are entering, at the rate of approximately 50,000 a month, as welfare reform kicks in. Happily, though, my fears turn out to be entirely unwarranted: during a month of poverty and toil, my name goes unnoticed and for the most part unuttered. In this parallel universe where my father never got out of the mines and I never got through college, I am "baby," "honey," "blondie," and, most commonly, "girl."

My first task is to find a place to live. I figure that if I can earn $7 an hour—which, from the want ads, seems doable—I can afford to spend $500 on rent, or maybe, with severe economies, $600. In the Key West area, where I live, this pretty much confines me to flophouses and trailer homes—like the one, a pleasing fifteen-minute drive from town, that has no air-conditioning, no screens, no fans, no television, and, by way of diversion, only the challenge of evading the landlord's Doberman pinscher. The big problem with this place, though, is the rent, which at $675 a month is well beyond my reach. All right, Key West is expensive. But so is New York City, or the Bay Area, or Jackson Hole, or Telluride, or Boston, or any other place where tourists and the wealthy compete for living space with the people who clean their toilets and fry their hash browns.[1] Still, it is a

[1]According to the Department of Housing and Urban Development, the "fair-market rent" for an efficiency is $551 here in Monroe County, Florida. A comparable rent in the five boroughs of New York City is $704; in San Francisco, $713; and in the heart of Silicon Valley, $808. The fair-market rent for an area is defined as the amount that would be needed to pay rent plus utilities for "privately owned, decent, safe, and sanitary rental housing of a modest (non-luxury) nature with suitable amenities."

shock to realize that "trailer trash" has become, for me, a demographic category to aspire to.

So I decide to make the common trade-off between affordability and convenience, and go for a $500-a-month efficiency thirty miles up a two-lane highway from the employment opportunities of Key West, meaning forty-five minutes if there's no road construction and I don't get caught behind some sun-dazed Canadian tourists. I hate the drive, along a roadside studded with white crosses commemorating the more effective head-on collisions, but it's a sweet little place—a cabin, more or less, set in the swampy back yard of the converted mobile home where my landlord, an affable TV repairman, lives with his bartender girlfriend.

No, this is a purely objective, scientific sort of mission. The humanitarian rationale for welfare reform—as opposed to the more punitive and stingy impulses that may actually have motivated it—is that work will lift poor women out of poverty while simultaneously inflating their self-esteem and hence their future value in the labor market. Thus, whatever the hassles involved in finding child care, transportation, etc., the transition from welfare to work will end happily, in greater prosperity for all. Now there are many problems with this comforting prediction, such as the fact that the economy will inevitably undergo a downturn, eliminating many jobs. Even without a downturn, the influx of a million former welfare recipients into the low-wage labor market could depress wages by as much as 11.9 percent, according to the Economic Policy Institute (EPI) in Washington, D.C.

But is it really possible to make a living on the kinds of jobs currently available to unskilled people? Mathematically, the answer is no, as can be shown by taking $6 to $7 an hour, perhaps subtracting a dollar or two an hour for child care, multiplying by 160 hours a month, and comparing the result to the prevailing rents. According to the National Coalition for the Homeless, for example, in 1998 it took, on average nationwide, an hourly wage of $8.89 to afford a one-bedroom apartment, and the Preamble Center for Public Policy estimates that the odds against a typical welfare recipient's landing a job at such a "living wage" are about 97 to 1. If these numbers are right, low-wage work is not a solution to poverty and possibly not even to homelessness.

It may seem excessive to put this proposition to an experimental test. As certain family members keep unhelpfully reminding me, the viability of low-wage work could be tested, after a fashion, without ever leaving my study. I could just pay myself $7 an hour for eight hours a day, charge myself for room and board, and total up the numbers after a month. Why leave the people and work that I love? But I am an experimental scientist by training. In that business, you don't just sit at a desk and theorize; you plunge into the everyday chaos of nature, where surprises lurk in the most mundane measurements. Maybe, when I got into it, I would discover some hidden economies in the world of the low-wage worker. After all, if 30 percent of the workforce toils for less than $8 an hour, according to the EPI, they may have found some tricks as yet unknown to me. Maybe—who knows?—I would even be able to detect in myself the bracing psychological effects of getting out of the house, as promised by the welfare wonks at places like the Heritage Foundation. Or, on the other hand, maybe there would be unexpected costs—physical, mental, or financial—to throw off all my calculations. Ideally, I should do this with two small children in tow, that being the welfare average, but mine are grown and no one is willing to lend me theirs for a month-long vacation in penury. So this is not the perfect experiment, just a test of the best possible case: an unencumbered woman, smart and even strong, attempting to live more or less off the land.

On the morning of my first full day of job searching, I take a red pen to the want ads, which are auspiciously numerous. Everyone in Key West's booming "hospitality industry" seems to be looking for someone like me—trainable, flexible, and with suitably humble expectations as to pay. I know I possess certain traits that might be advantageous—I'm white and, I like to think, well-spoken and poised—but I decide on two rules: One, I cannot use any skills derived from my education or usual work—not that there are a lot of want ads for satirical essayists anyway. Two, I have to take the best-paid job that is offered me and of course do my best to hold it; no Marxist rants or sneaking off to read novels in the ladies' room. In addition, I rule out various occupations for one reason or another: Hotel front-desk clerk, for example, which to my surprise is regarded as unskilled and pays around $7 an hour, gets eliminated because it involves standing in one spot for eight hours a day. Waitressing is similarly something I'd like to avoid, because I remember it leaving me bone tired when I was eighteen, and I'm decades of varicosities and back pain beyond that now. Telemarketing, one of the first refuges of the suddenly indigent, can be dismissed on grounds of personality. This leaves certain supermarket jobs, such as deli clerk, or house-keeping in Key West's thousands of hotel and guest rooms. House-keeping is especially appealing, for reasons both atavistic and practical: it's what my mother did before I came along, and it can't be too different from what I've been doing part-time, in my own home, all my life.

So I put on what I take to be a respectful-looking outfit of ironed Bermuda shorts and scooped-neck T-shirt and set out for a tour of the local hotels and supermarkets. Best Western, Econo Lodge, and HoJo's all let me fill out application forms, and these are, to my relief, interested in little more than whether I am a legal resident of the United States and have committed any felonies. My next stop is Winn-Dixie, the supermarket, which turns out to have a particularly onerous application process, featuring a fifteen-minute "interview" by computer since, apparently, no human on the premises is deemed capable of representing the corporate point of view. I am conducted to a large room decorated with posters illustrating how to look "professional" (it helps to be white and, if female, permed) and warning of the slick promises that union organizers might try to tempt me with. The interview is multiple choice: Do I have anything, such as child-care problems, that might make it hard for me to get to work on time? Do I think safety on the job is the responsibility of management? Then, popping up cunningly out of the blue: How many dollars' worth of stolen goods have I purchased in the last year? Would I turn in a fellow employee if I caught him stealing? Finally, "Are you an honest person?"

Apparently, I ace the interview, because I am told that all I have to do is show up in some doctor's office tomorrow for a urine test. This seems to be a fairly general rule: if you want to stack Cheerio boxes or vacuum hotel rooms in chemically fascist America, you have to be willing to squat down and pee in front of some health worker (who has no doubt had to do the same thing herself). The wages Winn-Dixie is offering—$6 and a couple of dimes to start with—are not enough, I decide, to compensate for this indignity.[2]

---

[2]According to the *Monthly Labor Review* (November 1996), 28 percent of work sites surveyed in the service industry conduct drug tests (corporate workplaces have much higher rates), and the incidence of testing has risen markedly since the Eighties. The rate of testing is highest in the South (56 percent of work sites polled), with the Midwest in second place (50 percent). The drug most likely to be detected—marijuana, which can be detected in urine for weeks—is also the most innocuous, while heroin and cocaine are generally undetectable three days after use. Prospective employees sometimes try to cheat the tests by consuming excessive amounts of liquids and taking diuretics and even masking substances available through the Internet.

I lunch at Wendy's where $4.99 gets you un-limited refills at the Mexican part of the Superbar, a comforting surfeit of refried beans and "cheese sauce." A teenage employee, see-ing me studying the want ads, kindly offers me an application form, which I fill out, though here, too, the pay is just $6 and change an hour. Then it's off for a round of the locally owned inns and guesthouses. At "The Palms," let's call it, a bouncy manager actually takes me around to see the rooms and meet the existing housekeepers, who, I note with satis-faction, look pretty much like me—faded ex-hippie types in shorts with long hair pulled back in braids. Mostly, though, no one speaks to me or even looks at me except to proffer an application form. At my last stop, a palatial B&B, I wait twenty minutes to meet "Max," only to be told that there are no jobs now but there should be one soon, since "nobody lasts more than a couple weeks." (Because none of the people I talked to knew I was a reporter, I have changed their names to protect their privacy and, in some cases perhaps, their jobs.)

Three days go by like this, and, to my cha-grin, no one out of the approximately twenty places I've applied calls me for an interview. I had been vain enough to worry about coming across as too educated for the jobs I sought, but no one even seems interested in finding out how overqualified I am. Only later will I realize that the want ads are not a reliable measure of the actual jobs available at any particular time. They are, as I should have guessed from Max's comment, the employers' insurance pol-icy against the relentless turnover of the low-wage workforce. Most of the big hotels run ads almost continually, just to build a supply of ap-plicants to replace the current workers as they drift away or are fired, so finding a job is just a matter of being at the right place at the right time and flexible enough to take whatever is being offered that day. This finally happens to me at one of the big discount hotel chains, where I go, as usual, for housekeeping and am

sent, instead, to try out as a waitress at the at-tached "family restaurant," a dismal spot with a counter and about thirty tables that looks out on a parking garage and features such tempt-ing fare as "Pollish [sic] sausage and BBQ sauce" on 95-degree days. Phillip, the dapper young West Indian who introduces himself as the manager, interviews me with about as much enthusiasm as if he were a clerk process-ing me for Medicare, the principal questions being what shifts can I work and when can I start. I mutter something about being woefully out of practice as a waitress, but he's already on to the uniform: I'm to show up tomorrow wearing black slacks and black shoes; he'll pro-vide the rust-colored polo shirt with HEARTH-SIDE embroidered on it, though I might want to wear my own shirt to get to work, ha ha. At the word "tomorrow," something between fear and indignation rises in my chest. I want to say, "Thank you for your time, sir, but this is just an experiment, you know, not my actual life."

So begins my career at the Hearthside, I shall call it, one small profit center within a global discount hotel chain, where for two weeks I work from 2:00 P.M. till 10:00 P.M. for $2.43 an hour plus tips.[3] In some futile bid for gentility, the management has barred employ-ees from using the front door, so my first day I enter through the kitchen, where a red-faced man with shoulder-length blond hair is throw-ing frozen steaks against the wall and yelling, "Fuck this shit!" "That's just Jack," explains Gail, the wiry middle-aged waitress who is as-signed to train me. "He's on the rag again"—a condition occasioned, in this instance, by the fact that the cook on the morning shift had

---

[3]According to the Fair Labor Standards Act, employers are not required to pay "tipped employees," such as restaurant servers, more than $2.13 an hour in direct wages. However, if the sum of tips plus $2.13 an hour falls below the minimum wage, or $5.15 an hour, the employer is required to make up the difference. This fact was not mentioned by managers or otherwise publicized at either of the restaurants where I worked.

forgotten to thaw out the steaks. For the next eight hours, I run after the agile Gail, absorbing bits of instruction along with fragments of personal tragedy. All food must be trayed, and the reason she's so tired today is that she woke up in a cold sweat thinking of her boyfriend, who killed himself recently in an upstate prison. No refills on lemonade. And the reason he was in prison is that a few DUIs caught up with him, that's all, could have happened to anyone. Carry the creamers to the table in a monkey bowl, never in your hand. And after he was gone she spent several months living in her truck, peeing in a plastic pee bottle and reading by candlelight at night, but you can't live in a truck in the summer, since you need to have the windows down, which means anything can get in, from mosquitoes on up.

At least Gail puts to rest any fears I had of appearing overqualified. From the first day on, I find that of all the things I have left behind, such as home and identity, what I miss the most is competence. Not that I have ever felt utterly competent in the writing business, in which one day's success augurs nothing at all for the next. But in my writing life, I at least have some notion of procedure: do the research, make the outline, rough out a draft, etc. As a server, though, I am beset by requests like bees: more iced tea here, ketchup over there, a to-go box for table fourteen, and where are the high chairs, anyway? Of the twenty-seven tables, up to six are usually mine at any time, though on slow afternoons or if Gail is off, I sometimes have the whole place to myself. There is the touch-screen computer-ordering system to master, which is, I suppose, meant to minimize server-cook contact, but in practice requires constant verbal fine-tuning: "That's gravy on the mashed, okay? None on the meatloaf," and so forth—while the cook scowls as if I were inventing these refinements just to torment him. Plus, something I had forgotten in the years since I was eighteen: about a third of a server's job is "side work" that's

invisible to customers—sweeping, scrubbing, slicing, refilling, and restocking. If it isn't all done, every little bit of it, you're going to face the 6:00 P.M. dinner rush defenseless and probably go down in flames. I screw up dozens of times at the beginning, sustained in my shame entirely by Gail's support—"It's okay, baby, everyone does that sometime"—because, to my total surprise and despite the scientific detachment I am doing my best to maintain, I care.

The whole thing would be a lot easier if I could just skate through it as Lily Tomlin in one of her waitress skits, but I was raised by the absurd Booker T. Washingtonian precept that says: If you're going to do something, do it well. In fact, "well" isn't good enough by half. Do it better than anyone has ever done it before. Or so said my father, who must have known what he was talking about because he managed to pull himself, and us with him, up from the mile-deep copper mines of Butte to the leafy suburbs of the Northeast, ascending from boilermakers to martinis before booze beat out ambition. As in most endeavors I have encountered in my life, doing it "better than anyone" is not a reasonable goal. Still, when I wake up at 4:00 A.M. in my own cold sweat, I am not thinking about the writing deadlines I'm neglecting; I'm thinking about the table whose order I screwed up so that one of the boys didn't get his kiddie meal until the rest of the family had moved on to their Key Lime pies. That's the other powerful motivation I hadn't expected—the customers, or "patients," as I can't help thinking of them on account of the mysterious vulnerability that seems to have left them temporarily unable to feed themselves. After a few days at the Hearthside, I feel the service ethic kick in like a shot of oxytocin, the nurturance hormone. The plurality of my customers are hard-working locals—truck drivers, construction workers, even house-keepers from the attached hotel— and I want them to have the closest to a "fine dining" experience that the grubby circumstances will allow. No "you guys" for me; everyone over twelve is "sir" or "ma'am." I ply them with iced tea and coffee refills; I return, mid-meal, to inquire how everything is; I doll up their salads with chopped raw mushrooms, summer squash slices, or whatever bits of produce I can find that have survived their sojourn in the cold-storage room mold-free.

Sometimes I play with the fantasy that I am a princess who, in penance for some tiny transgression, has undertaken to feed each of her subjects by hand. But the non-princesses working with me are just as indulgent, even when this means flouting management rules—concerning, for example, the number of croutons that can go on a salad (six). "Put on all you want," Gail whispers, "as long as Stu isn't looking." She dips into her own tip money to buy biscuits and gravy for an out-of-work mechanic who's used up all his money on dental surgery, inspiring me to pick up the tab for his milk and pie. Maybe the same high levels of agape can be found throughout the "hospitality industry." I remember the poster decorating one of the apartments I looked at, which said "If you seek happiness for yourself you will never find it. Only when you seek happiness for others will it come to you," or words to that effect—an odd sentiment, it seemed to me at the time, to find in the dank one-room basement apartment of a bellhop at the Best Western. At the Hearthside, we utilize whatever bits of autonomy we have to ply our customers with the illicit calories that signal our love. It is our job as servers to assemble the salads and desserts, pouring the dressings and squirting the whipped cream. We also control the number of butter patties our customers get and the amount of sour cream on their baked potatoes. So if you wonder why Americans are so obese, consider the fact that waitresses both express their humanity and earn their tips through the covert distribution of fats.

Ten days into it, this is beginning to look like a livable lifestyle. I like Gail, who is "looking at fifty" but moves so fast she can alight in one place and then another without apparently being anywhere between them. I clown around with Lionel, the teenage Haitian busboy, and catch a few fragments of conversation with Joan, the svelte fortyish hostess and militant feminist who is the only one of us who dares to tell Jack to shut the fuck up. I even warm up to Jack when, on a slow night and to make up for a particularly unwarranted attack on my abilities, or so I imagine, he tells me about his glory days as a young man at "coronary school"—or do you say "culinary"?—in Brooklyn, where he dated a knock-out Puerto Rican chick and learned everything there is to know about food. I finish up at 10:00 or 10:30, depending on how much side work I've been able to get done during the shift, and cruise home to the tapes I snatched up at random when I left my real home—Marianne Faithfull, Tracy Chapman, Enigma, King Sunny Ade, the Violent Femmes—just drained enough for the music to set my cranium resonating but hardly dead. Midnight snack is Wheat Thins and Monterey Jack, accompanied by cheap white wine on ice and whatever AMC has to offer. To bed by 1:30 or 2:00, up at 9:00 or 10:00, read for an hour while my uniform whirls around in the landlord's washing machine, and then it's another eight hours spent following Mao's central instruction, as laid out in the Little Red Book, which was: Serve the people.

I could drift along like this, in some dreamy proletarian idyll, except for two things. One is management. If I have kept this subject on the margins thus far it is because I still flinch to think that I spent all those weeks under the surveillance of men (and later women) whose job it was to monitor my behavior for signs of sloth, theft, drug abuse, or worse. Not that managers and especially "assistant managers" in low-wage settings like this are exactly the class enemy. In the restaurant business, they are mostly former cooks or servers, still capable of pinch-hitting in the kitchen or on the floor, just as in hotels they are likely to be former clerks, and paid a salary of only about $400 a week. But everyone knows they have crossed over to the other side, which is, crudely put, corporate as opposed to human. Cooks want to prepare tasty meals; servers want to serve them graciously; but managers are there for only one reason—to make sure that money is made for some theoretical entity that exists far away in Chicago or New York, if a corporation can be said to have a physical existence at all. Reflecting on her career, Gail tells me ruefully that she had sworn, years ago, never to work for a corporation again. "They don't cut you no slack. You give and you give, and they take."

Managers can sit—for hours at a time if they want—but it's their job to see that no one else ever does, even when there's nothing to do, and this is why, for servers, slow times can be as exhausting as rushes. You start dragging out each little chore, because if the manager on duty catches you in an idle moment, he will give you something far nastier to do. So I wipe, I clean, I consolidate ketchup bottles and recheck the cheesecake supply, even tour the tables to make sure the customer evaluation forms are all standing perkily in their places—wondering all the time how many calories I burn in these strictly theatrical exercises. When, on a particularly dead afternoon, Stu finds me glancing at a USA Today a customer has left behind, he assigns me to vacuum the entire floor with the broken vacuum cleaner that has a handle only two feet long, and the only way to do that without incurring orthopedic damage is to proceed from spot to spot on your knees.

On my first Friday at the Hearthside there is a "mandatory meeting for all restaurant employees," which I attend, eager for insight into our overall marketing strategy and the niche (your basic Ohio cuisine with a tropical twist?) we aim to inhabit. But there is no "we" at this meeting. Phillip, our top manager except for an occasional "consultant" sent out by corporate headquarters, opens it with a sneer: "The break room—it's disgusting. Butts in the ashtrays, newspapers lying around, crumbs." This windowless little room, which also houses the time clock for the entire hotel, is where we stash our bags and civilian clothes and take our half-hour meal breaks. But a break room is not a right, he tells us. It can be taken away. We should also know that the lockers in the break room and whatever is in them can be searched at any time. Then comes gossip; there has been gossip; gossip (which seems to mean employees talking among themselves) must stop. Off-duty employees are henceforth barred from eating at the restaurant, because "other servers gather around them and gossip." When Phillip has exhausted his agenda of rebukes, Joan complains about the condition of the ladies' room and I throw in my two bits about the vacuum cleaner. But I don't see any backup coming from my fellow servers, each of whom has subsided into her own personal funk; Gail, my role model, stares sorrowfully at a point six inches from her nose. The meeting ends when Andy, one of the cooks, gets up, muttering about breaking up his day off for this almighty bullshit.

Just four days later we are suddenly summoned into the kitchen at 3:30 P.M., even though there are live tables on the floor. We all—about ten of us—stand around Phillip, who announces grimly that there has been a report of some "drug activity" on the night shift and that, as a result, we are now to be a "drug-free" workplace, meaning that all new hires will be tested, as will possibly current employees on a random basis. I am glad that this part of the kitchen is so dark, because I find myself blushing as hard as if I had been caught toking up in the ladies' room myself: I haven't been treated this way—lined up in the corridor, threatened with locker searches, peppered with carelessly aimed accusations—since junior high school. Back on the floor, Joan cracks, "Next they'll be telling us we can't have sex on the job." When I ask Stu what happened to inspire the crackdown, he just mutters about "management decisions" and takes the opportunity to upbraid Gail and me for being too generous with the rolls. From now on there's to be only one per customer, and it goes out with the dinner, not with the salad. He's also been riding the cooks, prompting Andy to come out of the kitchen and observe—with the serenity of a man whose customary implement is a butcher knife—that "Stu has a death wish today."

Later in the evening, the gossip crystallizes around the theory that Stu is himself the drug culprit, that he uses the restaurant phone to order up marijuana and sends one of the late servers out to fetch it for him. The server was caught, and she may have ratted Stu out or at least said enough to cast some suspicion on him, thus accounting for his pissy behavior. Who knows? Lionel, the busboy, entertains us for the rest of the shift by standing just behind Stu's back and sucking deliriously on an imaginary joint.

The other problem, in addition to the less-than-nurturing management style, is that this job shows no sign of being financially viable. You might imagine, from a comfortable distance, that people who live, year in and year out, on $6 to $10 an hour have discovered some survival stratagems unknown to the middle class. But no. It's not hard to get my co-workers to talk about their living situations, because housing, in almost every case, is the principal source of disruption in their lives, the first thing they fill you in on when they arrive for their shifts. After a week, I have compiled the following survey:

- Gail is sharing a room in a well-known downtown flophouse for which she and a roommate pay about $250 a week. Her roommate, a male friend, has begun hitting on her, driving her nuts, but the rent would be impossible alone.

- Claude, the Haitian cook, is desperate to get out of the two-room apartment he shares with his girlfriend and two other, unrelated, people. As far as I can determine, the other Haitian men (most of whom only speak Creole) live in similarly crowded situations.

- Annette, a twenty-year-old server who is six months pregnant and has been abandoned by her boyfriend, lives with her mother, a postal clerk.

- Marianne and her boyfriend are paying $170 a week for a one-person trailer.

- Jack, who is, at $10 an hour, the wealthiest of us, lives in the trailer he owns, paying only the $400-a-month lot fee.

- The other white cook, Andy, lives on his dry-docked boat, which, as far as I can tell from his loving descriptions, can't be more than twenty feet long. He offers to take me out on it, once it's repaired, but the offer comes with inquiries as to my marital status, so I do not follow up on it.

- Tina and her husband are paying $60 a night for a double room in a Days Inn. This is because they have no car and the Days Inn is within walking distance of the Hearthside. When Marianne, one of the breakfast servers, is tossed out of her trailer for subletting (which is against the trailer-park rules), she leaves her boyfriend and moves in with Tina and her husband.

- Joan, who had fooled me with her numerous and tasteful outfits (hostesses wear their own clothes), lives in a van she parks behind a shopping center at night and showers in Tina's motel room. The clothes are from thrift shops.[4]

---

[4]I could find no statistics on the number of employed people living in cars or vans, but according to the National Coalition for the Homeless's 1997 report "Myths and Facts About Homelessness," nearly one in five homeless people (in twenty-nine cities across the nation) is employed in a full- or part-time job.

It strikes me, in my middle-class solipsism, that there is gross improvidence in some of these arrangements.[5] When Gail and I are wrapping silverware in napkins—the only task for which we are permitted to sit—she tells me she is thinking of escaping from her roommate by moving into the Days Inn herself. I am astounded: How can she even think of paying between $40 and $60 a day? But if I was afraid of sounding like a social worker, I come out just sounding like a fool. She squints at me in disbelief, "And where am I supposed to get a month's rent and a month's deposit for an apartment?" I'd been feeling pretty smug about my $500 efficiency, but of course it was made possible only by the $1,300 I had allotted myself for start-up costs when I began my low-wage life: $1,000 for the first month's rent and deposit, $100 for initial groceries and cash in my pocket, $200 stuffed away for emergencies. In poverty, as in certain propositions in physics, starting conditions are everything.

There are no secret economies that nourish the poor; on the contrary, there are a host of special costs. If you can't put up the two months' rent you need to secure an apartment, you end up paying through the nose for a room by the week. If you have only a room, with a hot plate at best, you can't save by cooking up huge lentil stews that can be frozen for the week ahead. You eat fast food, or the hot dogs and styrofoam cups of soup that can be microwaved in a convenience store. If you have no money for health insurance—and the Hearthside's niggardly plan kicks in only after three months—you go without routine care or prescription drugs and end up paying the price. Gail, for example, was

fine until she ran out of money for estrogen pills. She is supposed to be on the company plan by now, but they claim to have lost her application form and need to begin the paperwork all over again. So she spends $9 per migraine pill to control the headaches she wouldn't have, she insists, if her estrogen supplements were covered. Similarly, Marianne's boyfriend lost his job as a roofer because he missed so much time after getting a cut on his foot for which he couldn't afford the prescribed antibiotic.

My own situation, when I sit down to assess it after two weeks of work, would not be much better if this were my actual life. The seductive thing about waitressing is that you don't have to wait for payday to feel a few bills in your pocket, and my tips usually cover meals and gas, plus something left over to stuff into the kitchen drawer I use as a bank. But as the tourist business slows in the summer heat, I sometimes leave work with only $20 in tips (the gross is higher, but servers share about 15 percent of their tips with the busboys and bartenders). With wages included, this amounts to about the minimum wage of $5.15 an hour. Although the sum in the drawer is piling up, at the present rate of accumulation it will be more than a hundred dollars short of my rent when the end of the month comes around. Nor can I see any expenses to cut. True, I haven't gone the lentil-stew route yet, but that's because I don't have a large cooking pot, pot holders, or a ladle to stir with (which cost about $30 at Kmart, less at thrift stores), not to mention onions, carrots, and the indispensable bay leaf. I do make my lunch almost every day—usually some slow-burning, high-protein combo like frozen chicken patties with melted cheese on top and canned pinto beans on the side. Dinner is at the Hearthside, which offers its employees a choice of BLT, fish sandwich, or hamburger for only $2. The burger lasts longest, especially if it's heaped with gut-puckering jalapeños, but by midnight my stomach is growling again.

So unless I want to start using my car as a residence, I have to find a second, or alternative,

---

[5]Solipsism is a tricky concept—even if you are a philosophy major. It comes from the Latin *solus* (alone) and *ipse* (self); literally it means "only-oneself-ism." The extreme form of solipsism holds that there is no reality outside of one's mind. In this case, Ehrenreich is using the term loosely to suggest that her thinking was limited to the middle-class reasoning that holds it is improvident to spend $1200–$1800 a month for a motel room as long as there are apartments to be had for half that amount.

job. I call all the hotels where I filled out housekeeping applications weeks ago—the Hyatt, Holiday Inn, Econo Lodge, HoJo's, Best Western, plus a half dozen or so locally run guesthouses. Nothing. Then I start making the rounds again, wasting whole mornings waiting for some assistant manager to show up, even dipping into places so creepy that the front-desk clerk greets you from behind bullet-proof glass and sells pints of liquor over the counter. But either someone has exposed my real-life housekeeping habits—which are, shall we say, mellow—or I am at the wrong end of some infallible ethnic equation: most, but by no means all, of the working housekeepers I see on my job searches are African Americans, Spanish-speaking, or immigrants from the Central European post-Communist world, whereas servers are almost invariably white and monolingually English-speaking. When I finally get a positive response, I have been identified once again as server material. Jerry's, which is part of a well-known national family restaurant chain and physically attached here to another budget hotel chain, is ready to use me at once. The prospect is both exciting and terrifying, because, with about the same number of tables and counter seats, Jerry's attracts three or four times the volume of customers as the gloomy old Hearthside.

Picture a fat person's hell, and I don't mean a place with no food. Instead there is everything you might eat if eating had no bodily consequences—cheese fries, chicken-fried steaks, fudge-laden desserts—only here every bite must be paid for, one way or another, in human discomfort. The kitchen is a cavern, a stomach leading to the lower intestine that is the garbage and dishwashing area, from which issue bizarre smells combining the edible and the offal: creamy carrion, pizza barf, and that unique and enigmatic Jerry's scent—citrus fart. The floor is slick with spills, forcing us to walk through the kitchen with tiny steps, like Susan McDougal in leg irons. Sinks everywhere are clogged with scraps of lettuce, decomposing lemon wedges, waterlogged toast crusts. Put your hand down on any counter and you risk being stuck to it by the film of ancient syrup spills, and this is unfortunate, because hands are utensils here, used for scooping up lettuce onto salad plates, lifting out pie slices, and even moving hash browns from one plate to another. The regulation poster in the single unisex restroom admonishes us to wash our hands thoroughly and even offers instructions for doing so, but there is always some vital substance missing—soap, paper towels, toilet paper—and I never find all three at once. You learn to stuff your pockets with napkins before going in there; and too bad about the customers, who must eat, though they don't realize this, almost literally out of our hands.

The break room typifies the whole situation: there is none, because there are no breaks at Jerry's. For six to eight hours in a row, you never sit except to pee. Actually, there are three folding chairs at a table immediately adjacent to the bathroom, but hardly anyone ever sits here, in the very rectum of the gastro-architectural system. Rather, the function of the peritoilet area is to house the ashtrays in which servers and dishwashers leave their cigarettes burning at all times, like votive candles, so that they don't have to waste time lighting up again when they dash back for a puff. Almost everyone smokes as if his or her pulmonary well-being depended on it—the multinational mélange of cooks, the Czech dishwashers, the servers, who are all American natives—creating an atmosphere in which oxygen is only an occasional pollutant. My first morning at Jerry's, when the hypoglycemic shakes set in, I complain to one of my fellow servers that I don't understand how she can go so long without food. "Well, I don't understand how you can go so long without a cigarette," she responds in a tone of reproach—because work is what you do for others; smoking is what you do for yourself. I don't know why the antismoking crusaders have never grasped the element of defiant self-nurturance that makes the habit so endearing to its victims—as if, in the American workplace, the only thing people have to call their own is the tumors they are nourishing and the spare moments they devote to feeding them.

Now, the Industrial Revolution is not an easy transition, especially when you have to zip through it in just a couple of days. I have gone from craft work straight into the factory, from the air-conditioned morgue of the Hearthside directly into the flames. Customers arrive in human waves, sometimes disgorged fifty at a time from their tour buses, peckish and whiny. Instead of two "girls" on the floor at once, there can be as many as six of us running around in our brilliant pink-and-orange Hawaiian shirts. Conversations, either with customers or fellow employees, seldom last more than twenty seconds at a time. On my first day, in fact, I am hurt by my sister servers' coldness. My mentor for the day is an emotionally uninflected twenty-three-year-old, and the others, who gossip a little among themselves about the real reason someone is out sick today and the size of the bail bond someone else has had to pay, ignore me completely. On my second day, I find out why. "Well, it's good to see you again," one of them says in greeting. "Hardly anyone comes back after the first day." I feel powerfully vindicated—a survivor—but it would take a long time, probably months, before I could hope to be accepted into this sorority.

I start out with the beautiful, heroic idea of handling the two jobs at once, and for two days I almost do it: the breakfast/lunch shift at Jerry's, which goes till 2:00 P.M., arriving at the Hearthside at 2:10 P.M., and attempting to hold out until 10:00 P.M. In the ten minutes between jobs, I pick up a spicy chicken sandwich at the Wendy's drive-through window, gobble it down in the car, and change from khaki slacks to black, from Hawaiian to rust polo. There is a problem, though. When during the 3:00 P.M. to 4:00 P.M. dead time I finally sit down to wrap

silver, my flesh seems to bond to the seat. I try to refuel with a purloined cup of soup, as I've seen Gail and Joan do dozens of times, but a manager catches me and hisses "No eating!" though there's not a customer around to be offended by the sight of food making contact with a server's lips. So I tell Gail I'm going to quit, and she hugs me and says she might just follow me to Jerry's herself.

But the chances of this are minuscule. She has left the flophouse and her annoying roommate and is back to living in her beat-up old truck. But guess what? she reports to me excitedly later that evening: Phillip has given her permission to park overnight in the hotel parking lot, as long as she keeps out of sight, and the parking lot should be totally safe, since it's patrolled by a hotel security guard! With the Hearthside offering benefits like that, how could anyone think of leaving?

Gail would have triumphed at Jerry's, I'm sure, but for me it's a crash course in exhaustion management. Years ago, the kindly fry cook who trained me to waitress at a Los Angeles truck stop used to say: Never make an unnecessary trip; if you don't have to walk fast, walk slow; if you don't have to walk, stand. But at Jerry's the effort of distinguishing necessary from unnecessary and urgent from whenever would itself be too much of an energy drain. The only thing to do is to treat each shift as a one-time-only emergency: you've got fifty starving people out there, lying scattered on the battlefield, so get out there and feed them! Forget that you will have to do this again tomorrow, forget that you will have to be alert enough to dodge the drunks on the drive home tonight—just burn, burn, burn! Ideally, at some point you enter what servers call "a rhythm" and psychologists term a "flow state," in which signals pass from the sense organs directly to the muscles, bypassing the cerebral cortex, and a Zen-like emptiness sets in. A male server from the Hearthside's morning shift tells me about the time he "pulled a triple"—three shifts in a row, all the way around the clock—and then got off and had a drink and met this girl, and maybe he shouldn't tell me this, but they had sex right then and there, and it was like, beautiful.

But there's another capacity of the neuromuscular system, which is pain. I start tossing back drugstore-brand ibuprofen pills as if they were vitamin C, four before each shift, because an old mouse-related repetitive-stress injury in my upper back has come back to full-spasm strength, thanks to the tray carrying. In my ordinary life, this level of disability might justify a day of ice packs and stretching. Here I comfort myself with the Aleve commercial in which the cute blue-collar guy asks: If you quit after working four hours, what would your boss say? And the not-so-cute blue-collar guy, who's lugging a metal beam on his back, answers: He'd fire me, that's what. But fortunately, the commercial tells us, we workers can exert the same kind of authority over our painkillers that our bosses exert over us. If Tylenol doesn't want to work for more than four hours, you just fire its ass and switch to Aleve.

Management at Jerry's is generally calmer and more "professional" than at the Hearthside, with two exceptions. One is Joy, a plump, blowsy woman in her early thirties, who once kindly devoted several minutes to instructing me in the correct one-handed method of carrying trays but whose moods change disconcertingly from shift to shift and even within one. Then there's B.J., a.k.a. B.J.-the-bitch, whose contribution is to stand by the kitchen counter and yell, "Nita, your order's up, move it!" or, "Barbara, didn't you see you've got another table out there? Come on, girl!" Among other things, she is hated for having replaced the whipped-cream squirt cans with big plastic whipped-cream-filled baggies that have to be squeezed with both hands—because, reportedly, she saw or thought she saw employees trying to inhale the propellant gas from the squirt cans, in the hope that it might be nitrous

oxide. On my third night, she pulls me aside abruptly and brings her face so close that it looks as if she's planning to butt me with her forehead. But instead of saying, "You're fired," she says, "You're doing fine." The only trouble is I'm spending time chatting with customers: "That's how they're getting you." Furthermore I am letting them "run me," which means harassment by sequential demands: you bring the ketchup and they decide they want extra Thousand Island; you bring that and they announce they now need a side of fries; and so on into distraction. Finally she tells me not to take her wrong. She tries to say things in a nice way, but you get into a mode, you know, because everything has to move so fast.[6]

I mumble thanks for the advice, feeling like I've just been stripped naked by the crazed enforcer of some ancient sumptuary law.[7] No chatting for you, girl. No fancy service ethic allowed for the serfs. Chatting with customers is for the beautiful young college-educated servers in the downtown carpaccio joints, the kids who can make $70 to $100 a night. What had I been thinking? My job is to move orders from tables to kitchen and then trays from kitchen to tables. Customers are, in fact, the major obstacle to the smooth transformation of information into food and food into money—

---

[6]In *Workers in a Lean World: Unions in the International Economy* (Verso, 1997), Kim Moody cites studies finding an increase in stress-related workplace injuries and illness between the mid-1980s and the early 1990s. He argues that rising stress levels reflect a new system of "management by stress," in which workers in a variety of industries are being squeezed to extract maximum productivity, to the detriment of their health.

[7]Sumptuary laws (from Latin *sumptus*, or expense, and *sumere*, or to take, use, or consume) were quite common in England, European countries, and even colonial America through the seventeenth century. Sumptuary laws prohibited consumers from spending their money "foolishly" to purchase luxury or extravagant clothing, food, and so forth. The Constitution of the United States would seem to forbid sumptuary laws except in cases where the government seeks to protect the health of its citizens. Many regard the prohibition of alcohol sales in the early twentieth century as the last real example of a sumptuary law in the United States.—Ed.

they are, in short, the enemy. And the painful thing is that I'm beginning to see it this way myself. There are the traditional asshole types—frat boys who down multiple Buds and then make a fuss because the steaks are so emaciated and the fries so sparse—as well as the variously impaired—due to age, diabetes, or literacy issues—who require patient nutritional counseling. The worst, for some reason, are the Visible Christians—like the ten-person table, all jolly and sanctified after Sunday-night service, who run me mercilessly and then leave me $1 on a $92 bill. Or the guy with the crucifixion T-shirt (SOMEONE TO LOOK UP TO) who complains that his baked potato is too hard and his iced tea too icy (I cheerfully fix both) and leaves no tip. As a general rule, people wearing crosses or WWJD? (What Would Jèsus Do?) buttons look at us disapprovingly no matter what we do, as if they were confusing waitressing with Mary Magdalene's original profession.

I make friends, over time, with the other "girls" who work my shift: Nita, the tattooed twenty-something who taunts us by going around saying brightly, "Have we started making money yet?" Ellen, whose teenage son cooks on the graveyard shift and who once managed a restaurant in Massachusetts but won't try out for management here because she prefers being a "common worker" and not "ordering people around." Easy-going fiftyish Lucy, with the raucous laugh, who limps toward the end of the shift because of something that has gone wrong with her leg, the exact nature of which cannot be determined without health insurance. We talk about the usual girl things—men, children, and the sinister allure of Jerry's chocolate peanut-butter cream pie—though no one, I notice, ever brings up anything potentially expensive, like shopping or movies. As at the Hearthside, the only recreation ever referred to is partying, which requires little more than some beer, a joint, and a few close friends. Still, no one here is homeless, or cops to it anyway, thanks usually to a working husband or boyfriend. All in all, we form a reliable

mutual-support group: If one of us is feeling sick or overwhelmed, another one will "bev" a table or even carry trays for her. If one of us is off sneaking a cigarette or a pee,[8] the others will do their best to conceal her absence from the enforcers of corporate rationality.

But my saving human connection—my oxytocin receptor, as it were—is George, the nineteen-year-old, fresh-off-the-boat Czech dishwasher. We get to talking when he asks me, tortuously, how much cigarettes cost at Jerry's. I do my best to explain that they cost over a dollar more here than at a regular store and suggest that he just take one from the half-filled packs that are always lying around on the break table. But that would be unthinkable. Except for the one tiny earring signaling his allegiance to some vaguely alternative point of view, George is a perfect straight arrow—crew-cut, hardworking, and hungry for eye contact. "Czech Republic," I ask, "or Slovakia?" and he seems delighted that I know the difference. "Václav Havel," I try. "Velvet Revolution, Frank Zappa?" "Yes, yes, 1989," he says, and I realize we are talking about history.

I make the decision to move closer to Key West. First, because of the drive. Second and third, also because of the drive: gas is eating up $4 to $5 a day, and although Jerry's is as high-volume as you can get, the tips average only 10 percent, and not just for a newbie like

---

[8]Until April 1998, there was no federally mandated right to bathroom breaks. According to Marc Linder and Ingrid Nygaard, authors of *Void Where Prohibited: Rest Breaks and the Right to Urinate on Company Time* (Cornell University Press, 1997), "The right to rest and void at work is not high on the list of social or political causes supported by professional or executive employees, who enjoy personal workplace liberties that millions of factory workers can only daydream about. . . . While we were dismayed to discover that workers lacked an acknowledged legal right to void at work, [the workers] were amazed by outsiders' naive belief that their employers would permit them to perform this basic bodily function when necessary. . . . A factory worker, not allowed a break for six-hour stretches, voided into pads worn inside her uniform; and a kindergarten teacher in a school without aides had to take all twenty children with her to the bathroom and line them up outside the stall door when she voided."

me. Between the base pay of $2.15 an hour and the obligation to share tips with the busboys and dishwashers, we're averaging only about $7.50 an hour. Then there is the $30 I had to spend on the regulation tan slacks worn by Jerry's servers—a setback it could take weeks to absorb. (I had combed the town's two down-scale department stores hoping for something cheaper but decided in the end that these marked-down Dockers, originally $49, were more likely to survive a daily washing.) Of my fellow servers, everyone who lacks a working husband or boyfriend seems to have a second job: Nita does something at a computer eight hours a day; another welds. Without the forty-five–minute commute, I can picture myself working two jobs and having the time to shower between them.

So I take the $500 deposit I have coming from my landlord, the $400 I have earned toward the next month's rent, plus the $200 reserved for emergencies, and use the $1,100 to pay the rent and deposit on trailer number 46 in the Overseas Trailer Park, a mile from the cluster of budget hotels that constitute Key West's version of an industrial park. Number 46 is about eight feet in width and shaped like a barbell inside, with a narrow region—because of the sink and the stove—separating the bedroom from what might optimistically be called the "living" area, with its two-person table and half-sized couch. The bathroom is so small my knees rub against the shower stall when I sit on the toilet, and you can't just leap out of the bed, you have to climb down to the foot of it in order to find a patch of floor space to stand on. Outside, I am within a few yards of a liquor store, a bar that advertises "free beer tomorrow," a convenience store, and a Burger King—but no supermarket or, alas, laundromat. By reputation, the Overseas park is a nest of crime and crack, and I am hoping at least for some vibrant, multicultural street life. But desolation rules night and day, except for a thin stream of pedestrian traffic heading for their jobs at the Sheraton or 7-Eleven. There are not

exactly people here but what amounts to canned labor, being preserved from the heat between shifts.

In line with my reduced living conditions, a new form of ugliness arises at Jerry's. The next day, when I go for straws, for the first time I find the dry-storage room locked. Ted, the portly assistant manager who opens it for me, explains that he caught one of the dishwashers attempting to steal something, and, unfortunately, the miscreant will be with us until a replacement can be found—hence the locked door. I neglect to ask what he had been trying to steal, but Ted tells me who he is—the kid with the buzz cut and the earring. You know, he's back there right now.

I wish I could say I rushed back and confronted George to get his side of the story. I wish I could say I stood up to Ted and insisted that George be given a translator and allowed to defend himself, or announced that I'd find a lawyer who'd handle the case pro bono. The mystery to me is that there's not much worth stealing in the dry-storage room, at least not in any fenceable quantity: "Is Gyorgi here, and am having 200—maybe 250—ketchup packets. What do you say?" My guess is that he had taken—if he had taken anything at all—some Saltines or a can of cherry-pie mix, and that the motive for taking it was hunger.

So why didn't I intervene? Certainly not because I was held back by the kind of moral paralysis that can pass as journalistic objectivity. On the contrary, something new—something loathsome and servile—had infected me, along with the kitchen odors that I could still sniff on my bra when I finally undressed at night. In real life I am moderately brave, but plenty of brave people shed their courage in concentration camps, and maybe something similar goes on in the infinitely more congenial milieu of the low-wage American workplace. Maybe, in a month or two more at Jerry's, I might have regained my crusading spirit. Then again, in a month or two I might have turned into a different person altogether—say, the kind of person who would have turned George in.

But this is not something I am slated to find out. When my month-long plunge into poverty is almost over, I finally land my dream job—housekeeping. I do this by walking into the personnel office of the only place I figure I might have some credibility, the hotel attached to Jerry's, and confiding urgently that I have to have a second job if I am to pay my rent and, no, it couldn't be front-desk clerk. "All right," the personnel lady fairly spits, "So it's house-keeping," and she marches me back to meet Maria, the housekeeping manager, a tiny, frenetic Hispanic woman who greets me as "babe" and hands me a pamphlet emphasizing the need for a positive attitude. The hours are nine in the morning till whenever, the pay is $6.10 an hour, and there's one week of vacation a year. I don't have to ask about health insurance once I meet Carlotta, the middle-aged African American woman who will be training me. Carla, as she tells me to call her, is missing all of her top front teeth.

On that first day of housekeeping and last day of my entire project—although I don't yet know it's the last—Carla is in a foul mood. We have been given nineteen rooms to clean, most of them "checkouts," as opposed to "stay-overs," that require the whole enchilada of bed-stripping, vacuuming, and bathroom-scrubbing. When one of the rooms that had been listed as a stay-over turns out to be a checkout, Carla calls Maria to complain, but of course to no avail. "So make up the mother-fucker," Carla orders me, and I do the beds while she sloshes around the bathroom. For four hours without a break I strip and remake beds, taking about four and a half minutes per queen-sized bed, which I could get down to three if there were any reason to. We try to avoid vacuuming by picking up the larger specks by hand, but often there is nothing to do but drag the monstrous vacuum cleaner—it weighs about thirty pounds—off our cart and

try to wrestle it around the floor. Sometimes Carla hands me the squirt bottle of "BAM" (an acronym for something that begins, ominously, with "butyric"; the rest has been worn off the label) and lets me do the bathrooms. No service ethic challenges me here to new heights of performance. I just concentrate on removing the pubic hairs from the bathtubs, or at least the dark ones that I can see.

I had looked forward to the breaking-and-entering aspect of cleaning the stay-overs, the chance to examine the secret, physical existence of strangers. But the contents of the rooms are always banal and surprisingly neat—zipped up shaving kits, shoes lined up against the wall (there are no closets), flyers for snorkeling trips, maybe an empty wine bottle or two. It is the TV that keeps us going, from *Jerry* to *Sally* to *Hawaii Five-O* and then on to the soaps. If there's something especially arresting, like "Won't Take No for Answer" on *Jerry*, we sit down on the edge of a bed and giggle for a moment as if this were a pajama party instead of a terminally dead-end job. The soaps are the best, and Carla turns the volume up full blast so that she won't miss anything from the bathroom or while the vacuum is on. In room 503, Marcia confronts Jeff about Lauren. In 505, Lauren taunts poor cuckolded Marcia. In 511, Helen offers Amanda $10,000 to stop seeing Eric, prompting Carla to emerge from the bathroom to study Amanda's troubled face. "You take it, girl," she advises. "I would for sure."

The tourists' rooms that we clean and, beyond them, the far more expensively appointed interiors in the soaps, begin after a while to merge. We have entered a better world—a world of comfort where every day is a day off, waiting to be filled up with sexual intrigue. We, however, are only gatecrashers in this fantasy, forced to pay for our presence with backaches and perpetual thirst. The mirrors, and there are far too many of them in hotel rooms, contain the kind of person you would normally find pushing a shopping cart down a city street—bedraggled, dressed in a damp hotel polo shirt two sizes too large, and with sweat dribbling down her chin like drool. I am enormously relieved when Carla announces a half-hour meal break, but my appetite fades when I see that the bag of hot-dog rolls she has been carrying around on our cart is not trash salvaged from a checkout but what she has brought for her lunch.

When I request permission to leave at about 3:30, another housekeeper warns me that no one has so far succeeded in combining housekeeping at the hotel with serving at Jerry's: "Some kid did it once for five days, and you're no kid." With that helpful information in mind, I rush back to number 46, down four Advils (the name brand this time), shower, stooping to fit into the stall, and attempt to compose myself for the oncoming shift. So much for what Marx termed the "reproduction of labor power," meaning the things a worker has to do just so she'll be ready to work again. The only unforeseen obstacle to the smooth transition from job to job is that my tan Jerry's slacks, which had looked reasonably clean by 40-watt bulb last night when I handwashed my Hawaiian shirt, prove by daylight to be mottled with ketchup and ranch-dressing stains. I spend most of my hour-long break between jobs attempting to remove the edible portions with a sponge and then drying the slacks over the hood of my car in the sun.

I can do this two-job thing, is my theory, if I can drink enough caffeine and avoid getting distracted by George's ever more obvious suffering.[9] The first few days after being caught he seemed not to understand the trouble he

was in, and our chirpy little conversations had continued. But the last couple of shifts he's been listless and unshaven, and tonight he looks like the ghost we all know him to be, with dark half-moons hanging from his eyes. At one point, when I am briefly immobilized by the task of filling little paper cups with sour cream for baked potatoes, he comes over and looks as if he'd like to explore the limits of our shared vocabulary, but I am called to the floor for a table. I resolve to give him all my tips that night and to hell with the experiment in low-wage money management. At eight, Ellen and I grab a snack together standing at the mephitic[10] end of the kitchen counter, but I can only manage two or three mozzarella sticks and lunch had been a mere handful of McNuggets. I am not tired at all, I assure myself, though it may be that there is simply no more "I" left to do the tiredness monitoring. What I would see, if I were more alert to the situation, is that the forces of destruction are already massing against me. There is only one cook on duty, a young man named Jesus ("Hay-Sue," that is) and he is new to the job. And there is Joy, who shows up to take over in the middle of the shift, wearing high heels and a long, clingy white dress and fuming as if she'd just been stood up in some cocktail bar.

Then it comes, the perfect storm. Four of my tables fill up at once. Four tables is nothing for me now, but only so long as they are obligingly staggered. As I bev table 27, tables 25, 28, and 24 are watching enviously. As I bev 25, 24 glowers because their bevs haven't even been ordered. Twenty-eight is four yuppyish types, meaning everything on the side and agonizing instructions as to the chicken Caesars. Twenty-five is a middle-aged black couple, who

---

[9]In 1996, the number of persons holding two or more jobs averaged 7.8 million, or 6.2 percent of the workforce. It was about the same rate for men and for women (6.1 versus 6.2), though the kinds of jobs differ by gender. About two thirds of multiple jobholders work one job full-time and the other part-time. Only a heroic minority—4 percent of men and 2 percent of women—work two full-time jobs simultaneously. (From John F. Stinson Jr., "New Data on Multiple Jobholding Available from the CPS," in the *Monthly Labor Review,* March 1997.)

---

[10]I confess, I have never encountered the word "mephitic" in anything written later than the nineteenth century. A thing is mephitic if it has an offensive or noxious smell (hence, the term "mephitic weasel" was once used to refer to what we call skunks).—Ed.

complain, with some justice, that the iced tea isn't fresh and the tabletop is sticky. But table 24 is the meteorological event of the century: ten British tourists who seem to have made the decision to absorb the American experience entirely by mouth. Here everyone has at least two drinks—iced tea and milk shake, Michelob and water (with lemon slice, please)—and a huge promiscuous orgy of breakfast specials, mozzarella sticks, chicken strips, quesadillas, burgers with cheese and without, sides of hash browns with cheddar, with onions, with gravy, seasoned fries, plain fries, banana splits. Poor Jesus! Poor me! Because when I arrive with their first tray of food—after three prior trips just to refill bevs—Princess Di refuses to eat her chicken strips with her pancake-and-sausage special, since, as she now reveals, the strips were meant to be an appetizer. Maybe the others would have accepted their meals, but Di, who is deep into her third Michelob, insists that everything else go back while they work on their "starters." Meanwhile, the yuppies are waving me down for more decaf and the black couple looks ready to summon the NAACP.

Much of what happened next is lost in the fog of war. Jesus starts going under. The little printer on the counter in front of him is spewing out orders faster than he can rip them off, much less produce the meals. Even the invincible Ellen is ashen from stress. I bring table 24 their reheated main courses, which they immediately reject as either too cold or fossilized by the microwave. When I return to the kitchen with their trays (three trays in three trips), Joy confronts me with arms akimbo: "What is this?" She means the food—the plates of rejected pancakes, hash browns in assorted flavors, toasts, burgers, sausages, eggs. "Uh, scrambled with cheddar," I try, "and that's . . ." "NO,"she screams in my face. "Is it a traditional, a super-scramble, an eye-opener?" I pretend to study my check for a clue, but entropy has been up to its tricks, not only on the plates but in my head, and I have to admit that the original order is beyond recon-

struction. "You don't know an eye-opener from a traditional?" she demands in outrage. All I know, in fact, is that my legs have lost interest in the current venture and have announced their intention to fold. I am saved by a yuppie (mercifully not one of mine) who chooses this moment to charge into the kitchen to bellow that his food is twenty-five minutes late. Joy screams at him to get the hell out of her kitchen, please, and then turns on Jesus in a fury, hurling an empty tray across the room for emphasis.

I leave. I don't walk out, I just leave. I don't finish my side work or pick up my credit-card tips, if any, at the cash register or, of course, ask Joy's permission to go. And the surprising thing is that you can walk out without permission, that the door opens, that the thick tropical night air parts to let me pass, that my car is still parked where I left it. There is no vindication in this exit, no fuck-you surge of relief, just an overwhelming, dank sense of failure pressing down on me and the entire parking lot. I had gone into this venture in the spirit of science, to test a mathematical proposition, but somewhere along the line, in the tunnel vision imposed by long shifts and relentless concentration, it became a test of myself, and clearly I have failed. Not only had I flamed out as a housekeeper/server, I had even forgotten to give George my tips, and, for reasons perhaps best known to hardworking, generous people like Gail and Ellen, this hurts. I don't cry, but I am in a position to realize, for the first time in many years, that the tear ducts are still there, and still capable of doing their job.

When I moved out of the trailer park, I gave the key to number 46 to Gail and arranged for my deposit to be transferred to her. She told me that Joan is still living in her van and that Stu had been fired from the Hearthside. I never found out what happened to George.

In one month, I had earned approximately $1,040 and spent $517 on food, gas, toiletries, laundry, phone, and utilities. If I had remained in my $500 efficiency, I would have been able to pay the rent and have $22 left over (which is $78 less than the cash I had in my pocket at the start of the month). During this time I bought no clothing except for the required slacks and no prescription drugs or medical care (I did finally buy some vitamin B to compensate for the lack of vegetables in my diet). Perhaps I could have saved a little on food if I had gotten to a supermarket more often, instead of convenience stores, but it should be noted that I lost almost four pounds in four weeks, on a diet weighted heavily toward burgers and fries.

How former welfare recipients and single mothers will (and do) survive in the low-wage workforce, I cannot imagine. Maybe they will figure out how to condense their lives— including child-raising, laundry, romance, and meals—into the couple of hours between full-time jobs. Maybe they will take up residence in their vehicles, if they have one. All I know is that I couldn't hold two jobs and I couldn't make enough money to live on with one. And I had advantages unthinkable to many of the long-term poor—health, stamina, a working car, and no children to care for and support. Certainly nothing in my experience contradicts the conclusion of Kathryn Edin and Laura Lein, in

their recent book *Making Ends Meet: How Single Mothers Survive Welfare and Low-Wage Work*, that low-wage work actually involves more hardship and deprivation than life at the mercy of the welfare state. In the coming months and years, economic conditions for the working poor are bound to worsen, even without the almost inevitable recession. As mentioned earlier, the influx of former welfare recipients into the low-skilled workforce will have a depressing effect on both wages and the number of jobs available. A general economic downturn will only enhance these effects, and the working poor will of course be facing it without the slight, but nonetheless often saving, protection of welfare as a backup.

The thinking behind welfare reform was that even the humblest jobs are morally uplifting and psychologically buoying. In reality they are likely to be fraught with insult and stress. But I did discover one redeeming feature of the most abject low-wage work—the camaraderie of people who are, in almost all cases, far too smart and funny and caring for the work they do and the wages they're paid. The hope, of course, is that someday these people will come to know what they're worth, and take appropriate action.

Questions

1. Compare Ehrenreich's story of life as a waitress to Paules' account (reading 17) of being a waitress. Given that both studied similar subjects, one would expect there to be several similarities. However, did you spot important differences? Paules interviewed women working as waitresses while Ehrenreich lived the life. To what extent might this difference in methods explain the differences in their findings?

2. Imagine that tomorrow you had to postpone finishing college and survive in the "real world." How difficult would it be for you to put together enough money to get started out there? (Consider such things as transportation, housing [including first and last months' rent and security deposit], the cost of uniforms, etc.) (If your instructor assigns you to answer this question on paper and turn it in, take care not to reveal any details that are too personal!) Do you think that your parents or others would be happy to help you get started? What do you think happens to people whose relatives can't (or won't) help them out financially?

34
THE JOB GHETTO

Katherine Newman and Chauncy Lennon

One of my students expressed the conventional "wisdom" this way: "If people want to bad enough, they can get a job and make something of themselves. It might not be a great job, but at least it's a job. No one has to be poor in this society." In this 1995 article, Katherine Newman and Chauncy Lennon challenge such widely held assumptions about the availability of employment in our society.

To fix the welfare mess, conservatives say, we should stop making life on the dole so comfortable, cut benefits, and force overindulged welfare moms to go out and find honest jobs. Unskilled foreigners can find work, so why can't AFDC[1] recipients? With unemployment rates down, these expectations sound reasonable, particularly to middle-class Americans with stagnating incomes. The premise that jobs are available for those willing to take them is a great comfort to politicians with budget axes in hand and to conservative commentators calling on them to slash benefits. After all, they can claim they're not really casting poor women and children into the streets; they're just upholding the American work ethic.

But can just any warm body find a job? For the past two years, we have studied the low-wage labor market in Harlem, focusing on minimum-wage jobs in the fast-food industry, which are typical of the employment opportunities many reformers have in mind for welfare recipients. After all, these jobs presumably demand little skill, education, or prior work experience—or so the public believes.

The fast-food industry is growing more rapidly than almost any other service business and now employs more than 2.3 million workers. One in 15 Americans working today found their first job at McDonald's—not including Burger King and the rest. As a gateway to employment, fast-food establishments are gaining on the armed forces, which have long functioned as a national job-training factory. No wonder the average citizen believes these jobs are wide open! Yet, in inner cities, the picture looks different. With manufacturing gone, fast-food jobs have become the object of fierce competition.

Downward Pressures

Between 1992 and 1994, we tracked the work histories of 200 people working in fast-food restaurants in central Harlem, where according to official data about 18 percent of the population are unemployed and about 40 percent live below the poverty line. These numbers are typical of the communities where many long-term recipients of public assistance will have to look for work if their benefits are cut off. Some 29 percent of the households in Harlem receive public assistance.

---

[1]Aid to Families with Dependent Children, a form of welfare.—Ed.

Although the 200 workers in our study receive only the minimum wage, they are actually the victors in an intense competition to find work in a community with relatively few jobs to offer. At the restaurants where they work, the ratio of applicants to hires is approximately 14 to 1. Among those people who applied but were rejected for fast-food work in early 1993, 73 percent had not found work of any kind a year later, despite considerable effort. Even the youngest job hunters in our study (16- to 18-year-olds) had applied for four or five positions before they came looking for these fast-food jobs. The oldest applicants (over 25) had applied for an average of seven or eight jobs.

The oversupply of job seekers causes a creeping credentialism in the ghetto's low-wage service industries. Older workers in their twenties, who are more often high school graduates, now dominate jobs once taken by school dropouts or other young people first starting out. Long-term welfare recipients will have a tough time beating out their competition even for these low-wage jobs. They will be joining an inner-city labor market that is already saturated with better educated and more experienced workers who are preferred by employers.

Winners and Losers

We tracked nearly 100 people who applied for these minimum-wage jobs but were turned down, and compared them to the fortunate ones who got jobs. The comparison is instructive. Even in Harlem, African Americans are at a disadvantage in hiring compared to Latinos and others. Employers, including black employers, favor applicants who are not African American. Blacks are not shut out of the low-wage labor market; indeed, they represent about 70 percent of the new hires in these jobs. But they are rejected at a much higher rate than applicants from other ethnic groups with the same educational qualifications.

Employers also seem to favor job applicants who commute from more distant neighborhoods. The rejection rate for local applicants is higher than the rate for similarly educated individuals who live farther away. This pattern holds even for people of the same race, sex, and age. Other studies in the warehouse and dockyard industries report the same results. These findings suggest that residents of poor neighborhoods such as central Harlem are at a distinct disadvantage in finding minimum-wage jobs near home.

Mothers of young children face particular problems if they can't find jobs close to home. The costs and logistical complexities of commuting (and paying for longer child care hours to accommodate it) are a big burden.

In searching for jobs, "who you know" makes a big difference. Friends and family members who already have jobs help people get work even in the fast-food industry; those isolated from such networks are less likely to get hired. Personal contacts have long been recognized as crucial for getting higher-skilled employment. This research suggests that contacts are important at the bottom of the job ladder, too.

Native-born applicants are at a disadvantage compared to legal immigrants in securing entry-level work. In fact, even though central Harlem residents are nearly all African American, recent immigrants have a higher probability of being hired for Harlem's fast-food jobs than anyone else. Interviews with employers suggest that they believe immigrants are easier to manage in part because they come from countries where $4.25 an hour represents a king's ransom. Whether or not employers are right about the tractability of immigrants, such attitudes make it harder for the native-born to obtain low-wage jobs.

The people who succeed in getting these minimum-wage jobs are not new to the labor market. More than half of the new hires over the age of 18 found their first jobs when they were younger than 15 years of age. Even the people rejected for the minimum-wage positions had some prior job experience. Half of them also began working before they were 15 years old. Welfare recipients with no prior job experience, or no recent job experience, are going to be at a disadvantage in the competition.

"They Expect Too Much"

One explanation often advanced for low employment in poor communities is that the poor have unrealistic expectations. In this view, they are reluctant to seek (or take) jobs that fall below a "reservation wage," which is supposedly far above the minimum. We asked job seekers who were refused these entry-level jobs what they were hoping for and what wages they would accept. Their desires were modest: $4.59 per hour on average, which is quite close to the minimum wage. The younger the job-seeker, the lower was the expectation.

These job seekers were willing to accept even more modest wages. On average the lowest they would take was $4.17 per hour, which is less than the minimum level legally permitted for adult workers. It is striking that many applicants previously had higher salaries; the average wage for the best job they had ever held was $6.79 per hour. Many of central Harlem's job hunters are suffering from downward mobility, falling into the minimum-wage market even though they have done better in the past.

Comparing job seekers to jobholders shows the intensity of employment competition in the inner city, but it doesn't tell us how welfare recipients will fare. What assets do welfare recipients bring to the competition compared to other job hunters? The news is grim.

Nationally, one-third of the long-term welfare recipients have received high school diplomas. Recently hired fast-food workers in central Harlem have completed high school at a higher rate—54 percent. Almost 40 percent of welfare recipients have not held jobs in the year preceding their enrollment in welfare. Yet even the central Harlem applicants rejected for fast-food jobs have had more job experience. They have held an average of more than three jobs before applying for these positions.

In short, it is simply not the case that anyone who wants a low-wage job can get one. As is true for almost any glutted labor market, there is a queue of applicants, and employers can be fairly choosy. When conservatives point to the success of immigrants as proof that jobs are available for welfare moms, they are ignoring the realities of the inner city. Ethnic minorities of all kinds are already locked into a fierce struggle for scarce opportunities at the bottom.

When they go looking for jobs, welfare recipients go to the back of a long line. Policymakers should neither fool nor comfort themselves with the notion that welfare mothers can simply go out and get jobs. Investment in public employment and tax incentives for private employers will be needed on a massive scale if anything like that rosy scenario is to come about. Even then, the competitive hurdles facing the very poor will be high and many better-qualified people will be out there looking to leap over them.

Questions

1. According to Newman and Lennon's research, what sorts of factors distinguish jobholders and job seekers in Harlem?

2. How likely do Newman and Lennon think it is that welfare moms will be able to get off welfare and find jobs in the near future? Explain.

35

RACISM

Joe R. Feagin

If ever there comes a time that I want absolute silence in my classroom, I will simply announce, "Today, we are going to talk about racism."

It is hard to talk about race, let alone racism, in a public setting. White students confide that black students are "too sensitive" and "will think I'm a racist if I say anything." Black students mostly just say that white students "just don't get it," and "don't *want* to get it."

In his book, *Racist America: Roots, Current Realities, and Future Reparations*, Professor Feagin, one of today's most respected sociologists, offers us insight into why conversations about racism are so difficult. Whites and blacks, he has found, have very different understandings of the importance of race in U.S. society. Blacks experience racist behavior in schoolrooms, on the streets, in shops, at work, and even in health care settings. As Feagin notes, "being black in U.S. society means always having to be prepared for antiblack actions by whites—in most places and at most times of the day, week, month, or year." For black men and women, racism is an unfortunately large part of the present.

On the other hand, as far as most whites are concerned, "racism is a thing of the past"; thus, "black Americans who complain of it are paranoid or confused. There is a common saying among whites that a black person is 'playing the race card,' a comment generally used to suggest that person is making an illegitimate demand [or complaint] because antiblack racism is no longer thought of as a serious obstacle in the United States."

What follows is an excerpt from *Racist America*, in which Feagin explores the disjunction between race as it's seen by white and black Americans.

Soon after the 1960s civil rights movement declined in intensity, most whites were moving toward the view that racial discrimination is no longer an important problem for the nation. In a 1976 survey, for example, most (71 percent) whites agreed that "blacks and other minorities no longer face unfair employment conditions. In fact they are favored in many training and job programs." A meager 12 percent of whites agreed with the statement that "discrimination affects all black people. The only way to handle it is for blacks to organize together and demand rights for all." In a 1980 survey respondents were asked, "How much discrimination do you feel there is against blacks and other minorities in any area of life that limits their chances to get ahead?" Just over half of

Excerpts from *Racist America: Roots, Current Realities, and Future Reparations* by Joe R. Feagin. Copyright © 2000 by Routledge. Reproduced by permission of Routledge/Taylor & Francis Books, Inc.

blacks replied "a lot," compared to only a quarter of whites. In these surveys only a minority of whites viewed discrimination as a major hurdle (Kluegel & Smith 1986).

In more recent surveys, black and white Americans still differ dramatically in how they view discrimination. A 1990 NORC survey question asked why blacks have worse jobs, income, and housing than whites. Choosing among alternative explanations, two-thirds of black respondents said that it was "mainly due to discrimination," compared to only 35 percent of whites. Similarly, in a mid-1990s Pennsylvania survey researchers found that eight in ten black respondents thought inequality in jobs, housing, and income stemmed mostly from discrimination, while the majority of whites viewed this inequality as resulting from blacks' lack of motivation. Respondents were asked whether the quality of life for black Americans had gotten better in the last decade. Nearly six in ten whites said it had gotten better, compared to less than a third of black respondents (Smith 1996). Recent national polls have shown the same pattern. A 1997 ABC/*Washington Post* poll found that only 17 percent of the white respondents felt there was a lot of racial discrimination, compared to nearly half the blacks polled. In addition, several other surveys have found that on questions dealing with specific institutional areas such as housing, education, and jobs less than a majority of whites believe that blacks currently face discrimination (Blendon et al. 1986).

Several recent surveys have found that many whites think blacks are as well off as or are better off than whites in regard to education, health care, and jobs. For example, a Massachusetts survey found a majority of the white respondents saying that African Americans, Asian Americans, and Latino Americans now have *equality* in life chances with whites (Lehigh 1998). However, government statistical data indicate that such views are very much in error. Perhaps because of erroneous or misleading media reports, most whites do not understand just how much worse off blacks actually are than whites in most areas of political and economic life (Feagin & Feagin 1999).

"I AM NOT A RACIST": DENYING INDIVIDUAL RACISM

Clearly, a majority of whites do not see the United States as a nation that has a problem of serious and widespread racial discrimination. Apparently, most whites also do not view themselves as significantly racist in thought or action, often asserting "I am not a racist." In recent years many whites have also made such statements as "my family never owned slaves" or "my family did not segregate lunch counters." Many will say to black Americans something like, "Slavery happened hundreds of years ago—get over it." They do not know, or pretend they do not, that official slavery ended less than 140 years or so prior to their statements. In addition, whites making such assertions usually do not admit that they and their families have benefited greatly from slavery, segregation, and present-day discrimination.[1]

Many whites seem to mix negative views of black Americans with images of white innocence, thereby giving specific expression to elements of a broader racial ideology. Take this example of a white college student's reply to a question about her first experience with black Americans, in this case children: "I switched from a private school which had no blacks to a

---

[1]Elsewhere in his book, Feagin observes that "slaveholders were not the only beneficiaries of the slavery system; those who bought and sold products of plantations were also major beneficiaries. This latter group included merchants and consumers in many nations. In addition, many white workers in Britain and other parts of Europe owed their livelihood directly or indirectly to the slaves and plantation products. It seems unlikely that British and other European economic development would have occurred when it did without the very substantial capital generated by the slavery system" (51).—Ed.

Say discrimination doesn't exist, or doesn't exist in their lives but discriminate subconsciously.

Racism   341

public school, and I was thrown in the middle of a bunch of apes, no I'm just kidding. . . . And I don't know, my parents have always instilled in me that blacks aren't equal, because we are from [the Deep South]." In her interview she continues in this vein, making several negative comments about African Americans. Then at the end of her interview, she adds, "I don't consider myself racist. I, when I think of the word racist, I think of KKK, people in white robes burning black people on crosses and stuff, or I think of the Skinheads or some exaggerated form of racism" (Feagin & Vera 1995). We see here the imaging of the white self in positive terms.

It seems that most whites can assert that they are "not racist" because they see racism as something that *other* whites do. That is, they know other whites who are much more racist in thought or action than they are, and thus they see themselves as already beyond that racism. Jerome Culp has said, "To many white people, not being racist means having less racial animosity than their parents (something almost all can at least claim); having less racial animosity than someone they know (something all can claim); or not belonging to a white supremacist group. . . . For many white people, unless they believe overwhelmingly in the inferiority of black people, they are not collaborators with racism and are not racist" (Culp 1993). As we saw in white views of athletes and actors on "The Cosby Show," many whites hold some more or less positive images of selected black men or women. However, these usually superficial positive views reduce the ability of whites to see their own culpability in personal and institutional racism. Indeed, many a white person has a false consciousness that occurs when a white "believes he or she is identifying with a person of color, but in fact is doing so only in a slight, superficial way" (Delgado 1996). It is possible to hold that black Americans can be good entertainers, musicians, or sports figures, yet also believe

that most are inferior to whites in character, morality, or intelligence.[2]

Historical changes in racism have also been misperceived by whites. When the legal segregation era came to an end with the passage of civil rights laws in the 1960s, most whites apparently concluded that serious racism was being rapidly extinguished. Today, most whites, like the young woman interviewed above, seem to view what racism remains as a matter of isolated Klan-type bigotry and not as a system of racism cutting across U.S. institutions. As a result, they do not see their own racism. Moreover, the level at which racist attitudes are held can vary in degree of consciousness. Psychologist Patricia Devine has suggested that whites who reject overtly prejudiced views can still hold less consciously prejudiced thoughts that stem from prior socialization. For many whites this attitudinal racism is a persisting bad habit that keeps coming up in everyday thought and behavior. One reason for this is the fact that human beings are characterized by automatic information processing, which involves the unintentional activation of previously socialized attitudes such as racist stereotypes and prejudices (Devine 1989). Racist attitudes can thus be conscious, half-conscious, or even subconscious.

---

[2] Feagin introduced the racist stereotype of lazy black men and women earlier in the book and argued that it persists today: "A recent NORC national survey asked whites to evaluate on a scale just how work-oriented blacks are. Only a small percentage, 16 percent, ranked blacks at the hardworking end; just under half put blacks at the lazy end of the spectrum. . . . Notions of laziness are so strong as to overcome countering evidence. Researchers Justin Lewis and Sut Jhally had white subjects watch 'The Cosby Show,' a popular television show from the 1980s and 1990s that is still seen in reruns across the globe. Whites generally like the black Huxtable family portrayed on the show, yet many processed the images in a way that fit in with preexisting attitudes. They saw the success of the Huxtables as evidence that any black person could succeed if he or she would just work harder. As Lewis and Jhally concluded about white views, "The Huxtables proved that black people can succeed; yet in so doing they also prove the inferiority of black people in general (who have, in comparison with whites, failed)" (111).—Ed.

White Views on Government Action Against Discrimination

If antiblack discrimination is no longer regarded as a serious problem, then it is not surprising that most whites see less need, or no need, for strong antidiscrimination efforts by governments. From this perspective blacks pressing for continuing or enhanced antidiscrimination programs, such as aggressive affirmative action, are seen as making illegitimate demands. David Wellman has suggested that "the concrete problem facing white people is how to come to grips with the demands made by blacks while at the same time *avoiding* the possibility of institutional change and reorganization that might affect them" (Wellman 1977).

SYMBOLIC AND LAISSEZ-FAIRE RACISM

Some researchers have described a contemporary white perspective called *symbolic racism*. Whites often combine the notion of declining or eradicated blatant racism with the idea that blacks are making illegitimate demands for societal changes. As these researchers see the current situation, a majority of whites have shifted away from old-fashioned racist ideas and have accepted modest desegregation while strongly resisting aggressive government action for large-scale desegregation. This symbolic racism is grounded in white resistance to substantial changes in the status quo. Central to white concerns is a fear whites have of losing status and power because of black attempts to bring change. Deep-lying antiblack views—especially views of blacks violating traditional American work values—are still present, but white resentment of pressures for substantial change is central to the current racist ideology (Sears 1988). This symbolic racism perspective has been criticized by some scholars as playing down old-fashioned racism, when the latter still exists among

whites and is directly connected to negative views of programs to eradicate discrimination.

Lawrence Bobo, James Kluegel, and Ryan Smith have suggested a more historical approach. Since the 1950s, and shaped by structural changes in the society, they say white attitudes have shifted from an accent on strict segregation and overt bigotry to "laissez-faire racism,"[3] by which they mean whites' continuing stereotyping of blacks and blaming of blacks for their problems. Most ordinary whites have given up a commitment to compulsory racial segregation. Yet, they still strive to maintain white privilege and position. Survey data since the 1960s indicate a substantial discrepancy between white views on the *principle* of desegregation versus white views on the *implementation* of desegregation by government. While surveys in the mid-1960s indicated that nearly two-thirds of whites accepted integrated schooling in principle, just 38 percent accepted a role for government in pressing for more integration. By the mid-1980s white support for the principle of school integration had grown to 93 percent, while endorsement of government intervention had declined to 26 percent (Bobo et al. 1997). The survey data indicate similar discrepancies in white views of job and housing integration. Acceptance of the principle of racial integration does not mean that whites wish to see government intervene aggressively, or to personally have more contact with blacks. Whites maintain a positive sense of self and their claims to greater privileges and resources

---

[3]*Laissez-faire* (French, "let alone, don't interfere"). Laissez-faire capitalism thus is based on the premise that capitalism will work best if the government doesn't interfere by regulating. By extension, laissez-faire racism is racism that will continue and even flourish as long as the government does not attempt to push antiracist laws and policies (e.g., affirmative action).—Ed.

while fending off what whites see as illegitimate black demands for a fair share of those resources.

VIEWS ON AFFIRMATIVE ACTION

Affirmative action is a major example of a remedial program to deal with racial discrimination. Yet most whites, including most white leaders, have been opposed to *aggressive* affirmative action since at least the 1970s. In one 1977 survey of mostly white and male local and national leaders in business, farming, unions, the media, and academia, *most* were overwhelmingly opposed to affirmative-action quotas for black Americans in school admissions and jobs. Only 10 to 22 percent of the several leadership groups favored strong remedial quotas (Verba & Orren 1985). In addition, the overwhelming majority of these elites thought that equality of opportunity, not equality of results, was the best way to eradicate disparities. The white public seems to share this view.

Earlier we noted mid-1970s surveys suggesting that the white majority views blacks as no longer facing serious job discrimination and expresses opposition to an expanded effort for civil rights. Recent data show the same pattern: more than half of whites do not believe that government or private agencies should be making aggressive remedial efforts on behalf of black Americans or other Americans of color. In an ABC News/*Washington Post* survey only a quarter of whites thought minorities should receive some preferences in jobs and college admissions (Ladd 1995). And a late-1990s Gallup poll found that 70 percent of Republicans, a heavily white group, felt the federal government should not make special efforts to help Americans of color, because they should help themselves (Blendon et al. 1986). A majority of whites took the same position in a late-1990s survey in Massachusetts (Lehigh 1998). Most national surveys have shown the same pattern of white opposition to strong programs with special preferences or quotas as a means of aggressively remedying past discrimination. (Milder remedial programs may sometimes be acceptable.) Indeed, today many whites believe that they are likely to be the victims of governmental policies helping black Americans. One recent Pennsylvania survey asked a question as to how likely it would be that a white worker might lose a job or a promotion to a less qualified black worker. Most black respondents (57 percent) thought this was unlikely, while most whites (80 percent) thought it was likely (Smith 1996). National polls using such a question have gotten similar responses: The majority of whites seem convinced that antiwhite discrimination is now commonplace.

White elites have periodically expended substantial effort to shape the public's views of remedial programs. Researcher Robert Entman has examined trends in mass media reports of the controversy over affirmative action that recurred periodically in the 1980s and 1990s. He found significant peaking in media attention to affirmative action during the years 1987, 1991, and 1995—years that preceded presidential elections. This pattern suggests elite manipulation of the affirmative action issue for political purposes. The media elites and their white-collar employees tended to present the issue of affirmative action in white-framed ways or in terms of national controversy, using such phrases as the "tide of white anger" or the "growing white backlash." Entman concludes that "journalists, it seems, built their frame on claims by elite sources with an interest in promoting the impression of white arousal, filtered through the conflict norm that shapes story construction" (Entman 1997). The media attention accelerated concerns about affirmative action in the white public.

Related to opposition to strong affirmative action programs is the old individualistic ethic, especially the blame-the-victim version. Today, as in the past, many whites comment about the problems of blacks with such statements as, "Why can't they be like us?" The notion here is that if "they" will work harder and improve their personal and family values, then the normal assimilation processes will enable them to have greater socioeconomic mobility. One recent survey asked whether respondents agreed with this statement: "The Irish, Italians, and many other groups overcame prejudice and worked their way up, African Americans and other minorities should do the same without any special help from the government." Most whites (69 percent) agreed (Blendon et al. 1986). Most seem to perceive the black experience in terms of an individualistic mobility model. Black Americans, from this viewpoint, are little different from white immigrant groups, such as the southern and eastern European immigrants of the early 1900s. Like those immigrants, who are seen as having encountered discrimination, black Americans should be able to work themselves up the social ladder. If they do not make it, it is mostly their own fault.

Imaging the White Self

The racist ideas and attitudes of white Americans encompass *much more* than their antiblack views. Among these racist attitudes are positive views of white superiority and merit. Generally, the broad white-racist ideology sees white history as meritorious. Indeed, in the United States, group merit and individual merit are judged by standards created by the white majority. [Earlier in the book] we noted the images of white superiority and virtue in many Hollywood films. From the first years of movie-making to the present, when racial matters have been portrayed, whites as a group have almost always been portrayed as morally superior, intellectually superior, or otherwise meritorious. In these movies—including more

recent television movies—there may be a few white individuals who are racist bigots, but the society as a whole is not portrayed as racist. Some white person is typically a central hero, even in movies mostly about black Americans (for example, *Glory*).

Among elites and in the general public, whites have developed numerous sincere fictions that reproduce aspects of the broad racist ideology at an everyday level. Such fictions may describe whites as "not racist" and as "good people" even as the same whites take part in racist actions or express racist ideas. This moral privileging of whiteness may be conscious or it can be half-conscious or unconscious. Ruth Frankenberg found evidence of this unconsciousness in her research on white women: whiteness, she noted, is "difficult for white people to name. . . . Those who are securely housed within its borders usually do not examine it" (Frankenberg 1993). The sense of whiteness is often hidden deeply in individual psyches and practices. Being white, one might say, means rarely or never having to think about it. Whiteness is the national norm, and thus the white majority's views, practices, and culture are generally seen as normal.

Examining commentaries on racial inequality written by white students, Joyce King found that most were "unaware of how their own subjective identities reflect an uncritical identification with the existing social order." Only one student out of fifty-seven linked persisting racial inequality to the larger system of racial oppression (King 1991). Thus, while whites get many substantial advantages from systemic racism, they do pay a subtle and hidden price. This may include a lack of conscious awareness about certain critical aspects of social reality. Many have an uncritical mind that accepts the existing racial order with little questioning.

Perhaps most amazing is that a majority of whites today do not see the centuries of slavery and segregation as bringing whites substantial socioeconomic benefit. One survey found that

not a good
things yet do nothing
about it

nearly two-thirds of white respondents did *not* think that whites as a group had benefited from past and present discrimination against black Americans. Nor did they think whites should take significant action to remedy continuing discrimination (Blendon et al. 1991). Moreover, as we have seen, many whites have asserted their innocence with a torrent of comments such as "my family never owned slaves." This white guiltlessness is professed at all class levels, even by presidential candidates. Clearly, much work has gone into reframing the American history of racial oppression so that white Americans can appear blameless for the brutality and carnage they and their ancestors created.

Fostering and Learning Racist Attitudes

THE ROLE OF ELITES

[Elsewhere in this book] we examined how elites have fostered a racist ideology rationalizing the realities of unjust impoverishment and enrichment. This effort is a major source of the racist ideology and its associated attitudes that are held in the nonelite part of the white population. Through various means the white elites have manipulated ordinary white Americans to accept the racist ideology and its component parts. Moreover, after the elements of an era's racist ideology and structural arrangements are in place, ordinary whites need less manipulation, for they generally understand what is in their group interest. Indeed, groups of ordinary people often generate new permutations on old racist ideas, innovations that in their turn reinforce and reproduce the racist ideology.

The often hidden power of the elite works through propagating the racist ideology and its associated beliefs and images by means of the mass media and the educational system, as well as in workplaces and churches. Increasingly, the mass media are as important as family or school in creating and propagating racist images and attitudes. When blacks encounter whites in a broad array of contemporary settings, they often meet negative beliefs about their abilities, values, and orientations. Racial barriers persist today because a substantial majority of whites harbor antiblack sentiments, images, and beliefs and because a large minority are very negative in their perspectives. When most whites interact with black Americans at work, in restaurants, on the street, at school, or in the media they tend to think about the latter, either consciously or unconsciously, in terms of racist stereotypes inherited from the past and constantly reiterated and reinforced in the present.

The translation of antiblack attitudes into actual discrimination is shaped not only by these attitudes but also by subjective norms, such as what other people might think, and by perceived behavioral controls, such as what the response to discrimination will be. Most discrimination is thereby contextualized. Routinized discrimination in housing, employment, politics, and public accommodations is carried out by whites acting alone or in groups. Whites are usually implementing shared racist attitudes and norms of their families and other important social networks. The social norms guiding discrimination can be formal or legal, but most today are unwritten and informal. Moreover, much antiblack action is not sporadic but is carried out repeatedly and routinely by numerous dominant-group members influenced by the norms of their social networks. Whites have the power to discriminate as individuals, but much of their power to harm comes from membership in traditionally white networks and organizations.

EVERYDAY RACISM: SUBTLE, COVERT, AND BLATANT

The character of discrimination varies. Whites may actively persecute blacks, or they may engage in an array of avoidance behaviors. Discrimination can be self-consciously motivated, or it can be half-conscious or unconscious and deeply imbedded in an actor's core beliefs. At the level of everyday interaction with black Americans, most whites can create racial tensions and barriers even without conscious awareness they are doing so. Examples of this include when white men lock their car doors as a black man walks by on the street or when white women step out or pull their purses close to them when a black man comes into an elevator they are on.[4] Stereotyped images of black men as criminals probably motivate this and similar types of defensive action. Such practices represent, according to Philomena Essed, the "integration of racism into everyday situations" (Essed 1991). Systemic racism is thus a system of oppression made up of many thousands of everyday acts of mistreatment of black Americans by white Americans, incidents that range from the subtle and hard to observe to the blatant and easy to notice. These acts of mistreatment can be nonverbal or verbal, nonviolent or violent. Moreover, many racist actions that crash in on everyday life are, from the victim's viewpoint, unpredictable and sporadic. Such actions are commonplace, recurring, and cumulative in their negative impact. They are, as one retired black American in her eighties put it, "little murders" that happen every day (Feagin & Sikes 1994).

In a specific setting, such as an employment setting, a white person in authority may select another white person over an equally or better qualified black person because of a preconceived notion that whites are more competent or because of discomfort with people perceived as somehow different. This latter type of subtle discrimination includes, in John Calmore's words, "the unconscious failure to extend to a minority the same recognition of humanity, and hence the same sympathy and care, given as a matter of course to one's own group." The selectivity results "often unconsciously—from our tendency to sympathize most readily with those who seem most like ourselves" (Calmore 1989). Yet oppression is not less serious because it is more subtle.

The racist system is made even more complex by its reinforcement in many other aspects of the everyday behavior of white Americans. When whites make racist comments to other whites, or when they think or say racist things when watching television by themselves or with their families, they also reinforce and maintain the white-racist system, even though no blacks are present. Racism is systemic because it infiltrates most aspects of life.

WHO DOES THE DISCRIMINATING?

Antiblack discrimination comes from all levels and categories of white Americans. Most whites are involved in some way in creating, reinforcing, or maintaining the racist reality of U.S. society. Depending on the situation and the opportunity to discriminate, very large numbers of whites can and do discriminate. Judging from housing audit studies[5], perhaps half of all whites are inclined to discriminate in some fashion, whether subtly or blatantly,

---

[4]Elsewhere in the book, Professor Feagin notes the irony of this situation: "Federal surveys of white victims of violent crime have found that about 17 percent of these attackers are black, while about three-quarters are white. Most violent crime affecting whites is carried out by *white* criminals. Yet most whites do not take similar precautions when they are in the presence of those whites—disproportionately white men—who perpetrate most of the violent crime suffered by whites. The reason for this is that they do not see themselves as being in the presence of someone likely to commit a violent crime when they are around those socially defined as white" (114).—Ed.

[5]Audit studies are used to test the degree to which discrimination exists in a particular social arena. In a housing audit study, a white couple and a black couple might (separately) visit rental agencies to inquire about the availability of rentals. If antiblack discrimination exists, the study will show that black couples were more likely to be told that no appropriate rentals are currently available, whereas the white couple may discover that several rentals just happen to be available.—Ed.

in situations where they have housing to rent or sell to black individuals or families. It may well be that whites discriminate at similarly high levels in other major institutional arenas.

There are actively antiracist whites scattered across the nation. They consistently and regularly speak out against white racism, even to the point of risking personal injury, friendships, and jobs. However, in regard to racist practice, most whites seem to fall into three other categories of action. One large group of whites regularly engage in overtly racist behavior; some of these whites are greatly consumed by their racist hatreds, as can be seen in lynchings and hate crimes. A second, much larger, group of whites discriminate against blacks in a variety of ways, as the occasion arises, but they frequently discriminate in less overt or more subtle ways and may often not be consciously aware of their discrimination. A third group of whites are consistently bystanders, engaging in less direct discrimination but knowingly providing support for those who do. Whites in the latter two groups often reject the type of blatant discrimination in which some in the first group engage, and may speak out against it, even as they themselves are engaging in more subtle or covert types of discrimination. Most whites in these three groups routinely think in white-oriented terms when choosing mates, neighborhoods, schools, and business partners. The racist system is thereby reinforced in daily interactions among whites. A sense of white superiority, however dim, seems to be part of the consciousness of most whites, including those who are relatively liberal on racial matters.

Interestingly, when issues of racism are discussed in the mass media, it is often working-class whites, the Archie Bunkers of television fame, who get tagged as the serious racists by the news and other media programs. Blue-collar violence against black Americans often does get significant news attention. Yet elite and middle-class whites are less frequently the focus of attention in media discussions of racial problems, and media discussions of discrimination that do involve a few middle class or elite discriminators usually avoid making connections to broader issues of systemic racism. Indeed, most elite and middle class whites vigorously deny that they are racist.

The portrait of discriminatory practice that emerges from research is quite different. Judging from hundreds of interviews that I and my colleagues have conducted with black and white Americans over the last decade, as well as from numerous other field studies of discrimination in housing, employment, and public accommodations, the majority of whites who do the serious discriminating are those with some power to bring harm, such as white employers, managers, teachers, social workers, real estate agents, lenders, landlords and apartment managers, and police officers (Feagin & Sikes 1994; Feagin, Vera, & Imani 1996; St. Jean & Feagin 1998). Middle-income and upper-income men and women are heavily implicated in racial oppression, though it is likely that in most major institutional areas, such as corporate promotions and urban policing, white men account for the lion's share of discriminatory actions. Generally speaking, these middle-income and upper-income whites are the ones in a position to most significantly affect black lives. Certainly, whites with less social or economic power also discriminate against black Americans in all income categories. Blue-collar employees frequently harass black workers in the workplace, and blue-collar bigots may yell racist epithets or hurl beer cans at a black man, woman, or child on the street. And working-class whites do seem to predominate as perpetrators in violent attacks on blacks in public places.

Given the right circumstances, most whites in all income groups have the ability to put black Americans "in their place," to frustrate or sabotage their lives for racist reasons. However, the patterns of discrimination vary. Many in the employer class, for instance, may be most interested in the exploitation of black workers, whose lowest-paid members constitute a reserve army of workers. In contrast, those in the white working and middle classes may be more concerned about housing or educational competition with black Americans, and they appear to be the most likely to discriminate in these latter areas.

Facing Lifetimes of Racial Discrimination

Whether subtle, covert, or blatant, racist practices are commonplace and recurring in a great variety of settings, ranging from public accommodations to educational facilities, business arenas, workplaces, and neighborhoods. How frequent is the discrimination faced by black Americans? What forms does this discrimination take? We do not yet have full answers to these questions, but recent surveys are helpful.

Researchers Nancy Krieger and Stephen Sidney gave some 2,000 black respondents a list of seven settings, such as the workplace, where one can face discrimination. Seventy percent of the female and 84 percent of the male respondents reported encountering discrimination in at least one area. The majority reported discrimination in at least three settings (Krieger & Sidney 1996). Similarly, a survey in the Detroit area asked black respondents about facing discrimination in six situations. Thirty-two percent reported discrimination recently in at least one of the situations, and four in ten reported facing at least one form of discrimination frequently (Forman, Williams, & Jackson 1997). In addition, a recent Gallup survey inquired of black respondents if they had experienced discrimination in five areas (work, dining out, shopping, with police, in public transportation) during the last month. Just under half reported discrimination in one or

more of these areas, including 70 percent of black men under the age of 35 (Gallup 1977). Many black Americans frequently face racist barriers in an array of societal arenas.

Even these substantial data are likely to be serious underestimates of the frequency of racist obstacles. Short survey questions do not explore the great range of discrimination faced by black Americans in everyday life. Indeed, survey research on the black experience with discrimination is relatively recent and remarkably limited. Survey questions are usually brief and customarily deal with only a few of the many types of racial mistreatment in the society. Indeed, a few survey researchers have suggested that more detailed questioning would reveal a more substantial portrait of discrimination (Sigelman & Welch 1991).

There are other reasons why the existing survey data do not adequately describe the reality of everyday racism. Most black and white Americans are taught as children to focus on individual reasons for personal barriers or failures. Most are taught that blaming others, however legitimate that may seem, is generally not appropriate. The reasoning behind such socialization seems to be that a system-blame orientation makes a person seem weak to those she or he respects. Some black Americans who suffer from discrimination may thus feel that talking too much about racist barriers suggests that they as individuals are not capable of dealing with these difficulties. However, this reluctance to report to survey researchers some of the discrimination they experience does not mean that the discrimination is not harmful in the respondent's life.

In addition, the terminology used in most surveys leads to underestimates. The term "discrimination" itself is used by some black Americans only for very serious abuse by whites. Lesser forms of mistreatment, because they are so commonplace, may not be characterized as discrimination. For example, a young black college professor recently explained to me that he does not ordinarily think of certain everyday examples of differential treatment—such as white cashiers not putting money in his hand because they do not want to touch a black person—as "racial discrimination." It is the more serious incidents of racism that he would recall if asked a question by a pollster about having encountered racial discrimination recently. Racial obstacles are so much a part of black lives that they generally become a part of the societal woodwork. This "everydayness" of racist barriers means that for many black Americans a survey researcher's brief question about discrimination will bring quickly to mind primarily the more serious incidents that stay at the front of the mind—and sometimes not the many intrusions of more subtle racism that occur in one's life. A failure to recall some incidents with whites when questioned briefly does not mean these encounters are of little consequence. In order to survive in a racist society, black Americans cannot attend consciously to all the racist incidents that intrude on their lives. The personal and family cost of too-close attention to much discrimination is too great.

To my knowledge, there is no research on the frequency of the incidents and events of discrimination faced by individual black Americans over their lifetimes. In a few exploratory interviews with black respondents, I have asked a question about frequency and gotten large estimates in response. For example, I asked a retired printer from New York City how often he has faced discrimination over the course of his life. After some careful reflection, this man estimated that he confronts at least 250 significant incidents of discrimination from whites each year, if he only includes the incidents that he consciously notices and records. Blatant and subtle mistreatment by white clerks in stores and restaurants are examples he had in mind. Judging from

my own field studies using in-depth interviews with black Americans, this man's experience seems representative. Over the course of a lifetime, a typical black man or woman likely faces *thousands* of instances of blatant, covert, or subtle discrimination at the hands of whites. Today, this omnipresent and routinized discrimination remains a key mechanism in the social reproduction of systemic racism.

Racial Discrimination in Public Places

Racial oppression has a distinctive spatial dimension, and its character can vary as a black person travels from the private home site to more public spaces. In one study that interviewed a large number of middle-class black Americans, a professor at a major university noted the stress that comes from dealing with whites in public places:

> If I'm in those areas that are fairly protected, within gatherings of my own group, other African Americans, or if I'm in the university where my status as a professor mediates against the way I might be perceived, mediates against the hostile perception, then it's fairly comfortable. . . . When I divide my life into encounters with the outside world, and of course that's ninety percent of my life, it's fairly consistently unpleasant at those sites where there's nothing that mediates between my race and what I have to do. For example, if I'm in a grocery store, if I'm in my car, which is a 1970 Chevrolet, a real old ugly car, all those things— being in a grocery store in casual clothes, or being in the car—sort of advertises something that doesn't have anything to do with my status as far as people I run into are concerned. (Feagin & Sikes 1994)

The increase in unpleasant encounters that comes as this professor moves from her home into public arenas such as stores is attributed to the absence of mediating factors such as whites knowing that she is a professor. Much antiblack discrimination occurs outside social contexts where there are family or friends or symbols of status that may reduce the likelihood of discrimination. On the way to work or school there can be unpleasant contacts with white police-officers, white clerks who will not touch your hand, white teenagers at a traffic light, or white customers in stores who are rude. These racist practices are not limited to one setting but rather take place across many public arenas.

DISCRIMINATION IN PUBLIC PLACES

Psychological researchers have staged situations of possible discrimination in public places, and have discovered that white bystanders will often not respond to a black person's call for help in a staged emergency situation. In contrast, whites are much more likely to respond to calls for help from a white person (Dovidio 1993). One study found that when a black woman drops a bag of groceries in a public setting, a white person is less likely to help her than to help a white woman who has the same mishap (Crosby et al. 1980). The racial identity of the person needing help strongly affects white responses. Overt dislike of black people is one likely reason. One analyst has suggested yet another possible reason for the white reactions: The more whites see of black people suffering, such as in the media, the more they come to see that condition as normal, and the less sympathy they have for blacks in difficulty (Delgado 1996).

In a recent Gallup survey asking black respondents about discrimination in various settings in the preceding month, retail shopping was the area in which the largest percentage (30 percent) of the sample reported racial mistreatment. Indeed, 45 percent of the young men in this sample reported such discrimination. Twenty-one percent of the sample (and 32 percent of young men) also reported discrimination when dining out. Discrimination in dining includes very poor service that seems racially motivated and often being seated in an undesirable place, such as at the back of the restaurant near the kitchen. Discrimination in retail stores encompasses the extra surveillance often faced by black shoppers and other discrimination by white sales clerks. In this survey, moreover, those black respondents with higher incomes reported encountering more discrimination than those with lower incomes (Gallup 1997). Leanita McClain, a prize-winning black columnist for the *Chicago Tribune*, once suggested an important difference between contemporary racist practices and the old segregationist practices: "The old racism wouldn't let blacks into some stores; the new racism assumes that any black person, no matter how well dressed, in a store is probably there to steal, not to buy." Undoubtedly drawing on her own experience, she added that the old racism "didn't have to address black people; the new racism is left speechless when a black, approached condescendingly, has an eloquent comeback" (McClain 1986).

Black customers face discrimination in the buying process. One major Chicago study examined more than 180 buyer-salesperson negotiations at ninety car dealerships. Black and white testers, with similar economic characteristics and bargaining scripts, posed as car buyers. White male testers got much better prices from the salespeople than did white women or black men and women. Compared to the markup given to white men, black men paid twice the markup and black women paid more than three times the markup. The average dealer profit in the final offers to each category of tester was as follows: white men, $362; white women, $504; black men, $783; and black women, $1237. In another study the researchers used thirty-eight testers who bargained for some 400 cars at 242 dealers. Again, black testers were quoted much higher prices that white men, though this time black men were quoted the highest prices. In some cases racist language was used by salespeople, but the researchers concluded that the more serious problem was stereotyping about how much black customers will pay. The cost of this commonplace discrimination is high. Given that black customers pay two to three times the markup offered to white men—if this holds across the nation—then black customers "annually would pay $150 million more for new cars than do white males" (Ayres 1991).

Discrimination has also been found in professional services. Recently, one group of researchers used actors to portray black and white patients with certain coronary disease symptoms. A total of 720 physicians were asked to look at these recorded interviews and other patient data, to assess the probability of coronary artery disease, and to suggest treatment. The researchers found differences in proposed treatment: blacks, and especially black women, were less likely to be recommended for cardiac catheterization, compared to whites with the same dress, occupations, and medical histories (Schulman et al. 1999; Bach et al. 1999). Another recent study reported in the *New England Journal of Medicine* found that black patients with lung cancer were less likely to receive the best surgical treatment than white patients. The reasons for these patterns of differential medical treatment along racial lines are yet to be delineated, but they may include not only traditional racial stereotypes but also specific stereotypes shared by some white medical practitioners, such as the notion that black patients who get special or expensive treatments are not as likely as whites to take proper care of themselves after treatment. The explanation for differences in surgery may also include the reluctance on the part of some black patients to trust the recommendations of white physicians. More research remains to be done, but

there is no reason to expect that the racism of the larger society does not extend into the medical professions.

References

Ayres, Ian. 1991. "Fair Driving: Gender and Race Discrimination in Retail Car Negotiations." *Harvard Law Review* 104 (February).

Bach, Peter B. et al. 1999. "Racial Differences in the Treatment of Early-Stage Lung Cancer." *New England Journal of Medicine* (October 14).

Blendon, Robert J. et al. 1998. "The Public and the President's Commission on Race." *The Public Perspective*, February.

Bobo, Lawrence. 1988. "Group Conflict, Prejudice and the Paradox of Contemporary Racial Attitudes." In *Eliminating Racism*, Phyllis A. Katz and Dalmas A. Taylor, eds. New York: Plenum.

Bobo, Lawrence, James R. Kluegel, and Ryan A. Smith. 1997. "Laissez-faire Racism: The Crystallization of a Kinder, Gentler, Antiblack Ideology." In *Racial Attitudes in the 1990s: Continuity and Change,* Steven A. Tuch and Jack K. Martin, eds. Westport, CT: Praeger.

Calmore, John O. 1989. "To Make Wrong Right: The Necessary and Proper Aspirations of Fair Housing." In *The State of Black America 1989.* New York: The National Urban League.

Crosby, Faye et al. 1980. "Recent Unobtrusive Studies of Black and White Discrimination and Prejudice: A Literature Review." *Psychological Bulletin* 87.

Culp, Jerome M., Jr. 1993. "Water Buffalo and Diversity: Naming Names and Reclaiming the Racial Discourse." *Connecticut Law Review* 26 (Fall).

Delgado, Richard. 1996. *The Coming Race War?* New York: New York University Press.

Devine, Patricia G. 1989. "Stereotypes and Prejudice: Their Automatic and Controlled Components." *Journal of Personality and Social Psychology* 56: 15–16.

Dovidio, John F. 1993. "The Subtlety of Racism." *Training and Development*, April.

Entman, Robert M. 1997. "Manufacturing Discord: Media in the Affirmative Action Debate." *Press/Politics* 2.

Essed, Philomena. 1991. *Understanding Everyday Racism.* Newbury Park, CA: Sage.

Feagin, Joe R., and Clairece B. Feagin. 1999. *Racial and Ethnic Relations.* 6th ed. Upper Saddle River, NJ: Prentice-Hall.

Feagin, Joe R., and Melvin P. Sikes. 1994. *Living with Racism: The Black Middle-Class Experience.* Boston: Beacon Press.

Feagin, Joe R., and Hernan Vera. 1995. *White Racism: The Basics.* New York: Routledge.

Feagin, Joe R., Hernan Vera, and Nikitah Imani. 1996. *The Agony of Education: Black Students at White Colleges and Universities.* New York: Routledge.

Forman, Tyrone, David R. Williams, and James S. Jackson. 1997. "Race, Place, and Discrimination." In *Perspectives on Social Problems,* Carol Brooks Gardner, ed. Stamford, CT: JAI Press.

Frankenberg, Ruth. 1993. *White Women, Race Matters.* Minneapolis: University of Minnesota Press.

Gallup Organization. 1997. *Black/White Relations in the United States.* Princeton, NJ: Gallup Organization.

Hughes, Michael. 1997. "Symbolic Racism, Old-fashioned Racism, and Whites' Opposition to Affirmative Action." In *Racial Attitudes in the 1990s: Continuity and Change,* Steven A. Tuch and Jack K. Martin, eds. Westport, CT: Praeger.

Jhally, Sut, and Justin Lewis. 1992. *Enlightened Racism.* Boulder, CO: Westview Press.

King, Joyce E. 1991. "Dysconscious Racism: Ideology, Identity, and the Miseducation of Teachers." *Journal of Negro Education* 60.

Kluegel, James R., and Eliot R. Smith. 1986. *Beliefs about Inequality.* New York: Aldine de Gruyter.

Krieger, Nancy, and Stephen Sidney. 1996. "Racial Discrimination and Blood Pressure." *American Journal of Public Health* 86.

Ladd, Everett C. 1995. "Rethinking the Sixties." *The American Enterprise,* May/June.

Lehigh, Scott. 1998. "Conflicting Views of Massachusetts; Poll Shows a Sharp Racial Divide over the State of Equality." *Boston Globe,* June 14.

McClain, Leanita. 1986. "The Insidious New Racism." In *A Foot in Each World,* Clarence Page, ed. Evanston, IL: Northwestern University Press.

NORC. 1990. *General Social Survey.* Chicago, IL: National Opinion Research Center.

Schulman, Kevin A., et al. 1999. "The Effect of Race and Sex on Physicians' Recommendations for Cardiac Catheterization." *New England Journal of Medicine,* February.

Sears, David O. 1988. "Symbolic Racism." In *Eliminating Racism,* Phyllis A. Katz and Dalmas A. Taylor, eds. New York: Plenum.

Sigelman, Lee, and Susan Welch. 1991. *Black Americans' Views of Racial Inequality: The Dream Deferred.* Cambridge: Cambridge University Press.

Smith, Matthew P. 1996. "Bridging the Gulf Between Blacks and Whites." *Pittsburgh Post Gazette,* April 7.

St. Jean, Yanick, and Joe R. Feagin. 1998. *Double Burden: Black Women and Everyday Racism.* New York: M. E. Sharpe.

Verba, Sidney, and Gary R. Orren. 1985. *Equality in America: The View from the Top.* Cambridge, MA: Harvard University Press.

Wellman, David. 1977. *Portraits of White Racism.* Cambridge: Cambridge University Press.

Questions

1. Make a list of the varieties of antiblack racist acts that were described by black people in Feagin's article. Assume that these kinds of discriminatory acts are familiar to just about every black person in the United States. Which discriminatory acts on your list are of the sort that the average white person is likely to have many opportunities to personally observe and understand as racist?

2. It has been claimed that subtle bias can be as harmful as overt bids. Does Feagin's work tend to support this claim? Explain why or why not. Then, are there any circumstances under which subtle bias is even more harmful than overt bias?

36

"RACE DOESN'T MATTER, BUT . . ."

The Effect of Race on College Professors' Experiences and Emotion Management in the Undergraduate College Classroom

Roxanna Harlow

I hate to admit it, but as a college student I gave little thought to the difficulties of being a professor. Indeed, it seemed to me to be a pretty cushy job. Not surprisingly, I've since changed my mind. However, as a white college professor, it's clear that my job is easier than my colleagues of color. Professor Harlow discusses how the experience of being a college professor varies depending upon one's race.

Anyone who has taught at the college level probably can tell numerous stories about the rewards and exhilaration as well as the challenges and frustrations of teaching undergraduates. Many scholars have studied and discussed the college classroom in various ways (see, for example, Gallop 1997; Hendrix 1998; Jacobs 1999; Statham, Richardson, and Cook 1991); few, however, talk about it, other than anecdotally, as an emotional space where professors' multiple status characteristics shape their affective experiences in the classroom as they negotiate roles, expectations, and power dynamics through interaction with students. In this research I examine how race shapes

"'Race Doesn't Matter, but . . .' The Effect of Race on Professors' Experiences and Emotion Management in the Undergraduate College Classroom" by Roxanna Harlow from *Social Psychology Quarterly*, Vol. 66, No. 4 (December, 2003: pp. 348–363). Reprinted by permission of the American Sociological Association and the author.

professors' perceptions and experiences in the undergraduate college classroom, how they manage the emotional demands arising from these experiences, and how the management process affects the nature of their jobs overall.

Research has shown how black scholars' experiences differ from those of their white counterparts, particularly in regard to role conflict, isolation, and a lack of respect and legitimacy as scholars (Aguirre 2000; Baker 1991; Banks 1984; Fields 1996; Menges and Exum 1983; Phelps 1995; Sinegar 1987; Smith and Witt 1993). Surprisingly little of the research, however, addresses the degree to which a professor's race influences his or her experience in the classroom. When it is discussed, it is typically mentioned briefly and/or treated as a minor factor in the professor's routine. Smith and Witt (1993), for example, found that African Americans reported statistically significant higher levels of stress than white professors in regard to service and research, but not teaching. The scale used to measure teaching stress, however, measured the *tasks* of teaching, not the qualitative experience connected to professors' perceptions of the classroom climate, their relationship with students, their feelings about teaching, or the management of these views and feelings in order to teach effectively. Hendrix (1995), Rains (1995), and Moore (1996) found that black and white professors' experiences in the classroom indeed are qualitatively different. Yet because of scope limitations and small sample sizes (with Ns of 6 to 17), it is unclear whether these experiences are due to race or to gender, and the emotional component of teaching has been mostly unexplored.

As Goffman (1963) notes, race is an attribute that people consider when forming opinions about groups or individuals; therefore black professors may find themselves managing a racial stigma in the classroom. Such a stigma, as Feagin and Sikes (1994) explain, eventually can take an emotional toll. In this research I examine how the crediting[1] and the discrediting aspects of race differentially shape black[2] and white professors' experiences with undergraduate teaching and classroom emotion management. Because this area of research is largely unexplored, the answers to these questions provide greater insight into racial differences in faculty members' experiences in the classroom. They help us as well to understand how differences in emotional labor and management may create more and

_____

[1]Goffman (1963) defines a stigma as a discrediting attribute. It is difficult to fully understand the process of devaluing certain characteristics, however, without discussing how we come to value other characteristics. Crediting attributes, then, add or have the potential to add value or credibility to a person or a group of people. This concept is useful for understanding the relational nature of stigma, and how the valued and the devalued are integrally tied together. Jason Jimerson originally named and conceptualized this idea in personal discussions.

[2]In this study, the terms *black* and *African American* are used interchangeably to refer to black people acculturated in the United States.

different work for professors, depending on their social status characteristics.

EMOTIONAL LABOR AND MANAGEMENT

Hochschild (1983) discusses emotion as a workplace commodity, and estimates that one-third of the American workforce engages in emotional labor. While most jobs require us to deal with our emotions in some way (e.g., holding back anger at the boss), she distinguishes between this type of emotion work and emotional labor. Emotion work is the process of handling our daily, personal emotions; emotional labor involves evoking, performing, and managing emotions that are a required aspect of a job or occupation. Emotion management is the process of handling emotions in both personal (emotion work) and professional (emotional labor) spheres.

Emotional labor and management can be understood as a form of impression management (Goffman 1959; Wood 2000). According to Goffman (1959), impression management is the process through which people project a self-image that is consistent with how they want to be seen by others. Goffman believed that the ability to mask one's true emotions while providing the appropriate emotional display is the true test of a high-quality social performance. College teaching requires extensive emotional labor: professors try to perform and evoke emotions such as enthusiasm and excitement while also managing or suppressing their own immediate feelings and moods (Bellas 1999; Harlow 2002). These performances are affected, however, by the degree to which students and teachers begin their relationship with a mutual acceptance of the professor's status and identity.

IDENTITY AND AFFECT CONTROL THEORY

Identity theory states that a person's behavior is directly connected to her or his conception of self, and that these conceptions are shaped in part by responses from others through interaction (Stryker 1992). According to this theory, we all have multiple identities that are arranged hierarchically: that is, some identities are more relevant than others from situation to situation. For professors in the classroom, their identity as teacher tends to be one of the most central and most salient at that moment, and they perform in certain ways so as to reinforce that identity.[3] If it is not confirmed through interactions with students, a negative emotional effect may result. According to affect control theory, when our conception of self is not confirmed, our emotions provide the cue that things are going wrong. We then adjust our definition of a situation or change our behavior so as to correct the emotional dissonance (Heise 1989).

Similar to affect control theory, Burke (1991) discusses "the control-system view of the identity process" (p. 838). He explains that when a person's understanding of her or his own identity (the identity standard) in a social situation is inconsistent with feedback from others in that situation (inputs), that person becomes distressed. To resolve this feeling, the person changes her or his behavior (outputs) in an effort to alter the external feedback in a way that is consistent with the internally defined identity. Burke notes that matching one's identity standard with others' inputs can involve a complex cycle of interactions. Ultimately, however, these two must match; otherwise, high levels of stress result. In this paper I seek, in part, to explain what self-definitions professors are trying to establish with their classroom performances, and how these vary by race. If the definitions are not confirmed through interactions with students, what are the emotional consequences for professors, and how are they managed?

Race is what Cohen (1982) defines as a diffuse status characteristic: that is, even though a particular status may be irrelevant to a task, persons of high status are considered more competent. Therefore black professors' identity performances may involve providing "proof" in any number of ways to justify their presence in a high-status position. As Rakow (1991) observes, the statuses of white, male, and professor are all high, and thus are compatible and even anticipated. For African Americans, however, their racial status is inconsistent with their faculty status; therefore they may find themselves doing "tiring 'identity work'" (Rakow 1991:10) in order to reconcile students' perceptions with their own. The findings presented here show that race affects the amount of work professors do in the classroom; negotiating a racial stigma creates emotion work and labor for African American professors beyond that required of their white peers.

Data and Methods

From February through November 1999, I conducted 58 in-depth interviews with 29 white and 29 African American faculty members at a large Midwestern state university with a 91 percent white student population. Twenty-six respondents were female; 32 were male. They included 22 assistant professors, 27 associate professors, and nine full professors, ranging in age from 30 to 65 with a mean age of 44. Eighteen of the men and six of the women taught in traditionally applied fields such as business and health science; 14 men and

---

[3] An important aspect of identity theory is the concept of identity salience: the likelihood that an identity will be invoked at a particular point in time (Stryker 1992). I use the terms *central* and *salient* here because I am also referring to the concept of psychological centrality (Stryker and Serpe 1994). Psychological centrality pertains to the likelihood that an identity will be most important or most central for a person at a particular point in time. Centrality implies an awareness of the importance of the identity; salience does not (Stryker and Serpe 1994).

20 women were housed in the humanities or social sciences. I included only full-time tenure-track faculty members who taught at least one undergraduate course. I excluded professors in the School of Music because students were evaluated differently there. I targeted faculty members acculturated in the United States so that respondents' understandings of race and racial dynamics would be comparable.

The sample selection was based on the population of black professors meeting the above criteria; then I matched them with white participants of similar gender, rank, and department or area of study. Of the 30 black faculty members who qualified for the study, 29 agreed to participate. Of the corresponding white faculty members whom I contacted, only two did not participate. This response rate was extremely high (97% black and 94% white) in view of the time commitment asked of the participants.

The semistructured interview consisted of 37 open-ended questions and lasted, on average, 75 minutes. I (an African American) asked the professors about their anxiety on the first day of class, their teaching style, the level of students' energy in their classes, students' opinions of the respondents, how they would like to be viewed by students, and other subjects. Questions directly related to their social status were not raised until midway through the interview, when I asked about students' positive and negative views of the respondents, and whether they felt that their own race or gender affected any of those views. Because I kept the initial questions race-neutral (in regard to the professor), the race-related responses to those questions were generated on their own, and were a product of what was most important to the respondents at that time. The remainder of the interview dealt with topics such as challenges to authority, how the respondents handled those challenges, concerns about teaching, and job stress. I ended the interview with a general question about racism and sexism.

Findings

RACIAL DIFFERENCES IN FACULTY MEMBERS' PERCEPTIONS

"Race doesn't matter, but . . ." The black faculty members in my sample were aware of the negative stereotypes associated with their racial group, and often commented on the continued existence of racial problems in society today. Although they had a sophisticated understanding of macro social processes and how they affected racial inequality, almost half of the black professors were reluctant to claim that their race mattered to students, or that race influenced their classroom experience in any negative way. Problems related to racial issues were often internalized ("It's my own fault for thinking about it too much") or downplayed altogether (see Table 1). For example, one professor stated, "Race is always an issue," but then went on to emphasize regional differences that he felt were more important. He explained, "Just in general, getting over the, if you will, racial divide, I really haven't had any problems like that here. I just try to understand my students" (Respondent 25: black male).

Race was "always an issue" on a macro level, but this professor wanted to make clear that he personally had no problem with a "racial divide." Similarly, after pondering the effect of race on his teaching, another professor stated, "Uh, the race thing? In the sense that I'm aware that I'm black, but—I'm not sure . . . but I don't really think that it's going to make a difference in the classroom" (Respondent 23: black male).

Although these two professors expressed doubts about the significance of their race in the classroom, they also expressed an awareness of their subordinate racial status as well

Table 1 Self-Reported Classroom Experiences, by Race and Gender

	% of African American Professors			% of White Professors		
	Men (*n* = 16)	Women (*n* = 13)	Total (*N* = 29)	Men (*n* = 16)	Women (*n* = 13)	Total (*N* = 29)
Initially Downplayed or Internalized Their Racialized Classroom Experiences[a]	50	31	41	n/a	n/a	n/a
Believe Students Immediately Notice Their Racial Status	75	92	83	6	0	3
Believe Students Question Their Intellectual Authority (Competency/Qualifications)	94	54	76	6	8	7
Feel They Must Prove Their Competence/Intelligence	56	54	55	6	15	10
Received Inappropriate Student Challenges to Intellectual Authority	44	23	34	0	15	7
Racial Double Standard (White Advantage)	50	77	62	25	8	17

[a]This experience is not applicable to white professors because, for the most part, they did not interpret their classroom work in a racialized way.

as their rarity in the academy.[4] They believed that as soon as they stepped into the classroom, students were surprised by their race and/or noticed it immediately (see Table 1).

The data, then, produced seemingly contradictory statements about the effect of race on these professors' classroom experiences. After downplaying it initially, they then proceeded to explain how, in fact, race mattered significantly. Most of these professors felt that students stereotyped them: 76 percent of the black professors reported that students questioned their competency, qualifications, and credibility (see Table 1).

In essence, most black professors felt that their classes always contained at least some students who questioned their right to hold the status of professor. For example, immediately after Respondent 23 stated that he did *not* think his race made a difference in the classroom, he went on to explain that he *had* been concerned about his race because most of the students were white and had never seen a black professor before, especially in his discipline. As a result, he made an extra effort to appear qualified and knowledgeable:

> I wanted them to know that I know what I'm talking about, and that I'm really well qualified to teach what I teach. And I want them to know that I'm here because of my skills and my ability and that I can do a really good job. And so it's very important to me that when I teach, that comes across, because people will try to challenge you. (Respondent 23: black male)

---

[4]In 1997, black professors made up only 4.9 percent of the full-time faculty in degree-granting colleges and universities; 59 percent were at or below the rank of assistant professor. Whites made up 84 percent of the full-time faculty, with 53 percent at or above the rank of associate professor (National Center for Education Statistics 1997).

Similarly, after being asked, "Do you think your race or gender affects students' positive or negative views of you?" Respondent 25, who had said he had no problems with the "racial divide," added:

> Undoubtedly. Now exactly how, I'm not totally sure . . . but I did have a very, very interesting experience, though, my first semester with a black student. . . . And he said to me after about the third lecture of the class . . . "Dr. [his name], I'm so glad that you're here. I've never had a black professor before. And you're competent too." Well, I was glad that he was glad to see me . . . but his statement "and you're competent too" was very interesting coming from him. Now if that was coming from him, just think of what maybe some white kid from some rural farm town in [the state] is thinking when I stand up in front of him, [who] doesn't know me from Adam. (Respondent 25: black male)

Like Respondent 23, this faculty member may not have had problems with the racial divide, but he believed that his race influenced how students viewed him and his ability to teach. Although these responses from black professors initially sounded contradictory, the contradiction is resolved when understood in the context of a management strategy (to be discussed later), which enabled them to function effectively day to day.

In contrast to the black professors, some white male professors downplayed their intellectual presence in order to seem more approachable to students:

> I think that initially the main thing one's doing is not trying to make oneself seem knowledgeable because they're going to think that [I'll be that way] as a professor. I think it's a matter of trying to make oneself seem approachable and accessible, so for me there's a certain element of calculated self-deprecation. (Respondent 47: white male)

This difference in classroom reality for black and for white professors was illustrated in part by faculty members' reports of students' challenges to their classroom authority.

"I really do know what I'm talking about." Although few men of either race reported concerns about their physical authority in the classroom (the right to be in charge, organize the course, assign materials, and discipline students), black men reported that students resisted their intellectual authority—that is, their knowledge and competency (see Table 1). This was particularly the case for black assistant professors.

Black women also felt that their competency was questioned, but overall they were more likely to report challenges to their physical rather than their intellectual authority.[5] Young black women at the assistant and associate levels were the most likely to report challenges to both their competence and their control over the classroom. Explaining this dynamic, Respondent 34 (black female) noted that students do not usually see black people in positions of power, especially black women. As a result, they may doubt black women's academic and leadership capabilities. Commenting on the social structural factors shaping students' often unconscious attitudes about blackness, femininity, and intelligence, this professor went on to explain how looking young simply exacerbated the problem for such women.

This question of competency was an issue even for professors who taught predominantly nonwhite classes and/or classes on race-related topics. For example, when asked, "When students see you're their professor, what do you think they're thinking?" Respondent 32 (black

---

[5]Describing the "cult of true womanhood," Hill-Collins noted that "'true' women possessed four cardinal virtues: piety, purity, submissiveness, and domesticity" (1991:71). Thus, although black women (like black men) felt that students doubted their competence, they also struggled, in ways that the men did not, with issues of authority in regard to classroom presence (physical authority) as they tried to balance students' expectations of "submissiveness" and "domesticity" with power and control.

female) replied, "So when I walk into the class, they know it's a class dealing with black people. I walk in as a black professor. I think to some degree it probably legitimates the content. . . ." The remainder of her response was surprising, however:

> And I think when I walk in there, other things go through their minds. Probably whether or not I'm good, whether or not I'm tough, whether or not this is going to be a blow-off class for them, whether I'm an affirmative action professor, whether I'm going to be one of these attitudes kind of professor, whether I'm going to be a racist professor, whether I'm going to be the kind of professor who makes white people feel bad about what has happened to black people in America.[6]

Despite the course topic, this professor believed that her race triggered for students negative stereotypes about black people (in regard to competence and browbeating about racism), and black women in particular (in regard to anger and attitude). Another professor similarly explained that his blackness gave him credibility in teaching race-related topics. He then added:

> But then on the other hand there's always an undercurrent of "He's black, he couldn't possibly know what he's talking about." And a lot of that will come more from black students than white. 'Cause a lot of our people have internalized those kinds of ideas, you know. That's what they've been taught. (Respondent 30: black male)

He went on to explain how he states his credentials on the first day of class in an effort to counteract the negative stereotypes that students of all races have internalized.

---

[6]Several black professors used the term *affirmative action professor* or *affirmative action hire* to indicate that students thought they were unqualified. This is not to say that they themselves equated affirmative action with a lack of qualification. They seemed aware, however, that many students viewed affirmative action as the hiring of unqualified people of color.

The black professors' responses on these issues differed sharply from those of white faculty members. In reply to the question "When students see you're their professor, what do you think they're thinking?" one professor stated:

> I don't know if I've ever thought about what they were thinking. . . . I suspect that there is some response to the fact that I am still pretty young and female. I suspect perhaps now there is some feeling of "Is this a graduate student or professor?" I don't know if I ever thought about that. (Respondent 21: white female)

Similarly, another professor responded:

> I'm not sure I know exactly. I think I probably look a little young . . . but otherwise, I don't think that there's much about me that really makes me stand out specifically. . . . I don't think I make a very striking first impression or anything. (Respondent 28: white male)

Responses such as "I don't know" or "I never thought about that before" were common among white faculty members answering this question; these were followed by comments on how their age (and, in the case of women, their gender) might play a role in what students thought. White professors usually did not have to anticipate students' reactions to phenotypic cues, though such anticipation was commonplace for black professors. In contrast to the black faculty members, most white faculty members, especially white males, took students' confidence in them for granted: 76 percent of black professors felt that students called their qualifications into question, in contrast to only 7 percent of white professors (see Table 1).

The white professors had hardly considered how their racial status might shape students' personal and professional evaluations of them. When asked, "Do you feel that your race or gender affects students' positive or negative views of you?" white women were most likely to focus on their gender alone. White men often overlooked the crediting aspects of both their gender and their race. When Respondent

20, for example, was asked if his race and gender shaped students' attitudes, he replied:

> I don't think so. In my department, there's more women than men. . . . I mean there's a complex mix of faculty, and I don't think it makes any difference to any [students] really. . . . For example, we have black faculty, we have faculty from other countries, we have a lot of women [faculty], I told you. I think that for some of [the students] it's a fairly new experience, something they may not have thought about in their high school, especially, or their home towns. But . . . I don't think it matters a lot to them. (Respondent 20: white male)

In response to this question, another professor replied:

> Ohhh, I don't think so. I don't think so. I mean, it probably helps to be a white male but it's really hard to know. You know, the only reason why it may help is that they see me in them. . . . They look at me and say, well, this guy is kinda like me, so—I have no proof of that and I really have no way of knowing if that's really even to any great advantage. (Respondent 31: white male)

Although these professors were skeptical that there was any benefit to being a white male, many of the black faculty members in my sample felt that in fact it was a great advantage.

"THAT'S WRONG": CHALLENGES AND IMPRESSION MANAGEMENT

To resist negative stereotyping, the black professors in my sample often performed competence and authority by projecting a strict, authoritative demeanor, making students aware of their professional achievements, and (for black women) reminding students to call them Doctor or Professor rather than by their first name, Ms., or Mrs. Although women were more likely than men to describe their classroom style as authoritative, this distinction broke down along racial lines: 69 percent of white female respondents reported that they were authoritative in the classroom, while all of the black women did so. Among the men, 44 percent of the black faculty members considered their style to be authoritative, in contrast to only 19 percent of the white respondents (see Table 2). In addition, 69 percent of black women felt that they had to remind

Table 2 Self-Reported Presentation and Evaluation, by Race and Gender

	% of African American Professors			% of White Professors		
	Men ($n = 16$)	Women ($n = 13$)	Total ($N = 29$)	Men ($n = 16$)	Women ($n = 13$)	Total ($N = 29$)
Authoritative	44	100	69	19	69	41
Reminds Students to Call Them by Their Appropriate Title	13	69	38	0	31	14
Evaluated by Students as Cold/Mean/Intimidating	0	62	28	0	15	7
Evaluated by Students as Too Hard/Demanding	44	62	52	19	38	28
Felt Physically Threatened by a Student	0	31	14	0	8	3
Validation Regarding Classroom Performance Is Internal	56	46	52	19	0	10
Classroom Problems Decline with Age	25	54	38	6	54	28

students to call them Doctor or Professor, but only 31 percent of white women reported doing so.

In spite of their efforts to demonstrate competency, black professors reported more challenges to their intellectual authority than did their white counterparts (see Table 1). In most of these challenges, as described by the professors, students questioned their knowledge directly or indirectly in a way that was inappropriate or disrespectful. The challenges included arguments on basic points of the discipline (e.g., a student might argue that the sociological imagination is not defined as the professor defined it), questioning the validity of lecture material, and more indirect forms of resistance. Describing a challenge by a white student, one professor stated:

> First of all, he simply thought he knew everything, and that he certainly couldn't learn anything from me. And [he] went so far as to say, when I was trying to explain something, . . . "That's wrong, that's just wrong, that's not true.". . . This is very, very difficult because at the same time, you can't go off on him because you've got to be respectful and you've got to be this professional person and stuff, but it's very, very hurtful, you know, particularly from someone who was not an excellent student. (Respondent 45: black male)

While this professor was trying to manage his anger, he was also managing the frustration and "hurt" caused by the doubts to his competency from a student he believed was not even particularly bright.

In addition to direct challenges such as this, black professors discussed how students challenged them in indirect ways. In the following account, as in the situation described above, a student doubted the veracity of the class lecture material. The professor recounted what the student did to confirm her information:

> [The student] tells me that he was having trouble believing what I said, and that he went over to the [discipline] department to see if he could get that documented and validated. And I said, "And?" And he said, "Well, I asked some [discipline] professors and they said that such a document existed and that you were telling the truth." And I said, "Uh-huh." . . . Some students don't believe what I have to say and they will have to go and ask somebody white before they believe it. (Respondent 32: black female)

According to this respondent's account, although the student did not challenge her knowledge directly in class, the fact that he went to another professor in her discipline, specifically a white male professor, to confirm her information was an indirect challenge to her knowledge and intellectual authority over the class and the material. She added that she believed such double-checking of her material was quite frequent.

CONSEQUENCES OF RACIALIZED CLASSROOM EXPERIENCES

"I have to be perfect." For most of the black professors, one consequence of the challenges to their intellectual authority was a need to prove their competence to students (see Table 1). They were particularly conscious about doing well because they did not want to reinforce negative attitudes about black people's intelligence. This pressure to be a racial model often manifested itself in overpreparation and in a hyperawareness of speech patterns or mistakes of any kind. One professor stated:

> Given that I'm the only one [black female], you start to think, well God, you know, are people lookin' at what I do? And they've never seen a black female teaching in [the department]. [The discipline is] for white males. . . . So you always have that doubt. And it makes you a little nervous. Makes you want to do that much better so that you don't have to worry about it. . . . (Respondent 19: black female)

Another professor explained:

> When I first started teaching, I felt as though I had to be almost perfect. . . . And even the first couple of years here, if I would misspeak in

terms of making a mistake, I always felt as though students would stereotype me, so I always felt as though I couldn't make a mistake. I always felt as though I had to be perfect in terms of the content of the lecture, the delivery of the lecture. . . . And I just think that if we have more black faculty members who are here, Latino and otherwise, I could feel increasingly the freedom to not be perfect. (Respondent 33: black male)

These professors felt pressure not only to prove individual competence, but also, as reflected in the above quotes, to be perfect for the whole race because people might interpret any negative personal performance as a reflection on African Americans overall.

"If I were white . . ." In addition to the pressure to be perfect, black professors were coping with the frustration of receiving what they viewed as differential treatment by students: 62 percent of black professors raised the issue of a racial double standard (see Table 1). Overall they had the sense that white professors automatically commanded students' respect while black professors had to earn it. Respondents also felt that white professors were thought to be smarter, less biased, and more legitimate as faculty members. One professor explained:

I give my credentials the first day of class. And I do feel to some extent I have to, and I know nobody else [in this department] does. . . . So tomorrow I'll stand in front of class and tell them all that I've done and blah, blah, blah. . . . I've found if I don't do that, I don't get the respect that I would deserve. I'd get more people challenging what I say about [the discipline]. (Respondent 42: black male)

As the only nonwhite professor in his department, this respondent felt that the double standard lay in the need to prove his competence, unlike his white colleagues. The white professors in my sample tended to report that their intellectual authority over classroom material was assumed and taken for granted.

Another professor commented as follows on the double standard:

There are many black professors here at [the school] that think there's like a tax, OK—a black tax—on their course evaluations. So like say, if they got a 2.5 on their evaluation. That's equivalent to like a 2.8 for a white professor of comparable quality. That may be true and it may not be true; I don't really know.[7] (Respondent 25: black male)

Although he expressed his doubts about the actual existence of a "black tax," this respondent implied, at the very least, that the presence of a quantitative double standard was not implausible.

In addition to the frustration arising from a racial double standard, some black professors felt that their white colleagues did not understand how greatly their classroom experiences differed qualitatively:

[S]tudents expect the traditional hierarchy of society to prevail in the class. That is, white male on the top, and a black woman on the bottom. And they can't get ready for the fact that a black woman is teaching this class! And that the [white male teaching assistants] are not in charge . . . You know, I think that if I were white, that I wouldn't have to go through those sorts of things in my classroom . . . but at every turn I have to remind students that I am the professor. I'm not just the instructor . . . I have a PhD . . . I have to tell students, "Look. I graduated *summa cum laude*, I got my master's and my PhD . . . I published these books and these articles . . ." to let them know that, you know, I may be black, but what you think about in terms of what it means to be black is not necessarily what I am, if it's a negative perception . . . being uneducated and being illiterate and not able to think and basically being an affirmative action kind of a person. So those are the kinds of things that I think make my job more difficult. Much more difficult. And

---

[7]At this university, the items on the course evaluations are scored on a scale from 0 (lowest) to 4 (highest).

it's unfortunate that the so-called standardized evaluation process that we have been using in colleges and universities [does] not take these things into consideration. In fact, if you raise [the subject], the college will look at you like you're crazy because they don't deal with that. And they're actually being honest because they don't understand the sheer level of complexity on the part of the professor and the student in dealing with these kinds of issues. So I'm not blaming my colleagues. I'm just saying they're really very ignorant {pause} about what goes on in my classes, and the extent to which I have to use measures above and beyond what they have to use to even survive in the classroom. (Respondent 15: black female)

As stated above, some black professors sensed that people did not *get it*. They felt that people did not understand how being black made teaching a different job for them than if they had been white.

"THE ANGRY BLACK WOMAN": INTERSECTIONS OF GENDER AND RACE

While research has shown that white female faculty members struggle for respect and authority in the college classroom (Baker and Copp 1997; Harlow 2002; Martin 1984; Statham, Richardson, and Cook 1991),[8] black women confronted the burden of negotiating both femaleness and blackness. One respondent replied as follows to the question "Do you feel that your race or gender affects [students'] positive or negative views of you?":

I definitely believe that there's something to this business about me being angry and not opening up. I'm just so aware of this whole black woman as, you know, angry person kind of myth. Somehow that we're like 70 percent attitude. . . . But at the same time, I'm like look,

I'm not gonna be skinnin' and grinnin' Sambo every day. . . . I think they don't allow me the room to be serious, and I really do think that's about the "angry black woman with much attitude" myth, you know? . . . I do feel like some students expect that I'm gonna be more maternal, and if I don't live up to that, then the only place that's familiar to them that they can go in terms of judgments is "Oh, then she must have an attitude." So I'm not like "Oh come here, honey, let me hug you, feel my bosom" kind of thing, right . . . but I really do feel like I don't have options. That there are these sorts of two caricatures of black womanhood that they're familiar with, and that somehow I have to work within those. (Respondent 9: black female)

In other words, in the case of black women who do not fulfill the "motherly" expectation and who spend time doing serious work in class, students may interpret their seriousness or businesslike approach within the framework of stereotypical images of black femininity: that is, that black women are angry and have an attitude. Although both white and black women reported efforts to avoid being seen as mean or cold, black female faculty members were more likely to report actual evaluations by students as mean, cold, or intimidating. Black women also were more likely to report physical or verbal threats by students (see Table 2).

EMOTION MANAGEMENT STRATEGIES

For many professors, especially women, age and experience reduced some of the problems they faced in the college classroom (see Table 2). Negative constructions of blackness endure, however, so black professors had to rely on long-term strategies to manage the racial component of teaching.

"I don't have this problem, but . . ." As stated earlier, many black professors initially downplayed the effects of their race in the classroom; doing so helped them manage the overall

---

[8] I also found that women's emotional labor in the classroom is more extensive than men's. Emotional labor due to gender, however, functions differently than emotional labor due to race. This paper focuses only on the racial differences.

frustration of a double standard due to racism. By reconceptualizing a group problem such as racism as a problem unique to an individual's pedagogical strategies, black professors gained a greater sense of control over their classrooms and felt less like prisoners of students' negative social conditioning. One professor explained that some of his black peers faced racial difficulties in the classroom, but he did not experience this problem:

And I say this from the perspective of some of my peers, particularly black professors that I'm familiar with from all around the nation. Quite frankly they have a difficult time, some of 'em, dealing with large white classrooms. . . . Some of that, in my opinion, is not just the problem of dealing with a lot of white students. The problem is themselves! If they would just be themselves and stop trying to live up to some ideal that they think other people are looking for, they'd be fine in a lot of occasions. . . . I know [that] a lot of the white majority students, [when] they see a young black professor, they're gonna try 'em, OK. It's just that simple. . . . The question is, you know, is there a center there? Are you centered enough to just know that you have a job to do, and just go ahead and do it, and be yourself, and that should be enough, and if it's not, well, you're probably in the wrong profession. (Respondent 25: black male)

On the one hand, this professor acknowledged the structural constraints that are placed on black professors because of the stigmatization of blackness ("white majority students, they see a young black professor, they're gonna try 'em"). At the same time, however, he emphasized that such classroom dynamics did not pertain to him ("I say this from the perspective of some of my peers"). Thus it was a problem that ultimately depended on how an individual "centered" himself or herself, even though he heard such comments from black professors everywhere. Through this interpretation of the issue, he managed individually what would otherwise have been an insurmountable structural problem.

Similarly, when I asked Respondent 16, a black female, if she felt that her race or gender affected students' positive or negative views of her, she replied, "Oh I'm sure it does, but I don't know how. I'm sure it does. I'm certain it does." I then asked how she could be so certain if she was not even sure how students' views were affected. She replied:

Well, because in our society, race matters. It matters. And because it matters, then I think there are some students who probably do look at my race. However, I'm not a very race-conscious person. . . . I think I present myself such that people will see me as a friendly person, as an outgoing person, as a competent person, and for those reasons they would not then assume negative traits about me based on my ethnicity. And I think if I'm doing my work well in the classroom, that even though students might see me initially as being an African American teacher, that at the end they ought to see me as the professor, as a human agent in the classroom trying to bring about creative intellectual change. And I do think that I don't recall any of my students focusing unduly on my race. (Respondent 16: black female)

Once again, this professor acknowledged the social structural constraints of race ("in our society, race matters"), but then went on to exempt herself from these potential effects by saying that if she focused on doing her job well, students would not care about such things. Both by distancing herself from the structural impact of race and by not caring about what students thought (just "doing my work well in the classroom"), she alleviated some of the potential frustration of having to deal with stereotypes, the fear of being perfect, double standards, and the rest.

"I don't care what other people think." The idea of "just doing my job," "centering," and "looking internally" was common among most of the black faculty members (see Table 2). Many explained that as long as they did their job well, what they looked like would ultimately

be irrelevant to students. By adopting this attitude, they decreased the emotion management involved in worrying about stereotyping, credibility, and so forth. In explaining how he felt at the beginning of a new semester, one professor stated:

> [W]hen I walk into the classroom, I'm excited to get things started, and I feel very, very confident about my skills . . . and I don't worry about other people's politics anymore. Kind of like I have an internal focus, rather than an external focus about what other people think about me. It's more important how I feel about me. *I finally came to rest with that* (emphasis added). (Respondent 8: black male)

This professor later expressed pride in his new degree of emotional control in the classroom. Not only did he have to learn to reject consistently negative images of himself, he also had to learn how to suppress his anger in order to teach effectively.

Another professor explained that she *wanted* to stop caring about students' perceptions, but was continuing to struggle with this difficult form of emotion management. In reply to a question about how much she enjoyed teaching, she stated:

> I really try to do it the best way that I can do it. But sometimes it's pretty difficult because I just get tired of dealing with these issues. And I feel that I've been put upon. And I feel that [because] I have to deal with issues that other people don't have to deal with. . . . So I should just forget about it and go into the classroom and do the best job that I can. And that's what I try to do. But some days it is really a challenge. . . . Some of my colleagues just go into class and talk, and, you know, that's it. (Respondent 15: black female)

Frustrated by the fact that she could not, like her white colleagues, simply go into class and lecture without concerns about racism and stereotyping, this respondent realized that she had to stop caring so much about students' views. At the same time, she observed that just

doing the best job she could while ignoring her emotions was extremely difficult.

Analysis and Discussion

Consistent with findings by Feagin and Sikes (1994), many black faculty members were reluctant to say that their race mattered in the classroom, and looked for other reasons to explain their racialized experiences.[9] Ultimately, however, they expressed frustration about what they considered to be students' challenges to their intellectual authority. Yet despite this frustration, black professors also discussed how their race was beneficial to them in the classroom: many noted that black students were often happy to see that they had a black professor. In addition, they felt that their race increased their legitimacy when they were teaching on racial topics.

According to their reports, however, this legitimacy had rigid boundaries. Students may have felt that African American professors brought their personal experiences to topics of race, thus providing an "authentic" understanding of the issue. Yet at the same time, these professors discussed how their race detracted from their credibility in regard to students' perceptions of their *intellectual* knowledge of the material: that is, the scholarly, "objective" assessment of racial issues. Thus, although students might accept as legitimate certain experiential knowledge transmitted by the professor, black professors simultaneously might face doubts of their competency regarding their intellectual interpretations of the course work. Adding to the professors' frustration was the

---

[9]Half of the black men at some point downplayed the effect of their race in the classroom, but only one-third of the black women did so. This difference may exist because black women faced both gender and race discrimination, and so were less likely to downplay racial factors when the gender issues they faced were so widely acknowledged. Therefore their discussion of gender difference also integrated race: they discussed the experience of being *black* women in the classroom.

fact that both white and nonwhite students doubted their academic abilities.

Research by Chambers, Lewis, and Kerezsi (1995) adds credence to the view that students question black professors' competency. They found that white students generally continue to perceive African Americans negatively, particularly when "situations involve close social contact . . . or when African Americans are not cast in stereotypical roles" (p. 55). They argued that white students may view black professors as ineffective and may question their competency. In addition, after Hendrix (1998) interviewed students to explore the influence of race on professors' credibility, she found that overall, black professors were considered less credible than white professors, particularly when the course subject was not directly connected to their race.

Because of doubts about credibility, I found a heightened concern, particularly among black assistant professors, about making a mistake in class. Although some of this fear may have been due to lack of tenure, the junior professors stated explicitly that their concerns about tenure stemmed from their research, not their teaching. Their responses were consistent with findings by Aguirre (2000), who argued that because of nonwhite faculty members' small numbers and minority status, white students view them solely as affirmative action hires (which they interpret incorrectly as unqualified hires). These perceptions by students contribute to an environment in which faculty members of color may feel that they must "be overachievers in a context where [w]hite faculty are not themselves overachievers" (Aguirre 2000:72).

As a result of this pressure to overachieve, "minority faculty may perceive themselves as occupying a contradictory role in the academic workplace—outsiders but expected to be model citizens in academe," as they try to prove that they are equal to white faculty members (Aguirre 2000:51). The large amount of physical and emotional impression management involved in trying to convince students

of their competence and their right to be in charge would be eliminated if students identified immediately with the professor and associated that identity with intellect and professionalism. In this study, most white professors did not mention challenges to their competency, an indication that they did not need to constantly prove and project intellectual authority.

In contrast to their white colleagues, a mistake in class by black professors could be interpreted as incompetence; such an interpretation reinforces negative stereotypes and reflects negatively on black people as a whole. Not only did black professors carry the weight of knowing that their performance might symbolize the potential of an entire racial group, but many had white colleagues who might not have noticed or acknowledged the differences in their jobs due to race. Most of the white professors in the sample did not observe the possibility of racial differences in the classroom.

Being a credit to the race, while also experiencing the frustration of a racial double standard as well as denials from white colleagues that such a double standard exists, requires black professors to manage both personal and professional emotions far more extensively than their white peers. This is particularly the case for younger black professors: because they have less experience, they may struggle harder than their seasoned colleagues to win a sense of control over their ability to be effective. This challenge is intensified by the feeling that their knowledge as professors is already devalued because they are black. This dynamic is complicated further by gender: the black female respondents reported the effects of both gender and racial stereotypes as they worked to maintain their physical and intellectual presence in the classroom.

Hill-Collins (1991) discusses four cultural conceptualizations of black womanhood that historically have perpetuated black women's subordinate status. Two of these are relevant here. Probably the most common and most widespread is the mammy—the nurturing, obedient, asexual black woman. Another is the matriarch—the "overly aggressive, unfeminine women" (Hill-Collins 1991:74) who prevent the men in their lives from asserting their masculinity. According to Hill-Collins (1991), "the matriarch is essentially a failed mammy, a negative stigma applied to those African-American women who dared to violate the image of the submissive, hard-working servant" (p. 74). Thus the evaluations as mean, cold, angry, and attitudinal that so many of the black female respondents reported receiving (see Table 2) are consistent with this matriarch image: that is, their gender is also racialized. Black female professors seem to be allowed even less "room to be serious" (Respondent 9: black female) than their white female counterparts, who also struggle against stereotypical gender expectations. For those black women who did not succeed in walking the fine line between masculinity and femininity, students were even more likely to interpret their serious and/or professional behavior as overaggressive and insufficiently subservient.

To be effective in the classroom, black professors had to learn how to manage the frustration of a racial double standard and the pressure of representing an entire racial group. Trying not to care about students' stereotypical views emerged as a key management strategy. If they could ignore this type of negative feedback, the professors could gain a greater sense of control over the emotional and physical labor of the classroom.

If (as stated by identity theory) our conception of self is shaped in part by responses from others through interaction, and if our behavior is often shaped by our desire to have our conception of self reinforced (Stryker 1992), then professors' classroom performances are in part an effort to reinforce, through students, an identity as a good, knowledgeable professor. Many black faculty members, however, reported that such an identity was not reinforced for them through students, in part because of broader cultural understandings of blackness as inferior. Therefore, to function effectively in the classroom, they had to diminish or even eliminate the importance of interaction with students for defining and confirming their identity as teacher.

Thus the data showed that more than half of the black faculty members engaged in *selective identity construction*. This process can be defined as selectively incorporating responses from interactions that confirm conceptions of self, while rejecting responses that conflict with such conceptions, regardless of the significance of that interaction in defining a highly central or salient identity. For example, in spite of the centrality of the teacher identity in the classroom, many of the black professors learned to ignore identity cues from interactions with students that challenged their professorial identity. Instead they developed and reinforced their teacher identity through other means: positive interactions with students, interactions with friends, family, and peers, and internal strength. They emphasized selecting out interactions that contradicted their self-perceptions; meanwhile they maintained an internal focus so that their professor status was validated from within, not by students.

This process of maintaining an internal focus, however, involves extensive emotion management. According to affect control theory, as stated earlier, when our conception of self is not confirmed, we adjust our definition of a situation or change our behavior so as to relieve the resulting emotional tension (Heise 1989). The black professors who were the most satisfied with teaching, however, worked to ignore those emotional cues altogether instead of paying attention to the cues and trying constantly to change their behavior in order to correct students' perceptions of them. These professors learned to suppress and (in some cases) ultimately eliminate feelings of frustration, anger, or inadequacy in order to diminish the importance of those nonconfirming interactions; thus students' responses would no longer be integral to shaping their conceptions of self or their professorial identity.

Instead of adjusting their actions or the definition of the situation to change how they felt, as affect control theory would predict, these professors learned how to change how they felt in an effort to change, at some point, the definition of the situation. That is, by ignoring emotional cues from negative interactions with students, and by focusing solely on confirming their identity internally, they hoped, through their display of confidence and competence, to ultimately change how students viewed them and regarded black professors in general. Respondent 45 (black male) explained that this process required a movement from "conventional thinking" and "conventional reality" to "the new way of thinking."

For this professor, "conventional thinking" occurs when black professors accept as important the stereotypical ways in which students may view and/or interact with them. By changing their behavior in response to these interactions—by overpreparing, citing credentials, dressing up, or growing frustrated—professors give power and validation to that "conventional reality" and "conventional truth": that is, students will doubt the competence of black professors, and blackness will be stigmatized. The "new way" of thinking, however, requires such a firm grounding in one's sense of self and identity that interaction with students no longer serves to shape that identity. In other words, ideas about black inferiority ("conventional truth") are marginalized in that individual's reality and ultimately lose power.

Once this emotion management has been accomplished, the emotional labor in the classroom becomes much easier because one can focus on projecting excitement, enthusiasm, and friendliness without the need also to manage fear, frustration, and anger. When a professor can focus solely on the traditional aspects of the job, her or his feelings of enjoyment,

relaxation, and confidence can increase, with the effect of potentially undermining students' negative stereotypes about blackness. Contrary to Burke's (1991) notion of the identity process, selective identity construction saves professors from experiencing high levels of stress, even when students' perceptions do not match professors' self-concepts.

Although these black professors acknowledged racism as a systemic problem, by constructing their professorial identity selectively they were able to lessen the individual-level effect of race bias in order to function effectively in the classroom. When one professor was asked how racism and sexism influenced the way he thought about life in general, he replied:

> I think it influences it a lot. You know, despite my point that it seems silly to spend a lot of time and energy worrying about these things, these things do matter, especially in America. . . . So I think it matters a great deal, but it doesn't much matter to me. (Respondent 35: black male)

As this professor stated succinctly, people's preconceptions have the power, on a societal level, to affect the life chances of entire groups of people, and therefore are critically important. Yet although people are not insulated from the social and cultural effects of such judgments, they must live their lives as individuals. In that respect, in order to avoid paralysis by racism, other people's opinions must "not much matter."

Conclusion

When black and white faculty members teach, they function in disparate realities. White professors operate in a social space where whiteness is crediting and privileged, but is invisible and thus is taken for granted; African American professors function in a space where blackness is discrediting and devalued. The findings reported here suggest that these cultural and structural understandings of blackness and whiteness consequently shape the way in which black and white professors experience the college classroom and understand, interpret, and manage those experiences. Because these results are based on faculty experiences at a large, predominantly white university, further research is needed in settings that differ in size, region, and racial composition. In addition, an exploration of the classroom experiences of other nonwhite and international faculty members would be instructive.

The reality for many African American professors is that there will always be students who question their competency, credentials, and ability to teach and assess students' work. This reality, combined with the weight of representing the entire race, can be emotionally draining, particularly for young faculty members who may spend hours poring over lectures so as not to be anything less than perfect or totally prepared. To manage the frustrations resulting from a racial double standard, and to be effective in the classroom, my black respondents learned to stay cognizant of existing macro-level racial barriers while diminishing the importance of those barriers on the micro-level in order to prevent racism from debilitating them in their everyday lives.

References

Aguirre, Adalberto. 2000. *Women and Minority Faculty in the Academic Workplace.* San Francisco: Jossey-Bass.

Baker, Fostenia. 1991. "A Study of Black Faculty Perceptions of Hiring, Retention and Tenure Processes in Major White Universities." PhD dissertation, Department of Educational Leadership, George Washington University, Washington, DC.

Baker, Phyllis and Martha Copp. 1997. "Gender Matters Most: The Interaction of Gendered Expectation, Feminist Course Content, and the Pregnancy in Student Course Evaluations." *Teaching Sociology* 25:29–43.

Banks, William. 1984. "Afro-American Scholars in the University." *American Behavioral Scientist* 27:325–38.

Bellas, Marcia L. 1999. "Emotional Labor in Academia: The Case of Professors." *Annals of the American Academy of Political and Social Science* 561:96–110.

Burke, Peter. 1991. "Identity Processes and Social Stress." *American Sociological Review* 56:836–49.

Chambers, Tony, Jacqueline Lewis, and Paula Kerezsi. 1995. "African American Faculty and White American Students: Cross-Cultural Pedagogy in Counselor Preparation Programs." *The Counseling Psychologist* 23:43–62.

Cohen, Elizabeth G. 1982. "Expectation States and Interracial Interaction in School Settings." *Annual Review of Sociology* 8:209–35.

Feagin, Joe and Melvin Sikes. 1994. *Living With Racism.* Boston: Beacon.

Fields, Cheryl. 1996. "A Morale Dilemma." *Black Issues in Higher Education* 13:22–23, 25–26, 28–29.

Gallop, Jane. 1997. *Feminist Accused of Sexual Harassment.* Durham: Duke University Press.

Goffman, Erving. 1959. *The Presentation of Self in Everyday Life.* Garden City, NY: Anchor Books.

———. 1963. *Stigma.* New York: Simon and Schuster.

Harlow, Roxanna. 2002. "Teaching As Emotional Labor: The Effects of Professors' Race and Gender on the Emotional Demands of the Undergraduate College Classroom." PhD dissertation, Department of Sociology, Indiana University, Bloomington.

Heise, David. 1989. "Effects of Emotion Displays on Social Identification." *Social Psychology Quarterly* 52:10–21.

Hendrix, Katherine. 1995. "Professor Perceptions of the Influence of Race on Classroom Dynamics and Credibility." Presented at the annual meetings of the Western States Communication Association, February 10–14, Portland, OR.

———. 1998. "Student Perceptions of the Influence of Race on Professor Credibility." *Journal of Black Studies* 28:738–63.

Hill-Collins, Patricia. 1991. *Black Feminist Thought.* New York: Routledge.

Hochschild, Arlie R. 1983. *The Managed Heart.* Berkeley: University of California Press.

Jacobs, Walter. 1999. "Learning and Living Media Culture in the College Classroom: An Autoethnography of a Possible Postmodern Space." PhD dissertation, Department of Sociology, Indiana University, Bloomington.

Martin, Elaine. 1984. "Power and Authority in the Classroom: Sexist Stereotypes in Teaching Evaluations." *Signs* 9:482–92.

Menges, Robert and William Exum. 1983. "Barriers to the Progress of Women and Minority Faculty." *Journal of Higher Education* 54:123–44.

Moore, Valerie Ann. 1996. "Inappropriate Challenges to Professional Authority." *Teaching Sociology* 24:202–206.

National Center for Education Statistics. 1997. *1997 Integrated Postsecondary Education Data System, Fall Staff Survey.* Washington, DC: U.S. Department of Education.

Phelps, Rosemary. 1995. "What's in a Number? Implications for African American Faculty at Predominantly White Colleges and Universities." *Innovative Higher Education* 19:255–68.

Rains, Frances. 1995. "Views From Within: Women Faculty of Color in a Research University." PhD dissertation, Department of Educational Leadership and Policy Studies, Indiana University, Bloomington.

Rakow, Lana. 1991. "Gender and Race in the Classroom: Teaching Way out of Line." *Feminist Teacher* 6:10–13.

Sinegar, Lee Alton. 1987. "Coping With Racial Stressors: A Case Study of Black Professors in White Academe." PhD dissertation, Department of Counseling, George Washington University, Washington, DC.

Smith, Earl and Stephanie Witt. 1993. "A Comparative Study of Occupational Stress Among African American and White University Faculty: A Research Note." *Research in Higher Education* 34:229–41.

Statham, Anne, Laurel Richardson, and Judith Cook. 1991. *Gender and University Teaching.* Albany: SUNY Press.

Stryker, Sheldon. 1992. "Identity Theory." Pp. 871–76 in *Encyclopedia of Sociology,* edited by Edgar Borgatta and Marie Borgatta. New York: Macmillan.

Stryker, Sheldon and Richard Serpe. 1994. "Identity Salience and Psychological Centrality: Equivalent, Overlapping, or Complementary Concepts?" *Social Psychology Quarterly* 57:16–35.

Wood, Elizabeth Anne. 2000. "Working in the Fantasy Factory: The Attention Hypothesis and the Enacting of Masculine Power in Strip Clubs." *Journal of Contemporary Ethnography* 29:5–31.

Questions

1. What sort of emotion labor is involved in being a college professor? Why does Professor Harlow conclude that professors of color must do more emotion labor than white professors?

2. Reflect upon your experiences in school. What sort of emotion labor is required to play the student role? Do you think that the amount of emotion labor required from students tends to differ by race and gender?

3. Recall Mills' distinction (reading 1) between personal troubles and public issues. Do the professors studied by the author of this article tend to regard the extra effort they think they must make to prove themselves as professors, to be personal troubles or public issues?

   In your judgment, what are the differences in the experiences of white professors and professors of color—personal troubles or public issues?

4. Other research has shown that non-white professors generally have to work harder to get the same scores on their teaching evaluations. In view of the evidence presented by Professor Harlow, why do you think that is so?

37

CONFESSIONS OF A NICE NEGRO, OR WHY I SHAVED MY HEAD

Robin D. G. Kelley

No matter how much they distort reality, stereotypes exist and have an impact on people's lives. In this 1995 article, Robin Kelley recounts his experiences with what, to him, was a new stereotype.

It happened just the other day—two days into the new year, to be exact. I had dashed into the deserted lobby of an Ann Arbor movie theater, pulling the door behind me to escape the freezing winter winds Michigan residents have come to know so well. Behind the counter knelt a young white teenager filling the popcorn bin with bags of that awful pre-popped stuff. Hardly the enthusiastic employee; from a distance it looked like she was lost in deep thought. The generous display of body piercing suggested an X-generation flower child—perhaps an anthropology major into acid jazz and environmentalism, I thought. Sporting a black New York Yankees baseball cap and a black-and-beige scarf over my nose and mouth, I must have looked like I had stepped out of a John Singleton film. And because I was already late, I rushed madly toward the ticket counter.

The flower child was startled: "I don't have anything in the cash register," she blurted as she pulled the bag of popcorn in front of her for protection.

"Huh? I just want one ticket for *Little Women,* please—the two-fifteen show. My wife and daughter should already be in there." I slowly gestured to the theater door and gave her one of those innocent childlike glances I used to give my mom when I wanted to sit on her lap.

"Oh, god . . . I'm so sorry. A reflex. Just one ticket? You only missed the first twenty minutes. Enjoy the show."

Enjoy the show? Barely 1995 and here we go again. Another bout with racism in a so-called liberal college town; another racial drama in which I play the prime suspect. And yet I have to confess the situation was pretty funny. Just two hours earlier I couldn't persuade Elleza, my four-year-old daughter, to put her toys away; time-out did nothing, yelling had no effect, and the evil stare made no impact whatsoever. Thoroughly frustrated, I had only one option left: "Okay, I'm gonna tell Mommy!" Of course it worked.

So those five seconds as a media-made black man felt kind of good. I know it's a product of racism. I know that the myth of black male violence has resulted in the deaths of many innocent boys and men of darker hue. I know that the power to scare is not real power. I know all that—after all, I study this stuff for a living! For the moment, though, it felt good. (Besides, the ability to scare with your body can come in handy, especially when you're trying to get a good seat in a theater or avoid long lines.)

I shouldn't admit this, but I take particular pleasure in putting fear into people on the look-out for black male criminality mainly because those moments are so rare for me. Indeed, my *inability* to employ blackmaleness as a weapon is the story of my life. Why I don't possess it, or rather possess so little of it, escapes me. I grew up poor in Harlem and Afrodena (the Negro West Side of Pasadena/Altadena, California). My mom was single during my formative preadolescent years, and for a brief moment she even received a welfare check. A hard life makes a hard nigga, so I've been told.

Never an egghead or a dork, as a teenager I was pretty cool. I did the house-party circuit on Friday and Saturday nights and used to stroll down the block toting the serious Radio Raheem boombox. Why, I even invaded movie theaters in the company of ten or fifteen hooded and high-topped black bodies, coloniz-ing the balconies and occupying two seats per person. Armed with popcorn and Raisinettes as our missiles of choice, we dared any usher to ask us to leave. Those of us who had cars (we called them hoopties or rides back in that day) spent our lunch hours and precious class time hanging out in the school parking lot, running down our Die Hards to pump up Cameo, Funkadelic, Grandmaster Flash from our car stereos. I sported dickies and Levis, picked up that gangsta stroll, and when the shag came in style I was with it—always armed with a silk scarf to ensure that my hair was laid. Granted, I vomited after drinking malt liquor for the first time and my only hit of a joint ended abruptly in an asthma attack. But I was cool.

Sure, I was cool, but nobody feared me. That I'm relatively short with dimples and curly hair, speak softly in a rather medium to high-pitched voice, and have a "girl's name" doesn't help matters. And everyone knows that light skin is less threatening to white people than blue-black or midnight brown. Besides, growing up

with a soft-spoken, uncharacteristically passive West Indian mother deep into East Indian reli-gions, a mother who sometimes walked bare-foot in the streets of Harlem, a mother who in-sisted on proper diction and never, ever, ever used a swear word, screwed me up royally. I could never curse right. My mouth had trouble forming the words—"fuck" always came out as "fock" and "goddamn" always sounded like it's spelled, not "gotdayum," the way my Pasadena homies pronounced it in their Calabama twang. I don't even recall saying the word "bitch" unless I was quoting somebody or some authorless vernacular rhyme. For some unknown reason, that word scared me.

Moms dressed me up in the coolest mod outfits—short pant suits with matching hats, Nehru jackets, those sixties British-looking turtlenecks. Sure, she got some of that stuff from John's Bargain Store or Goodwill, but I al-ways looked "cute." More stylish than roguish. Kinda like W. E. B. Du Bois[1] as a toddler, or those turn-of-the-century photos of middle-class West Indian boys who grow up to become prime ministers or poets. Ghetto ethnographers back in the late sixties and early seventies would not have found me or my family very "authentic," especially if they had discovered that one of my middle names is Gibran, after the Lebanese poet Kahlil Gibran.

Everybody seemed to like me. Teachers liked me, kids liked me; I even fell in with some notorious teenage criminals at Pasadena High School because *they* liked me. I remem-ber one memorable night in the ninth grade when I went down to the Pasadena Boys' Club

---

[1]W. E. B. Du Bois (1868–1963) was the first African American to earn a Ph.D from Harvard University (1895). He taught sociology at several universities, was a strong advocate for racial integration, and in 1909 founded the National Association for the Advancement of Colored People. Ultimately, Du Bois lost faith in the possibility of integration and began to promote segregation. He was dismissed from the NAACP and moved to Ghana, where he lived until his death.—Ed.

to take photos of some of my partners on the basketball team. On my way home some big kids, eleventh-graders to be exact, tried to take my camera. The ringleader pulled out a knife and gently poked it against my chest. I told them it was my stepfather's camera and if I came home without it he'd kick my ass for a week. Miraculously, this launched a whole conversation about stepfathers and how messed up they are, which must have made them feel sorry for me. Within minutes we were cool; they let me go unmolested and I had made another friend.

In affairs of the heart, however, "being liked" had the opposite effect. I can only recall having had four fights in my entire life, all of which were with girls who supposedly liked me but thoroughly beat my behind. Sadly, my record in the boxing ring of puppy love is still 0–4. By the time I graduated to serious dating, being a nice guy seemed like the root of all my romantic problems. I resisted jealousy, tried to be understanding, brought flowers and balloons, opened doors, wrote poems and songs, and seemed to always be on my knees for one reason or another. If you've ever watched "Love Connection" or read *Cosmopolitan,* you know the rest of the story: I practically never had sex and most of the women I dated left me in the cold for roughnecks. My last girlfriend in high school, the woman I took to my prom, the woman I once thought I'd die for, tried to show me the light: "Why do you always ask me what I want? Why don't you just *tell* me what you want me to do? Why don't you take charge and *be a man?* If you want to be a real man you can't be nice all the time!"

I always thought she was wrong; being nice has nothing to do with being a man. While I still think she's wrong, it's an established fact that our culture links manhood to terror and power, and that black men are frequently imaged as the ultimate in hypermasculinity. But the black man as the prototype of violent hypermasculinity is as much a fiction as the happy Sambo. No matter what critics and stand-up comics might say, I know from experience that not all black men—and here I'm only speaking of well-lighted or daytime situations—generate fear. Who scares and who doesn't has a lot to do with the body in question; it is dependent on factors such as age, skin color, size, clothes, hairstyle, and even the sound of one's voice. The cops who beat Rodney King and the jury who acquitted King's assailants openly admitted that the size, shape, and color of his body automatically made him a threat to the officers' safety.

On the other hand, the threatening black male body can take the most incongruous forms. Some of the hardest brothas on my block in West Pasadena kept their perms in pink rollers and hairnets. It was not unusual to see young black men in public with curlers, tank-top undershirts, sweatpants, black mid-calf dress socks, and Stacey Adams shoes, hanging out on the corner or on the basketball court. And we all knew that these brothas were not to be messed with. (The rest of the world probably knows it by now, too, since black males in curlers are occasionally featured on "Cops" and "America's Most Wanted" as notorious drug dealers or heartless pimps.)

Whatever the source of this ineffable terror, my body simply lacked it. Indeed, the older I got and the more ensconced I became in the world of academia, the less threatening I seemed. Marrying and having a child also reduced the threat factor. By the time I hit my late twenties, my wife, Diedra, and I found ourselves in the awkward position of being everyone's favorite Negroes. I don't know how many times we've attended dinner parties where we were the only African Americans in the room. Occasionally there were others, but we seemed to have a monopoly on the dinner party invitations. This not only happened in Ann Arbor, where there is a small but substantial black population to choose from, but in the

Negro mecca of Atlanta, Georgia. Our hosts always felt comfortable asking us "sensitive" questions about race that they would not dare ask other black colleagues and friends: What do African Americans think about Farrakhan? Ben Chavis? Nelson Mandela? Most of my black students are very conservative and career-oriented—why is that? How can we mend the relations between blacks and Jews? Do you celebrate Kwanzaa? Do you put anything in your hair to make it that way? What are the starting salaries for young black faculty nowadays?

Of course, these sorts of exchanges appear regularly in most black autobiographies. As soon as they're comfortable, it is not uncommon for white people to take the opportunity to find out everything they've always wanted to know about "us" (which also applies to other people of color, I'm sure) but were afraid to ask. That they feel perfectly at ease asking dumb or unanswerable questions is not simply a case of (mis)perceived racelessness. Being a "nice Negro" has a lot to do with gender, and my peculiar form of "left-feminist-funny-guy" masculinity—a little Kevin Hooks, some Bobby McFerrin, a dash of Woody Allen—is regarded as less threatening than that of most other black men.

Not that I mind the soft-sensitive masculine persona—after all, it is the genuine me, a product of my mother's heroic and revolutionary child-rearing style. But there are moments when I wish I could invoke the intimidation factor of blackmaleness on demand. If I only had that look—that Malcolm X/Mike Tyson/Ice Cube/Larry Fishburne/Bigger Thomas/Fruit of Islam look—I could keep the stupid questions at bay, make college administrators tremble, and scare editors into submission. Subconsciously, I decided that I had to do something about my image. Then, as if by magic, my wish was fulfilled.

Actually, it began as an accident involving a pair of electric clippers and sleep deprivation—a bad auto-cut gone awry. With my lowtop fade on the verge of a Sly Stone afro, I was in desperate need of a trim. Diedra didn't have the time to do it, and as it was February (Black History Month), I was on the chitlin' lecture circuit and couldn't spare forty-five minutes at a barber shop, so I elected to do it myself. Standing in a well-lighted bathroom, armed with two mirrors, I started trimming. Despite a steady hand and what I've always believed was a good eye, my hair turned out lopsided. I kept trimming and trimming to correct my error, but as my flattop sank lower, a yellow patch of scalp began to rise above the surrounding hair, like one of those big granite mounds dotting the grassy knolls of Central Park. A nice yarmulke could have covered it, but that would have been more difficult to explain than a bald spot. So, bearing in mind role models like Michael Jordan, Charles Barkley, Stanley Crouch, and Onyx (then the hip-hop group of the hour), I decided to take it all off.

I didn't think much of it at first, but the new style accomplished what years of evil stares and carefully crafted sartorial statements could not: I began to scare people. The effect was immediate and dramatic. Passing strangers avoided me and smiled less frequently. Those who did smile or make eye contact seemed to be deliberately trying to disarm me—a common strategy taught in campus rape-prevention centers. Scaring people was fun for a while, but I especially enjoyed standing in the line at the supermarket with my bald head, baggy pants, high-top Reeboks, and long black hooded down coat, humming old standards like "Darn That Dream," "A Foggy Day," and "I Could Write a Book." Now *that* brought some stares. I must have been convincing, since I adore those songs and have been humming them ever since I can remember. No simple case of cultural hybridity here, just your average menace to society with a deep appreciation for Gershwin, Rodgers and Hart, Van Heusen, Cole Porter, and Jerome Kern.

Among my colleagues, my bald head became the lead subject of every conversation. "You look older, more mature." "With that new cut you come across as much more serious than usual." "You really look quite rugged and masculine with a bald head." My close friends dispensed with the euphemisms and went straight to the point: "Damn. You look scary!" The most painful comment was that I looked like a "B-Boy wannabe" and was "too old for that shit." I had to remind my friend that I'm an OBB (Original B-Boy), that I was in the eleventh grade in 1979 when the Sugar Hill Gang dropped "Rapper's Delight," and that *his* tired behind was in graduate school at the time. Besides, B-Boy was not the intent.

In the end, however, I got more questions than comments. Was I in crisis? Did I want to talk? What was I trying to say by shaving my head? What was the political point of my actions? Once the novelty passed, I began getting those "speak for the race" questions that irritated the hell out of me when I had hair. Why have *black men* begun to shave their heads in greater numbers? Why have so many black athletes decided to shave their heads? Does this new trend have some kind of phallic meaning? Against my better judgment, I found myself coming up with answers to these questions—call it an academician's reflex. I don't remember exactly what I said, but it usually began with black prizefighter Jack Johnson, America's real life "baaad nigger" of the early twentieth century, whose head was always shaved and greased, and ended with the hip-hop community's embrace of an outlaw status. Whatever it was, it made sense at the time.

The publicity photo for my recent book, *Race Rebels*, clearly generated the most controversy among my colleagues. It diverged dramatically from the photo on my first book, where I look particularly innocent, almost angelic. In that first photo I smiled just enough to make my dimples visible; my eyes gazed away from the camera in sort of a dreamy, contemplative pose;

my haircut was nondescript and the natural sunlight had a kind of halo effect. The Izod shirt was the icing on the cake. By contrast, the photograph for *Race Rebels* (which Diedra set up and shot, by the way) has me looking directly into the camera, arms folded, bald head glistening from baby oil and rear window light, with a grimace that could give Snoop Doggy Dogg a run for his money. The lens made my arms appear much larger than they really are, creating a kind of Popeye effect. Soon after the book came out, I received several e-mail messages about the photo. A particularly memorable one came from a friend and fellow historian in Australia. In the course of explaining to me how he had corrected one of his students who had read an essay of mine and presumed I was a woman, he wrote: "Mind you, the photo in your book should make things clear—the angle and foreshortening of the arms, and the hairstyle make it one of the most masculine author photos I've seen recently????!!!!!!"

My publisher really milked this photo, which actually fit well with the book's title. For the American Studies Association meeting in Nashville, Tennessee, which took place the week the book came out, my publisher bought a full-page ad on the back cover of an ASA handout, with my mug staring dead at you. Everywhere I turned—in hotel elevators, hallways, lobbies, meeting rooms—I saw myself, and it was not exactly a pretty sight. The quality of the reproduction (essentially a high-contrast xerox) made me appear harder, meaner, and crazier than the original photograph.

The situation became even stranger since I had decided to abandon the skinhead look and grow my hair back. In fact, by the time of the ASA meeting I was on the road (since abandoned) toward a big Black Power Afro—a retro style that at the time seemed to be making a comeback. Worse still, I had come to participate in a round-table discussion on black hair! My paper, titled "Nap Time: Historicizing the Afro," explored the political implications of competing narratives of the Afro's origins and meaning. Overall, it was a terrific session; the room was packed and the discussion was stimulating. But inevitably the question came up: "Although this isn't directly related to his paper, I'd like to find out from Professor Kelley why he shaved his head. Professor Kelley, given the panel's topic and in light of the current ads floating about with your picture on them, can you shed some light on what is attractive to black men about baldness?" The question was posed by a very distinguished and widely read African American literary scholar. Hardly the naif, he knew the answers as well as I did, but wanted to generate a public discussion. And he succeeded. For ten minutes the audience ran the gamut of issues revolving around race, gender, sexuality, and the politics of style. Even the issue of bald heads as phallic symbols came up. "It's probably true," I said, "but when I was cutting my hair at three-o'clock in the morning I wasn't thinking 'penis.'" Eventually the discussion drifted from black masculinity to the tremendous workloads of minority scholars, which, in all honesty, was the source of my baldness in the first place. Unlike the golden old days, when doing hair was highly ritualized and completely integrated into daily life, we're so busy mentoring and publishing and speaking and fighting that we have very little time to attend to our heads.

Beyond the session itself, that ad continued to haunt me during the entire conference. Every ten minutes, or so it seemed, someone came up to me and offered unsolicited commentary on the photo. One person slyly suggested that in order to make the picture complete I should have posed with an Uzi. When I approached a very good friend of mine, a historian who is partly my Jewish mother and partly my confidante and *always* looking out for my best interests, the first words out of her mouth were, "Robin, I hate that picture! It's the worst picture of you I've ever seen. It

doesn't do you justice. Why did you let them use it?"

"It's not that bad," I replied. "Diedra likes it—she took the picture. You just don't like my bald head."

"No, that's not it. I like the bald look on some men, and you have a very nice head. The problem is the photo and the fact that I know what kind of person you are. None of your gentleness and lovability comes out in that picture. Now, don't get a swelled head when I say this, but you have a delightful face and expression that makes people feel good, even when you're talking about serious stuff. The way you smile, there's something unbelievably safe about you."

It was a painful compliment. And yet I knew deep down that she was telling the truth. I've always been unbelievably safe, not just because of my look but because of my actions. Not that I consciously try to put people at ease, to erase conflict and difference, to remain silent on sensitive issues. I can't quite put a finger on it. Perhaps it's my mother's politeness drills? Perhaps it's a manifestation of my continuing bout with shyness? Maybe it has something to do with the sense of joy I get from stimulating conversations? Or maybe it's linked to the fact that my mom refused to raise me in a manner boys are accustomed to? Most likely it is a product of cultural capital[2]—the fact that I *can* speak the language, (re)cite the texts, exhibit the manners and mannerisms that are inherent to bourgeois academic culture. My colleagues identify with me because I can talk intelligently about their scholarship on their terms, which invariably has the effect of creating an illusion

---

[2]The concept of cultural capital has gained currency through the work of Marxist sociologist Pierre Bourdieu, who uses the term to refer to specific skills and competencies (for example, the ability to use language and other social skills) that middle- and upper-class parents are able to pass on to their children. Ownership of cultural as well as economic capital provides advantages to members of the middle and upper classes and increases the probability of their success.—Ed.

of brilliance. As Frantz Fanon said in *Black Skin, White Masks,* the mere fact that he was an articulate *black* man who read a lot rendered him a stunning specimen of erudition in the eyes of his fellow intellectuals in Paris.

Whatever the source of my ineffable lovability, I've learned that it's not entirely a bad thing. In fact, if the rest of the world could look a little deeper, beyond the hardcore exterior—the wide bodies, the carefully constructed grimaces, the performance of terror—they would find many, many brothas much nicer and smarter than myself. The problem lies in a racist culture, a highly gendered racist culture, that is so deeply enmeshed in the fabric of daily life that it's practically invisible. The very existence of the "nice Negro," like the model-minority myth pinned on Asian Americans, renders the war on those "other," hardcore niggas justifiable and even palatable. In a little-known essay on the public image of world champion boxer Joe Louis, the radical Trinidadian writer C. L. R. James put it best: "This attempt to hold up Louis as a model Negro has strong overtones of condescension and race prejudice. It implies: 'See! When a Negro knows how to conduct himself, he gets on very well and we all love him.' From there the next step is: 'If only all Negros behaved like Joe, the race problem would be solved'" (1946).

Of course we all know this is a bunch of fiction. Behaving "like Joe" was merely a code for deference and patience, which is all the more remarkable given his vocation. Unlike his predecessor Jack Johnson—the bald-headed prizefighter who transgressed racial boundaries by sleeping with and even marrying white women, who refused to apologize for his "outrageous" behavior, who boasted of his prowess in every facet of life (he even wrapped gauze around his penis to make it appear bigger under his boxing shorts)—Joe Louis was America's hero. As James put it, he was a credit to his race, "I mean the human race." (Re)presented as a humble Alabama boy, Godfearing

and devoid of hatred, Louis was constructed in the press as a raceless man whose masculinity was put to good, patriotic use. To many of his white fans, he was a man in the ring and a boy—a good boy—outside of it. To many black folks, he was a hero because he had the license to kick white men's butts and yet maintain the admiration and respect of a nation. Thus, despite similarities in race, class, and vocation, and their common iconization, Louis and Johnson exhibited public behavior that reflected radically different masculinities.

Here, then, is a lesson we cannot ignore. There is some truth in the implication that race (or gender) conflict is partly linked to behavior and how certain behavior is perceived. If our society, for example, could dispense with rigid, archaic notions of appropriate masculine and feminine behavior, perhaps we might create a world that nurtures, encourages, and even rewards nice guys. If violence were not so central to American culture—to the way manhood is defined, to the way in which the state keeps African American men in check, to the way men interact with women, to the way oppressed peoples interact with one another—perhaps we might see the withering away of white fears of black men. Perhaps young black men wouldn't feel the need to adopt hardened, threatening postures merely to survive in a Doggy-Dogg world. Not that black men ought to become colored equivalents of Alan Alda. Rather, black men ought to be whomever or whatever they want to be, without unwarranted criticism or societal pressures to conform to a particular definition of manhood. They could finally dress down without suspicion, talk loudly without surveillance, and love each other without sanction. Fortunately, such a transformation would also mean the long-awaited death of the "nice Negro."

Not in my lifetime. Any fool can look around and see that the situation for race and gender relations in general, and for black males in particular, has taken a turn for the worse—and relief is nowhere in sight. In the meantime, I will make the most of my "nice Negro" status. When it's all said and done, there is nothing romantic or interesting about playing Bigger Thomas. Maybe I can't persuade a well-dressed white couple to give up their box seats, but at least they'll listen to me. For now. . . .

Reference

James, C. L. R. 1946. "Joe Louis and Jack Johnson." *Labor Action,* July 1.

Questions

1. Have you ever been a victim of stereotyping—for example, based on your gender, race, ethnicity, sexual orientation, or social class? If you have, how did it make you feel?

2. Early in the article Kelley refers to the "media-made black man." What did he mean by this?

3. Does a shaved head have a different meaning for a black man than for a white man? In other words, would people find a white man with a shaved head to be scary? Why or why not?

4. Kelley says that "any fool can look around and see that the situation for race and gender relations in general, and for black males in particular, has taken a turn for the worse—and relief is nowhere in sight." To what extent do you agree with this assessment?

38

THE MODEL MINORITY MYTH

Asian Americans Confront Growing Backlash

Yin Ling Leung

In this 1987 article, Yin Ling Leung reveals something of a social paradox: Members of some groups in our society are singled out for discriminatory treatment because they are judged by the dominant group to be "inferior," whereas others are singled out for discrimination because they are judged "superior." Note that here, the terms *Asians* and *Asian Americans* refer to a wide range of peoples, including Cambodians, Chinese, Filipinos, Hmong, Japanese, Koreans, Laotians, Thais, and Vietnamese.

The once predominant media caricatures of Asians such as the effeminate Charlie Chan, the evil Fu Manchu, the exotic dragon-lady Suzy Wong or the docile, submissive Mrs. Livingston are giving way to a more subtle but equally damaging image. The emerging picture of Asians as hardworking, highly educated, family-oriented, and financially successful—in short, a "model minority"—appears benign at first, even beneficial. However, Asians are experiencing a growing backlash against their "model minority" status. The pervasive perception that Asian Americans are "making it," even surpassing whites despite their minority status, is resulting in discriminatory college admittance practices and a rise in anti-Asian sentiment.

What is now being coined the "model minority myth" began to take root in the late 1960s, after increasing numbers of Asian immigrants came to the U.S. under the Immigration Act of 1965.[1] A 1966 *U.S. News and World Report* article, entitled "Success Story of One Minority Group in the U.S.," portrayed Asian Americans as hardworking and uncomplaining, and implied that discrimination is not an obstacle for Asian Americans. A rash of similar articles followed, each attempting to reveal the "formula" responsible for Asian American success and prosperity.

The increased numbers of Southeast Asian refugees (the Hmong, Vietnamese, Laotian, and Kampuchean/Cambodians) and the increased immigration from Taiwan, Korea and Hong Kong have made Asians the second-fastest-growing minority population in the U.S. With this increase in numbers, the media has increased its focus on the "success stories" of Asian Americans as a whole. Articles in popular magazines such as *Newsweek, U.S. News and World Report* and others, with titles like "Asian-Americans: A 'Model Minority,'"

[1]Center for Third World Reporting. 1987. *Minority Trendsletter,* Winter, pp. 5–7.

"The Drive to Excel," "A Formula for Success," "The Promise of America," and "The Triumph of Asian Americans," perpetuate a distorted image of universal Asian-American success. One article in *Fortune* magazine portrayed Asians as a super competitive force, or "super minority," outperforming even the majority white population.

Myth Versus Reality

A closer examination of the facts, however, reveals holes in both the "model minority" and "super minority" myths. For example, 1980 census figures place the mean family income for Asian American families in the U.S. at $26,456—nearly $3,000 higher than white families. These figures dramatically change, however, if adjusted for the number of workers per family. Because Asians tend to have more workers per family, the total income of a family reflects less per individual. In addition, over 64 percent of Asian Americans live in urban areas of San Francisco, Los Angeles, New York and Honolulu, where the incomes and cost of living are correspondingly higher.

The model minority myth also masks the complexity of Asians in America and the different realities they face. In fact, Asian Americans come from sharply distinct backgrounds which determine their life in the U.S. Many of the "successful" Asian immigrants touted by the media as exemplifying the model minority phenomenon come from families that have been in the states for many generations or from aristocratic, elite, educated, economically advantaged backgrounds in their home countries. For example, the early Vietnamese refugee boat people were from wealthier and more educated communities than the more recent refugees from Vietnam. In addition, immigrants from China, Japan, and Korea tend to come from relatively more privileged backgrounds.

The more recent immigrants from Southeast Asia, like the Hmong, Laotian, Kampuchean/Cambodian, and the Vietnamese refugees arriving after 1976, do not mirror the image of instant success that the media perpetuates. These hundreds of thousands of Southeast Asian refugees suffer not only from language difficulties, but also from deep-seated emotional and psychological disorders, resulting from the trauma they experienced in the war-torn countries of Southeast Asia. Asian refugees also face limited work opportunities, substandard wages and lack of health benefits and unhealthy working conditions.

Another facet to [the] model minority myth is the belief that all Asians excel academically. There is no disputing that Asian Americans are "overrepresented" in the nation's colleges and universities. Asians make up approximately 3.7 million or 1.6 percent of the total U.S. population, but comprise 8 to 18 percent of enrollment in the nation's top colleges and universities. At the University of California at Berkeley, Asian students make up a quarter of the student population.

The media links Asian "success" in education with their strong familial bonds. This is, to some extent, an accurate portrayal. Many Asian cultures believe that social mobility is directly tied to education and therefore spend a disproportionate amount of family income on education, as compared to white families. Because it is a considerable sacrifice for most immigrant families to send their children to college, Asian students are often urged by their parents to pursue "safer" professions, such as medicine, engineering and other fields where the economic payback is proportionate to the number of years (and dollars) invested in education.

Even in these "safe" professions, however, Asians are discovering that quiet achievement and good job performance may not amount to promotions. A *Newsweek* article recently pointed to a phenomenon of Asian middle-management professionals, especially in corporate business fields, who "top-out," reaching a plateau beyond which their employers will not promote them.

Backlash: Asians Face Discrimination

Repercussions of the model minority myth on Asian Americans could be described as "the many being punished by the success of a few." Asians of all classes and generations are experiencing a rise in anti-Asian sentiment. This anti-Asian sentiment is expressed both through subtle, systematic discrimination, particularly in higher education, and through racially motivated violence.

Because of the disproportionate numbers of Asian Americans in the nation's universities, some colleges are denying Asians affirmative action consideration. At Princeton University, for example, where Asians make up approximately 8.5 percent of the entering class, admissions officials no longer consider Asian Americans as a minority group, despite federal regulations which define them as a protected subgroup.

Other prestigious colleges and universities are systematically excluding qualified Asians through the application of heavily subjective criteria. At the University of California at Berkeley, for example, despite a 14 percent rise in applications between 1983 and 1985, the number of Asian Americans admitted to UCB dropped 20 percent in 1984.

The Asian American Task Force on UC Admissions, which conducted a seven-month study, found that the university had temporarily used a minimum SAT verbal score to disqualify applicants. While Asian Americans excel on the math sections of the SAT, their national average on the verbal portion of the test was under 400. The Task Force also found that UCB now relies more heavily on subjective criteria for freshman admissions. For the fall of

1987, grades and test scores will determine only 40 percent of admittees, while 30 percent will be chosen by subjective factors which tend to operate against Asians.

According to Henry Der, executive director of Chinese for Affirmative Action: "Qualified Asian students are being excluded from the Berkeley campus in substantial numbers. It is apparent that UC policy changes are conscious attempts to limit the growth of Asian students, to the benefit of qualified white students."

Discriminatory practices at UC Berkeley point to a nationwide trend. At Harvard University, where Asians make up 10.9 percent of the first-year class, admitted Asian students had scores substantially higher than white students who were admitted. At Brown University, a study conducted by Asian American students found that Asian American admittance rates in the early 1980s had been consistently lower than the all-college admittance rate.

There is increasing evidence that these and other select schools are designing "hidden quotas" to exclude otherwise qualified Asian applicants. For example, a recent survey of Asian American applicants at Stanford demonstrated that popular images of Asians as narrowly-focused math and science students influenced how admissions officers judged Asians for entrance to college campuses. Just as "regional diversity" was used as a mechanism to keep Jews, who tended to be concentrated in metropolitan areas like New York and Los Angeles, out of elite institutions prior to World War II, "extra-curricular and leadership" criteria are functioning in a similar manner for certain Asians. The Stanford study found that although Asian Americans participated in nearly the same proportion as whites in high school sports, in equal numbers in music and in greater numbers in social, ethnic and community organizations, "intentional or unintentional" biases have made many applicants the victims of racial stereotypes.

Black conservative Thomas Sowell and other neoconservatives applaud the divorce of Asians from their minority status. Sowell believes that this will cause schools to be just as rigorous in selecting Asian students as they are at selecting majority white students. In this way, he continues, students will not be mismatched with their schools, a problem he attributes to quota requirements.

Anti-Asian Sentiment Rising

The model minority myth, coupled with the rising economic prowess of Pacific Rim Asian countries and the corresponding economic downturn in the U.S., has given rise to an increase in anti-Asian violence. In 1981, the Japanese American Citizens League recorded seven cases in which anti-Asian sentiment was expressed verbally, legislatively or physically; in 1982 they recorded four; in 1983, 20; in 1984, 30; in 1985, 48.

One explanation for this rise in anti-Asian violence is that Asians are being used as scapegoats[2] for the nation's economic problems. Both business and labor have waged explicitly anti-Asian media campaigns portraying Japanese competition as an explanation for the ills of American industry.

The case of Vincent Chin dramatically demonstrates the potential impact of such campaigns. Chin, a 27-year-old Chinese American resident of Detroit, was bludgeoned to death by two white unemployed auto workers. The two men, who were merely fined and put on

[2]The concept of scapegoat comes to us from the Old Testament. As told in Leviticus (16:10), on the day of Atonement, the sins of the Jewish people were heaped upon the head of a goat who was then "let go . . . into the wilderness." The term *scapegoat* thus literally means "escaping goat." Today, the concept is used to refer to people who, though they may be completely innocent of any offense, are singled out, blamed, and punished for the misfortunes of others.—Ed.

probation, mistook him for Japanese. They saw Chin as a representative of the Japanese automobile imports business, which they blamed for the loss of their jobs. Violence against Asian refugees and immigrants who compete for scarce resources in low-income communities has also dramatically increased.

The Asian Community Responds

Asian Americans are contradicting the very stereotype of the hardworking, uncomplaining minority by protesting the discriminatory practices in the nation's colleges and in the job market. For example, the Chinese American Legal Defense Fund, a Michigan-based organization, has filed suit against UC Berkeley and several other elite institutions, including Stanford, Princeton, Yale, and MIT. They charge that campuses have imposed "secret quotas" on Asians because of their growing enrollments. In another case, Yat-Pang Au, valedictorian of San Jose's Gunderson High School, with "top test scores and an impressive array of extracurricular activities," is threatening a civil rights suit against UC Berkeley for denying his entrance to the competitive College of Engineering.

At least one school has responded to this pressure by re-examining its admittance policies. A recent study of Asian student admission at Stanford, Brown, Harvard, and Princeton by John H. Bunzel and Jeffrey K. D. Au, both from Stanford, found that Stanford was the only university to buck the trend of declining Asian admissions. The 1986 entering class of Asian Americans increased from 119 last year to 245 this year. Asians at Stanford make up 15.6 percent of the class, still lower than UC Berkeley, where 26.5 percent of this year's entering class are Asian Americans.

Mobilizations against anti-Asian violence have also begun on the national and the community level. The Japanese American Citizens League, the Violence Against Asians Taskforce,

Chinese for Affirmative Action, and other Asian groups have monitored incidents of anti-Asian violence and pressured the U.S. Commission on Civil Rights and other government bodies to confront and investigate the problem. Projects such as the Coalition to Break the Silence and the Community Violence Prevention Project, both in Oakland, CA, are fighting to raise community consciousness on the issue through community forums and legislative testimony. The Coalition to Break the Silence has also developed ties with other organizations doing similar work in Los Angeles, New York, and Boston.

Questions

1. What does Leung mean by "backlash"? Can you think of any other examples of this phenomenon?

2. Some people who oppose affirmative action and quotas for blacks and Hispanics are nonetheless in favor of setting limits on how many Asian Americans should be admitted to colleges and universities. What could explain this apparent contradiction?

3. For individual Asian Americans, what difficulties might be caused by being stereotyped as a "model minority"?

39

TALES OUT OF MEDICAL SCHOOL

Adriane Fugh-Berman, M.D.

Research has shown that while boys and girls may sit in the same classrooms with the same teachers, they receive much different educations: "From grade school through graduate school Female students are more likely to be invisible members of classrooms" (Sadker and Sadker, *Failing at Fairness: How America's Schools Cheat Girls,* 1994). In this 1992 walk down memory lane, Adriane Fugh-Berman illustrates the nature of the invisibility and what happens when the "girls" try to change things.

[handwritten: women based on sexuality]

With the growth of the women's health movement and the influx of women into medical schools, there has been abundant talk of a new enlightenment among physicians. Last summer, many Americans were shocked when Frances Conley, a neurosurgeon on the faculty of Stanford University's medical school, resigned her position, citing "pervasive sexism." Conley's is a particularly elite and male-dominated subspecialty, but her story is not an isolated one. I graduated from the Georgetown University School of Medicine in 1988, and while medical training is a sexist process anywhere, Georgetown built disrespect for women into its curriculum.

A Jesuit school, most recently in the news as the alma mater of William Kennedy Smith, Georgetown has an overwhelmingly white, male and conservative faculty. At a time when women made up one-third of all medical students in the United States, and as many as one-half at some schools, my class was 73 percent male and more than 90 percent white.

The prevailing attitude toward women was demonstrated on the first day of classes by my anatomy instructor, who remarked that our

"Tales Out of Medical School" by Adriane Fugh-Berman, M.D. Reprinted with permission from the January 20, 1992 issue of *The Nation*. For subscription information, call 1-800-333-8536. Portions of each week's *Nation* magazine can be accessed at http://www.thenation.com.

elderly cadaver "must have been a Playboy bunny" before instructing us to cut off her large breasts and toss them into the thirty-gallon trash can marked "cadaver waste." Barely hours into our training, we were already being taught that there was nothing to be learned from examining breasts. Given the fact that one out of nine American women will develop breast cancer in her lifetime, to treat breasts as extraneous tissue seemed an appalling waste of an educational opportunity, as well as a not-so-subtle message about the relative importance of body parts. How many of my classmates now in practice, I wonder, regularly examine the breasts of their female patients?

My classmates learned their lesson of disrespect well. Later in the year one carved a tick-tack-toe on a female cadaver and challenged others to play. Another gave a languorous sigh after dissecting female genitalia, as if he had just had sex. "Guess I should have a cigarette now," he said.

Ghoulish humor is often regarded as a means by which med students overcome fear and anxiety. But it serves a darker purpose as well: Depersonalizing our cadaver was good preparation for depersonalizing our patients later. Further on in my training an ophthalmologist would yell at me when I hesitated to place a small instrument meant to measure eye pressure on a fellow student's cornea because I was afraid it would hurt. "You have to learn to treat patients as lab animals," he snarled at me.

On the first day of an emergency medicine rotation in our senior year, students were asked who had had experience in placing a central line (an intravenous line placed into a major vein under the clavicle or in the neck). Most of the male students raised their hands. None of the women did. For me, it was graphic proof of inequity in teaching; the men had had the procedure taught to them, but the women had not. Teaching rounds were often, for women, a spectator sport. One friend told me how she craned her neck to watch a physician teach a minor surgical procedure to a male student; when they were done the physician handed her his dirty gloves to discard. I have seen a male attending physician demonstrate an exam on a patient and then wade through several female medical students to drag forth a male in order to teach it to him. This sort of discrimination was common and quite unconscious: The women just didn't register as medical students to some of the doctors. Female students, for their part, tended (like male ones) to gloss over issues that might divert attention, energy or focus from the all-important goal of getting through their training. "Oh, they're just of the old school," a female classmate remarked to me, as if being ignored by our teachers was really rather charming, like having one's hand kissed.

A woman resident was giving a radiology presentation and I felt mesmerized. Why did I feel so connected and involved? It suddenly occurred to me that the female physician was regularly meeting my eyes; most of the male residents and attendings made eye contact with only the men.

"Why are women's brains smaller than men's?" asked a surgeon of a group of male medical students in the doctors' lounge (I was in the room as well, but was apparently invisible). "Because they're missing logic!" Guffaws all around.

Such instances of casual sexism are hardly unique to Georgetown, or indeed to medical schools. But at Georgetown female students also had to contend with outright discrimination of a sort most Americans probably think no longer exists in education. There was one course women were not allowed to take. The elective in sexually transmitted diseases required an interview with the head of the urology department, who was teaching the course. Those applicants with the appropriate genitalia competed for invitations to join the course (a computer was supposed to assign us electives, which we had ranked in order of preference, but that process had been circumvented for this course). Three women who requested an interview were told that the predominantly gay male clinic where the elective was held did not allow women to work there. This was news to the clinic's executive director, who stated that women were employed in all capacities.

The women who wanted to take the course repeatedly tried to meet with the urologist, but he did not return our phone calls. (I had not applied for the course, but became involved as an advocate for the women who wanted to take it.) We figured out his schedule, waylaid him in the hall and insisted that a meeting be set up.

At this meeting, clinic representatives disclosed that a survey had been circulated years before to the clientele in order to ascertain whether women workers would be accepted; 95 percent of the clients voted to welcome women. They were also asked whether it was acceptable to have medical students working at the clinic; more than 90 percent approved. We were then told that these results could not be construed to indicate that clients did not mind women medical students; the clients would naturally have assumed that "medical student" meant "male medical student." Even if that were true, we asked, if 90 percent of clients did not mind medical students and 95 percent did not mind women, couldn't a reasonable person assume that female medical students would be acceptable? No, we were informed. Another study would have to be done.

We raised formal objections to the school. Meanwhile, however, the entire elective process had been postponed by the dispute, and the blame for the delay and confusion was placed on us. The hardest part of the struggle, indeed, was dealing with the indifference of most of our classmates—out of 206, maybe a dozen actively supported us—and with the intense anger of the ten men who had been promised places in the course.

"Just because you can't take this course," one of the men said to me, "why do you want to ruin it for the rest of us?" It seemed incredible to me that I had to argue that women should be allowed to take the same courses as men. The second or third time someone asked me the same question, I suggested that if women were not allowed to participate in the same curriculum as men, then in the interest of fairness we should get a 50 percent break on our $22,500 annual tuition. My colleague thought that highly unreasonable.

Eventually someone in administration realized that not only were we going to sue the school for discrimination but that we had an open-and-shut case. The elective in sexually transmitted diseases was canceled, and from its ashes arose a new course, taught by the same man, titled "Introduction to Urology." Two women were admitted. When the urologist invited students to take turns working with him in his office, he scheduled the two female students for the same day—one on which only women patients were to be seen (a nifty feat in a urology practice).

The same professor who so valiantly tried to prevent women from learning anything unseemly about sexually transmitted diseases was also in charge of the required course in human sexuality (or, as I liked to call it, he-man sexuality). Only two of the eleven lectures focused on women; of the two lectures on homosexuality, neither mentioned lesbians. The psychiatrist who co-taught the class treated us to one lecture that amounted to an apology for rape: Aggression, even hostility, is normal in sexual relations between a man and a woman, he said, and inhibition of aggression in men can lead to impotence.

We were taught that women do not need orgasms for a satisfactory sex life, although men, of course, do; and that inability to reach orgasm is only a problem for women with "unrealistic expectations." I had heard that particular lecture before in the backseat of a car during high school. The urologist told us of couples who came to him for sex counseling because the woman was not having orgasms; he would reassure them that this is normal and the couple would be relieved. (I would gamble that the female half of the couple was anything but relieved.) We learned that oral sex is primarily a homosexual practice, and that sexual dysfunction in women is often caused by "working." In the women-as-idiots department, we learned that when impotent men are implanted with permanently rigid penile prostheses, four out of five wives can't tell that their husbands have had the surgery.

When dealing with sexually transmitted diseases in which both partners must be treated, we were advised to vary our notification strategy according to marital status. If the patient is a single man, the doctor should write the diagnosis down on a prescription for his partner to bring to her doctor. If the patient is a married man, however, the doctor should contact the wife's gynecologist and arrange to have her treated without knowledge of what she is being treated for. How to notify the male partner of a female patient, married or single, was never revealed.

To be fair, women were not the only subjects of outmoded concepts of sexuality. We also received anachronistic information about men. Premature ejaculation, defined as fewer than ten thrusts(!), was to be treated by having the man think about something unpleasant, or by having the woman painfully squeeze, prick or pinch the penis. Aversive therapies such as these have long been discredited.

Misinformation about sexuality and women's health peppered almost every course (I can't recall any egregious wrongs in biochemistry). Although vasectomy and abortion are among the safest of all surgical procedures, in our lectures vasectomy was presented as fraught with long-term complications and abortion was never mentioned without the words "peritonitis" and "death" in the same sentence. These distortions represented Georgetown's Catholic bent at its worst. (We were not allowed to perform, or even watch, abortion procedures in our affiliated hospitals.) On a lighter note, one obstetrician assisting us in the anatomy lab told us that women shouldn't lift heavy weights because their pelvic organs will fall out between their legs.

In our second year, several women in our class started a women's group, which held potlucks and offered presentations and performances: A former midwife talked about her profession, a student demonstrated belly dancing, another discussed dance therapy and one sang selections from *A Chorus Line*. This heavy radical feminist activity created great hostility among our male classmates. Announcements of our meetings were defaced and women in the group began receiving threatening calls at home from someone who claimed to be watching the listener and who would then accurately describe what she was wearing. One woman received obscene notes in her school mailbox, including one that contained a rape threat. I received insulting cards in typed envelopes at my home address; my mother received similar cards at hers.

We took the matter to the dean of student affairs, who told us it was "probably a dental student" and suggested we buy loud whistles to blow into the phone when we received unwanted calls. We demanded that the school attempt to find the perpetrator and expel him. We were told that the school would not expel the student but that counseling would be advised.

The women's group spread the word that we were collecting our own information on possible suspects and that any information on bizarre, aggressive, antisocial or misogynous behavior among the male medical students should be reported to our designated representative. She was inundated with a list of classmates who fit the bill. Finally, angered at the school's indifference, we solicited the help of a prominent woman faculty member. Although she shamed the dean into installing a hidden camera across from the school mailboxes to monitor unusual behavior, no one was ever apprehended.

Georgetown University School of Medicine churns out about 200 physicians a year. Some become good doctors despite their training, but many will pass on the misinformation and demeaning attitudes handed down to them. It is a shame that Georgetown chooses to perpetuate stereotypes and reinforce prejudices rather than help students acquire the up-to-date information and sensitivity that are vital in dealing with AIDS, breast cancer, teen pregnancy and other contemporary epidemics. Female medical students go through an ordeal, but at least it ends with graduation. It is the patients who ultimately suffer the effects of sexist medical education.

Questions

1. According to Fugh-Berman's account, the gender ratio was usually skewed at Georgetown's medical school. In your judgment, would there be less sexism if the ratio of men and women was more equal? Why or why not?

2. To what extent might it be said that the women medical students were victims of hate crimes? What would be the motive behind these attacks?

40
AFTERWORD

The Sociological Eye and Its Blinders

Randall Collins

As we neared the end of the twentieth century, many people paused to take stock of where we had come from and where we might be heading. Randall Collins was among those moved to such millennial musings. He was asked by the editors of *Contemporary Sociology* to answer some hard questions: Is there a core to sociology? Should there be? What do sociologists have in common that makes them members of the same discipline?

Does sociology have a core? Yes, but it is not an eternal essence; not a set of texts or ideas, but an activity.

This is not the same as saying the discipline of sociology will always exist. Sociology became a self-conscious community only in the mid-1800s, about five generations ago, and has been an academic discipline for four generations or less. Disciplines go in and out of existence. The very concept of disciplinary specialization as we know it was created in the Napoleonic period at the time of reorganization of the French Academies, as Johan Heilbron has shown in *The Rise of Social Theory* (1995). There is no guarantee that any particular discipline will remain fixed. Biology, a discipline first recognized by Auguste Comte, has repeatedly shifted its boundaries, combining with physics and chemistry, or spinning off genetics and ecology, making up a shifting array of new fields. Discoveries do not respect administrative boundary lines. Major advances in research or theory tend to pull followers after

them, who institutionalize themselves in turn for a while in some organizational form, if only until the next big round of discovery.

In much the same way, sociologists keep forming hybrid communities on their borders, for example, with economics, literary theory, or computer science. In recent decades, hybrid disciplines have split off from, overlapped with, or encroached upon sociology as criminal justice, ethnic studies, gender studies, management, science and technology studies (i.e., what was once "sociology of science"), and no doubt more to come. There is nothing to lament in this. A glance at the history of long-term intellectual networks, and of academic organizations, shows that branching and recombining are central to what drives intellectual innovation. (The pattern of such long-term networks is documented in my *The Sociology of Philosophies* [1998].)

Sociology, like everything else, is a product of particular historical conditions. But I also believe we have hit upon a distinctive intellectual activity. Its appeal is strong enough to keep it alive, whatever its name will be in the future and whatever happens to the surrounding institutional forms. The lure of this activity is what drew many of us into sociology. One

"The Sociological Eye and Its Blinders" by Randall Collins from *Contemporary Sociology*, Vol. 27, No. 1 (January 1998: pp. 2–7). Reprinted by permission of the American Sociological Association and the author.

becomes hooked on being a sociologist. The activity is this: It is looking at the world around us, the immediate world you and I live in, through the sociological eye.

There is a sociology of everything. You can turn on your sociological eye no matter where you are or what you are doing. Stuck in a boring committee meeting (for that matter, a sociology department meeting), you can check the pattern of who is sitting next to whom, who gets the floor, who makes eye contact, and what is the rhythm of laughter (forced or spontaneous) or of pompous speechmaking. Walking down the street, or out for a run, you can scan the class and ethnic pattern of the neighborhood, look for lines of age segregation, or for little pockets of solidarity. Waiting for a medical appointment, you can read the professions and the bureaucracy instead of old copies of *National Geographic*. Caught in a traffic jam, you can study the correlation of car models with bumper stickers or with the types of music blaring from radios. There is literally nothing you can't see in a fresh way if you turn your sociological eye to it. Being a sociologist means never having to be bored.

But doesn't every discipline have its special angle on all of reality? Couldn't a physicist see the laws of motion everywhere, or an economist think of supply curves of whatever happens in everyday life? I still think sociology is uniquely appealing in this respect. What physicists or chemists can see in everyday life is no doubt rather banal for them, and most of their discoveries in recent centuries have been made by esoteric laboratory equipment. Fields like economics, it is true, could probably impose an application of some of their theories upon a great many things. But for virtually all disciplines, the immediate world is a sideshow. For sociologists, it is our arena of discovery, and the source at which we renew our energies and our enthusiasm.

In saying this, I don't mean to say that the only true sociologists are the practitioners of ethnographic or participant observation, or that the core of sociology is limited to Goffman-style microsociology. I do think that all of us who are turned on by sociology, who love doing what we do, have the sociological eye. It is this that gives us new theoretical ideas and makes alive the theories that we carry from the past. The world a sociologist can see is not bounded by the immediate microsituation. Reading the newspaper, whether the business section or the personal ads, is for us like an astronomer training his or her telescope on the sky. Where the ordinary reader is pulled into the journalistic mode, reading the news through one or another political bias or schema of popular melodrama, the sociological eye sees suggestions of social movements mobilizing or winding down, indications of class domination or conflict, or perhaps the organizational process whereby just this kind of story ended up in print, defined as news. For us, novels depict the boundaries of status groups and the saga of social mobility, just as detective stories show us about backstages. Whatever we read with the sociological eye becomes a clue to the larger patterns of society, here or in the past. The same goes for the future: Today's sociologists are not just caught up in the fad of the Internet; they are already beginning to look at it as another frontier for sociological discovery.

I want to claim, in short, that all kinds of sociologists, microethnographers and statisticians, historical comparativists and theorists alike, have the sociological eye. I think that virtually all of the most productive sociologists among us do. We all went through a gestalt switch in our way of looking at the world, sometime early in our careers, that was the key moment in our initiation into sociology. Having become initiated, I suppose, one can also become burned out. The vision fades; everyday life becomes just everyday; the newspapers become just a little jolt of political clichés to go along with the morning orange juice;

sociology becomes just life at the office, number crunching or writing reviews on yet another meta-critique on the lives of dead Germans. Sure, we can lose the vision and the enthusiasm. But the initiation lingers; the gestalt switch is still there to be switched on. We can always reenergize ourselves by getting back to the source: Turn on the sociological eye and go look at something. Don't take someone else's word for what there is to see, or some common cliché (even a current trendy one), above all not a media-hype version of what is there; go and see it yourself. Make it observationally strange, as if you'd never seen it before. The energy comes back. In that way, I suspect, sociologists are probably more energized by their subject matter than practitioners of virtually any other discipline.

Now I want to thicken the plot. Turning on the sociological eye is the main way that many of us became sociologists, but it isn't the only way. There is another recruitment path, which also acts as a continuing source of energy and commitment. This is the path of social activism. Many, perhaps most of us, became interested in sociology because we belonged to social movements or had social commitments. We wanted to do something to change society, help people, fight injustice, and elevate the oppressed. This image of sociology has long been foremost in the public eye. In an earlier generation, people used to confuse "sociology" with "socialism," or more recently with "social work." The 1960s gave another radical jolt to this trajectory, along with a repetition of the pattern of putting down one's elders for not being up with today's crusade. We of the '60s generation have been experiencing the turn that comes, in time, of being on the receiving end of the same process.

There are complications in the career of activist commitment too; there can be burnout, and also institutionalization, so that researching one's favorite oppressed group also becomes just another day at the office. But here,

too, it remains possible to reawaken the old energy surge by making contact with the source: that is, get in touch with a movement that is still mobilized, feed one's energies into it, and receive back the stepped-up current that comes from solidarity and commitment. Old lefties (and, more precisely, old New Lefties) can get a surge in their commitment by intellectual action that carries forward the old targeting of opponents. World-system theory, for instance, is not just another academic specialty, for those who work in it; there is a political resonance that makes even such arcane topics as trade routes in the Ottoman Empire into opportunities to grapple with the history of the capitalist beast. Sociology is full of people who have passion, who care deeply about their subject, because so many of us came in through the activist side.

This is a second reason why sociology is so distinctive. Although politically committed persons and former or current activists work throughout the academic world, in few disciplines does activism mesh so directly with one's immediate work as in sociology. Sociology is nearly the most politicized and activist of all fields. (In recent years literature, which resembles sociology in several of the respects I have been discussing, has probably come to rival sociology in ideological intensity.) Probably the only disciplines that are even more thoroughly politicized than sociology are relatives of sociology, such as ethnic studies, black studies, and women's studies, which were created as hybrids between academic departments and activist movements.

Now to the crux of the drama. Sociology has two core commitments: what I have called the "sociological eye" and social activism. They can be combined; some people have both of them, simultaneously or in differing strengths at different times in their careers. And one can become burned out from both, so the entire population of those of us who are nominally called "sociologists" array ourselves all across this two-dimensional grid. Much of the conflict within sociology goes on between those who are at the peak intensities of the two different commitments.

In the late 1950s, C. Wright Mills' *The Sociological Imagination* castigated mere "abstracted empiricists" and "grand theorists" for losing what Mills regarded as the true sociological commitment to an activist critique and reconstruction of society. Today, James Rule in *Theory and Progress in Social Science* (1997) makes a parallel critique, charging that sociology is full of specialized intellectual movements caught up in self-generated problems, spinning technicalities of their own devising. For Rule, movements as diverse as rational choice, network analysis, and feminist theory all share the pathology of turning inward on themselves, surrounding themselves with a wall of esoteric vocabulary, and losing sight of the first-order questions of perennial concern: the conditions of stratification, social disruption, and violence. It is possible to be sympathetic to the spirit of Mills' and Rule's critiques and still to see the larger dimensions of the intellectual conflict. Mills' targets (Lazarsfeld, Parsons, Merton) and many of Rule's targets also had the sociological eye; these were (and are) sociologists who have turned on their vision, seeing something around us that the ordinary eye doesn't see, whether it be latent functions (in one of the older examples) or network structures (in one of the newer ones).

From the point of view of the committed activist, those sociologists who don't work on burning social problems seem like incomprehensible duffers or backsliding traitors to the cause; the activist commitment makes it hard to see that there is a driving commitment on the other side too, just an entirely different one. Erving Goffman, hiding out backstage in the mental hospital, was not merely seeing patients and psychiatrists through official or even counterofficial eyes, but was making his own distinctively sociological discoveries of how the construction of normalcy and of the self takes place. From the activist viewpoint, the judgment on other sociologists' work tends to be "if you're not part of the solution you're part of the problem." From the point of view of the voyager with the sociological eye, the activist is just someone who has already made up his or her mind and is no longer open to seeing anything new.

Perhaps the purest recent formulation of the viewpoint of the sociological eye is the preface to the second edition of Donald Black's *The Social Structure of Right and Wrong* (1998). Black regards the activist mentality as the biggest blinder to seeing the social pattern: For right and wrong, the categories by which the activist works are themselves socially variable attitudes arising from particular configurations of conflict, social control, and conflict management. For Black, categories such as crime, or ethnic or gender identity, are mere folk concepts that need to be dissolved into the analytical space of "pure sociology." Black is positively glowing from his sociological eye, almost like a Hindu tantric seer looking down and through us mere mortals below.

The two versions of sociological commitment, at their most intense, are like opposing gestalts; one impedes even bare awareness of what can be seen through the other. A recent example of the contretemps that can result is the public reception of Arlie Hochschild's *The Time Bind* (1997). Throughout her career, Hochschild's work has been a blend of the sociological eye and activist commitment, although (Hochschild is a student of Erving Goffman) the sociological eye tends to predominate. Hochschild treads on dangerous ground, because she chooses to study topics that are at the heart of current public controversy; yet she does not let the commitment dictate what she *sees*, and she goes willingly down the pathways opened by unexpected discoveries.

Research on *The Time Bind* began with a puzzle: Hochschild noticed that relatively few people were taking advantage of family-friendly employment policies allowing shorter hours, part-time work, parental leave, or flexible time. A politically conventional diagnosis today would be to blame economic pressure or subtle organizational coercion. Hochschild instead began to see the situation through a new gestalt: For many middle-class people, work and home were changing places. The successes of the middle-class women's movement were now producing unforeseen consequences. Home was becoming more of a hassle (already documented in Hochschild's previous book, *The Second Shift* [1989]), particularly as employed women work longer paid hours and still receive relatively little help from their husbands at home. One response, Hochschild perceived, was to gradually abandon the home battle, shifting the emotional center of one's life to one's work. Along with this has gone a large institutional shift: Family life has gotten de-skilled, dependent upon commercial services for everything from food preparation to child care and entertainment. The Taylorized factory of the early twentieth century, with its efficiency-oriented speed-up, has invaded the home just at the time that modern participative management techniques have made middle-class workplaces more emotionally friendly. Hochschild perceives that the spate of services for children, of how-to books and courses on dealing effectively with family situations, even the very concept of "quality time" with one's children, are a kind of speed-up in the home, putting scientific home management to work to manipulate emotions as well as diets and minutes. For Hochschild, the entire gestalt of work and family is shifting; the divorce rate of broken marriages needs to be seen in the light of "marriages" to a place of employment, with job terminations as a second, sometimes counterbalancing "divorce rate."

My point is that Hochschild's sociological imagination was lit up at some point in her research. The starting point involved fairly standard feminist issues in the public arena, but what she came to see was filled with ironic resonances of a prior history of sociological discovery: the industrial management movement of the earlier part of the century, the "emotion work" that Hochschild herself had earlier uncovered in her study of airline flight attendants (*The Managed Heart* [1983]), the interplay between the official frontstage ideals (in this case, of how a contemporary parent is supposed to deal with one's children) and the backstage reality of how people make out amid the pressure of institutions. It is exploring these resonances, I am sure, that drew Hochschild deeper and deeper into her research; the sociological eye has a way of pulling you down its wilderness paths. These same resonances give the book much of its appeal for sociologists.

At the same time, *The Time Bind* has been greeted with public controversy. Most people do not have the sociological eye; public political discourse is carried out in the language of parties and movements, and everything published is assessed as a move for or against a partisan position. Hochschild has been attacked for undermining the family leave act, for blaming working mothers for emotionally abandoning their children, for misperceiving the fight of working women against the pressures of corporate organization. Hochschild's response in the public press has been to stick to her vision: Her critics are closing their eyes on an unexpected reality they are afraid to see. Some of Hochschild's critics are sociologists, and some of the attack is not mere lay mentality against the professional sociologist: It is the perennial inner conflict of our discipline, the movement activist stance against the sociological eye. Some of the controversy over Hochschild's work mixes both dimensions; there are technical issues at stake involving research methods, the scope of interpretations based on Hochschild's particular slice of data, and underlying images of what kinds of families existed in an earlier historical period. Some of the activist critique of Hochschild's unwelcome findings is carried out on the terrain of technical argument. And indeed she may well be faulted in some of these aspects, such as the complexity of causes of why employees don't take off more time from work.

Yet the importance of Hochschild's vision remains; however specialized her research sample, she points to a cutting edge of social change. The puzzle over leave time was just the point of entry into a larger insight. Hochschild's sociological eye illuminates because it gives us a new gestalt, a way of making sense of what has happened to the entire complex of work-and-home as we pass a historical watershed. When examined analytically instead of moralistically, it is not a question of denouncing or defending contemporary outsourcing of child care, home care, entertainment, and emotional support; nor of nostalgia for another era in which indeed middle-class women were confined to craft work or domestic labor. I think Hochschild's critics are mistaken in assuming that she has merely warped the activist scale of evaluations, and in not understanding the seriousness of a commitment to seeing as much as one can with one's sociological eye, however unsettling the news may be.

The two sources of sociologists' commitment often struggle against each other. If we have to choose between them, I say we must choose the sociological eye; if that is lost, all is lost. Without it, even sociological activists lose their creativity and their credibility with the public, appearing only as purveyors of facts chosen by persons whose minds are already made up. But unless there is all-out war between the factions, we can live with the struggle, and even prosper from it. Sociology is fortunate that it has so much built-in energy, so much intellectual commitment—even if those commitments sometimes are at cross-purposes.

Yet it is not always so. Sometimes the intensities are at more moderate levels, where blending is easier. And sometimes both commitments are high, but the sociological eye is wonderfully appropriate for what the social activist wants to reveal. Good examples are the urban ethnographies of street life by Elijah Anderson, *Streetwise* (1990) and *The Code of the Streets* (forthcoming). Anderson has a Goffmanian eye for the nuances of signals and signs given off in public, at the same time that he presents the dilemmas of social interaction in a racially mixed, physically dangerous neighborhood. A good-hearted activist with no other resources than the best intentions, or an angry activist full of righteousness, could not have written these books; it takes a sociological eye. And what the sociological eye saw is now revealed to the rest of us who read Anderson's books. Probably the sociological eye will always be the possession of a little group of devotees within the larger society. But the border between sociologists and lay people isn't fixed, and some of what we see can cross over. Sometimes it expands other people's vision.

References

Anderson, Elijah. 1990. *Streetwise: Race, Class and Change in an Urban Community.* Chicago: University of Chicago Press.

———. forthcoming. *The Code of the Streets.*

Black, Donald. 1998. *The Social Structure of Right and Wrong.* 2d ed. Orlando: Academic Press.

Collins, Randall. 1998. *The Sociology of Philosophies: A Global Theory of Intellectual Change.* Cambridge, MA: Harvard University Press.

Heilbron, Johan. 1995. *The Rise of Social Theory.* Minneapolis: University of Minnesota Press.

Hochschild, Arlie. 1983. *The Managed Heart.* Berkeley: University of California Press.

———. 1989. *The Second Shift: Working Parents and the Revolution at Home.* New York: Viking.

———. 1997. *The Time Bind: When Work Becomes Home And Home Becomes Work.* New York: Metropolitan Books.

Rule, James B. 1997. *Theory and Progress in Social Science.* Cambridge: Cambridge University Press.

Questions

1. Collins says that the core of sociology is the "sociological eye." What is that?

2. Why does Collins say that activism can be a blinder to sociological eyes?

3. Based on all that you've learned in your sociology class, why is it so difficult for "lay people" to see the world through sociological eyes?